Peninsula & Silicon Valley Guide

AN INSIDER'S REFERENCE FOR NEWCOMERS, VISITORS, & RESIDENTS

GOOD LIFE PUBLICATIONS

CREDITS

Series Editor
Peter Massik

Contributing Writers and Editors, 3rd Edition
Julie Carlson, Heather Doherty, Susie Kramer, Daniel O'Donnell, Essan Ni,
Seleta Reynolds, Sharon Silva, Pat Smith, Christina Waters

Other Contributors
Jeremy Chipman, Rose Cremin, Elizabeth Dumanian,
Ryan Miziker, Jennifer Sandell, Eric Weaver

Maps
Ryan Miziker

Cover Design
Big Fish Books, San Francisco

Cover Image
Stock Agency/Photographer PNI

Good Life Silicon Valley Guide (An Insider's Reference
for Newcomer, Visitors, & Residents)
ISBN 0-886776-12-1 Softcover.
Third edition.
First edition published as Guide to the Good Life on the Peninsula.
Second edition published as Good Life Peninsula & San Jose Insider's Guide.

Please send all comments, corrections, and additions for future editions to:

Good Life Publications
580 Washington St. #306
San Francisco, California 94111
(415) 989-1844 or (888) 989-GOOD
(415) 989-3122 fax
comments@goodlifebooks.com
WWW.goodlifebooks.com

Special Sales

Good Life guides are available at bulk discounts for conventions, corporate gifts, fundrais-
ing sales premiums, and sales promotions. Special editions, including custom covers,
excerpts of existing guides, and corporate imprints, can be created for large orders. For
more information, contact Good Life Publications.

TABLE OF CONTENTS

INTRODUCTION

Welcome to the *Good Life Peninsula & Silicon Valley Guide*. This edition maintains the book's original purpose: providing information about the Bay Area customized specifically for the millions of people who live in and visit the Peninsula and Silicon Valley. In the never-ending search for comprehensiveness, we included as much as we could. If we overlooked some gem or gave you a bum steer, let us know! One cautionary note: prices are subject to change without notice (ditto hours of operation), so if you're watching your wallet or watch, play it safe and call ahead.

We hope that you have as much fun using the book as we did putting it together.

KEY TO RATINGS

This guidebook includes easy-to-understand stars and dollar signs for quality and price ratings. Keep in mind that things change. Even well-established businesses close, and changes in staff or ownership can greatly affect quality and price. The ratings in this book are based on information available at press time.

★ Stars

Sights and attractions are rated on the following popular scale of one to three stars.

★   Interesting.

★★   Worth a detour.

★★★   Worth the trip.

Restaurants are rated on the following scale of one to four stars. The star ratings are purely subjective, and based on an overall evaluation of the restaurant, with heavy emphasis on the quality and consistency of the food.

★   Fair to good. Has some interesting, satisfying features and dishes. Good if you are in the neighborhood.

★★   Very Good. Has some extraordinary dishes and features. Worth a detour.

★★★   Excellent. Has many extraordinary dishes and features. A worthy destination.

★★★★   Extraordinary. The best in its class, with consistently exceptional food, service, and atmosphere.

NR   Unable to rate at presstime. Restaurant is either not open yet, has just opened, or is in transition.

Restaurant Prices

Rating the price of a restaurant meal isn't a science: two groups can go to the same establishment and leave with wildly different checks. Our ratings are based on what it might cost each person to have a reasonable dinner (breakfast or lunch if that's all the restaurant serves) including tax and tip but excluding alcohol. Maybe enjoy one drink, split an appetizer, order an entrée, and share a dessert.

¢   A filling meal for $8 or less. Usually this refers to taquerias, burger joints, and other places with counter service.

$ $8 to $15 each for dinner. Typically, places that only serve brunch and lunch, ethnic restaurants, and other eateries where main dishes are under $10.

$$ You can get away with spending as little as $15 for dinner or easily go up to $25. Mostly places serving pasta, sushi, or moderately priced meat and seafood dishes ($10 to $15 entrées).

$$$ Meals run from $25 to $40 per person. Restaurants where most entrées are priced from $15 to $20, most items are à la carte, and most tables have a bottle of wine.

$$$$ At least $40 per person, but usually significantly more, especially with fine wine. Most entrées are over $20 or there is an expensive prix fixe menu. For that blow-out celebration meal.

San Francisco

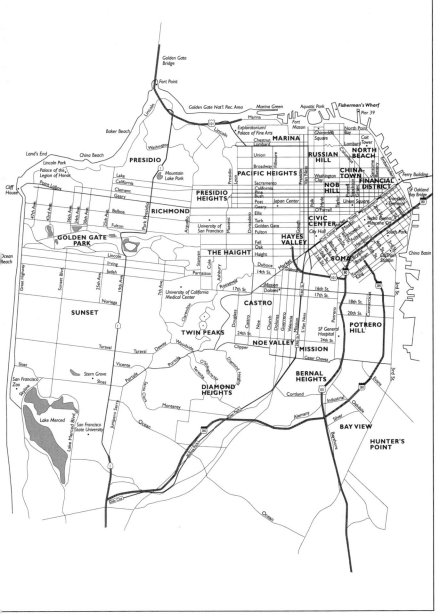

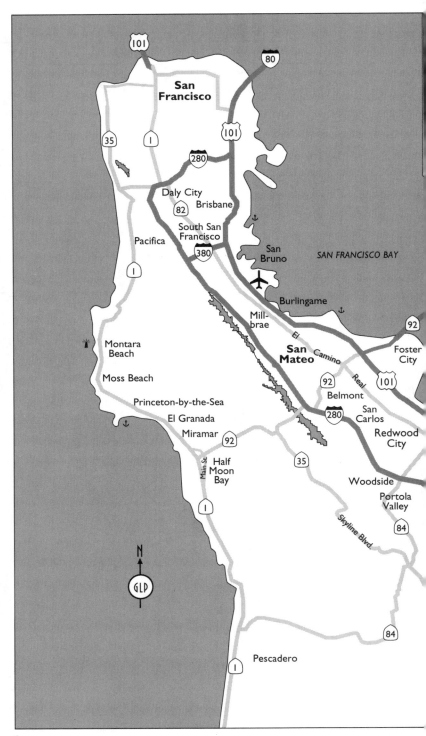

San Francisco

101

80

101

280

Daly City
82   Brisbane

South San
Francisco
380

San
Bruno

SAN FRANCISCO BAY

Pacifica

1

Burlingame

92

Mill-
brae

**San
Mateo**

El
Camino

Foster
City

Montara
Beach

Real

101

Moss Beach

92

Belmont

San
Carlos

Princeton-by-the-Sea

280

El Granada

Miramar   92

Redwood
City

Main St.   Half
Moon
Bay

35

Woodside

Portola
Valley

1

Skyline Blvd.

84

N

GLP

84

1   Pescadero

Peninsula & Silicon Valley Overview

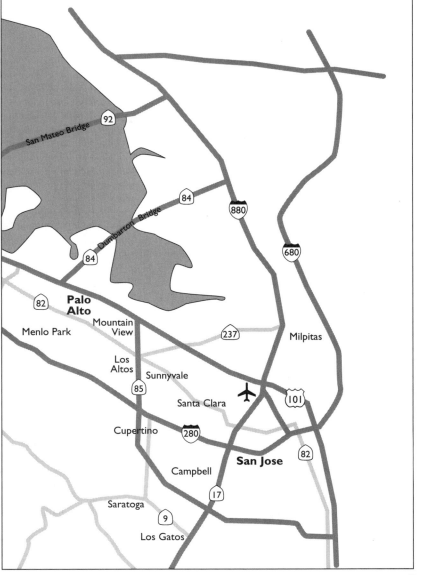

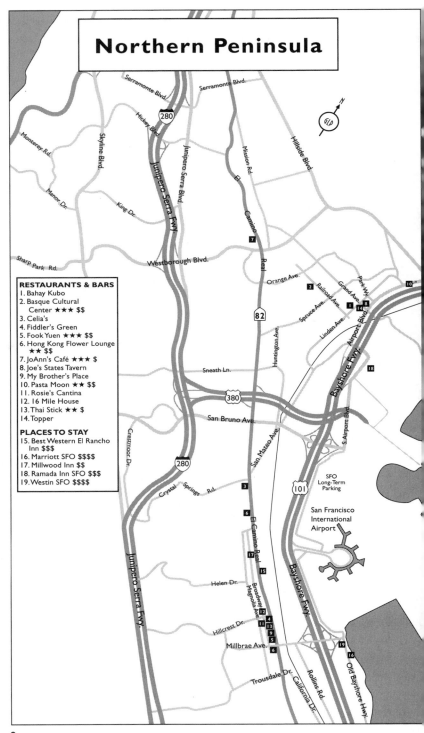

Northern Peninsula

RESTAURANTS & BARS
1. Bahay Kubo
2. Basque Cultural Center ★★★ $$
3. Celia's
4. Fiddler's Green
5. Fook Yuen ★★★ $$
6. Hong Kong Flower Lounge ★★ $$
7. JoAnn's Café ★★★ $
8. Joe's States Tavern
9. My Brother's Place
10. Pasta Moon ★★ $$
11. Rosie's Cantina
12. 16 Mile House
13. Thai Stick ★★ $
14. Topper

PLACES TO STAY
15. Best Western El Rancho Inn $$$
16. Marriott SFO $$$$
17. Millwood Inn $$
18. Ramada Inn SFO $$$
19. Westin SFO $$$$

Burlingame

RESTAURANTS & BARS
1. Alana's ★★ $
2. Brothers Delicatessen ★ $
3. Café La Scala ★★ $$
4. Chicken! Chicken! ★ $
5. Copenhagen Bakery & Café ★ $
6. Dicey Riley's Irish Pub
7. Ecco Café ★★ $$$
8. Elephant Bar
9. The Fisherman ★★ $$$
10. Grandview Restaurant ★★★ $$
11. Il Fornaio Cucina Italiana ★★ $$
12. Juban ★★ $$
13. Kincaid's ★★ $$$
14. Kuleto's Trattoria ★★ $$
15. La Piñata
16. Left at Albuquerque ★★★ $
17. Max's Opera Café ★★ $$
18. Moon McShane's
19. Narin ★★ $
20. Ramen Club ★★ $
21. Stacks ★★ $
22. Steelhead (Burlingame Station) Brewing Company ★★ $$
23. Sushi Bar Jun ★★ $$
24. Tavern Grill
25. World Wrapps ★ $
26. Yianni's ★★ $$

PLACES TO STAY
27. Doubletree Hotel SFO $$$
28. Embassy Suites Hotel $$$$
29. Hyatt Regency SFO $$$$
30. Park Plaza Hotel San Francisco $$$$

POINTS OF INTEREST
31. San Mateo County Convention and Visitors Bureau

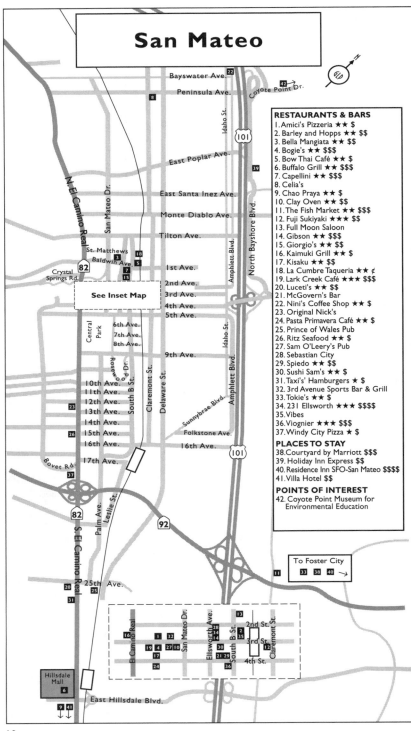

San Mateo

RESTAURANTS & BARS
1. Amici's Pizzeria ★★ $
2. Barley and Hopps ★★ $$
3. Bella Mangiata ★★ $$
4. Bogie's ★★ $$$
5. Bow Thai Café ★★ $
6. Buffalo Grill ★★ $$$
7. Capellini ★★ $$$
8. Celia's
9. Chao Praya ★★ $
10. Clay Oven ★★ $$
11. The Fish Market ★★ $$$
12. Fuji Sukiyaki ★★★ $$
13. Full Moon Saloon
14. Gibson ★★ $$$
15. Giorgio's ★★ $$
16. Kaimuki Grill ★★ $
17. Kisaku ★★ $$
18. La Cumbre Taqueria ★★ ¢
19. Lark Creek Café ★★★ $$$
20. Luceti's ★★ $$
21. McGovern's Bar
22. Nini's Coffee Shop ★★ $
23. Original Nick's
24. Pasta Primavera Café ★★ $
25. Prince of Wales Pub
26. Ritz Seafood ★★ $
27. Sam O'Leery's Pub
28. Sebastian City
29. Spiedo ★★ $$
30. Sushi Sam's ★★ $
31. Taxi's' Hamburgers ★ $
32. 3rd Avenue Sports Bar & Grill
33. Tokie's ★★ $
34. 231 Ellsworth ★★★ $$$$
35. Vibes
36. Viognier ★★★ $$$
37. Windy City Pizza ★ $

PLACES TO STAY
38. Courtyard by Marriott $$$
39. Holiday Inn Express $$
40. Residence Inn SFO-San Mateo $$$$
41. Villa Hotel $$

POINTS OF INTEREST
42. Coyote Point Museum for Environmental Education

To Foster City

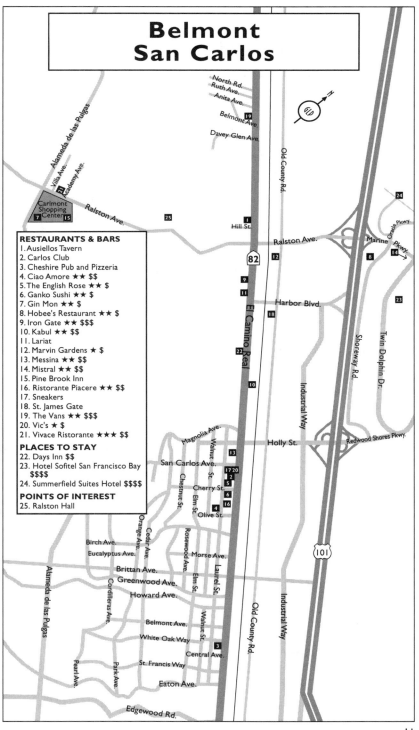

Belmont
San Carlos

RESTAURANTS & BARS
1. Ausiellos Tavern
2. Carlos Club
3. Cheshire Pub and Pizzeria
4. Ciao Amore ★★ $$
5. The English Rose ★★ $
6. Ganko Sushi ★★ $
7. Gin Mon ★★ $
8. Hobee's Restaurant ★★ $
9. Iron Gate ★★ $$$
10. Kabul ★★ $$
11. Lariat
12. Marvin Gardens ★ $
13. Messina ★★ $$
14. Mistral ★★ $$
15. Pine Brook Inn
16. Ristorante Piacere ★★ $$
17. Sneakers
18. St. James Gate
19. The Vans ★★ $$$
20. Vic's ★ $
21. Vivace Ristorante ★★★ $$

PLACES TO STAY
22. Days Inn $$
23. Hotel Sofitel San Francisco Bay $$$$
24. Summerfield Suites Hotel $$$$

POINTS OF INTEREST
25. Ralston Hall

Redwood City

RESTAURANTS & BARS
1. Bonsai Sushi ★★ $$
2. City Pub
3. El Grullense E&E ★ ¢
4. Estampas Peruanas ★★ $$
5. La Pachanga ★★ $
6. Las Parillas ★ $$
7. The Loading Zone
8. Max's ★★ $$
9. MiMe's Café ★★ $
10. Redwood Café and
    Spice Co. ★★★ $
11. Saddle Room
12. Shooters
13. Shouts Bar and Grill
14. Spanky's
15. Sports Club
16. Stacks ★★ $
17. Thanh's Restaurant ★ $
18. 2030 ★★ $$$
19. Villa Roma
20. Woodside Tavern
21. Woodside Thai Spot ★★ $

PLACES TO STAY
22. Best Western Executive
    Suites $$

POINTS OF INTEREST
23. San Mateo Historic Museum

Whipple Ave.

Hopkins Ave.

Brewster Ave.

Arguello St.

Winslow St.

Veterans Blvd.

E. Bayshore Rd.

Uccelli Blvd.

Winslow St.
Hamilton St.
Middlefield Rd.
Jefferson Ave.
Main St.

Sequoia Station

Jefferson Ave.

Broadway

Veterans Blvd.

101

Roosevelt Ave.

Middlefield Rd.

Chestnut St.

Bay Rd.

84

Charter St.

Spring St.

Broadway

Douglas Ave.

El Camino Real

82

Middlefield Rd.

1st Ave.

2nd Ave.

5th Ave.

Spring St.

Bay Rd.

Hudson St.

Woodside Rd.

Selby Ln.

5th Ave.

Stockbridge Ave.

Austin Ave.

Almendral Ave.

Tuscaloosa Ave.

Marsh Rd.

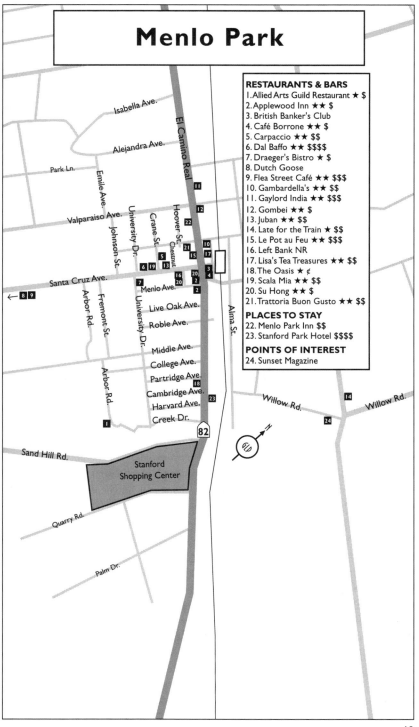

Menlo Park

RESTAURANTS & BARS
1. Allied Arts Guild Restaurant ★ $
2. Applewood Inn ★★ $
3. British Banker's Club
4. Café Borrone ★★ $
5. Carpaccio ★★ $$
6. Dal Baffo ★★ $$$$
7. Draeger's Bistro ★ $
8. Dutch Goose
9. Flea Street Café ★★ $$$
10. Gambardella's ★★ $$
11. Gaylord India ★★ $$$
12. Gombei ★★ $
13. Juban ★★ $$
14. Late for the Train ★ $$
15. Le Pot au Feu ★★ $$$
16. Left Bank NR
17. Lisa's Tea Treasures ★★ $$
18. The Oasis ★ ¢
19. Scala Mia ★★ $$
20. Su Hong ★★ $
21. Trattoria Buon Gusto ★★ $$

PLACES TO STAY
22. Menlo Park Inn $$
23. Stanford Park Hotel $$$$

POINTS OF INTEREST
24. Sunset Magazine

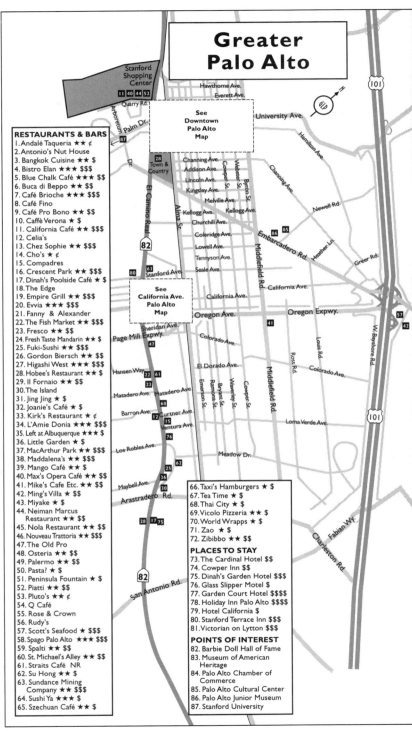

Greater Palo Alto

Stanford Shopping Center
11 40 44 52

Hawthorne Ave.
Everett Ave.

Quarry Rd.

Palm Dr.

University Ave.

Hamilton Ave.

See Downtown Palo Alto Map

28 Town & Country

Channing Ave.
Addison Ave.
Lincoln Ave.
Kingsley Ave.

Channing Ave.

Newell Rd.

Melville Ave.
Kellogg Ave.
Kellogg Ave.
Churchill Ave.

Coleridge Ave.

86 **85**

Lowell Ave.

Embarcadero Rd.
Heather Ln.

Greer Rd.

Tennyson Ave.

80 **63** Stanford Ave.
Seale Ave.

See California Ave. Palo Alto Map

California Ave.
California Ave.

Oregon Ave.
Oregon Expwy.

41

57
42

Sheridan Ave.
Page Mill Expwy.
47

Colorado Ave.

Louis Rd.

Colorado Ave.

Hansen Way
22 **61**

El Dorado Ave.

Ross Rd.

23

Matadero Ave.
Matadero Ave.
68

Barron Ave.
12 Curtner Ave.
15
Ventura Ave.
76

Bryant St.
Ramona St.
Emerson St.
Waverley St.
Cowper St.
Middlefield Rd.

Loma Verde Ave.

Los Robles Ave.

Meadow Dr.

25 **62**

Maybell Ave.
36
30

Arastradero Rd.

28 **17** **75**

82

San Antonio Rd.

Fabian Wy.

Charleston Rd.

RESTAURANTS & BARS

1. Andalé Taqueria ★★ ¢
2. Antonio's Nut House
3. Bangkok Cuisine ★★ $
4. Bistro Elan ★★★ $$$
5. Blue Chalk Café ★★★ $$
6. Buca di Beppo ★★ $$
7. Café Brioche ★★★ $$$
8. Café Fino
9. Café Pro Bono ★★ $$
10. Caffè Verona ★ $
11. California Café ★★ $$$
12. Celia's
13. Chez Sophie ★★ $$$
14. Cho's ★ ¢
15. Compadres
16. Crescent Park ★★ $$$
17. Dinah's Poolside Café ★ $
18. The Edge
19. Empire Grill ★★ $$$
20. Evvia ★★★ $$$
21. Fanny & Alexander
22. The Fish Market ★★ $$$
23. Fresco ★★ $$
24. Fresh Taste Mandarin ★★ $
25. Fuki-Sushi ★★ $$$
26. Gordon Biersch ★★ $$
27. Higashi West ★★★ $$$
28. Hobee's Restaurant ★★ $
29. Il Fornaio ★★ $$
30. The Island
31. Jing Jing ★ $
32. Joanie's Café ★ $
33. Kirk's Restaurant ★ ¢
34. L'Amie Donia ★★ $$$
35. Left at Albuquerque ★★★ $
36. Little Garden ★ $
37. MacArthur Park ★★ $$$
38. Maddalena's ★★ $$$
39. Mango Café ★★ $
40. Max's Opera Café ★★ $$
41. Mike's Cafe Etc. ★★ $$
42. Ming's Villa ★ $$
43. Miyake ★ $
44. Neiman Marcus Restaurant ★★ $$
45. Nola Restaurant ★★ $$
46. Nouveau Trattoria ★★ $$$
47. The Old Pro
48. Osteria ★★ $$
49. Palermo ★★ $$
50. Pasta? ★ $
51. Peninsula Fountain ★ $
52. Piatti ★★ $$
53. Pluto's ★★ ¢
54. Q Café
55. Rose & Crown
56. Rudy's
57. Scott's Seafood ★ $$$
58. Spago Palo Alto ★★★ $$$
59. Spalti ★★ $$
60. St. Michael's Alley ★★ $$
61. Straits Café NR
62. Su Hong ★★ $
63. Sundance Mining Company ★★ $$$
64. Sushi Ya ★★★ $
65. Szechuan Café ★★ $

66. Taxi's Hamburgers ★ $
67. Tea Time ★ $
68. Thai City ★ $
69. Vicolo Pizzeria ★★ $
70. World Wrapps ★ $
71. Zao ★ $
72. Zibibbo ★★ $$

PLACES TO STAY

73. The Cardinal Hotel $$
74. Cowper Inn $$
75. Dinah's Garden Hotel $$$
76. Glass Slipper Motel $
77. Garden Court Hotel $$$$
78. Holiday Inn Palo Alto $$$$
79. Hotel California $
80. Stanford Terrace Inn $$$
81. Victorian on Lytton $$$

POINTS OF INTEREST

82. Barbie Doll Hall of Fame
83. Museum of American Heritage
84. Palo Alto Chamber of Commerce
85. Palo Alto Cultural Center
86. Palo Alto Junior Museum
87. Stanford University

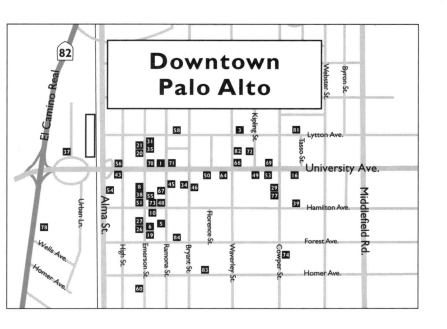

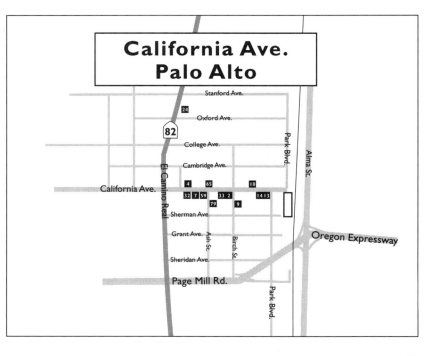

15

Mountain View
Los Altos

See
Downtown
Los Altos
Map

See
Castro
Street
Mountain
View Map

RESTAURANTS & BARS

1. Alberto's Club
2. Akane ★★★ $$
3. Amarin Thai Cuisine ★★ $
4. Applewood Inn ★★ $
5. Bandera Restaurant ★★ $$$
6. The Butler's Pantry ★ $
7. Chef Chu's ★★ $
8. Chez T.J. ★★★ $$$$
9. Country Gourmet ★ $
10. Don Giovanni (Ristorante) ★★★ $$
11. El Calderon ★ $
12. Fibbar Magee's
13. Francesca's
14. Frankie, Johnny and Luigi Too ★ $
15. Fred's
16. Fu Lam Mum ★★ $
17. Garden Fresh ★★ $
18. Hangen ★★ $
19. Hobee's Restaurant ★★ $
20. Hunan Home's ★★ $
21. I Fratelli ★★ $$$
22. Kamei Japanese House ★★ $
23. La Costeña ★★ $
24. La Fiesta ★★ $

25. Le Petit Bistro ★★ $$
26. Los Altos Bar & Grill ★ $$
27. Maharaja's ★★ $$
28. Mandarin Classic ★★ $$
29. Mei Long ★★★ $$
30. Molly McGee's
31. Pho Xe Lua ★ ¢
32. Royal Palace ★ $
33. Sono Sushi ★★ $
34. Sue's Indian Cuisine ★★ $$
35. Swagat Indian Cuisine ★★★ $$
36. Taqueria La Bamba ★★ ¢
37. Tied House
38. Tony and Alba's Pizza ★ $
39. Town Club
40. Tung Kee Noodle House ★★ ¢
41. Yakko ★★★ $

PLACES TO STAY

42. Best Western Mountain View Inn $$$
43. Crestview Hotel $$$
44. Residence Inn Mountain View $$$$

POINTS OF INTEREST

45. NASA/Ames Research Center

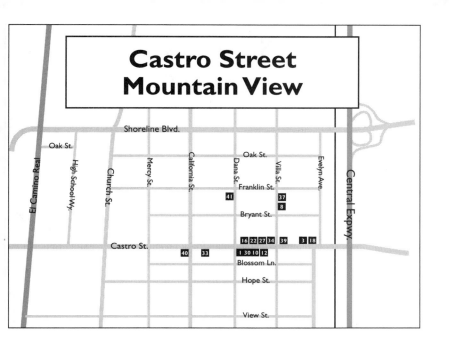

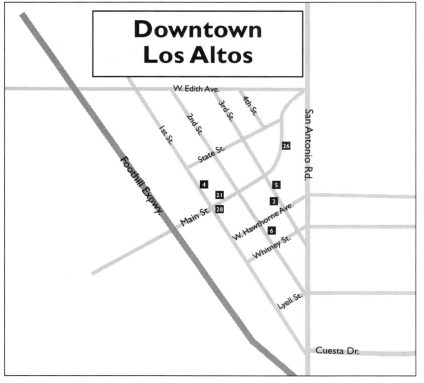

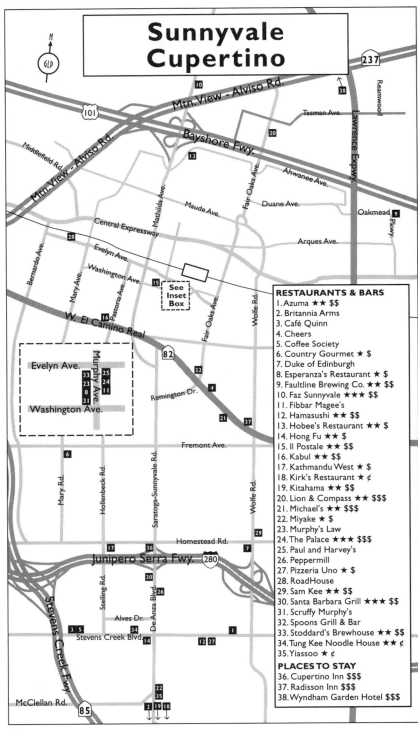

Sunnyvale Cupertino

RESTAURANTS & BARS

1. Azuma ★★ $$
2. Britannia Arms
3. Café Quinn
4. Cheers
5. Coffee Society
6. Country Gourmet ★ $
7. Duke of Edinburgh
8. Esperanza's Restaurant ★ $
9. Faultline Brewing Co. ★★ $$
10. Faz Sunnyvale ★★★ $$
11. Fibbar Magee's
12. Hamasushi ★★ $$
13. Hobee's Restaurant ★★ $
14. Hong Fu ★★ $
15. Il Postale ★★ $$
16. Kabul ★★ $$
17. Kathmandu West ★ $
18. Kirk's Restaurant ★ ¢
19. Kitahama ★★ $$
20. Lion & Compass ★★ $$$
21. Michael's ★★ $$$
22. Miyake ★ $
23. Murphy's Law
24. The Palace ★★★ $$$
25. Paul and Harvey's
26. Peppermill
27. Pizzeria Uno ★ $
28. RoadHouse
29. Sam Kee ★★ $$
30. Santa Barbara Grill ★★★ $$
31. Scruffy Murphy's
32. Spoons Grill & Bar
33. Stoddard's Brewhouse ★★ $$
34. Tung Kee Noodle House ★★ ¢
35. Yiassoo ★ ¢

PLACES TO STAY

36. Cupertino Inn $$$
37. Radisson Inn $$$
38. Wyndham Garden Hotel $$$

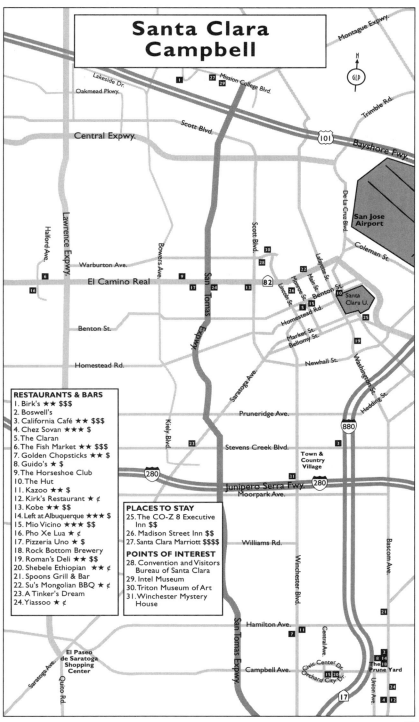

Santa Clara
Campbell

RESTAURANTS & BARS
1. Birk's ★★ $$$
2. Boswell's
3. California Café ★★ $$$
4. Chez Sovan ★★★ $
5. The Claran
6. The Fish Market ★★ $$$
7. Golden Chopsticks ★★ $
8. Guido's ★ $
9. The Horseshoe Club
10. The Hut
11. Kazoo ★★ $
12. Kirk's Restaurant ★ ¢
13. Kobe ★★ $$
14. Left at Albuquerque ★★★ $
15. Mio Vicino ★★★ $$
16. Pho Xe Lua ★ ¢
17. Pizzeria Uno ★ $
18. Rock Bottom Brewery
19. Roman's Deli ★★ $
20. Shebele Ethiopian ★★ ¢
21. Spoons Grill & Bar
22. Su's Mongolian BBQ ★ ¢
23. A Tinker's Dream
24. Yiassoo ★ ¢

PLACES TO STAY
25. The CO-Z 8 Executive Inn $$
26. Madison Street Inn $$
27. Santa Clara Marriott $$$$

POINTS OF INTEREST
28. Convention and Visitors Bureau of Santa Clara
29. Intel Museum
30. Triton Museum of Art
31. Winchester Mystery House

Downtown Saratoga

BARS & RESTAURANTS
1. The Bank
2. Bella Saratoga ★★ $$
3. La Fondue ★★ $$
4. La Mere Michelle ★★ $$$$
5. Le Mouton Noir ★★★ $$$$
6. Mandarin Chef ★★ $
7. Sent Sovi ★★★ $$$$
8. Viaggio ★★ $$$

PLACES TO STAY
9. The Inn at Saratoga $$$$

POINTS OF INTEREST
10. Savannah Channel Vineyards
11. Villa Montalvo
12. Youth Science Institute
13. Hakone Gardens

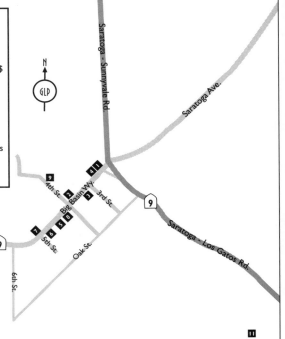

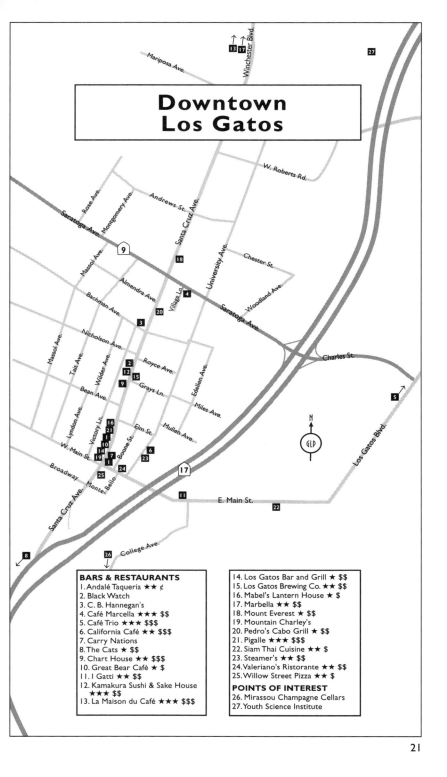

Downtown Los Gatos

BARS & RESTAURANTS
1. Andalé Taqueria ★★ ¢
2. Black Watch
3. C. B. Hannegan's
4. Café Marcella ★★★ $$
5. Café Trio ★★★ $$$
6. California Café ★★ $$$
7. Carry Nations
8. The Cats ★ $$
9. Chart House ★★ $$$
10. Great Bear Café ★ $
11. I Gatti ★★ $$
12. Kamakura Sushi & Sake House ★★★ $$
13. La Maison du Café ★★★ $$$
14. Los Gatos Bar and Grill ★ $$
15. Los Gatos Brewing Co. ★★ $$
16. Mabel's Lantern House ★ $
17. Marbella ★★ $$
18. Mount Everest ★ $$
19. Mountain Charley's
20. Pedro's Cabo Grill ★ $$
21. Pigalle ★★★ $$$
22. Siam Thai Cuisine ★★ $
23. Steamer's ★★ $$
24. Valeriano's Ristorante ★★ $$
25. Willow Street Pizza ★★ $

POINTS OF INTEREST
26. Mirassou Champagne Cellars
27. Youth Science Institute

RESTAURANTS & BARS

1. Agenda Restaurant ★★★ $$
2. Anh Hong ★★ $
3. Aqui ★★★ $
4. Bangkok Cuisine ★★ $
5. Bella Mia ★★ $$
6. B-hive Bar & Lounge
7. Britannia Arms
8. Cactus Club
9. Café Primavera ★ $
10. Caffè Goosetown ★★ $$
11. California Sushi ★★ $$
12. Casa Castillo ★ $
13. Casa Vicky ★ ¢
14. Chacho's ★★ $
15. Chez Sovan ★★ $
16. Cuban International ★ $$
17. Dac Phuc ★ ¢
18. Dos Locos
19. 840 North First ★★ $$$
20. Emile's ★★★ $$$$
21. Eulipia ★★★ $$$
22. Falafel Drive-In ★ ¢
23. The Fish Market ★★ $$$
24. The Flying Pig
25. Fuji ★ $
26. Garden City ★★ $$$
27. Germania at the Hochburg ★ $$
28. Gombei ★★ $
29. Gordon Biersch ★★ $$
30. Habana Cuba ★★ $$
31. Hamburger Mary's
32. Henry's World Famous Hi-Life ★ $
33. Hobee's Restaurant ★★ $
34. Hunan Taste ★★ $
35. Il Fornaio Cucina Italiana ★★ $$
36. Inca Gardens ★★ $
37. JJ's Blues Lounge
38. Katie Blooms
39. Kazoo ★★ $
40. Keystone Coffee Store
41. Kirk's Restaurant ★ ¢
42. Kitahama ★★ $$
43. Korea Buffet ★ $
44. Krung Thai ★★★ $
45. La Forêt ★★★ $$$$
46. La Pastaia ★★★★ $$$
47. La Tropicana
48. Lenny's
49. Le Papillon ★★★ $$$
50. Los Nicas ★ $$
51. Mike's
52. Mission Ale House
53. Ocean Harbor ★★ $
54. Okoyama ★ $
55. Original Joe's ★★ $$
56. Orlo's ★★ $$$
57. Pagoda ★★ $$$
58. Palermo ★★ $$
59. Paolo's ★★★ $$$
60. Patty's Inn
61. Picasso's ★ $
62. Quang Da ★★ $
63. Race Street Seafood Kitchen ★★ ¢
64. Red Sea Restaurant ★★ $
65. Rue de Paris ★★ $$$
66. Saddle Rack
67. Scott's Seafood ★★ $$$
68. Señora Emma's ★ $
69. 71 Saint Peter ★★ $$
70. Shamshiri ★★ $
71. Sousa's ★ $$
72. South First Billiards
73. Spiedo ★★ $$
74. Stratta ★★★ $$
75. Sue's Indian Cuisine ★★ $$
76. Suma Ching Hai International Association Vegetarian House ★★ $
77. Super Taqueria ★ ¢
78. Taiwan Restaurant ★ $
79. Taxi's Hamburgers ★ $
80. Teske's Germania House ★ $$
81. Thepthai ★★ $
82. Tied House
83. Tony and Alba's Pizza ★ $
84. Toon's
85. Tremors
86. Tung Kee Noodle House ★★ ¢
87. The Usual
88. Vaquero's ★★ $$
89. Vung Tao ★★★ $
90. Waves ★ $
91. White Dove Café ★★ $
92. White Lotus ★ $
93. White Rock Café ★★★ $$
94. Willow Street Pizza ★★ $

PLACES TO STAY

95. Best Western Downtown $
96. Doubletree Hotel San Jose $$$$
97. The Fairmont $$$$
98. The Hensley House $$$
99. Hotel De Anza $$
100. Hyatt Sainte Claire $$$$
101. Motel 6 San Jose South $
102. San Jose Hilton and Towers $$$$

POINTS OF INTEREST

103. Art Tech Silicon Valley Institute
104. Center for Beethoven Studies
105. Children's Discovery Museum
106. Chinese Cultural Gardens
107. d. p. Fong Galleries
108. Fallon House
109. Flea Market
110. J. Lohr
111. Japanese Friendship Gardens
112. Lick Observatory
113. Machu Picchu
114. Mirassou Vineyards
115. Municipal Rose Gardens
116. Peralta Adobe
117. Rosicrucian Egyptian Museum & Planetarium
118. San Jose Convention & Visitors Bureau
119. San Jose Historical Museum
120. San Jose Institute of Contemporary Art Galleries
121. San Jose Museum of Art
122. San Jose Museum of Quilts and Textiles
123. St. Joseph's Cathedral
124. Tech Museum of Innovation
125. Trinity Episcopal Church
126. Winchester Mystery House
127. Youth Science Institute

See Sunnyvale Map 41 42

280
Pruneridge Ave.
Stevens Creek Blvd.
Lawrence Expwy.
Prospect Ave.
Saratoga Ave.
4
88
Hamilton Ave.
Campbell Ave.
85
Winchester Blvd.
17
Union Ave.

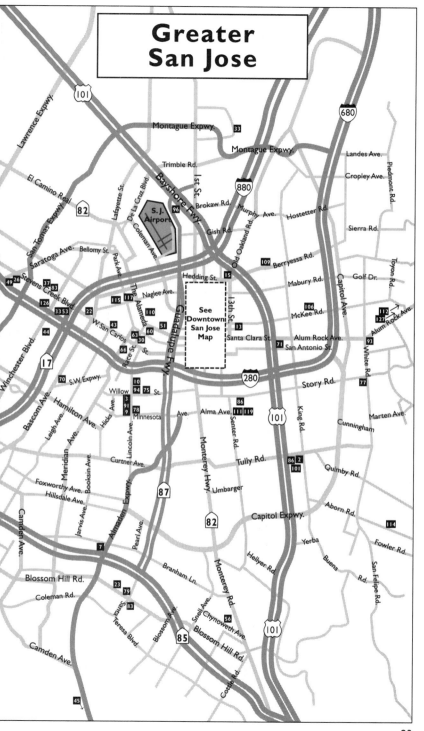

Greater San Jose

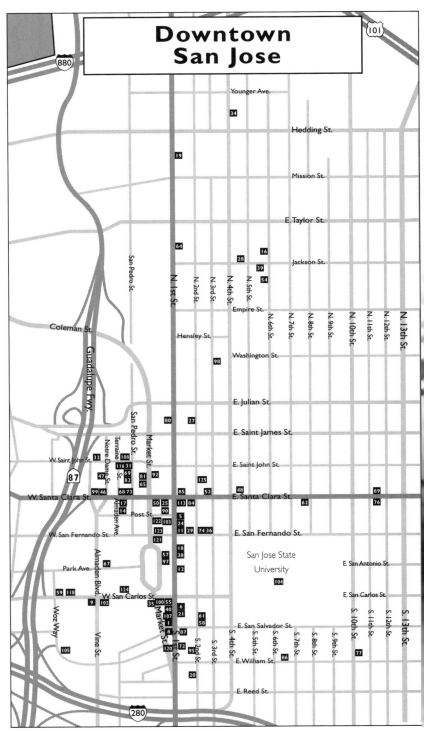

Downtown San Jose

880

101

280

Younger Ave.

Hedding St.

Mission St.

E. Taylor St.

Jackson St.

Coleman St.

San Pedro St.

N. 1st St.
N. 2nd St.
N. 3rd St.
N. 4th St.
N. 5th St.
N. 6th St.
N. 7th St.
N. 8th St.
N. 9th St.
N. 10th St.
N. 11th St.
N. 12th St.
N. 13th St.

Empire St.

Hensley St.

Washington St.

E. Julian St.

E. Saint James St.

E. Saint John St.

W. Saint John St.

Guadalupe Fwy.

San Pedro St.

Notre Dame St.

Terraine St.

Market St.

87

E. Santa Clara St.

W. Santa Clara St.

Almaden Ave.

Post St.

E. San Fernando St.

W. San Fernando St.

San Jose State University

E. San Antonio St.

Park Ave.

Almaden Blvd.

E. San Carlos St.

W. San Carlos St.

Woz Way

Vine St.

Market St.

E. San Salvador St.

S. 2nd St.
S. 3rd St.
S. 4th St.
S. 5th St.
S. 6th St.
S. 7th St.
S. 8th St.
S. 9th St.
S. 10th St.
S. 11th St.
S. 12th St.
S. 13th St.

E. San Salvador St.

E. William St.

E. Reed St.

Basics

The San Francisco Peninsula is many things: a cultural mecca, an economic power-house, a real-estate nightmare. But it is also a beautiful 42-mile stretch of land divid-ing San Francisco Bay from the Pacific Ocean, with the city occupying its narrow tip. From there the Peninsula widens on its way south, merging with the mainland below the bottom of the bay in San Jose. The shoreline is flat and low. Moving west, the ter-rain rises steeply into the Santa Cruz Mountains, which form the Peninsula's spine. Beyond the mountains, the land drops more gradually toward the Pacific.

For thousands of years the Peninsula was inhabited by the Ohlone Indians, who lived peacefully in small tribal settlements. Their way of life was decimated by European settlement, which began after Spanish explorer Don Gaspar de Portola's discovery of San Francisco Bay in October 1769 initiated mission development in the area. A community based on farming grew as Mexican land-grant settlement followed Mexican independence. This way of life expanded with the ousting of the Mexicans by U.S. forces, the Gold Rush in 1849, and statehood in 1850, and continued until World War II. The land was cleared for grazing and farming, the Santa Cruz redwood forests were harvested and milled to supply building materials for the growing city of San Francisco, and small towns sprang up along the railway linking San Francisco and San Jose.

Until World War II, the Santa Clara Valley was an agricultural community filled with orchards, while the northern Peninsula was a country playground for wealthy San Franciscans. During World War II, much of the area was used as a staging ground for troops on their way to the Pacific. After the war, many who had worked here or passed through decided to settle down on the Peninsula, and the population exploded. That sudden growth established much of the area's housing and deter-mined its largely suburban character. The aerospace industry fueled the expansion, spearheaded by major corporations such as Lockheed. Stanford University's proximi-ty gave the trend a technological bent and sowed the seeds for the emergence of Silicon Valley. Over the years, the success of companies like Hewlett-Packard, Apple, Intel, and Netscape has powered the Peninsula's continuing growth. As a result, San Mateo and Santa Clara counties now have some of the highest per capita incomes and housing prices in the nation.

Most of the region's residential development has taken place in the flatlands on the eastern half of the Peninsula. The corridor running south along Hwy 101 is densely settled, as is the stretch along El Camino Real (Hwy 82)—seemingly punctu-ated by a Taco Bell every few miles—which links Daly City with Santa Clara. Before World War II, each town between San Francisco and San Jose had its own unique identity. Rapid postwar population growth sent the communities sprawling into each other, with little of their individuality surviving. With the construction of I-280 paral-leling the foothills of the Santa Cruz Mountains, expansion is now also marching west, especially around San Jose. The Santa Cruz Mountains have been logged exten-sively over the last 150 years, but otherwise remain mostly undisturbed. On the Peninsula's Pacific Coast, development has been centered around Half Moon Bay. But for the most part, the area remains blessedly and primarily agricultural, especially south of Half Moon Bay.

Climate

California owes much of its dramatic population growth in the past 50 years to its attractive Mediterranean climate. Many say the Peninsula's weather is the best in the state, neither too warm nor too cool. In fact, Redwood City adopted the slogan "Climate Best by Government Test" after a local office for the National Climatic Data Center declared that the surrounding area won some sort of climatic beauty contest.

Generally, residents and visitors can look forward to warm days and cool nights year-round. But substantial variations exist from region to region, month to month, and year to year. The coastal areas bear the brunt of winter storms sweeping off the ocean and are cooled—chilled—by wind and fog the rest of the year. The Santa Cruz Mountains wring moisture from winter storms, getting significantly more rainfall than low-lying areas and even some occasional snow. Because the mountains shelter the bayside flatlands from the ocean, most Peninsula residents enjoy warm days and moderate rainfall. The weather gets hotter and drier farther south and east, meaning farther from the ocean. The average year-round daily Peninsula temperature is 70°F, while the nighttime low is 45°F. Daytime highs near 100°F are common during the summer, especially in the South Bay, while freezes happen occasionally during winter evenings in the low valleys. Almost all rainfall comes between October and April, except in El Niño years such as 1997-98. San Francisco and the northern Peninsula average just over 20 inches of rain per year; San Jose, under 14 inches; and Saratoga, almost 30 inches. Anyone familiar with the recent El Niño and prior drought knows how little these averages can mean for any specific year: between 1988 and 1990 San Jose received less than 10 inches each year, while during the winter of 1997-98, San Francisco received almost 50 inches.

Dress, Smoking, Tipping

Dress in California is generally casual. Business types wear their suits, but most high-tech companies allow employees to wear "Gap-casual" clothes, especially on Friday, often an official "dress-down" day. Very few restaurants require a coat and tie, although some may object to a full-blown grunge look. The only restaurants where you might feel out of place without formal dress are old-style Continental restaurants. Still, many people do dress up for a night out.

Smoking generates considerable controversy in California, but most local governments have passed regulations banning smoking in public buildings and work areas, while state law prohibits smoking in restaurants and even bars. (Some towns have even passed laws prohibiting smoking outdoors in areas such as waiting lines and restaurant patios.) Look for crowds of huddled people lighting up outside doorways, and expect clouds of smoke in areas that do allow smoking.

Unless otherwise noted on the menu or the check, restaurants do not include a gratuity on the bill. The standard tip is at least 15 percent of the tab, more for above-average service, less if the service was in some way offensive. (Double the tax for a quick tip calculation.) It is also customary to tip taxi drivers, airport baggage handlers, parking valets, and most hotel service staff.

Information

The following offices can supply you with additional information about the region.

Palo Alto Chamber of Commerce: 325 Forest Ave. (Bryant/Waverley), Palo Alto, 650/324-3121. • M-F 9am-5pm.

San Mateo County Convention and Visitors Bureau: 111 Anza Blvd. #410 (Airport Blvd.), Burlingame, 650/348-7600. • M-F 8:30am-5pm.

San Francisco Visitor Information Center: 900 Market St. lower level (Powell), SF, 415/391-2000; events hotline 415/391-2001. • M-F 9am-5:30pm; Sa 9am-3pm; Su 10am-2pm.

San Jose Convention and Visitors Bureau: 333 W. San Carlos St. #1000 (Almaden/Hwy 87), San Jose, 408/295-9600, 800/SAN-JOSE (726-5673). www.sanjose.org. • M-F 8am-5:30pm.

Convention and Visitors Bureau of Santa Clara: 1850 Warburton Ave. (Scott), Santa Clara, 408/244-9660. • M-F 8am-5pm.

Emergencies

If you are faced with an emergency that threatens life or property and demands immediate attention, dial 911 on any telephone. You will be connected with an emergency operator who will immediately direct your call to the appropriate place. Do not use this number if you do not have an emergency. To reach the police or some other agency for a nonemergency question, look up the number in your local phone book.

Special Resources

Resources for the Disabled

Adult Independence Development Center of Santa Clara County: 1601 Civic Center Dr. #100 (Lincoln/El Camino Real), Santa Clara, 408/985-1243.

Center for Independent Living: 355 Gellert Blvd. #256 (Hickey), Daly City, 650/991-5124. • 875 O'Neill Ave. (El Camino Real), Belmont, 650/595-0783.

Peninsula Center for the Blind & Visually Impaired: 2470 El Camino Real #107 (California), Palo Alto, 650/858-0202, 800/660-2009.

RCH Inc. (formerly Recreation Center for the Handicapped): 207 Skyline Blvd. (Lake Merced/Harding), SF, 415/665-4100.

Resources for the Elderly

Information and Referral Services, Inc.: 408/345-4532, 800/255-9333.

Retired & Senior Volunteer Program (RSVP): 1125 Quintara St. (20th Ave./21st. Ave.), SF, 415/731-3335. • 100 S. San Mateo Dr. (Peninsula), San Mateo, 650/696-4195. • 450 Bryant St. (University/Lytton), Palo Alto, 650/326-5362. • 1190 S. Bascom Ave. #220 (Stokes), San Jose, 408/277-4101.

San Mateo County Aging & Adult Services: 800/675-8437 (information and referral).

Senior Focus: Wellness Center in Mills Hospital, 100 S. San Mateo Dr. (Baldwin/2nd), San Mateo, 650/696-4190, 800/654-9966.

Resources for Gays and Lesbians

The best place to find out about gay and lesbian groups and activities is in San Francisco. Start by flipping through the *Bay Times*, the *Bay Area Reporter*, and *The Sentinel*, the three major free gay publications stocked by the city's gay cafés, bars, and bookstores. The Castro, with many gay-owned businesses, is the major meeting place in the city, although more so for gay men than for lesbians.

Bay Area Reporter: 395 9th St. (Harrison), SF, 415/861-5019.

The Lavender Pages: 800/440-4446, www.lavender.com.

Lyric Youth Talk and Info. Line: 800/246-7743.

New Leaf: 1853 Market St. (Guerrero), SF, 415/626-7000.

Resources for Women

Crisis Pregnancy Center of Santa Clara County: 2425 California St. (Showers), Mountain View, 650/964-8093.

Planned Parenthood: 219 South Gate Ave. (Lake Merced), Daly City, 650/991-3092. • 2211 Palm Ave. (25th/El Camino), San Mateo, 650/574-2622. • 1230 Hopkins Ave. (El Camino/Birch), Redwood City, 650/367-1933. • 170 Middlefield Rd. (Willow), Menlo Park, 650/328-1300. • 225 San Antonio Rd. (California), Mountain View, 650/948-0807. • 12345 El Monte Rd. (Moody), Los Altos Hills, 650/949-7243. • 604 E. Evelyn Ave. (Fair Oaks), Sunnyvale, 408/739-5151. • 1691 The Alameda (Naglee), San Jose, 408/287-7526. • 3131 Alum Rock Ave. (White) San Jose, 408/729-7600.

Rape Crisis Hotline: 415/647-7273, 408/779-2115.

Support Network for Battered Women: 650/940-7855. 24-hour hotline.

Women's Community Clinic: 696 E. Santa Clara St. (15th), San Jose, 408/287-4090.

Other Resources

Center for African and African-American Art & Culture: 762 Fulton St. (Webster), SF, 415/928-8546.

Chinese Cultural Center: Holiday Inn, 750 Kearny St., 3rd Fl., SF, 415/986-1822.

Jewish Community Information & Referral: 415/777-4545.

Mexican-American Community Services Agency: 130 N. Jackson Ave. (McKee/Alum Rock), San Jose, 408/928-1122.

Mission Cultural Center: 2868 Mission St. (24th St./25th St.), SF, 415/821-1155 (for Latino resources).

National Veterans Foundation: 800/366-8823.

North California Coalition for Immigrant Rights: 415/543-6769 for Chinese/Japanese/English, 415/543-6767 for Spanish/English.

North Peninsula Neighborhood Service Center: 600 Linden Ave. (California), South San Francisco, 650/588-8822.

Suicide Prevention Crisis Line: San Francisco 415/781-0500; north San Mateo County 650/692-6655; south San Mateo County 650/368-6655; Santa Clara County 650/494-8420; central San Jose 408/279-3312; south San Jose 408/683-2482.

United Way: 650/325-4636.

Notes for Foreigners

Passports/Visas

Visitors to the United States must have a valid passport and many must also have a U.S. visa, one for either a temporary stay or permanent residence. A visitor's visa allows the holder to come into the United States temporarily for business and/or pleasure (B-1) or for medical treatment (B-2). There are other visas for students, workers, and so forth (contact your consulate). The Visa Waiver Pilot Program exempts travelers who are coming to the United States for tourism or business for 90 days or less. Visitors to the United States from many nations can enter without a visa if they receive either a Waiver for Tourism (WT) or a Waiver for Business (WB). Visitors from other nations need to obtain a U.S. visa from the U.S. consulate in their home country. If you want to apply for an extension of your visa, contact the U.S. Justice Department's **Immigration & Naturalization Service**, 630 Sansome St., Rm. 200 (Washington/Jackson), SF, 415/705-4411. M-Tu 7am-3:30pm, W 7am-2:45pm, Th-F 7am-3:30pm; by phone M-F 8:15am-5:30pm.

Consulates

Many of the foreign consulates in San Francisco (and a few in San Jose and Los Angeles) are listed below. Consult the phone book for more listings.

Austria: 41 Sutter St. #207 (Sansome/Montgomery), SF, 415/951-8911.

Australia: 1 Bush St. (Market/Battery), SF, 415/362-6160.

Belgium: 625 3rd St. (Brannan), SF, 415/882-4648.

Brazil: 300 Montgomery St. #900 (Pine/California), SF, 415/981-8170. .

Canada: 550 S. Hope St., 9th Fl. (6th), Los Angeles, 213/346-2700.

China: 1450 Laguna St. (Geary), SF, 415/674-2900.

Denmark: 601 Montgomery St. #440 (Clay), SF, 415/391-0100.

France: 540 Bush St. (Grant/Stockton), SF, 415/397-4330.

Germany: 1960 Jackson St. (Gough/Octavia), SF, 415/775-1061.

India: 540 Arguello Blvd. (Geary/Anza), SF, 415/668-0683.

Ireland: 44 Montgomery St. #3830 (Post/Sutter), SF, 415/392-4214.

Israel: 456 Montgomery St. #2100 (California/Sacramento), SF, 415/398-8885.

Italy: 2590 Webster St. (Broadway), SF, 415/931-4924. • 95 S. Market St. #300 (Post), San Jose, 408/971-9170.

Japan: 50 Fremont St., 23rd Fl. (Mission/Market), SF, 415/777-3533.

Korea: 3500 Clay St. (Laurel), SF, 415/921-2251.

Mexico: 870 Market St. #528 (4th St./5th St.), SF, 415/392-5554. • 380 N. 1st St. #102 (Bassett), San Jose, 408/294-3414.

Netherlands: 1 Maritime Plaza (Clay at Front), SF, 415/981-6454.

New Zealand: 1 Maritime Plaza #700 (Clay at Front), SF, 415/399-1255.

Norway: 20 California St., 6th Fl. (Davis), SF, 415/986-0766.

Philippines: 447 Sutter St., 6th Fl. (Stockton/Powell), SF, 415/433-6666.

Russia: 2790 Green St. (Baker), SF, 415/202-9800.

Singapore: 1670 Pine St., 2nd Fl. (Van Ness/Franklin), SF, 415/928-8508.

Spain: 1405 Sutter St. (Franklin/Gough), SF, 415/922-2995 or 922-2996.

Sweden: 120 Montgomery St. #2175 (Sutter/Bush), SF, 415/788-2631.

Switzerland: 456 Montgomery St. #1500 (Sacramento), SF, 415/788-2272.

Taiwan (Coordinate Council for North American Affairs): 555 Montgomery St. #1002 (Clay/Sacramento), SF, 415/362-7680.

U.K.: 1 Sansome St. #850 (Sutter/Market), SF, 415/981-3030.

Money/Foreign Exchange

Changing money in America is more difficult than in most countries. Unlike banks in the rest of the world (or so it seems), most banks in the United States will not readily change foreign currency into U.S. currency. A bank's main branch in San Francisco's Financial District might offer currency exchange, especially if it is an international bank (a branch of a European or Asian operation). Otherwise, your most convenient option for the exchange of foreign currency, traveler's checks, or wire transfers is to try one of the dedicated exchange businesses like American Express or Thomas Cook (although these services usually have less favorable exchange rates than banks). The list below includes most local offices, but you'll notice that more often than not they are in San Francisco (or SFO airport). Before your arrival in the United States, you may want to consider buying traveler's checks in U.S. dollars.

If you (or a friend) has a local bank account, you have a few more exchange options. Most bank branches will buy your foreign currency, although they will not give you cash. Instead, they will deposit the cash into your account.

Consequently, the quickest way to get money in Silicon Valley is from one of the ubiquitous Automated Teller Machines (ATMs). Branches are plentiful, although most California banks charge a fee ranging from $1 to $3 for the service (in addition to any fee your own bank may charge). A few smaller banks are promoting No Surcharge ATMs; look for the label on the machine. On the plus side, when you use an ATM, you usually end up with a better exchange rate than if you change cash or traveler's checks.

San Francisco International Airport has two Bank of America branches, as well as B of A and American Express ATMs in every terminal. Foreign exchange is available at the B of A in the international terminal (departure level) daily from 7am to 11pm, 650/742-8081.

At **San Jose Airport**, you can find Thomas Cook, 800/287-7362, at Terminal C from 8:30am to 4:30pm weekdays, at Terminal A from 9am to 11:40am, at Baggage Claim 3 from 1pm to 3pm, and at Gate 16 from 11am to 12:30pm.

AFEX: 201 Sansome St. (Pine), SF, 415/781-7683.

American Express: 455 Market St. (1st St.), SF, 415/536-2600. • 560 California St. (Kearny/Montgomery), SF, 415/536-2600. • 124 Geary St. (Grant/Stockton), SF, 415/398-8578. • 333 Jefferson St. (Jones/Leavenworth), SF, 415/775-0240. • 250 University Ave. (Ramona/Bryant), Palo Alto, 650/327-3711. • 5155 Stevens Creek Blvd. (Lawrence), Santa Clara, 408/244-1015.

Thomas Cook: 800/287-7362. • 75 Geary St. (Kearny/Grant), SF. • 1 Powell St. (Eddy/Ellis), in the B of A, SF. • 86 Stanford Shopping Center (El Camino and Quarry), Palo Alto.

Pacific Foreign Exchange Inc.: 527 Sutter St. (Powell/Mason), SF, 415/391-2548.

Worldwide Foreign Exchange: 150 Cyril Magnin St. (Ellis/O'Farrell), SF, 415/392-7283.

Media

Newspapers

There's no shortage of media in the area. Nearly every town has its own free weekly that is delivered to all residents. (Palo Alto has the *Palo Alto Daily,* a relatively new paper with a feisty attitude designed to ruffle feathers at the more established *Palo Alto Weekly,* which is actually published twice a week.) The advent of desktop publishing has created a staggering number of other free publications that cover specific geographic areas and special interests (children, biking, children who bike, and so forth).

The *San Jose Mercury News* is San Jose's daily newspaper and the best place to find the inside scoop on Silicon Valley and other high-tech stories. The "Merc" tends to have in-depth stories actually written by its reporters, not just pulled from wire services. San Mateo County is served by the *San Mateo Times,* a smaller daily paper that was family run until it was recently acquired by a large chain.

Although San Francisco is the Bay Area's regional center, in the opinion of many people weaned on the *New York Times* and *Washington Post,* its two daily journalistic offerings suffer in comparison. Both read like small-town papers, heavy on local issues (especially political infighting) and sports. The larger circulation, morning-edition *Chronicle* is often called the "Comical" for its thin national and international news section, top-heavy with wire copy. The afternoon *Examiner* has struggled in recent years, with periodic rumors surfacing of a merger with the *Chronicle* or a shutdown, but it continues to grab readers with its screaming front page of bold, large-point headlines in the tradition of founder William Randolph Hearst. In recent years, the *Examiner* has worked at being a gadfly to city government, frequently running stories on mismanagement in city hall. The two papers combine to produce one Sunday edition, which includes the "Datebook" section (better known as the "pink pages"), one of the most comprehensive guides to arts and entertainment in the Bay Area.

Four major alternative free weeklies service the area. All provide extensive arts and entertainment listings as well as in-depth reporting with a leftist edge. The *Metro* covers Silicon Valley (there is also a Santa Cruz edition) and has done a lot to promote the region's identity as something distinct from San Francisco and even the Bay Area at large. The *San Francisco Bay Guardian* and *SF Weekly* attempt to outdo each other in their coverage of what's happening in San Francisco. The *East Bay Express* covers the East Bay scene, and is notable for its long but generally well-written cover stories.

Television

2	**KTVU**	Oakland (Fox)
4	**KRON**	San Francisco (NBC)
5	**KPIX**	San Francisco (CBS)
7	**KGO**	San Francisco (ABC)

9	**KQED**	San Francisco (PBS)
11	**KNTV**	San Jose (ABC)
14	**KDTV**	San Francisco (Univision/Spanish)
20	**KOFY**	San Francisco (WB)
36	**KICU**	San Jose (Ind)
44	**KBHK**	San Francisco (UPN)
54	**KTEH**	San Jose (PBS)
60	**KCSM**	San Mateo (PBS)

AM Radio

560	**KSFO**	Often-outrageous right-wing talk.
610	**KFRC**	Oldies from the '50s and '60s. Same as 99.7 FM.
680	**KNBR**	Mostly sports talk (NBC).
740	**KCBS**	Round-the-clock news, weather, and traffic. Solid reporting (CBS).
810	**KGO**	News/talk radio (ABC).
910	**KNEW**	"Real" country and western music, i.e., Garth *and* Merle.
1010	**KIQI**	Spanish-language programming.
1510	**KKHI**	Same as 100.9 FM.

FM Radio

88.5	**KQED**	SF's major public radio station. NPR, BBC, and local talk shows.
89.5	**KPOO**	SF community radio, with varied multiethnic music. Hard to pick up, worth finding.
89.7	**KFJC**	Foothill College radio. Diverse and progressive.
90.1	**KZSU**	Stanford University radio. Rock, rap, etc.
90.3	**KUSF**	University of San Francisco radio. Award-winning, diverse, lots of "college" rock.
90.7	**KALX**	University of California Berkeley radio. Eclectic.
91.1	**KCSM**	San Mateo public radio. Good jazz programming.
91.7	**KALW**	"Information Radio." Superb commercial-free programs; NPR, BBC, CBC, and local.
92.3	**KSJO**	Album-oriented rock, although more Nirvana than Van Halen.
92.7	**KZSF**	Nonmariachi Hispanic music.
93.3	**KYCY**	"Young" country music, i.e., Garth Brooks.
94.1	**KPFA**	Berkeley public radio and the flagship of the liberal Pacifica network. Diverse music and talk.
94.5	**KBAY**	"The Bay," soft rock.
94.9	**KYLD**	Rhythm and blues and hip hop. Was Wild 107 before it switched dial locations with KSAN.
95.3	**KRTY**	San Jose's "hot" country.
95.7	**KZQZ**	"Today's hits," meaning commercial club music.
96.5	**KOIT**	Light rock—*very* light rock—and love songs at night.
97.3	**KLLC**	"Alice," a new format going after the 20- to-34-year-old female demographic. Principally plays women vocalists and female-fronted rock bands (from Sarah McLachlan to Garbage).
98.1	**KISQ**	"Kiss FM." Motown, soul, "make-out music."
98.5	**KUFX**	"K-FOX", classic—Jurassic—rock in San Jose means Clapton and Credence.

98.9	**KSOL**	Spanish-language pop music.
99.7	**KFRC**	"More oldies." Enough said.
100.9	**KKHI**	Classical music.
101.3	**KIOI**	"K101." The closest thing to adult contemporary/Top 40 radio in San Francisco.
102.1	**KDFC**	Well-programmed commercial classical station. Lots of Lexus ads.
102.9	**KBLX**	"Quiet Storm." Another way of saying mellow adult contemporary.
103.7	**KKSF**	Easy listening jazz.
104.5	**KFOG**	Baby boomer–friendly contemporary and classic rock (Beatles to Dave Matthews) played by excellent, knowledgeable DJs. Lots of commercials.
105.3	**KITS**	"Live 105." Modern rock. Recently slanted programming towards a young, male audience. Howard Stern in the morning.
106.1	**KMEL**	"The People's Station." Rhythm-based dance and lots of rap.
107.7	**KSAN**	'60s and '70s popular rock (Bachman Turner Overdrive, Peter Frampton).

Phones

Pacific Bell, which was purchased by Southwest Bell Communications of San Antonio, Texas, is the local phone company throughout most of Northern California (GTE serves a very small portion of San Jose and much of the Gilroy area). Contact them at 800/750-2355 to establish new service, but be prepared to pay a setup fee of approximately $40 per line plus wiring charges for installation of jacks; you are free to do the wiring yourself or hire a third-party contractor.

Basic monthly service costs $11.25 for unlimited local calls (calls within 16 miles) and $6 for measured rate service (per-minute charges for all local calls). In addition, you will be charged various monthly access fees and taxes and for local toll calls (local "intraLATA" calls over 16 miles). Two-person households with an annual income of less than $16,000 may qualify for one of Pac Bell's discount plans; your customer service agent is not likely to volunteer this information without asking.

California is on the cutting edge of telephone deregulation. Thanks to the Telecommunications Act of 1996, the California Public Utilities Commission (CPUC) now allows competition among phone companies for local service. In addition to Pacific Bell, you can use AT&T, Sprint, MCI/Worldcom, or almost any other phone company for these calls. (Call the CPUC at 800/649-7570 for a complete list of approved carriers.) Comparing phone companies can be a bit confusing, as most offer a variety of savings deals based on which combination of services you use (local, long distance, cellular, internet, paging). Even if you stick with Pacific Bell for local service, you can still use these other companies for local toll calls, although you will probably have to dial an access code (10ATT, 10-10321, or similar) before dialing the number you are calling.

Public telephones were also deregulated as part of the 1996 Telecommunications Act. Scary as it sounds, there is no way of knowing what a call from a pay phone will cost these days, although most pay phones currently charge 35 cents for a local call of up to 15 minutes. Pay phone operators can also charge whatever they want for directory information (411) calls. More important, for local toll calls (calls over 16 miles) and long-distance calls, these phones can charge obscene rates. These charges can apply whether paid for with coins or charged to a calling card (unless you initiate your calling card call by dialing a special 800 number offering guaranteed rates). Pay phones owned and operated by Pacific Bell are typically more reliable than those run by other operators.

Utilities

Pacific Gas and Electric (PG&E) provides local gas and electric service to most homes in the area, with the exception of the towns of Palo Alto and Santa Clara. You can call PG&E at 800/743-5000 (they'll transfer you to your local office if need be) or consult the phone book for the office nearest you. Palo Alto is serviced by the Palo Alto Utilities Company; their customer service number is 650/329-2161. Santa Clara's gas service is handled by PG&E, and their electric company, Santa Clara Utilities, can be reached at 408/984-3044.

As with phones, California is pushing ahead with deregulation of gas and electricity. The general idea is that PG&E will continue to deliver the power, but you can purchase it from a variety of suppliers. For electricity, the California Public Utilities Commission (CPUC) keeps a list of registered Electric Service Providers (ESPs); you can verify a potential supplier's registration status by calling 800/555-7809 or checking out the CPUC web site at www.cpuc.ca.gov. Although natural gas follows a similar system, in practice it is primarily large companies and institutions taking advantage of buying gas on the open market. For more information about these changes, contact the CPUC at 800/555-7809 or 800/253-0500 or visit their web site www.cpuc.ca.gov. PG&E also maintains an information line at 800/743-0040. Customers of Palo Alto and Santa Clara's utility services are regulated by a separate deregulation timetable. Contact the utility directly to learn more.

Because the climate is moderate, many homes and apartments are poorly insulated, and you can expect to use heat intermittently from October to April, especially if you live in the hills. Air-conditioning is helpful on many summer days, particularly as you move south toward San Jose. Most cities are responsible for their own water and garbage services. Curbside recycling is common in most communities.

Seasonal Events

All of these events have loyal followings, attracting significant crowds. If you have to drive to reach an event, go early or prepare to get stuck in traffic.

January-February

Chinese New Year (San Francisco). Stretches over three weeks and culminates with the Golden Dragon Parade, which winds its way through Chinatown usually sometime in mid-February. Call the Chinatown Chamber of Commerce at 415/982-3000.

Cinequest, The San Jose Film Festival (San Jose). Call 408/995-5033 for information.

Clam Chowder Cook-Off (Santa Cruz). Held on the Beach Boardwalk. Find out more or enter your chowder at 408/423-5590.

March

St. Patrick's Day Parade (San Francisco). The parade takes place the Sunday before March 17 every year. Call the United Irish Cultural Center at 415/661-2700.

April

Coe Back Country Weekend (Gilroy). Call 408/848-4006 for information.

San Francisco International Film Festival (San Francisco). Call 415/931-FILM (3456).

May

Cinco de Mayo (San Jose). Details at 408/258-0663.

Cinco de Mayo (San Francisco). Call 415/647-8622.

Bay to Breakers (San Francisco). Takes place the third Sunday of May. Call 415/777-7770.

Carnaval (San Francisco). Call 415/826-1401.

June

Santa Cruz Mountains Winegrowers Vintners' Festival (Santa Cruz Mountains). Call the Winegrowers Association at 408/479-WINE (9463).

Monterey Bay Blues Festival (Monterey). Call 408/394-2652 for details.

San Francisco Lesbian, Gay, Bisexual, and Transgender Pride Celebration (San Francisco). Locally known as the Gay Parade. Call 415/864-3733 for more information.

July

California Rodeo (Salinas). The California Rodeo office can be reached at 800/771-8807.

San Jose International Mariachi Festival (San Jose). The Mexican Heritage Corporation at 408/292-5197 can give you details.

Santa Clara County Fair (San Jose). Call 408/494-3100 for dates and information.

Gilroy Garlic Festival (Gilroy). The Gilroy Garlic Festival has it all: garlic ice cream, people dressed as garlic, garlic art projects for kids. Call 408/842-6436.

Independence Day (San Francisco). If you've never seen fireworks in the fog, you've got to check it out. Call 415/777-8498.

August

San Jose Jazz Festival (San Jose). Call the San Jose Jazz Society at 408/288-7557.

Monterey County Fair (Monterey). Call 408/372-5863.

Tapestry in Talent's Festival of the Arts (San Jose). International cuisine, art, music, and other activities make this three-day event worth a visit. Call 408/293-9728 for details.

San Mateo County Expo and Fair (San Mateo). Carnival rides, farm animals, and cotton candy. Call 650/574-3247.

September

Fiestas Patrias (San Jose). Call 408/258-0663 for information.

Monterey Jazz Festival (Monterey). The folks who put it all together can be reached on weekdays at 408/373-3366.

Pacific Coast Fog Festival (Pacifica). Find out more at 650/359-1460.

SoFA Festival (San Jose). The San Jose Downtown Association at 408/279-1775 can give you dates and details.

Opera in the Park (San Francisco). Performed the Sunday after the first performance of the season. Call 415/861-4008.

Festival de las Americas (San Francisco). Held in late September. Call 415/826-1401.

SF Blues Festival (San Francisco). Call 415/826-6837 or 415/979-5588.

October

Half Moon Bay Pumpkin Festival and Great Pumpkin Weigh-Off (Half Moon Bay). Call 650/726-4485 for more information.

Half Moon Bay Bluegrass Festival (Half Moon Bay). Call 650/726-9652.

Return of the Monarchs/Welcome Back Monarchs Day (Santa Cruz). Call 408/423-4609 for details.

Halloween (San Francisco). Recently moved to the Civic Center. Show up in sequins or a serious costume or prepare to be ostracized as a lowly spectator.

November and December

For a local winter wonderland, check out San Jose's **Christmas in the Park**. It comes complete with Santa's village and the old bearded boy himself right in the middle of downtown San Jose. Call 408/277-3303 for more information. Palo Alto has its own celebration, on Fulton Street—known as **Christmas Tree Lane**—where the neighbors go all out decorating their houses with Christmas lights worthy of Las Vegas.

Transportation

DRIVING & AUTOMOBILES

Because California is the land of the automobile, it is also the land of automobile regulations. Bringing a car in the state from another state has its hassles, not the least of which is cost. Under state law, if you don't obtain California registration at the Department of Motor Vehicles (DMV) within 20 days of establishing California residency, you face a stiff fine. (You become a resident when you vote, your dependents attend public schools, you file for a home owner's property tax exemption, or you obtain any other privilege or benefit not ordinarily extended to nonresidents.) When you make your home here, you must also get a California driver's license within 10 days (see below). A word to the wise: California law requires wearing a safety belt, and police frequently issue tickets to violators.

Auto Registration

Perhaps you've already heard the horror stories about the DMV—long lines, endless forms, and bored, condescending staff. Well, it's all true. Going to the DMV is a long, complicated, and exceedingly frustrating exercise in bureaucracy. But you can save yourself some of the agony by calling ahead to make an appointment.

To register your car, you must fill out an application, present a California smog certificate, and show your out-of-state registration and title. Call ahead and the DMV will mail an application. Fill out the form carefully, since mistakes can cost you. For example, if you go to the DMV more than 20 days after the date you claim to have moved here, the DMV slaps you with a penalty. You should also know that your registration cost depends on your car's value. In other words, think twice before you brag that your 1971 bug is a priceless classic. In general, find out how the DMV will treat any information before you volunteer it. (But remember, making false statements to the DMV is a crime.)

You must also have your car's smog emissions checked no more than 90 days before you go to register. Many gas stations and repair shops perform this service. The fee varies from $20 to $50, but all shops must abide by certain rules regarding repairs and retesting on cars that fail the tests. Unfortunately, because California has the strictest auto emissions standards in the nation, most out-of-state cars don't comply with California smog regulations. Even after you get your smog certificate, you'll most likely be required to pay a $300 smog-impact fee. The certificate indicates that your car is as clean as it can be; the fee is because your car's best isn't good enough.

And as if this weren't enough, if you bought your car less than 90 days before you entered California, you'll also owe any difference between California's fairly hefty sales tax and the sales tax you paid in the state of purchase.

There's no escaping the DMV by purchasing a car within California either. If you purchase a car from a local dealer, he or she is responsible for collecting the fees and submitting the paperwork to the DMV. Within six to eight weeks of the purchase, you should receive a registration card from the DMV. If, however, you purchase a car from, say, your next-door neighbor, you are responsible for notifying the DMV of the transfer within 10 days of purchase (you must file an official form).

Driver's Licenses

Driving tests are normally waived for license renewals and holders of valid out-of-state licenses, so relax if you fit that bill. If you're applying for a new license and you're at least 18 years old, you will be required to pass a written test on road regulations, a vision test (bring your contacts or glasses), and a driving test. You must also prove you are a legal resident. Driving tests are given by appointment only, so call ahead. You supply the car for the test—in full working condition—as well as a licensed driver to accompany you to the test. The $12 application fee is good for three tries within 12 months. Once you've completed this obstacle course, you're photographed and thumbprinted (or fingerprinted, if you have no thumbs) and let loose on the road.

DMV Offices

Daly City: 1500 Sullivan Ave. (Southgate/Eastmoor), 650/994-5700. W 9am-5pm; Th 8am-6:30pm; Sa 8am-5pm (license issues only).

Gilroy: 8200 Church St. (1st/Welburn), 408/842-6488. M, Tu, F 8am-5pm; W 9am-5pm; Th 8am-6:30pm.

Los Gatos: 600 N. Santa Cruz Ave. (Blossom Hill/Roberts), 408/354-6541. M, Tu, F 7am-5pm; W 9am-5pm; Th 8am-6:30pm.

Mountain View: 595 Showers Dr. (El Camino/California), 650/968-0610. M, Tu, F 8am-5pm; W 9am-5pm; Th 8am-6:30pm.

Redwood City: 300 Brewster Ave. (Main/Veterans), 650/368-2837.

San Francisco: 1377 Fell St. (Broderick/Baker), 650/557-1179.

San Jose: 111 W. Alma Ave. (Almaden/Monterey), 408/277-1301. M 8am-6:30pm; Tu, Th-F 8am-5pm; W 9am-5pm.

San Jose/Santa Teresa: 180 Martinvale Ln. (Santa Teresa/Via del Oro), 408/244-4511. Tu, Th-Sa 8am-5pm; W 9am-5pm.

San Mateo: 425 N. Amphlett Blvd. (Poplar/Indian), 650/342-5332.

Santa Clara: 3665 Flora Vista Ave. (El Camino/Benton), 408/277-1640. M-F 8am-5pm.

AAA

You can probably save yourself plenty of grief by joining the American Automobile Association, better known nationwide as AAA, Triple A, or Three As and in Northern California as the California State Automobile Association (CSAA). CSAA helps you register your car and complete many DMV procedures. They also provide emergency road service: they'll tow your car, change your tire, deliver fuel if you run out, and get you into your vehicle if you lock yourself out, usually without asking embarrassing questions. You will, however, be asked to produce your AAA card, so keep it on you or in the car. Other benefits include an information service providing answers to technical questions, diagnostic clinics for low prices, auto maintenance classes, free maps, and traveler's checks. For help on the road, call 800/222-4357, 24 hours a day. Website: www.csaa.com. All the offices listed below are open 8:30am-5pm.

Cupertino: 1601 S. DeAnza Blvd. Suite 148 (Hwy 85/Prospect), 408/996-3553.
Daly City: 455 Hickey Blvd. (Gellert), 650/994-8400.
Palo Alto: 430 Forest Ave. (Waverley), 650/321-0470.
Los Gatos: 101 Blossom Hill Rd. (University), 408/395-6411.
Mountain View: 900 Miramonte Ave. (El Camino Real), 650/965-7000.
Redwood City: 20 El Camino Real (Edgewood), 650/364-0620.
San Francisco: 150 Van Ness Ave. (Hayes), 415/565-2012.
San Jose: 5340 Thornwood Dr. (Santa Teresa/Allen), 408/629-1911.
San Mateo: 1650 S. Delaware St. (16th), 650/572-1160.
Santa Clara: 80 Saratoga Ave. (San Tomas/Stevens Creek), 408/985-9300.
Sunnyvale: 755 S. Bernardo Ave. (El Camino/Remington), 408/739-4422.

Freeway Overview

Two major highways extend the length of the Peninsula, connecting San Jose to San Francisco. The primary commuter route, Hwy 101, slices through the heavily populated region along the bay and is generally crowded and subject to frustrating delays. I-280 rolls through the Santa Cruz Mountain foothills to the west of most settlements, providing beautiful views and high speeds most of the way, in part because access between I-280 and many Peninsula downtowns is via narrow, congested roads. Traffic becomes a problem north of I-380 and south from Cupertino to San Jose.

Only a few major roads connect Hwy 101 to I-280. I-280 traverses the Peninsula in the southern part of San Francisco. I-380 crosses at the narrowest point, near San Francisco International Airport. Hwy 92 runs through the middle of the Peninsula near San Mateo. Hwy 84 links the towns of Woodside and Redwood City (although traffic is stop and go through the traffic lights between Hwy 101 and Alameda de las Pulgas). Newly completed Hwy 85 provides a loop west of San Jose from Mountain View to south San Jose.

TravInfo: 817-1717 (no area code needed in Bay Area; outside Bay Area use 415) Provides transit information covering traffic, construction projects, car and van pooling, public transit, and airport transit.

Two major thoroughfares also connect the San Jose area to the East Bay: I-880 runs along the bay, and is often terribly congested; I-680 takes the inland route to Pleasanton, Walnut Creek, and beyond and is slightly less congested. Two bridges span the southern segment of the bay: Hwy 92, the San Mateo Bridge, connects Foster City on the mid-Peninsula to Hayward; Hwy 84, the Dumbarton Bridge, ties Palo Alto and Menlo Park with Fremont. Both bridges collect the $2 toll only in the westbound direction and have formidable rush-hour traffic. Hwy 237 crosses the mud flats at the southern end of the bay, connecting Santa Clara to Milpitas. Hwy 17 winds and climbs southwest across the mountains to the coastal community of Santa Cruz.

Automobile Rental

A quick glimpse in the phone book reveals no shortage of rental car agencies in the Bay Area. All of the major national organizations are well represented, as are many smaller agencies. Most companies have offices at the San Francisco and San Jose airports, but many maintain operations in downtown San Francisco and throughout the Peninsula as well.

When comparison shopping, remember that rental rates are as volatile as air fares; expect to pay more during the summer, for instance. Always ask about weekend, frequent flyer, student, and AAA discounts. Your rate is usually set when you make the reservation, not when you actually pick up the car, so book during a slow time. Also, many of the best rates are available only at airport locations (not hotel or downtown pickup sites). Be sure to get your confirmation number, in case the rental agency loses your reservation. If you're under 25, you're a special insurance liability, which may be reflected in an extra surcharge. And if you're under 21, most companies won't even talk to you. Many local governments levy additional car rental taxes of up to $5 per day.

Alamo: 800/327-9633.

Avis: 800/831-2847.

Budget: 800/527-0700.

Dollar: 800/800-4000.

Enterprise: 800/325-8007.

Hertz: 800/654-3131.

National: 800/227-7368.

Taxis

A number of taxi companies usually serve each city. Check the Yellow Pages under taxicabs in your area. Even companies with the same name (usually some variation on "yellow") operate independently from their kin in different areas. All cities regulate taxi fares, with the result that rates vary from community to community. In general, though, Bay Area cabs run about $2 per mile. Many companies offer flat and special rates for airport rides, long distances, and specific destinations, as well as senior and student discounts. Most companies encourage calling the night before to reserve a morning cab to the airport. Major operations take credit cards, but always double check when you call for a cab.

PUBLIC TRANSPORTATION

An extensive public transportation network with many interconnecting systems links Bay Area communities. This makes traveling without a car relatively easy, albeit slow. Since there's often more than one way to get someplace, take the time to find the most efficient option.

In terms of buses, Santa Clara Valley Transit Agency (VTA) and San Mateo County (SamTrans) together cover destinations from San Francisco to Gilroy, meeting midpoint at the Stanford Shopping Center. Alameda County Transit (AC Transit) serves the East Bay, while Golden Gate Transit serves the North Bay, each with links to San Francisco. MUNI serves San Francisco. Finally, the Dumbarton Express connects Palo Alto to the East Bay. As for trains, BART connects San Francisco and the northern Peninsula with the East Bay, CalTrain runs down the Peninsula between San Francisco and San Jose (and even Gilroy), VTA operates light rail trains in San Jose and Santa Clara, and MUNI operates some trains in San Francisco. Golden Gate Transit and the Blue & Gold Fleet operate ferries between San Francisco and the North Bay, while the Alameda/Oakland Ferry Service plies the waters between San Francisco and Oakland.

If you need to know more, call the numbers given under the different transportation agencies' listings. Once you get through the frequently busy phone lines, the operators are helpful, and most will send free timetables and maps within a couple of days. If you're stuck as to how to get from one place to another, try calling a visitor information center (see Basic Information section). Check out www.transitinfo.org for information on AC Transit, BART, CalTrain, Golden Gate Transit, SamTrans, MUNI, and VTA.

AC Transit: 817-1717 (no area code needed in Bay Area; outside area, add 415). AC Transit covers the East Bay from Richmond to Milpitas, with stops at every BART station. Transbay buses run from Oakland to San Francisco's Transbay Terminal via the Bay Bridge, mostly during rush hour. Although the buses are a bit run-down, they are the most effective way to cover short distances, such as from your home to a BART station. BART is faster for longer distances. Express routes, which operate only during rush hour, cover from downtown Oakland as far south as San Leandro and Hayward.

Fares for local or intercity express buses are $1.25 for adults and youths aged 13 to 17 (the fare for youths aged 5 to 12, seniors, and the disabled is 60 cents). Transbay routes cost $2.20 (youths, seniors, and the disabled travel for $1.10). Monthly passes for the East Bay only are $45 for adults, while a transbay pass is $75. Local passes can be upgraded to get across the bay for $1.10 round-trip. Books of 10 local bus tickets are priced at $10, and books of 10 transbay tickets run $18; both are sold at local stores. Request a transfer (an extra 25 cents) when you purchase your ticket. Purchase bus-BART transfers (valid only for the bus stop outside that particular BART station) for $1 in BART stations. Generally, buses run every 30 minutes during the day, every 15 minutes during commute hours, and every 30 or 60 minutes evenings and weekends. Passenger lifts are available on all AC Transit bus routes.

Alameda/Oakland Ferry Service: 510/522-3300. These ferries operate year-round between Oakland, Alameda, and San Francisco (Pier 39 and the Ferry Building). In Oakland they leave from Jack London Square and in Alameda from the Main Street Terminal; both locations have free parking.

On weekdays, ferries to San Francisco run every 30 to 60 minutes from 6am to 8:55pm. Ferries depart San Francisco from 6:30am to 8:25pm. Weekend ferries depart for San Francisco from 10am to 7:10pm, while ferries depart from San Francisco from 9:15am to 6:30pm. The journey is about 30 minutes.

Tickets and passes are purchased on the ferry or through the Regional Transit Connection (RTC) program at participating Bay Area businesses. The cost one way is $4.50 for adults, $3.25 for active military personnel, $2.75 for seniors and the disabled, and $1.75 for youths aged 5 to 12. Children under 5 are free. The 10-ticket package costs $35, 20 tickets cost $60, and the monthly pass is $115. All tickets include a free transfer on AC Transit or MUNI.

On summer weekends, the ferry operates from Oakland and Alameda to Angel Island State Park. Departures to the island are at 10:50am from Oakland and at 11am from Alameda. Arrival time at Angel Island is approximately 11:50am. The return trip departs from the island at 4:45pm, arriving at Alameda and Oakland at 5:35pm and 5:45pm, respectively. (*Note:* you should verify schedules as they are likely to change without notice.) Tickets include park admission and are purchased on the ferry. Fares are $13 for adults, $9 for seniors and juniors; $6 for children, and kids under 5 are free. Groups of 15 or more require reservations, which are available by calling 415/705-8214. Bicycles are allowed, although space is limited.

BART: 650/992-2278. Bay Area Rapid Transit is a quick, clean way to get from San Francisco to the East Bay. Five tracks go as far as Colma, Richmond, Dublin/Pleasanton, Fremont, and Pittsburg/Bay Point. BART plans to expand south of San Francisco through San Bruno and Millbrae to the airport and may also expand farther south in the East Bay to Warm Springs. Trains run every 15 to 20 minutes, more often during peak hours. Rail service runs daily until midnight starting at 4am on weekdays, 6am on Saturdays, and 8am on Sundays and major holidays.

Fares depend on the distance traveled and range from $1.10 to $4.70 for a one-way ticket. Kids under 4 ride free, and seniors, the disabled, and youths aged 5 to 12 receive a 75 percent discount (call 510/464-7133 for information). All BART trains, stations, and express buses accommodate elderly and disabled riders.

Blue & Gold Fleet: 415/773-1188 for information and 415/705-5555 for sales (www.blueandgoldfleet.com). Because of the recent Blue & Gold Fleet acquisition of the Red & White Fleet operations, all ferries between San Francisco and the East Bay now sail under the Blue & Gold flag. Their confusing menu of services includes both commuter runs and more tourist-oriented trips. Some boats leave from San Francisco's Ferry Building near downtown (especially commuter trips), some depart from Fisherman's Wharf (Pier 39 or Pier 41), and some hit both the Ferry Building and Fisherman's Wharf. Destinations include Sausalito, Tiburon, Oakland, Alameda, Vallejo, Alcatraz, Angel Island, Marine World Africa USA, Sonoma and Napa, and Muir Woods. The line also offers bay cruises.

There are too many schedules to list here, plus times change with the season (typically more service during the summer months); call for a current schedule or visit ticket locations at Pier 39 and Pier 41. The following should give you a rough outline of the operations: ferries between Oakland/Alameda and San Francisco ($4 each way) operate between 6am and 8:25pm on weekdays and 9:15am and 7:10pm on weekends. Between Tiburon and San Francisco ($5.50 each way), weekday service is from 6am to 7:15pm, and weekend service is from 9:30am to 7:30pm. Sausalito service ($5.50 each way) on weekdays is from 11am to 8pm and on weekends is from 10:40am to 7:10pm. Departures to Alcatraz are between 9:30am and 2:15pm. Bay cruises are from 10am to 4pm.

TRANSPORTATION

CalTrain: 800/660-4BUS (4287). Comfortable double-decker trains cruise the Peninsula between San Francisco and San Jose (and Gilroy on weekdays), stopping at stations every two to five miles. CalTrain runs approximately every hour from 5am to 10pm on weekdays, more often during commute hours (northbound in the morning, southbound in the afternoon). Saturday and holiday trains run hourly between 6am and 10pm; Sunday trains ply the same route every two hours from 7am to 10pm. On Friday and Saturday nights, the last train south from San Francisco leaves at midnight. The trip from San Jose to San Francisco takes 90 minutes, while the trip from Palo Alto to San Francisco takes 60 minutes. The journey from San Jose to Gilroy takes about 44 minutes. Rush-hour express trains cut these times significantly.

Fares are based on a zone system (the farther traveled, the more expensive the ticket). Riders can save with a variety of passes, including a 10-ride pass (valid for 60 days within the zones indicated), a monthly pass (call 415/508-7921 for information), and a weekend pass for $9. During the week, if you travel farther than your pass allows, you can pay to upgrade. Youths under 18 get discounts on tickets and monthly passes, and seniors and the disabled qualify for a roughly 50-percent discount. Children 5 to 11 ride for half the adult fare and, if accompanied by an adult, one child under 5 rides free. If you have a MUNI Fast Pass, you may ride CalTrain free on journeys within San Francisco. An important tip: buy your ticket at the station window if it's open, because CalTrain adds a surcharge if you pay your fare on the train when the station is open. Parking for a small fee is available at most stations outside of San Francisco. Each train can carry two wheelchairs and 15 stations have wheelchair lifts.

Dumbarton Express: 817-1717 (no area code needed in Bay Area; outside area, add 415). This small, moderately comfortable bus line runs across its namesake bridge, and is probably the most convenient way to get from the mid-Peninsula to the southern part of the East Bay. The single route connects Palo Alto and the Union City BART station in the East Bay, with a few stops along the way. It runs weekdays only between 5am and 7pm, hourly during the day, and every 15 minutes during rush hour. Local bus fares are $1 for adults, 35 cents for seniors and disabled, and 60 cents for youths. Transbay tickets are $2 for adults and $1 for seniors, youths, and the disabled. Bring exact change. Monthly passes are $65.

Golden Gate Transit: 415/923-2000. Buses run through Marin, Contra Costa, Sonoma, and San Francisco counties, with weekend routes to Stinson Beach and Point Reyes. Bus routes in San Francisco begin at the Transbay Terminal located at First and Mission streets. Basic service operates every 15 to 90 minutes, while commute routes from West Marin to San Francisco operate every 2 to 20 minutes. Bus fares are based on zones and vary from $1.40 to $5.30 for adults, 70 cents to $2.65 for seniors, and $1.05 to $4 for youths. Exact change is required.

Golden Gate Transit also operates two ferry routes, one between San Francisco and Larkspur and the other between San Francisco and Sausalito. Ferries depart San Francisco from the Ferry Building at the foot of Market Street. During commuter hours only, free shuttles are available to and from the ferry terminals and the surrounding areas in Marin and downtown San Francisco. On weekdays, the Larkspur ferry runs every 30 minutes to 2 hours from 5:30am to 8:25pm. On weekends and holidays, the ferry runs between 9:45am and 6:45pm. The Sausalito ferry departs every 75 minutes on weekdays from 7:05am to 8pm; on weekends and holidays it runs from 10:50am to 8:05pm. From Larkspur, the one-way fare is $2.50 on weekdays and $4.25 on weekends and holidays. The Sausalito ferry is $4.25 each way. Seniors receive 50 percent off, while youths aged 6 to 12 get 25 percent off. Discounts are also available for commuters and frequent riders.

Marguerite: 650/723-9362. Although primarily serving the Stanford University community, the red-and-white Marguerite shuttles are also free to the public. The buses run on weekdays only (excluding university holidays) from 6am to 7:45pm. Shuttles swing by every 15 minutes and are an efficient means of getting from CalTrain stations to campus. The Marguerite consists of lines A and B, the SLAC line, the Menlo line, and the downtown express. In addition to the CalTrain stations, other stops include the Stanford Shopping Center, the Stanford Linear Accelerator (SLAC) Center, and the Stanford Medical Center.

MUNI: 415/673-MUNI (6864). Grumbling about the fog and MUNI are two favorite pastimes of San Franciscans. Topping the list of MUNI complaints is the so-called banana service (a bunch of buses come all at once and then the next bus takes forever to arrive). Many buses are run-down, graffiti-covered, and dirty, although some sleek new models are in use. MUNI drivers take a lot of flack, but they generally do a good job coping with an incredibly stressful job. To MUNI's credit, the system it one of the most comprehensive transit systems in the country. Wherever you are in the city, at least one bus stop is within a few minutes' walk. MUNI not only covers San Francisco as thoroughly as the fog, it also ventures down to Daly City.

The system consists of electric buses, diesel buses, five light-rail train routes, and the famous cable cars. The real proof of MUNI's success is that many San Franciscans choose to live without a car. Most bus shelters have a map of the lines (although not every stop has a shelter). Maps of all routes are sold at convenience stores and drugstores; the *Official Street & Transit Map* is the best deal at only $2.

Most buses run from 6am to midnight. The OWL routes run all night from 1am to 5pm; the express (X) lines are fast routes straight downtown during rush hour. limited (L) buses only stop at every third or fourth stop. Buses run from every 2 minutes to every 30 minutes during the day; OWL routes usually run every 30 minutes or so. Sometimes timetables are available on the buses, but buses rarely operate on schedule, so most people just go to the bus stop and wait. Be forewarned: you may be in for the occasional 45-minute wait, especially in the evening.

The train routes (MUNI Metro) run from downtown west along Market Street, branching south and west to various parts of the city; the underground trains are typically faster than buses along equivalent routes, although unpleasantly crowded during rush hour.

Bus, light rail, and tram fare is $1 for adults, 35 cents for youths aged 5 to 17, seniors, and the disabled, and free for kids under 5. A ticket includes one transfer valid for the next 90 minutes. Exact change is required. A monthly Fast Pass costs $35 for adults and $8 for youths, seniors, and the disabled. The pass is also valid for CalTrain within San Francisco. Cable car fare is $2 but doesn't include a transfer (most passes can be used on cable cars).

All buses and rail stations are wheelchair accessible and some bus stops have wheelchair ramps. For the Accessible Services Program call 415/923-6142.

SamTrans: 800/660-4BUS (4287). Nicer than the MUNI or AC Transit, SamTrans provides service throughout San Mateo County with connecting service to San Francisco, San Francisco International Airport, and games at 3Com/Candlestick Park. It connects with BART, CalTrain, AC Transit, Golden Gate Transit, the Dumbarton Express, and the VTA. Passes and transfers from some of these companies are valid on certain SamTrans buses. AC Transit, Dumbarton Express, and VTA take SamTrans monthly passes as local fare credit on their systems at shared stops. A SamTrans monthly pass with a MUNI sticker gives unlimited rides on MUNI in the month indicated.

Buses generally run every 30 or 60 minutes beginning at 5am. Many lines stop around 6pm, although several continue until midnight. Express buses run during commute hours only. On Saturdays, the service is sparse and even more so on Sundays. Bikes are allowed on buses, and park-and-ride lots are found along some routes. All SamTrans buses are wheelchair accessible. The fare for local service is $1 for adults and 50 cents for youths, seniors, and the disabled. Express service is $2 or $2.50 for adults, with limited discounts for youths, seniors, and the disabled. Monthly passes for local buses are $36 for adults and $18 for youths, seniors, and the disabled. Express monthly passes are $72 or $90 for adults and $86 or $100 with a MUNI sticker.

Santa Clara Valley Transportation Authority (VTA): 408/321-2300, 800/894-9908. The VTA operates the buses, light rail system, and historic trolleys within Santa Clara County, branching out to Menlo Park, Milpitas, Saratoga, and Gilroy. Express buses, with park-and-ride lots, run between residential areas and Silicon Valley high-tech centers. Free shuttles serve the San Jose Arena from downtown, light rail stations, and parking garages. Buses also operate to 3Com Park for weekend 49ers games.

The regular adult fare is $1.10, or $1.75 for express commuter services. The youth fare is 60 cents, and seniors and the disabled pay 35 cents. Three children under four can ride free with an adult. Exact change is required. Day passes are also available for a bit more than twice these amounts. Monthly passes cost $35 for adults, $19 for youths, $8 for seniors and the disabled; the monthly express pass is $55. Bus service begins around 6am. Many buses continue until midnight and some until 2am, but a few stop after commute hours. Buses run every 15 to 30 minutes during the day and less frequently in the evening. On weekends and holidays, buses start between 6am and 9am; some run until around 6pm and others as late as midnight. Weekend buses run every 30 to 60 minutes.

Light Rail Transit (LRT) has eight routes: Old Ironsides/Great America, Lockheed, River Oaks, Metro/Airport, Santa Teresa/IBM, Kaiser, Creekside/Ridder Park, and McCarthy. The shuttle to Great America operates every 15 minutes when the park is open. Commuter routes generally operate every 15 minutes during rush hour; weekday service to the airport is every 10 to 15 minutes. The LRT connects to VTA bus lines, CalTrain, SamTrans, AC Transit, BART, Amtrak, and the Dumbarton Bridge Express. Tickets or passes from some of these companies may be accepted as part or full payment toward your VTA ticket, (SamTrans accepts VTA monthly and day passes as full fare at mutual stops.)

The six historic trolleys link the Civic Center and the San Jose Convention Center. They run from 11am to 5:30pm daily along a 1.5 mile route. From Memorial Day to Labor Day, the trolleys operate from 10:30am-6pm weekdays, 2:30-10:30pm weekends.

Most buses accommodate wheelchairs, and all light rail stations are wheelchair accessible (each train takes two wheelchairs).

Transportation for the Elderly and Disabled

Various public transportation agencies have alternatives for those who cannot utilize the regular facilities or vehicles. To secure eligibility, the elderly and disabled must meet each agency's requirements, apply in advance of need, and always call ahead to schedule rides. Check the public transportation listings above for additional information. As with most transportation options, it's wise to compare rates and services. You can also try taxicabs, as certain companies offer paratransit through taxis or vans.

A Firstcall Plus: 408/287-2273. South Bay.

Bay Trans. Co. Inc.: 408/565-9000. Peninsula.

Dial-A-Ride: 408/683-4151. South Bay.

East Bay Paratransit: 510/287-5000 or 800/555-8085. East Bay.

Leo's Paratransit: 415/822-7655. San Francisco.

MV Transportation: 415/468-4300. San Francisco.

On Lok: 415/292-8888 and 415/550-2210. San Francisco.

OUTREACH: 408/436-2865. South Bay.

Paratransit of San Francisco: 415/543-9651. San Francisco.

Redi-Wheels: 650/508-6341. Peninsula service offered through SamTrans.

Semax Transportation: 415/221-5961. San Francisco.

Yellow Paratransit Program: 415/282-2300. San Francisco.

GETTING AWAY

Air Travel

San Jose Airport (SJC) is one of the best-kept secrets around. It's close to most Silicon Valley companies and smaller and easier to navigate than San Francisco International Airport (SFO), but most people still fly into SFO, probably because there are many more flights. SFO travelers should be warned that the current construction of a massive new international terminal means that the airport is a mess, with traffic delays, bumpy roads, and ever-shifting traffic lanes evidence of the chaos. Oakland Airport (OAK) is less convenient but serves bargain airlines like Southwest.

San Francisco International Airport (SFO): 650/876-7809
Oakland Airport (OAK): 510/577-4000.
San Jose Airport (SJC): 408/277-4759.

Airport Transportation

Driving and Parking

San Francisco International Airport is located 14 miles south of San Francisco. Choose your route to SFO depending on your starting point and traffic; bad congestion, especially on Hwy 101 when there is a game at Candlestick/3Com Park, can cause severe delays. Take Hwy 101 to San Bruno; the airport exit is between Millbrae Avenue and I-380. Or take I-280 to I-380 to Hwy 101 south and follow the signs into the airport (you never actually get on Hwy 101). Allow extra time for current construction delays; call 650/635-4000 for a construction update.

SFO Parking Information Line: 650/877-0227. Call for information on parking rates, directions, valet service, and space availability. During busy holidays (especially Thanksgiving and Christmas), many parking lots fill up and turn away customers. You can call ahead for space availability, but the information is not always accurate, so allow extra time to look for parking.

SFO Short-Term Parking: Located across the street from the terminal buildings; signs direct you to the lot as you approach the terminals (it can be confusing, since it stands in the heart of the construction zone). Prices start at $2 for 20 minutes, with a maximum of $22 the first day and $35 a day thereafter. Walk to the terminal.

SFO Long-Term Parking: Located north of the terminal on McDonnell Road. From Hwy 101, take the North Access Road exit and turn left, then turn left again on South Airport Boulevard and follow the signs. From I-280, take I-380 to the South Airport Boulevard exit, take a right at the stoplight, and then follow the signs. (Construction in this area may affect access routes to the lot.) Free shuttles carry you from the lot to the terminal. Long-term parking rates are $11 per day for the first seven days and $14 per day after that.

Anza Park & Sky: 615 Airport Blvd. (Anza), Burlingame, 800/453-9056. Located along the bay south of the airport. From the south, take Hwy 101 north to the Anza exit, then make a right on Airport Boulevard. From the north, exit Hwy 101 onto Broadway eastbound. At the stoplight, turn right on Old Bayshore, and then turn left onto Airport Boulevard. The rate is $11.34 per day (plus tax).

Park N Fly: 101 Terminal Ct. (off Produce Ave.), South San Francisco, 650/877-0304. Located north of I-380 next to the frontage road on the west side of Hwy 101. From the north, take Hwy 101 to the South Airport Boulevard exit. At the stop sign, turn left onto Produce Avenue. Turn right on Terminal Court; the lot is on the left. From the south (including I-280/I-380) take Hwy 101 north to the South Airport

Boulevard exit. Turn left at the stoplight (onto South Airport Boulevard), left again at the next light (under Hwy 101), and left again at the next light (onto Produce Avenue). Turn right on Terminal Court; the lot is on the left. The shuttle-bus service seems more frequent than that of the competition. The rates are $11.25 per day (plus tax), $10.25 per day for seniors, and $67.50 per week.

PCA Parking: 160 Produce Ave. (Airport Blvd.), South San Francisco, 650/952-5730. Located north of I-380 on the frontage road on the west side of Hwy 101. From the north, take Hwy 101 to the Airport Boulevard exit. At the stop sign, turn left onto Produce Avenue. From the south (including I-280/I-380), take Hwy 101 north to the South Airport Boulevard exit. Turn left at the traffic light (onto South Airport Boulevard), left again at the next light (under Hwy 101), and left again at the next light (onto Produce Avenue). PCA Parking is on the right. PCA offers many discount coupons—look for them in the mail and at AAA offices—but their shuttle buses run less frequently than their competitors (especially from the terminal to the lot). The rates are $12.25 per day (plus tax) and $9 for seniors.

SkyPark: 1000 San Mateo Ave. (San Bruno Ave./Shaw), San Bruno, 650/875-6655. SkyPark is northwest of the terminal, located almost under I-380. From Hwy 101, exit west on San Bruno Avenue and turn right at the second light; SkyPark is on the other side of I-380 on the right. From I-280, take I-380 and exit on El Camino Real south. Turn left on San Bruno Avenue. At the first traffic light, turn right on Huntington Avenue. At the stop sign, take a sharp left onto San Mateo Avenue. The rates are $18 per day for indoor parking and $16 per day for outdoor parking ($1 per day discount for AAA members who show their cards when they drop off their cars).

San Jose International Airport is located along Hwy 101 just north of San Jose. Coming from the north, take Hwy 101 to just north of San Jose; you'll see the airport at Guadalupe Parkway. Turn right off Guadalupe onto Brokaw. Brokaw becomes Airport Boulevard and takes you to the airport. Coming from the south, exit Hwy 101 at First and Brokaw, turn left on Brokaw, and keep going until you reach SJC.

SJC Short-Term Parking: Located in the garage at Terminal A or in the hourly lot across from Terminal C. The charge is 75 cents per half hour, with a maximum of $20 per day. You can walk to the terminals.

SJC Long-Term Parking: Located in the "green" or "yellow" lot on Airport Boulevard north of Terminal A; the charge is 75 cents per half hour, with a maximum of $10 per day. Shuttles to the airport terminals are available.

Oakland Airport is located next to the bay in southwest Oakland, south of Alameda. Primary access is from Highway I-880 via the Hegenberger Road exit, located south of the Oakland Coliseum; Hegenberger Road takes you to the airport. From most points in the South Bay and Peninsula, take I-880 north, which can be reached from San Jose, Hwy 237, or the Dumbarton and San Mateo bridges. From San Francisco or the north Peninsula, take the Bay Bridge (I-80) east to I-880 south.

OAK Short-Term Parking: Located across the street from both terminals. The rate is $1 per 20 minutes with a maximum of $20 per day. It is an easy walk to the terminals.

OAK Long-Term Parking: Also located across the street from the terminal, next to the short-term lot. Still walking distance to the terminal, although there is also a shuttle bus. The rate is $5 per hour with a maximum of $10 per day.

OAK Economy Parking: Located to the right of the entrance road before you reach Terminal 1. This is the real long-term lot. The rate is $5 per hour with a maximum of $8 per day.

Airpark: 111 98th Ave. (Airport Rd.), Oakland, 510/568-1221. The rates are $7.50 per day and $45 per week. Seniors pay $6.50 per day and $39 a week.

Park N Fly: 82 98th Ave. (Airport Rd.), Oakland, 510/633-0700. The rates are $8 per day and $48 per week. Seniors receive $1 off the daily fee.

RBJ Airport Parking: Two locations, 106 Hegenberger Rd. (Airport Rd.) and 145 98th Ave. (Airport Rd.), Oakland, 510/562-3055. The rates are $6 per day and $36 per week. Seniors pay $5.50 per day.

Airport Public Transportation

See the Public Transportation section (above) for additional information on the companies and routes mentioned here.

Four SamTrans bus routes go to **San Francisco International Airport**: 7B, 7F, 3B, and 3X. From the south, the 7F express route stops at SFO on its trip between Palo Alto and San Francisco. Allow yourself a good hour for the ride from Stanford to SFO, or 40 minutes from Redwood City. The 7B local route stops at SFO on its trip between Redwood City and San Francisco. Allow yourself a little over an hour from Redwood City to SFO, 45 minutes from San Mateo. The adult fare for the 7F is $2.50 and for the 7B is $1 to San Francisco and $2 from San Francisco.

From San Francisco, both buses start at the Transbay Terminal at First and Mission streets. The 7B follows surface streets and takes an hour from San Francisco, while the 7F follows Hwy 101 and takes 40 minutes. The 7F only permits small hand luggage between San Francisco and the airport. Large baggage is permitted between the airport and Palo Alto and on the 7B. The buses run from 6am until midnight.

The 3B and 3X run from the Daly City and Colma BART stations, respectively, to the airport. The 3B travels surface streets to the airport. The 3X follows I-280 and I-380 for most of its route. The adult fare for both buses is $1. The 3X runs weekdays from 6am to midnight, Saturdays 7am to 9:20pm, and Sundays 7am to 8pm. The 3B runs from 6am to 7pm weekdays and from about 10am to 7pm Saturdays.

CalTrain also serves SFO. Hop a train to the Millbrae Station, then take the free CalTrain shuttle (operates until midnight) to the terminal building.

San Jose Airport can be reached by VTA Light Rail Transit (LRT) and buses, although it is a favorite gripe among South Bay denizens that the trains don't go directly to the airport, requiring a bus trip to complete the journey. From the Metro/Airport LRT Station in San Jose, catch the free Metro Airport Shuttle on the southbound side of First Street. The shuttle runs on weekdays every 10 minutes from 6am to 9am, then every 15 minutes until 4pm. From 4pm to 7pm, it runs every 10 minutes. After 7pm or on the weekend, you can catch the number 10 VTA bus, which runs from the Metro/Airport LRT and the Santa Clara CalTrain station to the airport. It leaves every 30 minutes during rush hour and every hour at other times. The number 10 runs from 6am to 10:30pm on weekdays and 7am to 10pm on weekends. Peninsula residents can reach the Santa Clara CalTrain station via either CalTrain or the 22 VTA bus, which travels down El Camino from Palo Alto. On weekdays from the Palo Alto Transit Center and CalTrain Station, you can take the 300 VTA bus with limited stops.

BART serves **Oakland Airport** via the Oakland Coliseum/Airport Station on the Fremont line. From the station, the AirBART shuttle costs $2 each way (50 cents for seniors) and runs about every 15 minutes, less frequently during evenings and weekends. The shuttle normally takes about 15 minutes to get to OAK and up to 30 minutes during rush hours. It runs from 6:05am to 11:35pm Mondays through Saturdays and 8:30am to 11:45pm on Sundays. Purchase a ticket *before* you board (buy it either inside the Coliseum/Oakland Airport BART station or inside the airport terminal near the door closest to the shuttle stop). Instead of the shuttle, you can take AC Transit bus 58, which leaves every 10 to 15 minutes during rush hours and every 17 minutes midday and weekends, and every 20 minutes from 7am to 1am. See the Public Transportation section above for information on how to reach BART.

Private Shuttles

Airport shuttles are usually faster and more convenient than pubic transportation, but more expensive. Research the different companies for the best deal, including asking other riders for recommendations, to avoid those with poor service.

(SuperShuttle in San Francisco has a good reputation.) Many shuttles offer discounts when they pick up more than one person at a location; some charge extra if you exceed a baggage limit. Always make reservations well in advance for rides to the airport, and when you do, let the shuttle service know if you have any special luggage requirements, such as a bike or ten bags.

A&R Transbay Connection: 408/263-5505. SFO, SJC, OAK.

Airport Connection: 510/841-0150. SFO, OAK, SJC.

Airport Service: 650/494-0200. SFO, OAK, SJC.

BayPorter Express: 415/467-1800. SFO, OAK.

Express Airport Shuttle: 408/378-6270.

San Jose Airport Shuttle: 800/957-4888. SFO, SJC.

South and East Bay Airport Shuttle: 800/548-4664, 408/225-4444. SFO, SJC.

Super Connection: 800/840-3133. SFO, SJC, OAK.

SuperShuttle: 415/558-8500. SFO.

VIP Airport Shuttle: 800/235-8847. SFO, SJC, OAK.

Land Travel

Amtrak: 800/USA-RAIL (872-7245). Amtrak connects the Bay Area to the rest of the United States from its depots in San Jose, Oakland, and Berkeley. The San Jose station stands conveniently next to the CalTrain station. Amtrak buses take passengers from San Francisco to Oakland and stop at the San Francisco CalTrain station. Those familiar with Amtrak train service between Boston and Washington, D.C. will be mystified by Amtrak's dizzying schedules and amazed at how few trains run on the West Coast routes; the majority of service is provided by buses. There are several trains a day from San Jose and Oakland to Sacramento and several others to the Central Valley. The *Coast Starlight* goes all the way up the Pacific Coast from San Diego and Los Angeles through San Jose to Seattle and Vancouver, Canada. Another train runs east from Oakland through Truckee and Reno—passing through spectacular Sierra scenery—on the way to Salt Lake City, Denver, and Chicago. Most long-distance trains require reservations.

Green Tortoise: 1667 Jerrold Ave., SF, 415/821-0803. Those who value novelty more than efficiency should look into the Green Tortoise. If a ten-day trip from San Francisco to New York with a merry band of interesting fellow passengers and a variety of stopovers strikes your fancy, the Tortoise could be for you. Passengers pile into a bus converted to sleeping quarters and hit the road. Green Tortoise travels as far as Alaska, Mexico, and Baja, and they also travel up and down California and the West Coast. The amenities are sparse—you shower at public facilities, eat cookout meals, and sleep in the bus on platforms with mattresses—but the experience is memorable.

Greyhound: 800/231-2222. Greyhound buses are a relatively inexpensive option. You won't get anywhere in a hurry, but you won't break the bank either. Greyhound has three main Bay Area depots: in San Francisco's Transbay Terminal at First and Mission streets, in downtown San Jose at 70 Almaden Avenue, and in downtown Oakland at 2103 San Pablo Avenue. There's also a minor Peninsula stop at 252 Mayfield Avenue in Mountain View near San Antonio Road and Alma Street. Greyhound's best deals are with the Ameripass, which gives you unlimited rides and an unrestricted schedule for a fixed fee. Make reservations more than two weeks in advance for discounts.

Neighborhoods & Housing

RESOURCES

Silicon Valley and the Peninsula have the hottest real-estate market in the United States. In other words, expect to have a hard time finding housing and expect to pay a lot for it. The best place to begin looking for a home or apartment is in the newspapers we've included below. (Since this is Silicon Valley, most listings are available on-line through the papers' web sites. New on-line listings spring up what seems like hourly.) Remember, plenty of other people are turning to these same listings, and the place that sounds perfect to you is bound to appeal to dozens—or even hundreds—of other renters or buyers.

If you're seeking a rental, it's a good idea to sign up with a rental or roommate referral agency; we've listed some below. Landlords with vacancies often list with them instead of in newspapers, because they are usually free to the property owner. You, the renter, pay for these services. One plus to the fee: it screens out some competition for vacancies. Also, agency listings are far more descriptive than newspaper ads—where every word costs the landlord—and include amenities, facilities, and roommate profiles.

The market is so hot, many landlords don't even advertise. They just stick up a For Rent or For Sale sign. This means that you have to scout your preferred neighborhood as often as possible. Finally, network with friends and coworkers. Company, college, and university bulletins boards—either traditional or on-line—are good sources, too, especially when the school year ends. Also, check out the notice boards at local cafés, bars, and Laundromats.

Whether you're buying or renting, be prepared to move fast. If you wait even a few hours to act on a place you like, someone else will snatch it up. Answer ads immediately and search daily for For Sale and For Rent signs in desirable neighborhoods. Carry your checkbook so you can make a payment on the spot if you find a place. Because the market is so tight, landlords can be very selective about their tenants. Consider visiting an apartment as if you're on a job interview: dress well and bring your resume (landlord references, credit report, and bank account number).

Finally, be prepared to pay more than the asking price, especially when buying. Bidding wars in Silicon Valley are as common as stock options, and many homes sell for more than the asking price. Likewise, if you find a must-have apartment, you may have to offer more than the competition is willing to pay.

Persevere and you'll find a place. In other words, avail yourself of every resource and allow at least three months for your search.

In addition to the newspapers listed below, there are numerous small, local papers—usually one per town—that usually carry a few listings.

Newspapers

Metro: Silicon Valley's independent arts and news weekly. Has a small section of classified ads covering the South Bay. The web site (www.metroactive.com) doesn't have rental listings, but it does have a lot of useful information about finding a rental, as well as good resource listings for everything from roommate services to fair-housing agencies (this information is also published in the annual "Almanack" edition).

Impressing A Landlord

The pairing between landlord and tenant is similar to that between employer and employee: both sides have a lot to offer and a lot to lose, so mutual suspicion is the rule. When the rental market is tight, as it is today, landlords often have the luxury of choosing among many qualified applicants. Renters have a better chance of getting the place of their dreams if they can impress a potential landlord right from the start, thereby ensuring an edge over other applicants. While landlords can't legally discriminate against a potential tenant based on race or religion, they can screen for whom they think will be stable and credit-worthy. Your reliability will boil down to a few key issues: references from former landlords (you don't want reports about trashing a previous apartment, then fighting an eviction), and proof you can and will pay rent, including a stable job profile, good income, and a solid credit history. Preparing a package with information addressing these concerns will show prospective landlords you will make an excellent tenant and are serious about finding a good place to live. Obtain a credit report far enough in advance to correct any mistakes, and be prepared to find a cosponsor if you have had a troubled past. Always carry all the information you'll need to fill out an application (bank account number, references, past landlord information). And don't forget to bring your checkbook so you can leave a deposit for that place you really love before 18 other people do.

Palo Alto Weekly: Palo Alto's local newspaper. Published twice a week, with the Friday edition heavily geared toward the real estate market. Check classified ads at www.service.com/paw.

San Francisco Chronicle and Examiner: San Francisco–based regional newspapers published daily. Check classified ads at www.sfgate.com. Best for listings north of Redwood City.

San Jose Mercury News: A regional newspaper published daily. Best for housing listings in the mid-Peninsula and South Bay. Check classified ads at www.sjmercury.com.

San Mateo County Times: A small daily newspaper read primarily on the northern Peninsula. Classified ads are found at www.newschoice.com.

Stanford Report: The employee newspaper of Stanford University is a good source for housing near the university. Go to www.stanford.edu and select "News Service," then select "Stanford Report." The student paper, the *Stanford Daily,* has a very small classifieds section, although the ads are not included on their web site.

Agencies and Related Operations

Bay Rentals: 3396 Stevens Creek Blvd. #3 (San Tomas/Winchester), San Jose, 408/244-4900; fax 408/244-0983; www.bayarearentals.com; email sales@bayarearentals.com. Claims to be the largest rental referral service in California. They have detailed listings in the immediate area for houses and apartments in Santa Clara, San Mateo, Santa Cruz, Alameda, and San Francisco counties. Fees are $88 for a 90-day membership and $98 if they send you email or fax updates. A $63 refund is issued if you don't find a place through their listings.

California Tenants Association: 478 W. Hamilton Ave. # 325 (San Tomas/Winchester), Campbell, no phone; www.catenants.com; email info@catenants.com. A membership-based tenants organization created in response to the housing crisis in the Santa Clara Valley. In addition to its lobbying and advocacy activities, the association provides tenants rights information, a move-in/move-out kit, information about alternative housing resources, and housing rights information. Many services require membership (basic $19.95 per year, full $38 per year). The web site has some good advice for renters.

Metro Rents: 2050 South Bascom Ave. (Campbell), Campbell 408/371-2011; fax 408/371-3537; www.metrorent.com; email newplace@metrorent.com. Extensive listings of apartments and houses for rent from San Francisco to San Jose, with some as far south as Santa Cruz (the San Jose operation used to be named Homerenters). It lists vacancies only and will refer you to a roommate referral agency if shared housing is sought. In-office search privileges cost $65. Web, email, and fax search privileges cost $85 for a 40-day membership in the Peninsula and $95 for a 60-day membership in the South Bay. Metro Rents will obtain and forward your credit report to landlords for $25. A $40 refund is issued if you don't find a place through their listings.

Roommate Express: Numerous locations are sprinkled throughout the Bay Area; call 408/295-5180 to make an appointment in San Jose and the South Bay and 650/322-6770 for the mid-Peninsula. Or sign up on-line at www.e-roommate.com. Roommate Express provides complete roommate services throughout the Bay Area. Using personality surveys completed by each applicant, a computer-matching system generates a list of compatible roommates for you. Listing a vacancy costs $69, seeking a vacancy is $129, and credit reports are $20. For an additional $10, you get 24-hour dial-in service. Membership runs for 60 days. A four-month roommate guarantee is included in case you run into that *Single White Female* situation.

CITY PROFILES

Keep in mind that many comments about Peninsula and South Bay communities are relative. For example, the fact that the area's median home price of $350,000 is considered affordable must be looked at in tandem with the fact that the counties' median income and median housing prices are the nation's highest. So what is acceptable by local standards would be labeled incredibly expensive on the East Coast or in the Midwest. History is relative as well. Although European settlement here dates back to the late 18th century, most development has occurred since World War II. Sunnyvale and Milpitas, which have boomed in the last 20 years, are looked upon as youngsters, while Palo Alto and Redwood City are seen as old-timers.

Describing school districts is even more relative. In general, schools in San Mateo and Santa Clara counties are better than average for California. (There was a time when the state's public schools were some of the best in the country, although that is no longer the case.) Although the schools in any city can vary significantly in facilities and rankings, hard-working students can get a good education in most of the area's classrooms. But for parents who went to Stanford and who want to make sure their children end up there, too, an above-average school isn't good enough. That's why they pay to live in a town like Palo Alto, where the schools are among the best in the country.

Yet, a few general rules do apply to the cities and towns of the Peninsula and the South Bay. As you climb from the bay up the Santa Cruz Mountain foothills, house size and housing prices rise with the elevation. And as prices increase, so does the average age of the community. This age gradation is not unique to California; after all, it takes time to save enough for a down payment and most people earn more as they get older. But since Proposition 13 was approved by the state's voters in the 1970s, any house owned prior to its passage has continued to be assessed at below market value for tax purposes until it is resold. Now many long-time homeowners are staying put because buying a new house would dramatically increase their property taxes.

The following towns are listed in roughly geographic order from north to south; estimated 1997 population is in parenthesis.

Brisbane (3,200)

This tiny blue-collar town is best known for its office complexes east of Hwy 101 and for San Bruno Mountain, the huge bald knob that straddles this part of the Peninsula. After years of debate and litigation, a large residential development was built on the northeast side of the mountain, adding a lot of residential units to a town filled primarily with commercial and industrial development. The moderately priced residential area—mostly pre-World War II single-family homes—is squeezed into an isolated valley on the steep slopes of the mountain and further cut off from neighboring towns by a lagoon.

Brisbane calls itself The City of the Stars, in honor of the holiday tradition of decorating houses with large star-shaped Christmas lights. Schools are above average for the northern Peninsula.

Daly City (101,300)

Although Daly City is San Mateo County's largest city, it seems more a part of San Francisco than the Peninsula. Located just south of the city, it exhibits an urban diversity rare on the Peninsula and even has a BART station, giving it excellent access to downtown San Francisco and the East Bay. A relatively recent influx of immigrants has given the bedroom community a large growth spurt, and it now boasts a young, mixed population, including northern California's largest Filipino community. Daly City has a long history as a refuge: in 1906, many San Francisco residents fleeing the destruction of the Great Quake and fire found safety on John Daly's ranch.

The city itself is located near a gap in the coastal mountains. Pacific-bound airplanes taking off from the nearby San Francisco International Airport cross this opening going west, while ocean winds and fog flow through it going east. Daly City has a broad mix of homes and, as is typical for the northern Peninsula, housing prices are reasonable (under $300,000 to purchase a three-bedroom house and monthly rent of $1,200 for a two-bedroom apartment). The ridges above I-280 have long been lined with countless rows of identical houses, looking like so many Monopoly pieces. Now, even newer construction follows this careful pattern. The schools fall into many districts and vary greatly in quality but are generally solid, especially considering the pressure the town's rapid growth and large immigrant population have put on the system.

Colma (1,200)

Very few people actually live in Colma, a town best known for its cemeteries: when San Francisco ran out of space, it banned such resting places and moved all its dead here. It has been burying them here ever since. Other than cemeteries, Colma is primarily home to commercial developments such as Auto Row on Serramonte Boulevard and the 280 Metro Center. If you need to pay your respects to the deceased or buy a car, BART has a station at 365 D Street.

South San Francisco (57,600)

Few people driving into San Francisco from the south have missed the huge white letters on San Bruno Mountain grandly proclaiming "South San Francisco—The Industrial City." (The name originated with a large meat-packing operation at the turn of the century.) Today you'll find more biotechnology companies, office parks, electronics firms, and airport hotels than heavy industry, but there are still a number of printing firms and warehouses that moved from San Francisco in search of cheaper real estate. Seventeen major construction projects are pending and could add 1.6 million square feet of office space, 1,620 new hotel rooms, and 882 houses. Some people might be disturbed by the ocean winds that blow through the gap near Daly City and then shoot through town, but South San Francisco's location near the airport and the intersection of Hwy 101 and I-380 makes transportation convenient, enhancing its commercial appeal.

The city's beautiful historic downtown, which stretches along Grand Avenue between Airport Boulevard and Chestnut Avenue, is currently being treated to a revitalization and landscaping project in an effort to attract more businesses. Most housing came along after World War II, and the neat, closely spaced, boxy homes and moderate prices (three-bedroom homes sell for about $300,000) resemble those in neighboring towns. Typical of the northern Peninsula, the quality of the schools varies. In recent years, South San Francisco has seen the arrival of many immigrants from Latin America and the Pacific, resulting in a diverse population that mirrors much of the rest of the state.

San Bruno (40,800)

Located on the narrowest point on the Peninsula, where I-380 connects Hwy 101 to I-280, San Bruno borders San Francisco International Airport on the east. As you might expect from a town at the center of the region's transportation system, commercial development dominates the area. San Bruno is home to three shopping centers within a mile of one another: Tanforan Park, Towne Center, and Bayhill Shopping Center. As its name implies, Towne Center serves as a de facto downtown, although there is a historic downtown of small-town-America storefronts and international grocery stores along San Mateo Avenue. Office parks and industrial areas, including a huge Gap corporate campus, are also well represented. Things will get even more commercial, and Tanforan Shopping Center will be redeveloped, when a BART line extension to the airport puts a station in San Bruno on Huntington Avenue. The tentative completion date for the extension is 2001.

San Bruno marks the dividing line between the northern Peninsula and the rest of it. The town resembles its northern neighbors in that housing is generally smaller, denser, and less expensive than in Millbrae and points south. Yet reflecting its status as a border town, San Bruno has both housing prices (about $350,000 to purchase a three-bedroom home and monthly rent of $1,300 for a two-bedroom apartment) and average incomes that are slightly higher than those farther north. As is common in the area, the most developed stretches lie along El Camino Real, and the more residential tracts sit in the hills toward I-280.

The town fits into three school districts, with the best schools associated with San Mateo and Millbrae to the south. Because it is less expensive than its southern neighbors and has grown faster, San Bruno is generally home to more young adults and young families.

Millbrae (21,400)

Standing in the shadow, if not the very flight path, of San Francisco International Airport, Millbrae has seen much industrial development associated with its noisy neighbor. The eastern half of town follows the normal Peninsula pattern of industrial and commercial development along Hwy 101, a mix of apartments and houses lies along El Camino Real, and larger single-family homes dot the hills toward I-280. The future will bring other changes related to the airport: a BART station, located immediately north of the Millbrae Avenue overpass and west of Hwy 101, will put that system, CalTrain, and SamTrans buses at a single location. The BART extension is scheduled for completion in 2001.

Action in Millbrae is on El Camino Real, a busy commercial strip with numerous Asian restaurants, including the celebrated Hong Kong Flower Lounge, a popular temple of Cantonese seafood. A small downtown shopping area on Broadway parallel to El Camino has made a major step in establishing its credibility: it now has a Starbucks coffee bar.

In most respects, Millbrae resembles neighboring bedroom communities like Burlingame in terms of housing, income, schools, and so forth. For example, most of the houses were built in the postwar boom, and are expensive ($550,000 and more for a three-bedroom home). One thing that sets the community apart from most of those around it is that nearly one-third of the population is over 55, something more typical in such exclusive nearby enclaves as Hillsborough and Atherton. The schools are variable but generally good.

Burlingame (28,600)

While most Peninsula cities struggle to maintain one downtown, Burlingame has two: one on Broadway, and the other on Burlingame Avenue, with a train station in each one. Admittedly, the retail strip on Broadway is pretty small, with just a few restaurants, Asian markets, and carpet stores. The real action is on Burlingame Avenue between El Camino Real and the CalTrain station. There you'll find a host of restaurants, cafés, and retail shops—the requisite Starbucks, Noah's, Peet's, and Gap—amidst a bustle of small-town energy. Around the two downtowns stand quiet suburban streets with a mix of houses and high-rise apartments.

The eastern side of Burlingame along Hwy 101 is filled with commercial development, much of it serving nearby San Francisco International Airport. Hotels, restaurants, and car-rental lots keep springing up. Hillsborough borders the western edge of Burlingame; north of Hillside Drive, Burlingame curves up to I-280.

Perhaps it's Hillsborough's influence, but Burlingame houses are anomalously big and expensive (a typical three-bedroom home is $600,000). Many of the city's charming older bungalows and Tudors have been demolished and replaced with pink-stuccoed Mediterranean-type mini mansions. For now the days of "monster homes" are numbered: the city counsel passed a ban, at least temporarily, on most second-story additions. Compared to Millbrae or San Mateo, real-estate costs are significantly higher, while rents and average incomes are lower. These housing prices limit new families, although the schools are generally good. Proximity to the airport makes Burlingame convenient for frequent travelers, although noise can be a problem.

Hillsborough (11,300)

As the northern Peninsula's stereotypically exclusive, hillside residential community, Hillsborough offers the conventional mix of large homes, quiet streets, low crime, and excellent schools. It is neck and neck with Atherton for highest average income and home prices (which run into the millions) on the Peninsula. Don't expect to see anybody strolling around town: sidewalks and streetlights are prohibited. Don't look for many young adults either. Established wealthy families come here for the excellent schools and stay for a safe old age.

San Mateo (92,200)

This is the city that made the county what it is today. Although Redwood City is older and the county seat, San Mateo plays a more central role: it's larger, located in the center of the county, has housing prices and incomes right at the county median, and boasts the region's main shopping center in Hillsdale Mall. The bustling downtown along Third and Fourth streets between El Camino Real and the CalTrain station has a good mix of restaurants, cafés, and shops, although competition from superstores and the mall has hurt some downtown businesses.

San Mateo's neighborhoods are predictably typical of the mid-Peninsula, with lots of quiet, tree-lined streets, a mix of houses and apartments from the last 100 years (with an abundance of units reflecting the postwar boom years), and commercial and industrial development along Hwy 101. Neighborhoods in the hills west of El Camino are generally more expensive. The neighborhoods along the train tracks near downtown have been attracting a diverse population of recent immigrants, especially Hispanics. Schools are generally pretty good, and the high school is especially well regarded.

Foster City (29,800)

The word *earthquake* carries a lot of weight in Foster City: this lagoon community was created almost 40 years ago on landfill, the same stuff that turned to Jell-O under San

Francisco's Marina District during the 1989 Loma Prieta tremor. Foster City residents, mostly highly educated professionals, insist that their enclave is constructed to withstand shaky ground: in fact, Foster City did survive the 1989 quake well. The city was built by one developer, T. Jack Foster, at the base of the San Mateo Bridge on what was then known as Brewer's Island. He created a clean, modern community with a centrally planned mix of bungalows, town houses, condominiums, offices, shopping centers, and parks. Because it's built on landfill, canals and sloughs wind through town. Leo Ryan Park is an excellent place to learn to sail or windsurf.

Since Foster City is barely four decades old, it has a decidedly youthful—some would say yuppie—character. Plenty of high-income professionals create high real-estate prices, especially high rents ($1,800 a month for a typical two-bedroom apartment). The schools are part of the San Mateo School District and are good. Foster City's location at the intersection of Hwy 101 and Hwy 92 makes it convenient to many points, but this central spot does mean a lot of other traffic passing through.

Belmont (25,200)

Sister city to neighboring San Carlos, Belmont sits at the geographic center of the Peninsula, halfway between San Francisco and San Jose, with easy access to Hwy 101. The community's wooded hillsides consist almost entirely of quiet upper-middle-class suburban neighborhoods. In addition to suburbanites, Belmont is home to the likes of Paul Revere, Molly Pitcher, and John Hancock (actually they're just fireplugs painted to look like heroes of America's past). State law recently threatened to paint over the 400 "happy hydrants," but they were saved by a unanimous vote in the Senate.

Belmont has even less commercial and industrial activity than San Carlos. Housing is slightly less expensive in Belmont (about $450,000 for a three-bedroom home) than in San Carlos, and apartments (which rent at about $1,200 a month for a two-bedroom unit) are more plentiful, although single-family homes rule the market. Perhaps it's because of the apartments, but Belmont has more young adults and fewer elderly residents than San Carlos. Schools are generally very good.

San Carlos (28,000)

This quiet spot epitomizes the upper-middle-class suburban bedroom community. Together with Belmont—even phone bills lump the two together as SNCRSBLM-NT—it provides a comfortable small-town haven in the heart of the mid-Peninsula. And as is the case with its neighbors, the residential areas lie primarily west of El Camino Real, while industrial and retail development dominates the land east of the roadway. The historic CalTrain station, built in 1888 in the style of architect H. H. Richardson, is now a state historic landmark. Nearby on Laurel Street, the tiny downtown is slowly reviving, with restaurants, bars, and cafés attracting pedestrian traffic.

Although San Carlos is a longtime Peninsula community, the population boom and much of the town's housing came after World War II. Housing is predominantly expensive suburban homes (running about $550,000 for a three-bedroom abode), and the population is generally established families. Schools, especially those in the elementary system, are good.

While San Carlos sits in the mid-Peninsula, traffic can be a problem: access to I-280 is slow, and Hwy 101 tends to clog up here. A project to raise the CalTrain tracks over Holly Street, Harbor Boulevard, and Ralston Avenue will fix some of the bottlenecks in Belmont and San Carlos. Although Harbor Boulevard has reopened, the entire project won't be completed until 2000.

Redwood City (73,200)

The history of this hard-working community goes back to the 1800s, when the city earned its name as a lumber town: redwood trees cut in the hills above what is now

Woodside were processed in Redwood City and shipped through its port to construction sites in San Francisco. For years, Redwood City has been piecing together a puzzle from which a revitalized downtown will emerge. The historic area around Broadway and Main streets got a facelift by buffing up the brick sidewalks and adding gas-lamp streetlights. City Center Plaza, an 81-unit apartment-retail complex was recently completed, and a University of California extension campus is on its way. Sequoia Station, a villagelike shopping center with a Safeway, Starbucks, Noah's, Barnes & Noble, and more, is right at the CalTrain station, a boon for public transit. Still, nobody will mistake this blue-collar community for tony Palo Alto.

Redwood City is the San Mateo County seat, and many government offices, from the DMV to the courthouse, are also near downtown. One of the Peninsula's more ethnically mixed communities, Redwood City has an especially large Hispanic population. The retail strip along Middlefield Road between Hwy 84 and Fifth Avenue is lined with Mexican restaurants and markets as evidence of their commercial influence.

The area near Hwy 101 is predominantly industrial, loaded with corporate offices, shopping centers, and warehouses; as you go southwest across El Camino Real into the hills, the area becomes increasingly suburban residential. As the oldest city in the area, Redwood City has the most diverse housing and well-established neighborhoods. Apartments are more plentiful to the northeast, houses to the southwest. Housing is abundant and generally less expensive (about $400,000 for a three-bedroom home) than in surrounding communities, making Redwood City popular with young singles and families. The schools are as diverse as the community.

Atherton (7,400)

One of the Bay Area's most exclusive towns, Atherton consists almost exclusively of large homes, many large enough to deserve the sobriquet "mansion." Homes have mansion-sized price tags to match their mass, ranging from $1 million to $4 million. Minimum lot sizes are strictly enforced, and absolutely no retail businesses are allowed. In fact, the only notable landmarks are The Menlo School and Menlo College.

Atherton sits quite unobtrusively on the flats between Menlo Park and Redwood City. Its elementary schools are very highly rated. Older students that stay in the public system attend Menlo Atherton High, which, although not as good as the elementary institutions, is still well above average. Prominent resident celebrities include Gap founder Don Fisher, investment tycoon Charles Schwab, and sports star Barry Bonds. Access to Hwy 101 and I-280 is pretty good, and Atherton's CalTrain station has a residents-only parking policy.

Woodside (5,500)

Nestled in the wooded valleys of the Santa Cruz Mountains, Woodside is best known as home to the horsey set, so don't be surprised if you see the local gentry riding their steeds down the main street. More of a village than a town, Woodside life is centered around the community's historic heart. Robert's Market sits in the middle of things along Woodside Road (Hwy 84) between I-280 and Kings Mountain Road; the town hall and the library are nearby. There's not much else to the actual town, but the large areas of open space that surround it—Huddart, Wunderlich, and Edgewood county parks—offer excellent trails for hiking, riding horses, and biking.

The houses are hidden in the woods and hills. Many are full-blown mansions, with pools and pool houses, tennis courts and tennis pavilions, and stables and even some stable boys. Despite the town's high price tags, Woodside is much quieter and less ostentatious than nearby Atherton. Indeed, residents prefer the seclusion afforded by their trees. There is an excellent elementary school, but older students attend Woodside High in Redwood City.

Menlo Park (29,500)

Downtown Menlo Park has a remarkable number of clock repair shops. Their customers must all come from other towns, because Menlo Park seems wholly committed to ignoring time, pinning its identity on a post-World War II vision of small-town America. Its modest heart, located on Santa Cruz Avenue, still boasts old-fashioned coffee shops serving grilled cheese sandwiches and independent pharmacies where pills and potions outnumber cosmetics. But times are changing, and Starbucks and its ilk have taken up residence.

This is also a town that enjoys peace and quiet. The city council banned noisy gas-powered leaf blowers despite protests from hundreds of gardeners and home owners fighting for their right to a well-tended lawn. This is serious stuff in these parts. Rebellious residents have responded by slapping bumper stickers onto their SUVs that say "When leaf blowers are outlawed, only outlaws will have leaf blowers." In resistance to another noisy machine, the automobile, the town has narrowed the main thoroughfare, El Camino Real, from three lanes to two, causing a modern inconvenience, the continuous traffic jam.

The central part of town between Middlefield Road and Alameda de las Pulgas consists primarily of quiet tree-lined streets, modest ranch homes, and small apartment complexes from the 1950s. The area is popular with senior citizens, but many young families are attracted by the housing prices (around $600,000 for a three-bedroom abode), which are below those of neighboring Palo Alto. Stanford University's influence is almost as strong here as in Palo Alto: many faculty families call Menlo Park home. The outstanding elementary schools are on a par with schools in Palo Alto, but the high school is not as good.

Heading east toward Hwy 101, apartments start to outnumber houses and the character becomes more blue collar. The area east of Hwy 101 resembles East Palo Alto, with plenty of recent industrial parks. Sun Microsystems has an enormous new corporate headquarters at the base of the Dumbarton Bridge. The western side of town has been developed into a modern town-house community, Sharon Heights, complete with landscaped lawns and golf courses. Sand Hill Road leads to I-280 and the famous office complexes housing America's largest concentration of venture capital firms.

Portola Valley (4,400)

This tiny enclave in the Santa Cruz Mountains above Stanford provides the ideal retreat for wealthy inhabitants who want tend their gardens and horses in seclusion. Surrounded by remote portions of the campus and acres of open space and parks, the privacy is disturbed only by the packs of bicyclists who wend their way along the twisting mountain byways. As you might expect, housing consists primarily of large, expensive modern homes set into the hillsides. When these houses are put up for rent, they are popular with groups of Stanford students, especially if a hot tub is part of the lease. Elementary schools are excellent, although the town is so small older kids must go off to Woodside High in Redwood City.

Palo Alto (59,900)

Ever since the *San Francisco Chronicle* named Palo Alto the best place to live in the Bay Area, residents have been referring to their community as Perfect Palo Alto. While it's supposed to be a joke, the phrase does embody a scarcely concealed smugness characteristic of the town. And why not? With its long-standing ties to neighboring Stanford University, Palo Alto has become a regional center, drawing visitors from all over the Peninsula to its many attractions. The vibrant downtown along University Avenue between Middlefield and Alma has a remarkable number of restaurants, cafés, bookstores, and movie theaters, including the beautifully restored Stanford Theatre. (Historic teetotaler Leland Stanford would be appalled to watch young singles flock to nighttime hot spots.) Visitors are also drawn to the glittering Stanford Shopping Center. Not many towns can offer their residents large parks like Arastradero Preserve, Foothills Park, and Palo Alto Baylands—each an oasis of solitude—but only Palo Alto would have the exclusive residents-only policy it enforces at Foothills.

Apparent perfection has a price, of course, and the cost per square foot for Palo Alto houses is among the highest anywhere. Three-bedroom shacks start at about $600,000, and prices for larger homes go into the millions. Monthly rent for a two-bedroom apartment is about $2,000. Palo Alto has mature neighborhoods with diverse housing, ranging from the stately shingled homes along the tree-lined streets south and east of downtown to boxy ranch homes and apartment complexes on both sides of El Camino Real.

The high real-estate prices provide a tax base that supports some of the best city services found anywhere. The school system is consistently top-rated (also reflecting Stanford's influence). A $143 million bond measure was passed in 1996 to remodel and upgrade all 15 district schools in the next few years. And at a time when most cities are paring back essential services, Palo Alto can afford to repave cracked sidewalks. Residents are predominantly tied to either Stanford or local high-tech and science-oriented employers such as Hewlett-Packard, Varian, and Digital. Residents range from Stanford students to yuppies to longtime natives, although housing costs exclude many young families from the area.

East Palo Alto (24,500)

Located at the base of the Dumbarton Bridge, East Palo Alto was primarily ranchland until World War II. Things look different today, as this small city struggles with urban problems such as crack and gangs. The school system is generally poor, and parts of East Palo Alto are dangerous and depressing. Not surprisingly given this profile, the city does provide affordable housing in a region that has almost none (many three-bedroom homes are under $200,000).

There are some bright spots in East Palo Alto's future. Vice President Al Gore is directing $1.6 million to the city for environmental cleanup and economic development. Marketing efforts to promote the low real-estate prices and ready access to the bridge have lured fast-growing high-tech firms to the office parks and warehouses on the border with east Menlo Park. Discussions continue with various developers to keep this trend going, with myriad plans in the works for corporate headquarters, malls, and more.

One of the Peninsula's most diverse communities, the residential areas house a mix of the people who migrated to the area in the last 50 years, especially Hispanics, Pacific Islanders, and African-Americans from the South. East Palo Alto also proves that neighbors can pull together in the face of adversity: residents have the strongest sense of community on the Peninsula. And the town's wealthy neighbors have helped with various social programs, including tutoring and teaching entrepreneurial skills.

Mountain View (73,000)

Recently, Mountain View remodeled its downtown along Castro Street between Central Expressway and El Camino Real. The makeover included brick sidewalks, gas-lamp streetlights, and newly planted street-side trees. The pink city hall, neighboring Center for the Performing Arts, and new public library form the architectural heart. A restaurant boom along Castro and surrounding streets arrived on the heels of the remodel. Most of the restaurants serve some sort of Asian cuisine—Chinese, Indian, Japanese, Thai—but other national tables are there for the serious seeker. The new downtown, combined with Mountain View's Shoreline Park—a reclaimed landfill with a large outdoor amphitheater, sailing lake, and miles of trails through marshland—is turning Mountain View into something of a regional attraction.

Mountain View's first boom occurred after World War II and was fed by employment at nearby Moffett Field Naval Air Station and NASA Ames Research Center. The Navy recently left Moffett and handed it over to NASA, but the war economy's legacy is an abundance of modest ranch homes and boxy apartment buildings. The plentiful housing stock is affordable ($500,000 for a three-bedroom home) compared to that of nearby Palo Alto and Los Altos and attracts a healthy mix of singles to its apartments (about $1,500 per month for a two-bedroom unit) and young families to its homes. Mountain View has been especially popular with many Hispanic immigrants. The more established neighborhoods west of El Camino Real and south of Castro Street resemble those in Palo Alto and Los Altos.

In line with its family-friendly character, Mountain View has good elementary schools (the high school is not as exemplary) and all the necessary modern conveniences in the plentiful new strip malls. Hwy 85 provides a key link from Mountain View to other parts of Silicon Valley, making the connection from Hwy 101 to I-280 in Cupertino a breeze. There are also two CalTrain stops.

Los Altos (28,000)

This archetypal upper-middle-class suburb is the kind of place you might see pictured in a driver's education film. Nice family homes with well-landscaped yards dot tree-lined streets. The quaint downtown village runs along Main Street across First, Second, and Third streets. The schools, especially the elementary ones, are excellent. Even the street signs are rustic carved wood.

But modern times have invaded Los Altos. The downtown coffee shops are Starbucks and Peet's, the bakery is Le Boulanger, and the real retail activity occurs in the strip malls along El Camino Real and San Antonio Road. Most important, current real-estate values are exorbitant (a three-bedroom house runs about $800,000), freezing out most young families and singles. As a result, nearly one-third of the population is 55 or older.

Los Altos Hills (8,000)

The rolling hills above Los Altos provide exquisite views for folks fortunate enough to live here. These lucky few—average household income is triple the county average—enjoy large homes on large lots surrounded by a ring of large open-space preserves. If you like the outdoors, you can choose from Arastradero Park to the north, Foothill and Los Trancos to the west, or Monte Bello and Rancho San Antonio to the south. Some residents keep their own horses for exploring the hills. This exclusively residential community has no town center or commercial activity. In fact, the only nonresidential spot in the area is Foothill College, which brings some nice performances to its auditorium. The K-12 school system also has a very good reputation. As is the case with the other exclusive communities, only a very few young adults are to be found here.

Sunnyvale (129,300)

Along with Cupertino and Santa Clara, Sunnyvale lies at the core of Silicon Valley. The city even maintains a patent library to keep the high-tech community pulsing. Vice President Al Gore singled out Sunnyvale as one of the best-run cities in America, an impressive credential given the fact that it is also the second-largest city in the county. The heart of this neat, well-kept community is a pair of shopping malls, TownCenter and Town & Country. For those who prefer a more old Main Street style, Sunnyvale's original downtown along Murphy Street (next to the CalTrain station) is experiencing a resurgence, with quite a few new restaurants and bars opening.

As with most fast-growing American cities, the dominant housing form is the multi-story condominium or town house, which is usually surrounded by enough strip malls to meet all the basic needs for food and clothing. These are mixed indiscriminately with the ubiquitous office complexes housing all those high-tech companies. While the city has a good assortment of residents, young singles and young families are the most visible, especially on the tennis courts and in the pools of those condominium complexes. Housing prices are moderate ($400,000 for a three-bedroom) by area standards (between Cupertino and Santa Clara), with enough of a range to allow most people to find something in their price range. Schools are a mixed bag.

Cupertino (44,800)

The influence of Apple Computer and the high-tech economy permeates Cupertino. There are no futuristic monorails; rather, much of Cupertino has the look of a functional suburban boomtown, with large blocks of "townhominiums" and wide boulevards lined with an endless string of strip malls. Apple's sprawling complex dominates a large area of town around De Anza Boulevard south of I-280. Perhaps because it includes the foothills at the base of the Santa Cruz Mountains, Cupertino is more upscale than Sunnyvale and Santa Clara: homeowners outnumber apartment dwellers, housing is more expensive ($550,000 for an average three-bedroom home), schools are better, and families are older. Some of the more established neighborhoods even have a traditional suburban feel: older trees, diverse one-story homes, and neighborhood shopping centers.

In addition to Apple and other members of the high-tech economy, Cupertino boasts De Anza College and its Flint Center for Performing Arts, an auditorium that hosts many of the region's performing arts companies and the occasional national act. Just west on Stevens Creek Boulevard you'll find Vallco Fashion Park, Cupertino's main mall. The newly completed Hwy 85 has eased some of the terrible congestion on town streets and made an easy link north to Hwy 101 and south around downtown San Jose.

Santa Clara (100,000)

When the Spaniards founded Mission Santa Clara in 1777 near what was to become San Jose, Santa Clara got a jump on the rest of Silicon Valley. Today, the mission site is home to the Jesuit-run Santa Clara University, located in a setting as close to downtown as suburbia allows. Nearby you'll find the city hall, the Triton Museum of Art, and a CalTrain station.

After World War II, the city readily embraced industrial development, as exemplified by local industrial giant FMC, once Farm Machinery Corporation and now a military contractor. Santa Clara even has its own convention center to compete with San Jose. The result of all this early activity is that the residential neighborhoods are older than those in Sunnyvale and Cupertino, and the area along Hwy 101 is heavily industrialized. The numerous ethnic restaurants and shops on El Camino Real reflect the residents' diverse backgrounds, including large Italian and Indian populations.

Perhaps related to its older neighborhoods, or maybe to its high level of industrial development and nearby San Jose Airport, housing (approximately $375,000 for a three-bedroom home) is more affordable than in Sunnyvale or Mountain View. The relatively affordable prices attract a wide range of residents, including young singles and families scarce in pricier towns. Families also like the fact that Santa Clara is convenient to what is arguably the area's best-known attraction, Great America, a giant amusement park north of Hwy 101. Schools generally lag behind those neighboring in Sunnyvale, Mountain View, and Cupertino.

San Jose (873,300)

While San Jose lacks San Francisco's cosmopolitan air and attitude, it actually outdoes San Francisco in many ways. San Jose was California's first city and first capital; it is now the Bay Area's biggest city, sprawling far and wide across the Santa Clara Valley where only orchards once flourished. Because there has been so much room to spread out, San Jose has maintained a rather suburban style and structure. Nevertheless, the ethnic diversity created by residents from all over the world, especially Latin America and Southeast Asia, makes the city a rich repository of culture and history.

Using wealth created by Silicon Valley's high-tech economy, San Jose created a glittering new downtown by redeveloping the area around Market and San Carlos streets. In addition to many good restaurants and a lively club scene, this refashioned area boasts a new arena that is home to the National Hockey League Sharks and has drawn such big names as Streisand and Pavarotti (neither of whom played in San Francisco). San Jose also has its own airport, museums, and performing arts companies. But along with size come the typical urban problems: crime, drugs, gangs, and deteriorating public schools.

As with any large city, housing is diverse. San Jose reflects its rapid post-World War II growth, with subdivisions sporting representatives from every era. That means that 1950s ranch homes share the landscape with 1990s town houses. Prices vary wildly from neighborhood to neighborhood (on average, expect to pay about $350,000 for a three-bedroom home and about $950 per month to rent a two-bedroom apartment) but are generally lower than those in other Peninsula and South Bay cities. North San Jose, known as Berryessa, is a middle- to upper-class bedroom community with many four-bedroom homes, town houses, and condos. Schools are average to above average. Most housing in culturally diverse Eastside is over 20 years old, with many apartments and some custom homes dotting the hills. Compared to schools in other San Jose neighborhoods, those in Eastside are average to below average. Evergreen in the southeast has rolling hills and 12- to 20-year-old subdivisions. Apartments abound and many new homes are going up. Schools here are very good. The south is divided among housing, industrial complexes, schools, and stores. Some homes were built in the 1950s and 1960s, but many are from the 1970s. Neighborhoods farther south have more of a country feel, and schools here are generally average to above average for the area. Homes in the west are less expensive and schools are generally average to poor. Central San Jose also has a wide variety of housing, from apartments to bungalows to mansions. Downtown schools vary greatly.

Perhaps reflecting its rapid growth, San Jose has far more children and far fewer older residents than its neighbors. All these children put pressure on the school system. Also typical of a sprawling city, San Jose has terrible traffic problems and attendant smog. Recent improvements include a new light rail system and Hwy 85, connecting southern San Jose with Cupertino and Sunnyvale.

Campbell (39,300)

A ragged border with San Jose, which almost surrounds it, makes Campbell look like a giant amoeba captured it. Nevertheless, it has carved out its own niche as an archetypal middle-class suburb. It offers more housing at lower prices (about $375,000 for a three-bedroom home) than is available in most other Silicon Valley towns, giving it a younger population than its neighbors. Schools are variable but adequate. Historically, the downtown's been sleepy, but lately an influx of new restaurants and pubs has hit. Another new addition is a farmers' market on Sundays. The name of the PruneYard shopping center is one of Campbell's few ties to its prewar life as a fruit-farming community.

Monte Sereno (3,400)

Both the smallest city and the southernmost prestige community in Santa Clara County, Monte Sereno occupies a protected enclave between Saratoga and Los Gatos. Most of the details on housing, demographics, and so forth from Saratoga and Los Altos Hills apply to Monte Sereno as well. Although its character is closer to those of Saratoga and Los Altos Hills, its commercial needs are met by nearby Los Gatos.

Saratoga (31,000)

This former logging and resort town has become one of the South Bay's most exclusive residential communities. Its location on the edge of the Santa Cruz Mountains, on the way to Saratoga Gap and Big Basin, once made Saratoga convenient for loggers and vacationers and now gives residents a nearby escape to the many parks along Skyline Drive. Downtown you'll find a quaint retail strip along Big Basin Way, with lots of pricey Continental restaurants, boutiques, and antique shops. In Saratoga, even the strip malls have wooden buildings instead of concrete slabs.

It's hard to tell what houses in Saratoga look like because they all seem to be hidden behind fences, especially in the flatter parts of town. While most seem to be expensive single-family homes, they are modest compared to the mansions common in other exclusive hillside communities. As you would expect in a community with few rental properties and high housing prices (about $700,000 for a three-bedroom and into the millions for more elaborate homes), the residents are mostly older. For those who can afford it, the schools are excellent. While Saratoga is a bit secluded at the edge of the Santa Clara Valley, Hwy 85 provides a quick route north to Cupertino and east to San Jose.

Los Gatos (29,700)

In its early days, Los Gatos was a rowdy logging town and stagecoach stop at the edge of the mountains, but it has quieted down since then. Fortunately, on its way to becoming a pricey bedroom community, it maintained many of its historic buildings, including those in the downtown area. Nature did try its own urban renewal when the 1989 Loma Prieta quake damaged many of the town's older structures, but most of the damage has been repaired. In keeping with the theme, Los Gatos puts its shopping malls in historic buildings: Old Town Shopping Plaza is housed in a one-time grammar school.

Most schools in Los Gatos have fared better, and today they are considered excellent. While housing is generally expensive, there is enough variety in the size and types of units available for rent and sale to allow access to newcomers. Consequently, you'll find more young adults in Los Gatos than in Saratoga or Los Altos. Improved access to the rest of the valley by way of newly completed Hwy 85 should make commuting easier but could threaten the town's funky individuality. Also threatened by development is the 1,145-acre Bear Creek Redwoods south of Los Gatos, which may be turned into a luxury housing and golf course complex.

Milpitas (61,200)

On the border between Santa Clara and Alameda counties stands Milpitas. As such, it represents a mix of high tech and blue collar. Historically a working-class community, it has attracted numerous high-tech production facilities to its ever-growing industrial parks, and median income is relatively high. Milpitas has also promoted unparalleled retail development. Wal-Mart is here, along with just about every other large American retailer, plus the town encouraged the conversion of an old Ford plant into the Great Mall of America, the Bay Area's biggest shopping mall.

Milpitas remains a rapidly growing, relatively new community, with plenty of housing at the lowest prices around (about $300,000 for a three-bedroom home and $1,200 a month for a two-bedroom apartment). This combination has resulted in a community with very few elderly residents, but what Milpitas lacks in age diversity it makes up for in ethnic diversity. Unfortunately, the town's transportation system has not kept up with its growth, and traffic on Hwy 880 and Hwy 237 is some of the worst in the entire Bay Area. As an unfortunate consequence of being on the border of two counties, BART stops just north in Fremont and Santa Clara Light Rail Transit only travels to the south, in San Jose. The schools are variable, but generally lag behind county averages.

HOTELS & INNS

Hotels and motels are scattered throughout the Peninsula and South Bay; most are generic but functional, with only a few historic or idiosyncratic entries in the market. We've tried to include all the interesting spots, plus a selection of generic ones to cover most locations and budgets. If none of these has suitable vacancies, keep the following in mind. You'll find the greatest concentration of corporate hotels along Hwy 101 (especially near San Francisco and San Jose airports) and along I-280 between Hwy 85 and downtown San Jose. With the boom in Silicon Valley, new ones are opening all the time. There are many, many smaller motels and hotels along the entire length of El Camino Real from San Bruno to Santa Clara.

With Valley business booming, hotels are attracting more and more guests. The result is that hotel prices, like housing prices, have skyrocketed. With hotels packed, make sure you have a reservation before you arrive. Unless otherwise noted, tariffs listed below are for the standard corporate rate during the week. Many hotels have a variety of rates, offering much more luxurious and expensive suites, as well as discounts for weekends, big corporations, frequent flyers, AAA members, and more.

Brisbane to Foster City

Best Western El Rancho Inn & Executive Suites $$$: 1100 El Camino Real (Center/Mateo), Millbrae, 650/588-8500. This large motor inn has the pink-flamingos look to go with the pools, but it's a pretty good location for those heading to SFO and is four blocks away from downtown Millbrae. In addition to palm trees, gazebos, fountains, and gardens, this California-mission-style establishment features a famous underwater view of the pool from the Terrace Café cocktail lounge, as seen in the movie *The Right Stuff.* $125-$180.

Courtyard by Marriott $$$: 550 Shell Blvd. (Hillsdale/Metro Center), Foster City, 650/377-0600, 800/321-2211. This Marriott is marketed to business travelers and has 147 rooms on three floors. Rooms are spacious and have separate sitting areas. A small gym is available, along with a pool and whirlpool/spa. The hotel's biggest plus is its location near companies like VISA, Federal Express, Microsoft, SAP America, Sprint, HBO, and Oracle. Su-Th $159; F-Sa $94.

Doubletree Hotel San Francisco Airport $$$: 835 Airport Blvd., (Anza off Hwy 101) Burlingame, 650/344-5500. A standard no-frills airport hotel, although the unique feature of complimentary chocolate chip cookies is rather nice. The pets-okay policy and baby-sitting service may come in handy. Su-Th $169-$179; F-Sa $109-$129.

Embassy Suites Hotel $$$$: 150 Anza Blvd. (Airport), Burlingame, 650/342-4600. A huge airport hotel on the bay. As the name implies, all rooms are suites with a separate living room area and a refrigerator, coffee maker, microwave, sink, and not one but two TVs—one in the living room and one in the bedroom. Enjoy a complimentary breakfast and two hours of free drinks in the evening. Su-Th $219-$234; F-Sa $159-$174.

Holiday Inn Express $$: 350 N. Bayshore Blvd. (off Hwy 101), San Mateo, 650/344-6376. Your basic motel, convenient to Hwy 101—right next to it, actually—and downtown San Mateo. Exactly what you'd expect in a regular room: a bed and a few pieces of furniture. $89-$95.

Hyatt Regency San Francisco Airport $$$$: 1333 Old Bayshore Hwy. (Millbrae Ave./Broadway), Burlingame, 650/347-1234, 800/233-1234. This classic Hyatt showcases a large ten-story atrium lobby with native greenery and waterfalls. A good place for the athlete-businessperson: it has a business center with audiovisual service, free shuttle to downtown San Francisco, fitness center and spa, and Knuckles Historical Sports Bar. Standard business-luxe rooms. Su-Th $270-$295; F-Sa $134.

Marriott San Francisco Airport $$$$: 1800 Old Bayshore Hwy. (Millbrae Ave./ Broadway), Burlingame, 650/692-9100, 800/228-9290. Perched right on the edge of San Francisco Bay, this large yellowish building may remind you of a Lego creation or chunk of cheese, but its interior is certainly much more promising. This comfortable upscale business hotel has a surprise: you can rent mountain bikes for local forays along the bay. Golf and tennis are also nearby. This Marriott has 133 rooms designed especially for business types and large meeting and banquet facilities. $189.

Millwood Inn $$: 1375 El Camino Real (Millwood/Center), Millbrae, 650/583-3935, 800/345-1375. White comes to mind upon encountering Millwood, as in white building with a white lobby that may remind you of a large bathroom (maybe it's the tiles). The typical pastel-drenched rooms are not overly flowery; the rooms with solid grays, browns, and whites are more attractive and modern looking. This is a family inn with free cable, breakfast bar, microwave and fridge, and even a pants presser. It has special family rooms with three or four beds that can accommodate six people. $84-$94; suite $139.

Park Plaza Hotel San Francisco Airport $$$: 1177 Airport Blvd. (off Hwy 101), Burlingame, 650/342-9200, 800/411-PARK. Beyond a lobby of warm colors, arches, and palms are 301 rooms and suites with a view of Peninsula hills or the San Francisco Bay. Take advantage of the indoor/outdoor heated pools, health and exercise center, bike rentals, nearby tennis and golf, and running paths along the bay. After exercising, dine at the Bay Lounge & Grill where you can watch others sweat it out (World Series, Superbowl, whatever sporting event is on). Café le Parc provides contemporary ambience and Sunday champagne brunches. $90-$180; suite $250-$500.

Ramada Inn San Francisco Airport North $$$: 245 S. Airport Blvd. (off Hwy 101), South San Francisco, 650/589-7200, 800/272-6232. After a $3.5 million renovation, this full-service hotel dwells in a unique garden setting next door to the South San Francisco Conference Center. The rooms have a nice lounging area and custom-designed cherrywood furnishings with rich colors. For water lovers, there is fishing nearby, although it's also tempting just to stay in with the On-Command Movie System, fitness/spa, and hair salon. $159-$169; suite $350.

Residence Inn San Francisco Airport-San Mateo $$$$: 2000 Winward Way (Mariners Island), San Mateo, 650/574-4700, 800/331-3131. Good for an extended stay, this 159-room hotel is one mile from downtown San Mateo. The suites have a full kitchen, living room area, and maybe a fireplace, and the penthouse is bilevel. Bonuses include Sport Court, a children's play area, and First Night Kit. Studio suites $179; penthouse $199.

Villa Hotel $$: 4000 S. El Camino Real (39th/41st), San Mateo, 650/341-0966. With soothing, pastel decor, the spacious suites include a living room area and work desk. This full-service 1950s-style hotel is near Hillsdale Mall and offers a fitness center, outdoor heated pool, and 10,000 square feet of meeting-banquet space. $109-$119.

Westin San Francisco Airport $$$$: 1 Old Bayshore Hwy. (Millbrae Ave.), Millbrae, 650/692-3500. A big airport conference hotel overlooking San Francisco Bay with a pool, spa, business services, and the like. Enter through a palm-lined driveway and take a swim in the indoor pool under a glass atrium. Su-Th $199-$234; F-Sa $109.

Belmont to Mountain View

Best Western Executive Suites $$: 25 5th Ave. (El Camino/Westmoreland), Redwood City, 650/366-5794, 800/528-1234. Comfortable and relatively affordable rooms in a building with sandstone-colored walls and red roofs located in a nondescript neighborhood on the border between Atherton and Redwood City. Amenities include an exercise and steam room, a sauna, and an outdoor hot tub. Among other niceties are complimentary Continental breakfast, coffee makers in each room, and cable TV. $99-$125; children under 12 free.

Best Western Mountain View Inn $$$: 2300 El Camino Real (Ortega), Mountain View, 650/962-9912, 800/528-1234. All the rooms and suites are outfitted with the basics and include a refrigerator, microwave, coffee maker, and sitting areas. Enjoy your complimentary Continental breakfast, sweat it off in the pool and fitness center, and come back for Chili's Bar & Grill. The location is convenient to many Silicon Valley companies, universities, Ames NASA Research Center, and Shoreline Amphitheater. $125-$250.

The Cardinal Hotel $$: 235 Hamilton Ave. (Ramona), Palo Alto, 650/323-5101. This hotel features a famous high-ceilinged Spanish-style great hall of a lobby with buffed tile floors and baronial light fixtures. The whole place was recently remodeled and the rooms sport a bright and cheerful look, not to mention that they're clean and well kept. It has a nice corner location and sits among a plethora of shops and sights. $65-$110; suite $170.

Cowper Inn $$: 705 Cowper St. (Forest/Homer), Palo Alto, 650/327-4475. Want sublime, leafy, antique-strewn New England ambience? The Cowper Inn provides porches for smokers and sherry in the parlor for everyone, as well as complimentary breakfasts and the mandatory cable TV. $65-$125.

Crestview Hotel $$$: 901 E. El Camino Real (Hwy 85/Mary), Mountain View, 650/966-8848, 800/95-HOTEL (4-6835). From the outside, it's a nondescript white building where the top half looks too heavy for the first floor. The hotel rests on the border between Mountain View and Sunnyvale and caters to corporate travelers. It provides free hot breakfast, kitchenettes, and a deli case in the lobby. Golf, parks, and Shoreline Amphitheater and Lake are nearby. $140-$155; suite $165.

Days Inn $$: 26 El Camino Real (F St.), San Carlos, 650/591-5771, 800/DAYS-INN (329-7466). There are only 29 rooms here, each one opening off the exterior hallways. Some suites have a Jacuzzi. You get Italian-tiled bathrooms, personal attention, breakfast, HBO, and limited room service. • $79-$89; suite $129.

Dinah's Garden Hotel $$$: 4261 El Camino Real (Charleston/San Antonio), Palo Alto, 650/493-2844. Set off of El Camino Real in a woodsy, landscaped setting that includes a pool, this hotel is a pleasant spot along the roadway. You can't get much more outdoorsy than these gardens and tropical lagoons. Everyone gets a private deck facing the lagoon or one of two pools, fresh fruit, and Ghirardelli chocolate. The rooms have fridges; for eating out, try the popular weekend brunch at the restaurant. For a real getaway, kick back in an international suite that sports an Asian, Mexican, or European theme. The exotic furniture will remind you why you're paying more. $160-$250.

Glass Slipper Motel $: 3941 El Camino Real (Page Mill/Charleston), Palo Alto, 650/493-6611. These Disneylandesque rooms are unquestionably the cheapest around. The exterior halls are lined with bright red doors in an apartmentlike complex, and at night the motel front is a wall of neon. Rooms are small and bare but neat. This kind of kitsch you should experience at least once. $44.

Garden Court Hotel $$$$: 520 Cowper St. (University/Hamilton), Palo Alto, 650/322-9000. With Mediterranean ambience and balconies, terraces, and patios, this is undoubtedly the executive choice in downtown Palo Alto. All those handsome young men in livery parking cars and hauling luggage will make any guest feel like a visiting dignitary. The pleasant oversized rooms are outfitted with expensive (if somewhat corporate) designer touches. Some rooms have canopy beds, fireplaces, and/or Jacuzzi spa tubs. This is a good place for wedding celebrations and corporate events. Best of all, the room service is catered by Il Fornaio, one of Palo Alto's better restaurants. $240-$295; suite $310-$450.

Hidden Villa Hostel ¢: 26870 Moody Rd. (off El Monte west of I-280), Los Altos Hills 650/949-8648. Nestled in the foothills of the Santa Cruz Mountains, the hostel is surrounded by rustic historic buildings, organic gardens, farm animals, and miles of hiking trails. Dorm rooms, private rooms, and a one-room furnished cabin called Josephine's Retreat are available. Dorm $11; private room $25-$31; Josephine's Retreat $40-$50.

Holiday Inn Palo Alto $$$$: 625 El Camino Real (University), Palo Alto, 650/328-2800. There's a splendid pool in the courtyard, as well as Japanese water gardens on the grounds. The inn is just across El Camino from Stanford and thus expensive and often booked up, so plan ahead. $189-$209.

Hotel California $: 2431 Ash St. (California/Sherman), Palo Alto, 650/322-7666. Located in a simple building with green awnings, the hotel features rooms attractively furnished with brass beds and the like, each a bit different from the others. Breakfast is purchased at Harlan's Bakery downstairs using vouchers given out by the hotel. There's a center patio, a communal kitchen complete with microwave, a coin-operated washer and dryer, and a place to iron. The facility is nonsmoking. $63-$73.

Hotel Sofitel San Francisco Bay $$$$: 223 Twin Dolphin Dr. (Redwood Shores/Marine), Redwood Shores, 650/598-9000, 800/763-4835. Bringing France (that means the country's culinary delights, too) to the Bay Area, this big corporate hotel is close to all the new industrial developments along the bay, especially Oracle (which gets special rates). The spa always looks good after a busy day. $239-$249; suite $279-$329.

Menlo Park Inn $$: 1315 El Camino Real (Valparaiso/Oak Grove), Menlo Park, 650/326-7530. Close to Stanford, with refrigerators, VCRs, and microwaves in the rooms and complimentary Continental breakfast. Modest and comfy. $115.

Residence Inn Mountain View $$$$: 1854 W. El Camino Real (El Monte), Mountain View, 650/940-1300. This 112-room hotel is all suites and penthouses with working fireplaces. The penthouses are on two stories with a living room and kitchen. Guests are coddled with complimentary cocktails, valet laundry service, a sports area, and a health club. You also get a kitchen, and there are facilities for barbecues and picnics. Designed and priced for an extended stay. 1-4 nights $229-$259; 5-11 nights $204-$234; 12 or more nights $189-$219.

Stanford Park Hotel $$$$: 100 El Camino Real (Harvard), Menlo Park, 650/322-1234. A shingled brick-and-oak building that conjures up images of ye olde English inn. Somehow this luxury hotel feels as quiet as a country inn, despite being smack dab on El Camino Real. It's convenient to the Stanford Shopping Center and campus, and the 163 rooms/suites are booked accordingly. $240-$365.

Stanford Terrace Inn $$$: 531 Stanford Ave. (El Camino/Yale), Palo Alto, 650/857-0333. You can't get much closer to Stanford University than this. The hallways are outdoors and the apartment-complexlike structure surrounds a small pool. Rooms are spacious enough and have typical but nice furnishings. Lots of Stanford visitors, no surprise, and a quiet, relaxed atmosphere. $135-$250.

Summerfield Suites $$$$: 400 Concourse Dr. (Island Pkwy. off Oracle Pkwy.), Belmont, 650/591-8600. The simple and elegant lobby of warm yellows and wood is inviting. All rooms are deluxe one- or two-room suites with recliner in the living room area, fully equipped kitchen, and complimentary breakfast buffet. $199-$300.

Victorian on Lytton $$$: 555 Lytton Ave. (Cowper/Webster), Palo Alto, 650/322-8555. This modern, sky-blue B&B, located in a residential area, is done up in faux-Victorian style. Its porch and a small but quaint garden with benches give it the look of an ornate house. Patchwork quilts and bolsters abound, the spacious rooms are stuffed with gorgeous antiques, and the bathrooms are nice and big. There are only a few rooms, however, and the tiny parlor is the only common area. Guests are mostly business types, although anyone up for the Victorian or pastel should swing by. $133-$220.

San Jose & the South Bay

Best Western Downtown $: 455 S. 2nd St. (William/San Salvador), San Jose, 408/298-3500. A basic downtown motel—more economical than the historic-landmark hotels nearby. A good deal for such niceties as complimentary Continental breakfast and fitness, spa, and steam facilities. $65-$75; kitchenette $85; suite $95.

The CO-Z 8 Executive Inn $$: 2505 The Alameda (El Camino/Bellomy), Santa Clara, 408/244-1040, 800/95-HOTEL (4-6835). This may be an unattractive, orange-hued inn, but it's one block from Santa Clara University, close to the heart of San Jose, decently close to Great America, and the rooms boast kitchenette, microwave, and fridge. Discounts for SCU faculty and students. $80-$90.

Cupertino Inn $$$: 10889 N. De Anza Blvd. (I-280/Homestead), Cupertino, 408/996-7700. Very convenient for trips to Apple Computer. Rates include breakfast and afternoon hors d'oeuvres. $135.

Doubletree Hotel San Jose $$$$: 2050 Gateway Pl. (Airport), San Jose, 408/453-4000. This large luxury hotel with stylish architecture is convenient to the airport. Features Maxi's Restaurant, California Sushi Bar, Coffee Garden, and Club Max for entertainment and dancing. $245-$275; suite $450-$650.

The Fairmont $$$$: 170 S. Market St. (Paseo de San Antonio), San Jose, 408/998-1900, 800/346-5550. The centerpiece to San Jose's downtown redevelopment boasts over 500 luxury rooms, a rooftop pool, fitness center, and a variety of restaurants. Museums, the convention center, and shops are nearby. With English tea in the afternoon, late-night music and dancing on the weekend, high-tech meeting rooms, two ballrooms, and even its own art gallery (Bingham Gallery), this impressive hotel caters to people who can afford it. $239; suite $500.

The Hensley House $$$: 456 N. 3rd St. (Hensley/Julian), San Jose, 408/298-3537. This three-story Victorian B&B in downtown San Jose offers private bathrooms, gourmet breakfasts, and afternoon hors d'oeuvres. Although its exterior consists of green walls and a green roof, inside you'll find chandeliers, stained-glass windows, and even 12-foot ceilings. The Hensley accommodates the business traveler with conveniences such as modem lines, but it's also good for Victorian weddings and parties. $125-$255.

Hotel De Anza $$$: 233 W. Santa Clara St. (Almaden), San Jose, 408/286-1000. A national historic landmark, this Art Deco hotel was recently restored as part of the renovation of downtown San Jose. The high ceiling in the lobby complements the inlaid marble floors below. The restaurant La Pastaia serves up some of the best California-Italian cuisine in the South Bay. Built in 1931, the hotel now offers fax machines, computers, cell phones, and secretarial and copying services. Known as The Grand Lady of San Jose, Hotel de Anza is still for the romantic, with nightly turndowned beds, terrycloth robes, and chocolates on the pillow. Stay in with the VCR and choice of videos or go for the live entertainment. $115-$249.

Hyatt Sainte Claire $$$$: 302 S. Market St. (San Carlos), San Jose, 408/295-2000, 800/233-1234. This remodeled historic hotel, a national landmark, is smaller than the Fairmont but quite luxurious. The Spanish-tiled interior courtyard offers a distinctive touch, and the hotel houses a branch of the Il Fornaio restaurant chain. Right across from the San Jose Convention Center, Saint Claire offers voice mail and down comforters. From the outside it looks old-fashioned (if not just old) and rather grungy, but just take one step inside and the elegant, shimmering arches and checkered floor prove that this hotel has not lost its spark. Su-Th $240-$250; F-Sa $125.

The Inn at Saratoga $$$$: 20645 4th St. (Big Basin aka Hwy 9), Saratoga, 408/867-5020, 800/543-5020. Both business travelers and vacationers looking for a spa retreat will enjoy this tasteful, romantic inn overlooking Saratoga Creek. In fact, all 45 rooms face one way—toward the creek. In the center of Saratoga, the inn is within walking distance to town essentials. Although, spoiled by wine, hors d'oeuvres, whirlpool, champagne, and complimentary breakfast, who would want to leave? $175; with whirlpool $240-$250.

Madison Street Inn $$: 1390 Madison St. (Lewis), Santa Clara, 408/249-5541. Period furnishings give this small Victorian B&B its charm, while modern touches such as a pool, hot tub, and excellent breakfasts add to the appeal. It's nestled within land-scaped gardens. $75-$115.

Motel 6 San Jose South $: 2560 Fontaine Rd. (Alvin off Tully), San Jose, 408/270-3131. Your basic cheap motel—it's south of downtown near Hwy 101 and Tully Road. $47-$50.

Radisson Inn $$$: 1085 E. El Camino Real (Lawrence/Wolfe), Sunnyvale, 408/247.0800. A full-service hotel with 136 rooms, including suites, and banquet and meeting facilities. $150-$170; suite $170-$190.

San Jose Hilton and Towers $$$$: 300 Almaden Blvd. (San Carlos), San Jose, 408/287-2100, 800/HILTONS (445-8667). One of the newest big hotels around, the San Jose Hilton was built to serve the new convention center. A modern white building with two high-rise towers, the Hilton is steps away from the Light Rail. For businesspeople, it has high-tech meeting rooms with teleconferencing. For them and everyone else, there are palm trees and a lap pool. $229-$274.

Sanborn Park Hostel ¢: 15080 Sanborn Rd. (off Hwy 9 west of downtown), Saratoga, 408/741-0166, 408/293-3787. Located 1,400 feet above sea level and surrounded by redwoods and windy roads, this 1908 log house in Sanborn Skyline County Park is a scenic getaway at a low price. Between the mother cottage and its baby cottage, the hostel has 39 beds, living room, dining room, meeting room, and stocked kitchen. It's located four miles from the town of Saratoga and eight minutes from many Silicon Valley freeways. $8.50-$11.50; half price for ages 18 and younger.

Santa Clara Marriott $$$$: 2700 Mission College Blvd. (off Great America Pkwy.), Santa Clara, 408/988-1500. If you're heading to a convention in Santa Clara, this big corporate hotel can easily take care of you. It's a plain, tall white building but has lighted tennis courts and indoor and outdoor pools. Although the hotel has 178 rooms designed for business types, Great America amusement park visitors love it, too, because it's close to the park. Su-Th $219; F-Sa $99.

Wyndham Garden Hotel $$$: 1300 Chesapeake Ter. (Hwy 237/Moffett Park), Sunnyvale, 408/747-0999. Craving a nice business hotel with a pool and spa? Try the Wyndham, located near Lawrence Expressway and Hwy 237, not far from Santa Clara Convention Center (and Great America). With modern architecture, this hotel has an impressive entrance as well as meeting and banquet facilities and the ever-popular heated pool. Su-Th $159; F-Sa $84.

Getting Settled

Every Peninsula town from South San Francisco to San Jose originated as a train stop. What began as the San Francisco–San Jose Railway in 1863 was purchased by the Southern Pacific Railroad in 1868. Wealthy San Franciscans rode the trains down the Peninsula to the large land tracts they had purchased for the price of a McDonald's Happy Meal. In most towns, Main Street retail districts surrounded the train depots. Many of these charming districts still exist and provide viable shopping options today. Take time from your hectic schedule and acquaint yourself with them. Each one provides a unique blend of shops, boutiques, restaurants, and cafés. The standouts are listed below. For those who prefer lots of parking and roofs with their shopping experience, there are plenty of large shopping centers, too. Hours vary widely from business to business, but a good general rule is to expect stores to be open Monday through Friday from 10am to between 6pm and 9pm (usually the bigger the store, the longer the hours), Saturdays from 10am to 6pm, and Sundays from noon to 5pm. For information on a single store, call the number provided in the listing. Most likely, a friendly recorded message will give you the details you need.

SHOPPING OVERVIEW

(Listed roughly Northwest to Southeast)

Serramonte Center: I-280 and Serramonte Blvd., Daly City, 650/992-8686. This ho-hum mall serves folks living at the north end of the Peninsula. Even San Franciscans have been known to wander beyond their beloved city limits to hit the sales at Macy's, Mervyn's, and Montgomery Ward.

Downtown Burlingame: Burlingame Ave. (between El Camino Real and California Dr.), Burlingame. The hottest downtown on the Peninsula attracts a bustle of strollers and shoppers. Unlike a number of its downtown neighbors, this historic area has welcomed big chains. Gap, Gap Kids, Banana Republic, Pottery Barn, Noah's, and Starbucks are all members of the retail community. Restaurants include Left at Albuquerque and Il Fornaio.

Downtown San Carlos: Laurel St. (between San Carlos and Arroyo aves.), San Carlos. This area gets better all the time. The small independently owned shops and boutiques are fun, but the restaurants are the scene-stealers. For no apparent reason, the area is fast becoming a Little Italy. Here are the winners: A Tavola, Piacere, Ciao Amore, and Café La Tosca. If you prefer a spot of tea, you can't beat The English Rose.

Hillsdale Shopping Center: El Camino Real and Hillsdale Blvd., San Mateo, 650/345-8222. Renovations have brought this enclosed mall into the '90s. Attractive architectural features complete with lush landscaping and Benjamin Bufano sculptures add to your shopping pleasure. Load your backpack with credit cards. The gang's all here: Macy's, Sears, Nordstrom, Mervyn's, and 150 specialty stores.

Downtown San Mateo: 3rd and 4th sts. (between Ellsworth Ave. and El Camino Real), San Mateo. This downtown is relatively large, so it lacks some of the charm of other downtown areas. Restaurants, cafés, and retail stores are spread out over three to four blocks in all directions. The big star is the new Draeger's Supermarket. Yes, a supermarket. In fact, a supermarket with an escalator. The Draeger family brings us the best of everything, from baked goods to wines. The facility also features a superb restaurant.

Stanford Shopping Center: El Camino Real and Quarry Rd., Palo Alto, 650/617-8585. For most of us, strolling Stanford Shopping Center is an event. For heavy-duty shoppers it is the entire Olympics. This upscale center just can't get any better, especially now that Bloomingdale's has moved in. This time, load your Gucci with credit cards. The big guns—Macy's, Saks Fifth Avenue, Nordstrom, and Neiman-Marcus—showcase a dazzling array of classic merchandise. Smaller retailers like The Gap, The Limited, and Banana Republic, offer a bit of funk for your wardrobe. Notice the outdoor mall plantings throughout the center: The seasonal displays are spectacular. The compound has grown, and getting around is no easy feat. Fortunately, there are coffee stops, candy shops, cafés, and full-scale restaurants for refueling. A favorite eatery is Max's Opera Café, where every waitperson is a Pavarotti wannabe.

Downtown Palo Alto: University Ave. (between Alma St. and Middlefield Rd.), Palo Alto. In the past three years, this college town has changed at a rapid rate. New restaurants, cafés, and retail stores seem to open up daily, all catering to gen-Xers and thirtysomethings. Stodgy longtime establishments are making way for the likes of Restoration Hardware, Starbucks, and Noah's. First-class restaurants line University Avenue and many nearby side streets. Eating and strolling take precedent here, especially in the evening when street performers offer cheap, darn good entertainment. Check out Stacey's, Borders, and Bell's for books.

Town & Country Village: El Camino Real and Embarcadero Rd., Palo Alto, 650/325-3266. • Stevens Creek and Winchester blvds., San Jose, 408/345-4670. • Washington and Mathilda aves., Sunnyvale, 408/736-6654. In contrast with the Bay Area super malls, these '50s-style open-air centers offer a mix of small retail establishments, ranging from women's and men's apparel shops to jewelry stores and delicatessens. There are two main reasons why these small operations continue to exist: customer service (most of the retailers are independents) and quality. For example, at the Palo Alto location, the Village Cheese House, which has been around for 40 years, makes up the best ham and Swiss on rye for taking to Stanford football games. The San Jose location offers the largest farmer's market in the area every Friday from 10am to 2pm and an Antique Collectibles Fair the first Sunday of every month.

Downtown Mountain View: Castro St. (between Central Expwy. and El Camino Real). Several years ago, Mountain View completely restored the downtown area. Now a bustling restaurant haven, Castro Street has earned the nickname Gourmet Gulch. Whatever kind of food your taste buds are craving, you'll find it here. Indian, Thai, Italian, and more Asian than you can shake a chopstick at. Newcomers Don Giovanni and Fibbar Magees have added a touch of class with their renovated, stylish interiors. Except for Printers Inc. bookstore, retail is considered sparse.

Downtown Los Altos: Main and State sts. (between El Camino Real and Foothill Expwy.). Charm, charm, and more charm. The very active Village Association has worked for years to keep the villagelike atmosphere alive and well. Starbucks and Le Boulanger have found their way in, but the majority of restaurants, trendy shops, and boutiques are all privately owned. Holiday season shines in Los Altos when the Parade of Lights marches down Main Street on the Sunday evening following Thanksgiving. Thousands of tiny glittering tree lights transform the area into a fairyland.

Sunnyvale Town Center: 2502 Town Center Ln. (Mathilda and Washington sts.), Sunnyvale, 408/245-6585. Macy's, J.C. Penney's, and Montgomery Ward are the major draws in this low-key enclosed mall.

Vallco Fashion Park: 1-280 and Wolfe Rd., Cupertino, 408/255-5660. Shopping and ice-skating go together like oil and water everywhere except this center. A large public skating rink, along with over 175 specialty stores, a video arcade, and an assortment of food establishments provide entertainment for every age group. J.C. Penney's and Sears are the anchors.

Downtown Saratoga: Big Basin Way (between Hwy 9 and 5th St.), Saratoga. This winding, tree-lined street beckons both shoppers and diners. Upscale specialty stops, clothing, and antique stores ensure a wealth of good choices. The dining is first-rate, from Bella Saratoga to Le Mouton Noir to Sent Sovi.

Valley Fair Shopping Center: Stevens Creek Blvd. and I-880, San Jose, 408/248-4451. This trendy mall is trying hard to catch up to the Stanford Shopping Center and succeeding nicely. Macy's and Nordstrom are the big names in this newly remodeled enclosed facility. There are 165 specialty stores, including a Super Gap with great pickings. A new parking structure is scheduled for completion by the '98 holiday shopping season—a real plus in overcrowded Silicon Valley.

Oakridge Mall: Santa Teresa Blvd. and Blossom Hill Rd., San Jose, 408/578-2910. This smaller, one-level mall features Macy's, Sears, and Montgomery Ward.

The Great Mall of the Bay Area: I-880 and Great Mall Pkwy., Milpitas, 408/945-4022. Burlington Coat Factory, Old Navy, and Oshman Super Sports USA are only three of the 180 tenants located at The Great Mall. Two themes run throughout this blend of outlets and retail-priced stores: bargains and more bargains. The value-oriented center measures about two-thirds of a mile, situated in a racetrack design. If you feel you're going in circles, you are.

BOOKSTORES

B. Dalton Bookseller: Serramonte Center, I-280 and Serramonte Blvd., Daly City, 650/994-1177. • Hillsdale Mall, El Camino Real and Hillsdale Blvd., San Mateo, 650/577-0910. • Eastridge Mall, Tully Rd. and Capitol Expwy., San Jose, 408/270-1070. • Oakridge Mall, Santa Teresa Blvd. and Blossom Hill Rd., San Jose, 408/226-0387. • Valley Fair Shopping Center, Stevens Creek Blvd. and I-880, San Jose, 408/246-6760. National chain. You'll find a good selection in these professional, well-organized stores.

Barnes and Noble: 1940 S. El Camino Real (Hwy 92), San Mateo, 650/312-9066. • Sequoia Station, 1091 El Camino Real (Jefferson), Redwood City, 650/299-0117. • 3600 Stevens Creek Blvd. (San Tomas), San Jose, 408/984-3495. • 1600 Saratoga Ave. (Campbell Ave.), San Jose, 408/370-0444. • PruneYard Shopping Center, Campbell and Bascom aves., Campbell, 408/559-8101. National chain. These bookstores are spacious and organized, giving off an elegant, almost erudite feel. You can basically find anything from computers to humor to pop culture. Bestsellers are always discounted. Some branches carry CDs and include cafés for the weary.

Books Inc.: Stanford Shopping Center, El Camino Real and Quarry Rd., Palo Alto, 650/321-0600. • North Terminal, near United Terminal in SFO, 650/244-0610. This local chain is one of the oldest booksellers in California (since 1851), and no wonder: one-quarter of the stock is always 50 to 90 percent off. Chefs should investigate the substantial cookbook selection. You can also browse through magazines and newspapers.

Borders Books & Music: 2925 El Camino Real (Hillsdale), San Mateo, 650/286-1895. • 456 University Ave. (Kipling), Palo Alto, 650/326-3670. • 15 Ranch Dr. (Hwy 237/McCarthy), Milpitas, 408/934-1180. • 50 University Ave. (Main/Elm), Los Gatos, 408/395-6622. A colossal bookstore, café, and record store all in one, Borders is a great place to relax for an extended period. You'll find an impressive and neatly decorated children's section, organized stacks, and a helpful staff. Although best known as a bookstore and café, Borders also boasts a substantial music inventory. For the most part, the selections are mainstream. Customers are welcome to take advantage of the listening stations.

Chimaera Books and Music: 165 University Ave. (High/Emerson), Palo Alto, 650/327-1122. Carries a fine selection of new and used books (specializing in literary and humanities titles), many unusual CDs, rare records, and much more. Don't look for technical books here: this is a hangout for literary folks. The selection of classical CDs, rock, and jazz is impressive. You'll find some rarities, new items, and used trade-ins. Buying, selling, and trading seven days a week for the past quarter century.

Crown Books: Super Crown, 1591 Sloat Blvd. (36th Ave.), SF, 415/664-1774. • Super Crown, 765 Broadway (Taylor/Hillcrest), Millbrae, 650/697-3224. • Super Crown, 590 Showers Dr. (El Camino), Mountain View, 650/941-4561. • Super Crown, 789 E. El Camino Real (Wolfe/Fair Oaks), Sunnyvale, 408/732-7057. • Super Crown, El Paseo de Saratoga, Saratoga and Campbell aves., San Jose, 408/871-2100. • Super Crown, Main St. Shopping Ctr., 858 Blossom Hill Rd. (Santa Teresa), San Jose, 408/629-1033. • Super Crown, 636 Blossom Hill Rd. (Hwy 17/Los Gatos Blvd.), Los Gatos, 408/358-4130. National chain started in Maryland in 1977, although with recent financial troubles, may not be around much longer. It specializes in discounted bestsellers (40 percent off *New York Times* hardcover bestsellers). Also a nice kids' section.

Heintzelman's Bookstore: 205 State St. (3rd), Los Altos, 650/941-1842. A friendly, attentive staff tends to customers at this small general bookstore. Despite its size, there are tons of books.

Kepler's Books: 1010 El Camino Real (Santa Cruz), Menlo Park, 650/324-4321. Kepler's boasts an enormous fiction selection that has attracted readers from all over the South Bay since 1955 and doubles as a hangout for literary types. Along with its many alternative and progressive sections, Kepler also offers a discount corner and children's area. Tables and chairs accommodate the hard-core browsers, while the more decisive can devour their purchases at the popular Café Borrone next door. Kepler's also sponsors frequent readings and book signings by visiting authors. If you really want to find out the latest around the world, Kepler's carries a slew of international magazines and newspapers. Among about 750 periodical titles, you're sure to encounter *Vogue Italia* and other intriguing imports.

Media Play: 940 Great Mall Dr. (Great Mall Pkwy. near Montague), Milpitas, 408/934-1844. This impressive complex is one stop for all the entertainment you'll need for a week and then some. You'll find a variety of discounted books, mainstream music, software, video games, and movie videos, all well organized.

Printers Inc.: 310 California Ave. (Birch), Palo Alto, 650/327-6500. • 301 Castro St. (Dana), Mountain View, 650/961-8500. Open since 1978, this revered pair of stores boasts a large literature collection offering titles both from mainstream and small presses, a separate room for poetry and literary theory that doubles as an evening venue for author appearances, and a large travel section. The store also stocks a select collection of unusual T-shirts, pens, cards, and gifts of a bookish nature. If you can't find what you're looking for, the staff will special order virtually any book in print. The Palo Alto shop has a spacious café next door, and the Mountain View shop has an outdoor patio. Printers Inc. sponsors frequent readings and book signings by visiting authors, all free and open to one and all.

Robert's Bookstore: 330 S. 10th St. (San Carlos/San Salvador), San Jose, 408/286-0930. Serving SJSU, Robert's has educational books categorized by majors. This store also has school supplies and a good section of study guides.

Stacey's Bookstore: 219 University Ave. (Emerson/Ramona), Palo Alto, 650/493-1222. • 19625 Stevens Creek Blvd. (Wolfe), Cupertino, 408/253-7521. The selection of business books is what gives this small local chain its reputation, although it stocks all kinds of books. Stacey's is among the nation's oldest (since 1923) and largest professional bookstores. Its specialty includes computer, technical, and medical books. As expected, the stores look professional.

Stanford University Bookstore: White Plaza, Stanford University, 650/329-1217. In addition to textbooks, the bookstore has an extensive selection of fiction, travel, technical, and language books; a small café; office and school supplies; a good newsstand; and a Stanford memorabilia and clothing section that occupies most of the second floor. There's also a section devoted to computers and software, printed music, CDs (mostly classical and current top hits), and children's literature. The bookstore regularly offers discounts on bestsellers and hosts readings, many by fellows at Stanford.

Long lines greet the beginning of an academic quarter but reduce in time. Unique gifts, free gift wrapping, and one-hour photo processing are additional plusses.

Tower Books & Records: 2727 S. El Camino Real (27th/28th), San Mateo, 650/570-7444. • 630 San Antonio Rd. (El Camino), Mountain View, 650/941-7300. • 871 Blossom Hill Rd. (Santa Teresa), San Jose, 408/363-1600. • 1900 S. Bascom Ave. (Campbell/Hamilton), Campbell, 408/371-5400. National chain of book and record stores. All bestsellers are discounted 30 percent. A computerized inventory system helps you find books, including good computer books. If technology isn't your definition of literary, an extensive alternative-titles subculture section is the sanctuary for you, or you can take an around-the-world cruise with international magazines and newspapers. Tower is still best known for its melodic side. Its operating hours are a plus: from 9am to midnight every day of the year. All locations house a wide selection of genres, from the obligatory Top 40 to soundtracks to jazz.

Waldenbooks: 106 Tanforan Park Shopping Center (El Camino/I-380), San Bruno, 650/583-7717. • 1354 Burlingame Ave. (Primrose/Park), Burlingame, 650/343-4231. • TownCenter, 2754 Town Center Ln. (Mathilda and Washington sts.), Sunnyvale, 408/739-9000. • Vallco Shopping Ctr., 10123 N. Wolfe Rd. (I-280/Stevens Creek), Cupertino, 408/255-0602. • Pavilion Mall, 150 S. 1st St. (San Fernando/San Carlos), San Jose, 408/292-6416. • Eastridge Mall, Tully Rd. and Capitol Expwy., San Jose, 408/274-1301. National chain with friendly, smaller stores. Offers the usual discounts and carries what you'd expect in a mainstream store.

Specialty

AACP Asian-American Books: 234 Main St. (2nd/3rd), San Mateo, 650/343-9408. This bookstore may be small, but it has a little bit of everything concerning Asian-American culture and literature, from origami and abacus instruction books to Amy Tan and Gus Lee. AACP also has reference, language, culture, history, and some poetry books. Catch up on Asian-American issues with periodicals, catalogs, and fly-ers. Call for hours during the summer, as the store may close for vacation.

Audio Book Central: 560 Masonic Way (Granada off Ralston), Belmont, 650/80-AUDIO (2-8346), 800/560-HEAR (4327). This spacious, well-organized store has over 5,200 audio book titles in numerous categories, including children's, *en español*, language, self-help, business, religion, and bestseller. You can also get books on CD. Books on cassette are on sale for 10 percent off the list price or for rent—$3.75 for 3 days, $7.50 for 7 days, $12.50 for 14 days, and $22.50 for 30 days. Discounted prepaid cards are available.

Computer Literacy Bookshops: 520 Lawrence Expwy. (Duane/Oakmead), Sunnyvale, 408/730-9955. • 2590 N. 1st St. (Trimble), San Jose, 408/435-1118. • 1 Infinite Loop (De Anza), Cupertino, 408/973-9955. These stores are for hard-core Silicon Valley types. If you want to know about anything from artificial intelligence to Java, networking to operating systems, you'll find it here, in over 20,000 titles. Look for bestsellers and hard-to-find titles. As the company name suggests, this is also a great place for people just starting to surf the net.

DigitalGuru Computer Bookshop: 546 Lawrence Expwy. (Duane), Sunnyvale, 408/720-6150, 800/800-1914. Since 1993, this bookstore has been supplying Silicon Valley with technical and computer books. As the Official Technical Bookshop for COMDEX and such information technology events as JavaOne, SeyBold, and DBExpo, you can be sure to find a book here for your specific needs.

East West Bookshop: 324 Castro St. (Dana/California), Mountain View, 650/988-9800, 800/909-6161. If you're looking for spiritual and New Age books and tapes, this is a great place to start. Sections include Realms Beyond, Ancient Traditions, Children's and Parenting, and The Mind, Consciousness, and Relationships. You can also find books in Spanish and some New Age music to take home and play while you read. Contact the store to find out about lectures, forums, classes, and other special events. Soothing music accompanies the gurgling of fountains throughout the store. You'll find lots of gift items, incense, and all you need to know to utilize *feng shui* the next time you feel like building a house. The store even has a small art gallery in the back.

Future Fantasy Books: 3705 El Camino Real (Page Mill/Charleston), Palo Alto, 650/855-9771. As you can guess, this is the place for sci-fi, fantasy, and mysteries. It hosts book signings, and you can even order a signed book ahead of time if you can't make it to the store to meet the author. The store also has a selection of horror items, T-shirts, and the Darwin fish you've seen on the back of cars.

Hicklebee's: 1378 Lincoln Ave. (Minnesota), San Jose, 408/292-8880. A children's bookstore extraordinaire. Fiction, activity books, poetry, in-the-car books, backyard books, can't-think-of-a-thing-to-do books—and that's just a start. Staffers know their inventory and are happy to share the knowledge.

Kinokuniya Bookstores: 675 Saratoga Ave. (Moorpark/Blackford), San Jose, 408/252-1300. Sister of the impressive San Francisco Japantown bookstore, this Kinokuniya doesn't match its kin's selection of English books on Japanese subjects. But the San Jose shop is a must for anyone looking for Japanese-language books.

Legal Recourse: 2431 Park Blvd. (California), Palo Alto, 650/324-2575. With lots of law books, legal forms, and software, this is the place for lawyers, law and paralegal students, and anyone getting sued or looking to sue. Legal Recourse is definitely a great resource for all your legal needs, with casebooks, outlines and other study aids, topical treatises, soft-cover code books, and CD-ROM–based research tools.

Linden Tree Children's Records and Books: 170 State St. (3rd/4th), Los Altos, 650/949-3390. Linden Tree runs neck and neck with Hicklebee's for the premier children's bookstore award. It offers a large collection of kids' reading books, song books, records, and tapes, as well as teaching tools for educators. The staff couldn't be better versed and more helpful if they tried. Adults will find tomes on early childhood and parenting.

M is for Mystery: 74 E. 3rd Ave. (El Camino/San Mateo Ave.), San Mateo, 650/401-8077. The wooden shelves are neatly stocked with new mysteries, plus some horror, true crime, spy, detective, and anything else vaguely mysterious, from Agatha Christie to Dean Koontz. Bestsellers are 20 percent off, and you'll also find some used books, books on tape, children and youth literature, collectibles, autographed copies, and classics.

Nolo Press Outlet Bookstore: 111 N. Market St. #115 (St. James), San Jose, 408/271-7240. Nestled in a rather hard-to-find location in downtown San Jose, Nolo offers business, legal, and consumer books. The space is not large, but it's packed with plenty of legal self-help, software, and Internet books, some at big discounts.

Phileas Fogg's Books, Maps & More for the Traveler: Stanford Shopping Center, El Camino Real and Quarry Rd., Palo Alto, 650/327-1754. If you're going on a journey, make this your first stop for its extensive map and guidebook selection. Just don't get lost among the 13,000 books, 5,000 maps, and a language section that includes 110 tongues. While you're here, pick up some travel accessories.

Psychic Eye Bookshop: 1128 W. El Camino Real (Shoreline), Mountain View, 650/964-2220. A large array of books on the metaphysical and the religious. A classroom in the back is regularly filled with instructors and students. Don't forget to visit the psychic reader to find out what's in store for you.

Two Sisters Bookshop: 605 Cambridge Ave. (El Camino), Menlo Park, 650/323-4778. Aside from tons of gift items such as candles and jewelry, this rather flowery shop has lesbian fiction and books on feminism, women's health, women's studies, biographies, and spiritualism, as well as a picture of the famed Xena. It's also a great place to get information on women's and lesbians' issues and events.

Used

Bell's Books: 536 Emerson St. (University/Lytton), Palo Alto, 650/323-7822. Search through several rooms of tightly packed floor-to-ceiling bookshelves (short—or vertically challenged—people who are afraid of heights may want more assistance than the ladders offered) for specialties like literary biographies and books on horticulture, history, and Christianity. Bell's, the oldest bookstore in Palo Alto (established in 1935), is a refined store—quality used and rare books live here; grungy paperbacks do not. Call first to sell.

The Bookbuyers: 317 Castro St. (California/Dana), Mountain View, 650/968-READ (7323). This huge place looks more like a library than a bookstore. The store has everything, including an ample fiction section that emphasizes mystery and sci-fi, plus books on tape, software, CDs, and records. You know they're serious about their used books when they have vintage paperbacks individually wrapped in plastic. You can spend a long time browsing through the aisles and aisles of fiction and nonfiction, and don't miss out on the old back issues of *Life* magazines. The CDs are mainly classical, jazz, and blues, as well as some salsa, Caribbean, and reggae, and the records are the good old stuff you'd expect on vinyl.

The Book-Go-Round: 14410 Oak St. (Saratoga-Los Gatos Rd.), Saratoga, 408/867-5552. You'll find virtually everything and anything here: thousands of used books, from history to children's, all donated and well organized. Search through paperbacks, hardcovers, records, CDs, and software. You may very well walk out with purchases of 25 cents or $1 per item.

Books Unlimited: 22 E. 25th Ave. (El Camino/Palm), San Mateo, 650/574-5377. You won't find a spot to sit down and read in this shop loaded—and in some cases literally piled—mostly with used books and lots of paperbacks priced at half off. It's a good idea to ask for help to sift through the assortment. There's plenty of mainstream fiction, a bit of nonfiction, some classics, and collectibles.

Curious Book Shoppe: 23 E. Main St. (College/University), Los Gatos, 408/354-5560. This general used bookstore has a large variety of everyday categories, as well as the rare—leather-bound volumes, obscure sets, various collectibles, and all sorts of other nostalgic goodies.

Feldman's Books: 1170 El Camino Real (Santa Cruz/Oak Grove), Menlo Park, 650/326-5300. Feldman's is a gigantic, multiroomed used bookstore. History books have a room to themselves, and you'll find a wide selection of art, cooking, philosophy, Eastern and Western religions, sciences, and entertainment. Walk through a courtyard to get to the fiction, sports, and psychology. You'll find collectibles, too.

Know Knew Books: 415 California Ave. (Ash/El Camino), Palo Alto, 650/326-9355. Aside from a clever business name, this bookstore offers a great selection of paperbacks and hardcovers, fiction and nonfiction. Look through a sizable section of collectibles and first editions.

Megabooks: 444 University Ave. (Kipling), Palo Alto, 650/326-4730. Stocked with used and new books, Megabooks is well organized and personable. Close to the entrance are many cookbooks and arts and crafts books. Also browse through a good selection of fiction, technical tomes, and textbooks.

Recycle Book Store: 138 E. Santa Clara St. (3rd), San Jose, 408/286-6275. This large store has an especially strong sci-fi selection and features a good collection of used hardcovers. It also houses videos and CDs.

A Time for Books: 733 Laurel St. (Olive/Cherry), San Carlos, 650/592-2665. This well-organized, professionally run store has mostly used books, with good sections of biography, history, science, science fiction, and mystery. You will find some rare and antiquarian tomes and autographed photos of celebrities.

Trade-A-Book: 2740 El Camino Real (Kiely/San Tomas), Santa Clara, 408/248-7598. The big red sign just says BOOKS, but the lettering on the window will tell you were you are, a bookstore with all paperbacks stacked horizontally instead of vertically. Everything is mainstream and modern fiction; don't look for classics here. Trade-A-Book is well stocked and organized, with lots of romance, horror, mysteries, and books for children and teens. There's only space for one or two people to sit and read, but you're likely to find a bargain to buy and enjoy at home in an easy chair.

Wessex Books & Records: 558 Santa Cruz Ave. (El Camino/Merrill), Menlo Park, 650/321-1333. This is home to an outstanding fiction selection, and the philosophy and history sections are also good. You'll find books by writers from more than 80 countries, literary criticism, collectibles, biographies, and university press titles. Books are mostly first editions, lots of American but also a sizable number of British. Prices run $5 to $15, but books are in good condition (there's a system rating the newness/usedness). After browsing through the books you can check out Wessex's classical, jazz, and blues used records.

Woodruff & Thush: 81 E. San Fernando St. (2nd/3rd), San Jose, 408/294-3768. Open since 1928, this downtown establishment is a bilevel warehouse crammed with old, rare, and used books. Arrive well before closing time, for the shop has been known to close a bit early and shut you out with its metal bars.

CDS, RECORDS, & TAPES

Also see bookstore section above for stores that sell both books and music.

Blockbuster Music: 5075 Junipero Serra Dr. (Serramonte), Colma, 650/997-0791. • 1087 El Camino Real (Hwy 84), Redwood City, 650/365-7468. • 645 San Antonio Rd. (El Camino/California), Mountain View, 650/941-1415. • 3785 Stevens Creek Blvd. (Saratoga Ave.), Santa Clara, 408/985-0461. • 868 Blossom Hill Rd. (Santa Teresa), San Jose, 408/224-4573. • 5255 Prospect Rd. (Saratoga Ave.), San Jose, 408/255-1660. • 187 Ranch Dr. (Hwy 237/I-880), Milpitas, 408/946-2042. As impressive and almost as ubiquitous as its video sidekick, Blockbuster Music carries everything from the common to the obscure in nearly every genre. Stores have helpful listening stations for the top-selling CDs, and you can bring any CD in the house to the central listening center, where an employee will help you hear a sample. As expected, Blockbuster Music also has movies on video and laser disc and video games for sale.

Camelot Music: 20 Serramonte Center, I-280 and Serramonte Blvd., Daly City, 650/755-9870. • Hillsdale Shopping Center, El Camino Real and Hillsdale Blvd., San Mateo, 650/571-0877. Established in 1956, this national chain plants outlets in malls and offers a spectrum of genres, from rap to classical to alternative. Although not as omnipresent in the Bay Area as other national chains, Camelot is a reliable place for basic music needs if you're near one of its two Peninsula locations.

Compact Disc Land: 477 University Ave. (Cowper/Kipling), Palo Alto, 650/324-3563. This sizable spot carries an excellent selection of new and used CDs in all categories. The new CDs are mostly rock, jazz, and classical, with a heavy emphasis on imports. You can check out new and used CDs at listening stations before purchasing. A fun gadget to look for here is the MUZE, an electronic catalog of all the CDs and cassette tapes available in the United States. If CD Land doesn't have what you're looking for, they'll happily special order it.

Compact Disc Warehouse: 470 E. El Camino Real (Saratoga Ave./Fair Oaks), Sunnyvale, 408/730-0991. Every inch of this store is devoted to CDs—new, used, and imports. Within the ocean of rock and pop selections float islands of ska/surf, Latin, country, reggae, rap, and folk. *Billboard*'s top albums are on sale, and the used section is more than promising. There are some listening stations with preselected CDs, although you can also listen to those of your own choice at one of the many stations.

Fiesta Latina: 591 Escuela Ave. (El Camino/California), Mountain View, 650/964-4530. • 217 E. Maude Ave. (Mathilda/Fair Oaks), Sunnyvale, 408/720-9644. Modest-sized but boasting a wide variety, Fiesta Latina has the Spanish CDs and tapes you want, whether it be Enrique Iglesias, traditional mariachi, or instrumental.

Flashback Records: 2090 Lincoln Ave. (Malone/Curtner), San Jose, 408/293-5274. Whip out the polyester and ogle over men with lipstick and teased hair. Flashback has Top 40 goodies from the 50s to the 80s and some 90s. Music lovers of all ages can find some great cheesy tune to be nostalgic about. You have lots of CDs, tapes, and singles to comb through, and a turntable is available for you to check out records before purchase.

The Groovesmith: 400 Florence St. (Lytton), Palo Alto, 650/FAT-LINE (328-5463). This unique store carries jazz, hip hop, soul, funk, blues, roots, dancehall, ska, reggae, and even more obscure genres such as acid jazz and triphop. You can still find good old vinyl here, as well as Groovesmith and other lines of T-shirts.

Hear Music: Stanford Shopping Center, El Camino Real and Quarry Rd., Palo Alto, 650/473-9142. The selection is inviting and extensive, and the store encourages you listen to music on the headphones that accompany all the displays. Hear sells an eclectic range of music—from hula melodies to Johnny Cash—and informative placards next to CDs describe in detail the artist or genre. The friendly staff doesn't mind if you stay for hours, moving from one set of headphones to another.

Musicland: 2449 Town Center Ln. (Mathilda and Washington sts.), Sunnyvale, 408/245-3875. • 10123 N. Wolfe Rd. (I-280/Stevens Creek), Cupertino, 408/257-6600. Music Land is affiliated with Sam Goody (see below), offering something for just about everyone.

Radio Free Records: 2626 Union Ave. (Bascom), San Jose, 408/559-7481. Located in a tiny room in downtown San Jose's historic Dohrmann Building, this shop is decoratively smothered with posters and flyers announcing the music it carries. The place specializes in punk, triphop, indies, and the like. Most of the CDs are new, with some at good prices. There is a small collection of used CDs.

Rasputin Music: 1820 S. Bascom Ave. (Hamilton/Arroyo Seco), Campbell, 408/371-8008. This Rasputin is an offspring of the majestic music mansion in Berkeley. The concept is the same, only smaller (one story instead of three). Aside from the mainstream in new and used packages, Rasputin houses good variety for people whose musical tastes lean toward the eclectic—indies, folk, reggae, ska, soul, international, gothic, industrial, and more.

The Record Man: 1322 El Camino Real (Jackson/Madison), Redwood City, 650/368-9065. Looking more like a bookstore than a music store, Record Man has wooden shelves crammed with over one million LPs, 45s, 78s, CDs, tapes, and laser discs. You'll find mostly records and tapes of rock, jazz, country, and easy listening. All the Elvis paraphernalia can only mean one thing—a section devoted to the King's music. The Planet Mix Annex DJ Shop has the hi-energy tracks—techno, hip hop, house, rap—in records, CDs, 45s, 12-inch singles. It also carries video games.

Rowe's Rare Records: 522 S. Bascom Ave. (San Carlos/I-280), San Jose, 408/294-7200. The quintessence of an organized mess, Rowe's overflows with records, including 78s, 45s, and 33s. Old posters of movies and bands hang from the tall ceiling, and all around are paraphernalia. The everyday records—rock, jazz, movie tunes—sit in white cardboard boxes, while the rare ones line the right wall. Some of the more ordinary offerings lounge in the sections marked 50 cents and $1.

Sam Goody: Serramonte Center, I-280 and Serramonte Blvd., Daly City, 650/994-1333. • 303-A Tanforan Park Shopping Center, El Camino Real and Sneath Ln., San Bruno, 650/589-2534. • 1311 Town Center Ln. (Mathilda and Washington sts.), Sunnyvale, 408/732-6234. • 893 Blossom Hill Rd. (Santa Teresa), San Jose, 408/629-7818. • Eastridge Mall, Tully Rd. and Capitol Expwy., San Jose, 408/223-6281.

Installments in a big chain, the Peninsula links in the Sam Goody empire are modest but reliable for mainstream of all genres.

Streetlight Records: 980 S. Bascom Ave. (Stokes/Fruitdale), San Jose, 408/292-1404. A large store with its own attitude, Streetlight Records caters to folks who appreciate progressive rock. But the shop also stocks rarities (think outdated technology) by the Beatles and other bands of yesterday for nostalgia buffs. Local music is another specialty, with wall space and a stage (for in-store concerts) dedicated to Bay Area artists. New and used CDs, 45s, 12-inch singles and even new and used CD-ROMs are sold. Don't miss out on collectibles and rare vinyl.

Vinyl Solution USA: 151 W. 25th Ave. (El Camino Real/Hacienda), San Mateo, 650/571-0440. The store name may convey either a feast for the vinyl hunter or just the opposite, but in any case this large music shop gives you the best of both worlds. After the poster-plastered walls greet you, you'll encounter a nice showcase of good old records. Deeper in is a decent section of new and used CDs and tapes. Although Vinyl Solution seeks to quench the thirst for rock and roll (it even has guitars sitting in the back), it also stocks some jazz, classical, international, and show tunes. Near the lone prelistening area is a great array of imports.

The Wherehouse: 280 Metro Center, Colma Blvd. and Junipero Serra Blvd., Colma, 650/755-7470. • 1950 S. El Camino Real (20th/Hwy 92), San Mateo, 650/571-8186. • 1932 El Camino Real (Woodside/Alameda), Redwood City, 650/364-2474. • 700 El Camino Real (Roble), Menlo Park, 650/322-0156. • 563 E. El Camino Real (Fair Oaks/Mathilda), Sunnyvale, 408/733-0644. • 1060 E. El Camino Real (Lawrence/Wolfe), Sunnyvale, 408/247-7433. • 21000 Stevens Creek Blvd. (Stelling), Cupertino, 408/725-1825. • 1337 Blossom Hill Rd. (Kooser/Coniston), San Jose, 408/267-4866. • 3127 Stevens Creek Blvd. (Winchester), San Jose, 408/244-0346. • 1705 E. Capitol Expwy (Silver Creek), San Jose, 408/270-4534. • 125 E. San Carlos St. (4th), San Jose, 408/971-9876. • 1087 Meridian Ave. (Willow), San Jose, 408/978-6667. • 543 E. Calaveras Blvd. (Milpitas Blvd.), Milpitas, 408/263-9063. Drive down El Camino long enough and you're bound to pass by one of these chain record stores. The Wherehouse has just the variety you'd expect from a store almost as mass produced as CDs are. It also has a small but often surprisingly fruitful used section. Plus, this well-organized space delivers a good of dose of videos, video games, and all kinds of accessories.

CHILDREN & MATERNITY

For children's bookstores, see bookstore section.

Baby on the Way Maternity Fashions: Vallco Fashion Park, 10123 N. Wolfe Rd. (I-280/Stevens Creek), Cupertino, 408/253-4675. The Bay Area's largest maternity store has fashions for the stylishly pregnant. Select from over 40 manufacturers for every phase of your lifestyle—business, casual, after five, lingerie, and nursing. Too tired? Preview the inventory on the web at www.babyonthewaymaternity.com.

FAO Schwarz Fifth Avenue: 48 Stockton St. (O'Farrell), SF, 415/394-8700. Trendy, high-priced and extravagant, this toy emporium is worth a trip into the city, especially during the holidays. Look for the store's famous selection of stuffed animals and dolls.

Hearth Song: 1344 Burlingame Ave. (Primrose/Lorton), Burlingame, 650/579-5711. Look for a wide assortment of quality nontoxic arts-and-crafts supplies, wooden toys and puppets, and dolls in this spot. The shop's ad promises, "Toys that run on imagination." Since many of the art supplies and toys include small pieces or sharp edges, the selection better suits older children.

Kiddie World Toys: 3640 Stevens Creek Blvd. (San Tomas), San Jose, 408/241-1100. Activities galore for the kiddies—games, toys, dolls, swimming pools, and gym sets. At least 10 high-quality redwood backyard structures are on display. Best selection and prices around.

Kiddie World Furniture: 3648 Stevens Creek Blvd. (San Tomas), San Jose, 408/984-8333. Stop here after Kiddie World if all of your needs haven't been met. Cribs, bathtubs, car seats, and all accompanying accessories are available under this one roof.

Kidio Homestore: 1952 W. El Camino Real (Escuela), Mountain View, 650/694-7975. Well-made, handsome wood furniture for children. Assembled room displays help you choose from a large selection of styles and colors. Brio toys are featured. Prices are reasonable but not discount.

Lullaby Lane: 556 San Mateo Ave. (San Bruno Ave.), San Bruno, 650/588-7644. • Furniture: 532 San Mateo Ave. (San Bruno Ave.), San Bruno, 650/588-4791. • Clearance Center: 570 San Mateo Ave. (San Bruno Ave.), San Bruno, 650/588-4878. A Peninsula institution, with three stores on one downtown San Bruno block, Lullaby Lane recently celebrated its 50th anniversary. The stores include a giant selection of furniture, especially cribs and rocking chairs. Other goods cover the gamut, from clothing, bedding, and toys to strollers, monitors, and car seats. Ask about the crib exchange program. Check out www.lullabylane.com for more information.

Once Upon A Child: Kids' Stuff with Previous Experience: 1929 W. El Camino Real (El Monte/Clark), Mountain View, 650/960-6822. • 1609 Meridian Ave. (Hamilton/Willowhurst), San Jose, 408/265-6800. • Monterey Plaza, 5530 Monterey Rd. (Monterey Hwy.), San Jose, 408/629-7245. An array of gently used, nearly new items. Includes clothing, play equipment, strollers, cribs, toys, and more. Come here to buy, sell, and trade. Now accepting maternity clothing. Price is always right.

Tiny Tots Togs and Nursing Mothers Resource: 200 E. Campbell Ave. (2nd), Campbell, 408/377-5350. Natural basics for babies and young ones. The shop features 100 percent cotton clothing, preemie to 6X or 7, and a wide variety of diaper coverings. A cloth diaper service, a complete line of breast feeding supplies, and a support system for nursing mothers are also found here. Educational toys from Brio and Lamaze round out the inventory.

Toys R Us: 555 9th St. (Brannan), SF, 415/252-0607. • 2675 Geary Blvd. (Masonic), SF, 415/931-8896. • 202 Walnut St. (Hwy 101/Veterans), Redwood City, 650/367-0186. • 130 E. El Camino Real (Saratoga-Sunnyvale Rd.), Sunnyvale, 408/732-0331. This chain offers a huge selection of mass-produced Saturday morning television toys at very reasonable prices, plus a nice array of fairly priced baby furniture and clothing. The stock is piled high on warehouse-type shelving, and the whole shopping experience can be overwhelming if the store is crowded. Customer service is possible if you can locate a salesperson. The Sunnyvale location has a resident ghost who has been known to roam the aisles and wreak havoc with toys.

FOOD & WINE

The local grocery scene is dominated by two giants, **Safeway** and **Lucky**. They each have stores in virtually every city on the Peninsula. Many branches of both chains are open 24 hours a day. Many neighborhoods still have independent grocers, and many cities hold weekend farmers' markets from spring through fall. Finally, virtually any store in California can sell alcoholic beverages, so don't be surprised to see a beer cooler in your drug store or rare, expensive wines in your neighborhood supermarket.

Specialty Markets

Andronico's: 1200 Irving St. (Funston), SF, 415/661-3220. • Stanford Shopping Center, El Camino and Quarry Rd., Palo Alto, 650/327-5505. • Los Altos Rancho Center, Foothill Expwy. and Magdalena Ave., Los Altos, 650/948-9265. Andronico's is one of the Bay Area's premier upscale grocers. There is an excellent selection of fresh seafood and meats. The produce section is among the best for a supermarket. The gourmet products are as good as you would expect in specialty stores.

Beltramo's: 1540 El Camino Real (Glenwood/Encinal), Menlo Park, 650/325-2806. Beltramo's claims to have "one of the world's largest and finest selections of wines and spirits," stocks over 3,500 wines, and has one of the broadest selections of beer around.

Beverages & More: 201 Bayshore Blvd. (Oakdale), SF, 415/648-1233. • 423 San Antonio Rd. (California), Mountain View, 650/949-1826. • 4175 Stevens Creek Blvd. (Kiely), Santa Clara, 408/248-2776. • 14800 Camden Ave. (Union), San Jose, 408/369-0990. This is the place for shoppers with champagne tastes and beer budgets. The prices here are some of the most competitive in the Bay Area, and the selection is out of this world. Beers can be found in an array of flavors along with a variety of hard liquors, snacks, and pastas and sauces.

Chaparral Super: 1001 E. Santa Clara St. (21st/22nd), San Jose, 408/998-8028. One of the most complete Latin American grocers in town, with Mexican, Central, and South American products. The meat, fish, and poultry counter is large and loaded. Produce includes all the usual goods. Packaged goods cover the basic sauces, spices, and chilies plus a complete line of South American goods.

Cosentino's Vegetable Haven: S. Bascom Ave. and Union Ave., San Jose, 408/377-6661. • 3521 Homestead Rd. (Bing), Santa Clara, 408/243-9005. For South Bay denizens, Cosentino's is *the* food emporium. In addition to high-quality vegetables, Cosentino's has a great selection of bulk items and gourmet goods. There are a few ethnic items and a good selection of gourmet mustards and olive oils. The meat, fish, and poultry counter features superior cuts, and many game meats, including quail, ostrich, and rattlesnake, are available.

Cost Plus: 785 Serramonte Blvd. (I-280), Daly City, 415/994-7090. • 68 Hillsdale Mall (El Camino/Hillsdale), San Mateo, 650/341-7474. • 1910 W. El Camino Real (Magdalena), Mountain View, 650/961-6066. • 4050 Stevens Creek Blvd., San Jose, 408/247-3333. • 1084 Blossom Hill Rd. and Almaden Expwy., San Jose, 408/267-6666. This bargain mecca offers an eclectic mix of gourmet and international foods. They sell many varieties of olive oil, vinegar, mustard, and pasta, boxed Italian tomatoes, and European cookies and chocolates. They also have a good mix of Asian sauces and noodles and some Mexican salsas. Their extensive spice collection features good prices. Selection varies from store to store and season to season.

Dobashi Market: 240 E. Jackson St. (5th/6th), San Jose, 408/295-7794. Although primarily Japanese (it is in the heart of Japantown), this small supermarket has a slightly pan-Asian feel to it. They sell produce, fish (both for cooking and sashimi), poultry, and meat (mostly cuts for shabu shabu and sukiyaki). Japanese staples line the shelves.

Draeger's Supermarket: 342 1st St. (Main), Los Altos 650/948-4425. • 1010 University Dr. (University), Menlo Park, 650/688-0677. • 222 S. 4th Ave. (B St.), San Mateo, 650/685-3730. An upscale food emporium with a full-service butcher (game birds available), an above-average produce department, and an extensive wine section. Draeger's has a wonderful selection of European goods, including a score of olive oils, gourmet mustards, fine vinegars (several brands of balsamic), and a stupendous deli with marinated olives, cold meats, and salads. They also carry an expensive selection of fine domestic and imported cheeses. When Draeger's added its San Mateo gourmet temple, it also made a commitment to serve a multiethnic cooking audience. The San Mateo store is the most complete, followed by Menlo Park.

Fiesta Latina: 1424 Cary Ave. (Norfolk/Patricia), San Mateo, 650/343-0193. A very complete Latin American produce and dry goods market. Fresh produce, a complete meat, fish, and poultry counter, and a deli case packed with Latin American cheeses keep local cooks coming back.

Halal Meats Deli & Grocery: 1538 Saratoga-Sunnyvale Rd. (Duckett/Prospect), San Jose, 408/865-1222. Although the highlight here is the halal butcher, there is more than meat. Packaged goods mix Indian and Middle Eastern staples. Various breads come fresh and frozen. Indian spices are well labeled.

India Food Mill: 650 E. San Bruno Ave. (San Mateo Ave./Hwy 101), San Bruno, 650/583-6559. • 460 Persian Dr. #1 (Fair Oaks/Hwy 237), Sunnyvale, 408/744-0777. A pair of small, well-organized warehouses filled with dried beans and lentils, rice, and flours. The spice selection is complete. Fresh nan, too, along with some cookware.

International Food Bazaar: 2052 Curtner Ave. (Union), San Jose, 408/559-3397. • 5491 Snell Ave. (Blossom Hill), San Jose, 408/365-1922. This fully stocked Mideast market has plenty of beans, lentils, rice, pickles, cheeses, and yogurts. There are also spices, teas galore, frozen halal meats and sausage, and lots of prepared salads. The bread selection is extensive, and there is even a little bit of basic produce.

K&L Liquors: 3005 El Camino Real (Selby), Redwood City, 650/364-8544. A San Francisco-style wine warehouse with cardboard boxes on the floor, good deals (especially on high-end wines), and some older vintages.

La Costeña: 2078 Old Middlefield Wy. (Rengstorff), Mountain View, 650/967-0507. La Costeña carries many hard-to-find Latin American products, especially Mexican and Salvadoran ones. La Costeña has an excellent selection of dried chilies and Mexican herbs and a small produce section with fresh yuca and plantains.

Marina Foods: 2992 S. Norfolk St. (Hillsdale), San Mateo, 650/345-6911. 10122 Bandley Dr. (Stevens Creek at De Anza), Cupertino, 408/255-2648. • 4140 Monterey Hwy. (Senter), San Jose, 408/224-8786. A large supermarket—Cheerios and all—oriented toward Asian customers. A highlight is the well-labeled produce section. A few aisles are dedicated to Chinese goods. Sections are also given over to Japanese, Southeast Asian, and Filipino items.

Mercadito Latino: 1726 El Camino Real (Hwy 84/Oak), Redwood City, 650/306-0105. After expanding some time ago, this busy store has become quite a complete Latin American grocer. The produce section is large. In addition to a full array of Mexican spices and packaged goods, there are many South American products. The deli counter has cheeses and sausages. To top it off, one aisle is lined with cookware.

Mi Pueblo: 40 S. Rengstorff Ave. (Middlefield), Mountain View, 650/967-3630. • 1114 S. King Rd. (Story), San Jose, 408/272-5370. A clean, well-organized Latin American store. The high-quality produce includes lots of fresh chilies, a few plantain varieties, and nopales and prickly pear cactus, all at good prices. The meat counter is well stocked and even has goat; they also have a good cheese selection, fresh *crema*, sausages, and housemade salsas. The dried chili and spice sections are extensive, and they have many South American products.

Monterey Market: 399 Stanford Shopping Center, El Camino Real and Quarry Rd., Palo Alto, 650/329-1340. People who seek out good produce and value prices swear by this festive market. The fresh, colorful offerings include Latin American staples like plantains and guava, and Asian essentials like bok choy and Chinese green beans (not to mention a good variety of exotic mushrooms). The prices are hard to beat for such top-of-the-line produce. Monterey Market also sells bulk nuts and large bags of basmati and rice.

Nak's Oriental Market: 1151 Chestnut St. (Santa Cruz/Oak Grove), Menlo Park, 650/325-2046. This tiny gem of a store is packed with Japanese and other Asian products, even fresh fish for sushi on Wednesdays and Fridays. Fresh produce includes Asian mushrooms, lemongrass, and snow peas. Japanese tableware also available.

Narayan Enterprises: 2520 California St. (Showers/San Antonio), Mountain View, 650/948-4777. Indian, Pakistani, Middle Eastern, and some Southeast Asian groceries. Fresh produce includes curry leaves, eggplant, okra, and beans. They also have a nice selection of frozen breads: nan and chapati.

New Castro Market: 340 Castro St. (California/Dana), Mountain View, 650/962-8899. One of the better Asian markets in the area. The produce section is decent and offers many choys, long beans, and lemongrass. The highlight of the store is perhaps the fish and meat department, which is as complete as any in the Bay Area. There is fresh fish and seafood especially for sushi and tanks with live shrimp, abalone, and many clams—all at great prices.

99 Ranch Market: 250 Skyline Plaza (Westmoor and Southgate), Daly City, 650/992-8899. • Cupertino Village, 10983 N. Wolfe Rd. (Homestead), Cupertino, 408/343-3699. • 1688 Hostetter Rd. (Lundy), San Jose, 408/436-8899. This chain has really nailed the assimilated Asian-American market with its modern supermarkets mixing traditional American goods with Asian specialty items. The fish department is a highlight, offering Chinatown-style low prices, variety, and live tanks in a comfortably sanitized environment. They even have some sashimi fish. Produce is another highlight, and items are well organized and well labeled in English. Packaged goods are grouped loosely by country. They even offer on-line shopping via their web site (www.99ranch.com).

Oakville Grocery: 715 Stanford Shopping Center, El Camino Real and Quarry Rd., Palo Alto, 650/328-9000. An upscale food emporium with a particularly nice wine selection (the proprietor owns the Joseph Phelps vineyard). The fine array of domestic and imported cheeses includes mascarpone, manchego, and fresh mozzarella, along with excellent breads and crackers for serving with them. Well over a dozen olive oils, other gourmet oils such as walnut and avocado, numerous vinegars, gourmet mustards, and exotic dried mushrooms, flours, and grains are stocked.

Race Street Fish & Poultry: 253 Race St. (Park/W. San Carlos) San Jose, 408/294-4857. An excellent fish and poultry market, Race Street carries crab, crawfish, shrimp and prawns, squid, octopus, oysters, mussels, live lobsters, chicken, duck, and rabbit. They'll handle special orders for game meats such as pheasant and quail. The attached fast-food restaurant does a booming business in fried and grilled fish.

Schaub's: The Street Market, Stanford Shopping Center, El Camino Real and Quarry Rd., Palo Alto, 650/325-6328. One of the best premium butcher shops on the Peninsula, offering a wide variety of fresh meats, including fish and seafood, as well as prepared rotisserie chicken and fajitas. They also carry a variety of terrific store-made sausages. Duck and rabbit are always on hand, while game meats such as pheasant, venison, and quail can be special ordered.

Senter Foods: 933 E. Duane Ave. (Lawrence/Fair Oaks), Sunnyvale, 408/735-7277. • 2889 Senter Rd. (Lewis), San Jose, 408/227-8771. A large pan-Asian supermarket, complete with a full meat, fish, and poultry department and Cheerios and Jell-O. Fresh produce includes lots of plantains and many kinds of basil and greens.

Sigona's Farmer Market: 2345 Middlefield Rd. (Hwy 84/Douglas), Redwood City, 650/368-6993. A wonderful produce market with a wide variety of fruits and vegetables, including lots of chilies, pea sprouts, and papayas and mangoes of all stripes. Sigona's boasts a complete selection of grains in bins. Some products are organic.

Suruki Japanese Foods: 71 E. 4th Ave. (San Mateo Dr.), San Mateo, 650/347-5288. A fairly large, well-equipped Japanese supermarket with a large produce section, a full meat and fish department (with sushi fish), a good little restaurant in a corner (Sozai Corner), and many premade salads.

Tin Tin Oriental Supermarket: 10881 S. Blaney Ave. (Bollinger), Cupertino, 408/255-7804. Similar to 99 Ranch Market, this complete supermarket sells both standard American and Asian specialty goods. Produce is fresh and varied (all labeled in English). The large meat, poultry, and seafood department has many tanks—lobster and spot prawns—as well as more familiar cello packs, some with sashimi cuts. Packaged goods are not as organized as the competition.

Trader Joe's: Various locations throughout Northern California. Call 800/746-7857 for the location and phone number of the store nearest you. A discount gourmet store with a decent assortment of domestic and imported cheeses. Salsas, chutneys, and various sauces are available, as well reasonably priced olives, nuts, and frozen fish. Some stores have even have fresh produce. Good cheap wines perfect for cooking.

Whole Foods: 774 Emerson St. (Homer), Palo Alto, 650/326-8666. • 15980 Los Gatos Blvd. (Blossom Hill), Los Gatos, 408/358-4434. • 20830 Stevens Creek Blvd. (De Anza/Stelling), Cupertino, 408/257-7000. • 1690 S. Bascom Ave. (Hamilton), Campbell, 408/371-5000. Whole Foods provides an abundant variety of organic foods in a soothing shopping experience. Among the goodies are a good fresh seafood section, organic and conventionally grown produce, a variety of bulk rices, whole grains and granolas, a bakery and deli, a meat market featuring organic meat and homemade sausages, and a great selection of wine and beer. Gourmet items include a full range of mustards, capers, and such, as well as a great selection of cheeses, olives, and other deli items. To top it all off, an on-site masseur at the Palo Alto store will relax you after you shop. (Really—no joke.)

Yaohan: 675 Saratoga Ave. (I-280/Blackford), San Jose, 408/255-6690, 408/255-6699. This American branch of a Japanese supermarket is large, modern, and targeted, with almost exclusively Japanese goods, an in-house sushi bar/quick restaurant, and an attached Japanese bookstore. This store has all you'll need for a Japanese meal. One corner is dedicated to seaweed salads and pickles. Of course, there are fish for cooking and for sashimi. Meats are primarily specialty cuts for shabu shabu and the like. The produce is also nice.

HOME FURNISHINGS

General Purpose

If one-stop shopping is all you have time for, there are a number of large department stores listed in the shopping overview that will suit your needs. For greater variety, browse the aisles of the stores listed below.

Bed, Bath and Beyond: 555 9th St. (Brannan), SF, 415/252-0490. Formerly known as the Bed and Bath Superstore. As the new name implies, you can now find enticing bargains for other rooms, too. You can also find that seldom-seen San Francisco commodity known as parking.

Butterfield West: 164 Utah St. (Alameda/15th St.), SF, 415/861-7500. If you're looking to inject a little drama into your shopping experience, or want to find something with a little more character than you'll discover at your average department or discount store, join the auction junkies that converge at Butterfield West approximately every third Monday of the month. The Monday sales are a clearinghouse for all of the items that don't merit being shown in one of Butterfield's Fine sales (where art experts buy for their galleries). Come to the warehouse on the weekend prior to the sale to view goods, which range from couches to paintings, books to china. You can leave a written bid on the weekend, which will be read off during the auction as though you were there. Better yet, come to the auction and fight it out in person with your competitors. There is no minimum bid, so you can pick up some great deals if you're diligent, but be warned: a 15-percent "buyer's commission" in addition to sales tax will be tacked onto whatever you bid, so do your math before you raise that paddle.

Costco Wholesale: 450 10th St. (Harrison/Bryant), SF, 415/626-4288. • 451 S. Airport Blvd. (off Hwy 101 at Beacon), South San Francisco, 650/872-2021. • 1340 El Camino Real (Sneath/Noor), San Bruno, 650/871-0460. • 2200 Middlefield Rd. (Charter), Redwood City, 650/369-3321. • 1000 N. Rengstorff Ave. (off Hwy 101 at Leghorn), Mountain View, 650/988-9766. • 150 Lawrence Station Rd. (Kifer), Sunnyvale, 408/730-1575. • 1601 Coleman Ave. (De La Cruz/Reed), Santa Clara, 408/567-9080. • 2201 Senter Rd. (Burke), San Jose, 408/275-1088. If you are flying solo and can't finish off a gallon can of baked beans, Costco is probably too much of a good thing. Just about everything is sold in bulk. If you are tending to a large family, a Little League team, or a company picnic, you will find terrific prices in this bare-bones wholesale warehouse. Stock is random: what is there today may not be there tomorrow. Checkout lines can be excruciatingly long, and there's no customer service. Despite the negatives, Costco is a great place to save money, although you must be a member.

Cost Plus World Market: 2552 Taylor St. (Bay/Northpoint), San Francisco 415/928-6200. • 785 Serramonte Blvd. (El Camino/Junipero Serra), Colma, 650/994-7090. • 1910 W. El Camino Real (Escuela/Rengstorff), Mountain View, 650/961-6066. • 4050 Stevens Creek Blvd. (Kiely/Saratoga Ave.), San Jose, 408/247-3333. Signs outside may read Cost Plus Imports, since the name change is recent. Inside you will find a discount import store with reasonably priced merchandise. Over the years, the inventory has grown along with the number of stores. A wide and interesting selection of tables, chairs, cabinets, patio and beach accessories, kitchenware, and decorative doodads are now available. Once the house is furnished, Cost Plus offers a bounty of international foods for your pantry and wines for your cellar. Baskets of all shapes and sizes are a specialty. Watch for colorful sales inserts in your newspaper.

Crate and Barrel: 125 Grant Ave. (Geary/Post), SF, 415/986-4000. • Stanford Shopping Center, El Camino Real and Quarry Rd., Palo Alto, 650/321-7800. • 2855 Stevens Creek Blvd. (off I-880 at S. Redwood), Santa Clara, 408/243-7500. Crate and Barrel targets a more fashion-oriented clientele than Cost Plus. You will find a complete selection of tableware, cooking utensils, and table linens, plus some furniture and patio items. Hand-painted dishes and bowls will make any bride and groom happy. Service and free gift wrapping are excellent. The new store at Stanford Shopping Center is an extravaganza. An entire floor is dedicated to furniture.

Fillamento: 2185 Fillmore St. (Sacramento), SF, 415/931-2224. Go to Fillamento for 10,000 square feet of the hippest home furnishings in town. If you prefer chintz on a four-poster bed, this mix of contemporary classics and high-style eclectic may not be for you. Some items may leave you wondering if they are serious. They are. And so are the price tags. A knowledgeable staff will lead you through a complete line of furnishings from dining room tables to bathroom soaps. Decorative candles are a specialty.

The Home Depot: 920 Blossom Hill Rd. (Santa Teresa), San Jose, 408/224-4900. • 2435 Lafayette St. (El Camino), Santa Clara, 408/492-9600. • 680 Kifer Rd. (Fair Oaks), Sunnyvale, 408/245-3686. Getting settled often means more than new kitchen towels and a hibachi. It can mean adding or replacing the nuts and bolts of your home. The Home Depot has it all in one place—fencing materials, garden tools, light fixtures, piping, paint, flooring, bathroom vanities and cabinets, doors, and every other unglamorous but necessary thing you need to be comfortable. Competitive prices.

Macy's: Union Square, Stockton and O'Farrell Sts., SF, 415/397-3333. • Stonestown Galleria, 19th Ave. and Winston Dr., SF, 415/753-4000. • 1 Serramonte Center, I-280 and Serramonte Blvd., Daly City, 650/994-3333. • Hillsdale Shopping Center, El Camino Real and Hillsdale Blvd., San Mateo, 650/341-3333. • 2838 S. El Camino Real (28th/31st), San Mateo, 650/341-3333 (furniture, rugs, and mattresses only). • Stanford Shopping Center, El Camino Real and Quarry Rd., Palo Alto, 650/326-3333. • 200 W. Washington Ave. (Mathilda/Sunnyvale Ave.), Sunnyvale, 408/732-3333. • 2210 Tully Rd. (Quimby/Capitol), San Jose, 408/238-3333. • Oakridge Shopping Center, Santa Teresa Blvd. and Blossom Hill Rd., San Jose, 408/224-3333. • Valley Fair Mall, Stevens Creek Blvd. and I-880, San Jose, 408/248-3333. A Bay Area staple, the stores in this large chain boast a department for everything you need, from clothing to home furnishings. Perpetual sales abound, but items can still be pricey. Leave ample time: you are more likely to win the lottery than find a salesperson to take your money. Don't miss **The Cellar at Macy's,** a housewares department with an excellent selection of cookware.

Pier 1 Imports: 3535 Geary Blvd. (Stanyan/Arguello), SF, 415/387-6642. • 101 Colma Blvd. (El Camino Real/Junipero Serra), Colma, 650/755-6600. • 2501 El Camino Real (Woodside), Redwood City, 650/364-6608. • 1255 W. El Camino Real (Bernardo/Sylvan), Sunnyvale, 650/969-8307. • 20610 Stevens Creek Blvd. (De

Anza/Stelling), Cupertino, 408/253-4512. • 1807 Saratoga Ave. (Lawrence), Saratoga, 408/255-3533. • 1009 Blossom Hill Rd. (Almaden/Winfield), San Jose, 408/978-9555. Pier 1 specializes in wicker baskets and wood furniture. Brass items are in abundance. A variety of basic but stylish glassware, dishes, rugs, and prints also grace the shelves. Higher priced than other import outlets.

Pottery Barn: 2100 Chestnut St. (Steiner), SF, 415/441-1787. • One Embarcadero Center, Battery and Sacramento sts., SF, 415/788-6810. • Stonestown Galleria, 19th Ave. and Winston Dr., SF, 415/731-1863. • 1230 Burlingame Ave. (California), Burlingame, 650/348-0668. • Stanford Shopping Center, El Camino Real and Quarry Rd., Palo Alto, 650/473-0449. • 2855 Stevens Creek Blvd. (Winchester), Santa Clara, 408/261-9882. Pottery Barn stocks everything necessary to outfit your space with the latest rustic styles and trendy upscale versions of the basics: glassware and dishware, lamps and rugs, candles, frames, vases, chests, wine racks, big cushy couches and chairs, and sturdy wood dining tables. Prices aren't cheap, but the offerings are stylish.

Restoration Hardware: Hillsdale Shopping Center, El Camino Real and Hillsdale Blvd., San Mateo, 650/577-9807. • 261 University Ave. (Bryant), Palo Alto, 650/328-4004. This Corte Madera–based chain mixes attractive furniture (heavy on updated Shaker and Mission styles), accessories (bar towels to picture frames), and the namesake do-it-yourself fixtures (furniture handles, towel bars, and the like).

Target: 5001 Junipero Serra Blvd. (off I-280, Serramonte Blvd. exit), Colma, 650/992-8433. • 2485 El Camino Real (Charter/Northumberland), Redwood City, 650/363-8940. • 555 Showers Dr. (El Camino/California), Mountain View, 650/965-7764. • 20745 Stevens Creek Blvd. (De Anza), Cupertino, 408/725-2651. • 3155 Silver Creek Rd. (Capitol), San Jose, 408/238-7800. • 1811 Hillsdale Ave. (Ross/Leigh), San Jose, 408/267-7900. Target is a treasure chest of reasonably priced household necessities, offering cheap towels, pots and pans, plastic anythings, and basic furniture. The furniture is along the line of shelving units, nightstands, and chairs made of lightweight pressboard or plastic, mostly unassembled. A computerized bridal and baby registry has proven very popular.

Whole Earth Access: 401 Bayshore Blvd. (Army/Cortland), SF, 415/285-5244. This well-known institution serves as something of a Sears for the New Age crowd. It carries everything the modern family needs, from jeans to housewares. A trip here can yield a cornucopia of stylish housewares, dishware and glasses, cutting boards, appliances, and so on. Whole Earth no longer stocks computers, but it still has a decent selection of audio, video, and communications gadgets. You can also order by phone (call the number listed above).

Z Gallerie: Stonestown Galleria, 19th Ave. and Winston Dr., SF, 415/664-7891. • 2071 Union St. (Webster/Buchanan), SF, 415/346-9000. • 2154 Union St. (Fillmore), SF, 415/567-4891. • 340 University Ave. (Waverley), Palo Alto, 650/324-0693. One of the Bay Area's premier purveyors of housewares and decorative items. The stylish and distinctive inventory includes dishware, glassware, flatware, overstuffed couches and funky chairs, beds, coffee and dining tables, bath products, and a wide variety of framed and unframed art posters. Great gift shopping.

Computers and Electronics

Anderson's: 901 El Camino Real (Jefferson/Broadway), Redwood City, 650/367-9400. • 999 El Camino Real (Wolfe/Poplar), Sunnyvale, 408/733-9820. • 606 Saratoga Ave. (Moorpark), San Jose, 408/554-1617. Go for the great selection of electronics at decent prices. Frequent warehouse sales will have you reaching for your wallet.

Circuit City: 303 Gellert Blvd. (off I-280, Serramonte Blvd. or Hickey exit), Daly City, 650/755-0101. • 1880 S. Grant Rd. (Hwy 101/Hwy 92), San Mateo, 650/578-

1400. • 1250 Grant Rd. (El Camino), Mountain View, 650/965-3500. • 1825 Hillsdale Rd. (Leigh/Ross), San Jose, 408/723-1500. • 4080 Stevens Creek Blvd. (Saratoga), San Jose, 408/296-5522. • 2217 Quimby Rd. (Tully/Capitol), San Jose, 408/223-1390. Circuit City is a chain store where you will find low- to mid-end electronics of every kind at competitive prices. Listening rooms for speakers, receivers, and car stereos are available to help you decide. The stores carry a large selection of TVs and VCRs, as well as some appliances and computer equipment. High-pressure salespeople tend to hover. You can arrange for installation of home security and car stereo systems.

ComputerWare: 343 Sansome St. (Sacramento), SF, 415/362-3010. • 487 S. El Camino Real (4th/5th), San Mateo, 650/375-5929. • 490 California Ave. (El Camino), Palo Alto, 650/323-7559. • 3215 Stevens Creek Blvd. (Winchester), Santa Clara, 408/345-0345. • 520 Lawrence Expwy. (Arques), Sunnyvale, 408/732-0200. Apple Macintosh computers, monitors, printers, peripherals, accessories, and software are what you find here. There is also a good selection of Mac software. Helpful staff will often let you load software on a machine for evaluation before purchase.

CompUSA: 1250 El Camino Real (Sneath), San Bruno, 650/244-9980. • 3561 El Camino Real (Lawrence), Santa Clara, 408/554-1733. This national chain of computer superstores specializes in PC computers, software, and accessories.

Fry's Electronics: 340 Portage Ave. (El Camino), Palo Alto, 650/496-6000. • 1177 Kern Ave. (Lawrence), Sunnyvale, 408/733-1770. • 600 E. Hamilton Ave. (Hwy 17), Campbell, 408/364-3700. • 600 E. Brokaw Rd. (I-880/Zanker), San Jose, 408/487-1000. Fry's is a Silicon Valley institution. The good news: The former-supermarket-turned-electronics-superstore carries Macs, IBMs, countless clones, printers and monitors, and enough parts and accessories to build your own computer. You can also find stereos, VCRs, TVs, CD players, fax machines, telephones, cameras, and answering machines. The bad news: You will find a Klystron tube on the shelf before you will find a shred of customer service. Bay Area folks come here for the unbeatable selection and prices.

Mateo Hi-Fi: 2199 S. El Camino Real (22nd), San Mateo, 650/573-6506. Serious audiophiles need to check out Mateo Hi-Fi. It specializes in custom home design and installation, as well as mid-fi with some high-fi and specialty products like in-wall speakers. You can always negotiate a deal with their competent salespeople.

The Good Guys: Serramonte Center, I-280 and Serramonte Blvd., Daly City, 650/301-8855. • 2727 El Camino Real (27th/28th), San Mateo, 650/574-5100. • 1247 W. El Camino Real (Bernardo/Hwy 85), Sunnyvale, 650/962-0101. • 3149 Stevens Creek Blvd. (Winchester), Santa Clara, 408/554-9700. • 1960 Tully Rd. (Quimby), San Jose, 408/274-1062. • 886 Blossom Hill Rd. (Santa Teresa), San Jose, 408/361-0300. The selection of audio/video/communications electronics is unsurpassed. Good Guys has a 30-day low "advertised" price guarantee, so if you are bargain hunting, you will want to compare prices. Listening rooms are available for your home and car stereo selections. As with all of the large electronics department stores, sales staff can be detrimental to your health.

Wireless World: 871 El Camino Real (Live Oak/Roble), Menlo Park, 650/322-0222. • 4646 El Camino Real (San Antonio), Los Altos, 650/941-3511. • 813 W. El Camino Real (Castro), Mountain View, 650/969-7200. • 956 Blossom Hill Rd. (Winfield), San Jose, 408/226-2230. • 1395 Winchester Blvd. (Hamilton/Payne), San Jose, 408/378-6990. • 4180 Stevens Creek Blvd. (Kiely), San Jose, 408/241-4300. • 1711 Branham Ln. (Hwy 85/Camden), San Jose, 408/448-6480. He who dies with the most toys wins—and this is the place to stock up on these toys. You can't be a bona fide Silicon Valley–type without your Motorola pager and Nokia digital cell phone. All the stores specialize in car audio and security systems, too. Helps to know what you want before you go in the door. Watch for sales.

Furniture

Cort Furniture Clearance Center: 2925 Meade Ave. (Bowers), Santa Clara, 408/727-1470. Cort has new and used furniture. Good buys can be found on dinged furniture.

Cort Furniture Rental: 626 San Antonio Rd. (El Camino/Fayette), Mountain View, 650/966-1758. • 4995 Stevens Creek Blvd. (Lawrence), Santa Clara, 408/984-0433. Need to impress your new boss and you don't even have a chair for her or him to sit in? Pay a visit to Cort Furniture Rental and have whatever you need delivered. Houseware packages are also available.

Designs in Wood: 251 W. El Camino Real (Mathilda/Sunnyvale Ave.), Sunnyvale, 408/730-1658. • 20149 Stevens Creek Blvd. (Blaney/De Anza), Cupertino, 408/253-6900. Formerly known as Oprah House, Designs in Wood features everything from custom-finished to unfinished pieces in pine, maple, oak, alder, and birch. It offers the South Bay's largest selection of wood furniture under one roof.

Flegel's: 870 Santa Cruz Ave. (Oak Grove/Menlo Ave.), Menlo Park, 650/326-9661. • 1654 2nd St. (G St./Shaver), San Rafael, 415/454-0502. Flegel's, which offers a complete home-design service, has been furnishing Bay Area homes since 1954. If the names Henredon and Brown Jordan mean anything to you, this is your place to shop. It helps to have an unlimited budget.

The Futon Gallery: 2951 El Camino Real (Olive/Page Mill), Palo Alto, 650/322-8193. • 998 El Camino Real (Poplar), Sunnyvale, 408/720-8036. The Futon Gallery, a small store that offers personal service, is a reliable place to buy a futon. It stocks an upscale line of futons, frames, and accessories.

The Futon Shop: 3545 Geary Blvd. (Stanyan/Arguello), SF, 415/752-9908. • 2098 El Camino Real (Stanford Ave.), Palo Alto, 650/329-1204. • 3390 Stevens Creek Blvd. (San Tomas/Winchester), San Jose, 408/296-8989. • 1080 Blossom Hill Rd. (Almaden), San Jose, 408/978-5696. The self-service atmosphere begs you to prepare your wish list before you arrive. Know what you want and what you are willing to pay before you enter these well-stocked emporiums.

Limn: 290 Townsend St. (4th St.), SF, 415/543-5466. The city's best-known location for cutting-edge designer furniture, Limn offers wares from Ligne Roset, Herman Miller, and many esoteric European manufacturers. Bargain hunters can find instant gratification and discounts on one-of-a-kind showroom items. Even if you can't afford a $5,000 couch, it's worth a visit here just to see some stunning art furniture.

Mancini Sleep World: 1450 Van Ness Ave. (Pine/Bush), SF, 415/447-1841. • 2034 W. El Camino Real (Rengstorff/Escuela), Los Altos, 650/988-1300. • 968 E. El Camino Real (S. Mary/Hollenbeck), Sunnyvale, 408/245-6251. • 50 N. Winchester Blvd. (Stevens Creek/Forest), Santa Clara, 408/261-7400. • 1086 Blossom Hill Rd. (Almaden/Sanchez), San Jose, 408/264-6100. You'll find a huge selection of bedding needs here, including mattresses in all sizes at all prices. The specialty is unique bed sets that save space and include storage; great for the kids' rooms.

Mattress Discounters: 1189 El Camino Real (Oak Grove), Menlo Park, 650/327-6288. • 1265 W. El Camino Real (Bernardo/Hwy 85), Sunnyvale, 650/694-4633. • 1033-A Blossom Hill Rd. (at Almaden Expwy.), San Jose, 408/445-2337. This mattress retailer is the nation's largest. They offer a bed frame free with a full, queen, or king set.

Mike Furniture: 2142 Fillmore St. (Sacramento), SF, 415/567-2700. Well-known designer Mike Moore sells his chic, California-style furniture here, nicely filling the furniture niche between department stores and studio designers. Moore specializes in overscale couches, armchairs, and clean-lined accessories.

Patioworld: 1310 W. El Camino Real (Mountain View Ave./Palo Alto Ave.), San Carlos, 650/592-9353. • 2124 W. El Camino Real (Ortega/N. Rengstorff), Mountain View, 650/964-4974. • Town & Country Village, Stevens Creek and Winchester blvds., San

Jose, 408/247-9992. To live the carefree California lifestyle, you must have your patio, deck, or balcony outfitted. And this premier patio furniture store is the place to start.

R.S. Basso: 355 University Ave. (Waverley/Bryant), Palo Alto, 650/322-6088. Home furnishings of an upscale nature with the accent on eclectic. A mix of Italian and European styles with American-made upholstery is the rule here, and there's something for every room in the house. Not for the faint of pocketbook.

Scandinavian Design: 317 South B St. (3rd/4th), San Mateo, 650/340-0555. Reasonably priced, good-quality furniture, including some children's furniture. Most pieces—lots of shelving, desks, dressers, and other basics—have a laminated look.

Thomas Moser Cabinetmakers: 3395 Sacramento St. (Presidio/Walnut), SF, 415/931-8131. This showroom displays the elegant, Shaker-inspired wooden furniture advertised in such magazines as the *New Yorker*. Only the well heeled need stop in.

Housewares

Lechters Housewares: Serramonte Center, I-280 and Serramonte Blvd., Daly City, 650/992-5047. • Stonestown Galleria, 3251 20th Ave., SF, 415/759-0528. • 10123 N. Wolfe Rd. (E. Homestead), Cupertino, 408/446-5785. • Eastridge Mall, Tully Rd. and Capitol Expwy., San Jose, 408/238-5688. • Oakridge Mall, Santa Teresa Blvd. and Blossom Hill Rd., San Jose, 408/365-1703. Lechters will satisfy your need for anything inexpensive for the kitchen and bathroom: plates, muffin pans, garlic presses, toothbrush holders, teapots, and small area rugs. Watch for sales.

Stroud's: 731 Market St. (3rd St./4th St.), SF, 415/979-0460. • 75 Serramonte Center, I-280 and Serramonte Blvd., Daly City, 650/991-9597. • 4 E. 4th Ave. (El Camino), San Mateo, 650/342-4743. • 700 El Camino Real (Roble/Middle), Menlo Park, 650/327-7680. • 1236 W. El Camino Real (Bernardo), Sunnyvale, 408/733-0910. • 3111 Stevens Creek Blvd. (Winchester), Santa Clara, 408/984-6090. • 5353 Almaden Expwy. (Hwy 85/Blossom Hill), San Jose, 408/978-0552. Stroud's has high-quality brands at reasonable discounts. Shelves are stocked with sheets, comforters, pillows, towels, bedroom and bathroom accessories, and decorative must-haves. Best to take some time and browse around a bit. Sales can be worthwhile.

Williams-Sonoma: Stonestown Galleria, 19th Ave. and Winston Dr., SF, 415/681-5525. • 150 Post St. (Kearny/Grant), SF, 415/362-6904. • Valley Fair Mall, Stevens Creek Blvd. and I-880, Santa Clara, 650/249-4424. • Stanford Shopping Center, El Camino Real and Quarry Rd., Palo Alto, 650/321-3486. Williams-Sonoma is for the Julia Child in all of us. Gorgeous copper pots, a wide variety of kitchen gadgets, tableware, and glassware are abundant in this specialty store. Cookbooks deserve a store of their own. Prices run high, but this fabulous stuff is worth it.

OUTLETS

American Tin Cannery: 125 Ocean View Blvd. (Eardley), Pacific Grove, 408/372-1442. Fish for bargains at Carole Little and Joan and David, among others.

Crate & Barrel: 1785 4th St. (Delaware/Virginia), Berkeley, 510/528-5500. The creative Crate & Barrel Outlet offers out-of-season, discontinued, and damaged goods (when available) from their retail stores. The markdowns aren't as significant as those at other outlets, but every little bit helps.

Esprit Factory Outlet: 499 Illinois St. (16th St. east of 3rd St.), SF, 415/957-2550. San Francisco's most dynamic outlet store is filled with high-tech displays and merchandise at prices from 30 percent to 70 percent off department-store markups.

Factory Stores at Vacaville: 321-2 Nut Tree Rd. (off Orange Dr. at I-80),Vacaville, 707/447-5755. Formerly known as the Factory Stores at Nut Tree. Nut Tree is long gone, but the outlets linger on. At this giant collection, you'll find stores such as **Bugle Boy, Casual Corner, Carter's, Oshkosh, Petite Sophisticates,** and **Reebok,** among at least 120 others.

Gunne Sax/Jessica McClintock: 35 Stanford St. (Brannan/Townsend), SF, 415/495-3326. If formalwear is your object of desire, this outlet is for you.

Marina Square in San Leandro: Marina Square, 1-880 at Marina Blvd., San Leandro. This East Bay mall has outlet stores for **The Gap, Eddie Bauer, Marshall's,** and **Nine West.** There is also a **Nordstrom Rack** clearance center replete with dresses and men's suits. Markdowns are generous.

North Face Outlet: 1325 Howard St. (9th St./10th St.), SF, 415/626-6444. • 1238 5th St. (Gilman), Berkeley, 510/526-3530. You can't miss the original North Face Outlet in Berkeley, featuring sportswear, outerwear, skiwear, and trustworthy equipment at discounted prices. But once you buy it, it's yours. There are usually no warranties on outlet goods, something to consider before making any serious investment.

Pacific West Outlet Store: Hwy 101 at Leavesley Rd. exit, Gilroy, 408/847-4155. This outlet has grown from a few select stores to 150 designer outlets. You could spend a week sifting through piles and racks of slightly imperfect items at **Anne Klein, Eddie Bauer,** and **Liz Claiborne.** When your feet give out, there's always the **Nike Factory Store** and **Adidas.**

THRIFT STORES

The thrift shops listed here carry used goods in decent condition. In general, "thrift" or "charity" stores rely on donations that vary widely in quality. Expect to pay little. Stores subtitled "consignment" or "resale" are more selective. Expect to pay more. Consignment shops will sell your unwanted things for a percentage. Also consider checking out one of **Butterfield West**'s auctions (see description under Home Furnishings, General Purpose stores, above). Finally, pick up a copy of *Rummaging Through Northern California*, a free directory of resale shops available at many thrift shops, for more ideas.

Discovery Shop: 746 Santa Cruz Ave. (El Camino/Crane), Menlo Park, 650/325-8939. • 243 Main St. (2nd/3rd), Los Altos, 650/949-0505. • 1451-A Foxworthy Ave. (Plummer/Cherry), San Jose, 408/265-5535. If you are in the market for a mink coat or a designer dress, visit a Discovery Shop. The offerings at these American Cancer Society resale shops are extremely tasteful and were once expensive. Clothing, jewelry, furniture, books, and antique collectibles can be found at decent prices.

Goodwill Industries: 1700 Haight St. (Cole/Clayton), SF, 415/387-1192. • 4085 El Camino Way (off El Camino Real near Charleston), Palo Alto, 650/494-1416. • 855 El Camino Real (Dale/Crestview), Mountain View, 650/969-3382. • 151 E. Washington Ave. (Sunnyvale Ave.), Sunnyvale, 408/736-8558. • 2800 El Camino Real. (Kiely), Santa Clara, 408/247-2800. • 1125 S. De Anza Blvd. (Stevens Creek), Cupertino, 408/252-3193. • 3060 Almaden Expwy. (Foxworthy), San Jose, 408/265-5692. • 1080 N. 7th Ave. (Commercial/Kinney), San Jose, 408/998-5798 (main offices). This national institution known for its large selection at good prices has many outlets. The Palo Alto store is chock-full of stuff, all of which is cheap and in good condition. In fact, the pickings are so good, a number of Goodwill executives have been indicted for skimming off the top. A few doors down from the main office at 950 N. 7th St. is the Goodwill wholesale "as is" warehouse. This is the last stop for all items that don't sell at the other outlets. Leftovers are sold off dirt cheap.

Pick of the Litter: 1801 S. Grant St. (Concar), San Mateo, 650/345-1024. The store takes its name from its beneficiary, The Peninsula Humane Society. You won't find many dogs among the merchandise. This big, well-organized store sells everything from furniture to books and records to clothes and housewares. Prices are low. Catch a special or sale and really save.

Ragtime Thrift Inc.: 2189 Leghorn Ave. (Park), Mountain View, 650/968-1941. A smallish thrift shop, Ragtime has become a hot spot for teenagers. Virtually undiscovered, it has a large inventory of retro clothing from the past three decades. A limited selection of records, tapes, and books; various appliances and utensils; and random household stuff fill up the rest of the store. Furniture shows up occasionally. Tag sales often reap a savings of 50 to 70 percent.

Salvation Army: 300 El Camino Real (Chapman), San Bruno, 650/583-3589. • 650 El Camino Real (Ralston/Davey Glen), Belmont, 650/591-5499. • 660 Veterans Blvd. (Whipple/Brewster), Redwood City, 650/368-7527. • 4140 Monterey Rd. (Senter), San Jose, 408/578-1288. Used clothing and secondhand couches, refrigerators, mattresses, desks, and more are found here, all at very low prices. Profits benefit the good works of the Salvation Army.

Savers: 875 Main St. (Stambaugh), Redwood City, 650/364-5545. • 60 S. Dempsey Rd. (Park Victoria), Milpitas, 408/263-8338. • 222 Business Cir. (S. Bascom), San Jose, 408/287-0591. Redwood City features furniture on the second floor and a huge, well-organized selection of clothing and housewares on the main floor. All items are purchased from Hope Rehabilitation, an organization that employs the disabled.

The Second Act: 12882 S. Saratoga-Sunnyvale Rd. (Herriman/Williams), Saratoga, 408/741-4995. The Second Act is the type of consignment shop you would expect to find in an upscale community like Saratoga. Cast-off clothes and furniture can be nicer than new purchases somewhere else. You might find Armani or Polo labels on the racks. Expect to pay a higher price.

This 'n' That Shop: 1336 5th Ave. (Broadway/O'Neill), Belmont, 650/591-6166. For over 30 years this bargain mecca has been reselling old clothes, housewares, books, and more to benefit the projects of Good Shepherd Episcopal Church. Low prices draw crowds in spite of limited hours.

Thrift Center: 1060 El Camino Real (Brittan/Morse), San Carlos, 650/593-1082. As big and ramshackle a thrift store as you will find anywhere, Thrift Center resells everything from furniture to clothing to appliances at very low prices.

Flea Markets

Classified ads in local newspapers will lead you to more flea market–type operations. Look for listings for secondhand goods, flea markets, and garage sales. Some papers even have a freebie section.

Capitol Flea Market: Capitol Expwy. and Snell Ave., San Jose, 408/225-5800. Entrance fees are 50 cents per person on weekdays (free on Fridays), $1.25 on Saturday, and $1.50 on Sunday; free parking. Th 6am-5:30pm; F 7am-5:30pm; Sa-Su 6am-5:30pm.

De Anza Flea Market: 21250 Stevens Creek Blvd. (off Hwy 85), Cupertino, 408/864-8414. No entrance fee, parking $3. First Saturday of every month, 8am-4pm. Over 800 stalls.

Foothill College Flea Market: 12345 El Monte Rd. (I-280), Los Altos Hills, 650/948-6417. Parking lot F. Third Saturday of every month. Profits benefit the Theater Guild.

The Flea Market Inc.: 1590 Berryessa Rd. (Commercial/Lundy), San Jose, 408/453-1110. No entrance fee, parking $1 W-F, $3 Sa-Su. Hours 7 am-6pm.

Restaurants

Agenda Restaurant Bar & Lounge ★★★ $$ 399 S. 1st St. (San Salvador), San Jose, 408/287-3991. Located in a sleekly renovated turn-of-the-century building, Agenda is a contemporary club and adult entertainment playground wrapped around a stylish restaurant. From its bold, minimalist decor to its gorgeous American cuisine—graced with hints of Asia and the Mediterranean—Agenda attracts a smart, young downtown crowd. This is the place to rendezvous for a serious cocktail or enjoy a late dinner of grilled portobellos and pan-seared Moroccan chicken. Everybody looks more attractive in this slick setting. Complimentary hors d'oeuvres served during happy hour (5-9pm daily). Reservations recommended. • Rest: Tu-Sa 5:30-10:30pm. Lounge: M-F 5:30pm-2:30am; Sa-Su 7pm-2am.

Akane Japanese Restaurant ★★★ $$/$$$ 250 3rd St. (Main/San Antonio), Los Altos, 650/941-8150. Frequented by purists and insiders, this distinctive Japanese restaurant offers superb sushi and an attractive setting for top-quality traditional dining. The gracefully crafted sushi rolls arrive with impeccable garnishes, and the sashimi of *maguro* competes with delicate soft-shell crab and hamachi *kama* for sheer beauty. Semiprivate booths with tatami seating surround a central area of tables and chairs. The wait staff are knowledgeable, but the jewellike portions served in this serene setting steal the show. • M-F 11:30am-2pm, 5-9:30pm; Sa 5-9:30pm; Su 5-9pm.

Alana's ★★ $ 1408 Burlingame Ave. (Primrose/El Camino), Burlingame, 650/348-0417. Alana's, a chichi little breakfast café imbued with the charm of a 1950s coffee shop, is straight out of a Martha Stewart decorating book. Swivel-chair counter seating surrounds the tiny open kitchen, but instead of sporting black vinyl, the stools are draped in bright pastel slipcovers. Tables covered in white linen, hardwood floors, and sponge-painted terra-cotta walls complete the decor. The menu covers all the breakfast bases—eggs Benedict, Swedish oatmeal pancakes with lingonberries, French toast—and offers a few light lunch choices. If you survey the crowd, you'll notice that the farmer's garden—eggs and vegetables heaped on a pan of potatoes—is by far the most popular dish. Alana's is definitely worth checking out—just don't tell your friends; the lines are already long enough. A café menu for dinner is a recent addition. • M-Tu 7am-3pm; W-F 7am-3pm, 5-9pm; Sa 8am-3pm, 5-9pm; Su 8am-2pm.

Allied Arts Guild Restaurant ★ $ 75 Arbor Rd. (Cambridge), Menlo Park, 650/324-2588. This genteel ladies' lunching spot is located in the lovely Allied Arts Guild compound. The restaurant is a beautiful example of Spanish Colonial style architecture. The prix fixe menu rotates such vintage 1950s fare as melon with strawberries, turkey roulade, and rice pilaf. The restaurant is staffed by volunteers and all the proceeds go to the Lucile Salter Packard Children's Hospital at Stanford. After lunch you can shop for crafts and wedding presents at the various boutiques housed in the compound and stroll through the well-tended flower gardens. The gardens are particularly spectacular in the spring. No credit cards. • M-Sa lunch seatings at noon, 12:30pm, and 1pm. Call ahead for Saturday lunch: they are often closed for wedding receptions.

Amarin Thai ★★ $ 156 Castro St. (Villa/Evelyn), Mountain View, 650/988-9323. Amarin, one of the better Thai restaurants on the Peninsula, draws crowds with a winning formula of friendly, efficient service and large portions of fresh, carefully prepared food. White tablecloths, fresh flowers, and Buddhas comprise the attractive decor, while the extensive menu features well-prepared curries, including the notable vegetable forest curry; authentic *mee krop* crispy Thai noodles; and numerous vegetarian options prepared with wheat flour or soybean. A wonderful lunch dish not listed on the menu but worth asking for is the barbecued honey pork with sticky rice and Thai salad. Next door, Amarin Thai Noodle House features two dozen different types of Thai noodles. Among the choices are excellent wide, flat rice noodles stuffed with black mushrooms, ground pork, and bamboo shoots and served with a flavorful sauce; a delicious curry noodle soup; and hearty yet delicately flavored ground beef and sweet basil with rice noodles. The decor is simple, bordering on unfinished. • M-Sa 11am-3pm, 5-10pm; Su 5-10pm.

Amici's East Coast Pizzeria ★★ $ 69 E. 3rd Ave. (El Camino/San Mateo Dr.), San Mateo, 650/342-9392. Amici's takes its cue from New York–style pizza parlors, offering thin-crusted pies baked in a wood-burning brick oven for extra crispiness. The varied toppings include fried eggplant (the best around), pesto, and three varieties of sausage. Pastas and salads are also available: a tangy Caesar antipasto salad makes an inexpensive meal for two. The shiny black-and-white-tiled space is popular with families; if you want a more adult surrounding, you can order Amici's at the Third Avenue Sports Bar a few doors down. (Customers are warned this option may take a little longer). A plus for the late-night crowd: Amici's is one of the very few Peninsula restaurants open until midnight every night. • M-F 11am-midnight; Sa-Su noon-midnight.

Andalé Taqueria ★★ ¢ 6 N. Santa Cruz Ave. (Bean/Main), Los Gatos, 408/395-4244. • 21 N. Santa Cruz Ave. (Main), Los Gatos, 408/395-8997. • 209 University Ave. (Ramona/Emerson), Palo Alto, 650/323-2939. Some say these are the best of the fresh-Mex restaurants. The brightly painted, festive interiors put you in the mood for the first-rate, reasonably priced food. If you're in a burrito rut, try the chicken tamale or one of the innovative daily specials. Be sure to sip an *agua fresca* through a neon-pink straw. Margaritas are made with wine rather than tequila; sangria and beer are also served. Cash only. • 6 Santa Cruz: Daily 11am-9pm. • 21 Santa Cruz: M-Th 11am-10pm; F 11am-11pm; Sa 9am-11pm; Su 9am-9pm. • Palo Alto: Su-Th 11am-10pm; F-Sa 11am-11pm.

Anh Hong ★★ $ 1818 Tully Rd. #150 (King), San Jose, 408/270-1096. Tucked into the back corner of a nondescript shopping center, Anh Hong, an authentic Vietnamese restaurant originally established in Saigon in 1954, is well worth seeking out. While the menu is extensive, most patrons opt for the *Bo 7 Mon*, a light, flavorful seven-course beef extravaganza. The seven courses include a tangy salad, a plate of paper-thin beef that you cook in your own fondue pot, a dish of grilled beef wrapped in a Hawaiian lot leaf, and more. As is common in Southeast Asian cultures, soup concludes the meal—in this case, a rice and beef soup that you will find yourself craving on cold and rainy days. Also recommended is the shrimp and squid marinated in lemongrass and barbecued at your table. Finish your meal with an excellent homemade flan. Reservations recommended on weekends. • M-Tu 2pm-10pm; F-Su 11am-11pm.

Applewood Inn ★★ $ 227 1st St. (Main/State), Los Altos, 650/941-9222. • 1001 El Camino Real (Menlo Ave.), Menlo Park, 650/324-3486. • To Go: 989D El Camino Real (Menlo Ave.), Menlo Park, 650/328-1556. This is a longtime favorite where the menu is concerned, but you may be less taken with the spare Mom-and-Pop surroundings. Nevertheless, try the heaped, thick-crusted, lovingly baked specialties. Ever had red caviar on your pizza pie? Polish sauerkraut? One popular model is the Nice with its onions, ricotta, and herb mixture. There's also an amazingly wide selection of imported beers. • LA: Sa-Th 4-9pm; F 4-10pm. • MP: M-Sa 5-10pm; Su 5-9pm. • To Go: Daily 5-9pm.

Aqui Cal-Mex Grill ★★★ $ 1145 Lincoln Ave. (Minnesota/Willow), San Jose, 408/995-0381. Postmodern cantina ambience and sparklingly fresh neo-Mex cuisine blend as smoothly as a handmade margarita in this sexy, high-concept eatery. Wildly popular with everyone who sips one of the fresh fruit *liquados* or samples the Cuban pork taco or amazing lime-dressed shrimp salads, Aqui offers healthy portions of fun, fiesta foods. Grilled meats, hearty beans, innovative vegetable accompaniments, and a hot-hotter-hottest salsa bar make this place a top draw. Casual and easily accessible, Aqui boasts a witty collection of colorful artwork and a miniature Wild West bar. • Su-Th 11am-9pm; F-Sa 11am-9:30pm.

Azuma ★★ $$ 19645 Stevens Creek Blvd. (Wolfe), Cupertino, 408/257-4057. Located near Hewlett-Packard, Apple, and Tandem, Azuma attracts a loyal clientele of Silicon Valley engineers at lunch and families at night. The tatami seating, fresh Japanese flower arrangements, and cheerful, kimono-clad servers have a calming influence on the diners, whether they're engineers tired of workplace politics or itchy four-year-olds. Most tables have tatami mats and walls, but you can also sit at the sushi bar or American-style tables. The traditional (but somewhat Americanized) Japanese menu is dependable and features the usual, from California rolls to hot sake. The sushi is fresh and top quality, and the tempura is always hot and crisp. • M-F 11:30am-2pm, 5:30-10pm; Sa 5:30-10pm; Su 5-9pm.

Bandera Restaurant ★★ $$$ 233 3rd St. (San Antonio/Main), Los Altos, 650/948-3524. Although Bandera is a chain restaurant, the bustling Los Altos outpost manages to escape that cookie-cutter feel. Locals flock here for the huge portions of delicious American-style comfort food and the stylish Southwestern interior. If the lines are long, relax at the large horseshoe-shaped bar with a glass of wine and sample one of the delicious appetizers—perhaps the New Orleans–style grilled artichoke, split and grilled over hardwood. The wood-fired spit-roasted chicken is about as good as chicken gets, and the mashed potatoes laced with scallions and garlic are worth the trip alone. All the barbecue items are great, and be sure to get a side of corn bread, chock full of corn kernels. Desserts are huge, including the delicious crème brûlée. • M-F 5-9:30pm; Sa-Su 4:30-10pm.

Bangkok Cuisine ★★ $ 407 Lytton Ave. (Waverley), Palo Alto, 650/322-6533. • 5235 Prospect Rd. (Lawrence/Saratoga), San Jose, 408/253-8424. The full complement of Thai dishes can be found here. Among them are an ocean of seafood-oriented specialties, including sautéed shellfish with curry, sweet basil, and coconut milk, as well as whole pompano deep-fried and topped with chili sauce. The portions are smallish and the tables packed together too tightly, but then again the food is well above average (although some claim quality is slipping). The small patio is great when the weather is nice. Polite service and inexpensive lunch specials are pluses. • MP: M-Sa 11am-3pm, 5:30-10pm; Su 5:30-10pm. • SJ: M-Th 11am-3pm, 5-9:30pm; F-Sa 11am-3pm, 5-10pm; Su 5-9:30pm.

Barley and Hopps ★★ $$/$$$ 201 South B St. (2nd), San Mateo, 650/348-7808. The name Barley and Hopps tells you that this is a brew pub. The atmospheric interior—exposed brick walls, dark wood furniture, and trademark alabaster light fixtures—tells you it's owned by the same group that runs Capellini and the Buffalo Grill (flatten the buffalo horns and voilà!). And the three-story dining-and-entertainment center concept hints at the success of Palo Alto's Blue Chalk Café. The beer is pretty good, especially the India pale ale, and complements the hearty menu: lots of smoky barbecue, gourmet deep-dish pizza, and a mixture of burgers, fish, and the like. They brew their own root beer here, too, so save room for dessert and order up a float. After dinner, head upstairs for a cigar and a game of pool, or downstairs to Blues on B, the basement blues club. • Su-M 5-9pm; Tu-Th 11:30am-2pm, 5-10pm; F 11:30am-2pm, 5-10:30pm; Sa noon-2pm, 5-10:30pm.

Basque Cultural Center ★★★ $$ 599 Railroad Ave. (Spruce/Orange), South San Francisco, 650/583-8091. It's worth tracking down this out-of-the-way institution in wind-blown South San Francisco. Simple, delicious French Basque specialties are served family style in the comfortable dining room decorated with country French furniture, crisp white tablecloths, and dark wood beams. Meals start off with a tureen of soup, followed by a salad and two entrées, which might include Basque style red snapper or pepper steak with a satisfying black-pepper crust. The portions are huge. Linger over coffee, and don't miss the display of pelota trophies (it's a court game) in the reception hall. Reservations recommended. • Tu-F 11:30am-2:30pm, 5:30-9:30pm; Sa 5:30-9:30pm; Su 5-9pm.

Bella Mangiata ★★ $$ 233 Baldwin Ave. (San Mateo Dr./Ellsworth), San Mateo, 650/343-2404. Bella Mangiata captures the way Italian restaurants looked and felt when the ideal eatery was on a Roman *viale* instead of in a Tuscan villa. The fully decorated interior is replete with umber tiles, bright murals, and white bentwood chairs. The extensive, old-fashioned menu features all the classic pasta, veal, chicken, and fish dishes, and the execution is solid, especially on the pastas. Even the warm-hearted wait staff will make you think you are in Rome. Although they sell beer and wine, they don't charge a corkage fee if you bring in your favorite bottle. Reservations recommended. • M-Sa 11:30am-10pm; Su 4:30-10pm.

Bella Mia ★★ $$ 58 S. 1st St. (San Fernando/Santa Clara), San Jose, 408/280-1993. Tailored and handsome, this contemporary Italian restaurant occupies a great Victorian space loaded with urban appeal. A prime mover-and-shaker lunch spot, the restaurant does a fine job with flame-broiled specialties, including a lovely hardwood-grilled lobster, spit-roasted Petaluma duck, and the full gamut of steaks and ribs. The pastas are quite good, and the salads are gargantuan. Bella Mia offers something for everyone, in a strategic, heart-of-the-city location. • M-Th 11am-9:30pm; F-Sa 11am-10pm; Su 10am-9pm.

Bella Saratoga ★★ $$ 14503 Big Basin Way (3rd/4th), Saratoga, 408/741-5115. Downtown Saratoga's most popular dining spot is located in a historic Victorian where you can enjoy a lazy Sunday brunch, complete with jazz and outdoor seating (weather permitting). The chef competes (and wins) in many of the pasta competitions held in the area. Some of his more stunning creations: salmon ravioli, oven-baked lasagna, and veal or chicken piccata. Indoors, the decor tends toward high Victorian—floral wallpaper, oak furniture, creaky stairs. A popular site for popping the question. • M-Th 11:30am-9:30pm; F 11:30am-11pm; Sa 10am-10pm; Su 10am-9pm.

Bella Vista Restaurant ★★ $$$ 13451 Skyline Blvd. (Hwy 92/Kings Mountain), Woodside, 650/851-1229. High up on top of Skyline Drive, the view from this woodsy retreat is unsurpassed, with the entire Peninsula and bay laid out before you. (Be sure to ask for a table with a view when you make your reservation.) A wood-burning fireplace, lots of rough-hewn wood, and white linen tablecloths create a rustic yet elegant ambience. The menu is classic Continental and expensive, and the place takes itself *very* seriously—some call it snooty—but the view is superb. • M-Th 5:30-9pm; F-Sa 5-10pm.

Birk's ★★ $$$ 3955 Freedom Cir. (Hichborn/Mission College), Santa Clara, 408/980-6400. The quintessential upscale California grill for Silicon Valley power lunchers. Birk's features a classic Pat Kuleto design—black-and-white tile, dark wood, and subdued lighting (similar to the Buffalo Grill but without the horns). The menu is big on simple grilled seafood, chicken, and meat, but with a heavy emphasis on the steak and ribs; it also covers smoked and sautéed dishes, as well as the ubiquitous pasta. There's a large wine selection and an even better assortment of beers on tap. Reservations recommended. • M-F 11:15am-2:30pm, 5-11pm; Sa-Su 5-11pm.

Bistro Elan ★★★ $$$ 438 California Ave. (El Camino/Ash), Palo Alto, 650/327-0284. If it's the Sixth Arrondissement you crave, Bistro Elan is the place to go. You are welcomed to this little storefront on bohemian California Avenue by candles flickering on Luxembourg Garden–style café tables, and it gets more Parisian from there. A zinc bar, a bustling open kitchen, and big bowls of fruit in season set the scene for a true bistro experience. The high-quality menu changes daily, and latecomers will likely find certain specials sold out. A small but strong wine list complements the delightful food, which combines traditional dishes with eclectic entrées based on seasonal ingredients: duck confit with potatoes and green beans, smoked salmon with wonton wrappers and wasabi, and pan-seared salmon with a Provençal artichoke ragout. The vegetable dishes and wicked French fries are worth ordering on the side. The coffee served in individual French press pots is superb. For a little Gallic culture, and a lot of charm and value, Bistro Elan beats a 15-hour flight to Orly any day. Reservations recommended. • Tu-F 11:30am-2pm, 5:30-10pm; Sa 5:30-10pm.

Blue Chalk Café ★★★ $$ 630 Ramona St. (Hamilton/Forest), Palo Alto, 650/326-1020. The Blue Chalk seats a huge crowd on two airy levels in a wood and stucco historic landmark. In warm weather, still more diners can enjoy the pleasant front patio. The Southern-influenced menu is superb; generously-portioned specialties might include a spicy seafood corn chowder, a blackened chicken Caesar salad, or grilled-vegetable sandwiches. There's also a good selection of local microbrews on tap. For gaming enthusiasts, pool tables and shuffleboard occupy one room, while upstairs there are dart boards and another shuffleboard table. This isn't your typical pool hall scene, however: on weekends it's packed with Silicon Valley singles and there's not a surly bartender or tough biker in sight. A popular place for group events and celebrations. • M-F 11:30am-2:30pm, 5-10pm; Sa 5-10pm (bar till 1:30am).

Bogie's ★★ $$/$$$ 60 E. 3rd Ave. (El Camino/San Mateo Dr.), San Mateo, 650/579-5911. Buried at the rear of a downtown San Mateo arcade, behind costume-jewelry and women's apparel shops, lies a swank, sophisticated throwback to an era when dining was intimate and a restaurant meal constituted an evening out. Bogie's looks like it belongs in a 1940s movie, with romantic lighting, black-and-white photos of old-time film stars, and lots of polished wood and mirrored surfaces. The old-fashioned elegance is not misleading. The service is impeccable and the food a winning mix of Continental classics and modern Cal-Asian creations. Entrées such as rack of lamb with rosemary-garlic flavored jus or braised tournedos with brandy and bernaise sauces are the stars of the menu, and the reasonably-priced homemade pastas merit a return trip. • Tu-F 11:30am-2:30pm, 5:30-10pm; Sa-Su 5:30-10pm.

Bonsai Sushi ★★ $$ 878 Jefferson Ave. (Middlefield/Broadway), Redwood City, 650/367-6547. Bonsai's interior looks like a postcard of a Kyoto restaurant: almost every surface in the cramped room is made from natural wood—the sushi bar, the tables, the walls, the bridge over the koi pond, even the ceiling. The sushi preparations are far less traditional, with an ever-changing array of chef's specials that combine ingredients with flair. The top-grade fish, while pricey, is extremely fresh and generously portioned. Other familiar menu items (*yakitori*, tempura, teriyaki, *udon*) are well prepared. The high-quality preparations draw steady crowds, which take their toll on the service. • M-F 11:30am-2pm, 5-10pm; Sa 5-10pm.

Bow Thai Café ★★ $ 43 South B St. (1st), San Mateo, 650/340-8424. Thai food served in a country-cottage-themed dining room (lace curtains, ceramic Peter Rabbit animals, and country-kitchen wood chairs)? What this sweet little restaurant lacks in decorative coherence it more than makes up for with authentic Thai cuisine. A perennial *San Mateo Times* Best Thai winner, Bow Thai serves up the standards as well as less common offerings such as spinach soup, Thai-style ravioli, and Bow Thai noodles—rice noodles stir-fried with curry, chicken, shrimp, and egg. Do as the natives do and sample one of the authentic fiery green curries—just be sure to order a Thai iced coffee to cool off your burning palate. • M-Sa 11am-10pm; Su 4-10pm.

Brandon's Restaurant ★★★ $$$ 1820 Barber Ln. (Montague/I-880), Milpitas, 408/432-6311. A cut above the usual hotel restaurant, Brandon's makes a designer statement with its soft linens and stylish decor, accented by large floral displays. Supertalented chef Clyde Griesbach brings Mediterranean flair to the sophisticated California cuisine served in this atmospheric setting. A great place to enjoy cocktails by the pool, Brandon's specializes in gorgeously presented fresh seafood, fine meats, and inventive salads starring locally grown seasonal produce. This versatile venue offers relaxed, upscale dining—perfect for a power lunch or a romantic evening. • M-F 6:30-10:30am, 11:30am-2:30pm, 5:30-10:30pm; Sa-Su 7am-2:30pm, 5:30-10pm.

Brothers Delicatessen and Restaurant ★ $ 1351 Howard Ave. (Primrose), Burlingame, 650/343-2311. If this were New York City, Brothers would be the authentic, dark-wood-paneled Carnegie Deli, while Max's would be the flashy, upscale Stage Deli. Catering to a predominantly older clientele, Brothers' interior features an old-fashioned suburban atmosphere of red vinyl booths, wood paneling, and threadbare red carpeting. The deli counter serves all the basics in respectable fashion: when you order a sandwich, nobody claims the corned beef is lean, and they have chopped liver and bulky rolls (even if they're not always the freshest). You'll also find a good selection of classic sandwiches as well as authentic plates of brisket, whitefish, lox, and even knockwurst. Service is comforting and familiar. • Daily 8am-8:30pm.

Buca di Beppo ★★ $$ 643 Emerson St. (Forest/Hamilton), Palo Alto, 650/FAW-ZOOL (329-0665). This casual, southern Italian restaurant brings an entertaining, tongue-in-cheek rendition of New York's Little Italy to Palo Alto. Beppo's kitchen turns out tasty, satisfying renditions of old favorites, including fried calamari, spaghetti and meatballs, homemade ravioli, eggplant parmesan, thin-crust pizzas, and *tiramisù*. The generous pizzas, salads, pastas, and desserts are served on platters for groups to share (in fact, parties of less than four are discouraged) as Frank Sinatra and Dean Martin croon familiar Italian-American tunes in the background; you'll leave feeling full and with a care package from "Nonni." *Note:* No reservations accepted, but you can call ahead up to an hour in advance Su-Th, and up to two hours in advance F-Sa, to get your name added to the waiting list. • M-Th 5-10pm; F-Sa 5-11pm; Su 4-10pm.

Bucks ★★ $/$$ 3062 Woodside Rd. (Cañada/I-280), Woodside, 650/851-8010. *Vanity Fair* dubbed Bucks "the Four Seasons of the venture capital set," and for good reason: This is the place to witness swaggering Silicon Valley execs making deals over plates of blueberry flapjacks. The interior looks like it was decorated by a cowpoke on peyote, with a talking bison over the bar and a general Wild West ambience. The salsa-on-your-burger menu has a California twist, with weekly specials like grilled swordfish with ancho butter to satisfy the expense accounts. But the real reason to mosey in is to watch the bucks trade hands at Bucks. • M-Th 7am-9pm; F 7am-10pm; Sa 8am-10pm; Su 8am-9pm.

Buffalo Grill ★★ $$$ 66 Hillsdale Mall (31st Ave. and El Camino), San Mateo, 650/358-8777. As its name suggests, this Pat Kuleto–designed destination departs wildly from his empire of Italian restaurants. The decor of this upscale (and perpetually packed) diner is over-the-top Western, with faux hunting trophies on the back wall and lighting fixtures shaped like buffalo horns alongside the booths. The food is equally tongue-in-cheek mock frontier with a Californian flourish. The entrées—such as grilled chicken club sandwich with smoked bacon on sourdough, or maple-cured pork chops with corn spoonbread and buttermilk onion rings—draw a never-ending stream of society mavens and power lunchers during the day and crowds from all over the Peninsula at night. Although the menu has lost its creative edge—they're in production mode these days—anything from the grill is a sure bet, as are the gargantuan homemade desserts, which two or three diners can happily share. Reservations are a must. • M-Th 11:30am-10pm; F-Sa 11:30am-10:30pm; Su 5-9pm.

The Butler's Pantry ★ $ 305 2nd St. (Main), Los Altos, 650/941-9676. This authentic English tearoom in the heart of downtown Los Altos is the perfect place to escape for a spot of tea. Despite the lace tablecloths, starched napkins, and fine bone china on the tables, the atmosphere is not quite as refined or formal as some tea places. The large selection of authentic English tea sandwiches includes cucumber and cream cheese, cheese and tomato, and egg and chive. Wonderful homemade scones are served with imported Devonshire cream (the real thing) and preserves. There are different tea combinations available (depending on how hungry you are and whether you're in the mood for sweets or savories), as well as authentic British fare such as Cornish pasties, Welsh rarebit, and shepherd's pie. There is even a Teddy Tea available for children. Tea lovers will be thrilled to know that they sell Taylors of Harrogate tea in bags as well as loose. • M-F 11am-5pm; Sa 10am-5pm; Su 10am-4pm.

Café Borrone ★★ $ 1010 El Camino Real (Santa Cruz), Menlo Park, 650/327-0830. This Menlo Park café is hugely popular—and justifiably so. Inside, expect to share a table and perhaps make a new friend; outside, relax at one of the umbrella-shaded patio tables. The wait staff are young and attractive, the atmosphere lively, and the prices typical for an upscale Peninsula café. Anything on the menu will please the palate: soups, salads, and sandwiches, as well as sinful pastries. After eating, you can browse at nearby Kepler's books. (Borrone recently expanded into Kepler's old discount annex.) On weekend nights, the teens come out to compare piercings and tattoos. • M-Th 7am-11pm; F 7am-midnight; Sa 8am-midnight; Su 8am-5pm.

Café Brioche ★★★ $$$ 445 California Ave. (El Camino/Ash), Palo Alto, 650/326-8640. Canvas umbrellas, walls decorated with trompe l'oeil stonework, and murals of antique French billboards give this splendid neighborhood bistro a South of France ambience and style. Lunch patrons linger over inexpensive salads and sandwiches—such as *croques monsieur*, of course—while dinner guests relax with expertly prepared French classics, such as sea bass Provençal or oven-roasted duck in a pomegranate-brandy sauce with rice-lentil pilaf. Blackboard specials might include veal scallops and chanterelle mushrooms. The desserts—long on old-fashioned favorites like fresh fruit *clafoutis* and dense chocolate tortes—are outstanding. Fine French and California wines are on offer—the perfect match for the authentic Provençal menu. • M 11am-3pm; Tu-Sa 11am-3pm, 5:30-9:30pm.

Café La Scala ★★ $$ 1219 Burlingame Ave. (Park/Lorton), Burlingame, 650/347-3035. Café la Scala, one of the more beloved Italian restaurants on the Peninsula, is loaded with over-the-top Tuscan ambience: a large and gregarious staff, faux marble plant beds and urns, Italian opera posters, swaths of lace hanging from ceiling lamps, and a trompe l'oeil view of an Italian countryside complete with peasant maid. The menu itself is less flamboyant—thank heavens—consisting of straightforward but thoughtfully prepared traditional dishes with an emphasis on garlic, garlic, and more garlic. Be careful not to overload on the bread served with garlic-scented Tuscan olive oil while you peruse the menu, which features a wide assortment of tasty pasta dishes. Try the *linguine alla Erbe*, a light pasta dish with garlic, olive oil, and lots of vegetables; or if you enjoy a cream sauce, *fettuccine a la Scala*. The kitchen usually features an array of nightly specials as well. La Scala is not above offering "ch-ch-chocolate" ice cream cake for dessert; opt instead for the light and fluffy *tiramisù*. If the weather permits, sit outside on the patio. • M-Th 11am-10pm; F-Sa 11am-11pm; Su 1-10pm.

Café Marcella ★★★ $$ 368 Village Ln. (off Hwy 9 at Santa Cruz), Los Gatos, 408/354-8006. The simple, unpretentious decor here can be a relief after too many visits to restaurants with ocher ombré walls and roaring brick ovens. White walls hung with French prints, light wood chairs, and a bar with chrome stools make for a modern feel and loud atmosphere. The food is well prepared and delicious; try the sensational appetizer plate of Brie, smoked salmon, prosciutto, and more. Roast duck, pastas, and pizzas are among the entrée options. A word to the wise: Don't pass up the desserts. • Tu-F 11:30am-2:30pm, 5-9:30pm; Sa 11:30am-2:30pm, 5-10:30pm; Su 5-10:30pm.

Café Primavera ★ $ 1359 Lincoln Ave. (Minnesota), San Jose, 408/297-7929. • 303 Almaden Blvd. (San Carlos), San Jose, 408/795-1200. California cuisine with a Mediterranean influence is served up at this charming little trattoria tucked into the edge of a San Jose suburb. Homemade pastas, delicately prepared vegetable entrées, and rich desserts make this low-key restaurant a pleasure. Tuck in with a favorite companion and a glass of local wine—the salads and soups offer as much comfort as flair, and everything tastes fresh. This is relaxed dining at its best. The downtown location offers a breakfast and lunch menu only. • Lincoln: M 11am-4pm; Tu-Sa 11am-9pm. • Almaden: M-F 7am-4pm.

Café Pro Bono ★★ $$/$$$ 2437 Birch St. (California/Sherman), Palo Alto, 650/326-1626. It's a pity the food at this traditional eatery isn't given away free for the public good. But patrons come anyway for the cozy decor, soft candlelight, hushed atmosphere, and solid preparations of regional Italian food. Start with carpaccio or grilled polenta with portobello mushrooms. Follow that with *penne al pesto* with sun-dried tomatoes or Susan's Downfall: ravioli with gorgonzola and toasted almond sauce. Entrées include a roast Cornish game hen with fresh fennel and cured olives and a succulent grilled king salmon with horseradish-herb crust. Stanford professors come here for a respite from Palo Alto's rampant trendiness. • M-F 11am-2:30pm, 5-10pm; Sa-Su 5-10pm.

Café Trio ★★★ $$$ 15466 Los Gatos Blvd. (Lark/Los Gatos-Almaden Rd.), Los Gatos, 408/356-8129. A welcome player in the South Bay restaurant scene. The modern black-and-white dining room is the setting for such culinary flights of fancy as grilled Anaheim peppers stuffed with goat cheese, panfried salmon cakes with mustard cream sauce, and a well-executed cioppino. Pasta dishes are delicious. Leisurely service accommodates the local gentry. • M-Th 11:30am-2:30pm, 5-9pm; F 11:30am-2:30pm, 5-10pm; Sa 5-10pm.

Caffè Goosetown ★★ $$ 1072 Lincoln Ave. (Willow), San Jose, 408/292-4866. Goosetown is the old nickname for this cozy suburb of San Jose. The neighborhood's namesake café, located in a refurbished saloon and restaurant (the saloon is still annexed), is currently showcasing the sensuous foods of southern Italy. This is the place to dine on knockout pasta sauces, seasonal fresh appetizers and antipasti, as well as complex game dishes. Fine desserts, impeccable espressos, and a long and unusual list of Sicilian wines make it a unique stop for those interested in Mediterranean-influenced California dining. The space is attractive and suited for romantic meals as well as family outings. • Tu-Th 11am-2:30pm, 5-9pm; F 11am-2:30pm, 5-10pm; Sa 5-10pm; Su 5-9pm.

Caffè Verona ★ $ 236 Hamilton Ave. (Emerson/Ramona), Palo Alto, 650/326-9942. The first and most famous of the great Peninsula cafés. Some call it home to Palo Alto's most ineffectual intellectuals, while others just call it home. Indeed, countless businesses and lifelong friendships have been born here. This place attracts a vagrant, trendy international crowd, so brush up on your foreign languages. Pick from plastic mock-ups of Italian dishes; the real McCoys come to your table looking amazingly similar but tasting good. The low-key Euro wait staff generally leaves you alone after seeing to your food and drink. • M-F 7am-11:30pm; Sa 8am-11:30pm; Su 8am-2:30pm (hours are usually shorter during Stanford summer break).

California Café Bar & Grill ★★ $$$ 50 University Ave. (Old Town), Los Gatos, 408/354-8118. • Stanford Barn, 700 Welch Rd. (off Quarry at Arboretum), Palo Alto, 650/325-2233. • Valley Fair Shopping Center, 2855 Stevens Creek Blvd. (Winchester/I-880), Santa Clara, 408/296-2233. A popular chain following the California-cuisine credo: imaginative food, pale drinks, pastel decor, and high prices. The Los Gatos branch is still basking in the glow of Bill Clinton's 1993 visit. What did the leader of the free world eat? Dungeness crab cakes with pink grapefruit *beurre blanc*, arugula, and crispy fried leeks, and, for dessert, chocolate whiskey cake with orange sauce and praline cream. *Note:* at presstime, the Los Gatos location was closed for remodeling and scheduled to reopen late fall 1998. • LG: Hours unavailable at presstime. • PA: M-Sa 11:30am-10:30pm; Su 10:30am-9:30pm. • SC: M-Sa 11am-10pm; Su 11am-8pm.

California Sushi and Grill ★★ $$ 1 E. San Fernando St. (1st/2nd), San Jose, 408/297-1847. • Doubletree Hotel, 2050 Gateway Pl. (Technology), San Jose, 408/436-1754. Fresh, creative sushi preparations and fine teriyaki and tempura emerge from the kitchen at California Sushi and Grill, one of downtown San Jose's more pleasant dining spots. The cheerful interior is done up in pink, black, and white, with a few bamboo accents. Sit upstairs and you overlook the Gordon Biersch beer garden. All this and karaoke, too. A second location in the Doubletree Hotel offers the same fare. • M-F 11:30am-2pm, 5-9:30pm; Sa 5-9:30pm.

Capellini ★★ $$$ 310 Baldwin (B St.), San Mateo, 650/348-2296. The high-ceilinged downstairs dining room (designed by Pat Kuleto), with its dark wood bar and gleaming fixtures, reverberates with the din of local patrons. Try to sit on the loft level for more audible conversation and a view of the goings-on. Bread served with excellent fruity olive oil starts things off while looking over the Cal-Italian menu; save space for the tasty pastas, salads, and main dishes. Good wine list. Reservations recommended. • M-F 11:30am-10pm; Sa 5-10:30pm; Su 5-9pm.

Carpaccio ★★ $$ 1120 Crane St. (Santa Cruz/Oak Grove), Menlo Park, 650/322-1211. A devoted clientele (including couples who refuse to celebrate their anniversaries anywhere else) flocks to this stylish restaurant. It's run by the same owners as San Mateo's Capellini and has a vaguely similar feel: dark 1940s ambience, two bar/counter areas, and large front windows that open onto the sidewalk in good weather. The menu features classic Italian antipasti, pizza, fresh pasta, seafood and veal dishes. Light eaters beware: Pasta portions are generous, and the cream sauces are a little heavy, so order carefully. Good wine list suitable for the many business lunchers. Incredible desserts, if you have any room left after the main courses. Reservations recommended. • M-F 11am-10pm; Sa 5-10:30pm; Su 5-9pm.

Casa Castillo ★ $ 200 S. 1st St. (San Fernando/San Carlos), San Jose, 408/971-8130. Casa Castillo turns out reliably well-made Mexican-American classics. Warm atmosphere and plenty of light make this bustling downtown Mexican dining room a mecca for those who like their enchiladas saucy and their salsa spicy. Run by an efficient and friendly staff, the local landmark caters to a busy professional clientele and visitors in search of a flawless chile relleno with rich refried beans. Add a chilled Bohemia beer and you have the start of a perfect afternoon. • M-F 9am-9pm; Sa 9am-10pm; Su 9am-4pm.

Casa Vicky ★ ¢ 792 E. Julian St. (17th), San Jose, 408/995-5488. One of the best values around. The delicious, spicy food at this self-service Mexican restaurant packs a lot of bang for the buck. You can eat solo for $2 to $4—an enormous tamale goes for $2, and a fiery chile relleno slathered in guacamole and sour cream is $3.50—or feed the entire family for just $13 with a whole mesquite-broiled chicken accompanied with rice, beans, chips, and salsa. Enjoy your meal outside on a nice day. • Daily 7am-10pm.

The Cats ★ $$ 17533 Highway 17 (Hwy 9), Los Gatos, 408/354-4020. An amiable jumble of a roadhouse. Originally a pit stop between Monterey and San Francisco during the logging boom, The Cats preserves its heritage with frontier food like barbecued beef and honey-glazed pork ribs grilled over an oak fire (and also with souvenir T-shirts for sale at the bar). The decor is equally low-key—mismatched wooden chairs, Tiffany lamps, and small tables fill the barroom and a separate dining room. The Cats is south of Los Gatos proper; look for the twin stone bobcats just off Highway 17. • Tu-Th 5:30-10pm; F-Sa 5:30-11pm; Su 5:30-10pm.

Chacho's ★★ $ 18 S. Almaden Ave. (Santa Clara St./Post), San Jose, 408/293-1387. The tacos, burritos, and salsas at Chacho's are a cut above the usual Mexican-American fare, and they are served in a simple cantina ambience. There's a definite *norteamericano* spin on this menu, which also includes burgers and fries, but the *horchata* (sweetened rice drink) and other *aguas frescas* are authentic. The chiles rellenos can be exceptional, and the shredded chicken soups are big and satisfying. This is a lively restaurant, filled with regulars who come for animated conversation and hearty helpings of food. The menu is inexpensive and has plenty of selection. • M 10am-7pm; Tu-W 10am-8pm; Th 10am-9pm; F-Sa 10am-11pm.

Chao Praya ★★ $ 4300 El Camino Real (43rd), San Mateo, 650/571-9123. Voted Best Thai by the *San Mateo Times*, Chao Praya draws mid-Peninsulans (even from restaurant-laden Palo Alto) to its small dining room. Cozy seating is available in the honeycomb of roomlets left over from a former life as a motel lobby. Lots of good salads to start things off; try the chicken *larb*. For a main course, the *gai prik sod*—chicken sautéed with fresh chili, bell pepper, and onion—is great. • M-Th 11:30am-2:30pm, 5-9:30pm; F 11:30am-2:30pm, 5-10pm; Sa 5-10pm; Su 5-9:30pm.

Chart House ★★ $$$ 115 N. Santa Cruz Ave. (Nicholson/Bean), Los Gatos, 408/354-1737. Good, simple food and attentive service make the   Chart House a popular dinner destination. The Los Gatos branch, located in a Victorian mansion in the center of town. The restaurant buys its excellent beef from Omaha—prime rib and "baseball sirloin teriyaki" (the tenderest part of the sirloin) are the best on the menu. The salad bar features seasonal fruits and a garlicky Caesar, as well as more traditional fare. Reservations recommended. • M-Th 5:30-9pm; F 5:30-10pm; Sa 5-10pm; Su 5-9pm.

Chef Chu's ★★ $ 1067 N. San Antonio Rd. (El Camino), Los Altos, 650/948-2696. Chef Chu's is a Peninsula institution, the kind of place where autographed photos of Brooke Shields and Gerald Ford hang on the wall. For every detractor who claims that standards have slipped, there's an equally adamant defender. We won't take sides, but we will say that there's still much here that's worth ordering, especially those old favorites, moo shu pork and wonton soup. Chef Chu's is always crowded; expect to wait most nights. • M-Th 11:30am-9:30pm; F 11:30am-10pm; Sa noon-10pm; Su noon-9:30pm.

Chez Sophie ★★ $$$ 201 California Ave. (Park), Palo Alto, 650/322-8586. This fanciful bistro, owned by longtime local restaurateur Sophie Nicolas, serves homestyle French fare in two cozy dining rooms. The charming interior contrasts formal touches like white tablecloths, fresh flowers, and striking cutlery with whimsical ceramic salt shakers and playful art. Start your meal with cold cucumber soup, which has a loyal local following, and choose from the rotating selection of entrées, which usually features a few traditional favorites like sweetbreads and rabbit as well as wonderful seafood and vegetarian entrées. All of the desserts are superb, particularly the *tarte Tatin*, the French version of apple pie. The wine list is comprehensive and includes many reasonably priced California and French choices. • Tu-F 11:30am-2:30pm, 6-9:30pm; Sa 6-10:30pm.

Chez Sovan ★★ $ 2425 S. Bascom Ave. (Dry Creek), Campbell, 408/371-7711. • 923 13th St. (Hwy 101/E. Hedding), San Jose, 408/287-7619. The original is located in a bleak San Jose neighborhood, but this shining star has additional quarters in a much tamer neighborhood in Campbell. Mme. Sovan, the chef, serves some of the best Cambodian food on the Peninsula. Try the amazing chicken salad crunchy with peanuts, shredded vegetables, and thin noodles in a beguiling sweet-and-sour hot sauce—you'll crave it for weeks afterward. Curries are fiery and flavorful; grilled skewers of beef, pork, or chicken are redolent of the Cambodian grill. Friendly service. • Campbell: Su-Th 11am-3pm, 5-9pm; F-Sa 11am-3pm, 5-10pm. • SJ: M-F 11am-2:30pm.

Chez T.J. ★★★ $$$$ 938 Villa St. (Castro/Shoreline), Mountain View, 650/964-7466. The interior of this restored Victorian bungalow is strictly Californian—peach walls, contemporary art, glass sculptures. Three prix fixe menus (from the seven-course *menu gastronomique* to the positively modest four-course *menu petit*) are offered nightly. Depending on the luck of the draw, you might be offered osso buco, venison with three-mushroom ragout, or monkfish in grape leaves. This is the type of place that serves palate-cleansing sorbets. Reservations required. • Tu-Sa 5:30-9pm.

Chicken! Chicken! ★ $ 234 Primrose Rd. (Burlingame/Howard), Burlingame, 650/344-4436. It doesn't take a lot of imagination to figure out what the specialty is here. But the Caribbean slant sets this cafeteria-style eatery apart from the Boston Chickens of the world. The decor is funky Caribbean cottage—brightly painted wooden furniture and a large patio—and the menu offerings reflect a Cayman Island slant. The deliciously moist and flavorful rotisserie chicken is basted in natural citrus, herbs, and spices from Grand Cayman, and the Jamaican Jerk chicken is tasty but not nearly as good as the rotisserie variety. The side dishes (salads, cornbread, mashed potatoes) also have a vaguely West Indian bent, but don't live up to the rotisserie chicken. The cheerful counterpeople will accommodate your wishes to eat in or take out. • Daily 11am-10pm.

Cho's ★ ¢ 213 California Ave. (Park), Palo Alto, 650/326-4632. Palo Alto's premier dive for inexpensive dim sum. Mr. Cho himself has been serving pot stickers and pork buns to a retinue of regular customers for years, and his tiny store is a local institution. He has recently expanded into the space next door but still has very few tables available; get your food to go and sit in the nearby public plaza. No credit cards. • M-Sa 11:30am-7:30pm; Su 11:30am-6:30pm.

Ciao Amore ★★ $$ 788 Laurel St. (Olive/Cherry), San Carlos, 650/802-8808. This is the kind of bare-bones haunt frequented only by locals in the know. The atmosphere certainly won't lure you into this brightly lit former deli with closely spaced tables, white lacquered chairs, linoleum floor, and cartoonish wall murals (one of Romeo and Juliet, the other of a Venetian covered bridge). Come instead for the delicious, bargain-priced renditions of authentic Italian dishes. The pasta is perfectly al dente, the meats are succulent and fork tender, and the fish preparations are fantastic (don't miss the nightly specials). Since Ciao Amore has no liquor license, you can bring your own wine; they don't charge a corkage fee. Save room for dessert, especially the *tiramisù* or the assortment of sorbets served in the fruit that lent its flavor (lemon in a lemon-peel cup, coconut in a half shell). • M-Sa 11:30am-2:30pm, 5-10pm; Su 5-10pm.

Clay Oven ★★ $$ 78 E. 3rd Ave. (El Camino/San Mateo Dr.), San Mateo, 650/342-9195. Clay Oven's narrow interior boasts dark, modernist decor. Walls are sponge painted blue-green with *trompe l'oeil* window images of the Indian countryside and the taj majal; high-backed chairs boasting Darth Vaderish black slip covers contrast with white table linens; and lilting Eastern music plays in the background. The lunch buffet is a good deal—for seven dollars, you can sample more than a dozen Indian dishes. Don't miss the spicy *aloo gobhi* (potatoes cooked with cauliflower), one of 13 vegetarian items on the menu. Your waiter will also brag about the tandoori chicken—trust him. Many other dishes inspire compliments, including the sublime *prawns sagwala,* prawns in a spicy spinach purée. • M-F 11:30am-2pm, 5:30-10pm; Sa-Su 5:30-10pm.

Copenhagen Bakery & Café ★ $ 1216 Burlingame Ave. (Primrose/Lorton), Burlingame, 650/342-1357. This perpetually packed café with a full-service bakery on one side and a breakfast and lunch restaurant on the other offers delicious pastries as well as classic breakfast dishes. Lunches have a distinctly Scandinavian slant, with lots of open-faced sandwiches and gourmet hams available. Save room for dessert. The café recently expanded and remodeled, and now sports a clean, Scandinavian look with lots of hardwood. • M-Sa 6am-6pm; Su 8am-4pm.

Country Gourmet ★ $ 2098 W. El Camino Real (Rengstorff/El Monte), Mountain View, 650/962-0239. • 1314 S. Mary Ave. (Fremont), Sunnyvale, 408/733-9446. Country cooking and a casual atmosphere are the hallmarks at this mini chain, where you can find dolphin-safe tuna salad on the menu alongside pastrami sandwiches and barbecued chicken. The interior features oak furniture, dried flowers, tin milk cans, and a collection of plants. A commercial feel manages to creep in, though. • M 7am-2:30pm; Tu-Th 7am-8pm; F 7am-9pm; Sa 8am-9pm; Su 8am-8pm.

Crescent Park Grill ★★ $$$ 546 University Ave. (Cowper/Webster), Palo Alto, 650/326-0111. The hackneyed real-estate dictum "location, location, location" applies perfectly to Crescent Park Grill, which hot San Francisco restaurateur John Cunin—of Cypress Club and 2223 Market fame—has opened in a notoriously high-turnover locale. Cunin just might break the curse, now that he has highly regarded chef Christopher Fernandez turning out plate after plate of delicious Mediterranean food: rich tomato soup, crisp-skinned roast chicken, earthy risotto, velvety lamb. But despite the elegant cherry-colored wood appointments, the decor is slightly schizophrenic. The light bar and café area has wood floors; opposite this are booths, dark carpeting, and a fireplace. No matter where you sit, you feel like you're in the wrong half. It's even worse if you end up in the Siberian isolation of the private-party room in back. The cheerfully unprofessional service is a world away from Cunin's other restaurants. Reservations recommended. • M-Th 11:30am-2:30pm, 5:30-10pm; F 11:30am-2:30pm, 5:30-11pm; Sa 5:30-11pm; Su 5-9pm.

Cuban International ★ $$ 625 N. 6th St. (Taylor/Jackson), San Jose, 408/288-6783. This restaurant was serving caramelized plantains long before the neighborhood became overrun by sushi bars. The small dining room is tropically outfitted, complete with a huge poster of a palm-lined beach. The menu focuses on Cuban meat dishes such as *ropa vieja*, Brazilian roast pork, and chicken stew, but also includes several seafood dishes, including an extravagant (and costly) paella. A recent change in ownership has regulars grumbling about a decline in food quality. • M-Th 11am-9:30pm; F 11am-10:30pm; Sa noon-10:30pm; Su noon-9:30pm.

Dac Phuc ★ ¢ 198 W. Santa Clara St. (Almaden), San Jose, 408/297-5517. This is a good safe bet if you're looking to try one of the many Vietnamese eateries sprinkled throughout downtown San Jose. Dac Phuc bustles with Vietnamese diners at lunchtime, when it can be hard to get a table or a waiter's attention. Dinner is a little more relaxed. The restaurant inhabits one of the few older buildings left downtown, and the look is so down-at-the-heels that it's kind of charming. An excellent version of *pho* (Vietnamese beef noodle soup with fresh mint and basil leaves) is served, along with a variety of rice dishes and rolled appetizers. Cash only. • Tu-Sa 10am-8pm; Su 10am-6pm.

Dal Baffo ★★ $$$$ 878 Santa Cruz Ave. (Crane/University), Menlo Park, 650/325-1588. Haute Italian food served in a hushed, formal (some might stay stuffy) dining room. This is one of the most expensive Peninsula restaurants—expect to drop a sizable wad—plus it boasts a wine list the size of *Webster's* that the *Wine Spectator* has called among the best in the world. Pasta and beef dishes are the high points of the menu. A good place for a celebration (say, a successful IPO). Wear your best dress-up clothes (jackets recommended for men). Reservations recommended. • M-F 11:30am-2pm, 5:30-10pm; Sa 5:30-10pm.

Dinah's Poolside Café ★ $ Dinah's Garden Hotel, 4261 El Camino Real (San Antonio/Charleston), Palo Alto, 650/493-4542. A Palo Alto weekend-brunch institution, Dinah's caters to a slightly older crowd than some of its upstart competitors. Although you need a map and a compass to find this unpretentious dining spot (just turn in at the tiny sign and proceed to the rear of the parking lot and around the building), the wait for a table on a Sunday morning is every bit as long as it is at Hobee's. The good news is that the wait is much more pleasant, since you can dangle your feet in the pool. The food is solidly American—fresh and plentiful, with a guaranteed lack of surprises. You'll leave satisfied, but it's the congenial surroundings and cheerful, family-style service that will keep you coming back. • Daily 6:30am-9:30pm.

Don Giovanni ★★★ $$ 235 Castro St. (Dana/Villa), Mountain View, 650/961-9749. Expert service and sophisticated ambience make dining here a terrific experience. Couples who stop in for a romantic evening will be served by skilled waiters, happy to offer suggestions but completely unobtrusive. Seafood in tomato, basil, and wine sauce; voluptuous *melanzane*; and generous spit-roasted entrées like a gloriously crisp Muscovy duck served with perfect vegetables are only some of the stars of this deeply rewarding menu. High ceilings, expansive lengths of terra-cotta wall, and exactly the right amount of candlelight make the dining room irresistible. The high-quality preparations and stylish Mediterranean setting make Don Giovanni a bargain at half the price. Savor a glass of Chianti Classico and you'll feel you've landed somewhere near Milan. • M-Th 11:30am-2:30pm, 5-10pm; F 11:30am-2:30pm, 5-11pm; Sa 11-11pm; Su 11am-10pm.

Draeger's Bistro ★ $ 1010 University Dr. (Santa Cruz/Menlo), Menlo Park, 650/688-0677. Draeger's, a food emporium for the rich and famous, opened this upstairs café in its Menlo Park store long before opening Viognier in San Mateo. European-style wicker chairs, slick granite-topped counters, lots of white tile, and heavy-duty espresso machines make for a striking, upscale atmosphere. Lattes and pastries are served at the coffee bar, while a menu of gourmet lunch and brunch items—hope for huckleberry pancakes—is served in the dining area. • Restaurant: Daily 7am-2:30pm.

Ecco Café ★★ $$$ 322 Lorton Ave. (Burlingame Ave./Bellevue), Burlingame, 650/342-7355. Self-taught chef Tooraj offers some of the most creative dining on the Peninsula. He serves *very* California-Continental dishes that meld fresh ingredients into subtle creations. The Tooraj salad, which includes baby greens, shrimp, hearts of palm, artichoke hearts, and fruit, is a best seller. Other inventive standouts might include a watercress and apricot soup and ahi tuna with an anchovy and olive compote. The dining room has a suburban Art Deco look, with well-spaced tables, crisp white linens, and lots of mauve. The subdued atmosphere attracts a steady flow of corporate types, Hillsborough ladies who lunch, and the Cadillac/cigar crowd, putting pressure on the small staff to keep up. • M-F 11:30am-2:30pm, 5:30pm-10pm; Sa 5:30pm-10pm.

840 North First ★★ $$$ 840 N. 1st St. (Mission/Hedding), San Jose, 408/282-0840. San Jose's power elite flock here at lunchtime—you might spot the mayor or a gaggle of lawyers on a lunch break from the courthouse. The sophisticated dining room, done up in grays and maroons with quirky modern light fixtures, is the ideal backdrop for business powwows. Italian and Asian influences prevail in the kitchen; pasta choices include shellfish linguine. Prawns with chili paste, sherry, and ginger are featured among the appetizers. The chef's upscale version of surf and turf is sautéed filet mignon with prawns served with sun-dried tomatoes and mushrooms. Reservations a must at lunch. • M-F 11:30am-10:30pm; Sa 5-10:30pm.

El Calderon ★ $ 699 Calderon Ave. (Church), Mountain View, 650/940-9533. The oldest and best Salvadorean restaurant on the Peninsula. Try the *pupusas,* El Salvador's national snack of thick corn tortillas filled with either cheese, chorizo, or chicken and then fried and served with an *encurtido de vegetales.* Another dish worth trying is the combination plate of *chicharrón*, plantains, *pupusas*, rice, and beans. • M-Th 11am-1:45pm, 5-8:45pm; F-Sa 5-9pm.

El Grullense E&E ★★ ¢ 2401 Middlefield Rd. (Charter), Redwood City, 650/369-9013. • 999 El Camino Real (Broadway/Jefferson), Redwood City, 650/568-3242. Got a craving for tacos at one in the morning? Have no fear—just head for El Grullense, which serves the best tacos around. The atmosphere is reminiscent of a fast-food restaurant, but the tacos and *sopitos* (soft, handmade corn tortillas) served open face with your choice of meat, are cheap and delicious. Of the seven types of fillings available, the *carne asada* (grilled beef) and the *al pastor* (barbecued pork) are particularly wonderful. Tacos are only $1, and the *sopitos* $1.50. Burritos are also offered, but stick to the tacos since it's what they do best (a word to the wise: opt for the mild sauce on your taco unless you have iron tastebuds—the hot sauce is truly incendiary). No credit cards. • Daily 8am-2am.

Emile's ★★★ $$$$ 545 S. 2nd St. (William/Reed), San Jose, 408/289-1960. Emile's has ruled the San Jose dining scene for nearly 20 years. Chef-owner Emile Mooser, the dapper Swiss-born and -trained chef, has a flair for public relations (expect to see him canvassing the dining room). The interior has a subdued elegance: an elaborate flower arrangement dominates the dining room, and an intricate, leaflike sculpture decorates the ceiling. Many of the dishes live up to Emile's vaunted reputation: grilled swordfish served with seafood risotto is perfectly cooked, and the osso buco is tender, rich, and flavorful. Finish off your meal with an ethereal Grand Marnier soufflé. Reservations recommended. • Tu-Th, Sa 6-10pm; F 11:30am-2pm, 6-10pm.

Empire Grill and Tap Room ★★ $$$ 651 Emerson St. (Forest/Hamilton), Palo Alto, 650/321-3030. The lovely vine-covered patio at the Empire Grill and Tap Room is the perfect spot for a relaxing lunch, weekend brunch, or romantic dinner, while the wood-paneled interior offers a completely different scene, packed with a boisterous crowd of singles and high-tech wheeler-dealers downing microbrewed beers and martinis. The menu leans toward well-prepared California cuisine, but the offerings are not overly remarkable and the portions sometimes leave you wanting more. Reservations recommended. • M-F 11:30am-10pm; Sa-Su 11am-10pm.

The English Rose ★★ $ 663 Laurel St. (San Carlos Ave.), San Carlos, 650/595-5549. An exceedingly ladylike English teahouse with surprisingly delicious food. The rigorously coordinated place settings include lavender napkins, pastel-patterned teacups, and floral tea cozies. Framed paintings of the English countryside, pictures of royalty, decorative plates, and all manner of bric-a-brac line the walls. The menu is inexpensive and authentic, if limited, with breakfast, lunch, and tea served all day. Noontime items include quiches, wonderful Cornish pasties, and banger and onion sandwiches, as well as tea plates and classic ploughman's lunches. No credit cards. • Tu-Sa 9am-3pm.

Esperanza's Restaurant ★ $ 173 S. Murphy Ave. (Evelyn/Washington), Sunnyvale, 408/732-3253. Excellent Mexican specialties at low prices. The cheery interior, decorated with trompe l'oeil scenes of Mexico and bright green tablecloths, makes a pleasant setting for a quick meal of fajitas, burritos, tamales, or enchiladas. Try the delicious *chilaquiles*—soft fried corn tortilla with eggs, onions, jalapeños, and tomatoes served with tangy *chile verde* sauce. No credit cards. • Su-Th 11am-8pm; F-Sa 11am-10pm.

Estampas Peruanas ★★ $$ 715 El Camino Real (Brewster/Broadway), Redwood City, 650/368-9340. If you have not been lucky enough to experience Peruvian food, Estampas Peruanas is the perfect place to discover it. Don't be put off by the nondescript exterior; inside you will find a relaxed and friendly atmosphere. Owner Carlos Enrique Shimabukuru serves up large portions of great food at moderate prices. Outstanding appetizers include *ceviche mixto*, fish marinated in lemon juice and spices; *chicharron de pollo*, crisply fried pieces of chicken served with an addictive tangy dipping sauce; and *camarones al ajillo*, prawns sautéed in garlic and wine. The *parihuela de mariscos*, described on the menu as "Peru's best soup," is sautéed shellfish with a light tomato broth and is a meal in itself. The *salpicada de mariscos*, seafood sautéed with onions and tomatoes, and the *bistec a la pobre*, a delicious broiled steak with sautéed onions, toasted bread, fried banana, fried eggs, and rice, are both standouts. The wine list is limited, so take advantage of the reasonable corkage fee and bring a bottle from home. Live Andean and Peruvian music is performed once a month. • Tu-Su 11am-9pm.

Eulipia ★★/★★★ $$ 374 S. 1st St. (San Carlos/San Salvador), San Jose, 408/280-6161. One of the first serious power-dining spots in the emerging downtown area, Eulipia has it all. The stylish interior features big booths, long brick walls, and striking artwork; the tiny bar pours a multitude of top California wines as well as definitive specialty cocktails. The wide-ranging American menu offers everything from delicious Southern classics (including the finest jambalaya in California) to distinctive charcoal-grilled Idaho river trout and New York steak with wild mushrooms. Desserts—especially the renowned lemon tart—are not to be missed. A lively setting for fine lunches and couples dining, Eulipia has a stellar location within walking distance of every major museum, theater, and hotel in downtown San Jose. • Tu-F 11:30am-2pm, 5:30-10pm; Sa 5:30-10pm; Su 4:30-9pm.

Evvia ★★★ $$$ 420 Emerson St. (University/Lytton), Palo Alto, 650/326-0983. Where do high-tech barons go to drop their hard-earned IPO money? Look no further than Evvia, located in an elegant yet rustic Mediterranean space featuring rough-hewn wood tables, colorful tilework, and striking Greek pottery. This is upscale Greek cuisine, ranging from *spanakopitta* and moussaka to seared ahi tuna salad, roast leg of lamb and chicken from the rotisserie, and pasta dishes with a Greek twist. The *meze* platter features an arrangement of three tasty spreads, crispy, crackerlike pita bread, and several different *dolmas* filled with subtly spiced rice. The dessert list includes several intriguing choices beyond the usual too-sweet baklava. The wine list combines California and Greek labels. Reservations recommended. • M-Th 11:30am-2:30pm, 5:30-10pm; F 11:30am-2:30pm, 5-11pm; Sa 5-11pm; Su 5-9pm.

Falafel Drive-In ★ ¢ 2301 Stevens Creek Blvd. (Bascom/I-880), San Jose, 408/294-7886. Although it looks like a burger joint given a recent make-over by immigrants from the Middle East, Falafel Drive-In has actually been in its present location in the Burbank area of San Jose since 1966. The drive-in's longevity can be attributed to a simple formula: darn good falafel at working-class prices. Order some fries or onion rings on the side for the perfect vegetarian grease fix. Indoor and outdoor seating is available, and the menu includes burgers for the meat-dependent. Cash only. • M-Sa 9am-8pm; Su 11am-6pm.

Faultline Brewing Company ★★ $$/$$$ 1235 Oakmead Pkwy. (N. Lawrence/Arques), Sunnyvale, 408/736-2739. This behemoth of a brew pub offers all the charm of a converted Rusty Scupper in an office park, which is exactly what it is. Fortunately, the target clientele (Silicon Valley engineers-with-no-lives) doesn't seem to mind the lack of ambience—what they want is a convenient place to drop some of their excess cash on high-quality beer and delicious food, and Faultline delivers. The food and beer are pricey but good, and the restaurant is only a stone's throw from most Silicon Valley cubicles. Weeknights between 6pm and 10pm Faultline is packed, and you can easily wait an hour for a table. Service can be slow during these times, too. • M-Tu 11am-10pm; W-F 11am-11pm; Sa-Su 5-10pm.

Faz Sunnyvale ★★★ $$/$$$ 1108 N. Mathilda Ave. (Moffett Park), Sunnyvale, 408/752-8000. Opulence was never so alluring as at this vibrantly decorated contemporary palace of Mediterranean and Middle Eastern cuisine. A gorgeous bar and exhibition kitchen rise above the multilevel seating, where an upscale clientele enjoys perfectly mixed cocktails and some amazing roast meats and spiced poultry classics. The *meze* platter—a beautiful array of world-class hummus, *dolmas*, *baba ghanoush*, pickled vegetables, and salty feta—is one of the finest versions of the genre. Very smart and stylish, the dazzling interior and attractive patio make Faz a prime deal-making venue. • M-F 6:30-9:30am, 11:30am-3pm, 5-10pm; Sa-Su 7:30-10am, 11:30am-3pm, 5-10pm.

The Fish Market ★★ $$$ 3150 El Camino Real (Page Mill/Matadero), Palo Alto, 650/493-9188. • 1855 S. Norfolk St. (Hwy 92/Roberta), San Mateo, 650/349-FISH (3474). • 3775 El Camino Real (Halford), Santa Clara, 408/246-FISH (3474). • 1007 Blossom Hill Rd. (Almaden/Santa Teresa), San Jose, 408/269-FISH (3474). The menu offers a huge selection of fresh seafood, mostly mesquite grilled, but also steamed, sautéed, or raw (sushi, ceviche, or half shell). Everything is simple but well done. The Palo Alto outpost of this chain looks like a nautical warehouse: it features polished brass and wood, photos of fishing piers, and exposed ventilation ducts. The San Mateo branch is the most upscale. • M-Th 11am-9:30pm; F-Sa 11am-10pm; Su noon-9:30pm.

The Fisherman ★★ $$$ 1492 Old Bayshore Hwy. (Broadway/Millbrae Ave.), Burlingame, 650/548-1490. Renovated after a fire a couple of years ago, the Fisherman sports crisp linen tablecloths, a stylish bilevel dining room, and sparkling views of the bay. All in all, a nice spot for business lunches (there is also a small banquet room upstairs for private parties). Seafood is clearly the highlight here, although the menu has pizza, pasta, chicken, and meats. Preparation can be inconsistent, but the Caesar salad, grilled fish, and crab cakes are usually reliable. One of the better restaurants on hotel row south of the airport. • M-Th 11:30am-2:30pm, 4:30-10pm; F 11:30am-2:30pm, 4:30-11pm; Sa noon-10pm; Su noon-10pm.

Flea Street Café ★★ $$$ 3607 Alameda de las Pulgas (Avy), Menlo Park, 650/854-1226. The ambience of a cozy country house and the cooking of enlightened chef and local celebrity Jesse Cool make this a must-visit. An omelet is not just an omelet here, but a concoction of stir-fried greens, roasted garlic, goat cheese, sun-dried tomato cream, and Yucatan sausage. Dinner selections include grilled salmon with buttermilk mashed potatoes and filet of beef in a wild mushroom port wine sauce. You get the satisfaction of eating organic ingredients, although good health comes at a fairly hefty price. Lunches are easier on the pocketbook. • Tu-F 11:30am-2pm, 5:30-9pm; Sa 5:30-9:30pm; Su 10am-2pm, 5:30-9pm.

Fook Yuen ★★★ $$ 195 El Camino Real (Millbrae Ave./Hillcrest), Millbrae, 650/692-8600. A convenient, commodious, family-oriented restaurant serving high-quality Hong Kong–style cuisine. Dim sum is famous, attracting crowds from miles around. Fish here is uniformly fresh (try the fabulous fried whole flounder), and barbecued meats are also recommended, while the Peking duck is done to perfection. At times, the brightly lit dining room can be loud and cacophonous, but the service doesn't suffer. Bring Grandma and the kids—no one will look askance. In fact, you'll fit in better. • M-Th 11am-2:30pm, 5:30-9:30pm; F 11am-2:30pm, 5:30-10pm; Sa 10am-2:30pm, 5:30-10pm; Su 10am-2:30pm, 5:30-9:30pm.

Frankie Johnnie and Luigi Too ★ $ 939 W. El Camino Real (Castro/Shoreline), Mountain View, 650/967-5384. A giant, popular 1950s-style Italo-American food factory owned by four sausage-magnate brothers. Students, families, and spooning couples come for the classic steam-table Italian fare (be warned, the pizza crust is so droopy it's dangerous). Sit in the open-air back room. Open late. • M-Th 11am-midnight; F-Sa 11am-1am; Su noon-midnight.

Fresco ★★ $$ 3398 El Camino Real (Page Mill/Charleston), Palo Alto, 650/493-3470. It's hard to fathom why the owner chose a former fast-food joint as the site of this popular California-cuisine eatery. It's even harder to fathom why numerous new menus and chefs later, it's still decorated with white tiles and pink vinyl booths. The menu offers pasta, salads, sandwiches, and some more ambitious meat, chicken, and fish dishes like achiote chicken and maple-cured pork chops. The roasted red pepper soup has a loyal following. Pleasant, casual service. • M 6am-10pm; Tu-Th 6am-10:30pm; F 6am-11pm; Sa 7am-11pm; Su 7am-10pm.

Fresh Taste Mandarin Cuisine ★★ $ 2111 El Camino Real (Oxford), Palo Alto, 650/324-8749. This Chinese restaurant on El Camino, right across from Stanford's soccer field, serves inexpensive food of unusually high quality. All the vegetables are fresh and unblemished. The *tsao liu* chicken has lean breast meat only. Try the tangerine beef, known for its tangy, citrus kick. The kitchen happily accommodates almost any substitution or special request, and the service is solicitous to a fault. • M-F 11:30am-2:30pm, 5-9:30pm; Sa-Su 5-9:30pm.

Fu Lam Mum ★★ $ 246 Castro St. (Dana/Villa), Mountain View, 650/967-1689. A Cantonese Chinese restaurant with an emphasis on seafood. There's not much missing from the menu, which includes that ancient aphrodisiac shark's fin soup as well as bird's nest with bamboo fungus. The walnut shrimp is definitely worth trying. A testament to its popularity and authenticity, there's rarely an empty table and the majority of patrons are Chinese families. The green carpets, green tablecloths, and fish tanks—some for food, some for decoration—add an aquatic overtone. • Daily 11am-2:30pm, 5pm-midnight.

Fuji ★ $ 56 W. Santa Clara St. (Market/1st), San Jose, 408/298-3854. Best known for its bento boxes (a Japanese sampler of teriyaki, tempura, and sashimi), Fuji provides quick service, fresh ingredients, and a filling meal for a fair price to a downtown lunch crowd. Fuji offers the usual Japanese menu amid the traditional decor of hanging globe lamps, oriental prints, and a small sushi bar. • M-Sa 11:30am-2pm, 5-10pm.

Fuji Sukiyaki ★★★ $$ 428 E. 3rd Ave. (Claremont), San Mateo, 650/348-7810. Fresh fish and creative combinations are the hallmarks of Fuji Sukiyaki, which serves up what is quite possibly the best sushi in San Mateo (the prices are as high as the quality). Cooked items include the usual range of noodles (*udon* and ramen), tempura, teriyaki, and sukiyaki, all available in a wide variety of combination dinners. The dining room features natural woods, gray carpet, and a long sushi bar in the front room, with small private rooms in back. • Tu-F 11:30am-2:30pm, 5-10pm; Sa-Su noon-2:30pm, 5-10pm.

Fuki-Sushi ★★ $$$ 4119 El Camino Real (El Camino Way), Palo Alto, 650/494-9383. A giant sushi spot with private tatami rooms: take off your shoes, sit on the floor (dangle your feet in the well), and sip sake served by a waitress in a kimono. Try the Japanese-style fondue called *shabu shabu*, which is a pot of boiling broth into which you dip cabbage, mushrooms, onions, and thinly sliced meat, and then dip the cooked morsels into a mustard sauce. Finish off the dish by drinking the broth. Open every day of the year. • M-F 11:30am-2pm, 5-10pm; Sa 5-10pm; Su 5-9:30pm.

Gambardella's ★★ $$ 561 Oak Grove Ave. (El Camino/Merrill), Menlo Park, 650/325-6989. Good, hearty southern Italian food served in an atmospheric wood-paneled dining room decorated with hundreds of old wine bottles. Specials might include lobster ravioli with Chardonnay cream sauce or petrale sole with spicy tomato sauce. A welcome respite from rampant trendiness, this place feels like it's been around for years. • Tu-Th 11:30am-2pm, 5:30-9:30pm; F 11:30am-2pm, 5:30-10pm; Sa 5:30-10pm; Su 5:30-9:30pm.

Ganko Sushi ★★ $ 1131 Cherry St. (El Camino/Laurel), San Carlos, 650/593-6843. A mom-and-pop sushi joint tucked away on a side street in downtown San Carlos. Service can lag when Ganko fills up—the sushi bar is a one-man show—but the fish is very fresh, the prices are reasonable, and they don't skimp on the portions. Adventurous types should try such creations as the carmen roll (eel, papaya, and avocado) and ganko roll (salmon skin, green onion, and cream cheese). *Donburi* (rice bowls), sukiyaki, *udon*, and other hot meals are a real bargain; the teriyaki chicken is delicious. • M-F 11:30am-2:30pm, 5-9pm; Sa 5-9pm.

Garden City ★★ $$$ 360 S. Saratoga Ave. (Stevens Creek), San Jose 408/244-4443. Las Vegas comes to San Jose at this legendary South Bay steakhouse. Located on the premises of San Jose's largest gambling and gaming venue, Garden City serves three-inch-thick prime rib, steaks, and grilled fish. Meat-and-potato cuisine is done to perfection here, hence the crowds of loyal patrons. The interior is dimly lit with a night-club ambience. During dinner hours a jazz band holds forth. • M-Th 11:30am-10pm; F 11:30am-11pm; Sa 5-11pm.

Garden Fresh ★★ $ 1245 W. El Camino Real (Shoreline), Mountain View, 650/961-7795. The fresh and delicious vegetarian food and the friendly service at this modest restaurant compensate for the uninspiring location and atmosphere. The owners are ever so nice (they give you free soup while you wait for your to-go order) and are very talented cooks. Even the mock meat dishes made from wheat gluten are wonderful: Don't miss the orange beef and the green boat. • Daily 11am-10pm.

Gaylord India Restaurant ★★ $$$ 1706 El Camino Real (Encinal/Valparaiso), Menlo Park, 650/326-8761. Years after closing its Stanford shopping center location, Gaylord has reopened on the mid-Peninsula, although the large, multiroomed cottage on El Camino is a far cry from the opulent Eastern decor of the former location. The new Gaylord's large main dining hall looks like it's in a country club, with a long bar, fireplace, and hardwood (dance) floor; the other rooms, which aren't always open, are smaller and more intimate. The food, however, remains as good and expensive as ever. Seekh Kabobs, chicken *tikka* and tandoori chicken cooked to perfection, garlic *nan* and onion *kulchas* warm from the oven—these are but a few of the highlights at this elegant Indian establishment. A very elaborate menu covers almost all North Indian dishes including a savory lamb curry served with a fragrant basmati and the most delectable cucumber yogurt *raita*. Treat yourself to some of the breads and appetizers, wash it all down with a Bombay beer, and have yourself a dinner fit for a Raj. • Daily 11:30am-2:30pm, 5-10pm.

Germania at the Hochburg ★ $$ 261 N. 2nd St. (St. James/Julian), San Jose, 408/295-4484. All the reliably hearty German classics have found a following at this venerable establishment housed in an old Victorian and highlighted by a bar with a vast collection of imported beers. The restaurant is filled with Teutonic memorabilia: suits of armor, coats of arms, and antique beer steins. Serviceable schnitzel and pork dishes, sides of authentic sauerkraut and creamy potatoes, and delectable warm apple strudels have pleased many a patron over the years. A comfy local rendezvous, with neither pretense nor unnecessary glamour. There is an outdoor patio and, on weekends, live music and dancing in the attached Austrian ballroom. • Tu-Su 11:30am-2pm, 5-9:30pm.

Gibson ★★ $$$ 201 E. 3rd Ave. (Ellsworth), San Mateo, 650/344-6566. Riding the retro-cocktail revival wave, this sleek Art Deco spot takes its name from a drink: Similar to a martini, a Gibson is garnished with a cocktail onion instead of an olive, and this restaurant marinates its own onions. Bathed in a pink glow, the understated dining room sports a long bar—the perfect spot for sipping a Gibson—well-spaced booths, and large, elegant chandeliers, with additional seating in an upstairs balcony and small front patio (both better bets for escaping the din in the main room).

Gibson's menu is considerably more modern, offering a delicious selection of inventive California cooking: grilled prawns with olives, tomatoes, and lemon oil; grilled halibut with tomato and onion gratin and saffron sauce; and pork loin with black bean sauce, roasted corn, and avocado salsa. Reservations recommended. • Daily 11:30am-2:30pm, 5:30-10:30pm.

Gin Mon ★★ $ Carlmont Center, 1079 Alameda de las Pulgas (Ralston), Belmont, 650/592-3663. Described by area residents as the only good Chinese food in the San Carlos-Belmont area, Gin Mon does a booming business. Expect a crowd in the tiny front area where people wait for tables or takeout. The small dining room is many steps above your typical dive: it's clean, comfortable, carpeted, and nicely lit. The long menu lists the usual array of familiar items, with particular raves for the pot stickers, walnut prawns, chow mein, and kung pao chicken. The friendly owners adroitly manage the crowds while they handle the continually ringing phone. • M-Sa 11:30am-9:30pm; Su noon-9pm.

Giorgio's ★★ $$ 30 South B St. (1st/Baldwin), San Mateo, 650/347-7000. Located in downtown San Mateo, Giorgio's is a promising Mediterranean bistro featuring a bright, airy bilevel room with high ceilings, hardwood floors, and an open kitchen (a bit of the spirit of JoAnne's B Street Café, Giorgios' predecessor, remains). The menu offers a wide variety of dishes, from pizza and pastas to Greek delights with a modern twist. You can't go wrong with the *horiatiki salata*, a Greek village salad, and the *linguine con vongole*. The friendly, formal-looking wait staff won't disappoint. • Tu-Su 11:30am-3pm, 5:30-10:30pm.

Golden Chopsticks ★★ $/$$ 1765 S. Winchester Blvd. (Hamilton/Campbell Ave.), Campbell, 408/370-6610. Learn how to cook Vietnamese at this do-it-yourself restaurant, where the specialties include an entrée of beef, chicken, shrimp, and calamari that you barbecue at your table on a rock heated to more than 450 degrees. The chef prepares the accompanying anchovy sauce and the vegetables wrapped in rice paper. Timid or lazy diners can choose from fried or sautéed beef, poultry, and seafood with accents of lemongrass and fish sauce, as well as a substantial variety of vegetarian dishes. The truly intrepid can order fried pigeon or eel soup with rice noodles. Start with an order of their wonderful spring rolls. Pink fluorescent lights give the dining room a warm glow; the waitresses are in elaborate traditional dress to match. • Daily 11am-10pm.

Gombei Japanese Restaurant ★★ $ 1438 El Camino Real (Glenwood), Menlo Park, 650/329-1799. • 193 E. Jackson St. (4th/5th), San Jose, 408/279-4311. You won't find any slimy, fishy things in these Japanese restaurants specializing in simple, light cooked dishes like teriyaki, tempura, *donburi* (rice bowls), and *udon* (noodle soup). A special salad of exotic Asian vegetables was a sculptural triumph one night, with a tangle of seaweed nestled among the various roots and unidentified vegetation. Looking into the open kitchen you'd think the meticulous chefs were assembling Swiss watches instead of meals. The waiting lines and largely Japanese crowd bode well for the food, but can often mean a wait. No credit cards. • MP: M-F 11:30am-2pm, 5-9:30pm; Sa 5-9:30pm; Su 5-9pm. • SJ: M-Sa 11:30am-2:30pm, 5-9:30pm.

Gordon Biersch Brewing Company ★★ $$ 640 Emerson St. (Hamilton/Forest), Palo Alto, 650/323-7723. • 33 E. San Fernando St. (1st/2nd), San Jose, 408/294-6785. This upscale beer hall continues to pack them in. The magic formula? Beer brewed on the premises, an attractive, on-the-prowl clientele, and an all-around stylish ambience. The long polished wood bar is favored by the young business set, especially on weekend evenings. In Palo Alto, a divider now separates the bar from the dining area; the front of the restaurant opens onto the sidewalk in warm-weather, making it a favorite summertime hangout. The California cuisine has a mixed reputation—chefs change regularly—but burgers are always a good wager, and the garlic fries are delicious, if potent. • PA: Su-W 11am-11pm; Th 11am-midnight; F-Sa 11am-1am. • SJ: Su-Th 11:30am-10pm; F-Sa 11:30am-11pm.

Grandview Restaurant ★★★ $$ 1107 Howard Ave. (California/Lorton), Burlingame, 650/348-3888. This glamorous Chinese restaurant has become a darling of the critics, ensuring that it will outlast its many predecessors at this location. Decorated like an upscale San Francisco dim sum house, with lots of mirrors, draped banquet tables, and bright flowers, Grandview has some atypical touches: an open kitchen facing a long counter (good for dining alone) and a small front patio. The restaurant specializes in Shanghaiese and Sichuan cooking, but the huge menu has something for everyone, including a smattering of vegetarian options; everything is grease-free and deliciously prepared. Even if you're predisposed to shy away from dessert at Asian restaurants, Grandview's sweet offerings are worth the risk. Cubes of rice pudding are particularly tasty. Or stop in for weekend dim sum: the dumplings are excellent. Service is accommodating, with advice freely given. • Su-Th 11am-3pm, 5-9:30pm; F-Sa 11am-3pm, 5-10pm.

Great Bear Café and Los Osos Diner ★ $ 19 N. Santa Cruz Ave. (Main), Los Gatos, 408/395-8607. Sensory overload. A rich coffee smell, loud Santa Cruz–style music, and bright oil paintings lining an exposed brick wall set the stage for the strongly flavored dishes at this self-service diner and espresso bar. The menu practically dares you to try a sandwich of spicy Italian sausage and peppers on a sourdough baguette or the garlic pizza with tomatoes, mushrooms, parmesan, and red onions. The glass case at the order counter contains a motley assortment of fruit salads, knishes, and gargantuan slices of truly amazing fruit pie. • Daily 6am-11pm.

Guido's ★ $ PruneYard Shopping Center, Campbell and Bascom avenues, Campbell, 408/377-7713. Simple, voluptuous Italian classics are the house specialty at this surprisingly atmospheric restaurant tucked behind a vintage shopping complex. The al fresco patio seating feels very Old World, and the menu involves comforting standards like calamari vinaigrette and minestrone soup, as well as crisp salads and celebrated pizzas. The fresh pastas are appealingly old-fashioned—this is the sort of place to satisfy that craving for marinara, garlic bread, and Chianti. Good *tiramisù* and fine espresso drinks finish the meal. • M-Th 11am-10pm; F 11am-11pm; Sa 8am-11pm; Su 8am-10pm.

Habana Cuba Restaurant ★★ $$ 238 Race St. (San Carlos/Park), San Jose, 408/998-2822. It's no longer necessary to go to Miami for authentic Cuban specialties served in an island atmosphere. If you're in the mood for yuca, sweet plantains, and black beans with rice, you'll love this family-run restaurant. Incredibly popular with the local Cuban community, the owners know many of the customers by name and make newcomers feel equally welcome. Choose from a selection of hearty pork and beef dishes served with white rice and sweet plantains, or opt for the wonderful *arroz con camarones a la Valenciana*, prawns cooked with saffron rice, onions, bell peppers, and green olives in a delicate tomato sauce. The homemade flan accompanied by strong Cuban coffee is the perfect finale. • M 11am-2:30pm; Tu-F 11am-2:30pm, 5-9:30pm; Sa noon-9:30pm.

Hamasushi ★★ $$ 20030 Stevens Creek Blvd. (De Anza/Wolfe), Cupertino, 408/446-4262. A conspicuous East-meets-West dropout, the former Chez Nous Hama renounced its short-lived French menu to return to its roots as a purveyor of traditional Japanese fare. Hamasushi is more elegant than the average sushi joint (although karaoke does make an appearance most nights), the sushi and sashimi are exquisitely fresh albeit pricey, and the long menu covers the full range of cooked dishes at more reasonable prices. • M-F 11:30am-2pm, 5:30-10:30pm; Sa 5-10pm; Su 5-9:30pm.

Hangen ★★ $ 134 Castro St. (Villa/Evelyn), Mountain View, 650/964-8881. Call the fire engines. The food at this Chinese restaurant is flaming hot. The unremarkable interior is clean, bright, and noisy, but the menu includes some of the best Sichuan plates around. Word is out, though, and dinner lines can be long. Recommended dishes include red oil wontons, heavenly sliced conch salad, tea-smoked duck, eggplant with sliced pork, and Hunan crispy fish. • Daily 11am-2pm, 5-9:45pm.

Henry's World Famous Hi-Life ★ $ 301 W. Saint John St. (Almaden), San Jose, 408/295-5414. Housed in a century-old roadhouse that was almost wiped out by the floods of '95, Henry's is a South Bay landmark. Smoky, white-oak barbecue is the specialty here. Choose from flavorful ribs served with a bowl of spicy sauce, teriyaki steak, or perhaps a side of mushrooms or barbecued onions. Pick a number and wait your turn in the dim, memorabilia-packed bar. • M 5-9pm; Tu-Th 11:30am-2pm, 5-9pm; F-Sa 4-10pm; Su 4-9pm.

Higashi West ★★★ $$$ 636 Emerson St. (Forest/Hamilton), Palo Alto, 650/323-9378. Higashi West's dramatic, tiny interior features an indoor waterfall and soaring shoots of black bamboo. The menu is equally striking, featuring many daring East-West preparations, all served in "Tsunami" plates (tapas-sized portions). Try the garlic-crusted pork chops with green apple essence and wasabi mashed potatoes, or the Higashi West roll—smoked salmon wrapped around tiger shrimp and baked. The traditional sushi is fresh, well prepared, enormous, and expensive. The menu lists 13 varieties of sake. Reservations recommended. • M-Sa 5:30-10pm.

Hobee's Restaurant ★★ $ 67 Town & Country Village (El Camino and Embarcadero), Palo Alto, 650/327-4111. • 4224 El Camino Real (Charleston/San Antonio), Palo Alto, 650/856-6124. • 2312 Central Expressway (Rengstorff), Mountain View, 650/968-6050. • 680 River Oaks Pkwy. (Montague), San Jose, 408/232-0190. • 920 Town & Country Village (Stevens Creek and Winchester), San Jose, 408/244-5212. • 1101 Shoreway Rd. (Hwy 101), Redwood Shores, 650/596-0400. • 800 Ahwanee Ave. (Mathilda), Sunnyvale, 408/524-3580. A country-style restaurant chain with a California health-food influence, Hobee's serves up legendary brunches on weekends in a cheery if precious atmosphere. Although breakfast is always available (don't miss the famed coffeecake), take a chance on the delicious daily specials and nonbreakfast standards like the flavorful black bean chili. A favorite breakfast spot of high-tech execs. The Palo Alto Town & Country location demonstrated customer loyalty when it finally reopened after it was destroyed by a fire. • PA T&C: M-F 7am-9pm; Sa-Su 8am-9pm. • PA Charleston: M 7am-2:30pm; Tu-F 7am-9pm; Sa 7:30am-9pm; Su 8am-2:30pm. • MV: M-F 6:30am-2:30pm; Sa-Su 7:30am-2:30pm. • SJ: M-F 6:30am-2:30pm; Sa-Su 8am-2:30pm. • SJ T&C: M 7am-2:30pm; Tu-F 7am-9pm; Sa 8am-9pm; Su 8am-3pm. • RS: M-F 7am-2:30pm; Sa-Su 8am-2:30pm. • Sunnyvale: M-F 7am-2:30pm; Sa-Su 8am-3pm.

Hong Fu ★★ $ 20588 Stevens Creek Blvd. (De Anza), Cupertino, 408/252-2200. Light, Cantonese-leaning seafood specialties served in an elegant, airy dining room decorated with jade statuettes set Hong Fu apart from the run-of-the-mill South Bay Chinese restaurant. Start with minced chicken in a lettuce cup, then try one of the well-prepared seafood dishes such as triple delight in bird's nest—shrimp, scallops, chicken, and vegetables in a lightly fried potato basket—or dry-braised scallops with broccoli. Vegetarians can choose from sizzling tofu Hong Fu style and a variety of braised and sautéed vegetable dishes. Reserve a table on weekend nights to avoid a wait. • M-Th 11am-2:30pm, 5-9pm; F-Sa 11am-2:30pm, 5-10pm.

Hong Kong Flower Lounge ★★ $$ 51 Millbrae Ave. (El Camino), Millbrae, 650/692-6666. • 1671 El Camino Real (Park), Millbrae, 650/588-9972. The Millbrae Avenue location is a celebrated tile-roofed temple with floor-to-ceiling windows on all three tiers. Ostentatious, yes, even gaudy, but somehow lovable. The Flower Lounge is best enjoyed by a group; reserve one of the round tables by the window. The specialty here is Cantonese seafood: live prawns, crab, lobster, catfish, and ling cod are fished out of huge tanks to appear only moments later on your plate. The kitchen doesn't stint. If you order prawns with walnut sauce or Sichuan conch and scallops, you'll get a plate piled high. The original location on El Camino is simpler. Service is aloof, to put it mildly, especially if you order in English. Dim sum every day. • Millbrae Ave.: M-F 11:30am-2:30pm, 5-9:30pm; Sa-Su 10:30am-2:30pm, 5-9:30pm. • El Camino: M-Th 11am-2:30pm, 5-9:45pm; F 11am-2:30pm, 5-10:15pm; Sa 10am-2:30pm, 5-10:15pm; Su 10am-2:30pm, 5-9:45pm.

Hunan Home's ★★ $ 4880 El Camino Real (Jordan), Los Altos, 650/965-8818. This unassuming Chinese restaurant serves some of the best hot and sour soup on the Peninsula—the broth is thin and savory, with thin strips of pork and crunchy mushrooms. Also not to be missed are the exceptional wontons in spicy broth. Main courses don't quite live up to the starters, but the quality is generally high. Decor is of the standard-issue Chinese-restaurant-with-pink-walls-and-fish-tank variety. • Daily 11:30am-2:30pm, 5-9:30pm.

Hunan Taste ★★ $ 998 4th St. (Hedding/I-880), San Jose, 408/295-1186. Another San Jose diamond in the rough, Hunan Taste is famous for its extra-hot versions of Hunan favorites. The restaurant's semi-shabby decor matches the down-at-the-heels character of the surrounding neighborhood, but that doesn't deter its fans, who pack the place at lunch and keep it humming at night. Perhaps it's the oddly appealing decor, featuring bunches of dried chilis hanging on the wall, Mexican style, or the marvelous Hunan tofu and Kung-Pao shrimp (a word to the wise: be sure to order your food "medium" unless you have a death wish) that keeps them coming. The kitchen is in full view behind glass, though we're not sure why. • M-Sa 11am-9pm.

I Fratelli ★★ $$$ 388 Main St. (1st/2nd), Los Altos 650/941-9636. Yet another offshoot from a San Francisco restaurant, no doubt looking to cash in on the IPO craze, although the menu is careful to point out that this is an "independently owned and operated" venture, and the offerings have been modified a bit. Like the San Francisco location, the Los Altos I Fratelli has been popular from its opening, drawing patrons with its convivial atmosphere, heaping plates of pasta, and simple grilled meats. Cream sauces can be on the heavy side, while lighter dishes such as a zesty ravioli with shrimp and asparagus show more finesse. Veal and swordfish dishes are also good bets. The bilevel dining room sports a soaring ceiling, red tile floor, yellow sponged walls hung with colorful original art, and loud acoustics. Good beer and wine selection. Reservations recommended. • Su-M 5-9:30pm; Tu-Th 11am-1:30pm, 5-9:30pm; F 11am-1:30pm, 5-10pm; Sa 5-10pm.

I Gatti ★★ $$ 25 E. Main St. (College/University), Los Gatos, 408/399-5180. Fashionable enough to be loud and lively, this attractive Italian restaurant offers some wonderful high-concept cooking as well as expertly grilled meats and sensuous pastas. Plates are prettily presented, taking their cue from the sunny decor. Menu highlights include salads of baby greens, tender braised lamb shank with porcini mushrooms, and a delightfully eclectic *antipasti misti* platter. Another Mediterranean bistro that has its act together, I Gatti is a popular couples dining venue. • Tu-F 11:30am-2:30pm, 5-10pm; Sa 5-10pm; Su 5-9:30pm.

Iberia ★★ $$$ 190 Ladera Shopping Center (Alpine off Hwy 280), Portola Valley, 650/854-1746. Regarded as one of the better restaurants on the Peninsula, Iberia prepares Spanish and Continental specialties in a beautiful setting. Spend a romantic evening in one of the indoor rooms or outside in the garden over large portions of terrific paella or seafood (you don't have to love garlic to love Iberia, but it helps). Many preparations, including flaming desserts, are orchestrated tableside, reinforcing an Old World feeling. Reservations recommended. • Daily 11:30am-2:30pm, 5:30-10pm.

Il Fornaio Cucina Italiana ★★ $$ 327 Lorton Ave. (Burlingame/California), Burlingame, 650/375-8000. • 520 Cowper St. (Hamilton/University), Palo Alto, 650/853-3888. • 302 S. Market St. (San Carlos), San Jose, 408/271-3366. The food is highbrow, the service is surly, and the wait is long at California's most glamorous restaurant chain. Pioneering pastas, carpaccio with arugula, and the occasional wild-boar ragout attract notables such as Joe Montana, the local Euro set, and anyone else who wants to be seen. The open counter affords a view of the frantic chefs at work, and the wood-burning ovens emit a delicious aroma—anything off the grill is a good bet. As with most chains, Il Fornaio lacks a certain soul, with both cooking and service consistently safe if not always inspired, so it's surprising how much residents either love or hate the place. • Burlingame: M-Th 11:30am-11pm; F 11:30am-midnight; Sa 10am-midnight; Su 10am-10pm. • PA: M-Th 7am-10:30am, 11:30am-11pm; F 7am-10:30am, 11:30am-midnight; Sa 8am-midnight, Su 8am-11pm. • SJ: M-Th 7am-10:30am, 11:30am-11pm; F 7am-10:30am, 11:30am-midnight; Sa 8am-midnight, Su 8am-11pm.

Il Postale ★★ $$ 127 W. Washington St. (Mathilda/Murphy), Sunnyvale, 408/733-9600. Bighearted and two-fisted, this robust restaurant likes to lavish its customers with generous portions and attentive service. Here is a place that turns out food Dean Martin would have loved. The marinara is perfection, and there's invariably some seafood pasta dish that will hit the exact al dente mark with plenty of pizzazz. The decor is classic Italian American and so is the menu. A place to be casual and get involved with the food. • M-Th 11am-10pm; F 11am-11pm; Sa 5-11pm; Su 5-9:30pm.

Inca Gardens ★★ $ 87 E. San Fernando St. (2nd/3rd), San Jose, 408/993-9793. Warm family-run atmosphere, a gleaming white interior, and a kitchen intent on bringing Peruvian specialties to North American palates all make Inca Gardens a satisfying place to eat. There are always reliable fresh grilled-fish specials, but truly adventurous diners will want to check out authentic dishes from the country where potatoes were first grown. Yes, there *are* many potato creations here—some stuffed with meat and eggs. An amazing fried-rice dish isn't to be missed. Everything is delicious, and some items wander into unforgettable territory. Lots of fun. • M 11am-3pm; Tu-F 11am-3pm, 5-9pm; Sa noon-9pm; Su noon-8pm.

Iron Gate ★★ $$$ 1360 El Camino Real (Harbor), Belmont, 650/592-7893. Elegant and expensive French cuisine in a romantic if slightly suburban setting. Take someone special, order the *crevettes bordelaise* or *veau à la saltimbocca* for two, and bask in the glow of the fireplace. A recent remodel has divided the dining area into smaller, more intimate rooms while streamlining the look with a soft, neutral palette and plush carpets, although it still has a traditional feel and the scent of heavy cologne. Waiters in tuxedoes provide discreet, formal service. The large cocktail lounge features an incongruously giant TV tuned to any available golf event. • M-F 11:30am-2:30pm, 5:30-10:30pm; Sa 5:30-10:30pm.

Jing Jing ★ $ 443 Emerson St. (University/Lytton), Palo Alto, 650/328-6885. The perennially popular Jing Jing serves up some of the spiciest Chinese food this side of San Francisco. If you're a fiery-food disciple, don't miss the orange peel beef and the *dahn dahn mihn* noodles. The simple whitewashed dining room is always packed, but the wait for a table is never very long because Jing Jing is also home to some of the speediest waiters and busboys around, who whisk you in and out before you can say chop suey. • M-Th 11:30am-2pm, 4:30-9:30pm; F-Sa 11:30am-2pm, 4:30-10pm; Su 11:30am-2:30pm, 4:30-9:30pm.

Joanie's Café ★ $ 447 California Ave. (El Camino/Ash), Palo Alto, 650/326-6505. Joanie's is a solid player in the breakfast league, serving up omelets, scrambles, pancakes, and waffles (great fresh berries on the last two). At lunch the line is out the door with people waiting for classic American fare like Cobb salads and tuna melts. On a cold day you can't beat their truly oniony French onion soup. Friendly, attentive service. • M-F 7am-2:30pm; Sa-Su 8am-2:30pm.

JoAnn's Café ★★★ $ 1131 El Camino Real (Arroyo), South San Francisco, 650/872-2810. This fabled Bay Area breakfast spot attracts hordes of omelet eaters on the weekends, so be prepared to wait for a table. The bright, airy interior is pleasant—try to snag a booth—and good background music (reggae, rock) serenades you as you peruse the long list of specialty egg dishes. Try the spectacular huevos rancheros or the seasonal berry hotcakes, or create your own omelet from a huge list of ingredients. This is home cooking like your mother never made. A popular spot for breakfast before heading to the ballpark for a Giants game. No credit cards. • M-F 7:15am-2:30pm; Sa-Su 8am-2:30pm.

John Bentley's Restaurant ★★★ $$$ 2991 Woodside Rd. (Cañada/I-280), Woodside, 650/851-4988. The namesake chef-owner's distinctive flair is evident from the moment you are seated in this intimate restaurant-cum-historic firehouse located in what was once known as Whiskey Hill. Bentley, a veteran of notable Bay Area kitchens, walks the line between contemporary and classical dishes, creating inventive combinations of the highest-quality ingredients. A light hand with seafood, intense aromatic infusions and sauces, and aerodynamic desserts are all signature touches from the hand of a master whose time—and audience—has come. You pay what you'd expect here, but you'll receive a very special evening in return. Reservations recommended. • Tu-F 11:30am-2:30pm, 5-9pm; Sa-Su 5-9pm.

Juban ★★ $$ 1204 Broadway (Laguna/Paloma), Burlingame, 650/347-2300. • 712 Santa Cruz Ave. (Chestnut/Crane), Menlo Park, 650/ 473-6458. This glamorous little restaurant specializing in *yakiniku*, a grill-at-your-table style of barbecue adopted from Korea, seems to have struck a chord—at lunch a steady stream of Asian businessmen pours in, and the restaurant has opened locations in San Francisco's Japantown and Menlo Park. The sleek interior, with its hardwood furnishings, peach walls, slate floors, and ample skylights, is bathed in warm, copper tones. Patrons sit in booths surrounding the grills, on which they cook bite-size morsels of beef, chicken, shrimp, scallops, and a variety of vegetables; the highlight is *wagyu*, better known as Kobe beef, a fantastically expensive, richly marbled (i.e., fat-laced) steak. Side dishes include kimchi and other pickled salads. Other menu items include soups, *donburi* rice bowls, and sukiyaki, all prepared with a Korean accent. Absentminded service matches the cook-it-yourself theme. • Burlingame: M-F 11:30am-2pm, 5-10pm; Sa 5-10pm; Su 4:30-10pm. • MP: M-F 11:30am-2pm, 5-10pm; Sa-Su 11am-10pm.

Kabul ★★ $$ 135 El Camino Real (Holly/Harbor), San Carlos, 650/594-2840. • 833 W. El Camino Real (Pastoria), Sunnyvale, 408/245-4350. Exotic Afghan cuisine with huge portions of kabob: tender chunks of meat charbroiled and served on a skewer with salad, Afghan bread, and rice. Vegetarian entrées, including the notable *challaw gulpi* (cauliflower stew), come with rice, bread, and salad. Despite the elegant atmosphere of dim lights and candles, jeans are acceptable attire. • SC: M-F 11:30am-2pm, 5:30-10pm; Sa 5:30-10pm; Su 5-9pm. • Sunnyvale: M-F 11:30am-2pm, 5:30-10pm; Sa-Su 5:30-10pm.

Kaimuki Grill ★★ $ 104 S. El Camino Real (2nd/3rd), San Mateo, 650/548-9320. A sister operation to Burlingame's Ramen Club, with a similarly eclectic Japanese menu combining sushi, noodles (*udon, soba*, and ramen), deep fry (*tonkatsu* fried pork cutlet), and *yakitori* grill (appetizer-sized skewers of meats and vegetables). Impeccably fresh sushi, hand-pulled noodles, and a delicate touch at the grill create a satisfying meal. The busy restaurant has a long sushi bar, a few tables, and a palette of white, gray, and natural wood. Expect an occasional wait for a table and lapses in service. • M, Sa 5:30-10pm; Tu-F 11:30am-2pm, 5:30-10pm.

Kamakura Sushi & Sake House ★★★ $$ 135 N. Santa Cruz Ave. (Main/Bean), Los Gatos, 408/395-6650. Smart, trendy ambience—lots of plush banquettes and a sexy little sushi bar—plus world-class sushi add up to another hit attraction for downtown Los Gatos. A great place to sample a wide range of cold and hot sakes, Kamakura does stellar *sunomonos* and teriyakis, as well as exceptional *gyoza* and many customized variations on sashimi. The sushi is truly beautiful. Everything comes in bright enamel boxes or on pretty hand-glazed pottery, garnished with elaborate fans of lemon and clouds of spun *daikon*. • M-Th 11am-2:30pm, 5:30-10pm; F 11am-2:30pm, 5:30-10:30pm; Sa noon-10:30pm; Su noon-9:30pm.

Kamei Japanese House ★★ $ 240 Castro St. (Villa/Dana), Mountain View, 650/964-6990. Located on downtown Mountain View's Castro Street strip, Kamei is a quiet, intimate retreat. Secluded booths ensure privacy, and the delicate paper lanterns dangling from the ceiling create a restful effect. If you get lost in the menu, which offers a wide variety of Japanese food, the wait staff will be happy to explain *unagi* and *tonkatsu* or the family dinner specials. If you're interested in sampling Japanese barbecue, check out the *robata* section of the menu, and if you're in the mood for comfort food Japanese style, order a soothing bowl of *udon* noodles in broth. • M-Th 11:30am-2:30pm, 5-10pm; F 11:30am-2:30pm, 5-10:30pm; Sa-Su noon-3pm, 5-10pm.

Kathmandu West ★ $ 20916 Homestead Rd. (Hollenbeck), Cupertino, 408/996-0940. Though the interior of this restaurant will make you think Indian, the menu has Nepalese specialties that you won't find elsewhere. Most of these dishes revolve around lentils, potatoes, and vegetables, which make up the national meal of *dahl bhat* (lentils and rice) many Nepalese eat twice a day. So it's no surprise that the lentil soup is tasty. Other good choices are *chara ko ledo* (chicken stir-fried with ginger and garlic) and the *mismas sekuwa* (marinated grilled meats and seafood). The low-price lunch buffet has plenty of vegetarian offerings as well. • M-F 11am-2pm, 5-10pm; Sa-Su 5-10pm.

Kazoo ★★ $/$$ 250 E. Jackson St. (6th), San Jose, 408/288-9611. • 10 E. Hamilton Ave. (Winchester), Campbell, 408/871-1250. On the corner of Japantown, this eatery boasts an unusually comprehensive display of plastic foods out front—a museum of sushi and tempura—to lure diners in. The interior surroundings are more understated, with the usual wooden shoji screens and Japanese prints. The emphasis is on sushi, and the chef proudly offers $1 sushi orders. The menu also includes curry dishes and chicken cutlets. A second location in Campbell adds sushi boats for entertainment. • SJ: M-Th 11:30am-2pm, 5-9:30pm; F 11:30am-2pm, 5-10pm; Sa noon-2pm, 5-10pm; Su noon-2pm, 4-9pm. • Campbell: M-F 11:30am-2pm, 5-9:30pm; Sa 5-9:30; Su 11am-2pm, 5-9pm.

Kincaid's ★★ $$$ 60 Bayview Pl. (Airport Blvd.), Burlingame, 650/342-9844. An enormous establishment overlooking San Francisco Bay on one side and a small lagoon on the other. Grilled steaks and shellfish are the stars of the menu; lunches are geared to the business set, with a "Chop Chop" salad consisting of lettuce and chopped up anitpasto-type items mixed together to create a healthy meal that won't ruin your tie. The chocolate indulgence dessert is decidedly messy and unhealthy. The swank bar features 15 beers, 30 single-malt scotches, and dozens of California wines. The valet parking and long-winded menu descriptions make Kincaid's a good place to impress out-of-towners, but if it's a bay view you're after, make sure it's a clear day before you book your reservation. • M-Th 11:30am-10pm; F 11:30am-11pm; Sa 5pm-11pm; Su 5pm-10pm.

Kirk's Restaurant ★ ¢ 361 California Ave. (Ash/Birch), Palo Alto, 650/326-6159. • 2388 S. Bascom Ave. (Union/Dry Creek), Campbell, 408/371-3565. • 1330 Saratoga-Sunnyvale Rd. (Hwy 85), San Jose, 408/446-2988. Some of the best, juiciest burgers around are served at these quintessential vinyl-and-cinder-block burger joints. The purists at Kirk's cook to order over mesquite charcoal and leave the garnishing up to you. Fixings are quirky; there is never lettuce, but there are always piles of onion and jalapeño peppers. Order a charbroiled steakburger, wash it down with a milk shake, and call the ambulance. • Daily 11am-9pm.

Kisaku ★★ $$ 47 E. 4th Ave. (El Camino/San Mateo Dr.), San Mateo, 650/347-4121. With nearly two hundred items on its menu, Kisaku, done up in a Japanese-country-inn decor, likely offers the most extensive selection of any Japanese restaurant on the Peninsula. This includes all the basics, plus a comprehensive sushi bar and even children's portions. Perhaps predictably, the quality is inconsistent, although tempura is delicious. Choose between traditional table seating in the large main room (with a sushi bar) or tatami mat seating (on the floor at low tables) in a series of private alcoves. Service is friendly. • M, W-F 11:30am-2pm, 5-10pm; Sa-Su 5-9:30pm.

Kitahama ★★ $$ 974 Saratoga-Sunnyvale Rd. (Bollinger), San Jose, 408/257-6449. At this rigorously serene sushi establishment, a spalike ambience pervades the many dining areas. The main room features a light-wood sushi bar with tatami tables on the periphery. Another wing houses private tatami rooms (some with telephones) where a $35 minimum per person is in effect. Yet another room houses a karaoke bar. Waitresses in traditional garb glide quietly through the restaurant, attending to your every need. The authentic sushi draws a crowd of appreciative Japanese who have made this into a private club of sorts for discriminating expatriates. • M-Sa 5pm-midnight.

Kobe ★★ $$ 2086 El Camino Real (Scott), Santa Clara, 408/984-5623. The large wooden badger guarding the door at Kobe is a tip-off that this is a restaurant big on spectacle. Take a moment to admire the suit of Japanese armor on display in the waiting area before taking a seat next to the delightful indoor stream backed by an impressive mural. If you prefer a more practical waterway, belly up to the sushi-boat bar, where sushi-laden craft float by for your perusal. Tables feature fresh-cut flowers, and the staff is friendly and attentive. Kobe offers a full range of Japanese delicacies, including teriyaki, tempura, *udon*, and *soba* noodles, generally very good, although the food doesn't quite hold its own against the decor. If you're in a hurry at lunchtime, certain dishes have been designated "extra quick meals," and bargain hunters can enjoy an early bird dinner special before 6:30. Kobe also features banquet facilities and private dining rooms. • M-F 11am-2:30pm, 5-9:30pm; Sa 5-9:30pm.

Korea Buffet ★ $ 1783 W. San Carlos St. (Leigh/Shasta), San Jose, 408/280-1866. Never again will you have to make that tough choice between going out for some exotic ethnic food or barbecuing on your back porch. Korea Buffet allows you to do both at once. Fill your plate with marinated beef or shrimp from the buffet, then toss it on the grill in the middle of your table. When your selection has been sizzled to perfection, wrap it up in a lettuce leaf with some rice and kimchi and munch away. The restaurant also features do-it-yourself soup, prepared in (you guessed it) a table-top saucepan next to the grill. The buffet features a variety of meats, seafood, vegetables, and salads. For one reasonable price you can refill your plate as many times as you like. Everything is fresh and delicious, and your food is guaranteed to be spiced to perfection and served piping hot—after all, you're the chef. • Daily 11am-3pm, 5-10pm.

Krung Thai ★★★ $ 642 S. Winchester Blvd. (Moorpark), San Jose, 408/260-8224. Adventurous diners in the South Bay are no doubt familiar with the strip mall genre of Asian restaurants. From the outside, Krung Thai seems a classic example: the cookie-cutter exterior and nondescript location promise little. Don't be fooled. There is no better Thai food to be found anywhere (at least on this side of the Pacific). If you don't believe us, ask the customers, most of whom are Thai. But the secret is out, and you will be met by long lines snaking out the door on weekend evenings and at lunchtime. Not even Krung Thai's expanded new location near I-280 has eased the crowds. Once the food arrives, however, nothing else seems to matter. Fortunately, success hasn't spoiled the serving staff, who are friendly and solicitous. • M-F 11am-3pm, 5-10pm; Sa-Su noon-10pm.

Kuleto's Trattoria ★★ $$ 1095 Rollins Rd. (Broadway), Burlingame, 650/342-4922. Is Pat Kuleto taking over the world? After conquering San Francisco, the master restaurateur/designer is making his mark all over the Peninsula. The giant sign outside the former Vanessi's in Burlingame announces this venture, done up like a huge yellow stucco Italian farmhouse. Inside, signature Kuleto touches abound: tortoise-shell-patterned light fixtures, softly buffed dark wood, and a roaring wood-fired oven. The three-tiered dining area affords views of the sauté chefs juggling pans over leaping flames, and a couple of different bar areas are ideal for solo diners. The menu reprises old favorites such as smoked-salmon-filled ravioli with asparagus and lemon cream sauce and risotto primavera. The homemade focaccia that comes with lunch and dinner is excellent, as are many of the specials, but pastas can be heavy. Service is usually quite professional and accommodating. • M-F 11:30am-10pm; Sa-Su 4-11pm.

L'Amie Donia ★★★ $$$ 530 Bryant St. (University/Hamilton), Palo Alto, 650/323-7614. Who would have imagined that a sterile café off University Avenue could be transformed into a warm, lively French bistro with little more than a bucket of yellow paint and the installation of a stylish wood and zinc bar? The perspicacious young Donia Bijan, who gained fame as chef at San Francisco's Sherman House and Brasserie Savoy, has savvy Peninsulans lining up for her expert renditions of traditional dishes like coq au vin, rabbit with mustard sauce, and *salade niçoise*. Desserts are a highlight. The front patio is pleasant on warm days. Reservations recommended. • Tu-F 11:30am-2pm, 5:30-11pm; Sa-Su 5:30-11pm.

La Costeña ★★ $ 2078 Old Middlefield Way (Rengstorff), Mountain View 650/967-0507. Listed in the *Guinness Book of World Records* for serving the largest and heaviest burrito in the world, La Costeña is in a class of its own. Great Mexican food and huge custom burritos are available at incredibly cheap prices. The different preparations of chicken, beef, and pork include an excellent *pollo borracho*, chicken stewed in vegetables and beer, *chile colorado beef*, and *chile verde pork*. There are also vegetarian options available, and a huge array of cheeses, beans, and salsas to choose from. The lines are long at lunch, so you may want to take *The Wall Street Journal's* advice and fax in your order. La Costeña also caters, offering specials such as the four-foot-long burrito. Food is only available for takeout. • M-F 6:30am-10pm; Sa-Su 8am-10pm.

La Cumbre Taqueria ★★ ¢ 28 North B St. (Baldwin), San Mateo, 650/344-8989. Long before designer burrito outlets proliferated, Peninsula residents in search of the best Mexican burrito made the trek up to La Cumbre in the city to wait in line for flame-grilled beef and fiery hand-cut cilantro salsa wrapped in an ultrafresh tortilla. Their prayers were answered when Eddie Duran, the fresh-out-of-business-school, quick-witted son of La Cumbre's proprietors, decided to open a second outlet in San Mateo. Authentic and healthy choices abound here, from no-lard refried, whole, or black beans to grilled chicken breast, top sirloin beef, and various handmade salsas, assembled to order into burritos, tacos, fajitas, or dinner plates. An exhaustive selection of fresh-squeezed juices, sodas, and beers, combined with a rowdy sound system, indoor-outdoor seating, and the erudite Eddie behind the register make La Cumbre a favorite with a highly diverse clientele in search of quality and value. • M-Sa 11am-9pm; Su 11am-8:30pm.

La Fiesta ★★ $ 240 Villa St. (Calderon/Castro), Mountain View, 650/968-1364. La Fiesta's drab exterior belies the festive interior, which features sombreros, piñatas, papier-mâché birds and fish, and a kitchenful of terra-cotta dishes suspended from the ceiling. A brightly colored, tiled bar occupies the center of the restaurant. Try the *mole poblano*, breast of chicken served with a heady mole sauce, or the *camarones picantes*, sautéed shrimp in a creamy *chipotle* and *guajillo* sauce. Portions are large. • Su-Th 11am-2pm, 5-9pm; F-Sa 11am-2pm, 5-10pm.

La Fondue ★★ $$/$$$ 14510 Big Basin Way, Suite 3 (3rd/4th), Saratoga, 408/867-3332. Just as bell bottoms and love beads are enjoying renewed popularity, fondue—that staple of the '70s dinner party—is back. The decor at La Fondue is strictly '90s, though, with sponge-painted walls, fleur-de-lis-printed banquettes, trompe l'oeil mosaics, and, in one of the three dining areas, midnight-blue walls spangled with gold stars and half-moon sconces. Diners can choose from more than 50 fondues prepared tableside, from classic Swiss Emmenthaler to tofu for vegetarians to wild game for meat lovers. Choices include pesto and cognac fondue and Cajun cheese with shrimp. Be sure to block out a couple of hours—this is not fast food. Monday and Tuesday are BYOB days: they don't charge corkage fees. Reservations recommended. • M-Th 5-9:30pm; F-Sa 5-11pm; Su 4-9:30pm.

La Forêt ★★★ $$$$ 21747 Bertram Rd. (Almaden), San Jose, 408/997-3458. Housed in an old two-story hotel overlooking Los Alamitos Creek, La Forêt is reminiscent of a more peaceful time. The country French atmosphere, with floral curtains, light-wood furniture, and crisp white tablecloths, is elegant yet relaxed. The menu changes seasonally, with a rotating selection of fish, poultry, and pasta. All dishes are expertly prepared and simply presented: the ahi tuna is perfectly seared, while the pork tenderloin is smooth and tender. For those with a frontiersman's palate, the wild-game offerings should appeal. Individual Grand Marnier soufflés are a dramatic ending. When making a reservation, request one of the tables overlooking the creek. • Tu-Sa 5:30-9:30pm; Su 10:30am-2pm, 5-9:30pm.

La Maison du Café ★★★ $$$ 14103-C Winchester Blvd. (Knowles), Los Gatos, 408/378-2233. Making use of a French-blue palette, the owners of this intimate café have created a warm, inviting atmosphere: blue lattice covers one wall, tables are draped in printed cloths, and decorative plates are set about. The classic French specialties include excellent *escargots à la Bourguignon*, grilled salmon hollandaise, and medallions of veal with morels, to name a few, as well as a crispy roast duck. Owner Ibrahim Guney will attend to your every whim. A classical guitarist serenades diners from the plant-filled balcony at lunch during the week and at weekend dinners. • Tu-F 11am-2:30pm, 5:30-9:30pm; Sa 5:30-9:30pm; Su 10am-2pm.

La Mere Michelle ★★ $$$$ 14467 Big Basin Way (3rd/Saratoga-Sunnyvale), Saratoga, 408/867-5272. On sunny weekend afternoons the outdoor patio at La Mere Michelle attracts leisurely lunchers with its blue-and-white-striped awning and potted red geraniums. The food is 1950s-style country-club fare—hearts of palm salad, shrimp Louie, and veal piccata—but well prepared. Not a place for culinary inventiveness, but for nostalgia's sake a worthy destination; plan to stay a while, service can be slow. • M 11:30am-2pm; Tu-F 11:30am-2pm, 6-10pm; Sa 11am-2pm, 6-10pm; Su 11am-2pm, 5:30-9pm.

La Pachanga ★★ $ 3102 Middlefield Rd. (4th), Redwood City, 650/364-7969. This small, brightly painted restaurant lures diners with its welcoming, casual atmosphere, featuring peach-colored walls, Mexican jukebox music, and embroidered tablecloths covered with plastic. The kitchen serves up authentic Mexican food all day long with an emphasis on fresh ingredients and spices, including unusual chilis and freshly shucked tamarind pods. While you can't go wrong with the tacos, burritos, and tostadas, the most popular dishes are the enchiladas and the *sopitos*, small handmade corn tortillas topped with meat, cabbage, Mexican cheese, and sauce. The extensive array of fresh seafood dishes is a bit more pricey. The adventurous should try the numerous interesting regional dishes not found at most restaurants (be sure to ask about the daily specials). There is a good selection of Mexican beer (the Negro Modelo is great) as well as an array of interesting *aguas frescas*. • Su-Th 8am-10pm; F-Sa 8am-11:30pm.

La Pastaia Hotel de Anza ★★★ $$$ 233 W. Santa Clara St. (Almaden), San Jose, 408/286-8686. Whether you choose the blue-tiled terrace by day or the boldly metropolitan dining room by night, La Pastaia consistently delivers great meals presented with confidence and flair. Ensconced within the jewellike Deco restoration of the Hotel de Anza, the restaurant is wildly popular with insiders and enlightened visitors alike. Wild mushrooms with creamy polenta, slow-simmered osso buco, and playful appetizers—such as deep fried baby artichokes with spicy aioli and poached-salmon salad—fuel the boldly romantic menu. Pastas are excellent, but the roasted poultry, braised shanks, and sautéed chops usually steal the show. Everyone looks attractive and interesting in this setting—just another plus to one of the top dining rooms in the area. • M-Th 11am-3pm, 5-10pm; F 11am-3pm, 5-10:30pm; Sa noon-2pm, 5-10:30pm; Su noon-2pm, 5-9pm.

Lark Creek Café ★★★ $$$ 50 E. 3rd Ave. (El Camino/San Mateo Dr.), San Mateo, 650/344-9444. This intimate, informal branch of celebrity chef Bradley Ogden's legendary Marin restaurant is a worthy successor to the well-regarded Café for All Seasons. Featuring Ogden's trademark upscale American fare, Lark Creek's menu mixes retro comfort foods like his legendary Yankee pot roast, chicken and dumplings, and iceberg lettuce salad with such classic California creations as salmon and rock shrimp cake with black bean salsa, and *soba* noodles with a baby white bean and vegetable stew. The California-cottage interior is light and elegant, with a pressed-tin ceiling, hardwood floors, and white linens. The pleasant bar makes a good spot for solo dining. Smart service. Reservations recommended. • M-Th 11:30am-2:30pm, 5:30-9pm; F 11:30am-2:30pm, 5:30-9:30pm; Sa 11am-2:30pm, 5-9:30pm; Su 10am-2pm, 5-9pm.

Las Parillas Restaurant ★ $/$$ 3282 Middlefield Rd. (6th/7th), Redwood City, 650/369-2040. This authentic Mexican restaurant serves wonderful, freshly prepared food in a cheerful, colorful dining room. The jukebox often blares *ranchera* music, photos of Mexican and American celebrities cover the walls, and groups of revelers crowd the picnic tables lacquered with maps of Mexico. The open kitchen turns out an array of authentic dishes, including extensive seafood options, as well as the popular *7 mares*, a seafood stew featuring seven different types of seafood and shellfish. Cash only. • Daily 8:30am-9:30pm.

Late for the Train ★ $$ 150 Middlefield Rd. (Willow/Roble), Menlo Park, 650/321-6124. Imaginative vegetarian fare in a countrified interior. The proprietors grow most of their own vegetables and use fresh ingredients in season. Brunch is worth getting out of bed for. Try the delicious buttermilk pancakes or one of the spectacular omelets. There's even outdoor patio seating, weather permitting. • M 7am-2:30pm; Tu-F 7am-2:30pm, 5-9pm; Sa 8am-2:30pm, 5-9:30pm; Su 8am-2:30pm.

Le Mouton Noir ★★★ $$$$ 14560 Big Basin Way (4th/5th), Saratoga, 408/867-7017. A perennial favorite, Le Mouton Noir serves imaginative French cuisine in a grandmother's parlor atmosphere. Pink and mauve accents and dried flowers abound. Despite a change in ownership, the restaurant hasn't skipped a beat. Start off with warm wild mushroom gateau (sautéed wild mushrooms in a light duck liver mousse) and move along to veal medallions and lobster tail served with a morel sauce, potatoes, artichoke hearts, and asparagus. If you can still see straight after such extravagances, order one of the deluxe desserts. • Daily 6-9:30pm.

Le Papillon ★★★ $$$ 410 Saratoga Ave. (Kiely), San Jose, 408/296-3730. A solicitous, tuxedoed maître d' greets you at the entrance, setting the tone for your meal at this tastefully understated French restaurant. The dining rooms are decorated with framed engravings and feature a neutral palette, and the pleasant bar overlooks a verdant garden. The Asian-influenced French cuisine wins raves from loyal patrons, although the ambience tends toward the corporate (Silicon Valley tycoons frequent the premises). Reservations recommended. • M-F 11:30am-2:30pm, 5-10pm; Sa 5-10pm; Su 5-9pm.

Le Petit Bistro ★★ $$ 1405 W. El Camino Real (El Monte/Shoreline), Mountain View, 650/964-3321. Mountain View's best-kept secret, this charming bistro serves reasonably priced French food. The wine list includes modestly priced French and California wines. Start with one of the delicious soups—a creamy lobster bisque or a fresh purée of spinach and asparagus textured with potatoes and leeks. Sauces are light and distinctive, flavored with cumin, saffron, hazelnuts, or citrus. The enthusiastic three-person staff (the waitress, busboy, and Jean Michel himself) will minister to your every need. • Tu-Th 5:30-9pm; F-Su 5:30-10pm.

Le Pot au Feu ★★ $$$ 1149 El Camino Real (Santa Cruz/Oak Grove), Menlo Park, 650/322-4343. The Gallic charm of this cozy restaurant—the Art Nouveau Parisian café decor (complete with Perrier umbrellas), the traditional French fare, and the friendly service—will convince you that not all French restaurants are snooty. The menu includes well-prepared versions of such favorites as escargots, Brie baked in pastry, and rack of lamb. The salmon in puff pastry is also a highlight. Lighting is dim for romantic trysts. The back patio makes for a pleasant lunch spot, even if it's next to a parking lot instead of the Seine. • Tu-Sa 5:30-9:30pm; Su 5:30-9pm.

Left at Albuquerque ★★★ $ 445 Emerson St. (University/Lytton), Palo Alto, 650/326-1011. • 1100 Burlingame Ave. (California), Burlingame, 650/401-5700. • PruneYard Shopping Center, Campbell and Bascom avenues, Campbell, 408/558-1680. The owners of the Blue Chalk Café have struck pay dirt again with this southwestern-style bar and restaurant. Bold desert art—black-and-white photos of rodeos and cowgirls, Navajo rugs, potted cacti, and more—and racks of tequila bottles furnish the space, which ends in an open kitchen against the back wall. The bar scene is wall-to-wall Silicon singles, with talk of mountain bikes and stock options filling the air. The contemporary southwestern menu is flavorful, varied, and less expensive than the Blue Chalk, with several tapas-sized dishes. The burritos are assembled from a wide range of meats, seafood, and grilled vegetables, and the specials come with appetizing side orders such as lightly breaded onion rings or *chipotle* mashed potatoes. For drinks, margaritas are popular, as is just about every other tequila drink. • PA: Daily 11:30am-10pm. • Burlingame: Daily 11am-10:30pm. • Campbell: M-F 11:30am-9pm; Sa-Su 11:30am-10pm.

Left Bank NR 635 Santa Cruz Ave. (Doyle), Menlo Park, 650/473-6543. When a chef as famous as Roland Passot, whose La Folie in San Francisco has been consistently rated one the city's best, opens a new restaurant, it's likely to attract notice. His Left Bank restaurant in Marin was an instant success: a large, casual brasserie (yellow walls, French posters, white tablecloths, and all) where simple classics dominate the menu—steak with *pommes frites,* roast chicken, duck confit, steamed mussels. The Menlo Park Left Bank, scheduled to open August 1998, replaces Yuen Yung, although all vestiges of the Chinese restaurant were removed. • Hours unavailable at presstime.

Lion & Compass ★★ $$$ 1023 N. Fair Oaks Ave. (Weddell), Sunnyvale, 408/745-1260. This high-tech haunt is starting to look a little faded around the edges, although Silicon Valley movers and shakers still make the pilgrimage at lunch. The white lattice exterior surrounded by birds of paradise and palm trees has a Florida resort feel. Inside, the tropical theme continues with terra-cotta floors, wicker chairs, and lazy ceiling fans. The seasonal menu includes such chichi fare as sautéed pork medallions in Marsala with a port fruit chutney. A good selection of ports by the glass. Reservations recommended. • M-F 11:30am-2pm, 5:30-9:30pm; Sa 5:30-9pm.

Lisa's Tea Treasures ★★ $$ 1145 Merrill St. (Oak Grove/Santa Cruz), Menlo Park, 650/326-8327. Located in a turn-of-the-century Victorian next to the Menlo Park train station, this traditional afternoon tearoom takes you back to a more genteel era. Each room is meticulously detailed, and tables are set with linen tablecloths, china, silver, and a small porcelain bell to ring should you need attention. The predominately female clientele comes for shower parties, birthdays, and intimate chats with old friends (although the tearoom welcomes children, it's best to leave the little darlings at home). The traditional afternoon teas include a pot of full-leaf tea, tea sandwiches, savories, and sweets. Portions are small and prices are a bit high, but the food is delicious and everything is beautifully prepared and presented. Each table is set with a jar of cookies and lemon curd. • Tu-Su 10am-5:30pm (seatings for full tea at 11:30am, 2pm, 4pm).

Little Garden ★ $ 4127 El Camino Real (El Camino Way), Palo Alto, 650/494-1230. Excellent Chinese-Vietnamese food in a Formica-table atmosphere. But where atmosphere is lacking, low prices usually follow, and you can dine sumptuously here on crackly imperial rolls and curried *kwo* noodle soup bristling with thread noodles and chicken, among other mysterious elements. Lemongrass chicken was a disappointment (the namesake ingredient was undetectable), but a healthy portion of moo shu pork made up for the omission. • M-Th 11:30am-2:30pm, 5-9:30pm; F-Sa 11:30am-2:30pm, 5-10pm; Su 5-9:30pm.

The Little Store ★ $ 3340 Woodside Rd. (Fox Hollow/Miramonte), Woodside, 650/851-8110. You wouldn't notice the circa 1930 white shack tucked under the oaks if it weren't for the adjacent parking lot filled with pickup trucks, Range Rovers, and horses hitched to the post. Hearkening back to the days when ranchers and loggers outnumbered software developers, The Little Store serves up hearty portions of okay burgers, grilled chicken, fries, and on-tap beer, along with plenty of authentic atmosphere, to locals and roadies. People come here for the scene, not the food, but you could do far worse at any fast-food joint farther down Woodside Road. The cooler stocked with made-in-Woodside wines is a highlight, as are the pies and brownies a la mode for dessert. Children friendly, despite the admonishing placard that greets customers: Children are welcome. Politeness and good manners are appreciated. No credit cards. • Tu-Sa 11am-3pm, 5:30-9pm.

Los Gatos Brewing Co. ★★ $$ 130 N. Santa Cruz Ave. (Grays), Los Gatos, 408/395-9929. A favorite haunt of business lunchers, beer drinkers, and beach types alike in Los Gatos. Indoors, singles mingle over pints of the brewed-on-site ales, including Dunkle, Los Gatos lager, and Nut Brown ale, as well as a rotating seasonal specialty. A long bar (salvaged from a St. Louis brothel) dominates one end of the soaring, barn-like space; another wall is occupied by a wood-burning oven for pizzas. The faux stone walls painted in earth tones add a rustic note. The menu features designer pizzas, pastas, and grilled meats, but beer is the draw here. • Su-Th 11:30am-3pm, 5-10pm; F-Sa 11:30am-3pm, 5-11pm.

Los Nicas ★ $$ 62 W. Santa Clara St. (1st/Market), San Jose, 408/294-7880. Downtown San Jose's collection of offbeat restaurants continues to grow. The newly opened Las Nicas captures not only the flavors but the look and feel of a genuine Central American restaurant: the food is festive and savory, but the place is a bit of a dump. If dingy carpeting and brown walls will spoil your appetite, stay away. If, on the other hand, you want to eat in a restaurant that mirrors its cousins to the south, Las Nicas is a good bet. Although surprisingly expensive, the food is very good, especially the seafood dishes and the Nicaraguan specialties. For a truly authentic dining experience, start with the fried pork with yuca and finish your meal with *maduros con crema* (sweet fried plantains with sour cream). • M-F 11:30am-9pm; Sa 1-9pm; Su 1-8pm.

Luceti's ★★ $$ 109 W. 25th Ave. (El Camino/Hacienda), San Mateo, 650/574-1256. A cozy, old-fashioned neighborhood restaurant and bar presided over by transplants from North Beach. The menu is northern Italian/continental, with various omelets, frittatas, and Americanish sandwiches thrown in at lunch and an expanded veal and fish selection at dinner. The carpaccio appetizer is one of the best around. A plate of fettuccine with veal, prosciutto, and mushrooms in a cream sauce served in the comfortably cluttered dining room is guaranteed to please. • M-Th 11am-2:30pm, 5-9:45pm, F 11am-2:30pm, 5-10:30pm; Sa 5-10:30pm, Su 5-9:30pm.

Mabel's Lantern House ★ $ 39 N. Santa Cruz Ave. (Main), Los Gatos, 408/354-1844. Kung pao calamari and red snapper are the standouts on the otherwise routine Chinese menu. Mabel's fills lots of take-out orders, but the redwood cane chairs, pink tablecloths, and paintings mounted on pink matting make for a pleasant if unexceptional atmosphere. • M-Th 11:30am-9:30pm; F 11:30am-10:30pm; Sa noon-10:30pm; Su 4-9:30pm.

MacArthur Park ★★ $$$ 27 University Ave. (El Camino), Palo Alto, 650/321-9990. Housed in a handsome, rustic barn designed by Julia Morgan, MacArthur Park is tucked away next to the Palo Alto CalTrain station. The restaurant gives fidgety diners the option of doodling with crayons on the paper-draped tables as they wait for giant platters of ribs or mesquite-grilled chicken, sausages, or fish. Fish entrées are fresh and cleanly grilled, while barbecue options from the oak-fueled smoker require a dentist-style bib. Entrée accoutrements are excellent; grilled pork loin is served with sautéed red cabbage and a delightful apple compote. Plentiful Sunday brunch buffet. • M-F 11:30am-2:30pm, 5:30-10:30pm; Sa 5-11pm; Su 10am-2pm, 5-10pm.

Maddalena's ★★ $$$ 544 Emerson St. (University/Hamilton), Palo Alto, 650/326-6082. This is one of the more formal restaurants in the mid-Peninsula, done up in dark wood paneling, antiques, and crystal chandeliers—the whole nine yards. Solicitous waiters in tuxes serve up luxury fare like rack of lamb, duck, and filet mignon. Popular with the Silicon Valley expense-account crowd. Despite the tony clientele, service is maddeningly inconsistent. • M 5:30-10pm; Tu-F 11:30am-2pm, 5:30-10pm; Sa 5:30-10pm.

Maharaja's ★★ $$ 236 Castro St. (Villa/Dana), Mountain View, 650/961-7382. One of many Indian restaurants on this stretch of Castro Street, Maharaja offers a wide array of specialties from all regions of the subcontinent, including an extensive vegetarian selection. For starters, try the vegetable *samosas* and the onion *bhaji*. The *biryanis*—rice dishes mixed with meat or vegetables—are a highlight, either as entrées or as side dishes. The decor features Indian artifacts layered on top of '50s diner furniture: brown Naugahyde booths and tubular metal chairs. Service is friendly, but not always speedy when the restaurant fills up. • Su-W 11am-2:30pm, 5-9:30pm; Th-Sa 11am-2:30pm, 5-10pm.

Mandarin Chef ★★ $ 14572 Big Basin Way (5th), Saratoga, 408/867-4388. Linen-clad tables, fresh flowers, and country-style decor distinguish the Mandarin Chef. Try the excellent (not too sweet) honey-roasted walnut prawns or the special beef, if it's available. Start off with the generous *pu pu* platter. • M-F 11:30am-2:30pm, 4:30-9:30pm; Sa noon-10pm; Su noon-9pm.

Mandarin Classic ★★ $$ 397 Main St. (1st), Los Altos, 650/948-8996. Framed oil paintings, lavish bouquets of silk flowers, a grand piano—this is not your average Chinese take-out joint. The menu, however, sticks to the tried and true, featuring all the usual suspects: spring rolls, hot and sour soup, moo shu prawns. The chef does have a couple of Shanghaiese specialties up his sleeve, like the snowflake seafood soup—minced shrimp, scallops, and crab in broth, topped with beaten egg white. The nightly happy hour features piano music and hors d'oeuvres. • M-Th 11:30am-3pm, 5-9:30pm; F-Sa 11:30am-3pm, 5-10pm; Su 5-9:30pm.

Mango Café ★★ $ 435 Hamilton Ave. (Cowper/Waverley), Palo Alto, 650/324-9443. Settle back in one of the huge fan-backed wicker chairs, order a dragon's mouth (tamarind, lime, and ginger) smoothie, and imagine you're in the West Indies. The spicy cuisine of Jamaica and Trinidad and Tobago is unusual and delicious. Try one of the patties (meat turnovers with a curried crust), a jerked joint (very spicy marinated chicken), or a delicate hearts of palm salad. For dessert, get the bread pudding, an exemplary rendition of the old classic. The background music is reggae and the service is friendly and hip. No liquor. • M-F 11am-2:30pm, 6-9:30pm; Sa 6-9:30pm.

Marbella ★★ $$/$$$ 14109 Winchester Blvd. (Knowles), Los Gatos, 408/374-1717. Ablaze with the seaside colors of the Riviera, the decor of this large and splashy restaurant makes a good match with the vibrant Mediterranean menu. Lamb shanks with white beans and asparagus join well-seasoned shish kabob, carpaccio, Niçoise salad and Spanish *zarzuela* shellfish soup to give an unusually broad glimpse of the regional cuisines of Spain, Greece, Italy, and France. There's even a fragrant Provençal vegetable stew with polenta to balance hearty dishes like roast chicken and Portuguese-style grilled pork chops. Very smart and yet accessible, this place attracts solo diners, after-work wine sippers, and those enamored of sun-drenched cuisine. • M-Th 11:30am-9:30pm; F 11:30am-10pm; Sa 5-10pm.

Max's (Opera) Café ★★ $$ 1250 Old Bayshore Hwy. (Broadway), Burlingame, 650/342-6297. • Sequoia Station, 1001 El Camino Real (Jefferson/Broadway), Redwood City, 650/365-6297. • 711 Stanford Shopping Ctr. (El Camino and Quarry), Palo Alto, 650/323-6297. Deli decor has never had it so good. In Palo Alto, the soaring ceilings, singing waitrons, and shelves stacked with cans of olive oil attract a done-to-the-nines crowd. (The Burlingame and Redwood City locations are more suburban.) The brassy, boastful menu starts with New York-deli-style chopped liver and corned beef sandwiches and then goes ballistic with pasta, barbecue, and Cajun prawns. Not everything works perfectly, but it's always tasty and interesting. Best to take a doggie bag for the main course to save room for Sweet Max's larger-than-life desserts. Singing waiters entertain the crowds in Palo Alto and Burlingame, earning the addition of Opera to the restaurant name. • Burlingame: M-Th 6:30am-11pm; F-Sa 6:30am-midnight; Su 6:30am-10pm. • RC: Daily 11:30am-2pm, 5-10pm. • PA: Su-Th 11:30am-10pm; F-Sa 11am-11pm.

Mei Long ★★★ $$ 867 E. El Camino Real (Bernardo/Hwy 85), Mountain View, 650/961-4030. The very gifted Renyi Liu cooks his way out of a paper bag and into the French/Chinese culinary hall of fame at this elegantly decorated restaurant hiding out in an ordinary strip mall. A fine wine list enhances the gorgeous Sichuan and Shanghai foods, which are given a new twist in dishes such as a tofu and beef appetizer infused with burnt orange peel. The seafood soups are tangy with black vinegar; the braised duck with red-wine sauce is joined with pea sprouts and steamed crescent buns. Definitely a romantic venue, where brilliant floral arrangements vie with the spectacular food for sheer visual dazzle. Mei Long is an incredible surprise, given the mundane location. • Tu-Th 11:30am-2pm, 5-9pm; F-Sa 11:30am-2pm, 5-9:30pm; Su 5-9pm.

Messina ★★ $$ 542 El Camino Real (Holly/San Carlos), San Carlos, 650/593-9116. The place to go if you're longing for unpretentious, overdecorated North Beach atmosphere without driving into the city. Heaping plates of pasta served in close quarters. The kind of place where the Italian waiter slams your pasta down on the red-and-white checked tablecloth before turning on his heels to attend to another bothersome customer. Crowded weekend nights, reservations recommended. • Tu-F 11am-2:30pm, 5-10:30pm; Sa-Su 5-10:30pm.

Michael's ★★ $$$ 830 E. El Camino Real (Wolfe/Fair Oaks), Sunnyvale, 408/245-2925. The long oak bar and leather wing chairs bring to mind a men's club, while the dining room features leather banquettes, plants, and etched-glass panels for a Belle Époque supper-club feel. "New England seafood specialties" are advertised, but the menu features Australian lobster tail, Maryland soft-shell crabs, and crab and shrimp cannelloni—not what you'd find at your average Maine clam house. Meat eaters will be relieved to find a New York steak sandwich and various veal preparations on the menu. • M-Th 11am-3pm, 5-10pm; F 11:30am-3pm, 5-10:30pm; Sa 5-10:30pm; Su 4-9pm.

Mike's Café Etc. ★★ $$ 2680 Middlefield Rd. (Oregon/Bryson), Palo Alto, 650/473-6453. This relaxed, unpretentious family-style eatery is a welcome addition to Palo Alto's midtown neighborhood. Presided over by the former headwaiter at Il Fornaio Palo Alto, the restaurant offers a wide-ranging menu including pastas, vegetarian options, and American classics like shrimp Louis, French dip sandwiches, and a 12-ounce New York steak. Try the outstanding grilled eggplant, provolone, and sun-dried tomato sandwich, and don't miss the homemade desserts. Friendly, knowledgeable staff. • M-F 11am-9pm; Sa-Su 8am-9pm.

MiMe's Café ★★ $ 2050 Broadway (Jefferson/Main), Redwood City, 650/568-2880. MiMe's slogan is "Great Service. Great Food. Great Cause." The cause and the service go together at this eatery, where low-income people are trained for jobs in the restaurant business. The kitchen turns out staple breakfasts, and lunch items such as individual pizzas, sandwiches, and salads. Heartier offerings might include a lamb stew, and there's always a quick lunch special for workers with a full docket at the nearby courthouse. MiMe's slogan should also read "Great-Looking Space": the yellow walls, high ceiling, and open kitchen make for a sunny, welcoming feel. • M-F 7:30am-2:30pm.

Ming's ★ $$ 1700 Embarcadero Rd. (E. Bayshore), Palo Alto, 650/856-7700. Ming's has been around for 30 years—since 1956, according to the logo. It feels like something of a throwback, with carved stone lions guarding the entrance and expansive, window-lined rooms lit by huge chandeliers. You expect traditional Chinese food, and that's what Ming's serves, although the menu holds a few surprises; in particular, you'll find many vegetarian dishes such as five-spice deep fried tofu and vegetarian kung pao chicken. Prices are also higher than at most Chinese restaurants. The excellent dim sum menu is a less expensive alternative and the highlight of any visit to Ming's: On weekends an army of waitresses wheel carts through the dining rooms, stopping at tables to offer tempting peeks under the lids of bamboo baskets. The steamed barbecue pork bun and the turnip cake are especially good. Ever-popular with the business lunch crowd, dinners and weekends are more relaxed. • M-F 11am-3pm, 5-9:30pm; Sa 11am-3pm, 5-10pm; Su 10:30am-3pm, 5-9:30pm.

Mio Vicino ★★★ $$ 1290 Benton St. (Monroe), Santa Clara, 408/241-9414. • 384 E. Campbell Ave. (Central), Campbell, 408/378-0335. A neighborhood joint where the smart-aleck staff joke among themselves and with guests (who are separated from the kitchen only by a small counter) and happily try to accommodate special requests.

Most important, the exotic pizzas and pastas are prepared to mouth-watering perfection. The house wine, Mio Red, is bottled exclusively for Mio Vicino by Bonny Doon Vineyard and is a great value. Mio Vicino is a bright corner space with lots of windows, simple yellow brick walls, and cheerful green-and-white-checkered tablecloths. A new Campbell location offers the same great pastas in more upscale surroundings that include a pleasant patio. • SC: M-Th 11am-10pm; F 11am-11pm; Sa 5-11pm; Su 5-9:30pm. • Campbell: M-Th 11am-10pm; F 11am-11pm; Sa 5-11pm; Su 5-9:30pm.

Mistral ★★ $$ 370-6 Bridge Pkwy. (Marine Pkwy.), Redwood Shores, 650/802-9222. Mistral *is* high-California cuisine: sun-dried tomatoes, portobello mushrooms, contrived pizzas, and the inevitable garlic mashed potatoes, as well as anything you can imagine coming out of a wood-fired oven (chicken, salmon, mussels, etc.). The barren dining room and bar overlook the water (a lagoon, to be exact), but for full romantic effect sit outside on the deck. Occasional special events like a Halloween costume contest cater to bored singles, but attracting patrons hardly seems necessary given the steady crowds of Electronic Arts programmers and Oracle sales reps. • M-F 11:30am-2pm, 5:30-10pm; Sa 5:30-10pm; Su 5:30-9pm.

Miyake ★ $ 10650 S. De Anza Blvd. (Bollinger), Cupertino, 408/253-2668. • 140 University Ave. (High), Palo Alto, 650/323-9449. A sushi joint with a riotous atmosphere created by the barking chefs, screaming waiters, and slaphappy clientele. Little boats in the mini moat around the bar float by laden with sushi; patrons grab when the urge hits. Lot's of fun, but the fish isn't always the freshest. • Daily 11:30am-10pm.

Mount Everest ★ $$ 412 N. Santa Cruz Ave. (Hwy 9/Andrews), Los Gatos, 408/354-2427. Indian food in Los Gatos? It can be found. Mount Everest may be buried in a down-at-the-heels strip mall along Winchester Boulevard, but it's worth discovering. The atmosphere is unexpectedly cheerful, considering the surroundings, with glittery fans hung upside-down on the soft pink walls and dense rows of track lighting adding a modern touch. The menu is traditional Indian and prices reasonable, but that's unique in Los Gatos. • M-Sa 11:30am-2pm, 5:30-10pm; Su 5-10pm.

The Mountain House ★★ $$$ 13808 Skyline Blvd. (King's Mountain/Hwy 92), Woodside, 650/851-8541. Located amid the redwoods of Skyline Boulevard, the Mountain House faces west into the woods and is best visited when there's still some daylight left. Stop off after a hike or bike ride and huddle by the giant fieldstone fireplace with a hot toddy; the delightful smell of wood smoke permeates the lodgelike bar area. Good bar menu in the front, with more traditional Continental dishes in the dining room. Go for the cooked-to-order meats, especially the monster veal chop. Reservations recommended. • W-Th 5:30-9pm; F-Sa 5:30-10pm; Su 5-9pm.

Narin ★★ $ 231 Park Rd. (Burlingame/Howard), Burlingame, 650/344-1900. This soothing, modernist Thai restaurant is clean and smart-looking, with crisp white linens, stylish lighting, and walls decorated with tasteful wood carvings. The food is uniformly delicious and presentations show a stylish hand. The extensive menu covers all the usual bases and offers plenty of seafood selections, including some nice claypot dishes. If it's offered, don't miss the chef's special fresh sea bass, lightly fried and served with garlic and white pepper or an incredible black bean sauce. Authentic, unusual noodle dishes with fresh vegetables complete the offerings. The restaurant is an offshoot of Narai Restaurant in San Francisco's Richmond district, but without Narai's Chinese menu selections. • M-Th 11:30am-3pm, 5-9:30pm; F-Sa 11:30am-3pm, 5-10pm.

Neiman Marcus Restaurant ★★ $$ Stanford Shopping Center (El Camino and Quarry), Palo Alto, 650/329-3329. Ladies who shop are often ladies who lunch, and when they're at the swank Stanford Shopping Center, Neiman's offers one of the most tasteful venues for a midday meal. Served in surroundings as elegant as the designer gowns in the windows, standout dishes here include sublime salads and perfectly prepared seafood and poultry specials. The chic setting makes you feel as rich as you'd like to be. A quiet and serene oasis from the spending frenzy. • M-Sa 11am-4pm.

Nini's Coffee Shop ★★ $ 1000 N. Idaho St. (Bayswater), San Mateo, 650/348-9578. If you happen to pass an obscure residential corner of San Mateo on a weekend morning and notice a line of hungry-looking suburbanites, you've found Nini's, a breakfast joint with the slogan "The outskirts of town, but the best around." This ancient, family-run diner offers hearty breakfasts that could fell a lumberjack, including all manner of eggs and scrambles packed with meat, cheese, and veggies, fluffy pancakes, and heaps of delicious home fries. Skip the eggs Benedict in favor of the Cajun pork chop or the teriyaki steak and eggs. Weekdays attract the kind of hungry men who earn a big breakfast: construction workers, firemen, and other hardworking laborers. The large back patio has heat lamps, making it a great all-season hangout. • M-F 6:30am-3pm; Sa-Su 7:30am-2:30pm.

Nola Restaurant ★★ $$ 535 Ramona St. (University/Hamilton), Palo Alto, 650/328-2722. This New Orleans–style restaurant is proving to be one of the area's livelier spots. The small bar, which faces the street, features several drinks embracing Nola's Mardi Gras atmosphere, including hurricanes and Nola's bug juice. The dining areas are set back from the street around a central courtyard, creating a French Quarter feel. Traditionalists might be surprised by the menu, which features a combination of Cajun, creole, and Caribbean influenced dishes ranging from authentic—jambalaya and gumbo—to highly eclectic—teriyaki skirt steak, barbecue chicken quesadilla, and grilled portobello mushroom tostada. The food is generally well-prepared, with the traditional dishes the best bets. Service has been extremely friendly but confused and bogged down by the madding crowds. Lunch is an on-and-off affair (currently it's off). • M-Th 5:30-10pm; F-Sa 5:30-11pm; Su 5:30-9pm.

Nouveau Trattoria ★★ $$$ 541 Bryant St. (Hamilton/University), Palo Alto, 650/327-0132. When you can't face the trendy crowd at Il Fornaio, Nouveau Trattoria offers an old-style European dining experience. Wine bottles line the walls, the lights are low, and the gracious wait staff won't make you feel stupid if you mispronounce the wine. Italian specialties like *penne al quattro formaggi* and *linguine alle vongole* never disappoint, but owner Annie Nunan adds a flip side featuring French classics such as *pâté de foie*, *salade niçoise*, and an excellent *steak au poivre*. (The bilingual menu explains that schizophrenic name.) Wednesday and Thursday evenings are dedicated to Basque specialties, hearty and delicious. Reservations recommended. • Tu-Su 5:30-10pm.

The Oasis ★ ¢ 241 El Camino Real (Cambridge), Menlo Park, 650/326-8896. This is the ultimate hangout: a slightly grubby and cheap old-fashioned sports bar, with hacked-up wooden booths (go ahead, add your initials), peanut shell–strewn floors, and a long bar for leaning, scoping, and imbibing. Hamburgers do the job, pizza has its share of devotées, and the beer list is long and eclectic. There's good TV-to-window ratio, and a variety of video games for the antisocial. Those under 21 years old are relegated to a small, heated outdoor patio equipped with picnic tables. Show up early if you plan to watch major sporting events. • Daily 11am-1am.

Ocean Harbor ★★ $ Town & Country Village, 370 S. Winchester Blvd. (Stevens Creek), San Jose, 408/243-3366. Cantonese seafood is the specialty here, although there should be enough meat, chicken, duck, and noodles to keep a squabbling family happy. Be sure to ask for the menu of house specialties to go beyond the ordinary. The open dining hall contains plenty of large round tables suitable for family-style dining; a side room has smaller tables for western-style dining. Dim sum is available for lunch every day. • M-F 7am-2:30pm, 5-9:30pm; Sa-Su 10am-3pm, 5-9:30pm.

Okayama ★ $ 565-A N. 6th St. (Jackson/Empire), San Jose, 408/289-9508. A pyramid scheme finally pays off at this low-key Japanese restaurant, where the best deals are the so-called pyramid dinners—various three-item combinations at low prices. The smallish, bare tables are closely spaced—no shoji screens separate them—but rice-paper window screens shield diners from the outside world, and the piped-in Japanese music will relax all but the most pressured business luncher, who can instead grab a bento box to go. • M-Th 11am-2pm, 5-8:30pm; F-Sa 10am-2pm, 5-9pm; Su 4:30-8:30pm.

Original Joe's ★★ $$ 301 S. 1st St. (San Carlos), San Jose, 408/292-7030. Yes, there is more than one Original Joe's in the Bay Area, but this is a *real* original. If the trendiness and healthy lifestyle of the Bay Area are getting you down, there's no better place to leave it all behind. This is the kind of joint where you feel a strong urge to order a martini for the first time in ten years. The waiters wear vests and bow ties, and you keep expecting to look up and see Robert DeNiro and Joe Pesci coming down the stairs. Dining options include steaks, huge burgers, and so-so pasta dishes. Not to be missed for connoisseurs of another time and another place. • Daily 11am-1:30am.

Orlo's ★★ $$$ Hayes Renaissance Conference Center, 200 Edenvale Ave. (Chynoweth/Branham), San Jose, 408/226-3200. Housed in the former dining room of one of the founders of South Bay society, Orlo's exudes turn-of-the-century elegance. Service isn't the least bit pretentious, however, and you'll feel comfortable whether you've chosen Armani or Gap attire. The menu is all-American, though touches of Mediterranean influence can be found in freshly conceived pastas, seafood paella, and intriguing seasoned specialties like Moroccan quail with grapes, ginger, and pilaf. It's a nice place to linger, starting with a glass of locally made wine on one of the terraces overlooking the palatial grounds. Updated dining in a historic landmark, yet not the least bit fussy. • M-F 11:30am-2pm, 5:30-9:30pm; Sa-Su 5:30-9:30pm.

Osteria ★★ $$ 247 Hamilton Ave. (Ramona), Palo Alto, 650/328-5700. Located in the heart of downtown Palo Alto, Osteria makes a congenial setting for a casual business meal. The food is more than adequate for a business lunch, but if you're looking for an exciting dining experience, you'll find the menu a bit uninspiring, focusing on traditional Italian salads, pasta, meat, and fish dishes. Tables in the brightly lit, colorfully decorated dining room are spaced a little close for comfort, making this a less than perfect choice for romantic dinners or confidential business discussions. Reservations recommended. • M-F 11:30am-2pm, 5-10pm; Sa 5-10pm.

Pagoda ★★ $$$ Fairmont Hotel, 170 S. Market St. (Park), San Jose, 408/998-3937. Located in the downtown Fairmont Hotel, this dark, elegant restaurant is done up in lots of glamorous black lacquer. A framed antique kimono hangs in the bar area, and design flourishes abound: even the enormous, jet-black service plates are eye-catching. In addition to well-executed, tasty Chinese dishes, a few Mongolian selections—lamb sautéed with leeks and served with onion bread, and a lamb *satay*—appear on the menu, as well as a few unusual choices—tea-smoked trout and a shark's fin soup for $20. Yes, there is takeout. • M-F 11:30am-2:30pm, 6-10pm; Sa-Su 6-10pm.

The Palace ★★★ $$$ 146 S. Murphy Ave. (Washington/Evelyn), Sunnyvale, 408/739-5179. Hotshot chef Joey Altman infuses the Palace's multicultural cuisine with an abundance of sass, style, and spice. Influences come from all corners—the Caribbean, Louisiana, the Mediterranean, and other places in between. The menu is suffused with West Indian spices, including some high-wattage hot sauces. Past offerings have included ahi tuna napoleon with crispy wontons, shiso, sprouts, and ponzu sauce, and olive-crusted sea bass with heirloom potatoes, fennel, and poached garlic merlot sauce. Located in a restored Art Deco movie theater, the soaring two-tiered interior is an architectural extravaganza, with biomorphic silver columns, wrought-iron accents, and sponge-painted orange walls. There's live jazz during dinner and DJ dancing on weekends. The whole sexy package adds up to a pulse-raising experience. Reservations recommended. • Tu-Sa 6pm-10pm.

Palermo ★★ $$ 452 University Ave. (Cowper/Waverley), Palo Alto, 650/321-9908. • 394 S. 2nd St. (San Salvador), San Jose, 408/297-0607. Big bites of garlic and ripe tomato punctuate most of Palermo's southern Italian dishes. Put simply, this is not subtle cuisine. The San Jose and Palo Alto locations differ wildly: The gargantuan San Jose facility encompasses three private banquet halls, a ballroom, a breezy outdoor courtyard, and even a wedding chapel, while the Palo Alto interior is small and cramped. • PA: M-F 11:30am-2pm, 5-10pm; Sa-Su 5-10pm. • SJ: Daily 11:30am-2pm, 5-10pm.

Paolo's ★★★ $$$ 333 W. San Carlos St. (Woz Way), San Jose, 408/294-2558. Among the notables who have dined on Paolo's acclaimed and inventive food are Joe DiMaggio, the Reagans, Frank Sinatra, and JFK. The chilled breast of rabbit stuffed with salsa verde and radicchio is one example of the kitchen's novel concoctions, but innovative touches enliven even the more staid dishes, like a beef tortellini in a béchamel sauce and a veal scaloppine with wilted spinach. In its current location (the decorating bill ran into the millions), Paolo's features European artwork on ocher sponge-painted walls and vaguely classical interior architecture. The atmosphere is more corporate than glitzy; at lunchtime there's even a *menu al professione.* Upstairs, you can enjoy an aperitif in the wine room or on the patio. Reservations recommended. • M-F 11am-2:30pm, 5:30-10pm; Sa 5:30-10pm.

Pasta? ★ $ 326 University Ave. (Bryant/Florence), Palo Alto, 650/328-4585. Since San Francisco has Pasta Pomodoro outlets opening almost as quickly as Starbucks franchises, it was only a matter of time before Palo Alto got its own fast, cheap, and trendy pasta joint. The terra-cotta sponge-painted walls and drop lighting belie the menu of six-dollar pastas, which, if you stick to the basics, are pretty darn good. The long lines of value seekers would indicate a chain in the making, but since a well-publicized "name-the-restaurant" contest failed to produce a winner, expansion may have to wait. • M-Th 11:30am-10pm; F-Sa 11:30am-11pm; Su 11:30am-10pm.

Pasta Moon ★★ $$ 315 Main St. (Hwy 92/Mill), Half Moon Bay, 650/726-5125. • 425 Marina Blvd. (Oyster Pt. Blvd.), South San Francisco, 650/876-7090. The South San Francisco branch of this Half Moon Bay favorite is located in the Oyster Point Marina complex. Overlooking the marina, the dining room is bright and comfortable, if a little institutional in feeling. (Outdoor tables with a view of the boat basin are preferable.) One of the better restaurants on the coast, the original location in Half Moon Bay is small and quaint, albeit a bit cramped, with small-town hospitality. Start with the antipasti plate, which might include generous servings of grilled eggplant, roasted peppers, frittata, and more. Pastas are always a good bet, as are the seafood dishes. • HMB: M-F 11:30am-2:30pm, 5:30-9:30pm; Sa-Su noon-3pm, 5:30-10pm. • SSF: M-F 11:30am-2:30pm, 5:30-9:30pm; Sa 5:30-9:30pm.

Pasta Primavera Café ★★ $ 34 E. 4th Ave. (El Camino/San Mateo Dr.), San Mateo, 650/548-9100. If you like pasta, this branch of the East Bay chain is the place for you. All pasta dishes, many of which are paired with chicken, veal, and/or seafood, are fresh, cooked to order, ample, and priced under $10. The cheese ravioli and ravioli Florentine are scrumptious, as is the penne with shrimp and chicken in dill sauce. Fresh salads include penne with tomatoes, spinach, and red onions in a pesto-lemon dressing, and a classic Caesar. The decor is basic 1980s corporate—with an open kitchen, a black-and-green color scheme, and lots of faux marble and mirrors—but the service is casual and assiduously friendly, and families with children are welcome. • Su-Th 11:30am-9:30pm; F-Sa 11:30am-10pm.

Pedro's Cabo Grill ★ $$ 316 N. Santa Cruz Ave. (Petticoat/Hwy 9), Los Gatos, 408/354-7570. A festive Mission-style Mexican restaurant with a perpetual din from the enthusiastic patrons, who range from large families to margarita-loving singles. The portions are filling and the ingredients are fresh, but the menu doesn't break new ground. Relax during the weekday happy hour from 4 to 6pm. • Daily 11am-10pm.

Peninsula Fountain & Grill ★ $ 566 Emerson St. (Hamilton), Palo Alto, 650/323-3131. You may experience the eerie feeling that you've stumbled onto the set of "Happy Days." The food recalls the '50s: juicy burgers, golden onion rings (delicious, if sometimes a bit on the greasy side), and tuna melts. The towering pies actually taste good (the apple in particular). Although the neon clock says "Eat and Get Out," the owners and the youthful wait staff are friendly to a fault. Service is snappy, the music is sock-hop cheery, and you can buy Pixie Stix at the cash register. • M-W 7am-10pm; Th 7am-11pm; F 7am-midnight; Sa 8am-midnight; Su 8am-10pm.

Pho Xe Lua Noodle House ★ ¢ 311 Moffett Blvd. (Central), Mountain View, 650/903-0698. • 1460 Halford Ave. (El Camino), Santa Clara, 408/244-9721. 82 S. Abel St. (Calaveras), Milpitas, 408/262-5751. This spacious, airy restaurant offers quick service, bargain prices, and great soup, attracting a brisk lunch business catering mostly to local Silicon Valley workers. The kitchen specializes in the delicious steaming Vietnamese noodle soup known as *pho* accompanied by condiment plates piled high with limes, mint, basil, hot peppers, and bean sprouts. Although the soup is traditionally made with beef, the menu here offers a chicken version as well. The kitchen turns out a good rendition of *bun thit nuong*, rice noodles with barbecued beef or pork. Try the fresh lemonade with your meal—add your own sugar to taste. • Daily 9am-9pm.

Piatti ★★ $$ Stanford Shopping Center (El Camino and Quarry), Palo Alto, 650/324-9733. The Peninsula branch of a chain with branches in the wine country and beyond, Piatti is spacious and bright, decorated with murals of giant vegetables and done up in warm shades of terra-cotta. Chef Aram Chakerian, from the Sacramento Piatti, prepares homemade pastas in garlicky sauces, pizzas from the wood-burning oven, and rotisserie chicken. A worthy player in the Peninsula Italian dining scene. Sit outdoors on the eminently pleasant patio. • M-Th 11:30am-10pm; F-Sa 11:30am-11pm; Su 11:30am-10pm.

Picasso's ★ $ 380 S. 2nd St. (San Carlos/San Salvador), San Jose, 408/298-4400. Charming atmosphere and a lively menu long on Spanish culinary favorites make this a fun stop in downtown San Jose. Lovely tapas are the top draw: a range of intriguing cheeses, cured meats, gloriously spiced seafood, and tangy, composed salads. The perfect outing when you crave a taste of the Mediterranean and are tired of pasta and *tiramisù*. • Tu-Th noon-2pm, 5-9pm; F noon-2pm, 5-10pm; Sa 5-10pm; Su 5-9pm.

Pigalle ★★★ $$$ 27 N. Santa Cruz Ave. (Main/Elm), Los Gatos, 408/395-7924. Murals of Parisian street scenes cover every inch of the walls here, transporting you to the City of Light. The authentic French specialties add to the illusion. Opt for the prix fixe menu; you get a mixed green salad, an entrée, vegetables, and dessert for far less than you would pay in Paris. A la carte specialties include a delicious grilled entrecôte with three-peppercorn port wine sauce and rabbit with mustard sauce. An abundance of Gallic charm makes for a memorable dining experience. • M-Sa 11am-10pm; Su 10am-10pm.

Pizzeria Uno ★ $ 19930 Stevens Creek Blvd. (Wolfe/De Anza), Cupertino, 408/973-1466. • 2570 El Camino Real (San Tomas), Santa Clara, 408/241-5152. Chicago-style deep dish pizza served in a bustling diner. Those who don't like the thick, flaky Chicago crust can opt for thin-crust "pizzettas." The menu also includes pasta, salad, and burgers, but the big attraction is the pizza. Beware: The large number of children makes for a high noise level. • Su-Th 11am-11pm; F-Sa 11am-midnight.

Pluto's ★★ ¢ 482 University Ave. (Cowper), Palo Alto, 650/853-1556. Pluto's serves truly healthy fast food: the portions are enormous, and the mouthwatering choices emphasize organic ingredients. You order cafeteria style at the counter—expect to wait in line—with most plates built around sandwiches or huge salads. Choose a Caesar or mixed greens, then pick up to seven mix-ins: nuts, corn, broccoli, peppers, fennel—the list is endless. If you are in a more carnivorous mood, top your salad off with fresh-roasted turkey, flank steak, or sausage, or have a sandwich instead. Then add your favorite side dishes: mashed potatoes with gravy, killer garlic potato rings, a variety of vegetables, even stuffing. After ordering, take a seat (if you can find one) in the cramped, minimalist-but-somehow-warm room. • Su-Th 11:30am-10pm; F-Sa 11:30am-11pm.

Quang Da ★★ $ 348 E. Santa Clara St. (8th), San Jose, 408/297-3402. This gem of a restaurant is simple, clean, and airy, with impeccable attention to detail. While the majority of Vietnamese restaurants in the Bay Area focus on Vietnam's Northern and Southern specialties, Quang Da (the restaurant's name means "center") specializes in central Vietnamese cuisine. Drawing from both the mountain-dwelling and fishing cultures, the kitchen offers an array of exotic dishes, including banana leaf rolls with ground pork and shrimp, steamed rice with clams central style, yellow egg noodle with crab meat, pork, and shrimp, and panfried cake with meat, bean sprouts, and shrimp. The atmosphere is casual, and the service is friendly. Finish off your meal with a crème brûlée. No credit cards. • Su-Tu 10am-10pm; Th-F 10am-10pm; Sa-Su 9am-10pm.

Race Street Seafood Kitchen ★★ ¢ 247 Race St. (W. San Carlos/Park), San Jose, 408/287-6280. A San Jose landmark, Race Street has been serving up flaky and delicious fish and chips for as long as anyone can remember. The lines can get long at lunchtime, especially on Fridays, when (according to a sign behind the counter) fried zucchini will not be served due to customer volume. (Who knows why?) The wait is worth it, though—everything on the menu is good, if not exactly good for you. Do-it-yourselfers can get fresh fish at the adjacent seafood market. No credit cards. • M-F 10:30am-8pm; Sa 10:30am-7pm.

Ramen Club ★★ $ 723 California Dr. (Oak Grove), Burlingame, 650/347-3690. An extremely authentic Japanese noodle house, straight out of the movie *Tampopo,* with little more than a counter and six tables. The house specialty, of course, is delicious *ramen:* thin noodles in broth, known in America as boil-and-serve dorm food. The freshly prepared version is infinitely tastier and makes a filling and inexpensive meal. Other menu items include a flavorful cold appetizer of spinach with sesame-seed dressing, reasonably priced sushi and sashimi, a variety of grilled meats, and teriyaki dishes. • Tu-F 11:30am-2pm, 5-10pm; Sa 5-10pm.

Red Sea Restaurant ★★ $ 684 N. 1st St. (Taylor), San Jose, 408/993-1990. Housed in a homey California bungalow, the Red Sea is attractively decorated with African crafts and tapestries. The excellent East African food is served in big colorful mounds on top of the tangy, spongy Ethiopian bread called *injera.* You tear off a piece and use it to scoop up a serving of meat, lentils, greens, or mixed vegetables. The drink menu is fun, with its Ethiopian honey wine and some obscure African beers (try Ngoma, a pilsner from Togo). Lots of good vegetarian options. Service is friendly. • M-F 11am-2pm, 5-9pm; Sa noon-10pm.

Redwood Café and Spice Co. ★★★ $ 1020 Main St. (Middlefield), Redwood City, 650/366-1498. Blink and you might miss this gem, which is tucked away in a tiny Victorian on the edge of downtown Redwood City. It offers scrumptious omelets—try the one with smoked salmon and cream cheese—but not much for those who steer clear of eggs. All breakfasts are served with a basket of delicious, piping-hot bread and muffins. Service is friendly and homey. A nice patio for sunny days. • Tu-F 7am-2:30pm; Sa-Su 8am-2pm.

Ristorante Piacere ★★ $$ 727 Laurel St. (Olive/Cherry), San Carlos, 650/592-3536. A relaxed alternative to the glitzy Italian restaurants of Palo Alto and San Francisco. The pastas and appetizers are all familiar, but a few of the *secondi,* like baked duck in a Grand Marnier sauce and veal scaloppine stuffed with ham and provolone in a red wine sauce, are more novel. The soothing modern interior is sectioned into various spaces with a dividing wall, a raised seating area, a small bar, and a sidewalk patio. Attractive decorative touches include light wooden arches, a sleek fireplace, funky semicircular booths, and the required sponge-painted walls. The look and menu match sibling restaurant Vivace in Belmont. Live jazz holds forth on weekend nights. Reservations recommended. • M-Sa 11am-2pm, 5-10pm; Su 5-10pm.

Ritz Seafood ★★ $ 1528 S. El Camino Real (15th), San Mateo, 650/571-6213. Everything else plays second fiddle to the seafood dishes at this popular Cantonese Chinese restaurant on El Camino, although during a brief period a few years ago they emphasized vegetarian food. Though the nonseafood offerings are just fine, the most extensive and inspired portion of the menu is devoted to such dishes as sautéed scallops with pine nuts and a variety of steamed whole fish. Ritz also serves dim sum daily and has a full bar. The modern interior is a classic upscale dim sum parlor with multiple dining areas, sponge-painted walls, framed art, and big chandeliers. Most importantly, the conspicuous fish tanks provide visual assurance to diners that their entrées are fresh. • Daily 11am-2:30pm, 5-9:30pm.

Roman's Deli ★★ $$ 71 Washington St. (Newhall), Santa Clara, 408/296-3864. From the outside, you wouldn't guess that a gourmet Italian restaurant lurked in the back of this storefront deli, and we suspect that the owners want to keep it that way. Roman's is a real neighborhood restaurant, where the proprietors know the customers by name and remember their favorite dishes. At lunch it's a deli; during dinner and Sunday brunch, there's no menu to speak of, just daily specials, which are uniformly good. Accompany your meal with any of the wines in the store—with only a tiny markup for restaurant service—or one of the extensive selection of beers. Full service catering also available. • M-Tu 8am-6pm; W-Sa 8am-10pm; Su 10am-2pm.

Royal Palace ★ $ 4320 El Camino Real (Los Altos Ave.), Los Altos, 650/941-8818. One of the best places around for good dim sum on a weekend morning. Despite its huge dining room, the place gets crowded, so make sure you arrive early, when the food is freshest. Dim sum is also available weekdays. Dinners are okay, but don't compare to the dim sum. • M-F 11am-2:30pm, 5-9:30pm; Sa 10am-3pm, 5-10pm; Su 10am-3pm, 5-9:30pm.

Rue de Paris ★★ $$$ 19 N. Market St. (Santa Clara), San Jose, 408/298-0704. Behind the floral-print curtains in this old-style dining room, an array of couples at various stages of romance—from first date to fiftieth anniversary—bill and coo. The menu, lettered in elaborate script, lists an array of French specialties, from *escargots de Bourguignon* to filet mignon with béarnaise sauce, with a few Italian standbys like fettuccine Alfredo thrown in. Order a glass of fine old port to prolong your meal. • M-Th 11:30am-2pm, 5:30-10pm; F 11:30am-2pm, 5:30-11pm; Sa 5:30-11pm.

Sam Kee ★★ $$ 1686 S. Wolfe Rd. (Homestead), Sunnyvale, 408/737-9976. You don't have to drive to San Francisco for delicious, authentic dim sum anymore. Sam Kee, a bustling Chinese restaurant specializing in seafood and dim sum, offers a huge array of choices, with weekend dim sum extravaganzas. The predominantly Chinese clientele usually includes a few huge family gatherings on weekends, who choose their selections from the heavily laden carts that whiz by. While many of the friendly servers speak limited English, they are willing to engage in the point-and-select option. The predictable decor offers a red, white, and gold color scheme, a large fish tank, and a glittering disco ball. • M-F 10:30am-9:30pm; Sa-Su 9am-10pm.

Santa Barbara Grill ★★★ $$ 10745 N. De Anza Blvd. (I-280/Stevens Creek), Cupertino, 408/253-2233. The very talented take-charge chef Patrick Clark has whipped this year-old grill into great shape. The island bar—an adult entertainment section and watering hole—attracts the young and the restless, while the beautifully appointed main dining room showcases generous American classics, from rotisserie chicken to down-home barbecue. There are plenty of superstar dishes, such as macadamia-crusted halibut and *tamari*-glazed salmon with scallion mashed potatoes. But don't miss the top-quality farmers market vegetables, which receive sensitive treatment here. Big, bold desserts to please any guy and delight any gal. For romantic dinners as well as family dining. • M-F 11:30am-10pm; Sa 5-10pm; Su 5-9pm.

Scala Mia ★★ $$ 820 Santa Cruz Ave. (Crane/University), Menlo Park, 650/323-3665. Sink into one of the comfortable upholstered booths with a bottle of the reasonably priced house Chianti and enjoy a garlic-laden meal at this small Northern Italian restaurant, sibling to Burlingame's Café La Scala. The fanciful decor (a multitude of angels, Miroesque lamps, and the mandatory peach-sponged walls) and huge portions of highly variable Italian cuisine keep the crowds coming, but what really distinguishes this place is the over-the-top friendly service. Start with a selection from the array of fresh salads—perhaps the *insalata scala mia*, spinach with goat cheese, oranges, tomatoes, onions, and extra virgin olive oil. The *fettuccine scala mia*, fettuccine with pancetta, shiitake mushrooms, and onions in a light cream sauce, is hearty and delicious. The linguine with clams is light, surprisingly spicy, and potentially addictive. As for dessert, if you are one of the few chestnut pie lovers in the world, you have found your home; otherwise stick to the cheesecake. • M-Th 11am-10pm; F-Sa 11am-11pm.

Scott's Seafood Grill and Bar ★ $$$ 2300 E. Bayshore Rd. (Embarcadero), Palo Alto, 650/856-1046. • 185 Park Ave. (Almaden/Market), San Jose, 408/971-1700. A Bay Area chain of elegantly furnished restaurants with tasteful maritime art on the walls and plenty of room between tables to allow for private conversation or just serious concentration on the well-stocked menu. The seafood sauté could feed a minor fleet, while the almond-crusted red snapper will please most seafood connoisseurs. Service is relaxed, to put it kindly, but you'll be glad for the extra time to savor every tender morsel. • PA: M 6:30am-9pm; Tu-F 6:30am-9:30pm; Sa 5-9:30pm; Su 5-9pm. • SJ: M-F 11:30am-10pm; Sa 5-10pm; Su 5-9pm.

Señora Emma's ★ $ 177 W. Santa Clara St. (Market/Notre Dame), San Jose, 408/279-EMMA (3662). The upstairs nightclub is a howling hot mecca for weekend singles and couples, while downstairs it's all about fast, counter-served Mexican specialties. Nothing fancy, the idea is to get your food and your drink—try the tangy tamarind *agua fresca*—and head for the outdoor patio, which provides a ringside seat for downtown people-watching. Cheese quesadillas are foolproof, the pork *chile verde* with red beans and rice is better than average. The burritos are huge, and the barbecued-chicken taco salads big enough for lovers to share. You pay at the counter and make a pit stop at the salsa bar; your order is delivered to your table. • Su-W 11am-9pm; Th-Sa 11am-2:30am.

Sent Sovi ★★★ $$$$ 14583 Big Basin Way (5th), Saratoga, 408/867-3110. When Adriatic closed, this small restaurant located in a quaint downtown house was taken over by David Kinch, a veteran of San Francisco's late, revered Ernie's. He's turned it into one of the South Bay's premier restaurants. The *tiny* dining room, a far cry from Ernie's opulence, manages to be both stylish and homey, with high ceilings, soft lighting, and French windows. The contemporary French food—look for accents from Spain and California—highlights fresh local ingredients—perhaps a delicate roast salmon or lusty braised shortribs. Reservations recommended. • Tu-Sa 5:30-9:30pm; Su 5-9pm.

71 Saint Peter ★★ $$ 71 N. San Pedro St. (St. John/Santa Clara), San Jose, 408/971-8523. This intimate downtown spot manages to be rustic and elegant at the same time, with brick walls, exposed rafters, linen tablecloths, and flowers on every table. Chef Mark Tabak conjures up specialties such as filet mignon with blue cheese, pork loin with an herb crust, and excellent polenta. A perfect setting for a romantic rendezvous. • M 11:30am-2pm; Tu-F 11:30am-2pm, 5-10pm; Sa 5-10pm.

Shamshiri ★★ $ 1392 S. Bascom Ave. (Stokes/Hamilton), San Jose 408/998-0122. Persian cooking with a family touch marks this ethnic eatery housed in a generic strip mall. You can't go wrong with the kabobs—available in simple, appealing combos—but the real delights are on the authentic side of the menu. Try items like braised poultry in walnut and pomegranate sauce or lamb shank stew with fava beans and dill. Plentiful *lahvosh* bread tastes great dipped in that ubiquitous Mediterranean blend of yogurt and cucumber, dusted here with dried mint. The feta and *dolmas* are reliably good, and some terrific stews long on eggplant, lemon, tomatoes, and lentils will delight adventurous diners. • Daily 11am-10pm.

Shebele Ethiopian ★★ ¢ 422 E. Campbell Ave. (Central/Civic Center), Campbell, 408/378-3131. A former soda fountain turned ethnic eatery, Shebele presents delicious and pungently flavored foods of Ethiopia, served on large rounds of the omnipresent fermented bread, *injera*. The menu offers stews of spiced meats and vegetables—lots of orange and yellow items—as well as fragrantly perfumed legume specialties. Most are designed to be scooped up with the soft bread, adding a sense of interactive play to the dining experience. Creamy, sweet desserts are subtly spiced with cinnamon, cloves, and coriander. Lovely service and a friendly environment. • M-Th 11:30am-10pm; F-Sa 11:30am-11pm; Su noon-10pm.

Siam Thai Cuisine ★★ $ 220 E. Main St. (University/Saratoga), Los Gatos, 408/354-1019. Attention culinary daredevils: The term *medium hot* is relative here. Fiery green chilis, garlic, and red curry paste season almost everything on the menu, from the acclaimed soups to the extensive seafood selection. The desserts, which emphasize coconut, are soothing but no less flavorful. The decor features mauve banquets, matching napkins, and diaphanous white curtains. • M-Th 11:30am-2pm, 5-9:30pm; F 11:30am-2pm, 5-10pm; Sa 5-10pm; Su 5-9:30pm.

Sono Sushi ★★ $ 357 Castro St. (Dana/California), Mountain View, 650/961-9086. Your basic sushi-boat joint, with a large center island surrounded by a moat full of floating sushi and a few hard, wooden booths around the edges. Unlike many sushi-boat restaurants, the fish is fresh and the variety is good. Prices are much lower than in other neighborhood Japanese eateries, especially for the cooked dishes, although there is not much beyond the basic tempura-teriyaki-sukiyaki standards. • Tu-Th 11:30am-2:30pm, 5-10pm; F-Su 11:30am-10pm.

Sousa's Restaurant ★ $$ 1614 E. Alum Rock Ave. (33rd/34th), San Jose, 408/926-9075. Located in San Jose's Little Portugal, Sousa's has been serving up Portuguese specialties for many years. The interior has a faded Old World feel, with its chandelier, white tablecloths, artificial flowers, and Air Portugal logo on the menu. *Porco Alentejano*, baked marinated pork and clams with cilantro, is a hearty combination of flavors that will transport you straight to Lisbon. *Bacalhau à Gomes de Sà* (baked codfish with potatoes and onions) and *arroz de mariscos* (seafood with rice) are good seafood options. If you have tried Portugal's *vinho verde*, translated as "green wine," you will be pleased to see three types listed on the menu. It may sound strange, but it's the perfect accompaniment to your meal. • Tu-F 11am-3pm, 5-9pm; Sa-Su 11am-9pm.

Spago Palo Alto ★★★ $$$/$$$$ 265 Lytton Ave. (Ramona/Bryant), Palo Alto, 650/833-1000. This fashionable Wolfgang Puck offspring brings the pulse of Los Angeles into the heart of Palo Alto: postmodern decor (long on riotous carpeting and primary colors) and a clamorous dining room perfect for celebrity-watching. The food is quite extraordinary given the high-volume business. Start with a cocktail at the glowing pavilion across the walkway, then work your way through the most exciting breadbasket in California. Appetizers are luxurious and full of contrasts: Maine day boat scallops with caramelized fennel, Hudson Valley foie gras with ginger and Calvados, or duck and shiitake potstickers with caramelized pear curry. Entrées run toward intricately spiced game dishes and sparklingly fresh Asian-influenced seafood. The dessert sampler for two offers a dazzling taste of the kitchen's best sweets. Puck's pizzas are served in the pavilion. If you want to eat before 9:30pm, book your reservations weeks in advance. • M-F 11:30am-10pm; Sa-Su 5-10pm.

Spalti ★★ $$ 417 California Ave. (El Camino/Ash), Palo Alto, 650/327-9390. This friendly restaurant is a wonderful addition to Palo Alto's California Avenue, with its traditional Northern Italian cuisine served in an elegant, spacious interior decorated with softly painted walls and matching light fixtures. Start with one of the delicious appetizers or fresh salads and choose from an array of classic pastas, veal dishes, seafood, lamb, and steaks. Outstanding dishes include *grigliata di polenta* (polenta with mushroom and wine sauce); *linguine con vongole* (linguine with clams); and *picatta di filetti sogliole* (sole in a lemon caper sauce). The large and reasonably priced desserts are delicious, in particular the homemade *tiramisù* and the crème brûlée. Spalti has developed a loyal clientele and reservations are recommended, especially on weekends. • M-Sa 11am-3pm, 5-10pm; Su 4:30-9pm.

Spiedo ★★ $$ 223 E. 4th Ave. (B St.), San Mateo, 650/375-0818. • 151 W. Santa Clara St. (San Pedro), San Jose, 408/971-6096. Located across from the Draeger brothers' shrine to gourmet cooking, this spacious San Mateo restaurant serves reasonably priced, hearty northern Italian fare. Most notable are the mesquite-grilled and spit-roasted (from which the name is derived) entrées including fresh fish, lamb chops, rabbit, duck, and more. Pastas and pizzas are also featured, as well as a wide selection of appetizers, although the wide-ranging menu makes consistency a problem. The interior is bright and attractive with lots of brass and glass, and the service is assiduous. The second location in San Jose faithfully replicates the original on two stories. • SM: M-Sa 11:30am-2:30pm, 4:30-10pm; Su 4:30-9pm. • M-Th 11:30am-3pm, 4-10pm; F 11:30am-3pm, 4-11pm; Sa 4-11pm; Su 4-10pm.

St. Michael's Alley ★★ $$ 806 Emerson St. (Homer/Channing), Palo Alto, 650/326-2530. Since St. Michael's Alley the restaurant closed a few years ago, St. Michael's Alley the café has expanded its food offerings and become a full-service restaurant. The small space still looks like a café, with the coffee bar, simple tables, and rotating local art (the full name includes "Art Café & Restaurant"). But the changing menu now includes an eclectic range of California-international dishes based on ingredients from the restaurant's own organic garden. Globe-trotting starters might include guacamole, Moroccan orange and mint salad, and designer pizzas. Main dishes jump from ricotta-filled spinach ravioli with sun-dried tomatoes and portobello mushrooms to Southwestern chicken breast with buttermilk mashed potatoes to paella. Weekend brunch, with its famous pastries and French toast, is a welcome carryover. Friendly atmosphere created by the hands-on owners. • Tu-Sa 7am-10pm; Su 7am-3pm.

Stacks ★★ $ 361 California Dr. (Lorton), Burlingame, 650/579-1384. • 314 El Camino Real (Whipple), Redwood City, 650/482-2850. Located near the Burlingame CalTrain Station, Stacks does a booming business with a local crowd of diehard pancake lovers who remain undaunted by the lengthy waits. Why do they persist? Stacks serves some of the Bay Areas finest pancakes, including blueberry, banana wheat-germ, and raisin walnut, as well as an impressive assortment of crepes, Belgium waffles, and other breakfast and lunch standards. Other pluses include the eggs Benedict, the full pot of coffee on the table, an extremely child-friendly atmosphere, and speedy service (once you finally get seated and place your order, the ETA for the food is usually under ten minutes). The bright, triangular space is lined with windows and filled with plants for a greenhouse effect. A recent expansion adds Redwood City to the empire with similar, if newer, decor. • Burlingame: Daily 7am-2:30pm. • RC: Daily 7am-2:30pm.

Steamers ★★ $$$ Old Town, 50 University Ave. (Main), Los Gatos, 408/395-2722. This festive seafood spot has a lively atmosphere. An aroma of garlic greets you at the door, foreshadowing good things to come. A glass block bar dominates the dining area, and curved wooden banquettes accommodate locals who come for well-prepared seafood specialties like grilled salmon, teriyaki mixed-fish grill, and steamed clams by the pound. • M-Th 11:30am-10pm; F-Sa 11:30am-11pm; Su noon-9pm.

Steelhead (Burlingame Station) Brewing Company ★★ $$ 333 California Dr. (Burlingame Ave./Bellevue), Burlingame, 650/344-6050. This trendy, renovated brew pub located across from the Burlingame CalTrain station attracts a steady stream of locals who don't feel like cooking; they're drawn to the large menu of California pub-grub staples (burgers, garlic fries, designer pizzas, dinner salads, and pastas). The cavernous space, styled with exposed brick walls and dark wood furnishings, is airy and open, and the youthful wait-staff is welcoming. Best to avoid happy hour dining, when the place teems with yuppies on the prowl (who let all of these guys out of their sales routes early?). But the swagger set loves it—the housemade beers, the pool table room, and the chance to find Mr. or Ms. Right among the many Wrongs having another pint of amber or stout before taking the train home. • Daily 11:30am-10pm (light menu until midnight).

Stoddard's Brewhouse ★★ $$ 111 S. Murphy Ave. (Washington/Evelyn), Sunnyvale, 408/733-7824. Opened by Bob Stoddard, former brew *meister* at the Tied House, the soaring two-story space houses a long, polished wood bar, wicker seating area, a downstairs dining room, and an upstairs aerie for quieter dining. Out back there's a beer garden in case you're restless. For starters, the hummus and eggplant with flat bread has become a quick success, while the roast chicken with garlic mashed potatoes and roasted corn is a good bet for an entrée. And, oh yes, the fresh-brewed ales are delicious. • M-Th 11:30am-2:30pm, 5:30-10pm; F 11:30am-2:30pm, 5-11pm; Sa 11am-3pm, 5-10pm; Su noon-3pm, 5-9pm.

Straits Café NR $$ 3295 El Camino Real (Page Mill/Matadero), Palo Alto, 650/494-7168. San Francisco's acclaimed Straits Café is joining the rush of San Francisco restaurateurs opening a Peninsula branch. The San Francisco locale serves Singaporean specialties (a blend of Malay, Indian, and Chinese dishes) in a hip, European-bistro atmosphere. The *ikam panggang,* a grilled boneless trout wrapped in banana leaf, is generally acknowledged to be one of the best seafood dishes anywhere. At presstime, the Palo Alto branch was planning an expanded menu with a French influence. • M-Th 11am-3pm, 5-10pm; F-Sa 11am-3pm, 5-11pm.

Stratta ★★★ $$ 71 E. San Fernando St. (2nd/3rd), San Jose, 408/293-1121. High on the list of both the upwardly mobile young and the old cultural guard, this stylish bistro is strategically positioned near theaters and movie houses in downtown San Jose. Housed in an old block of the city, the long brick walls and weathered hardwood floor lend an old-world patina to the wine bar and the gracious main dining area. If you're lucky, you'll get a seat in one of the burnished wooden booths. A good place to get a bit dressy and linger over some really fine pasta and rich meat entrées. Superior people-watching, yet intimate. • M 10:30am-2pm; Tu-F 10:30am-10pm; Sa-Su 5-10pm.

Su Hong ★★ $ 1039 El Camino Real (Menlo Ave./Santa Cruz), Menlo Park, 650/323-6852. • Take-out: 630 Menlo Ave. (Doyle), Menlo Park, 650/322-4631. • 4101 El Camino Way (Meadow), Palo Alto, 650/493-3836, take-out 650/493-4664. • Su Hong's flagship Menlo Park venue sports tasteful cream-and-lilac walls and white tablecloths for a soothing environment. The food is standard spicy Chinese, but it's extremely popular, especially the hot-and-sour soup, the pot stickers, and the minced chicken in lettuce with plum sauce. There's usually a wait on weekends, but with a bar inside and Kepler's Books across the street, killing time is no problem. If you're in a hurry, the take-out station is right around the corner. In south Palo Alto, there is another Su Hong just off El Camino. Same good food, but served in a more casual decor. • MP: M-Sa 11:30am-2:30pm, 4:30-9:30pm; Su 4:30-9:30pm. • TO: Su-Th 11:30am-3pm, 4-9:30pm; F-Sa 11:30am-3pm, 4-10pm. • PA: Su-Th 11:30am-2:30pm, 4:30-9:30pm; F-Sa 11:30am-2:30pm, 4:30-10pm; Su 11am-3pm, 4:30-9:30pm.

Su's Mongolian BBQ ★ ¢ 1111 El Camino Real (Main), Santa Clara, 408/985-2958. In a class by itself, this bustling and extraordinarily unpretentious Asian eatery specializes in quick, fresh stir-fried meals. The procedure is simple: you locate a table, then approach the selection of meats, veggies, and sauces—all fresh, raw, and waiting to be cooked—and make up your own combo. Perhaps you might mix thinly sliced chicken and fresh broccoli, mushrooms, and bean sprouts. Take your bowl to the grilling zone, where young chefs put on a show that Benihana would envy. Your meal is cooked before your eyes. You add sauces and rice. Drinks are delivered to the table, along with the check. For adventurous foodies looking for fun. • M-Sa 11am-2pm, 5-9pm; Su 5-9pm.

Sue's Indian Cuisine ★★ $$ 216 Castro St. (Villa), Mountain View, 650/969-1112. • 895 Willow St. (Bird/Lincoln), San Jose, 408/993-8730. The small dining room with crisp white linens and bright oil paintings makes a nice setting for Sue's delicious tandoori specialties, complete with *pilau* rice, vegetables, and *nan.* Order a variety of main dishes and share them around the table. Warning: The *gulab jaman* (fried milk balls in rose-flavored syrup) are overly sweet, even for an Indian dessert. The background music adds an authentic feel to the dining atmosphere. • MV: M-W 11am-2:30pm, 5-9:30pm; Th-F 11am-2:30pm, 5-10pm; Sa 11am-2pm, 5-10pm; Su 11am-2pm, 5-9:30pm. • SJ: Tu-Th 11am-2pm, 5-9:30pm; F-Sa 11am-2pm, 5-10pm; Su 5-9:30pm.

Suma Ching Hai International Association Vegetarian House ★★ $ 520 E. Santa Clara St. (11th/12th), San Jose 408/292-3798. The menu advertises "international gourmet vegetarian cuisine, healthy food, and spiritual information." The latter consists of books and videotapes by Suma Ching Hai, a self-proclaimed "enlightened being." If that doesn't spook you, you're in for a treat. Suma Ching Hai's followers serve exquisite vegetarian cuisine (no meat, poultry, fish, eggs, or MSG) with a pan-Asian flavor, including Vietnamese, Chinese, and Thai favorites, and even a few Indian and Italian dishes. The crisp salads are especially good. Service is attentive, and the dimly lit, stained glass–windowed dining room is generally tranquil, although the large-screen TV that continuously broadcasts Suma's lectures is initially a little hard to overlook. There's clearly more of an agenda here than the culinary one, but the casual diner is not subjected to a hard sell, and the food is worth the effort to try and ignore the boob tube proselytizing. • M-F 11am-2pm, 5-9:30pm; Sa-Su 11am-9:30pm.

Sundance Mining Company ★★ $$$ 1921 El Camino Real (Stanford Ave.), Palo Alto, 650/321-6798. Sundance Mining Company is celebrating over two decades of fine dining in Palo Alto. A traditional menu features steak, seafood, chicken, and pasta in a rowdy down-home atmosphere. Try the blackened swordfish and teriyaki chicken. A good place to hit if you're in the mood for certified Angus prime rib or an excellent grilled-to-order steak. Sundance has been voted best steakhouse on the Peninsula for many years. Reservations recommended. • M-Th 11:30am-2pm, 5-10pm; F 11:30am-2pm, 5-10:30pm; Sa 5-10:30pm; Su 5-9pm.

Super Taqueria ★ ¢ 1095 S. White Rd. (Story), San Jose, 408/272-7871. • 476 S. 10th St. (Williams), San Jose, 408/292-3470. Fast, authentic Mexican food with a fanatical following. The menu contains only five basic items—a taco, a burrito, and so on—but the selection of meat fillings, which runs from grilled chicken to barbecued pork to beef cheeks to tongue, provides sufficient variety. Colorful Latino murals make for a lively atmosphere. The speedy service, hefty portions, and low prices endear Super Taqueria to San Jose State students, who occupy at least a couple of tables at any given time. Cash only. • Daily 10am-10pm.

Sushi Bar Jun ★★ $$ 1355 Broadway (Capuchino/Paloma) Burlingame, 650/348-9188. Aki, the chef who has been turning out a dazzling selection of sushi at this hole-in-the-wall location for over 15 years, named the restaurant after his wife. There's not much to the decor, just a sushi bar, a mirror, and four small tables, but be sure to drop in for some of Aki's special hand rolls—the spicy tuna and hamachi are particularly good. Another favorite is the number 5 roll, an elaborate concoction built around tempura-fried squid, salmon, tuna, and carrot. The prices are standard for sushi (no bargains here) but the fish is perfectly fresh and well portioned, and the cooked dishes—tempura, teriyaki—are noteworthy as well. The back room with tatami-mat seating is perfect for a private party, but must be booked in advance. • M-F 11:30am-2pm, 5:30-10pm; Sa-Su 5:30-10pm.

Sushi Sam's ★★ $ 218 3rd Ave. (B St./Ellsworth), San Mateo, 650/344-0888. Crowds of young, lively Peninsulans queue up outside Sushi Sam's for some of the best raw fish around at reasonable prices (especially on the combination dinners) and the antics of Sam the owner, who is quite the cutup with his regular customers. The tiny interior features a cramped sushi bar on one side and a handful of small Formica-topped tables on the other. • Tu-Sa 11am-2pm, 5pm-10pm; Su 5pm-10pm.

Sushi Ya ★★★ $/$$ 380 University Ave. (Waverley/Bryant), Palo Alto, 650/322-0330. This tiny sushi bar serves excellent, still-quivering sushi and sashimi and is a favorite with visiting Japanese businessmen. If you're a sushi novice let Toshi, the sushi master, lead the way. He creates innovative presentations, and he'll put together a stunning sushi box to take out. There are only a few tables, so be prepared to wait or sit at the sushi bar. Sushi prices add up quickly, but cooked dishes—teriyaki, *donburi*, *udon*—are bargains. • M-F 11:30am-2pm, 5:30-9:30pm; Sa 5:30-9:30pm.

Swagat ★★★ $$ 2700 W. El Camino Real (Charleston/San Antonio), Mountain View, 650/948-7727. One of the best Indian restaurants on the Peninsula, Swagat's wide-ranging menu encompasses the different regional cuisines of India. Despite its location in a renovated motel dining room, the atmosphere is often festive, with many Indian families holding celebrations here. Don't miss the *dosas,* crepes made with lentil flour and stuffed with vegetable curry, the fresh curries, or the vegetarian entrées. The sweet *lassie,* a refreshing yogurt drink, is the perfect accompaniment to the scorching Vindaloo curries. Like many Indian restaurants, Swagat offers a large, reasonably priced lunch buffet that's popular with a Silicon Valley crowd. Reservations recommended. • Daily 11am-3pm, 5:30-10pm.

Szechwan Café ★★ $ 406 California Ave. (Ash), Palo Alto 650/327-1688. When you ask for a tip on a cozy neighborhood restaurant, you're probably not expecting Chinese food. But a local might well point you to the Szechwan Café. Service is attentive and friendly, there are fresh flowers on the tables, and the food is delicious and reasonably priced. Don't miss the wontons in chili sauce. There is also a large array of dishes made with tofu, all of which taste great. The cooks use oil sparingly and the food seems fresher and healthier than at many Chinese restaurants (although soups aren't a strong point). Szechwan even puts a premium on presentation: many of the dishes are served with elaborate carved-vegetable flowers. Lunches can be crowded. • M-F 11am-2:30pm, 4:30-9pm; Sa 4:30-9pm.

Taiwan Restaurant ★ $ 1306 Lincoln Ave. (Minnesota), San Jose, 408/289-8800. A landmark for well over a decade, this bustling Chinese restaurant cranks out a nonstop stream of Sichuan, Cantonese, and Taiwanese specialties. Every sweet-and-sour or hot-and-spicy dish you ever loved is given proper respect here in a cluttered dining room filled with mirrors and floral profusions. This place is a local institution and gets unbelievably busy at lunchtime, so plan accordingly. A great place for kung pao chicken and succulent potstickers. Especially fun to bring friends and dine family-style. • Su-Th 11:30am-3pm, 5-9pm; F-Sa 11:30am-3pm, 5-9:30pm.

Taqueria La Bamba ★★ ¢ 2058 Old Middlefield Way (Rengstorff), Mountain View, 650/965-2755. Huge burritos the size of a small loaf of bread, the Bay Area's best carnitas, and a limited menu with a Salvadorean touch are La Bamba's trademarks. The best strategy is to start with a *pupusa* (small, thick corn tortilla stuffed with cheese) and move on to the first half of a hard-to-find vegetarian burrito. Save the other half for your next meal. Expect a brief wait during the lunchtime rush—you may have to scramble for one of the few chairs. No credit cards. • M-F 10am-9:30pm; Sa-Su 10am-9pm.

Taxi's Hamburgers ★ $ 403 University Ave. (Waverley), Palo Alto, 650/322-TAXI (8294). • 2700 S. El Camino Real (27th), San Mateo, 650/377-1947. • Oak Ridge Mall (Blossom Hill and Santa Teresa) San Jose, 408/229-TAXI (8294). A perennial winner of the "Best Hamburger" award from the *San Mateo Times*, this popular local restaurant chain is decorated in the yellow, black, and white of a New York cab. The cheery interior, free balloons, and wide variety of kids' meals keep families coming back for more. In addition to the prize-winning burgers (not everyone agrees on their merits), Taxi's serves milkshakes, baked potatoes with assorted toppings, and various chicken dishes. • PA: M-Th 11am-11pm; F-Sa 11am-midnight; Su 11am-10pm. • SM: Daily 7am-10pm. • SJ: Daily 10am-9pm.

Tea Time ★ $ 542 Ramona St. (University/Hamilton), Palo Alto, 650/328-2877. Located in a historic stone building, this shop caters to tea connoisseurs and novices alike. The tea-happy owners offer more than a hundred types of teas, tisanes, and herbal blends and emphasize proper tea brewing methods (each pot of tea served is timed to the second for proper flavor). They're also more than happy to share their knowledge and encourage you to smell the different teas. While the tea is superb, the pastry offerings are unexceptional, although the scones served with lemon curd are a good bet. If you're interesting in steeping yourself in the culture of tea, sign up for one of the tea tastings scheduled throughout the year. • M-F 10:30am-6pm; Sa 11am-6pm.

Thai City ★ **$** 3691 El Camino Real (Page Mill/Charleston), Palo Alto, 650/493-0643. The aggressively red carpet and tablecloths might make you think you're at a Chinese restaurant, but the elegantly folded pink napkins tell you it's Thai all the way. The richly flavored sauces are pungent with spice but won't burn even a timid palate. While the soups are a joy, the curries can be heavy. Portions are on the small side. A large menu covers a variety of tastes at an equally wide range of prices: Bring a patron if you like prawns; the chicken you can finance on any budget. Vegetarians are catered to: the chef will substitute tofu, egg, and vegetables in any dish. • M-F 11am-2:30pm, 5-10pm; Sa noon-10pm; Su 5-10pm.

Thai Stick ★★ **$** 301 El Camino Real (Millbrae Ave./Hillcrest), Millbrae, 650/692-0414. With two branches in San Francisco and one in Millbrae, Thai Stick has clearly figured out a winning combination for serving Thai food. The *San Mateo Times* agrees, honoring Thai Stick with its "Best of..." award. The long menu covers most Thai dishes served in North America, and the preparation is uniformly good, although their peanut sauce and green curry merit extra praise. Portions, however, run small and prices high. Plate-glass windows on two sides brighten the coolly spacious room with its gray carpet and minimalist tapestries hung on the robin's-egg-blue walls. • M-F 11am-3pm, 5-10pm; Sa-Su 11am-10pm.

Thanh's Restaurant ★ **$** 3151 Middlefield Rd. (5th), Redwood City, 650/367-0567. Thanh's offers authentic Vietnamese and Chinese food. Start with the barbecued quail, flambéed before your eyes, and imperial rolls, the Vietnamese version of egg rolls. The beef and prawns in a claypot is a great hands-on meal: roll them in rice paper along with fresh mint, pickled garlic, and other vegetables. Other entrées worth trying are the coconut curried chicken and the spicy lemongrass chicken. Don't be put off by the no-nonsense linoleum floors and checkered tablecloths. • M-Tu, Th-F 11am-9pm; W 11am-2pm; Sa noon-9pm.

Thepthai ★★ **$** 23 N. Market St. (St. John/Santa Clara St.), San Jose, 408/292-7515. A roaring success. The decor at this modest downtown restaurant is minimal—a few Christmas lights, neon beer signs, and a pagodalike folly. The food is the point here, though, with some of the most delectable Thai dishes around emerging from the kitchen. Pad Thai is the specialty; crunchy red cabbage, sprouts, cilantro, and lime distinguish this rendition. Other hits are the fried tofu appetizer with peanut sauce, the ginger chicken, and all the soups. • M-F 11am-3pm, 5-10pm; Sa-Su noon-10pm.

Tokie's ★★ **$** 1058-G Shell Blvd. (Beach Park), Foster City, 650/570-6609. The basics, plain and simple. What this unassuming strip mall restaurant lacks in atmosphere it makes up for with satisfying, traditional Japanese fare: teriyaki, *udon, donburi*, and sushi with all the usual accompaniments. Despite the crowds of business lunchers on weekdays, the booths and tables are well spaced and you never feel rushed. Prices are low, service is cheerful, and the food is fresh. • Tu-F 11:30am-2pm, 5-9:45pm; Sa 5-9:45pm; Su 5-9pm.

Tony and Alba's Pizza and Italian Food ★ **$** 619 Escuela Ave. (Latham/El Camino), Mountain View, 650/968-5089. • 864 Blossom Hill Rd. (Santa Teresa), San Jose, 408/227-8669. • 3137 Stevens Creek Blvd. (Winchester), San Jose, 408/246-4605. These are the most authentic of authentic Italian pizza parlors. Everything you expect in a family-run pizza hangout is here: sports-blasting TVs; photos, pictures, and posters all over the walls; friends partying over pitchers; whole families chowing down; lovers sharing slices and sodas; and lots and lots of noise. So much of it, in fact, that many loyal customers prefer to take their pizza out. The crust is floppy, and the toppings are piled high. • Daily 11am-10pm.

Trattoria Buon Gusto ★★ **$$** 651-H Oak Grove Ave. (El Camino/Crane), Menlo Park, 650/328-2778. Italian is spoken here—in the kitchen, in the lively music that plays in the background, and in the menu that excels in the vernacular salads, antipasti, and flavorful pastas. The kitchen is family-run, and each dish is prepared to order with tangible pride. Dinner can be a lengthy affair—and is worth every minute. Fine Chiantis and fresh breads served with extra-virgin olive oil fill in any intervals between courses. Buon Gusto is a local secret, hidden in a parking lot behind the post office, but it's graced with so much warm Mediterranean atmosphere that everyone feels like a regular by the end of the evening. Small, unfussy, and great for a romantic rendezvous. • Tu-Th 11:30am-2:30pm, 5-9pm; F 11:30am-2:30pm, 5-10pm; Sa 5-10pm; Su 5-9pm.

Tung Kee Noodle House ★★ ¢ 401 Castro St. (California), Mountain View, 650/965-1488. • 20735 Stevens Creek Blvd. (De Anza), Cupertino, 408/257-9888. • 1818 Tully Rd. #162b (King), San Jose, 408/223-1688. • 930 Story Rd. (Senter/McLaughlin), San Jose, 408/298-1688, 408/298-3007. • 261 E. William St. (6th/7th), San Jose, 408/297-8888. With restaurants scattered throughout the South Bay, Tung Kee serves thousands of people a day; at lunchtime the lines snake out the doors. Their recipe for success: great noodles and low prices. A third of the 30 menu items cost $2.50, and there is nothing for over $5. The no-frills interiors have Formica tables with wooden benches and posters on the walls tracing the rise of this family-run business. Most entrées come in two sizes, small and large (the latter will satisfy even the heartiest of appetites). Popular dishes include wonton rice-stick noodle soup (#3), vermicelli duck curry soup (#13), and combination crispy fried noodles (#23). The fried flour cakes with dipping sauce are also a hit. No credit cards. • MV & Cupertino: 9am-9pm. • SJ: 9am-8pm.

2030 ★★ $$$ 2030 Broadway (Main/Jefferson), Redwood City, 650/363-2030. This chic dining spot has weathered a change in ownership and reestablished itself as a noteworthy mid-Peninsula destination, set apart from frantic downtown Palo Alto. The seasonal California menu might include such dishes as lobster ravioli with a sun-dried tomato and artichoke cream sauce, roast rack of lamb with cherry sauce, or New York steak with wild mushroom ragout. A well-priced wine list complements the food. The dining room is clean and simple, with exposed brick, a vaulted ceiling, and crisp black-and-white photographs on the walls. In warm weather, ask for a seat on the patio or at a sidewalk table. • M-Th 11:30am-2pm, 5-9pm; F 11:30am-2pm, 5-10pm; Sa 5-10pm; Su 5-9pm.

231 Ellsworth ★★★ $$$$ 231 S. Ellsworth Ave. (2nd/3rd), San Mateo, 650/347-7231. Sophisticated Peninsulans have come to rely upon the deft, discreet service and elegant California nouvelle cuisine that are the hallmarks of 231 Ellsworth. Improbably located in a downtown storefront, the Deco-ish dining room is a serene dining-out oasis in a cacophonous world, attracting a more mature crowd that doesn't need every meal to feel like an event. Proprietor Ken Ottobani's special source for exotic mushrooms is often evident in the day's specials, where morels and chanterelles regularly appear in showcase preparations. Don't resist the perfect pastry tray presented with a flourish: the lemon curd tart is tops. Excellent values are available on the wine list, which is occasionally highlighted in special wine and food dinners (ask to be put on the mailing list). The $11.50 prix fixe two-course luncheon makes a great impression on business clients, and the four-course dinner for $29.50 makes an important date memorable. Reservations recommended. • M-F 11:30am-2pm, 5:30-9:30pm; Sa 5:30-9:30pm.

Valeriano's Ristorante ★★ $$ 160 W. Main St. (Santa Cruz/Main), Los Gatos, 408/354-8108. A former bank on Los Gatos's main drag extravagantly transformed into a restaurant serving northern Italian cuisine. The soaring ceilings, terra-cotta walls, abundant brass accents, and hanging tapestries give a postmodern luxuriousness to the surroundings. Among the offerings are carpaccio, prosciutto with melon, designer pizzas, and brick-oven roasted chicken or game hen. Imaginative pasta preparations include *gnocchi alla salsa salvia*—gnocchi with fresh sage, Parmesan, and dry ricotta. A nice selection of California and Italian wines. • M-Th 11:30am-2:30pm, 5-10pm; F 11:30am-2:30pm, 5-11pm; Sa 5-11pm; Su 5-9pm.

The Vans ★★ $$$ 815 Belmont Ave. (El Camino), Belmont, 650/591-6525. One of the Bay Area's top ten places to pop the question, according to one poll. This hilltop restaurant and bar earned its romantic reputation largely for its breathtaking views of the East Bay hills and Mt. Diablo. The Vans has a colorful past, as befits the oldest bar on the Peninsula. It was built in 1915 in San Francisco as a Japanese teahouse, barged down the bay to Belmont, and then transformed by turns into a speakeasy and gambling den during Prohibition, a legal saloon in the '30s, and a full-scale restaurant in the '40s. The food today is classic Continental/American with an emphasis on mesquite-broiled meats and weekend brunches, but patrons come for the views. Reservations recommended. • M-F 11:30am-1am; Sa-Su 4pm-1am.

Vaquero's ★★ $$ 1010 El Paseo de Saratoga Shopping Center (Campbell Ave. and Saratoga Ave.), San Jose 408/871-1114. A cut above your average steakhouse, Vaquero's does witty spins on home-on-the-range cuisine. Nirvana for carnivores, this Southwestern-style dining room is long on rough-hewn ambience and border chophouse attitude. The salad accompaniments are better than average, and items like grilled chicken come garnished with salsa. The ribs are tasty and moist, and the side dishes inspired. When you're in the mood for something charbroiled, this is the perfect place to stop. • Su-Th 5-10pm; F-Sa 5-11pm.

Viaggio ★★ $$$ 14550 Big Basin Way (4th/5th), Saratoga, 408/741-5300. It's big, it's beautiful, and it's got everything you've ever wanted in the way of contemporary Italian specialty dining. Definitely one of those places that inspires diners to dress up and show off, Viaggio can range from thrilling to simply good. But the food is never boring, and it's always presented with panache. The dining room is ablaze with lots of white and gold accents, so you're surrounded with the most flattering atmosphere possible. A popular spot on the active peninsula restaurant scene. • M-Th 5-9pm; F-Sa 11am-2pm, 5-10pm; Su 11am-2pm, 5-9pm.

Vic's ★ $/$$ 1125 San Carlos Ave. (El Camino/Laurel), San Carlos, 650/595-2606. The breakfast hot spot of San Carlos. Every day hungry locals cluster around the lunch counter and in the booths to feast on hefty omelets and slog down institutional coffee. Vic's is almost as popular for lunch and dinner, when burgers, grilled sandwiches, and simple pastas and meats dominate the gargantuan menu. A stylish remodel added deep green carpeting, drop lighting, and earth-tone fabrics on the booths. The cost of the remodel is reflected in the prices. • M-F 6am-2:45pm, 5-9:30pm; Sa 7am-2:30pm, 5-9:30pm; Su 7am-2:30pm.

Vicolo Pizzeria ★★ $ 473 University Ave. (Cowper/Kipling), Palo Alto, 650/324-4877. The ultimate in gourmet pizza, with ultrarich cornmeal crust and scads of gorgeous toppings. (Escarole pizza comes decked out with mozzarella, sautéed greens, roasted red peppers, and feta.) Of course you pay for the exotic ingredients, but each slice is as filling as two anyplace else. The menu also includes focaccia sandwiches glistening with olive oil, several fancy salads, beer and wine, and a selection of desserts and coffee drinks. The little University Avenue storefront sports high ceilings with skylights, distressed-stucco walls, polished wood, and faux-marble tabletops. Partially baked pizzas are available for cooking at home. • Sa-Th 11:30am-10pm; F 11:30am-11pm.

The Village Pub ★★ $$$$ 2967 Woodside Rd. (Mountain Home/Cañada), Woodside, 650/851-1294. Don't let the folksy name deceive you. This is haute cuisine at the kind of high-rent prices you'd expect in Woodside. The interior is California-cottage style, with whitewashed walls and discreet framed prints. The menu changes frequently, but it might include such highly evolved fare as seared day boat scallops with foie gras, truffled potatoes, and foie gras butter sauce, or linguine with duck confit, wild mushrooms, roasted shallots, and herbed duck broth. Reservations recommended. • M-Th 11:30am-2:30pm, 5:30-9:30pm; F 11:30am-2:30pm, 5:30-10pm; Sa 5:30-10pm; Su 5:30-9:30pm.

Viognier ★★★ $$$/$$$$ 222 E. 4th Ave. (B St.), San Mateo, 650/685-3727. When the Peninsula's first family of food, the Draegers, expanded their super-upscale market empire to San Mateo, gourmet cooks clapped their oven mitts with glee.

With the simultaneous inauguration of their second-floor restaurant Viognier under the direction of national award-winning chef Gary Danko (formerly of the much-lauded Dining Room at the Ritz-Carlton), noncooks have an equal opportunity for delight. When Danko is on the line and on the mark, his dishes are truly superlative; unfortunately, the expansive menu lacks consistency, with ordinary offerings adjacent to glittering gems. Viognier seems to have trouble deciding whether it's a neighborhood bistro or a full-service restaurant, albeit among the best of either on the Peninsula. While the surrounding blond wood and banquette decor is simple and the views of downtown rooftops are underwhelming, the high-quality tabletop accessories will inspire you to buy something in the nearby housewares department. Service is uneven, but has been improving with age as Viognier achieves distinction. The restaurant boasts an extensive wine list by the bottle and glass. Reservations recommended well in advance. • M-F 11:30am-3pm, 5:30-10pm; Sa-Su 11:30am-3pm, 5:30-10pm.

Vivace ★★★ $$ 1910 Ralston Ave. (Alameda de las Pulgas/Academy), Belmont, 650/637-0611. An always-bustling trattoria, packed with locals and people who drive from as far away as Half Moon Bay, all willing to wait for a table, even with a reservation. The menu doesn't break any new ground with such appetizers as bruschetta and carpaccio, the basic pizzas and pastas, the grilled rib eye with green peppercorn sauce, or the veal scaloppine with a mushroom cream sauce, but execution is consistently good and service attentive. The modest-sized dining room features modern trattoria decor: cherry-toned woods, terra-cotta sponge-painted walls, and an open kitchen (very similar to its sibling restaurant Ristorante Piacere in San Carlos). • M-F 11:30am-2:30pm, 5-10pm; Sa-Su 5-10pm.

Vung Tao ★★★ $ 535 E. Santa Clara St. (12th), San Jose, 408/288-9055. • 1750 N. Milpitas Blvd. (Dixon Landing), Milpitas, 408/934-9327. Recent Vietnamese immigrants and trendy South Bay diners converge at this nondescript restaurant featuring updated 1970s coffee shop decor and some of the best, most authentic Vietnamese food in the South Bay. The mostly Southern Vietnamese menu includes many exotic dishes unavailable at other restaurants; try the shrimp cupcake with fish sauce (don't be put off by the translation), the steamed vermicelli with grilled onion beef accompanied by a platter of vegetable condiments, or the rice with grilled lemongrass chicken. Unless you are a diehard fan of Vietnamese desserts, opt instead for a sweet slow-drip Vietnamese iced coffee. A word to the wise: bring a sweater; they crank the AC here. There can be a wait on weekends. A second location in Milpitas is more suburban. • SJ: Su-Th 9am-9pm; F-Sa 9am-10pm. • Milpitas: Daily 9am-9pm.

White Dove Café ★★ $$ 1167 Lincoln Ave. (Willow), San Jose, 408/280-5297. Simple and unpretentious, White Dove is an earthy alternative hangout that specializes in contemporary California cuisine with some eclectic, natural-food tendencies. Lovely seafood entrées showcase the kitchen's expertise. Sparkling fresh salads and innovative vegetable dishes add to the overall effect. There's a lively neighborhood bar just through the back exit of the restaurant, but the main dining room is serene, intimate, and overseen by caring staff. A good setting for a quiet, healthy, and delicious meal. • Daily 10am-9pm.

White Lotus ★ $ 80 N. Market St. (Santa Clara/St. John), San Jose, 408/977-0540. The menu at this Chinese restaurant sends mixed messages, proclaiming that "all food items are meatless" and yet listing dishes like spicy pork with lemongrass and meat loaf with shredded tofu over rice. But perplexed vegetarians can breathe easy: all the "meats" at White Lotus are merely substitutes fashioned from tofu, wheat gluten, and vegetables. Several more traditional dishes with no pretensions to animal origins will satisfy purists who object even to imitation flesh, and vegetarians who prefer meat-free diner food to meat-free Chinese food can enjoy the mock ham sandwiches and beef stew. The fish tank at the back is purely decorative. No alcohol. • Tu-F 11am-2:30pm, 5-9pm; Sa 11am-9:30pm; Su 11am-9pm.

White Rock Café ★★★ $$ 3116 Alum Rock Ave. (White), San Jose, 408/729-4843. Outside downtown San Jose on the way to Alum Rock Park, this tiny out-of-the-way bistro shines with the talents of a dazzling mother/daughter cooking team. The nightly prix fixe menu is the way to go here, since whatever the chef is interested in on a given evening will doubtless prove amazing. Opening courses of creative sushi can lead to perfect soups, generous salads, and entrées that seem to have come straight out of a Parisian café. On Friday nights the specials are especially interesting, and the straightforward service makes it a pleasure to linger. Worth looking for if you're heading east of downtown. Reservations preferred. • Tu-F 11:30am-2pm, 5-9pm; Sa 5-9pm.

Willow Street Wood Fired Pizza ★★ $ 1072 Willow St. (Lincoln), San Jose, 408/971-7080. • 20 S. Santa Cruz Ave. (Main), Los Gatos, 408/354-5566. Gourmet pizzas emerge from the roaring ovens at this bustling neighborhood dinner spot. Toppings include goat cheese and barbecued chicken, plus upscale versions of the basics, like plum tomatoes and basil. Pastas round out the offerings. Finish off your meal with an excellent *tiramisù*. • Su-Th 11:30am-10pm; F-Sa 11:30am-11pm.

Windy City Pizza ★ $ 35 Bovet Rd. (El Camino), San Mateo, 650/591-9457. Unbelievable deep-dish Chicago-style pizza, along with smoky barbecued ribs and hot links. Allow some time to choose from the zillions of toppings. There's even a dessert pizza with cream, chocolate, cheese, and fruit. Stick to the basics, though, for the most expert execution. Windy City offers a comfortable blue-collar atmosphere and the friendliest wait staff for miles. We advise passing on the free delivery, which can make for soggy pizza. • Su-Th 11am-10pm; F-Sa 11am-11pm.

Woodside Bakery and Café ★★ $/$$ 3052 Woodside Rd. (Cañada), Woodside, 650/851-7247. This is the neighborhood noshery for the Ralph Lauren set, serving the manicured and the muscular who ride their Beemer, hog, or steed to Cañada and Woodside roads. Fast-moving self-service and to-go lines at all hours confirm the reputation of the bakery's superior pastries and breads. From noon until night, the full-service restaurant stokes the wood-fired brick oven to produce mouthwatering focaccia and imaginatively concocted chewy crusted pizzas, along with Italian-influenced salads, creative pastas, and grilled fish, meat, or fowl main courses. The Californian-Mediterranean menu changes quarterly, and the chalkboard of specials changes with the market, but can't-miss favorites like the Parmesan-flavored Basegio Burger remain. Tuscan terra-cotta and marble decor inside and a dining patio outside bolster the casual but stylish scene. • Bakery: Daily 6am-6pm. Café: Su-W 11:30am-2:30pm, 5-9pm; Th-Sa 11:30am-2:30pm, 5-10pm.

Woodside Thai Spot ★★ $ 593 Woodside Rd. (Hudson), Redwood City, 650/365-4079. Despite the unpromising exterior (in a former life it could have been a biker bar), excellent, fiery Thai food served on white linen tablecloths is found within. *Tom kha gai*—hot-and-sour soup with chicken, lemongrass, and coconut milk—is a masterpiece. *Yum ta lay*—silver noodles with shrimp, chicken, red onion, peanuts, and chili in a lemon dressing—will have you calling the fire engines. • M-F 11:30am-2:30pm, 5-10pm; Sa-Su 5-10pm.

World Wrapps ★ $ 201 University Ave. (Emerson), Palo Alto, 650/327-9777. • 1318 Burlingame Ave. (Park/Primrose), Burlingame, 650/342-9777. The fresh-Mex scene faces serious competition from this rigorously international chain. World Wrapps' elaborate—some would say bizarre—variations on the homely burrito include enormous tomato, spinach, and low-fat tortillas holding mounds of rice (jasmine or Spanish), black beans (fat free is an option), exotic salsas (mango, red pepper and corn, or tomato basil), and multicultural fillings like curried vegetables or creole snapper. A nice addition for those who believe in maintaining burrito authenticity, you can order the fillings as salads or on rice instead of wrapped. The unlikely accompaniment to this fare is a selection of fruit smoothies laced, if you choose, with the usual assortment of healthy add-ins: wheat germ, bee pollen, and the like. A word to the wise: consider takeout during peak hours, when seating is scarce and the noise level is high. • PA: Daily 11am-11pm. • Burlingame: Daily 11am-10pm.

Yakko ★★★ $/$$ 975 W. Dana St. (Franklin), Mountain View, 650/960-0626. A high-intensity sushi scene attracts devoted locals, who thrill to the gorgeous fresh creations and creatively spiced hot entrées at this very popular Japanese eatery. The pace is brisk, the service fast, and the huge menu ranges from familiar classics to the exotic. The daily specials are terrific and the pulsating ambience makes this an upbeat dining experience in the heart of Silicon Valley. • M-F 11:30am-2pm, 5:30-9:30pm; Sa 5:30-9:30pm.

Yianni's ★★ $$ 224 Primrose Rd. (Burlingame/Howard), Burlingame, 650/347-2088. A taste of the Aegean just off the Avenue. Yianni's menu offers an extensive range of Greek dishes, from *spanakopitta* and *dolmas* to lamb chops with brandy sauce and sautéed calamari. For dessert, bypass the baklava in favor of the *galaktoboureco*, a citrus-tinged custard with a filo crust. The upscale suburban interior is done entirely in blue and white, Mykonos style. The service is gracious and attentive. • Tu-Th 11:30am-2:30pm, 5-9pm; F 11:30am-2:30pm, 5-10pm; Sa noon-3pm, 5-10pm; Su 5-9pm.

Yiassoo ★ ¢ 2180 S. Bascom Ave. (Campbell), Campbell, 408/559-0312. • 10660 S. De Anza Blvd. (Bollinger), Cupertino, 408/253-5544. • 2372 El Camino Real (San Tomas), Santa Clara, 408/983-1008. Greek grub at low prices. A few genuinely exotic dishes supplement the usual selection of gyros, *spanakopitta,* and the like. The blue-and-white-tiled interior is bright and clean, although a fast-food ambience prevails. Yiassoo is a fun spot for a quick meal—just don't expect to be transported to a Mediterranean isle. No credit cards at Cupertino and Santa Clara locations. • Daily 11am-9:30pm.

Zao ★ $ 261 University Ave. (Ramona/Bryant), Palo Alto, 650/328-1988. "Health and wisdom in a bowl" is the motto at this trendy Pan Asian noodle bar, which has captured the fancy of the novelty-craving Peninsula set. Noodles are available any which way: tossed in cool salads, sautéed, and served in broth, while the minimalist decor (think exposed concrete), affordable prices, and friendly service all add to the restaurant's appeal. Take a seat by the large open windows, order a noodle-wrapped crab cake to start, and watch the crowds pass by. Popular entrées include shrimp and seasonal vegetables served in a light soy-tamarind dressing with wheat noodles, and sesame-crusted salmon and buckwheat noodles in a miso broth. While many dishes soar, some verge on bland (the flavor is greatly enhanced by the *sriracha* and soy sauce available on each table). Tea aficionados will be charmed by the full-leaf teas served in French press pots. • Su-Th 11:30am-10pm; F-Sa 11:30am-10:30pm.

Zibibbo ★★ $$ 430 Kipling St. (University/Lytton), Palo Alto, 650/328-6722. Perhaps because the owners chose a tongue-twister of a name, many people still refer to Zibibbo as LuLu Palo Alto. And why not? Although the menu is not identical, when Jody Denton and Marc Valiani of Restaurant LuLu in San Francisco made their move south, they kept enough of LuLu's look and feel to earn the sobriquet: the sunny, yellow-and-blue Provençal color scheme, the rotisserie, the buzz of the crowd. Zibibbo—which is the Sicilian name for the Muscat grape—features dishes with a more pan-Mediterranean feel, freely adding elements of Spanish, Moroccan, and Italian cooking to LuLu favorites like iron skillet–roasted mussels and rosemary chicken. The restaurant is a stunning hodgepodge of dining areas, stretching nearly an entire block and mixing in a bar, open kitchen, courtyard patio, mezzanine, and more. While service can show some suburban amateurism, the food is usually San Francisco professional, making it one of bustling Palo Alto's better meals. • M-Th 11:30am-10:30pm; F 11:30am-11:30pm; Sa 9am-11:30pm; Su 9am-10:30pm.

CITY INDEX

BELMONT
Gin Mon ★★ $
Iron Gate ★★ $$$
The Vans ★★ $$$
Vivace Ristorante ★★★ $$

BURLINGAME
Alana's ★★ $
Brothers Delicatessen ★ $
Café La Scala ★★ $
Chicken! Chicken! ★ $
Copenhagen Bakery & Café ★ $
Ecco Café ★★ $$$
The Fisherman ★★ $$$
Grandview Restaurant ★★★ $$
Il Fornaio Cucina Italiana ★★ $$
Juban ★★ $$
Kincaid's ★★ $$$
Kuleto's Trattoria ★★ $$
Left at Albuquerque ★★★ $$
Max's Opera Café ★★ $$
Narin ★★ $
Ramen Club ★★ $
Stacks ★★ $
Steelhead (Burlingame Station)
   Brewing Company ★★ $$
Sushi Bar Jun ★★ $$
World Wrapps ★ $
Yianni's ★★ $$

CAMPBELL
Chez Sovan ★★ $
Golden Chopsticks ★★ $
Guido's ★ $
Kazoo ★★ $
Kirk's Restaurant ★ ¢
Left at Albuquerque ★★★ $
Mio Vicino ★★★ $$
Shebele Ethiopian ★★ ¢
Yiassoo ★ ¢

CUPERTINO
Azuma ★★ $$
Hamasushi ★★ $$
Hong Fu ★★ $
Kathmandu West ★ $
Miyake ★ $
Pizzeria Uno ★ $
Santa Barbara Grill ★★★ $$
Tung Kee Noodle House ★★ ¢
Yiassoo ★ ¢

FOSTER CITY
Tokie's ★★ $

LOS ALTOS
Akane ★★★ $$
Applewood Inn ★★ $
Bandera Restaurant ★★ $$$
The Butler's Pantry ★ $
Chef Chu's ★★ $
Hunan Home's ★★ $
I Fratelli ★★ $$$
Mandarin Classic ★★ $$
Royal Palace ★ $

LOS GATOS
Andalé Taqueria ★★ ¢
Café Marcella ★★★ $$
Café Trio ★★★ $$$
California Café ★★ $$$
The Cats ★ $$
Chart House ★★ $$$
Great Bear Café ★ $
I Gatti ★★ $$
Kamakura ★★★ $$
La Maison du Café ★★★ $$$
Los Gatos Brewing Co. ★★ $$
Mabel's Lantern House ★ $
Marbella ★★ $$
Mount Everest ★ $$
Pedro's Cabo Grill ★ $$
Pigalle ★★★ $$$
Siam Thai Cuisine ★★ $
Steamers ★★ $$
Valeriano's Ristorante ★★ $$
Willow Street Pizza ★★ $

MENLO PARK
Allied Arts Guild Restaurant ★ $
Applewood Inn ★★ $
Applewood Pizza 2 Go ★★ $
Café Borrone ★★ $
Carpaccio ★★ $$
Dal Baffo ★★ $$$$
Draeger's Bistro ★ $
Flea Street Café ★★★ $$$
Gambardella's ★★ $$
Gaylord India ★★ $$$
Gombei ★★ $
Juban ★★ $$
Late for the Train ★ $$
Le Pot au Feu ★★ $$$
Left Bank NR
Lisa's Tea Treasures ★★ $$
The Oasis ★ ¢
Scala Mia ★★ $$
Su Hong ★★ $
Su Hong Take-out ★ $
Trattoria Buon Gusto ★★ $$

MILLBRAE
Fook Yuen ★★★ $$
Hong Kong Flower ★★ $$
Thai Stick ★★ $

MILPITAS
Brandon's Restaurant ★★★ $$$
Pho Xe Lua ★ ¢
Vung Tao II ★★★ $

MOUNTAIN VIEW
Amarin Thai Cuisine ★★ $
Chez T.J. ★★★ $$$$
Country Gourmet ★ $
Don Giovanni ★★★ $$
El Calderon ★ $
Frankie Johnny and Luigi Too ★ $
Fu Lam Mum ★★ $
Garden Fresh ★★ $
Hangen ★★ $
Hobee's Restaurant ★★ $

Kamei Japanese House ★★ $
La Costeña ★★ $
La Fiesta ★★ $
Le Petit Bistro ★★ $$
Maharaja's ★★ $$
Mei Long ★★★ $$
Pho Xe Lua ★ ¢
Sono Sushi ★★ $
Sue's Indian Cuisine ★★ $$
Swagat ★★★ $$
Taqueria La Bamba ★★ ¢
Tony and Alba's Pizza ★ $
Tung Kee Noodle House ★★ ¢
Yakko ★★★ $

PALO ALTO
Andalé Taqueria ★★ ¢
Bangkok Cuisine ★★ $
Bistro Elan ★★★ $$$
Blue Chalk Café ★★★ $$
Buca di Beppo ★★ $$
Café Brioche ★★★ $$$
Café Pro Bono ★★ $$
Caffè Verona ★ $
California Café ★★ $$$
Chez Sophie ★★ $$$
Cho's ★ ¢
Crescent Park Grill ★★ $$$
Dinah's Poolside Café ★ $
Empire Grill ★★ $$$
Evvia ★★★ $$$
The Fish Market ★★ $$$
Fresco ★★ $$
Fresh Taste Mandarin ★★ $
Fuki-Sushi ★★ $$$
Gordon Biersch ★★ $$
Higashi West ★★★ $$$
Hobee's Restaurant ★★ $
Il Fornaio Cucina Italiana ★★ $$
Jing Jing ★ $
Joanie's Café ★ $
Kirk's Restaurant ★ ¢
L'Amie Donia ★★★ $$$
Left at Albuquerque ★★★ $
Little Garden ★ $
MacArthur Park ★★ $$$
Maddalena's ★★ $$$
Mango Café ★★ $
Max's Opera Café ★★ $$
Mike's Café Etc. ★★ $$
Ming's ★ $$
Miyake ★ $
Neiman Marcus ★★ $$
Nola Restaurant ★★ $$
Nouveau Trattoria ★★ $$$
Osteria ★★ $$
Palermo ★★ $$
Pasta? ★ $
Peninsula Fountain & Grill ★ $
Piatti ★★ $$
Pluto's ★★ ¢
Scott's Seafood ★ $$$
Spago Palo Alto ★★★ $$$
Spalti ★★ $$

St. Michael's Alley ★★ $$
Straits Café NR
Su Hong ★★ $
Sundance Mining Co. ★★ $$$
Sushi Ya ★★★ $
Szechuan Café ★★ $
Taxi's' Hamburgers ★ $
Tea Time ★ $
Thai City ★ $
Vicolo Pizzeria ★★ $
World Wrapps ★ $
Zao ★ $
Zibibbo ★★ $$

PORTOLA VALLEY
Iberia ★★ $$$

REDWOOD CITY
Bonsai Sushi ★★ $$
El Grullense E&E ★★ ¢
Estampas Peruanas ★★ $$
La Pachanga ★★ $
Las Parillas Restaurant ★ $$
Max's Café ★★ $$
MiMe's Café ★★ $
Redwood Café & Spice Co. ★★★ $
Stacks ★★ $
Thanh's Restaurant ★ $
2030 ★★ $$$
Woodside Thai Spot ★★ $

REDWOOD SHORES
Hobee's Restaurant ★★ $
Mistral ★★ $$

SAN CARLOS
Ciao Amore ★★ $$
The English Rose ★★ $
Ganko Sushi ★★ $
Kabul ★★ $$
Messina ★★ $$
Ristorante Piacere ★★ $$
Vic's ★ $

SAN JOSE
Agenda Restaurant ★★★ $$
Anh Hong ★★ $
Aqui Cal-Mex Grill ★★★ $
Bangkok Cuisine ★★ $
Bella Mia ★★ $$
Café Primavera ★ $
Caffè Goosetown ★★ $$
California Sushi and Grill ★★ $$
Casa Castillo ★ $
Casa Vicky ★ ¢
Chacho's ★★ $
Chez Sovan ★★ $
Cuban International ★ $$
Dac Phuc ★ ¢
840 North First ★★ $$$
Emile's ★★★ $$$$
Eulipia ★★★ $$$
Falafel Drive-In ★ ¢
The Fish Market ★★ $$$
Fuji ★ $
Garden City ★★ $$$

Germania at the Hochburg ★ $$
Gombei ★★ $
Gordon Biersch ★★ $$
Habana Cuba Restaurant ★★ $$
Henry's Hi-Life ★ $
Hobee's Restaurant ★★ $
Hunan Taste ★★ $
Il Fornaio Cucina Italiana ★★ $$
Inca Gardens ★★ $
Kazoo ★★ $
Kirk's Restaurant ★ ¢
Kitahama ★★ $$
Korea Buffet ★ $
Krung Thai ★★★ $
La Forêt ★★★ $$$$
La Pastaia ★★★ $$$
Le Papillon ★★★ $$$
Los Nicas ★ $$
Ocean Harbor ★★ $
Okoyama ★ $
Original Joe's ★★ $$
Orlo's ★★ $$$
Pagoda ★★ $$$
Palermo ★★ $$
Paolo's ★★★ $$$
Picasso's ★ $
Quang Da ★★ $
Race Street Seafood ★★ ¢
Red Sea Restaurant ★★ $
Rue de Paris ★★ $$$
Scott's Seafood ★ $$$
Señora Emma's ★ $
71 Saint Peter ★★ $$
Shamshiri ★★ $
Sousa's Restaurant ★ $$
Spiedo ★★ $$
Stratta ★★★ $$
Sue's Indian Cuisine ★★ $$
Suma Ching Hai Vegetarian
    House ★★ $
Super Taqueria ★ ¢
Taiwan Restaurant ★ $
Taxi's' Hamburgers ★ $
Thepthai ★★ $
Tony and Alba's Pizza ★ $
Tung Kee Noodle House ★★ ¢
Vaquero's ★★ $$
Vung Tao ★★★ $
White Dove Café ★★ $$
White Lotus ★ $
White Rock Café ★★★ $$
Willow Street Pizza ★★ $

SAN MATEO
Amici's East Coast Pizzeria ★★ $
Barley and Hopps ★★ $$
Bella Mangiata ★★ $$
Bogie's ★★ $$$
Bow Thai Café ★★ $
Buffalo Grill ★★ $$$
Capellini ★★ $$$
Chao Praya ★★ $
Clay Oven ★★ $$
The Fish Market ★★ $$$

Fuji Sukiyaki ★★★ $$
Gibson ★★ $$$
Giorgio's ★★ $$
Kaimuki Grill ★★ $
Kisaku ★★ $$
La Cumbre Taqueria ★★ ¢
Lark Creek Café ★★★ $$$
Luceti's ★★ $$
Nini's Coffee Shop ★★ $
Pasta Primavera Café ★★ $
Ritz Seafood ★★ $
Spiedo ★★ $$
Sushi Sam's ★★ $
Taxi's' Hamburgers ★ $
231 Ellsworth ★★★ $$$$
Viognier ★★★ $$$
Windy City Pizza ★ $

SANTA CLARA
Birk's ★★ $$$
California Café ★★ $$$
The Fish Market ★★ $$$
Kobe ★★ $$
Mio Vicino ★★★ $$
Pho Xe Lua ★ ¢
Pizzeria Uno ★ $
Roman's Deli ★★ $$
Su's Mongolian BBQ ★ ¢
Yiassoo ★ ¢

SARATOGA
Bella Saratoga ★★ $$
La Fondue ★★ $$
La Mere Michelle ★★ $$$$
Le Mouton Noir ★★★ $$$$
Mandarin Chef ★★ $
Sent Sovi ★★★ $$$$
Viaggio ★★ $$$

SOUTH SAN FRANCISCO
Basque Cultural Center ★★★ $$
JoAnn's Café ★★★ $
Pasta Moon ★★ $$

SUNNYVALE
Country Gourmet ★ $
Esperanza's Restaurant ★ $
Faultline Brewing Co. ★★ $$
Faz Sunnyvale ★★★ $$
Hobee's Restaurant ★★ $
Il Postale ★★ $$
Kabul ★★ $$
Lion & Compass ★★ $$$
Michael's ★★ $$$
The Palace ★★★ $$$
Sam Kee ★★ $$
Stoddard's Brewhouse ★★ $$

WOODSIDE
Bella Vista Restaurant ★★ $$$
Bucks ★★ $
John Bentley's ★★★ $$$
The Little Store ★ $
The Mountain House ★★ $$$
The Village Pub ★★ $$$$
Woodside Bakery & Café ★★ $

TYPES OF CUISINE

AFGHANI & NEPALESE
Kabul ★★ $$
Kathmandu West ★ $

AMERICAN
Agenda Restaurant ★★★ $$
Alana's ★★ $
Allied Arts Guild Restaurant ★ $
Bandera Restaurant ★★ $$$
Barley and Hopps ★★ $$
Birk's ★★ $$$
Blue Chalk Café ★★★ $$
Brothers Delicatessen ★ $
Bucks ★★ $
Buffalo Grill ★★ $$$
Café Marcella ★★★ $$
Café Primavera ★ $
The Cats ★ $$
Chart House ★★ $$$
Chicken! Chicken! ★ $
Copenhagen Bakery & Café ★ $
Country Gourmet ★ $
Crescent Park Grill ★★ $$$
Dinah's Poolside Café ★ $
Draeger's Bistro ★ $
Faultline Brewing Co. ★★ $$
The Fish Market ★★ $$$
The Fisherman ★★ $$$
Fresco ★★ $$
Garden City ★★ $$$
Guido's ★ $
Joanie's Café ★ $
JoAnn's Café ★★★ $
Kincaid's ★★ $$$
La Mere Michelle ★★ $$$$
Lark Creek Café ★★★ $$$
Late for the Train ★ $$
Left Bank NR
Los Gatos Brewing Co. ★★ $$
MacArthur Park ★★ $$$
Max's Opera Café ★★ $$
Michael's ★★ $$$
Mike's Café Etc. ★★ $$
MiMe's Café ★★ $
Neiman Marcus ★★ $$
Nini's Coffee Shop ★★ $
Nola Restaurant ★★ $$
Original Joe's ★★ $$
Orlo's ★★ $$$
Peninsula Fountain & Grill ★ $
Redwood Café & Spice Co. ★★★ $
Santa Barbara Grill ★★★ $$
71 Saint Peter ★★ $$
St. Michael's Alley ★★ $$
Stacks ★★ $
Steelhead (Burlingame Station)
   Brewing Company ★★ $$
Sundance Mining Co. ★★ $$$
The Vans ★★ $$$
Vic's ★ $

ASIAN
Su's Mongolian BBQ ★ ¢

Zao ★ $

BARBECUE
Barley and Hopps ★★ $$
The Cats ★ $$
Henry's Hi-Life ★ $
MacArthur Park ★★ $$$
Windy City Pizza ★ $

BASQUE
Basque Cultural Center ★★★ $$
Nouveau Trattoria ★★ $$$

BREW PUBS
Barley and Hopps ★★ $$
Faultline Brewing Co. ★★ $$
Gordon Biersch ★★ $$
Los Gatos Brewing Co. ★★ $$
Steelhead (Burlingame Station)
   Brewing Company ★★ $$
Stoddard's Brewhouse ★★ $$

BURGERS/PUB FOOD
Bucks ★★ $
Kirk's Restaurant ★ ¢
The Little Store ★ $
The Oasis ★ ¢
Taxis' Hamburgers ★ $
Vaquero's ★★ $$

CAFÉ
Café Borrone ★★ $
Café Brioche ★★★ $$$
Caffè Verona ★ $
Copenhagen Bakery & Café ★ $
Draeger's Bistro ★ $
Great Bear Café ★ $
The Little Store ★ $
MiMe's Café ★★ $
Neiman Marcus ★★ $$
Pluto's ★★ ¢
Tea Time ★ $
White Dove Café ★★ $$
Woodside Bakery & Café ★★ $

CALIFORNIA/FUSION
Aqui Cal-Mex Grill ★★★ $
Bistro Elan ★★★ $$$
Brandon's Restaurant ★★★ $$$
Café Trio ★★★ $$$
California Café ★★ $$$
Chez T.J. ★★★ $$$$
840 North First ★★ $$$
Empire Grill ★★ $$$
Eulipia ★★★ $$$
Flea Street Café ★★ $$$
Gibson ★★ $$$
Gordon Biersch ★★ $$
Higashi West ★★★ $$$
John Bentley's ★★★ $$$
Lion & Compass ★★ $$$
Mistral ★★ $$
The Palace ★★★ $$$
Spago Palo Alto ★★★ $$$
Stoddard's Brewhouse ★★ $$
2030 ★★ $$$
231 Ellsworth ★★★ $$$$

The Village Pub ★★ $$$$
Viognier ★★★ $$$
Woodside Bakery & Café ★★ $
World Wrapps ★ $

CAMBODIAN
Chez Sovan ★★ $

CARIBBEAN
Chicken! Chicken! ★ $
Cuban International ★ $$
Habana Cuba Restaurant ★★ $$
Mango Café ★★ $

CHINESE
Chef Chu's ★★ $
Cho's ★ ¢
Fook Yuen ★★★ $$
Fresh Taste Mandarin ★★ $
Fu Lam Mum ★★ $
Garden Fresh ★★ $
Gin Mon ★★ $
Grandview Restaurant ★★★ $$
Hangen ★★ $
Hong Fu ★★ $
Hong Kong Flower ★★ $$
Hunan Home's ★★ $
Hunan Taste ★★ $
Jing Jing ★ $
Mabel's Lantern House ★ $
Mandarin Chef ★★ $
Mandarin Classic ★★ $$
Mei Long ★★★ $$
Ming's ★ $$
Ocean Harbor ★★ $
Pagoda ★★ $$$
Ritz Seafood ★★ $
Royal Palace ★ $
Sam Kee ★★ $$
Su Hong ★★ $
Su's Mongolian BBQ ★ ¢
Szechuan Café ★★ $
Taiwan Restaurant ★ $
Tung Kee Noodle House ★★ ¢
White Lotus ★ $
Zao ★ $

CONTINENTAL
Bella Vista Restaurant ★★ $$$
Bogie's ★★ $$$
Copenhagen Bakery & Café ★ $
Dal Baffo ★★ $$$$
Ecco Café ★★ $$$
Iron Gate ★★ $$$
La Mere Michelle ★★ $$$$
Maddalena's ★★ $$$
The Mountain House ★★ $$$
Paolo's ★★★ $$$
The Vans ★★ $$$

DELI
Brothers Delicatessen ★ $
Max's Opera Café ★★ $$
Roman's Deli ★★ $$

ENGLISH & TEA
The Butler's Pantry ★ $

The English Rose ★★ $
Lisa's Tea Treasures ★★ $$

ETHIOPIAN/ERITREAN
Red Sea Restaurant ★★ $
Shebele Ethiopian ★★ ¢

GERMAN
Germania at the Hochburg ★ $$

FRENCH
Basque Cultural Center ★★★ $$
Bistro Elan ★★★ $$$
Café Brioche ★★★ $$$
Chez Sophie ★★ $$$
Chez T.J. ★★★ $$$$
Emile's ★★★ $$$$
Iron Gate ★★ $$$
L'Amie Donia ★★★ $$$
La Forêt ★★★ $$$$
La Maison du Café ★★★ $$$
Le Mouton Noir ★★★ $$$$
Le Papillon ★★★ $$$
Le Petit Bistro ★★ $$
Le Pot au Feu ★★ $$$
Nouveau Trattoria ★★ $$$
Pigalle ★★★ $$$
Rue de Paris ★★ $$$
Sent Sovi ★★★ $$$$
White Rock Café ★★★ $$
Zibibbo ★★ $$

GREEK
Evvia ★★★ $$$
Giorgio's ★★ $$
Yianni's ★★ $$
Yiassoo ★ ¢

HEALTHY
Aqui Cal-Mex Grill ★★★ $
Country Gourmet ★ $
Flea Street Café ★★ $$$
Hobee's Restaurant ★★ $
Late for the Train ★ $$

INDIAN
Clay Oven ★★ $$
Gaylord India ★★ $$$
Maharaja's ★★ $$
Mount Everest ★ $$
Sue's Indian Cuisine ★★ $$
Swagat ★★★ $$

ITALIAN
Bella Mangiata ★★ $$
Bella Mia ★★ $$
Bella Saratoga ★★ $$
Buca di Beppo ★★ $$
Café La Scala ★★ $$
Café Primavera ★ $
Café Pro Bono ★★ $$
Caffè Goosetown ★★ $$
Capellini ★★ $$$
Carpaccio ★★ $$
Ciao Amore ★★ $$
Dal Baffo ★★ $$$$
Don Giovanni ★★★ $$
840 North First ★★ $$$

Frankie Johnny and Luigi Too ★ $
Gambardella's ★★ $$
Guido's ★ $
I Fratelli ★★ $$$
I Gatti ★★ $$
Il Fornaio Cucina Italiana ★★ $$
Il Postale ★★ $$
Kuleto's Trattoria ★★ $$
La Pastaia ★★★ $$$
Luceti's ★★ $$
Messina ★★ $$
Mio Vicino ★★★ $$
Nouveau Trattoria ★★ $$$
Original Joe's ★★ $$
Osteria ★★ $$
Palermo ★★ $$
Paolo's ★★★ $$$
Pasta? ★ $
Pasta Moon ★★ $$
Pasta Primavera Café ★★ $
Piatti ★★ $$
Pizzeria Uno ★ $
Ristorante Piacere ★★ $$
Roman's Deli ★★ $$
Scala Mia ★★ $$
Spalti ★★ $$
Spiedo ★★ $$
Stratta ★★ $$
Trattoria Buon Gusto ★★ $$
Valeriano's Ristorante ★★ $$
Viaggio ★★ $$$
Vivace Ristorante ★★★ $$
Zibibbo ★★ $$

JAPANESE
Akane ★★★ $$
Azuma ★★ $$
Bonsai Sushi ★★ $$
California Sushi and Grill ★★ $$
Fuji ★ $
Fuji Sukiyaki ★★★ $$
Fuki-Sushi ★★ $$$
Ganko Sushi ★★ $
Gombei ★★ $
Hamasushi ★★ $$
Higashi West ★★★ $$$
Juban ★★ $$
Kaimuki Grill ★★ $
Kamakura ★★★ $$
Kamei Japanese House ★★ $
Kazoo ★★ $
Kisaku ★★ $$
Kitahama ★★ $$
Kobe ★★ $$
Miyake ★ $
Okoyama ★ $
Ramen Club ★★ $
Sono Sushi ★★ $
Sushi Bar Jun ★★ $$
Sushi Sam's ★★ $
Sushi Ya ★★★ $
Tokie's ★★ $
Yakko ★★★ $
Zao ★ $

KOREAN
Juban ★★ $$
Korea Buffet ★ $

LATIN AMERICAN/ MEXICAN
Andalé Taqueria ★★ ¢
Aqui Cal-Mex Grill ★★★ $
Casa Castillo ★ $
Casa Vicky ★ ¢
Chacho's ★★ $
El Calderon ★ $
El Grullense E&E ★★ ¢
Esperanza's Restaurant ★ $
Estampas Peruanas ★★ $$
Inca Gardens ★★ $
La Costeña ★★ $
La Cumbre Taqueria ★★ ¢
La Fiesta ★★ $
La Pachanga ★★ $
Las Parillas Restaurant ★ $$
Left at Albuquerque ★★★ $
Los Nicas ★ $$
Pedro's Cabo Grill ★ $$
Señora Emma's ★ $
Super Taqueria ★ ¢
Taqueria La Bamba ★★ ¢

MEDITERRANEAN
Brandon's Restaurant ★★★ $$$
Crescent Park Grill ★★ $$$
Marbella ★★ $$
Orlo's ★★ $$$
Zibibbo ★★ $$

MIDDLE EASTERN
Falafel Drive-In ★ ¢
Faz Sunnyvale ★★★ $$
Kabul ★★ $$
Kathmandu West ★ $
Shamshiri ★★ $

OTHER
La Fondue ★★ $$
Left at Albuquerque ★★★ $
Su's Mongolian BBQ ★ ¢
World Wrapps ★ $

PIZZA
Amici's East Coast Pizzeria ★★ $
Applewood Inn ★★ $
Café Marcella ★★★ $$
Frankie Johnny and Luigi Too ★ $
Giorgio's ★★ $$
Guido's ★ $
Il Fornaio Cucina Italiana ★★ $$
Los Gatos Brewing Co. ★★ $$
MiMe's Café ★★ $
Mistral ★★ $$
The Oasis ★ ¢
Pizzeria Uno ★ $
Spiedo ★★ $$
Tony and Alba's Pizza ★ $
Valeriano's Ristorante ★★ $$
Vicolo Pizzeria ★★ $
Willow Street Pizza ★★ $

Windy City Pizza ★ $
Woodside Bakery & Café ★★ $

PORTUGUESE
Sousa's Restaurant ★ $$

SEAFOOD
Chart House ★★ $$$
The Fish Market ★★ $$$
The Fisherman ★★ $$$
Fook Yuen ★★★ $$
Fu Lam Mum ★★ $
Hong Fu ★★ $
Hong Kong Flower ★★ $$
Kincaid's ★★ $$$
Michael's ★★ $$$
Ocean Harbor ★★ $
Race Street Seafood ★★ ¢
Ritz Seafood ★★ $
Scott's Seafood ★ $$$
Steamers ★★ $$

SINGAPOREAN
Straits Café NR

SPANISH
Iberia ★★ $$$
Picasso's ★ $

STEAK, RIBS, & CHOPS
Garden City ★★ $$$
Original Joe's ★★ $$
Sundance Mining Co. ★★ $$$
Vaquero's ★★ $$

THAI
Amarin Thai Cuisine ★★ $
Bangkok Cuisine ★★ $
Bow Thai Café ★★ $
Chao Praya ★★ $
Krung Thai ★★★ $
Narin ★★ $
Siam Thai Cuisine ★★ $
Thai City ★ $
Thai Stick ★★ $
Thepthai ★★ $
Woodside Thai Spot ★★ $

VEGETARIAN
Amarin Thai Cuisine ★★ $
Garden Fresh ★★ $
Kathmandu West ★ $
Late for the Train ★ $$
Pluto's ★★ ¢
Red Sea Restaurant ★★ $
Suma Ching Hai Vegetarian
    House ★★ $
White Lotus ★ $

VIETNAMESE
Anh Hong ★★ $
Dac Phuc ★ ¢
Golden Chopsticks ★★ $
Little Garden ★ $
Pho Xe Lua ★ ¢
Quang Da ★★ $
Thanh's Restaurant ★ $
Tung Kee Noodle House ★★ ¢
Vung Tao ★★★ $

SPECIAL FEATURES

OPEN FOR BREAKFAST/ BRUNCH
Alana's ★★ $
Andalé Taqueria ★★ ¢
Bella Mia ★★ $$
Bella Saratoga ★★ $$
Brandon's Restaurant ★★★ $$$
Brothers Delicatessen ★ $
Bucks ★★ $
Buffalo Grill ★★ $$$
Café Primavera ★ $
Caffè Verona ★ $
California Café ★★ $$$
Casa Castillo ★ $
Casa Vicky ★ ¢
The Cats ★ $$
Copenhagen Bakery & Café ★ $
Country Gourmet ★ $
Dinah's Poolside Café ★ $
Draeger's Bistro ★ $
Empire Grill ★★ $$$
The English Rose ★★ $
Falafel Drive-In ★ ¢
Faz Sunnyvale ★★★ $$
Flea Street Café ★★ $$$
Fresco ★★ $$
Great Bear Café ★ $
Guido's ★ $
Hobee's Restaurant ★★ $
Il Fornaio Cucina Italiana ★★ $$
Joanie's Café ★ $
JoAnn's Café ★★★ $
La Costeña ★★ $
La Forêt ★★★ $$$$
La Maison du Café ★★★ $$$
La Mere Michelle ★★ $$$$
La Pachanga ★★ $
Lark Creek Café ★★★ $$$
Las Parillas Restaurant ★ $$
Late for the Train ★ $$
MacArthur Park ★★ $$$
Max's Opera Café ★★ $$
Mike's Café Etc. ★★ $$
MiMe's Café ★ $
Nini's Coffee Shop ★★ $
Peninsula Fountain & Grill ★ $
Pho Xe Lua ★ ¢
Pigalle ★★★ $$$
Quang Da ★★ $
Redwood Café & Spice Co. ★★★ $
Roman's Deli ★★ $$
Sam Kee ★★ $$
St. Michael's Alley ★★ $$
Stacks ★★ $
Super Taqueria ★ ¢
Taxi's' Hamburgers ★ $
Tung Kee Noodle House ★★ ¢
The Vans ★★ $$$
Vic's ★ $
Vung Tao ★★★ $
White Dove Café ★★ $$

Zibibbo ★★ $$

BUSINESS MEALS
Agenda Restaurant ★★★ $$
Azuma ★★ $$
Barley and Hopps ★★ $$
Bella Mia ★★ $$
Bella Vista Restaurant ★★ $$$
Birk's ★★ $$
Bistro Elan ★★★ $$$
Blue Chalk Café ★★★ $$
Bucks ★★ $
Buffalo Grill ★★ $$$
Café Trio ★★★ $$$
California Café ★★ $$$
Capellini ★★ $$$
Carpaccio ★★ $$
Chart House ★★ $$$
Chef Chu's ★★ $
Chez T.J. ★★★ $$$$
Crescent Park Grill ★★ $$$
Dal Baffo ★★ $$$$
Ecco Café ★★ $$$
840 North First ★★ $$$
Emile's ★★★ $$$$
Eulipia ★★★ $$$
Evvia ★★★ $$$
Faz Sunnyvale ★★★ $$
The Fish Market ★★ $$$
The Fisherman ★★ $$$
Gaylord India ★★ $$$
Gibson ★★ $$$
Gombei ★★ $
Gordon Biersch ★★ $$
Hamasushi ★★ $$
Hobee's Restaurant ★★ $
Hong Fu ★★ $
Iron Gate ★★ $$$
John Bentley's ★★★ $$$
Juban ★★ $$
Kabul ★★ $$
Kincaid's ★★ $$$
Kisaku ★★ $$
Kitahama ★★ $$
Kobe ★★ $$
Kuleto's Trattoria ★★ $$
La Mere Michelle ★★ $$$$
La Pastaia ★★★ $$$
Lark Creek Café ★★★ $$$
Le Papillon ★★★ $$$
Left at Albuquerque ★★★ $
Lion & Compass ★★ $$$
Los Gatos Brewing Co. ★★ $$
MacArthur Park ★★ $$$
Maddalena's ★★ $$
Mandarin Classic ★★ $$
Max's Opera Café ★★ $$
Michael's ★★ $$$
MiMe's Café ★★ $
Ming's ★ $$
Mistral ★★ $$
Neiman Marcus ★★ $$
Nouveau Trattoria ★★ $$$
Pagoda ★★ $$$

Paolo's ★★★ $$$
Pasta Primavera Café ★★ $
Pedro's Cabo Grill ★ $$
Piatti ★★ $$
Ristorante Piacere ★★ $$
Ritz Seafood ★★ $
Scott's Seafood ★ $$$
71 Saint Peter ★★ $$
Shamshiri ★★ $
Spago Palo Alto ★★★ $$$
Spiedo ★★ $$
Stoddard's Brewhouse ★★ $$
Stratta ★★★ $$
Su Hong ★★ $
Sundance Mining Co. ★★ $$$
Szechuan Café ★★ $
Thai Stick ★★ $
Tokie's ★★ $
2030 ★★ $$$
231 Ellsworth ★★★ $$$$
Valeriano's Ristorante ★★ $$
The Village Pub ★★ $$$$
Viognier ★★★ $$$
Zibibbo ★★ $$

CHILDREN FRIENDLY

Allied Arts Guild Restaurant ★ $
Amarin Thai Cuisine ★★ $
Amici's East Coast Pizzeria ★★ $
Andalé Taqueria ★★ ¢
Anh Hong ★★ $
Applewood Inn ★★ $
Aqui Cal-Mex Grill ★★★ $
Azuma ★★ $$
Bandera Restaurant ★★ $$$
Bella Mangiata ★★ $$
Bella Mia ★★ $$
Bow Thai Café ★★ $
Brothers Delicatessen ★ $
Buca di Beppo ★★ $$
Buffalo Grill ★★ $$$
The Butler's Pantry ★ $
Café Borrone ★★ $
Café Primavera ★ $
Casa Castillo ★ $
Casa Vicky ★ ¢
Chacho's ★★ $
Chao Praya ★★ $
Chart House ★★ $$$
Chef Chu's ★★ $
Chicken! Chicken! ★ $
Copenhagen Bakery & Café ★ $
Dinah's Poolside Café ★ $
Draeger's Bistro ★ $
El Calderon ★ $
El Grullense E&E ★★ ¢
Esperanza's Restaurant ★ $
Estampas Peruanas ★★ $$
The Fish Market ★★ $$$
Fook Yuen ★★★ $$
Frankie Johnny and Luigi Too ★ $
Fresco ★★ $$
Fresh Taste Mandarin ★★ $
Fu Lam Mum ★★ $

Gin Mon ★★ $
Giorgio's ★★ $$
Gombei ★★ $
Grandview Restaurant ★★★ $$
Great Bear Café ★ $
Habana Cuba Restaurant ★★ $$
Hangen ★★ $
Hobee's Restaurant ★★ $
Hong Fu ★★ $
Hong Kong Flower ★★ $$
Hunan Home's ★★ $
Il Postale ★★ $$
Inca Gardens ★★ $
Jing Jing ★ $
Joanie's Café ★ $
Kamei Japanese House ★★ $
Kirk's Restaurant ★ ¢
Kisaku ★★ $$
Kuleto's Trattoria ★★ $$
La Cumbre Taqueria ★★ ¢
La Pachanga ★★ $
Las Parillas Restaurant ★ $$
Lisa's Tea Treasures ★★ $$
Little Garden ★ $
The Little Store ★ $
Mabel's Lantern House ★ $
MacArthur Park ★★ $$$
Marbella ★★ $$
Max's Opera Café ★★ $$
Mike's Café Etc. ★★ $$
MiMe's Café ★★ $
Ming's ★ $$
Nini's Coffee Shop ★★ $
Ocean Harbor ★★ $
Pasta Primavera Café ★★ $
Pedro's Cabo Grill ★ $$
Peninsula Fountain & Grill ★ $
Pho Xe Lua ★ ¢
Pizzeria Uno ★ $
Quang Da ★★ $
Race Street Seafood ★★ ¢
Redwood Café & Spice Co. ★★★ $
Ritz Seafood ★★ $
Royal Palace ★ $
Sam Kee ★★ $$
Señora Emma's ★ $
Sono Sushi ★★ $
Spalti ★★ $$
Stacks ★★ $
Su Hong ★★ $
Su's Mongolian BBQ ★ ¢
Super Taqueria ★ ¢
Sushi Bar Jun ★★ $$
Swagat ★★★ $$
Szechuan Café ★★ $
Taiwan Restaurant ★ $
Taqueria La Bamba ★★ ¢
Taxi's' Hamburgers ★ $
Thai City ★ $
Thai Stick ★★ $
Thanh's Restaurant ★ $
Tony and Alba's Pizza ★ $
Trattoria Buon Gusto ★★ $$

Tung Kee Noodle House ★★ ¢
Vic's ★ $
Vicolo Pizzeria ★★ $
Vung Tao ★★★ $
Willow Street Pizza ★★ $
World Wrapps ★ $
Yiassoo ★ ¢
Zao ★ $

OPEN LATE (AFTER pm)

Agenda Restaurant ★★★ $$
Amici's East Coast Pizzeria ★★ $
Andalé Taqueria ★★ ¢
Anh Hong ★★ $
Barley and Hopps ★★ $$
Birk's ★★ $$$
Brandon's Restaurant ★★★ $$$
Buca di Beppo ★★ $$
Café Borrone ★★ $
Café La Scala ★★ $$
Café Marcella ★★★ $$
Caffè Verona ★ $
The Cats ★ $$
Chacho's ★★ $
Crescent Park Grill ★★ $$$
Cuban International ★ $$
Don Giovanni ★★★ $$
El Grullense E&E ★★ ¢
Evvia ★★★ $$$
Faultline Brewing Co. ★★ $$
Frankie Johnny and Luigi Too ★ $
Fresco ★★ $$
Fu Lam Mum ★★ $
Garden City ★★ $$$
Gibson ★★ $$$
Giorgio's ★★ $$
Gordon Biersch ★★ $$
Great Bear Café ★ $
Guido's ★ $
Hamasushi ★★ $$
Il Fornaio Cucina Italiana ★★ $$
Il Postale ★★ $$
Iron Gate ★★ $$$
Kamakura ★★★ $$
Kincaid's ★★ $$$
Kitahama ★★ $$
Kuleto's Trattoria ★★ $$
L'Amie Donia ★★★ $$$
La Fondue ★★ $$
La Pachanga ★★ $
La Pastaia ★★★ $$$
Left at Albuquerque ★★★ $
Los Gatos Brewing Co. ★★ $$
Luceti's ★★ $$
MacArthur Park ★★ $$$
Max's Opera Café ★★ $$
Messina ★★ $$
Michael's ★★ $$$
Mio Vicino ★★★ $$
Nola Restaurant ★★ $$
The Oasis ★ ¢
Original Joe's ★★ $$

PENINSULA & SILICON VALLEY RESTAURANTS

Pasta? ★ $
Peninsula Fountain & Grill ★ $
Piatti ★★ $$
Pizzeria Uno ★ $
Pluto's ★★ ¢
Rue de Paris ★★ $$$
Señora Emma's ★ $
Shebele Ethiopian ★★ ¢
Steamers ★★ $$
Sundance Mining Co. ★★ $$$$
Taxi's' Hamburgers ★ $
Valeriano's Ristorante ★★ $$
The Vans ★★ $$$
Vaquero's ★ $
Willow Street Pizza ★★ $
Windy City Pizza ★ $
World Wrapps ★ $
Zao ★ $
Zibibbo ★★ $$

OUTDOOR SEATING
Akane ★★★ $$
Allied Arts Guild Restaurant ★ $
Aqui Cal-Mex Grill ★★★ $
Bella Mangiata ★★ $$
Bella Mia ★★ $$
Bella Saratoga ★★ $$
Bistro Elan ★★★ $$$
Blue Chalk Café ★★★ $$$
Brandon's Restaurant ★★★ $$$
Café Borrone ★★ $
Café La Scala ★★ $$
Café Primavera ★ $
Café Trio ★★★ $$$
Caffè Goosetown ★★ $$
Caffè Verona ★ $
California Café ★★ $$$
Casa Castillo ★ $
Casa Vicky ★ ¢
Chicken! Chicken! ★ $
Country Gourmet ★ $
Crescent Park Grill ★★ $$$
Dinah's Poolside Café ★ $
Don Giovanni ★★★ $$
Empire Grill ★★ $$$
Esperanza's Restaurant ★ $
Falafel Drive-In ★ ¢
The Fish Market ★★ $$$
Flea Street Café ★★ $$$
Germania at the Hochburg ★ $$
Gibson ★★ $$$
Grandview Restaurant ★★★ $$
Guido's ★ $
Iberia ★★ $$$
Il Fornaio Cucina Italiana ★★ $$
Il Postale ★★ $$
Joanie's Café ★ $
John Bentley's ★★★ $$$
Kirk's Restaurant ★ ¢
L'Amie Donia ★★★ $$$
La Cumbre Taqueria ★★ ¢
La Mere Michelle ★★ $$$$
La Pastaia ★★★ $$$
Late for the Train ★ $$

Le Mouton Noir ★★★ $$$$
Le Pot au Feu ★★ $$$
Lion & Compass ★★ $$$
The Little Store ★ $
MacArthur Park ★★ $$$
Marbella ★★ $$
Mike's Café Etc. ★★ $$
MiMe's Café ★★ $
Mistral ★★ $
The Mountain House ★★ $$$
Nini's Coffee Shop ★★ $
Nola Restaurant ★★ $$
Nouveau Trattoria ★★ $$$
The Oasis ★ ¢
Orlo's ★★ $$$
Palermo ★★ $$
Paolo's ★★★ $$$
Pasta? ★ $
Pasta Primavera Café ★★ $
Piatti ★★ $$
Pizzeria Uno ★ $
Pluto's ★★ ¢
Red Sea Restaurant ★★ $
Redwood Café and Spice Co.
　★★★ $
Ristorante Piacere ★★ $$
Roman's Deli ★★ $$
Santa Barbara Grill ★★★ $$
Scott's Seafood ★ $$$
Señora Emma's ★ $
Sent Sovi ★★★ $$$$
71 Saint Peter ★★ $$
Spago Palo Alto ★★★ $$$
Spalti ★★ $$
Stacks ★★ $
Steamers ★★ $$
Steelhead (Burlingame Station)
　Brewing Company ★★ $$
Stoddard's Brewhouse ★★ $$
Taxi's' Hamburgers ★ $
Tony and Alba's Pizza ★ $
2030 ★★ $$$
Vaquero's ★★ $$
Viaggio ★★ $$$
Vicolo Pizzeria ★★ $
Willow Street Pizza ★★ $
Woodside Bakery & Café ★★ $
Zibibbo ★★ $$

ROMANTIC
Allied Arts Guild Restaurant ★ $
Basque Cultural Center ★★★ $$
Bella Mia ★★ $$
Bella Saratoga ★★ $$
Bella Vista Restaurant ★★ $$$
Bogie's ★★ $$$
Brandon's Restaurant ★★★ $$$
The Butler's Pantry ★ $
Café Brioche ★★★ $$$
Café Pro Bono ★★ $$
Caffè Goosetown ★★ $$
California Sushi and Grill ★★ $$
Capellini ★★ $$$
Chez Sophie ★★ $$$

Chez T.J. ★★★ $$$$
Don Giovanni ★★★ $$
Emile's ★★★ $$$$
Empire Grill ★★ $$$
The English Rose ★★ $
Faz Sunnyvale ★★★ $$$
Flea Street Café ★★ $$$
Gambardella's ★★ $$
Gibson ★★ $$$
Hamasushi ★★ $$
I Gatti ★★ $$
Iberia ★★ $$$
Il Fornaio Cucina Italiana ★★ $$
Iron Gate ★★ $$$
John Bentley's ★★★ $$$
Kabul ★★ $$
Kamei Japanese House ★★ $
Kitahama ★★ $$
L'Amie Donia ★★★ $$$
La Fondue ★★ $$
La Forêt ★★★ $$$$
La Maison du Café ★★★ $$$
La Pastaia ★★★ $$$
Le Mouton Noir ★★★ $$$$
Le Papillon ★★★ $$$
Le Petit Bistro ★★ $$
Le Pot au Feu ★★ $$$
Lisa's Tea Treasures ★★ $$
Mandarin Classic ★★ $$
Mei Long ★★★ $$
Michael's ★★ $$$
The Mountain House ★★ $$$
Narin ★★ $
Nouveau Trattoria ★★ $$$
Orlo's ★★ $$$
The Palace ★★★ $$$
Pasta Moon ★★ $$
Pigalle ★★★ $$$
Redwood Café & Spice Co. ★★★ $
Ristorante Piacere ★★ $$
Rue de Paris ★★ $$$
Santa Barbara Grill ★★★ $$
Sent Sovi ★★★ $$$$
71 Saint Peter ★★ $$
Spago Palo Alto ★★★ $$$
Spalti ★★ $$
Stratta ★★★ $$
231 Ellsworth ★★★ $$$$
The Vans ★★ $$$
Viaggio ★★ $$$
Vivace Ristorante ★★★ $$

VIEWS
Bella Vista Restaurant ★★ $$$
Chart House ★★ $$$
The Fisherman ★★ $$$
Kincaid's ★★ $$$
La Forêt ★★★ $$$$
Mistral ★★ $$
The Mountain House ★★ $$$
Pasta Moon ★★ $$
The Vans ★★ $$$

Sights & Attractions

SIGHTSEEING

In general, the Peninsula and San Jose lack the famous tourist destinations San Francisco offers. Most of this book is filled with interesting and exciting activities, from highbrow arts to lowbrow amusements, from bars to sports. But for those hard-to-please guests who want real tourist attractions, the kind that come with colorful brochures and their own postcards, we've compiled the following list. Even hardened locals might be surprised to discover something new here.

Chinese Cultural Gardens: Overfelt Park, McKee Rd. and Educational Park Dr., San Jose, 408/251-3323, 408/27-PARKS (277-2757). Linking to Tainan, Taiwan, one of four San Jose sister cities, this garden is guarded by a large, ornamental Friendship Gate. A 30-foot statue of Confucius by a reflective pond, a memorial, and pavilions are among the nongreen attractions. • 10am-sunset. Free.

Fallon House: 175 W. St. John St. (San Pedro), San Jose, 408/993-8182. Enclosed by a beige picket fence, this 15-room pre–Civil War home belonged to one of San Jose's earliest mayors. A brick path winds through a quaint garden, and the Victorian-style rooms are luxuriously decorated. • Tu-Su 11am-3:15pm. $6 general, $5 seniors, $3 children 6-17, children under 6 free. Includes tour of both Fallon House and Peralta Adobe (see below).

Filoli House and Gardens: Cañada Rd., Woodside, 650/364-2880. Built as a country retreat by San Francisco silver magnate William B. Bourn, Filoli (as in "To **FI**ght, to **LO**ve, to **LI**ve") became famous as the mansion in the opening shot of the 1980s television series "Dynasty." Designed by well-known San Francisco architect Willis Polk and completed in 1917, the clematis-draped brick building was deeded to the National Trust for Historic Preservation in 1975. Guided and self-guided tours of the 43-room mansion on its 654-acre estate allow you to roam through the house and linger in the various grand salons. The gardens, now reaching maturity, are laid out as a succession of "rooms," each having its own design and personality. Throughout the seasons, the plantings provide an ever-changing palette of brilliant color nestled against the Santa Cruz Mountains. • Guided tours by reservation Tu-Th at 9:30am, 11:30am, and 1:30pm. Self-guided tours (no reservation required) F-Sa 10am-2pm. $10 adults, $1 children under 12.

The Flea Market: 1590 Berryessa Rd. (Hwy 101/King), San Jose, 408/453-1110. With 120 acres of bargains, international food operations, and unusual sights and sounds (and maybe smells), this is a flea market, carnival, and foreign bazaar all rolled into one. Stroll past as many as 2,700 vendors, a quarter-mile long row of farm-fresh produce, and 35 restaurants. After the live entertainment, auctions, arcade, and antique merry-go-round, take advantage of the tree-shaded parks. Don't forget to show off your bartering prowess (or at least try it out). • W-Su 7:30am-5pm. Parking: $1 weekdays, $3 weekends.

Japanese Friendship Gardens: Kelley Park, 1300 Senter Rd. (Keyes), San Jose, 408/295-8383, 408/277-5254. Modeled after the Korakuen Gardens of Okayama, San Jose's sister city, here you'll find a serene and rather exotic setting. Don't miss the rare koi (carp) in four heart-shaped lakes. Wander down paths that pass knolls and ponds; visit the foot bridges and moon bridge. • Daily 10am-sunset. Free.

Lick Observatory: Mount Hamilton Rd. (off Alum Rock Rd.), San Jose, 408/274-5061. The observatory was created over 100 years ago by James Lick, a millionaire obsessed with the idea of life on the moon and intent on gathering his own proof. After San Francisco rejected his plans, he built the observatory on Mount Hamilton. It takes about an hour by car to climb the windy road to the observatory, but the guided tours of the telescopes and their views are quite interesting. • M-F 12:30pm-5pm; Sa-Su 10am-5pm. Free. Guided tours every half hour until 4:30pm.

Municipal Rose Garden: Corner of Naglee and Dana aves., San Jose, 408/277-4191, 408/27-PARKS (7-2757). As "San Jose's Pride and Joy," this six-acre ocean of roses has been a treat for the senses since 1937. With more than 189 varieties and 3,500 shrubs, new blossoms pop up every six to eight weeks. • Daily 8am-sunset.

NASA/Ames Research Center: Moffett Field (off Hwy 101), Mountain View, 650/604-6497, 650/604-5000. With 430 acres, Ames is one of NASA's major aeronautical research facilities. Tour the field laboratory and see a wind tunnel, a gigantic flight hangar (big enough for a dirigible), and a flight simulator laboratory. The two-hour tour covers about two miles. • Tours by reservation only, M-F 7am-5pm. Free.

Peralta Adobe: 184 W. St. John St. (San Pedro), San Jose, 408/993-8182. Built in approximately 1797, this is San Jose's oldest structure and last remnant of El Pueblo de San Jose de Guadalupe. The adobe is a small white building with cacti for its garden and an outdoor working oven. Inside, period pieces and artifacts give you a good idea of the pueblo lifestyle. • W-Su 11am-4pm. $6 general, $5 seniors, $3 children 6-17, children under 6 free; includes tour of both Peralta Adobe and Fallon House.

Ralston Hall: College of Notre Dame, 1500 Ralston Ave. (El Camino/Alameda de las Pulgas), Belmont, 650/508-3501. This 80-room mansion dating from 1849 is now part of the College of Notre Dame. The first floor is filled with authentic 19th-century antiques. Crystal chandeliers, ceiling mirrors, etched glass between rooms, and more makes this one of those houses that looks too good to live in—so it's just perfect to visit. • Tours for groups of 4 to 40 by appointment (call weeks in advance), M-F 10am-2pm. $5.

St. Joseph's Cathedral: 80 S. Market St. (Post/San Fernando), San Jose, 408/283-8100. Step inside and you'll think you've landed in a historic European cathedral. Extremely ornate and colorful, this spacious building displays hand-painted murals, stained-glass windows, near life-size statues, and a custom-made organ. Built in the 1870s, the cathedral is also a historic site. You may get a neck ache looking up at the

Historic San Jose

San Jose is the oldest European civil settlement in California, established in 1777 as El Pueblo de San Jose de Guadalupe. Through the years, the city has lost a few words in its name and grown into Northern California's largest city. Historic Downtown Tours sponsored by the San Jose Historical Museum every Thursday and first Saturday of the month cover 200 years of history. Five different tours are offered, all starting at noon at different locations, so it's a good idea to call first (408/287-2290). Lasting about 45 minutes, the tours highlight historic buildings, architecture, and facts. Knowledgeable volunteer docents explain "what used to be here," "what it was like," and, of course, "what happened to it" on the St. James Park Tour, Early Pueblo Town Tour, Old Business District Tour, Old City Plaza Tour, and East Santa Clara Street Tour.

The Old Plaza Tour, for instance, starts at St. Joseph's Cathedral and winds along Market and San Fernando streets. The tour shows you the location of California's first capitol, gives you a brief history of the once-extant Chinatown and its occupants, and takes you to historic sites such as Hotel Saint Claire, Dohrmann Building, and Fox California Theatre. You can't help but see San Jose in a different light afterward. It may make you wish that the nearby high-tech folks could build a time machine.

art that completely covers the high dome ceilings and walls. Although the gift shop next door tells you this place is touristy, you'll nonetheless encounter people dropping in for a moment of prayer. • Call the gift shop, 408/275-6090, to arrange a tour.

Stanford University

Tourist Information, Memorial Auditorium, inside main lobby, Serra and Galvez sts., Stanford Campus, 650/723-2560. A good place to begin your exploration of Stanford is the information window inside Memorial Auditorium. The booth, located in the main lobby, is a source of maps and information on tours and campus attractions. An **official tour** of the Stanford campus from one of the student guides is a great way to familiarize yourself with the campus. Tours, which last about one hour, leave at 11am and 3:15pm from the front steps of Memorial Auditorium daily except during finals week, between quarters, and on some holidays. For groups of fewer than nine people, tours are free and no reservations are needed. Larger groups should contact 650/723-2560 for reservations and fees. Also call this number to arrange a one-hour golf-cart tour. It leaves at 1pm daily, costs $5, and accommodates up to seven people.

• **The Hoover Institution** on War, Peace, and Revolution, at the corner of Serra and Galvez sts., 650/723-1754, was founded by President Hoover in 1919 (although construction on the building wasn't begun until 1941). It researches current world political events, supplies policy recommendations and advisors to Washington, D.C., and remains a conservative hotbed in a more or less liberal college community. • Daily 10am-4:30pm.

• **Hoover Tower,** corner of Serra and Galvez sts., 650/723-2053. For $2 ($1 children, free with current Stanford ID), you can ride to the top of this campus landmark and check out the immense vista; on a clear day you can see from the foothills to the bay. • Daily 10am-4:30pm.

• **Memorial Church** is in the heart of **The Quad** (site of the president's office and many department offices). The church is the most photographed object on campus. It's open to the public for sightseeing (Monday through Friday, tours on Friday), weddings (most Saturdays), and services (Sundays). The stunning mosaic was imported from Europe over a century ago.

• **Rodin Sculpture Garden**, somewhat hidden and northwest of **The Oval** (where Palm Drive loops around in front of The Quad), features numerous works by the namesake sculptor, including the haunting "Gates of Hell." Don't limit yourself to a daytime visit; the lighting at night dramatizes the passionately intertwined muscles of Rodin's sculptures and the young lovers who often enjoy the garden's beauty—and darkness.

• **Stanford Museum** Closed until 1999 owing to damage from the 1989 earthquake.

• **Stanford Linear Accelerator (SLAC),** 2575 Sand Hill Rd. (Sharon Park), Menlo Park, 650/926-2204. Get a crash course in particle physics at SLAC. The two-hour free tour begins with an orientation meeting and slide presentation in the auditorium, followed by a bus tour of the 426-acre world-famous facility. • Visitors center is open M-F 8am-5pm, but tour reservations are required (make them months in advance).

Sunset Magazine: 80 Willow Rd. (Middlefield), Menlo Park, 650/321-3600. Follow a self-guided tour of the magazine's test kitchens and gardens. The editorial offices are located in Spanish-style buildings. Seven full-time gardeners keep the lovely gardens with 300 native West Coast plants well manicured. • M-F 9am-4pm. Free.

Trinity Episcopal Church: 81 N. 2nd St. (Santa Clara/St. John), San Jose, 408/293-7953. Established in 1863, this is San Jose's oldest church and looks it. A rustic wooden building, it is modest and more than authentically ancient, although it still holds services. • Tours by appointment Su 9am-3pm; or see the "Historic San Jose" sidebar for tour information.

Villa Montalvo: 15400 Montalvo Rd. (off Hwy 9 heading towards Los Gatos), Saratoga, 408/961-5800. An Italian Renaissance-style villa built in 1912 in the redwoods for

Senator James Phelan, who bequeathed it for use as an artists' sanctuary. The gallery, open to the public, displays some of the resident artists' works and pieces by other contemporary Bay Area artists in rotating exhibits. Outside, nature trails wind through redwood groves where a regular performance series is held in an outdoor amphitheater. There is even a love temple on the grounds. • Hours vary. Free.

Winchester Mystery House: 525 S. Winchester Blvd. (Stevens Creek/I-280), San Jose, 408/247-2101. This 160-room Victorian maze of a house underwent 24-hours-a-day construction from 1884 to 1912, at the behest of firearms heiress Sarah Winchester. She was convinced that the nonstop construction would appease evil spirits she held responsible for the deaths of her husband and baby daughter. You haven't seen odd architecture until you behold stairs leading to the ceiling, windows in the floor, doors opening to walls, and chimneys climbing up four stories only to stop 18 inches from the ceiling. Not only is this place fascinatingly weird, it's also quite luxurious; over $5 million (in Winchester's time) was spent on the finest wood, Tiffany glass, and other ingredients in this superstitious concoction. In addition to the regular one-hour house tour, there's a 50-minute behind-the-scenes tour of areas of the house that were formerly off limits to the public. • Su-Th 9am-5pm; F-Sa 9am-8pm. Regular tour: $13.95 adults, $10.95 seniors, $7.95 ages 6-12, free ages 5 and under. Behind-the-scenes tour: $10.95 adults, $9.95 seniors (children under 12 not allowed). Admission for both tours is $21.95 adults, $18.95 seniors.

Woodside Store Historic Site: Corner of Tripp and Kings Mountain rds., Woodside, 650/851-7615. Established in 1854 by Matthias Alfred Parkhurst, this was the first store between San Jose and San Francisco. In the good old days, it was also a library, post office, and dental office for workers in the redwood industry. Today it still operates as a general store, and its museum showcases antique supplies and packaged goods from the 1850s and such appliances as an apple press, a working antique scale, and a bean sorter. Original furnishings and equipment such as blacksmith tools are preserved. • Tu-Th 10am-4pm; Sa-Su noon-4pm. Tours by appointment. Free.

Wineries

While they lack the notoriety of wineries in Napa and Sonoma, South Bay wineries offer a good opportunity to taste a variety of excellent wines in a more intimate setting. And don't underestimate the quality of these wines—Ridge in particular is known for its world-class reds. For additional information, contact the **Santa Clara Valley Wine Growers Association** at 408/778-1555 or the **Santa Cruz Mountain Winegrowers Association** at 408/479-9463.

Cooper-Garrod Estate Vineyards: 22600 Mt. Eden Rd. (off Pierce), Saratoga, 408/741-8094. This family-owned and -operated winery started with Garrod in 1893. After a sample of Chardonnay, Cabernet Franc, or Cabernet Sauvignon in the his-

What a Long Strange Trip

Sleepy, suburban Palo Alto and Menlo Park don't seem like the kind of towns to give rise to the Grateful Dead and LSD culture. But between 1961 and 1965, the original members of the band met one another, played in a variety of combinations under a couple of different names, and eventually became the Dead. In fact, when the Dead hooked up with Ken Kesey and his Merry Pranksters, they gave their first "Acid Test" party in Palo Alto. Many band members were locals: drummer Billy Kreutzman attended Palo Alto High, as did harmonica player Ron "Pigpen" McKernan; guitarist Bob Weir lived in Atherton and spent a little time at Menlo-Atherton High. Although most of the places where they hung out are long gone, some still exist, albeit in new locations. Kepler's original location across El Camino was a hotbed of the Beat scene, and a favorite spot for Jerry Garcia and Pigpen. St. Michael's Alley has moved and changed names, but Palo Alto's original coffeehouse was one of the Dead's first venues. The VA hospital in Menlo Park where Kesey served as a guinea pig in army LSD tests still exists, although the drug research program, we presume, does not.

toric "Fruit House" tasting room, view some historic exhibits or picnic under eucalyptus trees while enjoying a great view. • Tasting Sa-Su 11am-4:30pm. Free.

Cronin Vineyards: 11 Old La Honda Rd. (Portola/Preston), Woodside, 650/851-1452. A tiny winery overlooking San Francisco Bay and Portola Valley, Cronin nurtures small quantities of their wines using very low-tech, alternative wine-making techniques. Wine tasting is a casual affair in the family's living room, and the wine cellar is in the house basement. Ask to be put on the mailing list if you would like to attend an open house. • Tasting and tours by appointment. Free.

David Bruce: 21439 Bear Creek Rd. (off Hwy 17), Los Gatos, 408/354-4214, 800/397-9972. Doctor Bruce was a dermatologist who experimented with wine making and came up with national success. His Pinot Noir is especially well regarded. With a view of Monterey Bay, this is a good place for a picnic. • Tasting daily noon-5pm. Free.

Hallcrest Vineyards and The Organic Wine Works: 379 Felton Rd. (off Hwy 9), Felton, 408/335-4441, 800/OWW-WINE (699-9463). According to the owners, this is the only place in the country certified as a maker of organic wine. That means no preservatives or sulfites: People with allergies can enjoy the reds and whites here and not worry. • Tasting daily 11am-5:30pm. Tours by reservation, $3.50 including tasting.

J. Lohr: 1000 Lenzen Ave. (The Alameda), San Jose, 408/288-5057. Of all places to establish a winery, why not downtown San Jose? This winery is not only unique for its location, but also its method of vinification: it has an outdoor tank farm. • Tasting daily 10am-5pm; free. Tours Sa-Su 11am, 2pm.

Mirassou Champagne Cellars: 300 College Ave. (Prospect), Los Gatos, 408/395-3790. In a beautiful setting overlooking Los Gatos, you'll find locally made champagne, dinners, and complimentary events. • Tasting W-Su noon-5pm. Tours Sa-Su at 2pm, unless production is in progress. Free.

Mirassou Vineyards: 3000 Aborn Rd. (White/Ruby), San Jose, 408/274-4000. Founded by Pierre Pellier of France in 1854, Mirassou is the oldest family-operated winery in North America. Enjoy tours, tastings, candlelight dinners, and Sunday afternoon concerts in a historic setting. • Tasting M-Sa noon-5pm; Su noon-4pm. Tours daily at 2pm (call ahead). Free.

Page Mill Winery: 13686 Page Mill Rd. (west of I-280), Los Altos Hills, 650/948-0958. The self-proclaimed "best-kept secret on the Peninsula" is indeed obscure because it has no regular business hours. In the foothills behind Stanford University, this winery is open for tasting in May and November—call for information.

Ridge Vineyards: 17100 Monte Bello Rd. (off Stevens Canyon), Cupertino, 408/867-3233. One of the first small, fine California wineries, Ridge was established 1959 and overlooks San Francisco Bay. Award-winning Cabernet, Zinfandel, and Chardonnay attest to the emphasis on good wine. A visit is a good time to join one of Ridge's subscription programs that gives members access to hard-to-find wines (usually unavailable in stores). • Tasting Sa-Su 11am-3pm. Free.

Savannah Chanel Vineyards: 23600 Congress Springs Rd. aka Hwy 9 (west of downtown), Saratoga, 408/741-2930. Although the name sounds more like a perfume than a wine, you'll find only a historic turn-of-the-century winery here with hundreds of small oak barrels and casks. Founded by Pierre Pourroy in 1892. You can now enjoy wine in the 1912 Redwood Tasting Room, a Mediterranean-style chateau with a great view. Facilities for picnics, barbecues, private parties, weddings, and conferences. • Tasting daily 11am-5pm, $3. Tours by appointment.

Sunrise Winery: 13100 Monte Bello Rd. (off Stevens Canyon), Cupertino, 408/741-1310. Built in the 1880s, Sunrise is one of the last winery ranches. Along with premium varietal wines, you'll find picnic facilities and maybe a peacock in the scenic surroundings. • Tasting F-Su 11am-3pm. Free.

Thomas Fogarty Winery and Vineyards: 19501 Skyline Blvd. (Hwy 84/Page Mill), Woodside, 650/851-6777. Specializing in handmade wines from the Burgundian varietals of its estate, Thomas Fogarty has a beautiful 2,000-foot-high setting offering wonderful views. Good for conferences and events, too. • Tasting Th-Su 11am-5pm. $5 (keep the glass).

Woodside Vineyards: 340 Kings Mountain Rd. (off Woodside Rd.), Woodside, 650/851-3144. One of the smallest and oldest vineyards in California, Woodside has estate-bottled Chardonnay, Zinfandel, and Cabernet wines for tasting. Tour the winery, cellars, and vineyards. • Open three times a year for tasting and tours—call for dates.

MUSEUMS

Art Tech Silicon Valley Institute of Art and Technology: 89 S. 1st St. (Post), San Jose, 408/971-9100. Put the San Jose Museum of Art together with the Tech Museum of Innovation and you get Art Tech, the only San Jose gallery devoted to the fusion of art and technology. Featuring high-tech art created with computer technologies, electronics, optics, and such, the long white walls of this gallery house often strange and always fascinating pieces. • Tu-F noon-6pm; third Th noon-8pm. Free.

Barbie Doll Hall of Fame: 433 Waverley St. (University/Lytton), Palo Alto, 650/326-5841. Come examine one of the most famous of contemporary cultural icons in a newly expanded collection of over 16,000 pieces—the largest in the world. Check out nearly every Barbie product created since 1959 (the year of her birth), and see how the world of Barbie reflected almost every change in our popular culture. Don't miss Hippie Barbie, the first black Barbie, Ken, and of course Barbie's financially unlimited wardrobe—clothes that exemplify America's own fashion trends. • Tu, Th 1:30-4pm; W, F 1:30-4:30pm; Sa 10am-noon, 1:30-4:30pm. $6 adults, $4 children under 12.

Center for Beethoven Studies: San Jose State University, Wahlquist Library North Room 318, (San Fernando/4th) San Jose, 408/924-4590. All classical music pilgrims must visit this shrine to the great composer. The only center in North America devoted only to Beethoven, this humble room in a university library showcases the area's largest Beethoven collection, including original manuscripts, first editions, memorabilia, books, recordings, and videos. Right by the door is the obligatory bust of the man himself. • M-F 1-5pm and by appointment. Free.

Children's Discovery Museum: 180 Woz Way (Almaden/San Carlos), San Jose, 408/298-5437. Get involved in the wonderful world of science, arts, technology, and humanities in this participatory science museum with over 150 hands-on exhibits. It is the largest children's museum on the West Coast, and it includes a walk-through model of San Jose's streets and underground, complete with traffic controls and waste-disposal systems that children can operate. Learn about life before electricity, explore the properties of water, and dive into cultures of the past. The building itself is quite a sight: a purple Ricardo Legorreta creation with spectacular angles. • Tu-Sa 10am-5pm; Su noon-5pm. $6 adults, $5 seniors, $4 ages 2 to 18, children under 2 free. Parking $2.

Coyote Point Museum for Environmental Education: 1651 Coyote Point Dr. (off Hwy 101), San Mateo, 650/342-7755. Includes the two-acre Wildlife Habitat filled with badgers, otters, and other native animals; and the Environmental Hall, an 8,000-square-foot simulated walk from the San Francisco Bay to the Pacific Coast. The traveling exhibits change every three or four months. • Tu-Sa 10am-5pm; Su noon-5pm. $3 adults, $2 seniors and ages 13 to 17, $1 ages 4 to 12, children under 4 free. Free first Wednesday of month. Parking $4.

d. p. Fong Galleries: 383 S. 1st St. (San Salvador/San Carlos), San Jose, 408/298-8877. The only thing within the white, almost unfinished-looking walls is contemporary art from the Bay Area, Southern California, New York, and/or Asia. The rotating displays feature only a few artists at a time. • W-Su 1-6pm; third Th 5-8pm. Free.

Intel Museum: 2200 Mission College Blvd. (Montague/Great America Pkwy.), Santa Clara, 408/765-0503. After you're greeted by a figure in a bunny suit (the kind people wear in chip-making factories, not a fuzzy costume with pointed ears), try out the hands-on exhibits to learn how computer chips are made and used. Check out the 3,500-square-foot giant microprocessor. Roam at your leisure; tours are available by reservation. • M-F 8am-5pm. Free.

Machu Picchu (Galleria y Museo de las Americas): 42-D S. 1st St. (Post/Santa Clara), San Jose, 408/280-1860. Tucked upstairs in the rear of El Paseo Court, the gallery houses art and folk art from Mexico, Central and South America, and the American Southwest. Colorful tapestries, sculptures, ceramics, jewelry, clothing, artifacts, textiles, and more pack this small, homey space. Also a good place to attend Andean-music concerts and find out about Latin American events. • M-F 11am-5pm; Sa 1-5pm; Su by appointment only. Free.

Museum of American Heritage: 351 Homer Ave. (Waverley/Bryant), Palo Alto, 650/321-1004. Historically minded Silicon Valley denizens will love this showcase of precomputer technology. Travel through the past in the 1930s kitchen, turn-of-the-century attorney's office, and 1920s grocery store. See what technology meant in the 1800s and early 1900s with the displays of radios, typewriters, electric trains, and other appliances and artifacts. • F-Su 11am-4pm, or by appointment. Free during regular hours.

Palo Alto Cultural Center: 1313 Newell Rd. (Embarcadero), Palo Alto, 650/329-2366. In a quiet, parklike setting, this center displays contemporary artwork, local and beyond. The exhibits are temporary but indelible. This facility also offers art classes. • Tu-Th 10am-5pm, 7-9pm; F-Sa 10am-5pm; Su 1-5pm. Free ($1 donation).

Palo Alto Junior Museum: 1451 Middlefield Rd. (Embarcadero), Palo Alto, 650/329-2111. Features a zoo of small animals representative of each phylum of the animal kingdom, as well as rotating exhibits on topics like forests and underwater life. Trainers show off the animals on weekends. Natives include raccoons, foxes, ravens, and reptiles. Learn about natural history, astronomy, and environmental issues as well. The Play Spot is a hands-on area for preschoolers. • Tu-Sa 10am-5pm; Su 1-4pm. Free.

Rosicrucian Egyptian Museum & Planetarium: Park and Naglee aves., San Jose, 408/947-3636. Ancient history buffs and anyone who still believes in King Tut's curse will want to explore this museum, which contains more than 4,000 artifacts from Egypt, Assyria, and Babylonia. This is the largest ancient Egyptian collection on display in the western United States. Highlights include human and animal mummies and a full-size replica of a nobleman's tomb, but also check out the jewelry, scarabs, scrolls, utensils, and textiles. Outside statuary includes the sphinx and some obelisks. The Planetarium holds shows on astronomy and ancient cultures—mythology as well as modern astronomical findings—providing insight into humanity, the universe, and history. • W-M 10am-5pm. $7 adults, $5 students and seniors, $3.50 ages 6 to 15, children under 6 free. Planetarium show: W-M 2pm. $4 adults, $3.50 students and seniors, $3 ages 6 to 15, children under 6 free.

San Jose Historical Museum: Kelley Park, 1600 Senter Rd. (Phelan/Alma), San Jose, 408/287-2290, 408/27-PARKS (7-2757). Original and replica buildings of turn-of-the-century San Jose sprawl over 25 acres at this unique outdoor museum, where you can visit a re-creation of San Jose's original main street, inspect an old firehouse, or sip a soda at O'Brien's Candy Factory—the place that served the first ice cream soda west of Detroit. Many buildings were transported from their original sites. Docent-led tours will give you a quick history lesson. See the historic working trolley and enjoy special events year-round. • M-F 10am-4:30pm; Sa-Su noon-4:30pm. $4 adults, $3 seniors, $2 ages 5 to 17, children under 5 free. Hours and fees may change—call ahead.

San Jose Institute of Contemporary Art Galleries: 451 S. 1st St. (William/San Salvador), San Jose, 408/283-8155. Gallery space for changing exhibitions of cutting-edge visual artists. Exhibits spotlight artists who focus on the Bay Area and cultural diversity. Works are unique but not too far into the deep end. • Tu-Sa noon-5pm; third Th until 8pm. Free.

San Jose Museum of Art: 110 S. Market St. (San Fernando), San Jose, 408/294-2787. Focusing on art from the 20th century, this modern-looking, two-story building houses only a small permanent collection. The museum hosts some spectacular traveling exhibitions in its new 45,000-square foot wing, however. Sculpture courts house three-dimensional art. • Tu-W, F-Su 10am-5pm; Th 10am-8pm. $7 adults, $4 students and seniors, $4 ages 6 to 17, children under 6 free. Free first Thursday of the month for general admission, first Tuesday of the month for seniors, and first Sunday of the month for children and their escorts.

San Jose Museum of Quilts and Textiles: 60 S. Market St. (Santa Clara/San Fernando), San Jose, 408/971-0323. Full of rotating exhibits on contemporary and traditional quilt making and textile design, the American Museum, featuring fiber arts from around the world, is the only one of its kind in the state and the first in the country. Although this place may sound like a granny museum, the modern pieces are great works of abstract art that any art lover can appreciate. • Tu-W, F-Su 10am-4pm; Th 10am-8pm. $6.50 general admission, $4 students and seniors, free to children under 13. Free first Thursday of the month.

San Mateo County Historic Museum: 777 Hamilton St. (Broadway/Marshall), Redwood City. Telephone not available at presstime. As of September 1998, the museum will be in its new location in Redwood City. Exhibits rotate twice a year and document the history of San Mateo County. Carriages from the 1800s, old photos, Native American artifacts, fossils, and more are the storytellers of the county's past. • M-Th 9:30am-4:30pm; Su 12:30-4:30pm. Free. Note: hours subject to change.

Tech Museum of Innovation: 145 W. San Carlos St. (Almaden/Market), San Jose, 408/279-7150. *Note:* The museum will be located at 201 S. Market St. after November 1998. During the move, it will be closed from July 6 to October 31, 1998. A Silicon Valley highlight, the museum is designed to help visitors understand how technology works. Visitors can drive a Land Rover over a simulated Martian landscape, man the controls of life-size robots, and perform calculations on a nine-square-foot computer chip. Learn about genetics, bikes, and the universe. The hands-on focus is educational and fun as you find out your particle count or measure your static voltage. When the new location on the corner of Park and Market streets opens, the huge facility will include four main galleries, an interactive section, and a 300-seat IMAX theater. • Tu-Su 10am-5pm. $6 adults; $4 students, seniors, and ages 6 to 18; children under 6 free.

Triton Museum of Art: 1505 Warburton Ave. (Lincoln), Santa Clara, 408/247-3754. Devoted to modern art, the museum hosts changing exhibitions that focus on works by contemporary California artists but also mounts shows of art from around the world. • Tu 10am-9pm; W-Su 10am-5pm. Donation requested.

Youth Science Institute: Alum Rock Park, 16260 Alum Rock Ave. (east of White), San Jose, 408/258-4322. Rotating natural history exhibits and hands-on displays accompany live animals such as birds of prey and reptiles. Puzzles and books are fun and educational, and you may run into a skeleton or two. • Tu-Sa noon-4:30pm; also open Su noon-4:30pm during the summer. 50 cents adults, 25 cents children.

Youth Science Institute: Vasona Park, 296 Garden Hill Dr. (off Lark btwn. Hwy 17 and Winchester), Los Gatos, 408/356-4945. Visit land and aquatic animals in this nature center and revisit the dinosaurs in a small exhibit. Lots of hands-on stuff for kids. • M-F 9am-4:30pm. Free admission but parking is $4.

Youth Science Institute: Sanborn-Skyline Park, 16055 Sanborn Rd. (access from Hwy 9 west of Saratoga), Saratoga, 408/867-6940. Natural science displays, insect zoo, and reptiles in a redwood forest in the Santa Cruz Mountains. Visit the geology room and learn about earthquakes and volcanoes. The building itself used to be an old mansion. • Tu-F 9am-4:30pm; Sa-Su 12:30-4:30pm. Donations requested. Parking $4.

AMUSEMENTS

Action Zone Indoor Paintball Center: 111 Uranium Rd. # A (Kifer/Mead), Sunnyvale, 408/738-2255. Enjoy this modern game of two teams battling with guns that fire exploding sacs of paint. The Center has lots of hidden corners, a three-story castle, and even a 50-foot slide to make the combat scene more adventurous. • Tu-F 6pm-midnight; Sa noon-midnight. $10/first hour (including equipment); $5 for each additional hour; must be 12 or older.

Diamond Billiards: 4700 Almaden Expwy. (Hillsdale/Cherry), San Jose, 408/266-POOL (7665). Another addition to the upscale pool hall scene. This one has a suburban angle: it's open to all ages and has darts and an arcade for when you're tired of being hustled. • M-Th 4pm-midnight; F-Sa noon-2am; Su noon-midnight.

Bay Meadows: 2600 S. Delaware St. (25th), San Mateo, 650/574-7223. Is Custer's Revenge going to place or show in the fourth? Put your money where your mouth is. When the sun shines and the field is tight, you can't beat the fun and excitement: only a crowd with money on the line can cheer like this one does. Horse races are run on the track throughout the year, but call for a schedule (racing alternates with sister track Golden Gate Fields in Berkeley). Watch a simulcast when they're not running live.

Belmont Iceland: 815 Old County Rd. (Ralston), Belmont, 650/592-0532. Public sessions held Thursdays, Fridays, and Saturdays only. • Call for hours. Admission $6 for adults, $5 children during the day, $6 evenings; skate rental $2.

Eastridge Ice Arena: Eastridge Mall, 2190A Tully Rd. (Capitol), San Jose, 408/238-0440. Day and evening public sessions in addition to figure skating and hockey. • Hours vary, call ahead. Admission $5.50; skate rental $2.50.

(Paramount's) Great America: Great America Pkwy. (north of Hwy 101), Santa Clara, 408/988-1776. Invertigo, a suspended roller coaster, is the newest toe-curling addition to this full-blown amusement park in Santa Clara. Top Gun also turns the traditional roller coaster on its head and has you dangling below the tracks rather than resting on top. Other variations on the theme are the Vortex, an enormous roller coaster that you ride standing up, and the 360-degree Tidal Wave roller coaster. For those likely to lose their lunch, there's instead Rip Roaring Rapids, a simulated white-water rafting ride (you'll get *very* wet). Folks looking for more leisure in their attractions have plenty from which to choose. The park features shows with live singing and dancing, a seven-story movie screen and Nickelodeon's Splat City for kids. Films in the IMAX theater are included in the price of admission. Great America occasionally hosts popular music concerts, which cost $9 in addition to general admission. • Open March-October. Summer: Su-Th 10am-9pm; F-Sa 10am-11pm. Spring and fall: Sa-Su 10am-9pm. $31.99 ages 7 to 54; $18.50 ages 3 to 6; free ages 2 and under; $20.99 seniors. Season passes $65. Parking $6.

Great Entertainer: 2028 El Camino Real (20th), San Mateo, 650/349-0811. Try your hand at one of 26 pool tables available. When you get tired of that, take a turn into the full arcade and play until your thumb can do no more. They also have several foosball tables. With a selection of beer and grub, you may pass the whole night right here. • Su-Th 11am-2am; F-Sa 11am-3am.

Ice Center of San Jose: 1500 S. 10th St. (Alma), San Jose, 408/279-6000. Dual ice rink. Group lessons, figure skating, and hockey. • Hours vary; call for session and lesson information. General skating: $6 adults; $5 children; $2.50 skate rental.

Ice Chalet: Vallco Fashion Park, 10123 N. Wolfe Rd. (Stevens Creek/I-280) Cupertino, 650/574-1616. Adult and youth hockey classes offered. Public skating, lessons, and other programs at various times every day. • $6 to get on the ice, $3 to rent skates.

Ice Oasis: 3140 Bay Rd. (5th), Redwood City, 650/364-8090. They have various public sessions for skating and scheduled open hockey games for people over 18. They also have a skating school for all levels and adult and youth hockey leagues. • Hours vary, so call ahead. $6 adults; $6 seniors; and $5 children 12 and under. Skate rental $2.

Magic Edge: 1625 N. Shoreline Blvd. (Hwy 101/Charleston), Mountain View, 650/254-7325. Where else but Silicon Valley could you expect to find a virtual reality restaurant and bar? Look out Red Baron, and pray the flight simulators don't make you air sick. Reservations strongly recommended. • M noon-11pm; Tu-Th 11am-11pm; F 11am-midnight; Sa 9am-midnight; Su 9am-10pm. $14.75 for a 12-minute "flight" and $19.75 for 20 minutes; additional $2 "membership" fee for first timers.

Malibu Castle: 320 Blomquist St. (Hwy 101 to Seaport Blvd. exit, then east to Blomquist), Redwood City, 650/367-1905. Rent some clubs and take a whack at one of the three 18-hole miniature golf courses, or grab a bat and take a few practice swings in the electronic batting cages. Replenish your energies at the snack bar; hot dogs and Velveeta-covered nachos never tasted so good. Malibu Castle also has a mini prix for kids between 4'6" and 3'2". • Su-Th 10am-10pm; F-Sa 10am-midnight. $6 adults; $5 under 14 for golf; $1.50 for 20 pitches.

Malibu Grand Prix: 340 Blomquist St. (Hwy 101 to Seaport Blvd. exit, then east to Blomquist), Redwood City, 650/366-6442. A dream come true for would-be Indy 500 racers (and fun for everyone else as well). Malibu has a fleet of turbo charged go-carts and several different tracks of varying difficulty for child drivers and regular cars for older speed demons. After you've satisfied the speed demon in you, wander inside and regress for a while in the video arcade. • Su-Th 10am-10pm; F-Sa 10am-midnight. $3.19 for first lap; $2.95 for each lap after that. Requirements: 8 years old and 4'6" for go-carts; 18 years old and valid driver's license for regular cars.

Mar Vista Stables: 2152 Skyline Blvd. (John Daly), Daly City, 650/991-4224. For $20 per person per hour, you're fixed up with a trusty steed and a guide and set loose to ride along the coast. • Daily 9am-5pm.

Marine World: I-80 and Hwy 37, Vallejo, 707/643-6722. After 30 as the Bay Area's pre-mier marine life park, 1998 marks a paramount change to this theme park with the investment of $50 million in thrill rides and new attractions. The new Dolphin Harbor show expands on the park's previous main attraction, the Killer Whale show. Their much-touted Shark Experience does indeed give you a new angle on these solemn, graceful creatures as you walk along a Plexiglas walkway right under them. Sea lions, walruses, and a variety of sea life live in the aquariums and tide pools. The 16 new rides include two raucous roller coasters, the 3-D virtual reality Dinosphere, and plenty of others to get you upside down and soaking wet. Unfortunately, it seems the land ani-mals have not benefited from the new improvements. • Summer daily 10am-10pm; spring and fall F-Su 10am-8pm. $28.99 adults; $19.99 ages 4 to 12; free ages 3 and under; $23.99 seniors. Parking $6.

Moonlight Lanes: 2780 El Camino Real (Kiely), Santa Clara, 408/296-7200. Check out the Saturday night rock and bowl: all the balls you can bowl from 10pm to 1am with full rock-club sound and light. Regular bowling the rest of the week.

Planet Granite: 2901 Mead Ave. (Bowers/Uranium), Santa Clara, 408/727-2777. This large indoor climbing facility features fully contoured structures that look like rocks. The 14,000-square-foot facility has 75 ropes, an enormous bouldering area, and a full range of weights and fitness equipment. Classes and programs for people of all ages and abilities available. • M-F 11am-10pm; Sa-Su 10am-6pm.

Raging Waters: Lake Cunningham Regional Park, 2333 S. White Rd. (Tully/Capitol), San Jose, 408/270-8000. If it's summer and you're looking for a way to cool off, head to Raging Waters in San Jose. This water park, with lots of neon bathing suits and teenyboppers, is especially fun with a large group of people. Slides with names like White Lightning, Blue Thunder, Rampage, and Serpentine will twist you, turn you, and finally throw you into a huge pool. The new Barracuda Blaster is a four-person toboggan water ride. Changing rooms, showers, and lockers available. • Mid-June until late-September daily 10am-7pm. Spring and fall open weekends only. General admission $20.99; children under 4'2" $16.99; free ages 3 and under.

Santa Clara Billiards: 4525 Stevens Creek Blvd. (Kiely), Santa Clara, 408/296-3333. • Su-W 11am-2am; Th-Sa 11am-4am.

The Winter Lodge: 3009 Middlefield Rd. (Colorado/Loma Verde), Palo Alto, 650/493-4566. The only permanent outdoor ice rink west of the Sierra Nevada is found right in Palo Alto. Call for session and lesson information. • Open October-April. Admission $5; skate rental $2.

Entertaining Children

The Bay Area offers plenty of old-fashioned ways to keep the loved ones amused. Below is a selective sampling of activities (for kids and adults) that get everyone out of the house and away from the computer or TV. Look for many more activities listed in other sections of this guide. (We've also cross-referenced some favorites here.)

Many of the activities listed in the Amusements section above are surefire kid pleasers, as are many museums, both on the Peninsula and in San Francisco and beyond. Many entertaining family destinations are found just a short distance from the Peninsula and South Bay, too, from San Francisco to Marin. For example, try majestic Muir Woods (Marin section). Monterey Bay Aquarium (Monterey section) is another favorite family destination, as are the many other beautiful parks in our area (Vasona in Los Gatos is a favorite—see Oak Meadow Park, below). Consult the front section of your yellow pages for a list of community parks with playgrounds near you. For a day trip, Golden Gate Park (San Francisco section) offers many activities.

Don't overlook your town's community programs. Almost every library has story hours. Check the phone book for one near you and call for the story schedule. During summer, the parks are filled with a variety of kid's programs, from puppet shows to concerts. Finally, most towns have extensive recreation programs with soccer, t-ball, swimming, and more.

Academy of Sciences (includes Steinhart Aquarium, Morrison Planetarium, and the Natural History Museum): Tea Garden Dr., Golden Gate Park, SF, 415/750-7145. Morrison Planetarium: 415/750-7141. Laserium: 415/750-7138. See San Francisco Museums section for additional information.

Ardenwood Historical Farm: 34600 Ardenwood Blvd. at Hwy 84, Fremont, 510/796-0663. A historic California farm where you can learn about California in the early days of European settlement. Staff and volunteers wear Victorian clothing and culti-vate the same crops that were grown 100 years ago. Visitors can see demonstrations of farm chores and ride in horse-drawn trains and wagons. • April-November: Th-Su 10am-4pm, plus Memorial Day, Independence Day, Labor Day, and the first weekend in December. $5 adults; $4 ages 13 to 17 and seniors; $3.50 ages 4 to 12; free ages 3 and under. Tu-W, Sa grounds are open but no trains, wagon rides, or house tours. $1 adults; 50¢ children.

Bamboola: 5401 Camden Ave. (Kooser), San Jose, 408/448-4FUN (4386) An enor-mous and relatively new children's activity center with a toddler play area, a soft play-ground, an outdoor jungle garden, a climbing rock, arts-and-crafts studios, and more. • Tu-Th 11am-8pm; F 11am-9pm; Sa 10am-8pm; Su 10am-6pm. Free under 1 year; $3.95 ages 12 to 36 months; $8.95 ages 3 to 12; $1.95 adults.

Barbie Doll Hall of Fame: 433 Waverley St. (University/Lytton), Palo Alto, 650/326-5841. See Peninsula Museums section for additional information.

Bay Area Discovery Museum: 557 East Fort Baker (Alexander Ave. to East Rd.), Sausalito, 415/487-4398. See Marin chapter.

Children's Discovery Museum: 180 Woz Way (Almaden/San Carlos), San Jose, 408/298-5437. See Peninsula Museums section for additional information.

Coyote Point Museum for Environmental Education: 1651 Coyote Point Dr. (off Hwy 101), San Mateo, 650/342-7755. See Peninsula Museums section.

Discovery Zone: 2541 S. El Camino Real (Hwy 84/5th), Redwood City, 650/568-4386. • 217 Ranch Dr. (McCarthy/Hwy 237), Milpitas, 408/934-8600. Children absolutely love these basic indoor fun centers. Each is filled with soft, brightly colored structures that kids can jump on, crawl through, slide down, or play with. Toddlers even have their own area. Socks are required. • M-Th 10am-8pm; F-Sa 10am-9pm; Su 11am-7pm. Admission $5.99 ages 3 to 12; $3.99 ages 1 to 3; free under 1 year and parents.

Emma Prusch Farm Park: 647 S. King Rd. (Story/I-280), San Jose, 408/27-PARKS (7-2757). This San Jose park started as a farm. Today it highlights the area's agricultural history with a rare fruit orchard (see a raisin tree), a Victorian farmhouse, a barn, and a small animal area with ducks, chickens, pigs, and sheep. Also includes a large grassy area for picnicking and kite flying and a multicultural arts center. • Daily 8:30am-sunset. Free.

Exploratorium: 3601 Lyon St. (Marina Blvd.), SF, 415/561-0360 (recorded information); Tactile Dome 415/561-0362. An incredible hands-on science museum. See San Francisco Museums section for additional information.

Gymboree: General Bay Area information 800/265-5018. • St. Paul's Episcopal Church, 415 El Camino Real (Burlingame Ave./Bellevue), Burlingame, 650/358-9943. • Laurelwood Shopping Center, 3180 Campus Dr. (Hillsdale), San Mateo, 650/358-9943. • Woodside Methodist Church, 2000 Woodside Rd. (Alameda de las Pulgas), Redwood City, 650/949-5798. • Los Altos Rancho Center, Foothill Rd. and Springer Rd., Los Altos, 650/949-5798. • Town & Country Village, Stevens Creek Blvd. and Winchester Blvd., San Jose, 408/296-2109. • Oakridge Mall, Blossom Hill Rd. and Santa Teresa Blvd., San Jose, 408/629-5813. While parents complain about the prices and relentless corporate marketing, kids love it here. Lots of classes for babies (with their parents) through preschoolers are offered. Basically, it's a padded room with tons of toys and things to climb to help your child's physical development. Teachers lead classes in songs and games; there is also free time for you and your child to explore in a soft environment. • Call for latest class schedule. First class free. Class enrollment is for three months: $120 one class a week; $140 more than one class a week.

Happy Hollow Park and Zoo: Kelley Park, 1300 Senter Rd. (Keyes), San Jose, 408/295-8383. Part of Kelley Park, right in the heart of the city. You'll find a miniature train and a few other rides, a small petting zoo, and a play area where kids can go wild. Also within Kelley Park is the San Jose Historical Museum (see Peninsula Museums section). • Happy Hollow: Daily 10am-5pm. $4.50. Historical Museum: M-F 10am-4:30pm; Sa-Su noon-4:30pm. $4 adults; $2 ages 4 to 17; $3 seniors.

Hidden Villa: 26870 Moody Rd. (off El Monte), Los Altos Hills, 650/949-8660. An educational working farm nestled on the edge of Rancho San Antonio park. Check out the crops, learn how farms work, and pet the animals. Also houses an AYH Youth Hostel and a multicultural summer camp. • Tu-Su 9am-dusk. Parking fee $5 per car.

The Jungle Fun and Adventure: 555 9th St. (Brannan/Bryant), SF, 415/552-4386. • El Paseo de Saratoga, Saratoga Ave. and Campbell Ave., San Jose, 408/866-4386. Kids go wild in this adventurous (and safe) indoor play facility, where they can fly on track glides and swim through ball pools. A café features pizzas (look for specials where admission is free with purchase of pizza). Socks are required and parents must stay on the premises. • Su-Th 10am-8pm; F 10am-9pm; Sa 9am-9pm. M-F before 5pm $6.95 ages 4 to 12; $4.95 ages 3 and under (Tu $2.48 ages 3 and under). Su-Th after 5pm $3.95 all ages. F-Sa after 5pm $6.95 for 2 hours all ages.

Lawrence Hall of Science: Middle Centennial Dr., (Piedmont Ave./Grizzly Peak), Berkeley, 510/642-5133. Perched high on the hill behind UC Berkeley, this famed science museum looks like an ancient Greek temple paying worship to the gods. Views of the Bay and civilization below are spectacular. Inside, the special robotics exhibitions (in the past they've included huge insects and dinosaurs that stomp, screech, and roar) immediately command a youngster's attention. Other highlights of this interactive museum are hairy tarantulas that crawl on your arm (kids like this), computers that psychoanalyze, and electricity globes that make anyone's hair fit for the 1970s. • Daily 10am-5pm. $6 adults; $2 ages 3 to 6; $4 students and seniors.

Oakland Zoo: 9777 Golf Links Rd. (I-580), Oakland, 510/632-9523. Stresses the presentation of animals in their natural habitat. It features an island habitat for monkeys, an acre of roaming territory and a mud bath for the elephants, and a eucalyptus grove for the romping lions, plus a train ride, picnic areas, and a great sky ride. • Daily 10am-4pm. $5.50 adults; $3 ages 2 to 14 and seniors. Car parking $3 additional. Rides are also charged individually.

Oak Meadow Park: Blossom Hill Rd. at Garden Hill Dr., Los Gatos, 408/354-6808, 408/395-RIDE (7433). Attached to Vasona Lake County Park. Ride the restored carousel and the steam railroad. • During spring and fall, the railroad is open weekends only (closed during winter). $1 rides; $5 parking.

Palo Alto Cultural Center: 1313 Newell Rd. (Embarcadero), Palo Alto, 650/329-2366. Although it's run largely by the city of Palo Alto, you don't have to be a resident to sign up for the many art classes at the center. Children's classes cover ages 18 months to 18 years and range from one-day workshops to multiweek sessions. Subjects include drawing, sculpture, crafts, and more. Unfortunately, the combination of heavy local demand and a challenging registration system can make it tough to get into the class you want (call for a current schedule and registration information). *Note:* not all classes are held at the center. • Tu-Th 10am-5pm, 7-10pm; F-Sa 10am-5pm.

Palo Alto Junior Museum: 1451 Middlefield Rd. (Embarcadero), Palo Alto, 650/329-2111. See Peninsula Museums section for additional information.

Purple Crayon: 301 Cornwall St. (4th Ave.), SF, 415/831-0693. This arts-and-crafts studio helps children express their creativity through classes, birthday parties, and a summer art camp. It provides a warm, inviting space where free expression and messiness are encouraged (perfect for parties). The ongoing-enrollment classes change from time to time but usually include drawing, sculpture, and painting, as well as programs geared toward younger children (even 20-month-old kids) that emphasize skills development and exploration of materials. Popular birthday party projects include making glitter globes, spaceships, picture frames, and masks. • Call for latest class schedule. Classes (10 weeks): $200 ages 5 and up (2 hours), $140 ages 2 to 5 (1 hour); walk-in classes $15 per hour. Parties (2 hours) $200 for up to 10 people, $10 per additional person, includes art project, instructors, and studio time.

Rosicrucian Egyptian Museum & Planetarium: Park and Naglee aves., San Jose, 408/947-3636. See Peninsula Museums section for additional information.

San Francisco Zoo: Sloat Blvd. (45th Ave. next to Lake Merced), SF, 415/753-7061. Increasingly, this zoo features animals in re-creations of their natural habitats, although the older exhibits are on the small side and unadorned. The Primate Discovery Center is a centerpiece of the zoo. Whether by flaw or fluke, there seems to be an escape every few years. Other highlights include penguins, lions, tigers, koala bears (oh my!), and a petting zoo. • Daily 10am-5pm. Nonresidents: $9 adults; $6 ages 12 to 17 and seniors; $3 ages 3 to 11; free ages 3 and under. Residents: $7 adults; $3.50 ages 12 to 17 and seniors; $1.50 ages 3 to 11; free ages 3 and under.

San Jose Museum of Art: 110 S. Market St. (San Fernando), San Jose, 408/294-2787. This museum offers a number of programs geared specifically toward children and their parents. See Peninsula Museums section for additional information.

Serra Park: 730 The Dalles Ave. (Hollenbeck), Sunnyvale, 408/730-7506. Local park with soft lawns, a wading creek, and an excellent playground with monkey bars, slides, and tubes galore. The spray pool is a hot-weather highlight.

Tech Museum of Innovation: 145 W. San Carlos St. (Market/Almaden), San Jose, 408/279-7150. See Peninsula Museums section for additional information.

Underwater World: Pier 39, Embarcadero and Beach sts., SF, 415/623-5300. Although opened in April 1996, the aquarium is still not well known. It takes you on a moving walkway through see-through tunnels for a fish-eye view of the local aquatic life. • Daily 9am-9pm. $12.95 adults; $9.95 seniors; $6.50 ages 3 to 11; free ages 3 and under.

Youth Science Institute: Alum Rock Park, 16260 Alum Rock Ave. (Penitencia Creek), San Jose, 408/258-4322. • Vasona Park, 296 Garden Hill Dr. (off Lark btwn. Hwy 17 and Winchester), Los Gatos, 408/356-4945. • Sanborn-Skyline Park, Hwy 9 west of Saratoga, 408/867-6940. See Peninsula Museums section for additional information.

Pro and College Sports

Baseball

Oakland Athletics: Oakland Coliseum (I-880 to Hegenberger Rd. exit or BART to Coliseum station), Oakland, 510/638-0500. www.oaklandathletics.com.

San Francisco Giants: 3Com/Candlestick Park, (Hwy 101 to 3Com/Candlestick exit on the southern edge of San Francisco), SF, 415/467-8000; www.sfgiants.com. Watch them here until the new downtown ballpark is completed.

Basketball

Cal Bears: Harmon Gym, UC Berkeley Campus, Bancroft St. at Telegraph St., Berkeley, 800/GO BEARS (462-3277). www.berkeley.edu. Also plays three games at San Francisco's Cow Palace.

Golden State Warriors: New Arena at the Oakland Coliseum, (I-880 to Hegenberger Rd. exit or BART to Coliseum station), Oakland, 510/986-2236. www.nba.com/warriors.

Summer Pro-Am League: Kezar Pavilion, at Stanyan and Beulah sts. (near Golden Gate Park), SF. On weekday evenings during the summer, watch some present and future NBA stars (past participants include Jason Kidd and Gary Payton) take on local playground legends. Free admission.

Stanford Cardinal: Maples Pavilion, Stanford Campus, 800/BEAT CAL (232-8225). www.stanford.edu.

Football

Cal Bears: Memorial Stadium, UC Berkeley Campus, Stadium Way off Piedmont Ave., Berkeley, 800/GO BEARS (462-3277). www.berkeley.edu.

Oakland Raiders: Oakland Coliseum, (I-880 to Hegenberger Rd. exit or BART to Coliseum station), Oakland, 800/949-2626. www.raiders.com.

San Francisco 49ers: 3Com/Candlestick Park, (Hwy 101 to 3Com/Candlestick exit on the southern edge of San Francisco), SF, 415/468-2249. www.sf49ers.com.

Stanford Cardinal: Stanford Stadium, Stanford Campus, 800/BEAT CAL (232-8225). www.stanford.edu.

Hockey

San Jose Sharks: San Jose Arena (W. Santa Clara and Autumn sts.), San Jose, 800/366-4423. www.sj-sharks.com.

Soccer

San Jose Clash: Spartan Stadium, at 7th St. and Alma Ave., San Jose State University, San Jose, 408/241-9922. www.clash.com.

San Francisco Bay Seals: Kezar Pavilion, at Stanyan and Beulah sts. (near Golden Gate Park), SF, 415/39-SEALS (7-3257). www.sfbayseals.com.

Arts and Entertainment

MOVIE THEATERS

Multiplexes dominate the mainstream-movie scene. Those who can wait awhile after hot new movies are released can see them at a substantial discount at many theaters. Next to San Francisco, the Palo Alto area has the most theaters showing alternative flicks: foreign, independent, art, or classic. In an effort to cope with sellouts, many theaters allow customers to purchase tickets in advance over the phone using a credit card. Call your local theater for additional information on these programs. You can also always dial 408/777-FILM (3456) for a quick listing of the next and nearest show time of your favorite flick, yours without even finding the paper. Finally, don't forget to check out movies playing in alternative venues like universities and libraries: you may find movies well beyond the mainstream, often at bargain prices.

Daly City to San Carlos

Burlingame Drive-In: Burlingame Ave. off Old Bayshore Hwy., Burlingame, 650/343-2213. A funky, penny-wise option. Double features of first-run films play at this relic with outmoded prices for those who are willing to forego state-of-the-art sound. $5.25 general admission.

Century Hyatt 3: 1304 Old Bayshore Hwy. (Broadway/Millbrae Ave.), Burlingame, 650/340-1516. First-run multiplex. $7.75.

Century Plaza 8: 410 Noor Ave. (off El Camino Real north of I-380 and Tanforan), South San Francisco, 650/742-9200. First-run multiplex. $7.75.

Hillsdale Cinema: 3011 S. El Camino Real (Hillsdale), San Mateo, 650/349-4511. First-run multiplex. $7.

Tanforan Discount: Tanforan Shopping Ctr., El Camino Real and Sneath Ln., San Bruno, 650/588-0291. Discount first-run multiplex. $3.50.

UA Metro Center: 200 Colma Blvd. (Junipero Serra/El Camino), Colma, 650/994-1065. First-run multiplex. $8.

Redwood City to Mountain View

Aquarius Cinemas: 430 Emerson St. (University/Lytton), Palo Alto, 650/32MOVIE (6-6843). Aquarius shows foreign films that are hard to track down elsewhere. $7.50.

Century Cinema 16: 1500 N. Shoreline Blvd. (Hwy 101), Mountain View, 650/960-0970. Huge first-run multiplex. Parking lot fills up and popular movies frequently sell out. $7.75.

Century Park 12: 557 E. Bayshore Rd. (Whipple), Redwood City, 650/365-9000. First-run multiplex. $7.

Guild Theater: 949 El Camino Real (Live Oak/Menlo Ave.), Menlo Park, 650/32MOVIE (6-6843). The Guild shows artsy and foreign films in a slightly down-at-the-heels Art Deco auditorium adorned with frayed velvet curtains and giant chevrons. Bring a sweater on a cool night; this theater is mercilessly under-heated. $7.50.

Palo Alto Square: 3000 El Camino Real (Page Mill), Palo Alto, 650/32MOVIE (6-6843). A spacious duplex showing a mix of commercial and art-house flicks, Palo Alto Square is the South Bay's participant in the San Francisco International Film Festival held each spring. $7.50.

Park Theater: 1275 El Camino Real (Oak Grove/Valparaiso), Menlo Park, 650/32MOVIE (6-6843). Almost identical to its neighbor, the Guild. $7.50.

The Stanford Theater: 221 University Ave. (Emerson/Ramona), Palo Alto, 650/324-3700. The remodeled Stanford Theater presents double features of classic movies (along with a few old clunkers) in an elaborate Art Deco setting complete with live organ music. Showings follow monthly themes—Sinatra, for example—and features change every few nights. $6 for double feature.

UA Redwood Six: 305 Walnut St. (Veterans), Redwood City, 650/367-9090. Last chance for first-run films at a multiplex. $7.

Sunnyvale to San Jose

Almaden Cinema 5: Willow Glen Shopping Ctr., 2306 Almaden Rd. (Almaden Expwy./Curtner), San Jose, 408/265-7373. Older first-run films. Recently remodeled. Discounts.

AMC Mercado 20: Mercado Santa Clara Center, 3111 Mission College Blvd. (Great America), Santa Clara, 408/919-0248. First-run multiplex. $7.50.

AMC Milpitas 10: 577 E. Calaveras Blvd. (I-880), Milpitas, 408/946-5050. First-run multiplex. $6.75.

AMC Oakridge Six: Oakridge Mall, 913 Blossom Hill Rd. (Santa Teresa), San Jose, 408/227-6660. First-run multiplex. $6.

AMC Saratoga 14: El Paseo de Saratoga, Campbell and Saratoga aves., Saratoga, 408/871-1441. First-run multiplex. $7.50.

AMC Sunnyvale Six: Sunnyvale Town Center, McKinley and Mathilda aves., Sunnyvale, 408/746-3800. First-run multiplex. $6.

AMC Town & Country: Town & Country Shopping Ctr., Stevens Creek and Winchester blvds., San Jose, 408/243-4262. First-run multiplex. $7.50.

Camera One: 366 S. 1st St. (San Carlos/San Salvador), San Jose, 408/998-3005. Art and foreign flicks. $7.50.

Camera Three: 288 S. 2nd St. (San Carlos), San Jose, 408/998-3300. Art and foreign flicks. $7.50.

Capitol Drive-In: Capitol Expwy. and Monterey Rd., San Jose, 408/226-2251. Double features of first-run films with FM radio sound. $5.75 per person.

Campbell Plaza 4: 2501 Winchester Blvd. (Campbell Ave./San Tomas), Campbell, 408/378-2425. Discount first-run multiplex. $3.

The Cellar: Agenda Lounge, 399 S. 1st St. (San Salvador), San Jose, 408/287-3991. Alternative 16mm films every Thursday night. Free.

Century Capitol 16: Capitol Expwy. and Snell Ave., San Jose, 408/972-9276. First-run multiplex. $7.50.

Century 10 Berryessa: 1171 N. Capitol Ave. (Berryessa), San Jose, 408/926-7091. First-run multiplex. $7.75.

Century 21-24: 3161 Olsen Dr. (Winchester), San Jose, 408/984-5610. First-run multiplex. $7.75.

Century 25: Westgate Shopping Ctr., Campbell and Saratoga aves., San Jose, 408/984-5610. First-run multiplex. $7.75.

Meridian Six: 4400 Stevens Creek Blvd. (Kiely/Lawrence), San Jose, 408/246-6710. First-run multiplex. $6.

Oaks Cinema Five: 21275 Stevens Creek Blvd. (Hwy 85), Cupertino, 408/446-0472. Pass holders can see older first-runs films for $1.50 Mondays through Thursdays and $3 on the weekends. Membership $2.

Towne Theatre: 1433 The Alameda (Naglee/Race), San Jose, 408/287-1433. Art, independent, and foreign flicks (part of the Camera chain). $7.50.

UA Pavilion Theaters: 201 S. 2nd St. (San Carlos), San Jose, 408/277-0114. First-run multiplex. $7

UA PruneYard: PruneYard Shopping Center, Campbell and Bascom aves., Campbell, 408/371-3020. First-run multiplex. $7.

PERFORMING ARTS

To find out what's playing where and when, check out the following resources:

sanjose.phone: 408/295-2265. Events line for San Jose activities. www.sanjose.org.

Silicon Valley Classics: www.classicalmusic.org. Online calendar of events.

Classical Music and Opera

California Youth Symphony: 650/325-6666. Since 1952 the Youth Symphony has maintained a variety of programs for training future stars. The award-winning group performs in the San Mateo Performing Arts Center, the Flint Center, and Foothill College (where some performances are free).

Opera San Jose: Montgomery Theatre, W. San Carlos and S. Market sts., San Jose, 408/437-4450. The company of young and talented professionals regularly performs works by Verdi, Rossini, Mozart, and others at the Montgomery Theatre. • Box office M-F 9am-6pm.

Palo Alto Chamber Orchestra: 650/856-3848. An excellent group of young Peninsula musicians that performs chamber and symphonic works, mostly in Spangenberg Theatre at Gunn High School.

Peninsula Civic Light Opera: San Mateo Performing Arts Center, 428 Peninsula Ave. (Delaware), San Mateo, 650/579-5568. This popular community theater company appears at the San Mateo Performing Arts Center.

Peninsula Symphony Orchestra: 650/574-0244. The orchestra performs at the Flint Center and the San Mateo Performing Arts Center. An annual holiday concert is held in conjunction with the Stanford University chorus in Stanford Memorial Chapel in late November.

Pocket Opera: 415/575-1102. Features operas translated into English by Donald Pippin. A small chamber orchestra accompanies the vocalists. The company, which delivers a light touch to an often very serious art form, performs throughout the Bay Area, including in the Mountain View Center for the Performing Arts.

Redwood Symphony: Cañada College (exit I-280 at Farm Hill Blvd.), Redwood City, 650/366-6872. Based at Cañada College, the Redwood Symphony performs its own casual brand of orchestral music throughout the area. During family concerts children can sit on stage with the orchestra.

San Jose Symphony Orchestra: 408/288-2828. Attracts excellent soloists and guest conductors. Tickets tend to be a little less expensive than those for the San Francisco Symphony. Performances are held in the Flint Center, the San Jose Center for the Performing Arts, and the San Jose Civic Auditorium.

San Jose Chamber Orchestra: 408/286-5111. San Jose's resident chamber music company.

Stanford University: Braun Music Center, Stanford University, 650/723-3811. The **Stanford Symphony Orchestra** and the **Symphonic Chorus** are excellent groups, particularly when they perform together. The **Chamber Chorale** is a smaller chorus that performs chamber music of every period from the Renaissance to the 20th century.

West Bay Opera: 650/843-3900. The second oldest opera company in the Bay Area, the West Bay Opera appears at the Lucie Stern Theatre in Palo Alto. The highly acclaimed group performs three fully staged operas per year, plus the occasional shorter piece. Watch for student discounts on Thursday nights.

Dance

Lively Arts at Stanford: Press Courtyard, Santa Teresa St., Stanford University, 650/723-2551. The Lively Arts at Stanford routinely brings such well-known and innovative groups as MOMIX, Bebe Miller Dance Company, and Pilobolus to various campus venues. Also, the Dance Division of the Stanford Athletics Department presents ballet, modern, jazz, and ethnic dance concerts throughout the year; the annual Spring Migration is a highlight. • Information M-F 8am-5pm.

Peninsula Ballet Theatre: San Mateo Performing Arts Center, 600 N. Delaware St. (Peninsula), San Mateo, 650/343-8485. The only professional ballet company in the mid-Peninsula area draws consistently good notices for favorites such as *The Nutcracker* and *Giselle*.

San Jose Cleveland Ballet: Center for the Performing Arts, Almaden Blvd. and Park Ave., San Jose, 408/288-2800. This joint venture between the cities of San Jose and Cleveland has received critical acclaim for its performances of new ballets and elegant renditions of the classics. The company performs from October to April at the San Jose Center for the Performing Arts.

San Jose Dance Theater: 408/293-5665. Performs *The Nutcracker* at the San Jose Center for the Performing Arts.

Theater

American Musical Theatre: 408/453-7100. Performs traditional Broadway musicals on a large scale at the San Jose Center for the Performing Arts.

City Lights Theater Company: 529 S. 2nd St. (William/Reed), San Jose, 408/295-4200. A talented small company that produces an eclectic variety of contemporary plays.

Mountain View Center for the Performing Arts: Mercy and Castro sts., Mountain View, 650/903-6000. Hosts community theaters, professional touring companies, and international artists and attractions. Look out for free summer events.

Palo Alto Players: 650/329-0891. The oldest group around; they put on five shows a year, notable for their consistent quality and reasonable ticket prices.

Venues

Burgess Theater: 601 Laurel St. (Willow/Ravenswood), Menlo Park, 650/323-9365.

City Lights Theater: 529 S. 2nd St. (William/Reed), San Jose, 408/295-4200.

Cubberley Theatre: 4000 Middlefield Rd. (San Antonio/Charleston), Palo Alto, 650/329-2418.

Flint Center: De Anza College, 21250 Stevens Creek Blvd. (Hwy 85), Cupertino, 408/864-8816.

Foothill College: 12345 El Monte Rd. (I-280), Los Altos, 650/948-4444.

Fox Theatre: 2215 Broadway (Middlefield), Redwood City, 650/363-0149.

Hillbarn Theatre: 1285 E. Hillsdale Blvd. (Foster City Blvd.), Foster City, 650/349-6411.

Lucie Stern Theatre: 1305 Middlefield Rd. (Melville), Palo Alto, 650/329-2526.

Montgomery Theater: S. Market and W. San Carlos sts., San Jose, 408/277-3900.

Mountain View Center for the Performing Arts: Mercy and Castro sts., Mountain View, 650/903-6000.

San Jose Center for the Performing Arts: 255 S. Almaden Blvd. (San Carlos), San Jose, 408/277-3900.

San Jose Repertory Theatre: 101 Paseo de San Antonio (Market), San Jose, 408/291-2255.

San Mateo Performing Arts Center: 600 N. Delaware St. (Peninsula), San Mateo, 650/762-0258.

Santa Clara University Theatre: Mayer Theater, Santa Clara Univ. (The Alameda and Palm Dr.), Santa Clara, 408/554-4015.

Sunnyvale Community Center Theater: 550 E. Remington Dr. (Saratoga-Sunnyvale/El Camino), Sunnyvale, 408/733-6611.

Spangenberg Theatre: Gunn High School, 780 Arastradero Rd. (Foothill), Palo Alto, 650/354-8220.

Villa Montalvo Center for the Arts: 15400 Montalvo Rd. (Saratoga-Los Gatos Rd.), Saratoga, 408/961-5858.

San Jose Repertory Theatre: 408/291-2255. A professional company producing a combination of classics, old favorites, and some original plays in a stunning new blue-paneled theater.

Saratoga Drama Group: 408/255-0801. This group has been putting on two musicals a year for the past three decades and has developed a considerable following.

Silicon Valley Shakespeare Festival: 415/422-2221. It's free. The players perform on summer weekends in outdoor venues throughout the Bay Area—call for locations. Don't forget your blanket and picnic.

Stage One Theatre: 408/293-6362. Produces cutting-edge contemporary theatre. Highlights include the South Bay premiere of *Jeffrey*.

Teatro Vision: 408/947-8227. This San Jose theater group challenges audiences to think about issues that confront Chicanos and Latinos.

TheatreWorks: 650/903-6000. A highly regarded and extremely popular local company that produces everything from Broadway musicals to staged readings of new works, TheatreWorks performs primarily at the Lucie Stern in Palo Alto and the Mountain View Center for the Performing Arts.

BARS & CLUBS

The Peninsula and Silicon Valley are home to a huge array of nightspots that cater to the many different tastes of the eclectic residents. Beer drinkers rejoice: a growing number of bars brew their own beer, and many others serve great selections on tap. Great sources for finding out what's happening each weekend are the *Metro*, the "Eye" section in Friday's *San Jose Mercury News*, Sunday's *San Francisco Examiner-Chronicle* "Datebook" section (the pink pages), the *Bay Guardian*, and the *SF Weekly*. You might want to call **BASS Tickets** at 510/762-2277 or 408/998-2277 for information on ticket availability for bigger shows and a listing of events. You can also buy tickets on line through ticketweb: www.ticketweb.com. See Major Venues sidebar for descriptions of the most popular places for large shows.

Closing time is 2am (although some places close earlier, especially weeknights) and the legal state drinking age is 21 (most bars and clubs check identification religiously). Some nightspots, especially those with live entertainment, have All Ages nights, when the age requirement drops to 18 and customers over 21 can get their hands stamped for liquor purchase.

Agenda Restaurant Bar & Lounge: 399 S. 1st St. (San Salvador), San Jose, 408/287-3991. Located in a sleekly renovated turn-of-the-century building, Agenda is a three-story contemporary club and adult-entertainment playground wrapped around a stylish restaurant. With its bold decor, this popular destination attracts a smart, young downtown crowd in search of a serious cocktail or a late dinner. Upstairs, live music favors jazz—trad, acid, Latin, or swing—and reggae. Downstairs, a DJ spins dance tunes. Complimentary hors d'oeuvres are served during happy hour (daily 5-7:30pm).

Alberto's Club: 736 W. Dana St. (Castro/Hope), Mountain View, 650/968-3007. Cross the threshold and you'll receive a first-rate introduction to Latin American dance music. Alberto's has DJ dancing to salsa most nights (Mondays are reserved for tango, Saturdays for live Spanish rock) and lessons are included with the cover charge for early arrivals. Occasional Fridays live Salsa acts make an appearance.

Alpine Inn: 3915 Alpine Rd. (Arastradero), Portola Valley, 650/854-4004. A former stagecoach stop and longtime standby that's still known primarily by its old nickname, Zott's (the full name used to be Risotti's). Today, the name has changed, but the burgers are still acclaimed all over the Peninsula, and the outdoor picnic tables are a great (if dusty) place to hang with friends. Gather up 10 of your closest chums, plant yourselves in the sun on a Saturday afternoon, and order a couple of pitchers of beer.

Antonio's Nut House: 321 California Ave. (Birch), Palo Alto, 650/321-2550. For knee-deep nutshells, peek into Antonio's Nut House (it's unclear whether the name refers to the snacks or the clientele). Snarl hello to barmaids Melinda and Barb and drink a beer while watching the big-screen TV, or take in a game of pool—if the regulars will let you play.

Ausiello's Tavern: 864 El Camino Real (Ralston), Belmont, 650/595-9531. Have a beer where the athletes themselves drink. Too many bars hang up memorabilia, turn on a football game, and call themselves a sports bar. At Ausiello's the passion for sports is real. Just ask any one of the pool-shooting baseball players still dressed in their grass-stained trousers. And forget the cocktails, because there are none: true sports fans swig cold beer and munch on salted peanuts.

Bahay Kubo: 203 Linden Ave. (Grand), South San Francisco, 650/583-6683. A Filipino bar that serves traditional food and bottles of cold beer to a hungry and thirsty "industrial city" workforce. There's nothing pretentious about this friendly place, as empty beer boxes are stacked next to the old Formica tables and plastic chairs. Monday through Friday from 4pm to 6pm is happy hour. Come then for free Filipino appetizers and 50 cents off already low-priced drinks.

The Bank: 14421 Big Basin Wy. (Saratoga-Sunnyvale), Saratoga, 408/867-5155. The Bank, which really was a bank, has been deemed a historic landmark by the city of Saratoga. The charm of the venerable brick building attracts an older crowd, the elegance of the flock wallpaper lures well-dressed couples, the comfort of the plush couches brings in a younger crew, and the tackiness of hundreds of knickknacks appeals to everyone else out for a casual evening of fun.

Barley and Hopps: 201 South B St. (2nd), San Mateo, 650/348-7808. The name Barley and Hopps tells you that this is a brewpub. The beer is pretty good, especially the India pale ale, and complements the hearty menu: lots of smoky barbecue, gourmet deep-dish pizza, and the like. After dinner, head upstairs for a cigar and a game of pool, or downstairs to Blues on B, the basement blues club.

The B-hive Bar & Lounge: 372 S. 1st. St. (San Carlos/San Salvador), San Jose, 408/298-2529. As they like to say at the B-hive, they're buzzing. You have to be 21 years old or older to get in, but this dance club above the Olympia restaurant finds plenty of candidates. The doors open at 9pm, but the place doesn't really get going until around eleven. The heavy bass from the dance music, the brightly colored lights spinning and flashing throughout the room, and the crowded dance floor make this club one of San Jose's hottest. But don't leave home in your blue jeans: the shiniest, tightest club gear seems to be the unspoken dress code. Drink specials run early.

Black Watch: 141½ N. Santa Cruz Ave. (Nicolson), Los Gatos, 408/354-2200. Watch out or you'll be waiting in line, both to get inside Black Watch and for a taxi home. The bar has long been known for it's $5 pint-size kamikazes, which are served with a strainer and as many short-stemmed glasses as you need to send your entire table spinning out of control. Since driving after a couple rounds like this is suicidal, catch a cab home.

Blue Chalk Café: 630 Ramona St. (Hamilton/Forest), Palo Alto, 650/326-1020. One of downtown Palo Alto's most popular hangouts, Blue Chalk has something to keep everyone entertained far into the evening. The airy, two-level hall features an excellent restaurant, three pool tables rented by the hour (or one "challenge" table for the hustlers), dart lanes, a shuffleboard table, and a sports TV section. If you're thirsty, pick from the good selection of local microbrews on tap. A healthy mix of singles-scene energy and neighborhood-hangout comfort coexists here.

Boswell's: PruneYard Shopping Center, Campbell and Bascom aves., Campbell, 408/371-4404. The dimly lit Anglophile yard-sale theme sets Boswell's apart from its bright American surroundings. Sibling to Woodside's venerable Pioneer Saloon, anonymous local bands keep the joint jumping with solid rock covers nightly.

Britannia Arms: 5027 Almaden Expwy. (Hwy 85/Cherry), San Jose, 408/266-0550. • 1087 Saratoga-Sunnyvale Rd. (Bollinger/Prospect), Cupertino, 408/252-7262. The pints-and-darts folks fill this pair of British theme pubs. You won't forget you're in Silicon Valley, but listening to a good band or watching a soccer game with a delicious black and tan in hand is a good way to catch your breath.

British Bankers Club: 1090 El Camino Real (Santa Cruz), Menlo Park, 650/327-8769. Sink into an overstuffed parlor chair, order a round of Guinness, and imagine you're hanging out in a posh English drawing room straight out of *Brideshead Revisited*. A wide selection of English brews is offered on tap, and British fare such as shepherd's pie is served at the bar. In the evenings, the BBC swarms with fortysomething divorcés making their first forays back into the dating scene. The plush atmosphere is a refreshing change from the noise of other bars, although it does occasionally heat up courtesy of live blues bands.

C.B. Hannegan's: 208 Bachman Ave. (N. Santa Cruz), Los Gatos, 408/395-1233. The ground floor houses a dinerlike restaurant with a well-lit counter, a few booths, and a large glass-enclosed patio. Upstairs, a darker spruced-up bar offers lively action and a top-notch list of beers and single-malt scotches to a mostly singles crowd.

Cactus Club: 417 S. 1st St. (San Salvador), San Jose, 408/4919300. This SoFA (South of First Area) dance club serves up live rock and alternative music part of the week, while DJs spin a mix of hip hop, house, top 40, gothic, and industrial the other days. Admission without alcohol for those 18 to 21.

Café Borrone: 1010 El Camino Real (Santa Cruz), Menlo Park, 650/327-0830. Inside this hugely popular spot you'll probably have to share a table. Outside, relax at one of the umbrella-shaded patio tables and enjoy espresso drinks, beer, and wine. Staffers are young and attractive, and the atmosphere is lively. On weekend nights, the teens come out to compare piercings and tattoos.

Café Fino: 544 Emerson St. (University/Hamilton), Palo Alto, 650/326-6082. With its antique cash register, mahogany bar, and ceiling murals, the lively Café Fino is reminiscent of an amusing 1940s-style Art Deco piano bar. Come in for the great jazz (starting nightly around 7pm) but stay for the delicious food.

Café Quinn: Oaks Ctr., 21269 Stevens Creek Blvd. (Mary), Cupertino, 408/252-CAFÉ (2233). Food and service are quirky in this airy café, but tall windows and an outdoor patio make it a winner in warm weather. Espresso drinks, smoothies, beer, and wine cater to healthy and unhealthy tastes alike.

The Carlos Club: 612 El Camino Real (San Carlos Ave.), San Carlos 650/593-8985. Voted the best bar on the Peninsula in 1998 by the *San Mateo Times,* this Las Vegas–style lounge still attracts the same seasoned drinkers that have been frequenting it for the past 25 years, but a younger crowd is beginning to make its mark. Something about the dim red lighting, the lava-rock wall behind the bar, the fireplace, the huge couch, the piano, and the padded black-vinyl bar top—perfect for drinks and elbows—has made this into the town's hottest spot. On Thursdays, Fridays, and Saturdays the place heats up with the most entertaining karaoke scene on the Peninsula.

Carry Nations: 8 N. Santa Cruz Blvd. (Main), Los Gatos, 408/354-1771. The modern upscale decor, complete with small overhead lights accenting the restored brick and a single couch in back, attracts local professionals on weekdays. On weekends, the same atmosphere draws a younger, louder crowd. No bar places more importance on the quality of the drinks and the service and delivers accordingly.

Celia's: 3740 El Camino Real (Curtner), Palo Alto, 650/843-0643. • 504 Peninsula Ave. (Delaware/Claremont), San Mateo, 650/343-5886. • 201 El Camino Real (San Felipe), San Bruno, 650/877-8245. This growing chain serves up the usual Mexican-American food in a faux ranchero setting of tiles, stucco, open beams, and bright flags. The food is adequate, but the potent margaritas and the festive bar atmosphere are worth a visit.

Cheers: 685 E. El Camino Real (Fair Oaks), Sunnyvale, 408/749-1288. Dollar drink nights (Sundays and Wednesdays) pack in the bargain hunters. The music is a combination of dance singles mixed with classic rock. On Thursdays and Fridays you'll also find a large crowd, even though the drink specials aren't as generous. But the cowboys don't seem to mind as long as the music—sometimes live—stays country. An added benefit is the free line-dancing lessons, if you can find room on the large dance floor. When things heat up, get some fresh air on the patio.

Cheshire Pub and Pizzeria: 1494 El Camino Real (White Oak), San Carlos, 650/592-0607. The Cheshire is an unobtrusive neighborhood bar with all kinds of imported beers, including Guinness and Harp on tap. At first glance, you might not even know pizza is served, but you'll soon discover hungry regulars ordering up the popular pies. A handy take-out service and pleasant open-air patio make pizza eating even more pleasurable.

City Pub: 2620 Broadway (El Camino), Redwood City, 650/363-2620. A hip and happening hangout in Redwood City's revived downtown, the City Pub draws trendy Peninsulans sporting the latest Doc Martens and Gap flannels. Designer lighting shines on the restored brick, requisite fireplace, and mod copper bar. Decent pub grub and an excellent selection of beer on tap—24 varieties at last count, including Tied House Amber, Lighthouse Ale, and Pilsener Urquell—keep customers coming.

The Claran: 1251 Franklin Mall (Benton/Homestead), Santa Clara, 408/296-9558. This no-frills student bar is usually pretty quiet until about midnight. Then small groups of three or four people wander in for that much-needed break from studying. The black-and-white-checkered floor and the Formica bar contribute a little character to the place but not much. The modern-rock jukebox adds a little life, and the cheap drinks add a little pleasure.

Coffee Society: Oaks Shopping Center, 21265 Stevens Creek Blvd. (Hwy 85), Cupertino, 408/725-8091. While Nike-clad Apple employees type on PowerBooks inside, their chain-smoking, nose-pierced kids monopolize the tables outside. Weekends and evenings can be packed and loud. Service can be slow and sloppy, but it's the only lively café in Cupertino.

Compadres Mexican Bar and Grill: 3877 El Camino Real (Curtner/Arastradero), Palo Alto, 650/858-1141. Summer or winter, people fill the courtyard tables at Compadres, munching chips and salsa and downing huge, frosty margaritas (some of the best around). Check it out on your birthday and you might walk away with a piñata and a photo of yourself in an oversize Mexican sombrero.

Dicey Riley's Irish Pub: 221 Park Rd. (Burlingame Ave./Howard), Burlingame, 650/347-7656. If you're in Burlingame and want to enjoy a pint or sip a smooth Irish whiskey, then roll into Dicey's. Sporting a large bar and plenty of Naugahyde, this roomy, casual, brightly lit place is more a blue-collar American bar than an Irish pub. Try your hand at darts, show off your pool skills, watch a soccer match on one of the clearest big-screen TVs in the Bay Area, or simply talk the night away in one of the booths scattered throughout the room.

Dos Locos: 150 S. 1st St. #F2 (Paseo de San Antonio), San Jose, 408/993-9616. You almost feel as if you're in a glass when you sit at the small bar here. Surrounded by windows, the inside of Dos Locos is not much bigger than a San Jose State classroom—where many patrons spend time. There's a seating area outside the actual bar, but not actually outside: the small tables are crowded onto a tile floor and roped off inside a mall—for lack of a better word—surrounded by shops and another bar. This is also home to one of the tastiest margaritas in town. And at 32 ounces, it's one of the biggest, too.

Duke of Edinburgh: 10801 N. Wolfe Rd. (Homestead), Cupertino, 408/446-3853. This Silicon Valley watering hole for would-be Brits dispenses eight brews on tap, including Watneys, Harp, Fullers, and Newcastle brown ale, and serves quintessential "English fayre" such as fish-and-chips (crispy and not too oily), bangers and mash, and a good ploughman's lunch. The interior, from the carpeting to the lamps, was imported from England. On warm afternoons, sit on the outdoor patio and enjoy a classic English refreshment such as a black and tan or a shandy.

The Dutch Goose: 3567 Alameda de las Pulgas (Avy), Menlo Park, 650/854-3245. Push through the creaky screen door into this dark hole-in-the-wall with pinball machines, pool tables, and a small patio in the back. The carvings in the tabletops and the peanut shells on the floor finger the place as an old-timer. Ask the bartender to pull you an Anchor Steam from the tap, try some deviled eggs, toss your peanut shells on the floor, and relax.

The Edge: 260 California Ave. (Birch/Park), Palo Alto, 650/324-EDGE (3343). Primarily a dance club playing modern rock of the Live-105 variety (dress in black if you really want to fit in), The Edge also puts on concerts by hip local bands or even national acts as diverse as Black Uhuru and Hole. Although this is one of the few places where the under-21 set can go for a good time, it's not exclusively a teenybopper hangout.

The Elephant Bar: 1600 Old Bayshore Hwy. (Broadway/Millbrae Ave.), Burlingame 650/259-9585. If you show up here, you'd probably be nuts to try the Coco Loco. It's a 48-ounce tropical fruit concoction with a punch that could bring an elephant to its knees. The decor is just as wild as the drinks are. Your best bet is to follow the tiger-print carpet past the circular bar—where you'll be greeted by countless small brass elephant heads—and over to a booth. Then slide back on the leopard-skin seat cushion and enjoy one of the most spectacular views of the Bay you'll find anywhere. The Elephant draws much of its clientele from nearby airport hotels

Empire Grill and Tap Room: 651 Emerson St. (Forest/Hamilton), Palo Alto, 650/321-3030. The lovely vine-covered patio is the perfect spot for a quiet and relaxing lunch, weekend brunch, or romantic dinner, while the wood-paneled interior appeals to a boisterous crowd of singles and high-tech wheelers and dealers in search of microbrewed beers and martinis.

Fanny & Alexander: 412 Emerson St. (University/Lytton), Palo Alto, 650/326-7183. Inside, this Scandinavian beer garden looks more like an upscale big-city pub, with shiny hardwood floors, deep ocher walls, and lots of open space. Then the crowds descend and you know you're in Palo Alto. If the weather is warm, enjoy the spacious back patio where a crowd grooves to live music on weekends.

Faultline Brewing Company: 1235 Oakmead Pkwy. (N. Lawrence/Arques), Sunnyvale, 408/736-2739. This behemoth of a brewpub offers all the charm of a converted Rusty Scupper in an office park, which is exactly what it is. Fortunately, the customers don't seem to mind the lack of ambience. What they want is a convenient place for high-quality beer and delicious food, and Faultline certainly delivers. Weeknights between 6pm and 10pm Faultline is a sardine can.

Fiddler's Green: 333 El Camino Real (Taylor/Hillcrest), Millbrae, 650/697-3419. The smooth, creamy, black Guinness that pours from the overworked Fiddler's Green tap has most of the other local Irish pubs green with envy. It's the closest you'll come to the real thing on the Peninsula. Dark wood accents, a warm atmosphere, and an excellent pub menu make it easy to see why Irish immigrants consider this their home away from home.

Fibbar Magee's: 156 S. Murphy Ave. (Washington/Evelyn), Sunnyvale, 408/749-8373. • 223 Castro St. (Dana/Villa), Mountain View, 650/964-9151. In recent years, this newish Irish pub, complete with stone fireplace and plenty of beers on tap, has become the hottest spot on Murphy Avenue. Weeknights primarily are rosy-cheeked Irish laughing it up while they chat the night away. On the weekends, much louder and younger American weekend warriors join the Irish. Attracted by the live music, which can be anything from traditional Irish to modern rock to disco, the weekenders dance the night away. The second Fibbar Magee's opened in 1996 to accommodate the hoards of people at the Sunnyvale location, and everything was done right. There are hidden booths tucked away for privacy, knowledgeable bartenders who can make almost any drink imaginable, a diverse array of live bands, and a large parquet dance floor.

The Flying Pig: 78 S. 1st St. (San Fernando/Santa Clara), San Jose, 408/298-6710. This is one of downtown's hippest hangouts, enjoying a large student following from San Jose State and the neighboring community colleges. The bar is exceptionally clean for a college hangout (there's even a cozy fireplace), and some of the regulars are dressed to impress (they must be downtown workers). Outside seating makes it possible to escape the decibel level of the modern music blasting inside this classy bar.

Francesca's: 2135 Old Middlefield Way (Rengstorff), Mountain View, 650/965-1162. On the outside it looks like an Italian restaurant. Inside, it's a great place to relax. The casual atmosphere and the semicircular padded booths in the back room—they hold six comfortably—make group conversations possible. The average customer age is 40ish, consequently the jukebox is stocked primarily with easy rock selections from the '70s and '80s.

Major Bay Area Venues

Concord Pavilion: Ygnacio Valley Rd. (off Hwy 680), Concord, 510/671-3100, 510/676-8742. Large, outdoor amphitheater featuring major-label performers spring through fall. Attracts country western acts in addition to traditional rock. Capacity: 12,500.

The Fillmore: 1805 Geary Blvd. (Fillmore), SF, 415/346-6000, show info; 415/346-3000, office. It is hard to conceive of the '60s ever having happened without the psychedelic extravaganzas that occurred here: the Grateful Dead, Janis Joplin, Jefferson Airplane, and many more. These days, the bilevel ballroom with great acoustics continues to draw big-time rockers on occasion (e.g., Tom Petty's twenty-night engagement), while providing an encouraging setting for young bands on their way up. Many shows are all ages, which brings out the teenagers in force. Capacity: 1,100.

Great American Music Hall: 859 O'Farrell St. (Polk/Larkin), SF, 415/885-0750. There may not be a better place in the city to see live music than this gorgeous, ornate venue in a seedy block of the Tenderloin. A 19th century vaudeville hall restored to its former glory, the club has red velvet drapes, marble columns, a wraparound horseshoe balcony, and a gold-leaf, molded ceiling. The size is just about perfect—not too large, not too small—and as long as you're not sitting behind one of those ground-floor columns, the sight lines are excellent. Best of all, the wooden floor and the high ceiling make the acoustics consistently superb, no matter what kind of music is being performed. Capacity: 600.

Greek Theatre: Gayley Rd. (Hearst/Bancroft), UC Berkeley Campus, Berkeley, 510/642-9988, 510/642-0527. A very pretty outdoor amphitheater. Hosts a popular spring and summer concert series featuring major-label acts, with an emphasis on folk-rockers like Tracy Chapman. The seating is designed so that each audience member has a killer view of the stage. Bring a blanket to cushion the concrete seats. Better acoustics down low. Capacity: 8,500.

Kaiser Arena: 10 10th St. (Fallon), Oakland, 510/238-7765. A fairly large arena that highlights rhythm and blues acts and standbys like Tower of Power. Capacity: 8,000.

Lively Arts at Stanford: Stanford Univ., Stanford, 650/723-2551. The Stanford Concert Network brings professional acts like Shawn Colvin to campus every year, usually at very low prices. The intimate, outdoor **Frost Amphitheater** holds occasional concerts, but most well-known groups play at gloomy **Memorial Auditorium** when they come to campus. Capacity: Frost 3,000; Memorial Auditorium 1,700.

Oakland Coliseum and Stadium: 7000 Coliseum Way (off Hwy 880 at Hegenberger), Oakland, 510/569-2121. Major Bay Area concerts come to the Oakland Coliseum (the indoor basketball arena) and the Oakland Stadium (the huge outdoor stadium). Accessible via BART. Capacity: Arena 15,000; Stadium 65,000.

Shoreline Amphitheatre: Shoreline Blvd. (Amphitheatre), Mountain View, 650/967-4040. Large outdoor amphitheater hosting a varied lineup of major acts performing spring through fall. Reserved seating down low, general admission on the lawn further back, with large video monitors set up so you can see the band. Generally pleasant, but it was built on landfill, and you can occasionally smell it. Capacity: 20,000.

Slim's: 333 11th St. (Folsom/Harrison), SF, 415/522-0333. A big-time venue for live music, Slim's is a large, airy space that hosts a wide variety of performances, mostly rock but also blues, country, and ska. When a nationally known act comes here it's usually SRO on the expansive floor, which means those stuck behind one of the numerous support columns are SOL. The high ceiling muddles the sound, which makes the already-distracted crowd even less attentive, which often makes for an unsatisfying concert experience. To escape the scene, head for the balcony.

Villa Montalvo: 15400 Montalvo Rd. (Saratoga-Los Gatos Rd.), Saratoga, 408/961-5800. Smaller outdoor amphitheater on historic estate. Hosts a variety of summer performances, from music to drama to children's shows. Capacity: 800.

The Warfield: 982 Market St. (5th St./6th St.), SF, 415/775-7722, general info;. 415/775-9949, directions; 415/567-2060, office. One could easily mistake The Warfield for one of the Tenderloin strip joints that surround it, so (relatively) nondescript is its marquee. Step inside from the grime, however, and behold a beautiful old theater. The recently remodeled hall with old-style decor offers table seating with an oh-so-tiny mosh pit on the stage level and traditional theater seating (reserved) in the balcony. The Warfield has hosted everyone from Dylan to Dinosaur Jr., although in recent times it has done a heavy trade in the modern rock acts that are too big for the clubs, yet not quite ready to sell out the Coliseum. Folks with general-admission tickets should arrive very early to guarantee a good seat. Capacity: 2,000.

Fred's: 2534 Old Middlefield Way (San Antonio/Rengstorff), Mountain View 650/940-9838. Set back from the street, Fred's might be missed if you blink while driving by. It's a small dive with a local assemblage of liverless patrons who know where to go to get a stiff drink. Don't worry if you are not a regular. Most people who hang here love to talk. If they're not chatting, it's probably because they're involved in an intense game of dominos or someone is about to win a game of liar's dice. Don't be surprised if you find yourself playing in the next round.

Full Moon Saloon: 129 South B St. (1st/2nd), San Mateo, 650/340-8182. If you're a young and restless creature of the night, this is the bar for you. Nightly live music runs the gamut from techno to alternative to various forms of rock and roll, all played under the warm rays of multicolored spotlights. The crowd varies with the music. Two pool tables—one shares space with the dance floor—are nearly always in use. The lighting is dim red and the walls are black, except for a mural above the bar that depicts the universe with a giant full moon at its center.

Garden City: 360 S. Saratoga Ave. (Stevens Creek), San Jose 408/244-4443. Las Vegas comes to San Jose at this legendary South Bay steakhouse, located on the premises of the city's largest gambling and gaming venue. The dimly lit interior has a nightclub ambience. The traditional jazz bands that play here are usually a cut above average.

Gordon Biersch Restaurant/Brewery: 640 Emerson St. (Forest/Hamilton), Palo Alto, 650/323-7723. • 33 E. San Fernando St. (1st/2nd), San Jose, 408/294-6785. Gordon Biersch helped launch the Peninsula microbrewery and was the first of the crowd to cater directly to the yuppie market. Rampant competition has cut the crowds a little, but no one else attracts as many suits after work. Beer brewed on the premises is fresh and delicious, and the upscale food is pretty good, especially in San Jose. San Jose has live jazz Wednesday through Sunday nights and a nice patio.

Henry's World-Famous Hi Life: 301 W. Saint John St. (Almaden), San Jose, 408/295-5414. Henry's was known primarily for barbecued ribs and steak before the Sharks came to town. It's now known among hockey fans as *the* place to go before, during (if you don't have tickets), and after a game at the tank (the arena is just two blocks away). The full bar might appeal to dinner patrons, but it's the beer that sends the energetic fans into a frenzy. Show up early, as this memorabilia-packed bar fills up. On slow nongame nights, Henry's closes around 10pm.

The Horseshoe Club: 2655 El Camino Real (San Tomas/Kiely), Santa Clara, 408/248-4100. The only criterion for becoming a drinking member of the Horseshoe Club is that you have to like country music. It doesn't hurt to have a large cowboy hat, too, just like almost everyone else does. Every night except Mondays a country music band plays on the large stage against the back wall. The round bar, red lighting, and the never-empty dance floor add character to this urban saloon.

The Hut: 3200 The Alameda (Franklin), Santa Clara, 408/296-6024. A mostly mellow dive that sits in the shadows of Santa Clara University, The Hut is done up in furniture suitable for a motor home. There's a full bar, cheap drinks, a bartender named Coach (who actually is a coach and looks like one), a daily happy hour from 4pm to 7pm, and a pool table, darts, and pinball for entertainment. In other words, it's the classic college hangout. Wednesday nights, when well drinks and beers are $1.50, the place is loaded with bad-tipping students intent on setting new speed records for alcohol consumption.

The Island: 4141 El Camino Real (El Camino Way), Palo Alto, 650/493-9020. The Island has been hit by a lot of hurricanes recently. A small service window now links it to a new restaurant next door called Café Dee's, which specializes in New Orleans cuisine. Since the merger, curious new customers have ventured into this dive to sample the fruity rum hurricanes that the regulars—middle-aged, seasoned drinkers who line up at the *long*, padded, curved bar—don't drink. The jukebox still plays light rock classics from the '70s; and the wood paneling on the walls has never looked better.

JJ's Blues Lounge: 3439 Stevens Creek Blvd. (Winchester), San Jose, 408/243-6441. JJ's is the South Bay's premier blues dive. The only survivor of the trio of JJ's venues, the Stevens Creek spot is narrow and unembellished. Nightly drink specials and terrific blues bands, both local and national, keep the joint jamming.

Joe's States Tavern: 200 Grand Ave. (Linden), South San Francisco, 650/588-7073. Recognized as a South San Francisco landmark, this old-fashioned joint was a hot destination in the 1950s, although no longer. The televisions aren't bad for watching games, if you can manage to stop your eyes from wandering around the large, airy room. Everything from a 20-foot anaconda skin to giant crab legs to stuffed animal heads hangs from the walls and sits on the shelves.

Katie Blooms: 150 S. 1st St. (San Fernando), San Jose, 408/294-4408. Spacious and dark, this Irish pub gets very crowded at times. Urban professionals from nearby offices, students from SJSU, and twenty- and thirtysomethings from the surrounding suburbs are all found drinking at one of the two fully stocked bars. When the crush is less, these same people duck in to enjoy some great pub grub.

Keystone Coffee Store: 321 S. 1st St. (San Carlos), San Jose, 408/292-4698. The crowd at this downtown San Jose café is more entertaining than most Hollywood movies—androgynous teens, baby boomers on dates, spandex-clad rockers. On weekend nights the line for coffee streams out the door. Fortunately, the servers work well under pressure. The calico walls are lined with a cluttered assortment of junk that adds to the shabby, eccentric feel of the place.

La Piñata: 1205 Burlingame Ave. (Lorton), Burlingame, 650/375-1070. Stylish, young Burlingame singles sipping large glasses of bright red planter's punch feel right at home around the cozy tables here. The colorful corner cantina has plenty of windows, permitting you to check out the action (and the game on TV) before deciding to join the fun.

La Tropicana: 47 Notre Dame St. (Santa Clara/St. John), San Jose, 408/279-2340. Wear your best jeans, boots, and cowboy hat and you'll fit right in at this downtown hot spot for Mexican *banda* music and dancing. A command of the Spanish language is helpful, too. Plan to spend some time waiting in the line that almost always curls around the building. A cover charge applies when there's live music.

Lariat: 1428 El Camino Real (Harbor), Belmont, 650/593-7201. Don't get roped into going back to the same old bar again. Do what a lot of people who frequent other bars in the area do, and go to the Lariat for a change of pace. It's an unpretentious neighborhood joint with a clientele as diverse as the area around it. There are 21-year-old kids playing pinball, longer-haired, thirty-year-old pool players in concert T-shirts from the mid-'80s, and, possibly, some middle-aged parents (or their friends) at the bar. Adding to the laid-back neighborhood feel is the menu of simple home-cooked food (returning after a three-year absence).

Left at Albuquerque: 445 Emerson St. (University/Lytton), Palo Alto, 650/326-1011. • 1100 Burlingame Ave. (California), Burlingame, 650/401-5700. • PruneYard Shopping Center, Campbell and Bascom aves., Campbell, 408/558-1680. The owners of the Blue Chalk Café have struck pay dirt again with these southwestern-style combination bar-restaurants. Bold desert art and racks of tequila bottles furnish the space. The bar scene is wall-to-wall Silicon singles, with talk of mountain bikes and stock options filling the air. For drinks, margaritas are popular, as is just about every other tequila drink. (The bar has the best selection of the blue agave liquor around.) If you stay for dinner, the contemporary southwestern dishes are flavorful, varied, and inexpensive.

Lenny's: 171 E. Santa Clara St. (4th/5th), San Jose, 408/292-4581. Despite its cheap, strong drinks, this small, narrow bar has never really caught on with younger people (even starving students from nearby San Jose State). Have two here and you'll be done. The brown walls have nothing on them, the music playing on the jukebox is nondescript '70s stuff, and the patrons are just regular folks.

The Loading Zone: 2048 Broadway (Main), Redwood City, 650/299-9117. Load up your equipment Sunday nights. The Loading Zone provides the amps and you provide the instrument. Open jam night is a great way to meet other musicians and hear some excellent improvised sets of blues, rock and roll, or whatever comes out of the speakers. If it sounds too cutting edge to you, then drop by to hear one of the professional rock-and-roll bands that appears every weekend.

The Los Altos Bar & Grill: 169 Main St. (3rd/State), Los Altos, 650/948-4332. This neighborhood venue, which plays everything from jazz to dance music, has all the hallmarks of a combination singles and sports bar: flashing lights, a wide-screen TV, potato skins. Local bands and swingles take over on the weekends.

Los Gatos Bar & Grill: 15½ N. Santa Cruz Ave. (Main), Los Gatos, 408/399-5424. A lively, sophisticated sports-bar ambience, good vibes, and little in the way of pretense characterize this upstairs food-and-drink arena. Catering to a healthy young crowd that enjoys microbrews during the game and then settles into conversation over spicy bar food or burgers, the menu has something for everyone. A fun place to see and be seen.

Los Gatos Brewing Co.: 130 N. Santa Cruz Ave. (Grays), Los Gatos, 408/395-9929. A favorite haunt of business-lunch seekers, beer drinkers, and beach types alike. Indoors, singles mingle over pints of the brewed-on-site suds, including Dunkle, Los Gatos lager, and Nut Brown ale. A long bar (salvaged from a St. Louis brothel) dominates one end of the soaring, barnlike space; another wall is occupied by a wood-burning pizza oven. The faux stone walls painted in earth tones add a rustic note.

Marvin Gardens Alehouse and Grill: 1160 Old County Rd. (Ralston), Belmont, 650/592-6154. Marvin Gardens attracts an industrial workforce crowd of all ages and from all walks of life. Some finish their shifts and come in filthy, while others come in with their top button open and silk tie loosened. Either way, the spongy, worn, maroon barstool cushions reject no one. Nor do the 15 or so wooden picnic tables out back that are especially popular during warm summer evenings. Choosing one of the 30 beers offered (or a glass of wine) is about the hardest decision you'll have to make here. But you better make it quick, because that same industrial workforce must also go to work every morning, which means that Marvin Gardens closes at 10pm.

McGovern's Bar: 215 E. 4th St. (Ellsworth), San Mateo, 650/375-8435. Ever wondered where snowboarders go when they're not snowboarding? Take a peek into McGovern's and you'll see a warehouse bar full of them. With a pretty even ratio of single men to single women, this dim, one-step-below-casual bar can fill up quickly. The jukebox cranks out music that's modern, guitar based, and not as loud as the hundreds of conversations taking place around it. The most popular area of the bar is near the pool table and foosball setup. Unless you're a seasoned pro, forget about winning at either.

Mike's Sports Tavern: 950 The Alameda (Morrison/Almaden), San Jose, 408/938-0903. A great spic-and-span place to watch a weekend game with the family, complete with pool tables, a couple of video games, and dartboards (which can be hard to get during the day, but are usually free at night). The clientele consists primarily of Latinos from the neighborhood; the diner-style menu fulfills cravings for good game food.

Mission Ale House: 97 E. Santa Clara St. (3rd), San Jose, 408/292-4058. You'll find a college-student atmosphere here, but perhaps more suited to master's-degree candidates than undergrads. Instead of beer-guzzling yahoos out to get drunk fast, patrons here consume cocktails and spirits at a mellow pace. The long bar and polished bottles sparkle under modern overhead lights. If you're not into exploring the singles scene, a dance floor (with disco ball), loud modern rock and dance music, and a few pool tables with bright red felt will entertain you.

Molly McGee's: 241 Castro St. (Dana/Villa), Mountain View 650/961-0108. Molly McGee's has the best patio in the area for enjoying a drink. There's even a fully stocked bar right on the tiled terrace. Although the patio is covered, a refreshing breeze makes its way through the tables and into the main bar area on hot evenings, cooling off the always large and wild group of fashionably dressed weekend drinkers.

Moon McShane's: 269 Primrose Rd. (Burlingame/Howard), Burlingame 650/348-6666. Recent renovations have transformed Moon McShane's from a dark, smoke-filled Irish pub into a fresher, brighter, livelier hangout. Black wooden chairs, blinding white walls, and snazzy hardwood floors set the tone of the new look. Plus, the floors are great for a little late-night dancing to live rock and roll.

Mountain Charley's: 15 N. Santa Cruz Ave. (Main), Los Gatos, 408/395-8880. A hot spot for trendy rockers to hear local bands. The weekend crowds can be enormous. In fact, the crush on some occasions has been so great that half of the dancers have had to vacate to guard against the floor collapsing under the weight.

Murphy's Law: 135 S. Murphy Ave. (Washington/Evelyn), Sunnyvale 408/736-3822. Most locals describe Murphy's Law as a cross between a neighborhood dive and a trendy sports bar. The customers are primarily men whose athleticism doesn't extend past lifting their beer mugs. Pool and shuffleboard add a little life to the place, but nothing compared to the emotion of a home run or touchdown shown on the big screen TV. Live blues bands rock the joint Friday and Saturday nights.

My Brother's Place: 213 El Camino Real (Hillcrest), Millbrae, 650/697-2403. You'd never know where you were if you didn't read the sign before you entered this almost-sinister spot. My Brother's Place is one of the darkest bars on the Peninsula. It's so dark that it's impossible to walk in without every head in the place turning toward the light that spills through the opened door. This dive attracts middle-aged barflies who've been around long enough to like strong, simple drinks. The jukebox is usually blaring some heavy guitar-based tune.

Oasis Beer Garden: 241 El Camino Real (Cambridge), Menlo Park, 650/326-8896. Generations of graffiti carved into the hardwood tables and booths of The O attest to its longtime popularity, especially with Stanford students. Beer by the pitcher and several TVs eternally tuned to sporting events make this a great place to hang out any night of the week. A variety of video games are provided for the antisocial. A small, heated outdoor patio equipped with picnic tables, a favorite haunt of local softball teams, is a good spot to bring companions under 21 years old.

Old Pro: 2865 El Camino Real (Page Mill/Olive), Palo Alto, 650/325-2070. Once you enter this Quonset hut, you'll find nothing surprising about this always-busy sports bar. Like most such places, the Old Pro has taken the sports theme to the extreme: every inch on the walls is occupied by either a pennant, framed photograph, or a TV tuned to—you guessed it—a sporting event. What is surprising, however, is the wine list filled with reasonably priced selections. The loyal clientele includes Stanford students (no breathing space here before and after games).

Original Nick's: 1214 S. El Camino Real (12th), San Mateo, 650/574-1530. The sign outside advertises pizza, deli, and sandwiches, but Nick's is first and foremost a sports bar. The first floor recalls an old-time, slightly shabby pizza parlor, with nondescript furniture and a TV stuck on the sports station. The pool tables upstairs attract a rowdy frat-brother crowd who come in for the large choice of beers on tap—22 at last count—from north coast microbrews to rare imports.

The Palace: 146 S. Murphy Ave. (Washington/Evelyn), Sunnyvale, 408/739-5179. A swanky supper club in a restored Art Deco movie theater, the soaring two-tiered Palace is an architectural extravaganza, with silver columns, wrought-iron accents, and sponge-painted orange walls. Live jazz accompanies dinner—the menu is a fantastic multiethnic melange—and DJ dancing is on the weekend bill. The whole sexy package adds up to a pulse-raising experience.

Patty's Inn: 102 S. Montgomery St. (San Fernando), San Jose, 408/998-4566. The decor of this sports bar is the usual: home-team jerseys, autographed hockey sticks, and photos of ex-Raiders. Regulars stop in after work for a cheap beer or to watch the end of a game on one of the small television sets. Pool is only 50 cents a game, and the house team belongs to a bar league. Before the Sharks play, a large rabid crowd gathers.

Paul and Harvey's: 130 S. Murphy Ave. (Washington/Evelyn), Sunnyvale, 408/736-5770. On weekends, most of the other bars on Murphy Avenue host musicians whose booming efforts spill out the front doors. Paul and Harvey's meets this clamorous onslaught head on with a jukebox programmed with old rock and roll. Preaching to a small congregation of regular customers, the jukebox here has never let any outside music steal the attention of its captive audience. There's a table for pool players, too.

Peppermill: 10690 N. De Anza Blvd. (Mariani), Cupertino, 408/996-7750. Here is where you find all of the excitement of Las Vegas served in a drink. That's because the bar is owned and operated by a Nevada casino chain, which makes this home to the flashiest, most colorful cocktails on the Peninsula. Order from an elegant waitress dressed in black satin, then settle back into one of the many couches that clutter the lounge. If you're lucky, you'll be able to snag one near the large flaming fountain.

Piacere Ristorante: 727 Laurel St. (Olive/Cherry), San Carlos, 650/592-3536. On weekends, the bar here stays open long after the restaurant closes. The marble floor, the glazed dark bar top, and the soft funky beat of the jazz quartet attract an upscale San Carlos crowd. Dressed to kill in elegant evening gowns and expensive suits, prestigious couples enjoy chic cocktails or finish off the night with a glass of Chardonnay.

Pine Brook Inn: 1015 Alameda de las Pulgas (Ralston), Belmont, 650/591-1735. At the bar, 30- to 50-year-old, casually dressed men and women drinking everything from wine to beer to vodka tonics hang out. They are the Pine Brook's younger regulars. Come Saturday night, the dance floor hosts snappily dressed, high-energy 60-year-old couples who tear up the place to the sounds of a top-40 cover band. On Fridays, a DJ spins top-40 platters for a somewhat younger dance crowd.

Pioneer Saloon: 2925-A Woodside Rd. (Whiskey Hill), Woodside, 650/851-8487. One of the best of the local joints, the Pioneer features a different band every night, and the tiny dance floor is usually jammed with urban cowboys. Cover charge is around $3, but the beer is cheap and the atmosphere is relaxed.

Prince of Wales Pub: 106 E. 25th Ave. (El Camino), San Mateo, 650/574-9723. San Mateo's oldest pub, with darts, foosball, and plenty of beer (it's regularly featured in the *Celebrator Beer News*). The habanero hamburger and an outdoor patio for warm-weather lounging push up the beer sales.

Q Café: 529 Alma St. (University/Hamilton), Palo Alto, 650/322-3311. You'll find none of those dodgy pool sharks hustling anyone at this giant place, a stylish industrial-chic conglomeration of exposed brick and ductwork. And although it started off as a pool hall, some nights you'd be hard-pressed to even find a game of pool. On Thursdays, Fridays, and Saturdays, there's usually a $5 cover charge, and the place crawls with people who look like they jumped directly out of *GQ* or *Cosmo*. Some pack the dance floor as they bounce around to the latest dance tunes, while others choose to mix and mingle in the bar area. The focus during the other evenings of the week is on the food (glorified pub grub but well prepared).

RoadHouse: 1102 W. Evelyn Ave. (Bernardo/Mary), Sunnyvale, 408/739-7939. Even if you don't bring your motorcycle, put on your best leather and head over to this fun biker bar. The numerous square tables with black-and-white-checkered cloths are good sites for pairing a bottle of Bud with some idle chat. If it's late on a Thursday through Saturday, you might catch the sounds of a local rock band singing the blues while you shoot some pool.

Rock Bottom Brewery: PruneYard Shopping Center, Campbell and Bascom aves., Campbell, 408/377-0707. Boulder Creek Pale Ale and Raccoon Red are just two of the five beers regularly served here. Once you taste them, you'll know why this

Colorado-based chain of brewpubss has become popular among young and old beer connoisseurs alike, with the result that it is largest brewery chain in the United States. Thursdays and Fridays you can count on Rock Bottom being busy, Saturdays vary, and the rest of the week you'll find a more mellow scene. The unfinished wooden walls and hardwood floor and the denim-shirted staff combine to give the place a real homey feel. If you get too comfortable, move outside onto the large patio and revive in the fresh air.

Rose & Crown: 547 Emerson St. (University/Hamilton), Palo Alto, 650/327-ROSE (7673). The friendly English staff, the great selection of British ales on tap, and the dart room are all big draws here. Seating can be cramped at the tiny tables, but that's part of the fun. The reasonably priced menu features traditional pub fare—fish-and-chips, ploughman's lunch, and Stilton burgers. This is one of the least pretentious eateries and watering holes around, and it's often chock-full, especially on weekends.

Rosie's Cantina: 333 Broadway (Hillcrest/Millbrae Ave.), Millbrae, 650/697-7825. If you're in the mood for a refreshing drink, plant yourself in a seat at Rosie's. On warm summer evenings, sit on the small tiled terrace and watch people stroll by while you sip a frozen margarita. Or make your way to the bar inside and follow your fellow drinkers: chase your shot of tequila with a cold beer.

Rudy's: 117 University Ave. (Alma), Palo Alto, 650/329-0922. Although the name doesn't sound German, Rudy's definitely shows off plenty of Bavarian influence with its list of beers. Southern Germany makes the best sweet, creamy *weissbier* (wheat beer) in the world, and one of the most popular brands, Franziskanner, is on tap at Rudy's.

Saddle Rack: 1310 Auzerais Ave. (Meridien), San Jose, 408/286-3393. Urban cowboys and real rednecks meet at the Saddle Rack, a country music club that features a mechanical bull and free dance lessons Wednesday through Friday. Rumor has it that the bar once brought in a real bull but it escaped.

Saddle Room: 1607 Woodside Rd. (Alameda de las Pulgas/Belmont Ave.), Redwood City, 650/361-9756. One of the few joints left in the area where you still might see a round bought for the bar. The television set and video golf game are the primary objects of attention in this small blue-collar hangout, and everyone is treated equally except the man who has won the "coveted green jacket" in the yearly makeshift golf tournament and drink fest. So if you're looking for some new old golf and drinking buddies, wander in.

Sammy O'Leary's Pub: 76 E. 3rd Ave. (San Mateo Ave.), San Mateo, 650/579-6160. This is the home of the Thirsty Thursdays $1 pint night, an event that attracts a fair amount of people. Most of the time the pub is filled with neighborly suburbanites out to share a story over a pint. Although the shiny bar doesn't have a lot of unused space, a small stage is occasionally set up on weekends for local bands.

Scruffy Murphy's: 187 S. Murphy Ave. (Washington/Evelyn), Sunnyvale, 408/735-7394. One of the newest bars in downtown Sunnyvale, Scruffy Murphy's is still a little ragged around the edges in terms of character. A quiet Irish pub on weeknights—a great place to catch up on the day's events with a friend—it becomes a bustling hub of excitement and music on weekend nights, with the roar of the crowd and the pounding of feet on the dance floor dashing all hope for normal conversation.

Sebastian City: 215 S. Ellsworth St. (2nd/3rd), San Mateo, 650/347-8525. Yet another hip and happening place in San Mateo for slumming local professionals to hear some live blues that will knock their socks off (not literally; a dress code is enforced Thursday through Saturday evenings). Sebastian City is a trendy dance club and bar, a glorified pool hall with seven immaculate tables, and a trendy venue for live rhythm and blues all under one roof. Mondays through Sunday from 4pm to 7pm is happy hour; go for the $2 well drinks and microbrews and $2 appetizers. The live music starts later, when drinks are full price.

Shooters: 2411 Broadway (Winslow), Redwood City, 650/363-0888. Miss the days of disco? The ball is still hanging over the dance floor at Shooters. The live music can vary, but it continues to attract a die-hard contingency of middle-aged ex–disco clubbers who haven't forgotten how to boogie. There are no pool tables and no dartboards limiting the space in the bar, leaving plenty of room to move and mingle. Whether you're dancing or people watching, you'll enjoy the well-stocked bar.

16 Mile House: 448 Broadway (Hillcrest), Millbrae, 650/692-4087. As soon as you walk through the heavy oak door, you feel the presence of time. It's the type of room that the ghost of a late eccentric millionaire might choose to haunt. The high ceiling, red flock wallpaper, dark wood accents, and large antique mirror all reflect the bar's age. It began as a stagecoach stop 16 miles from San Francisco and has remained in business for the last 120 years. The primarily gray-haired clientele huddled at the bar adds to the old-time atmosphere. Although it will never be a wild hangout for 21 year olds, it is a great place to watch an afternoon game or to bring a date for an after-dinner drink.

Sneakers: 1163 San Carlos Ave. (El Camino/San Carlos Ave.), San Carlos, 650/802-0177. It's too bad there's no college close to Sneakers. Much like a campus pub, the floors are wood and the walls saturated with jerseys, photographs, game balls, and television sets. Bowls of pretzels sit on the bar, and the focus of the beverage menu is 18 draft beers. Look familiar yet? It should to most patrons and employees, because it couldn't have been too long ago that they were in college.

South First Billiards: 420 S. 1st St. (San Salvador), San Jose, 408/294-7800. The San Jose outpost of San Francisco's successful South Beach Billiards follows the same formula: a clean, well-lit pool hall that rents tables by the hour, serves up decent bar food, and pours lots of good beer from the tap.

Spanky's: 2114 Broadway (Jefferson), Redwood City, 650/365-4330. Spanky's has changed from the scary rocker bar it used to be to a flashy California neon palace. If you're in the mood to show off your tightest pants and shiniest shirt and want to dance to a heavy beat, you're found the right place. With an almost even ratio of men to women, this destination for twentysomethings is getting more and more popular.

Spoons: 1555 S. Bascom Ave. (Hamilton), Campbell, 408/559-7400. • 725 Fair Oaks Ave. (El Camino), Sunnyvale, 408/720-0136. Whoever dreamed up the Spoons concept hit pay dirt with the sports bar–taqueria theme. The chain draws crowds on weekend nights with its festive frat-party atmosphere, mugaritas (frozen margaritas served in mugs), and abundant bar food. The taproom is decked out with sports pennants and athletically inclined patrons, and the dining room is done up in high-Mexican knickknack. Party on.

Sports Club: 840 Main St. (Broadway), Redwood City, 650/366-6019. Don't spend all night hunting for an empty shuffleboard or pool table. Most likely there's a free one at the Sports Club, even on a weekend night. This sports bar is actually far more popular during the day. The big, airy room can seem barren at night. On holidays such as Memorial Day and the Fourth of July, a free barbecue is usually held. Not surprisingly, beer-guzzling sports fans of all ages (above 21, that is) show up.

St. James Gate: 1410 Old County Rd. (Harbor), Belmont, 650/592-5923. Two types of patrons show up here. First, there are the overworked Americans and Irish immigrants who take refuge together indoors after working outside all day. The second group is made up of corporate types who, after being inside all day, crowd themselves onto the patio for a chance to feel the unfamiliar warmth of the sun and quaff microbrews. When darkness descends and the band gets going, the two worlds come together to listen to the music.

Steelhead Brewery: 333 California Dr. (Burlingame Ave./Bellevue), Burlingame, 650/344-6050. Settle into this trendy, renovated brewpub for the evening. With up to eight delicious beers brewed on-site, you'll never run out of options. A youthful staff welcomes everyone to the airy, cavernous space of exposed brick walls and dark wood furnishings. Other appealing features include the pool room, the small patio, and the chance to find Mr. or Ms. Right. (After work, the place teems with locals on the prowl.)

Stoddard's: 111 S. Murphy Ave. (Washington/Evelyn), Sunnyvale, 408/733-7824. Former Tied House brewmeister Bob Stoddard created this soaring monument to well-heeled South Bay culture. The trendy brewpub is outfitted with a long, polished wood bar, wicker seating, Jackson Pollock wall paint, and a steady stream of after-work singles. Excellent beer and good (if expensive) food are served. If you're restless, head for the beer garden out back.

Tavern Grill: 1448 Burlingame Ave. (El Camino Real/Primrose), Burlingame, 650/344-5692. The Tavern Grill attracts a weekend crowd that's just as sophisticated as the clubby bar. Well-dressed business financiers moving up the social and financial ladders sip martinis and microbrews. The black-framed artwork, jazz music (live on Tuesdays), and elegant lighting add to the Wall Street ambience. On Monday nights all the elegance and sophistication are forgotten when an in-house DJ keeps the place jumping.

Teske's Germania House: 255 N. 1st St. (Julian/St. James), San Jose, 408/292-0291. An authentic German beer hall in San Jose? Strange but true. Teske's delivers a hunting-lodge atmosphere of dark wood, stuffed birds, antlers, wagon-wheel lights, and an electric train running around the bar. The menu features heavy German specialties such as Wiener schnitzel and sauerbraten, as well as a great selection of beer from the old country. Sit in the lovely beer garden out back on warm evenings.

3rd Avenue Sports Bar & Grill: 77 E. 3rd Ave. (El Camino/San Mateo Ave.), San Mateo, 650/340-9872. Not much more than a pizza parlor for 21 year olds, this place can fill up. The '90s music that bounces off the bright white walls and hardwood floors can be heard from way down the street. The noise seems to have less effect on conversation than the soundless sports program on the extra-large television screen does.

Tied House Café and Brewery: 954 Villa St. (Shoreline/Bryant), Mountain View, 650/965-BREW (2739). • 65 N. San Pedro Sq. (Santa Clara), San Jose, 408/295-BREW (2739). These are some of the best brewpubs around, each one large enough to accommodate an entire fraternity. A big-screen TV, darts, shuffleboard, kegs to go—what more could a frat brother ask for? Eight great beers are served on tap, from Alpine Pearl pale to Ironwood dark. Order a sampler if you can't decide. The beers are absolutely delicious, and you can watch their creation in giant gleaming vats onsite. Pub grub is passable (stick to the basics), but the kitchen stays open late.

Toon's: 52 E. Santa Clara St. (2nd), San Jose, 408/292-7464. A downtown club featuring live music and a sense of humor—you'll know what we mean when you see the ads. Lots of early drink specials.

Topper: 249 Grand Ave. (Linden), South San Francisco, 650/588-7770. Considering the neighborhood, this is a surprisingly clean—almost sophisticated—blue-collar bar. Even the shiny black-tile facade and neon sign stand out in an otherwise industrial area. Inside, you'll find wall-to-wall red carpet, dark green walls, nicely finished dark wood accents, and crystal chandeliers. Topper even closes at a respectable midnight.

Town Club: 180 Castro St. (Villa/Evelyn), Mountain View, 650/967-2425. A neighborhood dive without them, the Town Club is perhaps most rewarding to its longtime regulars. The bar, popular among those 40 and up, has the second oldest liquor license in Mountain View, and there's a wall filled with black-and-white photographs of longtime regulars (most dressed in armed service uniforms). Loyalty that's measured in decades is what the Town Club was founded on, and what keeps it going today. It also has a pool table, a jukebox, a full bar, and all kinds of local characters.

Tremors: 31 E. Santa Clara St. (1st/2nd), San Jose, 408/971-7260. Watch this bar. It's going to be a good one. Opened in April 1998, it has the potential to be the new hot spot. Downstairs are a full bar well stocked with lots of draft beers, a jukebox, a fish tank (left from the previous restaurant), and a large dance floor. Upstairs are pool tables, video games, and an air hockey table. To attract people, the pool and video games are free of charge and the drinks are inexpensive and proportioned generously.

The Usual: 400 S. 1st St. (San Salvador), San Jose, 408/535-0330, 408/298-9375. From the outside this place, with a giant billboard above its door, looks more like the movie theater it once was than a hip club. The billboard lists the bands that will be performing that week: big names in the Bay Area and even national acts like Hot Tuna and Smashmouth. DJs spin records on nights that aren't booked for live performances. Music includes hip hop, retro '70s and '80s stuff, and alternative dance tracks, sometimes played simultaneously in the front and back rooms. Most of the time the college-age crowd is casually dressed. Tickets are sold for the live performances, but prices never run too high. On DJ nights, a minimal cover is charged.

Vibes: 223 South B St. (2nd/3rd), San Mateo, 650/348-8423. Swing yourself into one of the best rhythm-and-blues clubs around. The food from the kitchen is good, the oysters from the oyster bar a little better, and nothing is more satisfying than the music. Although live bands are featured every night, there isn't always a cover charge, and if there is, it's usually nominal. People pack this place after 9pm, so arrive early and enjoy a heavy-handed cocktail before the show. If you play an instrument, show up Sunday evenings for the open jam session. You might learn something.

Villa Roma: 593 Woodside Rd. (Hudson/Central), Redwood City, 650/365-5060. This quiet Roman-inspired institution, complete with a miniature statue of David, marble columns, and marble bar, is housed in a single dark and dingy room. The brightest spot is a beautiful 25-year-old mural of a Roman bathhouse. There's a small selection of bottled beers—none on tap—but the bar is fully stocked for the established spirits drinkers who have been coming to Villa Roma for years.

Waves Smokehouse and BBQ: 65 Post St. (1st/Market), San Jose, 408/885-9283. The old Feremin Building (a state historic landmark built in 1873) has been transformed into an attractive restaurant and saloon serving barbecued ribs, sandwiches, and salads. Tucked in an alley on quirky Post Street, Waves features a beautiful 19th-century antique bar and a rooftop patio. The beer list is impressive, but the food and the service have yet to measure up to the charming setting. Until that happens, enjoy the lively reggae bands that play on weekends.

Woodside Tavern: 768 Woodside Rd. (Gordon), Redwood City, 650/366-6560. If you're in the mood to sit and talk—or even shout—over a pitcher of beer, then head for the Woodside Tavern. Not because there are plenty of draft beers to choose from. And not because you and a friend can yell an entire conversation and no one would even notice. You want to go here because you can actually sit down. The Woodside Tavern is so big, you're almost always guaranteed a perch.

Gay and Lesbian Clubs

Not surprisingly, most of the Bay Area's gay and lesbian clubs are located in San Francisco. Silicon Valley does have a few watering holes.

A Tinker's Damn: 46 N. Saratoga Ave. (Stevens Creek), Santa Clara, 408/243-4595. A welcoming bar popular with a younger crowd, complete with dance floor, pool table, bar, and friendly patrons.

Hamburger Mary's: 170 W. Saint John St. (San Pedro), San Jose, 408/947-1667. Of the South Bay gay clubs, Hamburger Mary's is the largest, with an outdoor patio, pool tables, and a good-size dance floor—usually full. Wednesdays are prime dance nights, and strippers show up on Sundays. Call for current happenings on other nights (open daily).

Shouts Bar: 2034 Broadway (Main), Redwood City, 650/369-9651. Redwood City's only gay bar, offering dancing, as well as pool Mondays through Wednesdays.

Sports & the Great Outdoors

EXTREME SPORTS

Sometimes you just want to do something really wild, really extreme, and really stupid. When this mood hits you, try out one of the many extreme sports practiced in the Bay Area. Imagine the tension released when you leap off an 11-story bridge and are snatched from the jaws of death by the equivalent of a rubber band on steroids. Imagine how petty everyday concerns become when you're hanging from the strut of a plane, 3,000 feet above the ground, wearing a glorified bedspread on a string. But fear not: these sports are all taught and practiced by professionals under whose guidance the apparently insane is, in all probability, quite safe. In fact, you're more likely to be seriously injured while driving to the site of the sport than you are once you get there.

Bungee Jumping

Bungee jumping is sort of the quick-fix of adventure sports. You don't have to have any skills, any preparation, or even any brains. The basic concept is to get some significant distance above the ground (at least 100 feet), attach yourself firmly to a very strong elastic band, and then jump from this suicidal height and hope that the elastic will stop you before the ground does. In practice, the launching platform is a crane, a balloon, or a bridge. The elastic band is actually multiple strands of a cord originally designed to absorb the shock of a tank parachute—in other words, these are damn strong cords. The cords are attached to the jumper by both a chest and pelvis harness system. The net result of all the redundancy is that although bungee jumping is one of the craziest-looking of the thrill sports, in many ways it is probably the safest, at least at the beginner level.

Now that your brain is convinced that bungee jumping is totally safe, try telling that to your body when it's teetering over a 100-foot drop with only a fat string to save it from going "splat." Even if you *know* it's safe, bungee jumping is still a huge rush.

Bungee Adventures: 2218 Old Middlefield Way (at Shoreline Amphitheater), Mountain View, 650/903-3546. The granddaddy of the business is owned by the Kockelman brothers of the banned Reebok commercial fame. They specialize in crane jumps. The latest, something called the ejection seat, is essentially a giant slingshot: the victim or victims (it can accommodate two) are strapped into a chair attached to the cord and catapulted into space. • Sa 10am-3pm and before most concerts. $49 for 150-foot jump; $69 for 220-foot jump. $10 extra for ankle harness.

Icarus Bungee: 510/521-5867. Run by Dan Roza out of his home, although you'll have to travel a little to jump with this banzai bungee master. Mr. Roza specializes in bridge jumping. • $85 for two jumps off a 100-foot bridge, spring and summer; $75 winter and fall; group discounts.

Hang Gliding and Paragliding

For those who haven't seen paragliding, it looks like hang gliding with a rectangular parachute. Unlike hang gliding, paragliding equipment doesn't require complicated setup procedures or special roof-racks. You can pack all the gear necessary for gliding—a harness, glider, and helmet—in a pack that's smaller than most camping packs. Preparation time is negligible: it takes 10 minutes to find yourself soaring aloft among our feathered friends.

So how do you get involved? There are a variety of gliding schools around San Francisco that teach paragliding to the beginner. It takes about four days to soar and from five to eight days to get a "class one" rating that officially entitles you to fly solo. Even if you have no intentions of pursuing the sport, the first day is nonetheless great fun and well worth the effort. You get to glide just like the experts, but not for quite as long.

What hang gliding demands in skill and preparation it gives back in speed and maneuverability. Paragliders go 20 to 25 miles an hour, while the speed of a hang glider can approach 65 or 70 miles per hour. Where paragliders float, hang gliders soar and swoop. When the wind becomes too strong for paragliders, the hang gliders are just coming into their element.

The first day of hang gliding is a lot like the first day of paragliding. Cast aside those fears of launching off sheer cliffs; as a novice, you'll be learning on gently sloping sand dunes where you'll reach an altitude of no more than a few feet. After learning the rudiments of flight, you'll progress to larger and larger hills and glides until you can finally soar off cliffs, usually after around ten days of training.

Air Time of San Francisco: 3620 Wawona St. (47th Ave./48th Ave.), SF, 415/759-1177. Offers lessons for paragliding (never more than three people), a ground school to understand how it all works, and sells paragliding and hang gliding equipment. Reservations required for all lessons. • Call for hours. One-day lesson $169, tandem flight $150.

A Place of Wings: 408/736-1222. Gregg Pujol, the owner, recognizes the need for small classes, so he guarantees no more than four to a class. Classes include "ground school" where instructors teach principles of flight and aerodynamics in order to give students the best understanding of the intricacies of paragliding. • Call for appointment.

Mission Soaring: 1116 Wrigley Way (Sinclair/Frontage), Milpitas, 408/262-1055. Mission Soaring, one of the most complete hang gliding shops anywhere, offers lessons for beginners at competitive rates and throws in extensive ground-school training. The shop also sells, rents, and services equipment. • Shop hours: W 11am-5:30pm; Th 11am-9:30pm; F 11am-6:30pm; Sa 9am-6:30pm. Hang gliding on weekends and most weekdays. One-day lesson $120, five-lesson package $500. Web site: www.hang-gliding.com.

Skydiving

Skydiving may be the granddaddy of all airborne adventure sports, but don't think that it's been overtaken by its younger relatives. The total terror generated by hurling yourself out of a speeding plane miles off the ground is still unmatched. And perhaps because skydiving is older and more established, or perhaps because it really *is* dangerous, the preparation involved is much greater than that for the above-mentioned thrill sports (especially considering the actual time elapsed during the sport). When you sign up to "do a jump," you're in for a half-day of thorough training. After four hours of land training, which includes working with a simulated chute and learning every possible emergency procedure, you strap on the gear, crawl into a tiny plane, and take off for your drop.

Note that there are essentially three approaches to the first day of skydiving. The basic approach is the **solo static-line jump**, which means that when you finally leave the safety of the plane, your rip cord (which activates the chute) is attached by a 30-foot cord to the plane. The second approach is the **accelerated free-fall jump**. This jump involves six, rather than four, hours of training, but it allows you to jump solo and to free fall for about 60 seconds. You are not simply left to survive on your own, however; two instructors jump with you. The final approach is a **tandem free-fall**

jump. You and an instructor (strapped to your back) free fall for about 60 seconds. You don't pull your own rip cord, and the tandem jump does not directly lead toward becoming certified. Skydiving is not taught in population centers (for obvious reasons), so teaching areas are a trek.

Adventure Center: Hollister Airport, Hollister, 408/636-0117. The closest and the most expensive place to go, but people who have learned here seem satisfied with their experience. • Daily 9am-sundown. Accelerated free fall $270 first jump, or $1,199 for seven-lesson package. Tandem $160 per jump; groups of 10 or more $10 off per person. Certified jumpers $18 per jump and $20 for rig rental.

Parachute Center: 23597 N. Hwy 99, Acampo, 209/369-1128. Located at a private airport way out in Lodi. They recommend their bargain-rate tandem jumps for the first time to get you acquainted with skydiving and see if you're really interested. • M-Su 9am-sundown. Static-line course $500 for 10 jumps. Tandem jumps $100. Accelerated free fall $1,000 for seven jumps. Certified jumper $3, plus $1 for every 1,000 feet ($15 from 13,000 ft.). $10 for equipment rental.

Skydance Skydiving: Davis Airport, Davis, 800/752-3262. Run by Alasdair Boyd, an Englishman who treats jumpers in a most civilized fashion. Skydance features substantial group discounts. • W-Su 8am-sundown. Discounts available for groups of eight or more. Static-line jump $196 (but not encouraged). Accelerated free fall $294 first jump. $1,129 for seven-lesson package. Tandem (9,000 feet) $139 and (14,000 feet) $179 per jump. Special seven-jump package, the first three jumps of which are tandem $999.

BICYCLING

Mountain Biking

The sport of mountain biking was invented just north of San Francisco on the slopes of Mt. Tamalpais, and the Bay Area has a reputation as a riding mecca; reality falls somewhat short of reputation. The good news for mountain bikers is that the surrounding area is loaded with parks and open-space preserves with extensive, well-maintained trail networks. The bad news is that mountain bikers are not welcome in many of these areas. In an act of "eco-Buchananism," landowners, hikers, and equestrians unhappy with the dramatic growth in trail use occasioned by the sport are dedicated to eradicating it from "their" playground. The following rides are just a sampling of what's available locally; most bike stores carry a good selection of detailed books and maps showing which trails are open to bikers.

Of the park agencies on the Peninsula, San Mateo County is the least friendly toward mountain bikers, limiting them to major service roads with few exceptions. California State Parks limits bikes primarily to fire roads (bikes are allowed on some trails). The Mid-Peninsula Open Space District and Santa Clara County allow bikes on many of their single-track trails, especially in the less-busy parks.

Long Ridge Open Space Preserve: This small preserve offers some of the best legal single-track riding on the Peninsula. The trails roll along a ridge parallel to Skyline Boulevard between Page Mill Road and Hwy 9 through a mix of oak-filled canyons and grassy knolls, reaching overlooks with terrific views. Parking and the trailhead are on the west side of Skyline Boulevard, three miles south of Page Mill. Look for the Long Ridge/Peters Creek Trail. The trails wind and roll along the ridgetop to an intersection with Skyline Boulevard. Strong riders can continue across Skyline into Upper Stevens Creek County Park to make a long loop ride.

Montebello Road: The views on this ride are spectacular. Park at Stevens Creek Reservoir off Stevens Canyon Road in the hills above Cupertino. From the parking lot, Montebello Road is a sharp right turn off Stevens Canyon Road another quarter mile up. The first stretch is a good indicator of what lies ahead: grades as steep as 15 percent. Nestled among the acres of vineyards at the top is Ridge Winery, vintner of some of California's best reds. The paved portion of Montebello comes to an end not far above the winery and gives way after a few bends to real dirt. The trail climbs approximately 2,000 feet in eight miles up to the top of Black Mountain, one of the highest points on the Peninsula. To return, continue along Montebello to a junction with the Indian Creek Trail—a long, bumpy traverse down a steep hillside. At the bottom, turn left on the Canyon Trail toward Stevens Canyon and Saratoga Gap. The final thrill of this trail is where it cuts across a washed-out section of old Stevens Canyon Road. Crossing really isn't difficult, but don't look down until after you're across. A short way down you'll hit paved Stevens Canyon Road—a great wind-down road along a shaded creek. The road joins Mt. Eden Road, which cuts sharply off to the right. Turn left to stay on Stevens Canyon.

Purisima Creek Redwoods Open Space Preserve: This large park offers some long, steep descents—and return climbs—through redwood, tan oak, and madrona groves. The preserve is on the west side of Skyline Drive, less than half a mile north of Kings Mountain Road and Tunitas Creek Road. Purisima Creek Trail drops rapidly down from the ridge to wind westward along the banks of Purisima Creek. On your descent you'll pass lumbermen's clearings now filled with lilacs and tan oak trees. When you reach the preserve's western entrance, turn right to take Harkins Trail up to chaparral-covered Harkins Ridge, then turn right on Soda Gulch Trail to return to Purisima. Turn left and climb back to your car.

Upper Stevens Creek County Park: This park offers steep canyons in a remote and beautiful valley. Park at the Grizzly Flat trailhead on the east side of Skyline three miles north of Hwy 9. The two-mile, 1,000-foot vertical descent down the Grizzly Flat Trail is a beautiful glide through a canopy of mixed evergreen and hardwood forest; look out for some tricky rocks and ruts that cut across the wide trail. At the bottom, pass a lovely clearing and cross Stevens Creek. Turn right on the Canyon Trail and begin your loop back via Table Mountain Trail to Charcoal Road. At the top of Charcoal Road, turn right on a connector trail to get back to Skyline.

Road Biking

One the nation's premier road riding spots, the winding roads west of I-280 provide an incredible array of challenging routes for bikers.

Cañada Road: Flat, expansive Cañada Road is a cruising ground for beginners and a proving ground for triathletes and time trialists. Running parallel to I-280 from Hwy 84 in Woodside north to Hwy 92 near San Mateo, this out-and-back route clings to the eastern edge of the San Andreas Rift with views of the Santa Cruz mountains and Crystal Springs Reservoir. Begin at Woodside Road (Hwy 84) about one mile west of I-280. Cañada Road is closed to cars on the first and third Sunday of the month from April to October, making it a fine stretch for an exhaust-free ride. (15 miles to Hwy 92)

Kings Mountain Road: Kings Mountain Road climbs to Skyline Boulevard from Woodside to the north of Hwy 84. It is ideal for fast descents and relaxed climbs. Begin on Hwy 84 in Woodside and head west until you see Kings Mountain Road branching off to the right (about 0.7 miles). The climb begins after you pass the historic Woodside Store at Tripp Road, and winds upward past hidden mansions and through Huddart Park. From the summit at Skyline, descend the way you came or consider taking Skyline five miles south to Hwy 84. (10 miles to the top from Woodside Rd.).

Old La Honda Road: An area favorite, narrow Old La Honda Road climbs from Portola Valley to Skyline Boulevard. It heads west from Portola Road about a mile south of Sand Hill Road, making a twisting ascent through stands of oak and redwood to Skyline. Minimal traffic and patched, uneven pavement combined with dense vegetation make for a peaceful, if strenuous, climb. At the top, enjoy panoramic views of the bay and ocean from Windy Hill (0.3 miles south on Skyline), then go north on Skyline to Hwy 84. Turn right on Hwy 84 to Portola Road (first right at the bottom) back to your starting point. (19 miles)

Old La Honda Road (west): This route makes either a short, rustic loop on its own or an extension to any of the other rides that reach Skyline Boulevard. From the intersection of Skyline Boulevard and Hwy 84, take Hwy 84 west approximately three miles. Look for Old La Honda Road on the left (if you see a big red barn, you've just missed it). The ascent back to Skyline from the west is dramatic, with a view over the surrounding hills to the ocean. (5.5 miles round-trip)

Portola Valley Loop: Probably the area's best-known cycling route, the Portola Valley loop is a pleasant, mildly hilly circuit passing along the stables and woods of this tranquil community. Due to its popularity, Portola Road's wide shoulders generally whir with the passage of shiny, spandex-clad cyclists. Start at the intersection of Alpine Road and Sand Hill Road. Follow Sand Hill west across I-280 and around the western edge of Jasper Ridge Preserve, where it merges into Portola Road. Pass through Portola Valley and go left onto Alpine Road, which leads back to Sand Hill Road. (12 miles)

Resources

Regional Bicycle Advisory Committee (REBAC): 510/452-1221.
East Bay Bicycle Coalition: 510/530-3444.
Mid-Peninsula Bicycle Coalition: 650/342-9677 (San Mateo)
San Francisco Bicycle Coalition: 415/431-2453.
Silicon Valley Bicycle Coalition: 650/965-8456 or 408/867-9797.

GOLF

Golfers the world over maintain that playing the courses of Northern California is an experience just this side of heaven. The San Francisco Peninsula abounds with courses both affordable and breathtaking, while the Monterey Bay area is home to the most famous places: Pebble Beach, Cypress Point, and Spyglass.

Blackberry Farm Golf Course: 22100 Stevens Creek Blvd. (Foothill), Cupertino, 408/253-9200. A nine-hole par three course; short and tight, but enjoyable. It's ideal for beginners, but you'll feel at home whatever your level of expertise. • Public, 9 holes, par 29. Greens fee: M-F $9; Sa-Su $11; seniors, juniors (16 and under) $1 off weekdays.

Crystal Springs Golf Club: 6650 Golf Course Dr. (I-280/Skyline), Burlingame, 650/342-0603. A public course located at the edge of the Santa Cruz Mountains overlooking the San Francisco Watershed. • Public, 18 holes, par 72. Greens fee: M-Th $35; F-Su $50. Cart fee: $26 for double; $13 for single.

Cypress Golf Course: 2001 Hillside Blvd. (Serramonte), Colma, 650/992-5155. An extra-long nine-hole course, with a lake and lots of trees to keep things interesting. Public, 9 holes, par 37, driving range. Greens fee: M-F $12; Sa-Su, holidays $15; seniors M-F before 9am $10. Cart fee: $12.

Deep Cliff Golf Course: 10700 Clubhouse Ln. (McClellan), Cupertino, 408/253-5357. Perfect for the golfer who wants to graduate from his or her first nine-hole experience. Yet, this course has some interesting holes and can still capture the interest of the more experienced golfer. It tends to play rather slow on weekends. • Public, 18 holes, par 60. Greens fee: M-F $23; Sa-Su $30. No carts available.

Del Monte Golf Course: 1300 Sylvan Rd. (Sloat), Monterey, 408/373-2700. The oldest course this side of the Mississippi (dating back to the 1870s), Del Monte has recently been improved. The greens are small, but you have to be dead center to sink those putts. It has some very interesting and difficult holes, as well as good package deals with privileged tee times for hotel guests. • Public, 18 holes, par 72. Greens fee: $80. Cart fee: $18 per person.

Glen Eagles International Golf Course: 2100 Sunnydale Ave. (Persia), SF, 415/587-2425. A challenging Scottish Links-style course, with rolling hills, tight fairways, and tricky greens. Conditions are often complicated by fog and wind. Tee times not accepted for play during the week, but are accepted for the weekend beginning on Monday morning. • Public, 9 holes, par 72 for 18 holes. Greens fee: M-Th $11 for 9 holes, $17 for 18 holes; F $12 for 9 holes, $20 for 18 holes; Sa-Su, holidays $14 for 9 holes, $24 for 18 holes. Cart fee: $8 per player based on 2 players for 9 holes; $11 per player for 18 holes. Golf spikes are mandatory.

Golden Gate Park Golf Course: Golden Gate Park (at 47th Ave.), SF, 415/751-8987. This short, par-three course in Golden Gate Park is a great place for beginners to try out their swing and for more experienced players to sharpen up their short game. The tight fairways require a steady hand. Fog often becomes a factor in this ocean-side course, as does the wind when you shoot toward the ocean off the fifth tee. Play is first come, first served. • Public, 9 holes, par 27. Greens fee: M-F $10; Sa-Su $13; with resident card M-F $6; Sa-Su $8. No carts available.

Half Moon Bay Golf Links: 2000 Fairway Dr. (Hwy 1), Half Moon Bay, 650/726-4438. In addition to the original Links course designed by Arnold Palmer, a new Ocean course has recently been added, designed by Arthur Hills. Both courses are as beautiful as they are challenging. Truly a pleasure to play. • Public, 18 holes, par 72. Links course greens fee: M-Th $85; F-Su, holidays $105. Ocean course greens fee: M-Th $95; F-Su, holidays $115. Prices include cart fee. Ocean course may be walked. Metal spikes are prohibited.

Harding Park: Harding Park Rd. (Skyline), SF, 415/664-4690. One of the busiest courses in Northern California, Harding is a challenging 18-hole course surrounded by Lake Merced. It's fairly flat, but heavily guarded by trees. They accept reservations one week in advance of play. • Public, 18 holes, par 72, driving range. Greens fee: M-F $26; Sa-Su $31; with resident card M-F $17; Sa-Su $20. Cart fee: $22.

Lincoln Park Golf Course: 34th Ave. and Clement St., SF, 415/221-9911. With a prime location overlooking the Golden Gate, this course wraps around the Legion of Honor and runs along the cliffs over the ocean. Between the hills, the curves, and the wind, you'll have your hands full. Run by the city of San Francisco, there has been a growing chorus of complaints about poor upkeep. A breathtaking view off of the 17th tee makes it all worthwhile. Call 415/750-GOLF (4653) six days in advance for reservations. • Public, 18 holes, par 68. Greens fee: M-F $23; Sa-Su $27; with resident card M-F $15; Sa-Su $18. Cart fee: $11 per player.

Mission Bay Golf Center: 1200 6th St. (Channel), SF, 415/431-PUTT (7888). This is *not* a golf course, but with a double-decker driving range, putting green, and pitching green, it's a great place to come to sharpen up your skills. They offer group or private lessons for every level. On soggy weekends, this place is packed with disgruntled golfers. • Tu-Su 7am-11pm; M 11:30am-11pm. $7 for bucket of balls.

Olympic Club: 599 Skyline Blvd. (John Muir/John Daly), SF, 415/587-4800. If you know someone who is a member of this private club, it would be worth your while to make nice with them to get you on the course. Three striking courses are included within this immaculately maintained club, where the pros play when they come to town. The Lake Course is among the top ten in the country and has hosted many U.S. Opens. The Ocean Course is shorter and tighter, with the added challenges of wind and fog. The scenic, nine-hole Cliffs Course is a new addition to the club. • Private, Two 18-hole courses, One 9-hole course, driving range. Members and guests only.

Pacific Grove Golf Links: 77 Asilomar Blvd. (Del Monte), Pacific Grove, 408/648-3175, 408/648-3177. A fun public course with two different nines. With some noteworthy holes along the ocean, Pacific Grove is reasonably priced compared to its close neighbors on 17-Mile Drive. • Public, 18 holes, par 70. Greens fee: M-Th $25; F-Su, holidays $30. Cart fee: $25. Reservations taken seven days a week beginning at 7am.

Palo Alto Golf Course: 1875 Embarcadero Rd. (east of Hwy 101), Palo Alto, 415/856-0881. On the bay next to the Palo Alto Baylands, this moderately priced muni course is for long hitters. Like a number of courses in this area, it often takes on a totally different character in the afternoon when the wind can really blow. If you don't like high winds, play in the morning—especially in a tournament. Greens fee: M-F $22; Sa-Su $26. Cart fee: $20.

Pebble Beach Golf Links: 17-Mile Dr., Pebble Beach, 408/624-6611. Words cannot really do justice to the experience of playing this world-famous course. With eight holes skirting the ocean, lush fairways, tough and very fast greens, and breathtaking scenery, golfers travel from all over the world to fulfill their dreams of playing at Pebble, and really pay for it. Probably the only course in the world where the experience is more important than the score. • Resort/public play accepted, 18 holes, par 72. Greens fee: $255 for resort guests (includes cart); nonguests $295 to walk, $320 to ride. Reservations highly recommended but can be made only one day in advance. Web site: www.pebblebeach.com.

Presidio Golf Club: 300 Finley Rd. (off Arguello Blvd. in the Presidio), SF, 415/561-4653. In the fall of 1995, this course opened to the public for the first time since its creation in 1895. Since the army has relinquished control of the course, it has been run by Arnold Palmer's management company, which is in the process of making some major improvements, including a new clubhouse and irrigation system. The course commands dramatic views of the city and is surrounded by eucalyptus and cypress trees. The layout is hilly and challenging, with fog and wind frequently sweeping over the course. People will come from far and wide to play this course, so make a reservation early. • Public, 18 holes, par 72, driving range. Greens fee: M-Th $35; F $45; Sa-Su $55. Cart fee: $13 per player.

Sharp Park: Hwy 1, Pacifica, 650/359-3380. A great oceanside location makes this a very scenic course, with the front nine set inland and the back nine running along the ocean. Tight fairways, sand, water hazards, and the wind make this a challenging course. Reservations required at least a week in advance. • Public, 18 holes, par 72. Greens fee: M-F $23; Sa-Su $27. Cart fee: $22.

Shoreline Golf Links: 2600 N. Shoreline Blvd. (Amphitheatre), Mountain View, 650/969-2041. A moderately priced public course which takes on another character when the afternoon winds blow. This course, with two different nines, can be tough. The tenth hole skirts the beautiful windsurfing lake. Public, 18 holes, par 72. Greens fee: M-Th $30; F $35; Sa-Su $42. Cart fee: $24.

(The Links at) Spanish Bay: 2700 17-Mile Dr., Pebble Beach, 408/624-6611. The newest addition to the wonders of the 17-Mile Drive. This public course was designed in the style of the famous British Links courses. If you like a difficult course, with lots of sand, wind, and rough, a game here is a must. There are plenty of accommodations for vacations or overnight stays. • Public/resort, 18 holes, par 72. Greens fee: $165 for guests, $210 nonguests. Prices include cart fee. Reservations recommended two months in advance.

Spyglass Hill Golf Course: Stevenson Dr. and Spyglass Hill Rd., Pebble Beach, 408/624-6611. Part of the renowned trio from the old Crosby Clambake (together with Pebble Beach and Cypress Point), Spyglass Hill is semiprivate, with public play accepted. From challenging holes to very fast tricky greens, to say nothing of the weather, this course can humble the best. A must for the avid golfer. • Semiprivate/resort. 18 holes, par 72. Public play accepted. Greens fee: $195 guests, $250 nonguests. Price includes cart fee.

Stanford University Golf Course: 198 Junipero Serra Blvd. (Campus Dr. West), Stanford University, 650/323-0944. A green splash set in the foothills. This private course ranks with the best; each hole is distinctive. It's a course you'll remember and to which you'll certainly want to return—a true but fair test of your golfing prowess. Members, students, and faculty can invite guests. • Private, 18 holes, par 71. Guest fees: M-F $55; Sa-Su $65. Stanford students $20. Stanford faculty: M-F $45; Sa-Su $55; Cart fee: $28. No metal spikes.

Sunnyvale Golf Course: 605 Macara Ln. (Maude), Sunnyvale, 408/738-3666. This muni course is one of the best values around and one of the most played. Recently improved, this course is forgiving and favors the uncontrolled fade (slice). It's also fun to play and good for the intermediate golfer. • Municipal, 18 holes, par 70. Greens fee: M-F $25; Sa-Su $34. Cart fee: $23.

PARKS & OPEN SPACE

The Peninsula has some of the Bay Area's most extensive open space, offering a wide variety of terrain from deep redwood forests to sere, grassy slopes. To the west, you can enjoy beautiful coastline and beaches and redwood forests. To the east, abundant and exotic waterfowl live on the shores of the San Francisco Bay. Area parks fall roughly into four classes: City Parks, County Parks, Regional Open Space Preserves, and State Parks. Each government agency has its own rules and the different classes of parks have different levels of development—highest in State Parks and lowest in Regional Open Space Preserves.

The following information covers the major Peninsula parks, but there are always more gems out there. For more information, you can contact any of the managing agencies or the **Trail Center** at 3921 E. Bayshore in Palo Alto, 650/968-7065 (open M-F 11am-3pm); they can tell you about local trails and trail activities and sell you some excellent maps. Most of our daytrips and weekend getaways include information on outdoor excursions beyond the immediate area. A final word of caution: poison oak grows abundantly in most of these parks. Learn to recognize it.

City Parks

In addition to the many local neighborhood parks (check the front of your yellow pages for more information), some cities maintain larger parklands with regional appeal. Please remember, Palo Alto's Foothills park is open only to Palo Alto residents and their guests.

Alum Rock: Alum Rock Ave. (east of I-680) or Penitencia Creek Rd., San Jose, 408/259-5477. Mineral springs, picnicking, hiking, biking, and horseback riding through dry ranchland all beckon park visitors to this 700-acre canyon east of San Jose.

Foothills Park: 3300 Page Mill Rd. (entrance between Altamonte and Moody Rds.), Palo Alto, 650/329-2423. Located halfway up Page Mill Road, this 1,400-acre nature preserve is *open only to Palo Alto residents and their guests*. Nature trails, hiking, picnicking, fishing, playing fields, car camping, and an interpretive center make Foothills a popular spot. Day use fee is $3 per automobile, $1 per bicycle. Bikes are prohibited on trails. Dogs on leash only.

Hakone Gardens: 21000 Big Basin Way (just west of downtown), Saratoga, 408/741-4994. This city park actually consists of four separate gardens. The Japanese pond garden was designed by one of the emperor's former gardeners and built in 1917. Since that time a tea garden, a Zen garden, and a bamboo garden have been added. Admission is free but parking is $5. M-F 10am-5pm; Sa-Su 11am-5pm.

Palo Alto Baylands: Left at the east end of Embarcadero Rd., Palo Alto, 650/329-2506. A beautiful spot for an easy walk or bicycle ride through 2,000 acres of salt marsh and sloughs. There is an astonishing variety of bird life here, and the sight of a great blue heron is impressive and far from rare. An interpretive center shows you what to look for.

Shoreline Park: 3070 N. Shoreline Blvd. (Amphitheatre), Mountain View, 650/903-6392. A small man-made park on a reclaimed landfill with Shoreline Amphitheatre, a golf course, a sailing lake, and many trails along the bay.

County Parks

Most county parks include picnic areas, bathrooms, a visitors center or park head-quarters, comprehensive maps, the occasional playing field or playground, and readily-available rangers. **San Mateo County Parks and Recreation Department**, which covers the northern portion of the Peninsula and most of the coast north of Santa Cruz, can be reached at 590 Hamilton St., Redwood City, 650/363-4020; reservations 650/364-5811. **Santa Clara County Department of Parks and Recreation**, encompassing San Jose and the southern Peninsula, can be reached at 298 Garden Hills Dr., Los Gatos, 408/358-3741; reservations 408/358-3751.

Coyote Point County Recreational Area (San Mateo): Coyote Point Dr. from N. Bayshore Blvd., San Mateo, 650/573-2592. A small, bayside park with windsurfing, swimming, trails, a children's area, marina, boat ramp, and nature museum. Parking fee is $4. No dogs or pets. Open daily until 8pm.

Huddart County Park (San Mateo): King's Mountain Rd. 2 mi. west of Hwy 84, Woodside, 650/851-1210. Once the hub of an extensive logging operation, Huddart Park is now heavily forested with second-growth redwoods. Shady trails wind through steep redwood canyons, evergreen and oak forests, and flat chaparral and meadows. There are picnic grounds with barbecue pits, and a unique playground designed for the physically handicapped. Other attractions include hiking, equestrian trails, a whole-access trail, and hike-in group campsites. No dogs.

Memorial Park (San Mateo): Pescadero Rd., 6 mi. west of Alpine Rd., 650/879-0212. One of the most beautiful of the inland coast-side parks. Particularly inviting is the swimming hole made from Pescadero Creek, which is kept stocked with trout during the spring and summer. Enjoy the hiking, biking, and equestrian trails, as well as pic-nicking and car camping areas and a nature museum. No dogs or pets.

Pescadero Creek County Park (San Mateo): Camp Pomponio Rd. off Alpine Rd. west of Skyline Dr. (trails connect with Memorial and Sam McDonald County Parks and Portola State Park), 650/879-0238. By far the largest of this cluster of three county parks with 7,500 acres. The hillsides are quite steep and feature lush redwood groves and open ridgetops with views of the ocean. Bicycles are allowed on fire roads. Trail camping is first come, first served.

Sam McDonald County Park (San Mateo): Pescadero Rd., 3 mi. west of La Honda, 650/879-0238. Sam McDonald borders **Heritage Grove**, a stately 27-acre stand of old-growth redwood, and offers hiking and camping (car and trail). This park offers hik-ing on 42 miles of trails, biking on some fire roads, picnicking, and camping. Large group reservations and administrative offices 650/363-4020. The **Sierra Club Hikers' Hut** is a great place for group overnights (book far in advance through the Sierra Club, 650/390-8411).

San Pedro Valley County Park (San Mateo): Linda Mar Blvd. east to Oddstad Blvd., Pacifica, 650/355-8289. Small park in a deep canyon just inland from Pacifica. Visitors center and hiking, including whole-access trails. Parking $4 year-round. No dogs or pets. Bring water.

Sanborn Skyline County Park (Santa Clara): Access from Hwy 9 west of Saratoga and Skyline Blvd. between Hwy 9 and Hwy 17, 408/867-9959. Steep forested slopes set the background for hiking, biking, camping, an outdoor theater, and a youth hostel.

Stevens Creek County Park (Santa Clara): Stevens Canyon Rd., Cupertino, 408/867-3654. Wooded canyons surrounding a reservoir offer good hiking, biking, horseback riding, and picnicking.

Upper Stevens Creek County Park (Santa Clara): Skyline Blvd., 1.5 mi. north of the Hwy 9 intersection, 408/867-9959. Offers 1,200 undeveloped acres with trails descending from Skyline Boulevard into Stevens Canyon and adjoining Open Space Preserves. Trails are open for hiking, biking, and horseback riding.

Open Space Preserves

There is an extensive green belt stretching along Skyline Boulevard (Hwy 35) from Hwy 92 west of San Mateo south to Los Gatos. Trails run through grassy plains and scrub oaks and descend to chaparral, pine, and madrona forests, and redwood-filled canyons. Trail maps can be obtained at the **Midpeninsula Regional Open Space District Office** at 330 Distel Circle in Los Altos, 650/691-1200 (M-F 8:30am-5pm). Or you can try **The Trail Center** in Palo Alto at 3921 E. Bayshore, 650/968-7065 (M-F 11am-3pm).

There are two classes of preserves. **Group A Preserves** have fully developed parking areas, well-maintained trails, and good signs. Printed brochures and maps are available at the preserve entrance. **Group B Preserves** have little or no developed parking facilities and trails are limited; maps are available only from the district office. *Note:* Preserves are located outside of city limits, so park addresses do not include a city.

El Corte de Madera (B): Skyline Blvd. (4 mi. north of Hwy 84), parking at Skeggs Point Overlook. Boasts a massive sandstone outcropping (accessible only on foot) and the Methuselah Tree, one of the oldest redwoods in the area. Due to recent logging, many of the trails here are dead-ends, and signage is insufficient at best, so prepare for a potentially long and confusing—but definitely beautiful—outing.

Long Ridge (B): Skyline Blvd. (3 mi. north of the intersection of Hwy 9 and Skyline Dr.), parking on the east side of Skyline or the southeast corner of the intersection of Hwy 9 and Skyline. The rolling terrain along Skyline has a mix of oak, madrona, and fir, as well as grasslands with spectacular views of surrounding parklands. (And don't forget some of the best legal single-track mountain biking trails in the area.)

Los Trancos (A): Page Mill Rd., parking 1 mi. east of Skyline Blvd. on the north side of Page Mill. Small preserve with deep woods, rolling grasslands, and great views from San Francisco to Mt. Diablo. Enjoy the hiking and equestrian trails—the most famous is the San Andreas Fault Trail, which features a self-guided explanation of earthquakes.

Monte Bello (A): Page Mill Rd., parking 1 mi. east of Skyline Blvd. on the south side. The largest MROSD preserve boasts excellent views of Santa Clara Valley from Black Mountain, which at 2,800 feet is the highest peak on the mid-Peninsula. The sag ponds formed along the San Andreas fault by the 1906 earthquake are no less admirable. A sign in the Page Mill parking area will help you identify local summits, while a nature trail will help you identify natural inhabitants. Reservations required for the trail camp near Black Mountain.

Purisima Creek Redwoods (A): Skyline Dr., parking 4 mi. south of Hwy 92, parking for disabilities-access trail 6 mi. south of Hwy 92. (Alternate access from Hwy 1, one mile south of Half Moon Bay on Higgins-Purisima Rd.) This large park offers two magnificent redwood-filled canyons facing Half Moon Bay, plus a quarter-mile handicap-accessible trail with restrooms and picnic tables.

Rancho San Antonio (A): Cristo Rey Dr. off Foothill Rd. (south of I-280), parking at Rancho San Antonio County Park. Accessible through Rancho San Antonio County Park, this preserve has excellent hiking trails up the foothills, with spectacular views of the Santa Clara Valley from the grassy plains at the summit. Bicycling is not permitted.

Camping Spots

The region's many parks offer a variety of camping opportunities, from drive-in areas with showers and flush toilets to backpacking camps with no facilities. Trail camps rarely have a water supply, so you'll have to pack in what you'll need. Campground policies and fees vary from park to park; call for up-to-date details. Many parks require reservations, especially for car camping during the summer. Trail camps are more frequently first come first served, and much less likely to fill up.

Big Basin Redwoods State Park: 408/338-8860.

Butano State Park: 650/879-2040.

Castle Rock State Park: 408/867-2952.

Coyote Lake County Park: 408/842-7800.

Foothills Park: 650/329-2423.

Half Moon Bay State Beach: 650/726-8820.

Henry Cowell Redwoods State Park: 408/335-4598.

Henry W. Coe State Park: 408/779-2728 or 408/848-4006.

Joseph D. Grant County Park: 408/274-6121.

Memorial County Park: 650/879-0212.

New Brighton State Beach: 408/464-6329.

Portola State Park: 415/948-9098.

Sanborn-Skyline County Park: 408/867-9959.

Seacliff State Beach: 408/685-6442.

Sunset State Beach: 408/763-7063.

Uvas Canyon County Park: 408/779-9232.

Skyline Ridge (B): Skyline Blvd. (just south of Alpine Rd.), parking less than 1 mi. south of Page Mill Rd. This park along Skyline features an interpretive center, wheelchair-accessible trails, excellent mountain biking trails, and a Christmas tree farm.

Windy Hill (A): Skyline Blvd., parking 2 mi. south of Hwy. 84 on the east side. The most prominent bald spot along Skyline Ridge, the grassy knolls atop this park feature spectacular views of both the ocean and the bay. Hike one of three trails down the steep hillside into the lush creekside valley above Portola Valley.

State Parks

State Parks are the most well-known preserves in the area, visited by tourists and locals alike, and provide all the amenities required by the RV set. Expect campsites, tour buses, well-maintained visitors centers, comprehensive maps, and guided tours. The agency responsible for these parks is the **California Department of Parks and Recreation**, P.O. Box 2390, Sacramento, 95811, 916/653-6995. They also have local district offices in San Francisco 415/330-6300 and Santa Cruz 408/429-2850. Reservations for camping at these parks or for other restricted programs are generally handled by **Park.Net**, 800/444-PARK (7275) or www.park-net.com. Trail camps are usually first come first served, otherwise reservations are made directly through the park.

Año Nuevo State Reserve: Hwy 1, 30 mi. south of Half Moon Bay, 650/879-0227. Between December and March, Año Nuevo is the breeding ground for a large colony of northern elephant seals. Guided tours are necessary during these months: park officials don't want tourists wandering freely while bull elephant seals as large as mini-vans fight for territory. Walks last over two hours and cover three miles; tickets must be purchased in advance through Park.Net (800/444-7275 or www.park-net.com). During the off-season, elephant seals are less numerous and more sedate, and the preserve provides excellent birdwatching, fishing, and surfing. Parking is $5. Reserve closes at 6pm. Call for current information. No fishing or claming.

Big Basin Redwoods State Park: Hwy 236 (runs right through the park), headquarters 9 mi. south of Boulder Creek, 408/338-8860. Big Basin is California's first state park, now comprising 18,000 acres of magnificent old-growth redwoods. There is a hiking trail connecting Big Basin to Castle Rock State Park, 14 miles to the northeast, and another trail leading from the park headquarters down a rough but scenic drop to the ocean (together forming the Skyline to the Sea Trail). Another long hike leads to idyllic Berry Creek Falls. The park also offers bike roads, camping (car and trail), a visitors center, and food service. Parking is $6.

Butano State Park: Cloverdale Rd., 3 mi. east of Hwy 1 and 5 mi. south of Pescadero, 650/879-2040. Nearly 2,200 acres of steep coastal canyon with redwood forests, banana slugs, and chaparral ridges. Hiking here can be strenuous: the Año Nuevo Trail (not for the weak of heart) leads to an overlook with a panoramic view of the ocean and Año Nuevo Island. The park offers camping (car and trail), picnicking, and hiking trails. Parking is $5.

Castle Rock State Park: 15000 Skyline Blvd., 2 mi. south of the intersection with Hwy 9 in Los Gatos, 408/867-2952. Located on the crest of the Santa Cruz Mountains, Castle Rock boasts amazing sandstone formations popular with rock climbers, waterfalls, and canyons. It also has trail camping on a first come, first served basis. Day use $5 per vehicle. Dogs and smoking are prohibited.

Henry Coe State Park: Dunne Ave. east from Hwy 101 in Morgan Hill, 408/779-2728. An enormous park of over 80,000 acres of great views over rugged ranchland in mountains east of Morgan Hill. The large size makes it good for mountain biking. The park has a friendly ranger station, a small museum, and first come, first served camping (car and trail). Day use $5 per vehicle.

Portola State Park: Portola State Park Rd., off Alpine Rd. 3 mi. west of Skyline Dr., 650/948-9098. Deep in the folds of the Santa Cruz mountains, wander among second-growth redwoods in this isolated park. Features include hiking, camping (car and trail), picnicking, a nature trail, museum, and visitors center. Parking is $6, day use only.

RIVER RAFTING

The first questions of rafting are which rivers and which seasons to choose. All rivers are rated on an international scale of rafting difficulty from I to V (Class I means barely moving, and Class V is for experts only). The rafting season as a whole extends from March or April until September or October, depending on snow melt and reservoir release. Trips can run from an afternoon to a month, and multiple-day trips often combine rafting with camping, hiking, or other wilderness activities. No matter what kind of trip you take, reservations should be made well in advance. In preparation, talk to your guide about what you'll need to pack. For a free directory of California river outfitters, call **California Outdoors** 800/552-3625.

Access to Adventure: 800/441-9463. This outfit runs rivers throughout Northern and Central California as well as rivers in Oregon. The variety of excursions include a half-day trip for $55. One- to two-day runs range from $80-$380; group discounts available.

All Outdoors Whitewater Trips: 1250 Pine St., #103, Walnut Creek, 510/932-8993, 800/247-2387. A large, interesting outfit with trips to ten rivers in Northern California. Local trips offer wilderness camping with runs on the American, Stanislaus, Klamath, Merced, Tuolumne, and Salmon Rivers. $79-$270; group discounts available.

American River Recreation: 916/622-6802, 800/333-RAFT (7238). Charters from the Bay Area for large groups. Trips include the South, Middle, and North Forks of the American River as well as the Merced. $59-$500; group discounts available.

Beyond Limits Adventures: 209/869-6060, 800/234-RAFT (7238). Beyond Limits runs tours in California's Gold Country on the American, Merced, Kaweah, Stanislaus, and Yuba Rivers. $49-$229; group and midweek discounts available.

Cache Canyon River Trips: 800/796-3091. Absolutely the best deal in the Bay Area if you're just looking for a day trip—the two-person raft, courtesy transportation, even a free Budweiser (after the trip) is $30 per person. More involved, more expensive two-day trips also available. Self-guided, Class III river, and beautiful scenery to boot. $25-$125. Web site: www.cachecanyon.com.

Cal Adventures: 5 Haas Clubhouse, Berkeley, 510/642-4000. Cal Adventures always has competitively priced trips, including a one-day trip to the South Fork of the American River. It can get overcrowded, but the well-trained guides will maneuver your boat through any sticky situation. $65-$85; group discounts available. Web site: www.caladventures.com.

Environmental Traveling Companions (ETC): Fort Mason Center, Bldg. C, Buchanan St. at Marina Blvd., SF, 415/474-7662. This fascinating all-volunteer operation organizes a variety of water adventures for people with disabilities (as well as the able-bodied), ages 12 and up. ETC will take you on trips all over Northern California as well as Colorado and Utah. $45 and up; reservations required.

OARS: 800/346-OARS (6277), 209/736-4677. OARS is a well-reputed outfit with rafts on many rivers throughout the western United States, such as the Tuolumne, Merced, Kern, and Rogue Rivers. $49-$2,600.

Tributary Whitewater Tours: 800/672-3846, 530/346-6812. They offer over 20 trips that cover most of the major Northern California waterways. Student and group discounts are available. $79-$380. Web site: www.whitewatertours.com.

Whitewater Connections: 800/336-7238, 530/622-6446. Unusual trips combining rafting with sailing, horseback riding, parasailing, and hot-air ballooning. They will arrange a charter bus for Bay Area groups. $59-$489. The $489 "ultimate trip" includes horseback riding, hot-air ballooning, and paragliding; group discounts available.

SAILING

The Bay Area provides some of the best sailing in the world. The Bay's major **harbors—San Francisco, Sausalito, Alameda, Berkeley, Richmond**—provide the best access to the central part of the bay; from the South Bay, it's a lot quicker to drive than to sail. San Francisco, of course, has access to the heart of the bay. Richmond has easy access to San Pablo Bay, where conditions are shallower and less windy. Alameda presents some challenges—including a lengthy estuary and a large wind hole just south of the Bay Bridge. Heading south from the city onto the Peninsula, you'll find many access points: try **South Beach** (just south of the Bay Bridge), **Oyster Point** (South San Francisco), **Coyote Point** (San Mateo), and **Redwood City**. Across the bay, check out the **Ballena Bay Harbor** just south of the Alameda Naval Air Station, and the **San Leandro Harbor** further to the south.

Some protected areas of the bay and outlying lagoons are ideal for sailing smaller boats: **Shoreline, Parkside Aquatic,** and the **Leo Ryan Parks** on the Peninsula; **Berkeley Marina's South Sailing Basin;** and Oakland's **Lake Merritt.**

There are many different programs available for those interested in sailing. Yacht clubs are operated for the benefit of members and their guests, but **private sailing clubs** own boats which are available for charter, either skippered or bareboat. With a skippered charter, the charter company supplies both the skipper and boat. Most can only carry six passengers, but Chardonnay Charters has a vessel qualified to carry a greater passenger load. Experienced skippers can reserve a bareboat charter, which lets you control your own day on the bay. (Many clubs require American Sailing Association Certification or equivalent experience; it's best to get checked out a couple of days before you intend to sail.) The least expensive charters are those which take place at regularly scheduled times and set their prices on a per-person basis. Reserve early. **Sailing schools** that aren't club-affiliated also provide a viable introduction to sailing, although they are typically reserved for small boats (ideal for learning the basics). One of the best ways to get plugged into the local sailing network is to pick up an edition of *Latitude 38* (415/383-8200), which publishes lists of crews looking for boats, and skippers looking for crews.

Resources

U.S. Coast Guard NorCal Region: Yerba Buena Island, 415/399-3400.

Private Sailing Clubs and Schools

Note: Clubs and associations should be contacted before visiting in person.

Cal Sailing Club: Berkeley Marina, University Ave., Berkeley, 510/287-5905. This organization is run by volunteers, including their instructors. It is the least expensive way to get out on the bay, so call for details. Their membership rates are excellent, they give lessons, and run the organization like an aquatic co-op.

Cass Charters and Sailing School: 1702 Bridgeway, Sausalito, 415/332-6789. They offer lessons on 22- to 35-foot boats, and offer rentals on a range of sizes.

Chardonnay Charters: 704 Soquel Ave., Santa Cruz, 408/423-1213. They offer a whale-watching charter as well as rent a Santa Cruz 70 but do not offer lessons.

Club Nautique Sausalito: 100 Gate Six Rd., Sausalito, 415/332-8001.

Foster City Recreational Department: 650 Shell Blvd., Foster City, 650/345-5731. The department holds small-boat sailing classes during the summer months. Classes are taught in the nicely landscaped Leo Ryan Park, although they are not offered as frequently as those run by outfits solely dedicated to sailing; no rental service.

Lake Merritt Sailboat House: Lakeside Park, 568 Bellevue Ave., Oakland, 510/444-3807. Located on Lake Merritt in Oakland's Lakeside Park, this quaint setting seems totally removed from the nearby downtown. There's a year-round rental and lesson programs for small boats.

O.C.S.C. San Francisco Bay Sailing School: 1 Spinnaker Way, Berkeley, 510/843-4200. Located at the western end of University Avenue. They teach on bigger boats from 24 to 44 feet.

Pacific Yachting: 790 Mariner Pkwy., Santa Cruz, 408/423-7245. This club has a fleet of 17 sailing yachts ranging from 26 to 43 feet that certified sailors can take out bareboat. (You can also rent skippered charters for any occasion.) The club offers various instruction programs that will take an inexperienced sailor through to certification. One of the most popular programs is the six-day live-aboard instructional vacation.

Rendezvous Charters: Pier 40, South Beach Harbor (The Embarcadero at Townsend), SF, 415/543-7333. Bareboat, skipper, and private charters available, as are a variety of scheduled cruises, including brunch and sunset trips that cost only $23 per person for two hours. A unique cruise boat is the Rendezvous, a 78-foot replica of a 19th century square-rigged Brigantine. Reservations required for cruises. Lessons are offered on 22- to 40-foot boats.

Spinnaker Sailing Mountain View: 3160 N. Shoreline Blvd., Shoreline Regional Park, Mountain View, 650/965-7474. Spinnaker offers rentals, children's sailing camps, and small-boat courses at Shoreline Park in Mountain View. Web site: www.spinnsail.com.

Spinnaker Sailing Redwood City: 451 Seaport Ct., Redwood City, 650/363-1390. This is the place where Spinnaker teaches big-boat sailing courses and rents charters on the bay. Web site: www.spinnsail.com.

Spinnaker Sailing San Mateo: 1 Seal St., Parkside Aquatic Park, San Mateo, 415/570-7331. In Spinnaker's San Mateo location, look for rentals, children's sailing camps, and small-boat courses at Parkside Aquatic Park. Web site: www.spinnsail.com.

Universities

UC Berkeley's Cal Adventures: 5 Haas Clubhouse, Berkeley, 510/642-4000. Their flexible and inexpensive programs are open to all, even nonstudents. Classes and rentals are available through the UC Aquatic Center (at the Berkeley Marina); the rental program is open to those who have completed their intermediate course or the equivalent. Sailing privileges are open to graduates of more advanced courses. Web site: www.caladventures.com.

UC Santa Cruz: E. Field House, Santa Cruz, 408/459-2531. Similar to Cal Adventures, UCSC also allows certified skippers to bring along guests for a small fee. Or call the UC Boating Center in Santa Cruz Harbor 408/425-1164.

SCUBA DIVING

Some excellent diving can be found off the Northern California coast—the cold water, rich in nutrients, supports a wide variety of marine life. Our giant kelp forests are famous throughout the world, and there's even a good chance that a friendly seal might bump into you on your next dive.

Monterey Bay Harbormaster: 408/646-3950.

Park.Net California State Park Reservation System: 800/444-PARK (7275). www.park-net.com.

Divers Alert Network (DAN), National Hotline: (919) 684-8111 or (919) 684-4326.

Where to Dive

Some of the best and most convenient dive sites in the Bay Area are in Monterey, Pacific Grove, and Carmel. There is also some great diving along the north coast in Sonoma and Mendocino Counties. The diving along the north coast is generally at an intermediate to advanced level, with trickier entries than the dives in Monterey. Diving for abalone is also a very popular sport in this region. As a general rule, the further north you go, the thinner the crowds and the more abundant the abalone, so stay over and make a weekend of it. When deciding where to make a dive, be sure to consult *Diving and Snorkeling Guide to Northern California and the Monterey Peninsula*, by Steve Rosenberg, which gives detailed descriptions of dives all along the coast. Also worth a look is *California Diver*, available at local dive shops.

Shore Diving

Point Lobos State Reserve, four miles south of Carmel on Hwy 1, is a great place to begin diving. The shore entry into **Whaler's Cove** is easy, and the cove itself has a nice kelp bed and wonderful trough covered with invertebrates. **Bluefish Cove** is right nearby, a deeper dive. Diving is limited, and during the summer months weekend reservations should be made three weeks in advance. Reservations are made directly through the reserve 408/624-4909. The reservation fee is $7 per team (2-3 divers). Entry to the reserve is an additional $7 per automobile.

    Lover's Point is one of the safest and easiest dives in the Monterey Bay area, although no diving is allowed after 11:30am in the summer, making it a popular night diving spot. There are three places to enter from the beach, but Lover's Point

Beach is the safest and easiest entry and exit. Another calm spot to dive in Monterey is the **Breakwater**, but it is often crowded. At its deepest, it descends to about 60 feet off the rock reef down to the sandy sea floor and is teeming with life—sea lemons are a common sight. To get there, go to Foam Street at the start of Cannery Row. Parking is available at the dock and costs $1.

Only those experienced with surf entries and exits should try **Monastery Beach**. There is a large kelp forest community at both ends of this reef, and a plenitude of wildlife, but absolutely don't dive if it's rough and choppy—the area is known as Mortuary Beach.

Along the northern coast, **Timber Cove**, 13 miles north of Jenner on Hwy 1, has some kelp beds which are often frequented by seals. With a small dive shop and warm showers, this spot is well-appointed for the diver. Abalone are abundant here. Further north along Hwy 1 in Little River, **Van Damme State Park** has clear waters and an impressive fern canyon. The protected cove makes for an easy entry, and the ocean swell is generally calm. Camping and showers are available. **Russian Gulch**, 10 miles south of Ft. Bragg on Hwy 1, is a protected cove with an abundance of legal-sized abalone (those over seven inches in diameter). Call 707/937-5804 for camping reservations.

Boat Diving

If you can't find a protected entry and are tired of braving the surf and the surge, most of the area dive shops have boat trips or listings for companies operating in the area.

Wharf #2 and the **Eel Grass Bed** is an easy, shallow dive at the north end of Figueroa Street in Monterey. Access is by boat only and requires the permission of the harbormaster. Be sure to check out the Eel Grass Beds, which are some 30 feet from the pilings. Located between Pescadero Point and Cypress Point, **the Pinnacles** is a boat dive site regarded as one of the best in the area. On a sunny day, the combination of kelp and rocky pinnacles make the scenery quite dramatic. The area is part of the Carmel Bay Ecological Reserve, so no collecting or spear fishing is permitted.

Cemetery Reef, north of Timber Cove on Hwy 1 in Sonoma County, is a long off-shore reef accessible by boat. Only advanced divers should attempt this dive, but those who are up for the challenge will be well-rewarded.

Equipment and Lessons

Prices listed at end of each listing are for weekend scuba rental (all gear included).

Any Water Sports: 1344 Saratoga Ave. (Payne), San Jose, 408/244-4433. Offers three-week certification classes that move you from pool to ocean. $75.

Aquarius Dive Shop: The Breakwater, 32 Cannery Row, Monterey, 408/375-6605. • Rental: 2240 Del Monte Ave., Monterey, 408/375-1933. A good supply of rentals, though reservations are recommended for weekend use. They sponsor a chocolate abalone dive each March. $70.

Bamboo Reef: 584 4th St. (Bryant/Brannan), SF, 415/362-6694. • 614 Lighthouse Ave., Monterey, 408/372-1685. The oldest dive shop in Northern California carries a complete spectrum of diving gear. They offer instruction certified by both NAUI, SSI, and PADI, and continuing diving programs for advanced divers. $60-$85.

Cal Dive & Travel: 1750 6th St. (Delaware), Berkeley, 510/524-3248. Offers both NAUI and PADI certification and carries most brands of equipment. Performs routine maintenance on regulator and tanks, and organizes diving trips. $72.

Diver Dan's: 2245 El Camino Real (Scott/San Tomas), Santa Clara, 408/984-5819. The folks at Diver Dan's can help you get Five-Star PADI certification or show you one of the largest lines of scuba gear in the area. Ask about their annual gear swap. • $60-$75.

Monterey Bay Dive Center: 225 Cannery Row, Monterey, 408/656-0454. The place to receive three-week lessons (about 40 hours) for PADI lifetime certification. Five-Star

PADI certification allows the center to certify up to the instructor level. They have their own pool, classroom, and boat for lessons. • $60-$90.

Monterey Bay Wetsuits: 207 Hoffman Ave. (Lighthouse/Foam), Monterey, 408/375-7848. Monterey Bay makes custom wet- and dry-suits for all water sports and even does repairs and mending.

Scuba Unlimited: 651 Howard St. (2nd St./3rd St.), SF, 415/777-DIVE (3483) • 517 E. Bayshore Rd. (Whipple/Bair Island), Redwood City, 650/369-DIVE (3483). A PADI Five-Star Instructional Dive Center with classes ranging from entry level to instructor level certification. The center carries one of the broadest ranges of scuba equipment in the Bay Area, and also features well-maintained rental equipment and repair services. $70-$80.

SEA KAYAKING

Sea kayaking is a sport that you can do safely with a minimum of instruction—sea kayaks are both stable and easy to paddle. If you already know what you're doing, check out the sites listed below. If you want to try it out before committing, many operators have basic programs that will put you and your friends out on the water with a minimum of hassle. As you improve, you can join organized trips to a variety of destinations throughout Northern California. The full moon trips are quite popular.

Kayaking Sites

With the ocean and the bay all around us, kayaking sites are abundant. For beginners, the sheltered bays and coves of San Francisco Bay are convenient starting points. The generally quiet waters of **Richardson Bay** between Sausalito and Tiburon and the **Oakland Estuary** both work well. Other typically calm areas include **Bolinas Lagoon** (near Stinson Beach in Marin) and **Tomales Bay** (by Point Reyes). Also look for kayaking operations on the **Russian, Gualala, Albion,** and **Big Rivers.** From these sites you can move on to more exposed parts of the bay and ocean. (Don't overestimate your ability: the huge swells, tidal currents, and huge ships all pose a formidable challenge. **Half Moon Bay** has a core group of enthusiasts. In **Santa Cruz**, the ocean is beautiful: blue, clear, and almost warm. One of the most popular kayaking destinations, **Monterey Bay**, offers excellent opportunities to view the area's abundant wildlife.

Kayak Rentals and Instruction

Adventure Sports: 303 Potrero St., Santa Cruz, 408/458-DO-IT (3648). Rents kayaks, along with other water toys, and offers lessons for paddlers of all levels. Beginners are required to take an introductory class in basic paddling and safety before going out in a enclosed boat. Rentals $30 for 24 hours off-site for experienced kayakers.

Adventures by the Sea: 299 Cannery Row (Dickman), Monterey, 408/372-1807. $25 per person per day; includes lessons and equipment.

BlueWaters Ocean Kayak Tours: Point Reyes National Seashore (beach site at Tomales Bay), Inverness, 415/669-2600. BlueWaters specializes in tours but will rent their boats. Their tours include one-day or overnight trips throughout Northern California and special moonlight paddles for $49. Tours $49-$79 per day; discounts for groups of six or more. Rentals are $25-$45 for singles and $35-$65 per boat for doubles. Web site: www.bwkayak.com.

Cal Adventures: 5 Haas Clubhouse, Berkeley, 510/642-4000. Rowing center at South Basin of the Berkeley Marina. Cal Adventures offers instruction and equipment for reasonable prices, a variety of classes for all levels, and even off-site rentals. Introductory classes are offered almost every weekend and cover basic equipment, safety, paddling techniques, and rescues. Call for class dates and times. $55 for students, $65 for the community. Reservations recommended. Web site: www.caladventures.com.

California Canoe and Kayak: 409 Water St. (Washington), Oakland, 510/893-7833. Also provides instruction and equipment for reasonable prices, a variety of classes for all levels, and off-site rentals. Introductory classes are offered almost every weekend, which cover basic equipment, safety, paddling techniques, and rescues. Classes given on the bay for all levels. Then take one of their guided group paddles, especially to Angel Island. $89 intro safety class required for renting. Reservations accepted. Web site: www.calkayak.com.

Environmental Traveling Companions (ETC): Fort Mason Center, Bldg. C, Buchanan St. at Marina Blvd., SF, 415/474-7662. This fascinating all-volunteer operation organizes a variety of water adventures for people with disabilities (as well as the able-bodied). "Benefit trips" available for students and others (prices vary). Tours start at $38 per day.

Monterey Bay Kayaks: 693 Del Monte Ave. (Estero), Monterey, 800/649-KELP (5357). Offers excellent instruction and a full line of kayaks for rent or purchase. Marine biologist-led classes are designed to elevate you beyond mere paddling to enjoying the water and wildlife. The company also organizes special outings—whale watches, trips to bird and wildlife sanctuaries. $25 per day with 20-minute orientation. Reservations recommended on weekends. Web site: www.montereykayaks.com.

Sea Trek Ocean Kayaking Center: Schoonmaker Point Marina, Sausalito, 415/488-1000. Will qualify you to paddle at any kayaking location after a full day of lessons. They teach formal safety lessons on the quiet Richardson and Tomales Bays; from there you can move on to novice and expert daytime trips and night tours of the bay under the full moon. Full-day introductory lessons $95; tour prices vary.

Tamal Saka, Tomales Bay Kayaking: Hwy 1, Marshall (8 miles north of Pt. Reyes Station), 415/663-1743. Located on the shores of Tomales Bay across from scenic Point Reyes National Seashore, where overnight camping spots are peaceful and plentiful. They rent single and double kayaks—both open and closed deck—and offer classes, guided trips, and rentals. Special guided trips include full-moon paddles, nature tours, and trips outside Tomales Bay to places such as Drakes Bay, the Russian River, Mendocino Coast, and Mono Lake. Prices are on the high side, but the equipment is good and the locale unique. Rentals are $35-$55 for singles and $45-$75 per boat for doubles; Tuesdays are discount days. Web site: www.tamalsaka.com.

WINDSURFING

Few areas in the United States have as many breezy days, abundant launch spots, terrific views, and well-stocked windsurfing shops as the Bay Area; it's an ideal place for the avid windsurfers who regularly color our waters. As a general rule, winds pick up in mid to late afternoon and die down as the sun starts to set. The best wind is usually on the leading edge of an advancing fog bank; once the fog settles in, it tends to choke off the wind. The summer season (May-July) sees the best wind. You'll need a wet suit year-round in the bay and the Pacific, as water temperatures are low enough to induce hypothermia.

Places to Sail

Most of the beginner and intermediate spots listed will have good wind on clear days in the late spring and summer. On those days when San Francisco's famous fog just refuses to recede, you'll have better luck finding the breezes inland. Call the on-site rental locations for water, wind conditions, and the hours best suited to your skill level.

Beginning to Intermediate

Alameda's Crown Memorial State Beach: 510/521-7090. This sheltered location with side-onshore winds that push you back to shore has an easy launch that leads directly to the sandy-bottomed sailing site—a great place to practice waterstarts. A concessionaire rents boards on the beach, call 415/440-5405 for information. From I-880 exit west on High Street. Take a right on Hwy 61, then a left on Shoreline Drive, which turns into Westline Drive. Crown Beach is on the left side of the road.

Lake Del Valle State Park (Livermore): 925/455-4008. This inland lake is a beginner's paradise with rentals, lessons, and facilities on-site. Take I-580 east to Livermore Avenue, which turns into Tesla Road. Go right at Mines Road and follow the signs.

Intermediate to Advanced

Berkeley Marina: A tricky launch from the sheltered pier at the marina leads to the main sailing area. Full facilities and plenty of parking can be found at the west end of University Avenue in Berkeley, with on-site lessons and rentals by Cal Adventures. Launch from the piers adjacent to the Cal Adventures yard (follow the signs).

Candlestick Point: The flat-water speed sailing conditions here are ideal for learning and refining jibing technique, although the gusty winds that tend to blow side-off-shore can be hazardous, and the rocky launch spot is a minor nuisance. Take the 3Com/Candlestick Park exit off Hwy 101 and stay right until you see the park entrance. The sailing area is at the south end of the parking lot.

Coyote Point Regional Park: 650/573-2592. Some of the most consistent winds in the bay, with conditions that vary from moderate winds and flat water near shore to powerful wind-driven chop further out. Excellent facilities with a $4 per car entry fee. Hwy 101 to the Dore Avenue exit, left at off-ramp and follow signs to entrance.

Crissy Field: This is a thrilling spot to sail with large swells and amazing views of the city and the Golden Gate Bridge. Expect to contend with frigid waters, strong tides, howling winds, and immense ships. A concessionaire rents boards on the beach, call 415/440-5405 for more information. Enter the Presidio in San Francisco from Marina Boulevard across from the St. Francis Yacht Club and continue straight. Once inside the gate, take the first street to your right and follow it to the beach.

Gazos Creek: 408/425-1218. A lesser-known remote spot with wavesailing conditions. Don't sail alone here. On Hwy 1 about 35 to 40 minutes south of Half Moon Bay; look for signs.

Half Moon Bay Harbor: 650/726-4382. Flat-water sailing during the winter and summer months. Head south for wavesailing. In Half Moon Bay, a few miles north of the Hwy 92 intersection.

Natural Bridges State Beach: 408/423-4609. Summer thermal winds make it possible to push through the moderate shorebreak. Once beyond the break, two large kelp beds create a flat-water sailing area. Just north of Santa Cruz on Hwy 1. Go West on West Cliff Drive. The Park will be to the right along the water's edge.

Rio Vista/Sherman Island: A great place to learn or practice high-wind technique. Take I-680 north to Hwy 242 west to Hwy 4 west toward Antioch/Stockton. Cross the Antioch toll bridge, take the first left at Sherman Island Road. Ascend a short grade to the levee road and go left along the levee, to any of the sailing spots along the river. Parking on the bank to the right anywhere along the river is forbidden.

Rio Vista/Windy Cove: This warm-weather, fresh-water sailing spot gets crowded at early morning. The best winds blow from dawn to 10am, and again in the late afternoon. Take I-680 north towards Concord to Hwy 242 west to Hwy 4 west toward Antioch/Stockton. Cross the Antioch toll bridge and continue until the next bridge (Brannan Isl. State Bridge). Windy Cove is located just across this second bridge on the left side of the road.

San Luis Reservoir: Expect high (15 to 40 knots) winds from 5am to 10am at this popular freshwater site. The reservoir is approximately 20 miles east of the Hwy 101/152 interchange in Gilroy; just follow the signs.

Waddell Creek State Park: 408/425-1218. Check out one of Northern California's most celebrated wavesailing playgrounds. Only advanced sailors should try; you must pay an admission fee from Memorial Day through Labor Day. Located about 45 minutes south of Half Moon Bay on Hwy 1; watch for the signs.

Lessons and Retail Shops

ASD: 302 Lang Rd. (Airport Blvd.), Burlingame, 650/348-8485. Caters to the high-end sailor with custom board manufacturing and repairs. $50 for board rental on Coyote Point.

Berkeley Boardsports: 843 Gilman St. (San Pablo), Berkeley, 510/527-7873. This store has a wide selection but limited to retail and demos only. No lessons or rentals.

Cal Adventures: 5 Haas Clubhouse, Berkeley, 510/642-4000. One of the best buys in the area, Cal Adventures is located on the UC campus but opens all courses to the public at low prices. After completing a beginner's course, students are eligible to buy a two-month, $100 pass that provides unlimited use of all equipment during recreational hours. Web site: www.caladventures.com.

City Front Sailboards: 2936 Lyon St. (Lombard), SF, 415/929-7873. A small, well-stocked shop with custom and retail equipment. Hours vary according to season.

California Windsurfing: 650 Shell Blvd. (Hillsdale), Foster City, 650/594-0335. On the Foster City Lagoon next to the San Francisco Bay. Board rental is $15. Lessons are available. Summer hours begin in April and run through October.

Delta Windsurf Company: 3729 West Sherman Island Rd., Rio Vista, 916/777-2299. A great retail store and launch site on the shore of one of Rio Vista's most popular sailing spots. Rentals are available.

Helm Ski & Windsurf: 333 N. Amphlett Blvd. (Indian/Santa Inez), San Mateo, 650/344-2711. A full-service shop that hosts swap meets in the summer. One day rental is $35 for longboard and $40 for short board.

San Francisco School of Windsurfing: Lake Merced (off of 19th Ave.), SF (beginner and intermediate); or Candlestick Point (advanced), SF, 415/753-3235. A complete range of lessons are available, as well as a week-long windsurfing camp. One-day $70 basic course for WIA beginner certification is required for rental. Advanced classes are offered at Candlestick, where there are also on-site rentals.

Spinnaker Sailing: Shoreline Lake, Shoreline Park (N. Shoreline Blvd. at Amphitheatre), Mountain View, 650/965-7474. • Port of Redwood City, Seaport Blvd. east of Hwy 101, 650/363-1390. • Parkside Aquatic Center, Roberta Dr. (Norfolk), San Mateo, 650/570-7331. Complete WIA certification facilities with a great rental program, besides the two-day weekend course for $135 they offer advanced lessons, and instructor-certification courses. Rentals are $14 during the week and $17 on the weekend.

Windsurf Bicycle Warehouse: 428 S. Airport Blvd. (Utah/N. Access Rd.), South SF, 650/588-1714. Production and hybrid equipment, high-end hardware, and an attentive staff. Retail only.

Windsurf del Valle: Lake del Valle, 1 Del Valle Rd. (Mines), Livermore Hills, 925/455-4008. Beginning and intermediate sailors are taught in lessons geared to new participants of the sport. Open daily in the summer.

Windcraft Sailboard Center & Academy: 17124 Sherman Island Rd., Rio Vista, 916/777-7067. A full-service shop with a windsurfing academy that holds beginner's classes at Rancho Seco Lake and intermediate to advanced lessons on the windy delta waters.

San Francisco

People flock to San Francisco. It was the gold that first brought them here in droves, but it is the distinctive beauty, the weather, the spirit of diversity and acceptance, the cultural history and rich cultural present that keeps them coming.

For thousands of years before the first European sailed through the Golden Gate, the area was inhabited by Coast Miwok and Ohlone Indians. When the Spanish finally stumbled upon the bay in 1775, they quickly claimed the area for Spain and established a community dubbed "Yerba Buena," or "good herb," for the wild mint that grew in the region. In 1835, after the Spanish had lost control of Mexico, Andrew Jackson made an unsuccessful bid to the newly created Mexican government to purchase Yerba Buena for the U.S. What could not be won with financial negotiations was won with force. The U.S. claimed Yerba Buena in 1846 as a result of its success in the Mexican-American War.

Official U.S. control over tiny Yerba Buena (renamed San Francisco by the Americans) came in 1848, just a week after gold was discovered in the Sierra Nevada Mountains. Although San Francisco was far from the gold mines, the mad rush west boosted its population from several hundred to over 25,000 in under a year. Those were San Francisco's boom years, when the quickly growing city gained a seamy reputation for the scoundrel-filled saloons and brothels crowded into the port area known as the Barbary Coast. By the 1870s, the boom years were over, the Sierra mined out. Nevertheless, the completion of the transcontinental railroad in 1869 assured the city's continued growth.

Yet tumult lay ahead. The Big One hit on April 18, 1906, while the city was sleeping. Estimated at over an eight on the Richter scale, the earthquake and the resulting fires demolished almost the entire city between the port and Van Ness Avenue. The public works projects of the Depression era gave the city its two main bridges: the Bay Bridge, which opened in 1936, quickly followed by the Golden Gate Bridge, which opened in 1937.

The onset of World War II brought another boom to San Francisco, as it became the major stepping-off point for military operations in the Pacific. New jobs created by the shipyards drew thousands of people to the area, and many military families that passed through the area returned to settle at the close of the war.

During the post-war years, the city continued its freewheeling ways, becoming the birthplace of the 1950s Beat movement in North Beach and the 1960s hippie scene in Haight-Ashbury. San Francisco's gay community stepped forward to be recognized with the Gay Pride movement, which took off during the 1970s. Elements of all of these movements still flourish throughout the city. Intellectuals and poets crowd the cafés and bars of North Beach and beyond. Along Haight Street, hippies still linger; some have been there since the Summer of Love, others were born during the Reagan years. Rainbow flags shout Gay Pride from rooftops in the Castro, and the community takes over the city once a year during the Gay Pride Parade. This tolerance and diversity has created a modern city that reveals elements of its past at every turn.

San Francisco's weather will keep you guessing—not only day to day, but hour to hour. A sunny, 80-degree afternoon in the city can quickly turn into a gray 50 degrees when thick banks of fog roll in, leaving many a scantily clad tourist shivering. The unpredictability of the weather means it's always a good idea to dress in layers. The fog occurs most often during the summer: It is created offshore when warm, moist air meets the chilly Pacific Ocean. Hot weather inland creates thermal updrafts that draw the fog through the Golden Gate and over the hills. The oceanside half of the city sees more fog than the bayside half: North Beach may enjoy sunny weather while the Richmond shivers under a mantle of fog. Spring and fall are the best seasons, with September and October the most spectacular months.

SIGHTSEEING

The real sights and attractions of San Francisco are not the museums and monuments, but the neighborhoods themselves, each with its own character and identity. To glimpse the unique charm of each area, and to avoid parking nightmares, travel by foot—and be ready to climb the city's famous hills.

Chinatown ★★★

The **Dragon's Gate**, an elaborate structure with photogenic dragons, marks the main entrance to Chinatown at the corner of Grant Avenue and Bush Street. Beyond the gate, the streets suddenly take on the bustle, color, and richness of Asia. Chinatown developed when virulent racism from the late 1800s to 1950s confined all Chinese in San Francisco to the blocks bordered by California, Stockton, Broadway, and Kearny streets. Today, Chinatown is the largest Chinese enclave outside of Asia, and street life here has a decidedly foreign feel, with many conversations and signs in Chinese.

Chinese Cultural Center: Holiday Inn, 750 Kearny St. (Clay), 415/986-1822. Stop by to get your bearings and pick up listings of sights and current events. • Tu-Su 10am-4pm.

Portsmouth Square: Kearny St. between Clay and Washington. Originally a social center of the Spanish village Yerba Buena, Portsmouth Square is still a neighborhood center. Many older men gather to smoke, gossip, and play Chinese chess, while young families come to enjoy the playground. The parking lot under the square has the lowest prices around, and there are often lines to get inside.

Grant Avenue ★★: between Bush and Broadway. Although now largely geared toward tourists, Grant Avenue is the main thoroughfare in Chinatown. Outstanding Chinese architecture and many interesting shops filled with everything from tourist trinkets and housewares to cameras and electronics line its blocks. Some particularly intriguing spots are the **Chinatown Kite Shop** (717 Grant) and the **Wok Shop** (718 Grant). Farther up the street is **Ten Ren's** (949 Grant), a distinguished tea store with a vast storehouse of leaves, roots, and flowers. **Li Po Lounge** (916 Grant) and **Buddha Lounge** (901 Grant) are just two of the local hangouts, both with friendly bartenders. **Golden Gate Fortune Cookie Factory** (56 Ross Alley, enter from Jackson or Washington between Stockton and Grant) is a fun spot to explore the making of these crunchy treats; the x-rated fortunes are guaranteed to bring a blush and an adolescent laugh. To see Chinatown locals, poke around Grant Avenue between Jackson Street and Broadway among the many food markets.

Stockton Street ★★: between Sacramento and Vallejo sts. Here you can pick up all kinds of fresh seafood and produce, as well as anything from live frogs and Chinese pornography to ginseng.

Tin How Temple ★: 125 Waverly St. (off Clay between Stockton and Grant). To view a truly authentic centerpiece of Chinese culture, climb the long staircase to visit this temple, which was founded in 1852 to honor the Goddess of Heaven, the protectress of travelers. It is open to visitors; leave a small donation before you descend.

Chinese Telephone Exchange Building: 743 Washington St. (Kearny/Grant). Although it looks like a pagoda, the building was originally the Pacific Telephone and Telegraph Exchange serving Chinatown; now it is a branch of the Bank of Canton.

Chinese Historical Society of America Museum: 650 Commercial St. (Kearny/Montgomery), 415/391-1188. Museum dedicated to Chinese pioneers in California and to the establishment of Chinese-American culture in America. • M 1-4pm; Tu-F 10am-4pm. Free.

Old St. Mary's Cathedral: 600 California St. (Grant). Built in 1854, this quaint brick building was California's first cathedral and one of the few buildings in this part of the city to survive the 1906 earthquake and fire.

Union Square/Financial District ★

Union Square, framed by Geary, Powell, Post, and Stockton streets, is an enclave of palm trees and park benches swarming with tourists, shoppers, pigeons, and homeless people. Named for the pro-Union rallies held here during the Civil War, the looming Dewey Monument at its center commemorates a Spanish-American War victory. A recent redecoration that included the removal of the formal Italianate hedges made this square much more inviting. For a quick overview of downtown, ride the **glass elevators ★** to the top of the posh **St. Francis Hotel** on the Powell side of the square.

The **Cable Car Turnaround** at Powell and Market streets serves as ground zero for the area's many tourists. Appropriately, the **San Francisco Visitor Information Center** 415/391-2000 is located nearby on the plaza's lower level. Driving and parking in this congested area are difficult at best. Fortunately, public transit options are plentiful. If you do drive, the best parking deal is at the **Sutter-Stockton Garage** (entrances on Stockton and Bush streets); the **Ellis-O'Farrell Garage** (entrances on Ellis and O'Farrell streets) has similar rates. The **Union Square Garage** (entrances on Post and Geary streets) has reasonable night rates.

Union Square Shopping ★★: Most people come to Union Square to stay in the many hotels and to shop. Historically, large department stores and small, unique boutiques dominated the area, but an increasing number of chain specialty operations have moved in, making the area resemble a downtown shopping mall. Among the famous stores on the square are **Macy's**, **Neiman-Marcus**, **Saks Fifth Avenue**, **Hermes**, **Tiffany**, **Bally**, and—just so you don't think it's all high fashion—a **Disney Store, Borders Books & Music,** and **Niketown.** Nearby entries include San Francisco's own **Gump's** (135 Post), plus **F.A.O. Schwartz** (48 Stockton), **Williams-Sonoma** (150 Post), **Virgin Megastore** (2 Stockton), and **The Gap** (890 Market). The best way to experience this area is to start early (ensuring a space in the Sutter-Stockton parking garage) and walk the streets radiating from Union Square. To complete the scene, visit the stylish **San Francisco Centre** (Market and 5th streets), which features a spiral escalator and anchor tenants **J. Crew, Ann Taylor,** and **Nordstrom.**

Other notable spots found around Union Square include the city's own **Wilkes-Bashford** (375 Sutter), which suits many of the city's business elite and celebrities, and **Emporio Armani** (1 Grant), located in a striking Roman-style building that once housed a bank. The latter also features Armani-designed food at a chic café within the store. For more expensive Armani, visit the **Giorgio Armani Boutique** (278 Post), one of the few stores in America showcasing Armani's top-of-the-line Black Label line. Drop in at the world-class **Fraenkel Gallery** and the interesting **Stephen Wirtz Gallery,** as well as several others located in the building at 49 Geary. These galleries host a variety of modern work, including some interesting photography. Serious gallery goers should pick up the *Gallery Guide,* a free publication that lists exhibition schedules for the city's major galleries, some located around Union Square.

Theater district: centered around Geary St. west of Union Square. Many of San Francisco's theaters are located near Union Square. Make sure to see what's on the bill at the renowned **American Conservatory Theater.** Check any of the following San Francisco publications for a comprehensive listing of shows and information on how to buy tickets: *The Bay Guardian, SF Weekly, Arts Monthly,* or the "Datebook" section of the Sunday *San Francisco Examiner and Chronicle.* For low-priced tickets, try **TIX Bay Area** on the east side of Union Square, 415/433-STBS (7827), where half-price tickets for some shows are available the day of the show; note that half-price ticket sales are *cash only.*

San Franciscans make money to spend on Union Square's posh shops and theaters in the **Financial District**. A leisurely stroll through these streets can uncover a treasure trove of architectural and historical gems. For, despite its sheer wall of modern edifices, this district holds more artifacts of the city's early history than any other area. Driving and parking here during the day, especially at rush hour, can be all but impossible—don't do it. Fortunately, the area is also the hub of San Francisco's public transportation network.

In the days when gold coming down from the Sierra had to be measured and valued, San Francisco's early bankers established themselves along Montgomery Street, and they have never left. Today, Montgomery is known as Wall Street of the West for the numerous financial and banking giants to be found here.

Transamerica Building ★: Montgomery Street between Washington and Clay. By far the most famous downtown landmark, this 48-story pyramid gives the city's skyline its most distinctive landmark. Locals who at first hated the building (after all, it was built by a Los Angeles firm), have by now adopted it as their own. From an economic standpoint, the structure was disastrously planned: its tapering shape allows for only a few choice offices on the pricey upper floors, and the top 212 feet are purely ornamental—beautifully lit at night, but unrentable. In a move to get a little more out of the building, the Transamerica Corporation converted a public lookout point on the 27th floor into office space. Uninvited visitors are politely but firmly shown the elevator down to the lobby, where they can view the city through a "Virtual Viewing Platform," TV monitors connected to rooftop cameras. The adjacent **redwood park** is a cool and quiet place to picnic.

Embarcadero Center: Four blocks from Drumm to Battery between Clay and Sacramento sts. Consisting of four office towers, the lowest three levels of this center have shops and restaurants that cater to downtown workers, and increasingly, building managers hope, to tourists. **Skydeck**, 415/772-0555, is an indoor/outdoor viewing area on the 41st floor of Embarcadero One. • Daily 9:30am to sunset. $5 adults; $3.50 students and seniors; $3 ages 5-12; free for children under 5.

Jackson Square: After a visit to the frenetic Financial District, wandering here offers a return to tranquillity. Not actually a square, but rather the area bordered by Montgomery, Battery, Jackson, and Gold streets, it is best approached by aimless wandering, rather than rigid sightseeing. This area was the Barbary Coast of San Francisco's early days, known for its brothels and bars (where soldiers were often Shanghaied into involuntary service on ships headed for the Orient). Today, it contains some of the few downtown buildings to survive the 1906 quake, appropriately filled with antique shops—great for window shopping even if you can't afford the $20,000 Persian rug on display.

Nob Hill and Russian Hill ★★

A few words may come to mind when first asked to describe **Nob Hill**: pretentious, diverse, quaint. This is a charming residential area offering true urban living with a European flair. These qualities emanate not only from the architecture of the buildings nestled along narrow streets, but also from the local businesses. While Nob Hill is bustling with hotels, **Russian Hill** is a quiet, residential neighborhood full of wonderful restaurants, shops, and cafés.

Top of Nob Hill ★★: California St. between Mason and Taylor. The site of the Big Four hotels: **Stanford Court, Mark Hopkins, Fairmont,** and **Huntington**, named for the railroad and silver barons whose mansions graced the hill until their demise in the 1906 earthquake and fire. **The Pacific-Union Club**, an elegant brownstone at the top of Nob Hill, is the only remnant of those elite structures, and is now a private club for old-money San Franciscans. For an amazing view, visit the **Top of the Mark ★★** atop the **Mark Hopkins Hotel** or the **Crown Room ★★★** atop the **Fairmont Hotel ★** (the exterior **glass elevator ★★★** to the Crown Room is incredible, if slow) and relax in comfort by the piano bar with an expensive cocktail. If you go to either one during a slow time, you can usually rubberneck without staying for a drink or a meal. While you're in the Fairmont, stop in at the campy **Tonga Room ★** and enjoy the mechanical tropical storm and floating band while sipping exotic drinks (see Bars & Clubs section). Many of the hotel's halls display interesting historical photos and painting with an emphasis on images showing destruction from the 1906 quake. Across from the Huntington Hotel, play on the swing sets or relax on the grass in **Huntington Park.**

Grace Cathedral ★: 1100 California St. (Taylor), 415/749-6310. This Episcopalian cathedral is one of San Francisco's greatest architectural jewels. Climb the grand staircase that leads you to a copy of Ghiberti's bronze doors to the Baptistry in Florence, Italy. The interior walls are covered with the usual gilded saints and other religious figures, as well as less typical murals and stained glass depicting the history of San Francisco and America from Sir Francis Drake to astronaut John Glenn. Extremely informative tours can be arranged by appointment. Go to the 11am service on Sunday to catch the choir's amazing performances.

Cable Car Museum: 1201 Mason St. (Washington), 415/474-1887. A small museum of cable-car history (see Museums section).

Russian Hill Walkways ★: Macondray Lane is a woodsy lane with delightful cottage houses made famous in Armistead Maupin's *Tales of City* books; enter from Jones between Union and Green streets and go south. Both Green and Vallejo streets have **stairways ★** between Jones and Mason streets (use caution when passing at night); a park at the top of Vallejo Street just east of Jones offers incredible **views ★★** and a tiny patch of grass for a picnic.

Lombard Street ★★: between Hyde and Leavenworth sts. The primary tourist attraction in the area is a drive or walk down what's known as The Crookedest Street in the World, a serpentine brick road lined with magnificent flower gardens and beautiful homes. It's best to walk the block, but if you drive, go early or risk a long wait in traffic sure to burn your clutch: the backup can extend all the way to Van Ness Avenue. (You can usually sneak around the waiting line by entering Lombard off Hyde Street heading northbound.)

San Francisco Art Institute ★★: 800 Chestnut St. (Jones), 415/771-7020. San Francisco's oldest art school is also a great place to visit: enjoy student exhibits while wandering through the Spanish courtyard, check out the mural by former institute teacher Diego Rivera (follow the signs), visit the two galleries with regularly changing shows, and then go up to the rooftop café for an inexpensive lunch surrounded by angular art students and incredible bay **views ★★★**.

North Beach/Telegraph Hill ★★

North Beach is San Francisco's little Italy, where sand and parking are a state of mind—you'll find neither today—the city's cradle of cafés, its repository of restaurants (and a bevy of bars). The Italian population dates back to the late 1800s, and, although Chinatown has expanded into North Beach, the old influence remains. In the 1950s and 1960s, Beats such as Lenny Bruce, Jack Kerouac, and Allen Ginsberg came for the cheap rents—long gone—hung out at places like **Vesuvio Café** (255 Columbus) and were published by Lawrence Ferlinghetti's **City Lights Bookstore** next door (261 Columbus). Throw a balled-up napkin over your shoulder in a North Beach café and you'll hit a writer. Although tourism is a neighborhood mainstay, tourist attractions are few. Other than visiting Coit Tower (see below), most people come to soak up the neighborhood atmosphere and enjoy the cafés, restaurants, and bars.

Columbus & Grant Avenues ★★: Columbus Avenue is a main drag in North Beach, lined with countless cafés, pastry shops, and Italian restaurants. Grant Avenue is another major thoroughfare, with plenty of blues bars, cafés, restaurants, and eclectic retail stores. **Quantity Postcards** has both streets covered with two locations (1441 Grant and 507 Columbus). It has the best selection of postcards in the city, with subjects ranging from the historical to the perverse, as well as wacky funhouse props to play with. Grant Avenue between Vallejo and Filbert streets is home to some of the city's finest women's clothing boutiques for casual but stylish wares.

Washington Square Park ★: Union St. and Columbus Ave. North Beach's patch of green, where neighborhood residents mingle with park residents (homeless) and tourists. The park is dominated by **Saints Peter and Paul Catholic Church**, which was founded in 1884 and was the first Italian parish established in the United States, as well as the backdrop for Joe DiMaggio and Marilyn Monroe's wedding photos. The church towers are beautifully lit at night. **Liguria Bakery** (1700 Stockton) makes the city's best focaccia (go early in the day before they run out).

Telegraph Hill ★★★: Access via Lombard, Filbert, and Greenwich sts. The hill, which stands northeast of the neighborhood's restaurants and cafés, is named for the semaphore that operated on the summit between 1850 and 1890 to announce approaching ships. The **views ★★★** from the top are spectacular. **Coit Tower**, 415/362-0808, one of the city's great landmarks, stands atop the hill. The tower was funded by a bequest of Lillie Hitchcock Coit and honors San Francisco's fire fighters (she was an honorary member of a Engine Company No. 5). The lobby walls are covered with **WPA murals ★★** by local artists, many students and associates of Diego Rivera. The social realist murals depict life in California. Many of them present strong critiques of contemporary society, and they caused quite a row before the tower's opening. A short elevator ride costing $3 ($2 for seniors and $1 for children) takes you to the tower's summit; the vantage point is spectacular, but the views are generally better from outside, where they are unobstructed by dirty windows. Open 10am-6pm. Like everything in North Beach it's better to walk than to drive—the small parking lot fills quickly, creating massive traffic jams on the approach roads—but the view is worth the huff up the hill.

Filbert Steps ★★★: To enjoy the real secret of North Beach and get a taste of San Francisco's uniqueness, take one of the paths leading down the east side of Telegraph Hill to the Embarcadero piers. Although generally called the Filbert Steps, both Filbert and Greenwich streets descend the hill in a series of quaint stairways through Hobbit-like houses surrounded by gardens bursting with flowers and hiding friendly cats (and sometimes the city's flock of wild parrots). This is the only part of North Beach to survive the 1906 quake. At the corner of Filbert and Montgomery streets, Humphrey Bogart fans can see the Art Deco building that was featured in the film *Dark Passage*. Levi's Plaza sits at the bottom of the hill.

Embarcadero/The Waterfront ★★★

The **Embarcadero** (Spanish for "wharf") is a sunny palm-lined esplanade filled with joggers, bikers, and skaters. The walk between the Ferry Building and Pier 39 is pleasant.

Ferry Building: Embarcadero at the foot of Market St. The building's elegant clock tower (modeled on the cathedral tower in Seville, Spain) was once the tallest structure in the city. For years after the 1989 quake, the hands remained frozen at 5:01 and the flagpole skewed at an odd angle, a reminder of the temblor's effects.

Fisherman's Wharf: Throngs of tourists can always be found in the area surrounding Fisherman's Wharf—the city's most popular tourist attraction—shopping or waiting in line for ferries to **Angel Island**, **Alcatraz**, and **Sausalito**. If crowds aren't to your liking, stay away. While most of the land-based sights are decidedly tacky, the bay offers some fascinating activities: a bay cruise, a sea lion colony, and historical ships.

Alcatraz ★★★: One of the most frequented tourist attractions in San Francisco, Alcatraz has held many of the most infamous prisoners in our nation's history. During the period between 1937 and 1963, this tiny island housed Al Capone, Machine Gun Kelly, and Robert "Birdman" Stroud, among many others.

Set in the center of the bay, The Rock has always had an eerie quality. In 1963, as the cost of upkeep for the decaying prison skyrocketed, the government shut it down. In the second half of the decade, the island was occupied for a short period by a group of Native Americans who claimed an inherent right to the land. Today, however, The Rock is owned by the National Park Service and open to the public.

Tickets for the ferry ride and for the tour are available from the **Blue and Gold Fleet,** 415/773-1188 for information and 415/705-5555 for sales. A ferry ticket alone costs $7.75 adults, $6 seniors, and $4.50 ages 5-11, but most people choose to purchase the ferry and audiotour together for $11 adults, $9.25 seniors, and $5.75 ages 5-11. Available in several languages, the 35-minute, self-guided audiocassette tour is well worth the cost. It includes accounts by former inmates and prison guards, as well as an overview of the history of the island. Tickets should be purchased several days in advance either by reporting to the offices at Pier 39 or 41 between 8:30am and 5pm (8am to 7pm during the summer) or by phone (there is a $2 service charge for tickets ordered over the phone). Ferries depart from Pier 41 at half-hour intervals between 9:30am and 2:15pm (4:15pm, June through August). You are invited to stay as long as you like on the island; the last returning day-time ferry departs at 6:30pm.

You can also visit Alcatraz on a special night tour; however, some sections of the island open during the day are not open to the public at night. Departures are Thursday through Sunday at 6:15pm and 7pm. The price is $18.50 adults, $15.75 seniors and youth, and $9.25 for children.

Bay Cruise ★★★: Though more expensive than a ferry ride to Marin, a cruise around the bay can give you a beautiful view of the city and surrounding area. There are two ferry lines that offer rides beneath the bridge, along the bay, and around Alcatraz: **Red & White Fleet** 800/229-2784 boats depart from Pier 43½ beginning at 10am and run every 30 to 45 minutes until 6:15pm. The fares run $16 for adults; $12 for youth aged 12-18, seniors aged 62 and over, and active military; and $8 for children 5-11. Fares include rental of an audiocassette tour—available in a variety of languages—lasting just under an hour. Tickets can be purchased at the pier. **Blue and Gold Fleet** 415/773-1188 boats depart from Pier 39 every 30 to 45 minutes from 10am to 6:45pm. The fares run $16 for adults; $12 for seniors, ages 12-18, and active military; and $8 for children 5-11. Boat trips include a narrated tour on the sights you pass. Tickets can be purchased at the pier or by phone 415/705-5555 between 8am and 7pm (there is a $2 charge for phone orders). It is not necessary to purchase tickets in advance, although it is a good idea in the summer. *Note:* Bring warm clothes on any bay trip, the frigid winds off the water can be bone chilling.

Sea Lions ★★★: One of the most popular and interesting sights here is the sea lions that have taken over a number of docks in the marina on the west side of Pier 39. The animals drive the boatkeepers crazy with their incessant barking and pungent odor. A thrilling sight in the middle of a busy city.

Fisherman's Wharf: Embarcadero between Stockton and Polk sts. At one time, Fisherman's Wharf was the center of San Francisco's commercial fishing industry. Today, you can still spot fishing boats plying the harbor or unloading their catch at the docks, but for the most part the wharf area, with its Wax Museum, Guinness Book of Records display, and innumerable T-shirt and souvenir shops, serves the tourist industry. **Pier 39** itself is a modern shopping area built on an old pier. It looks like a boardwalk and is a favorite spot to watch street performers. The stores sell mostly tourist items of the T-shirt-and-cotton-candy variety. **Underwater World** is a new aquarium.

Across the street, **Boudin's Bakery** (156 Jefferson) continues to turn out sourdough bread as it has since 1849—although not originally in this space. A large window lets you view the process. A short distance west on Jefferson, you can pick up small, pricey samples of crab, squid, and other seafood from a group of retail fish peddlers. Continue west on Jefferson to **The Cannery** (2801 Leavenworth), a former Del Monte peach canning plant converted into a shopping center. **Ghirardelli Square** is nearby at 900 North Point. Originally a woolen mill during the Civil War, it later became the chocolate factory for which it is named. The current **Ghirardelli Chocolate Manufactory** is an old-fashioned ice cream parlor with long lines, high prices, great fudge, and examples of historic chocolate-making machines—the real factory is now in the East Bay. Ghirardelli Square itself offers yet another shopping center, although this one is much more upscale than Pier 39. Beach Street and **Victorian Park** are popular with tourists and peddlers (and hustlers) catering to tourists.

Maritime National Historic Park ★: Much of the waterfront west of Pier 43 is part of an outdoor historic park with restored ships, a World War II submarine, and a museum (see Museums below). **Aquatic Park ★**, on the shore just north of Ghirardelli Square, is a protected cove with a beach used primarily by the members of the Dolphin Club, a group of ocean swimmers who take a famous cold dip every New Year's. For a good view of the city and a peek at the salty fishermen of the wharf, take a walk along the **municipal pier** several hundred yards west of Aquatic Park at the foot of Van Ness Avenue.

The Marina ★★

The Marina's sunny weather and trendy shops, restaurants, and bars attract San Francisco's swinging twenty- and thirtysomethings. (The beautiful people are settling down, though, and the neighborhood is becoming more family oriented as evidenced by the Baby Gap on Chestnut Street.) The best way to enjoy the Marina is to hang out at an outdoor table at a café or on the Marina Green.

Fort Mason ★: at the foot of Laguna St. at Marina Blvd. Although it was under the watchful eye of U.S. Army from the 1850s until the 1970s, Fort Mason is now part of the **Golden Gate National Recreational Area** (GGNRA is headquartered here). The long warehouse-type buildings that line the water's edge house numerous crafts stores, theaters, and museums showcasing the ethnic diversity of the city (see Museums section for more on the **African-American Cultural Society** and the **Craft and Folk Art, Italo-American,** and **Mexican museums**). Start your exploration with a wonderful vegetarian meal at **Greens** (see review). **Book Bay Bookstore** 415/771-1076 sells inexpensive used books to raise money for the San Francisco Public Library. Inland up the hill, you'll find a beautiful **park ★** good for picnicking and sunbathing, as well as an **AYH Youth Hostel** popular with budget tourists.

Marina Green ★★: waterfront between Fort Mason and Baker St. Starting from Fort Mason, jump on your bike or Rollerblades—walking also works—and head west along the Marina Green pathway toward the Golden Gate Bridge. From kite flyers to runners, dog walkers, bike riders, and boat lovers, this strip has something for everyone. Take a walk out on the peninsula behind the Yacht Club and look for **the wave organ**, a series of benches and ceramic tubes embedded in the rocks that magnify the sounds of the sea. The shoreline continues west into the Presidio (see below).

Palace of Fine Arts ★★: Lyon St. and Marina Blvd., 415/561-0360. San Francisco built the Palace for the 1915 Panama-Pacific International Exposition to show the world how well it had recovered after the 1906 quake. Ironically, it was constructed on landfill and was never intended for permanent settlement—even today's structure is a reconstruction of the plaster-and-wood original. The Palace and surrounding lagoon and fountain are beautiful but in need of maintenance. The area is equally popular with visitors, wedding photographers, folks seeking a spot to snooze for a bit, pigeons, seagulls, and ducks. The **Exploratorium ★★** (see Museums section) is a hands-on science and technology museum with something for everyone.

Chestnut Street ★: between Fillmore and Broderick sts. To experience the upscale side of San Francisco's neighborhood street life, wander past the many restaurants, cafés, and shops along the Marina's main retail strip.

Pacific Heights ★★

Pacific Heights, a ritzy residential neighborhood perched atop one of San Francisco's hills, is a favorite place to see the San Francisco Bay in panorama and to view some of the city's most dazzling architecture. The north side of the hill leads down to the Marina, passing through an area centered around **Union Street** known as Cow Hollow, a bucolic pasture in the 1800s.

If you like to walk (or climb), the **Lyon Street Stairs** ★ on Lyon Street between Green Street and Broadway connect the Marina with Pacific Heights. From the top, the view of the Palace of Fine Arts, the Golden Gate Bridge, and the bay is stunning.

Victorians ★★: You can walk for hours through Pacific Heights, gawking at the many well-preserved homes and sprawling mansions. The area boasts many Victorians because it was primarily developed in the late 1800s—the height of the Victorian period—and it was behind the main fire line when the 1906 quake burned almost everything east of Van Ness Avenue. Although California, Pine, and Bush streets are busy thoroughfares, they have many nice examples of this architectural style.

Haas-Lilienthal House ★: 2007 Franklin St. (Washington/Jackson), 415/441-3004. Short of befriending a wealthy local, your best chance of seeing the inside of a Victorian is to visit this Queen Anne mansion built in 1886. Presently owned by the Foundation for San Francisco's Architectural Heritage, it's the only Victorian house open to the public, and comes complete with period furniture. You can visit the house for an hour-long tour on Wednesday noon-4pm and on Sunday 11am-5pm. The admission fee is $5 adults, $3 children under 12 and seniors. Walking tours of the neighborhood leave from the museum entrance at 12:30pm on Sundays. The fee is $5 adults, $3 children and seniors.

Shopping ★: Fillmore, Union, and Sacramento streets are the main retail strips in the area—each a boutique browser's paradise. Fillmore between Sutter and Jackson is where yuppie comfortably meets upscale grunge, with a mix of cafés, restaurants, and shops. Union Street between Gough and Steiner has a mix of jewelry, clothing, and furniture stores suited to Pacific Heights' gentry. Sacramento Street between Presidio and Spruce has many antique stores. Starbucks and other chains have moved in, though, taking away some of these neighborhoods' uniqueness.

The Golden Gate ★★★

Although the bridge is San Francisco's most recognizable landmark, its natural surroundings are also impressive. Much of the land ringing the entrance from the ocean to the bay remained relatively undeveloped as part of military installations guarding the area since the late 1700s. Over the years, a sizable chunk of these installations has been converted to parkland; the Presidio, a vast military expanse surrounding the bridge's south anchor, is still in the process of being handed over to the Park Service; much of this area's future remains uncertain.

Golden Gate Bridge ★★★: The Art Deco suspension bridge, constructed from 1933 to 1937, stretches 1.86 miles. Parking areas on both sides accommodate the hordes of tourists who come to enjoy the beautiful views of the bay, the city, and the surrounding hillsides from the bridge (parking areas on the west side of the bridge are less congested, and it's easy to walk under the span to the other side). Most tourists congregate around the **Visitors Center** located at the southeast entrance near the toll booths. A sidewalk along the east side of the bridge lets pedestrians **walk** ★★★ across the bridge (bring warm clothes, as the winds can be fierce). While the views are great, the noise and exhaust can be overwhelming when traffic is heavy.

Presidio ★★★: This military-base-turned-park has the potential to be an incredible resource for San Francisco visitors and residents. Although the National Park Service runs it now, many funding issues remain to be worked out. The Park Service is currently in the process of cleaning up the military's toxic waste sites, tearing down structurally unsound buildings, and restoring many areas to their natural habitat. While the construction can be a bit disconcerting, there are still acres of shady groves and miles of shoreline offering beaches and spectacular views, as well as a golf course.

The northeast section of the Presidio along **Crissy Field** ★ features a long stretch of beach along the bay: a favorite launch spot for windsurfers and an excellent spot for a jog, picnic, or sunset stroll. The Park Service has made restoring this area to its natural habitat a priority (so far, not much has happened). Mason Street, the road running parallel to the beach, is a favorite flat spot for beginning in-line skaters. Crissy Field continues west to the Golden Gate Bridge. Although the trail directly up to the bridge is closed, you can follow the road up to the bridge.

Fort Point ★: 415/556-1693. A historic structure located under the southern end of the bridge. You can take an audio tour of this site, the only Civil War fort on the West Coast. Watch daring surfers catch precarious waves off the point. • W-Su 10am-5pm. Audio tour $2.50 adults, $1 ages 12 and under.

Lincoln Boulevard ★★★: This busy thoroughfare skirts the Presidio's western edge, providing spectacular **views ★★★** of the Golden Gate. From the small parking areas located on the boulevard, you can head off on one of the many narrow pathways that meander along the cliffs. Lincoln Boulevard becomes El Camino del Mar when you leave the Presidio and enter Sea Cliff, a district that contains many elegant Mediterranean-style homes. As you head west, stop at **Baker Beach** or **China Beach** for a little sunbathing.

Lincoln Park ★★★: This park, which occupies the northwest corner of San Francisco, has two faces: the perfectly manicured golf course and the rugged coastline. **The Coastal Trail ★★★** runs west from El Camino del Mar at the park's eastern edge—where it borders the golf course—winding around a rugged point called **Lands End** to Seal Rocks near the Sutro Baths, ending at Ocean Beach. It offers exquisite **views ★★★** of the Golden Gate Bridge and the Marin Headlands. Lincoln Park is also home to the newly restored **Palace of the Legion of Honor ★★★** (see Museums section). In addition to a reputable collection, the museum boasts a stunning exterior and a beautiful setting. Be sure to walk around the parking lot to see the moving **Holocaust sculpture ★** and more views.

Expansive **Ocean Beach ★** occupies the city's western edge. Perched at the northern end of Ocean Beach is the classic **Cliff House,** 1090 Point Lobos Ave., at the end of Geary Boulevard, 415/386-1170, oozing with San Francisco history and trivia. The original Cliff House was built in 1863, only to burn and be rebuilt two more times. Today the Cliff House building houses touristy restaurants with **beautiful views ★★** (a good place for a drink), a camera obscura, the **Musée Mecanique**, and a **Park Service Visitor Center** 415/556-8642 open daily 10am-5pm. Also in the late 1800s, Adolph Sutro built a huge indoor-outdoor swimming pool called **Sutro Baths** right next to the Cliff House. Its ruins are visible today. **Sutro Heights Park**, across the Great Highway and up the hill, harbors a charming Victorian kiosk. Despite its cobbled-together state, the area remains an attraction for tourists and locals alike.

Golden Gate Park ★★★

Who would have thought it possible in 1870 that a 1,017-acre plot of windswept sand dunes could be transformed into a lush green park? With the vision and guidance of William Hammond Hall, a young civil engineer, and his successor, planner John McLaren, a whole new ecological system was born and has grown to become a verdant wonderland. Spanning three miles east to west and nine blocks north to south, Golden Gate Park is a city treasure, inviting enthusiasts of life to sample nature, sports, and culture: in addition to verdant pathways, the park houses some of the city's largest museums as well as an eclectic collection of attractions and sports facilities. If in-line skating or biking is your thing, visit the park on Sundays when traffic on John F. Kennedy Drive east of 19th Avenue is blocked off so those on man-powered wheels can glide down the park streets in peace.

The park has more than 50 entryways, from the Great Highway at the west end of the park to the eastern boundary at Stanyan Street. The best way to start is with the *Map & Guide to Golden Gate Park*, found at the **McLaren Lodge Visitors Center** 415/831-7200 on John F. Kennedy Drive near Stanyan Street on the eastern edge of the park. Open M-F 8am-5pm. (Most of the bike rental or sport shops on Haight and Stanyan streets also sell the map.)

The centrally located Music Concourse is flanked by two of Golden Gate Park's most famous attractions: the **California Academy of Sciences** and the **M.H. de Young Memorial Museum**. The de Young building houses both the **Asian Art Museum** (which is slated to move when its new Civic Center home has finished undergoing retrofitting) and a large collection of American and British art (see Museums section). As the park was originally created for strollers who wanted a respite from the frenetic pace of city life, there are hundreds of paths to explore.

Japanese Tea Garden ★★: Music Concourse, 415/752-1171. The famous—and popular—garden offers a beautiful setting where you can lose yourself in Zen contemplation of pagodas, bonsai trees, and expensive tea. It's best visited on a rainy spring day.
• Open 9am-6pm daily; $2.50 adults, $1 children and seniors.

Strybing Arboretum ★: M.L. King, Jr. Dr. between 9th and 19th aves., just south of the Music Concourse, 415/661-1316. A walk through the countless varieties of plants and flowers here can be particularly pleasant on a spring day. Vision-impaired visitors will enjoy the **Garden of Fragrance**; its plants are specifically selected for scent and texture.

Rose Gardens ★: J.F. Kennedy Dr. near 8th Ave. A wonderful collection of these flowering beauties in a variety of colors and sizes.

Stow Lake ★: located near the middle of the park just west of the Music Concourse. An artificial lake popular with strollers and those who like taking a rowboat out on the water (boats available for rent). **Strawberry Hill**, a rise in the middle of Stow Lake, is the highest point in the park. An attractive waterfall cascades down the hill into the lake.

Children's Playground: off Kezar Dr. A favorite spot to climb, swing, and slide (make sure to visit the Herschel-Spillman carousel, restored to its original splendor, complete with horses, frogs, and zebras). • Open June-September daily 10am-5pm and October-May on F-Su 9am-4pm. $1 adults and 25 cents kids.

Other Park Attractions: The **Shakespeare Garden** (behind the Academy of Sciences) contains plants and flowers figuring in Shakespeare's works. The **Buffalo Paddock**, on John F. Kennedy Drive at the west end of the park, is a large section of land reserved for a small bison herd. Just east of the paddock you'll find **Spreckels Lake**, where you can watch members of the Model Yacht Club sail their miniature boats. Continuing west on Kennedy Drive, you reach the **Dutch Windmill** surrounded by a colorful tulip garden. The windmill originally drove a pump used for irrigating the park. If you continue on the drive and cross the Great Highway, there's parking along **Ocean Beach**. The **Beach Chalet Brewery and Restaurant** has marvelous views of the Pacific Ocean and a small museum covering the park's history. The **Polo Field** fills the middle of the western half of the park. Forget any images of idle gentry lounging here; this area has been home to musical gatherings since the great Human Be-In and the Summer of Love.

The Haight ★★

The Haight Ashbury was the center of the mid-1960s hippie utopia, but a lot has changed in 30 years. The Haight's heyday was in 1967, when the Human Be-In and the Gathering of the Tribes were held at the Golden Gate Park Polo Field. Over 20,000 people gathered to listen to Timothy Leary, Jerry Rubin, Jefferson Airplane, and the Grateful Dead. The Haight has gradually matured since those days—there's a Gap store on the corner of Haight and Ashbury—but it hasn't lost its 1960s feel. When Grateful Dead guitarist Jerry Garcia died in 1995, the streets filled with groups of fans—many of whom weren't even born by the Summer of Love—grieving around makeshift shrines. You'll also find a mix of local residents: students; young, affluent professionals and homeowners; black-clad, pierced hipsters; and an enclave of 1960s holdouts, petty drug dealers, and aggressive panhandlers.

The Upper Haight runs along Haight Street from Golden Gate Park to Central Avenue and contains the famous intersection of Haight and Ashbury. Part of the area's charm lies in the large, ornate Victorian homes, many of which have been beautifully restored in luscious color schemes. The best house viewing is actually on the blocks north and south of Haight; cross-street Masonic Avenue is also a good spot. Most famous of the lot is 710 Ashbury Street, former communal home of the Grateful Dead. Country Joe McDonald and Janis Joplin both lived right up the street, at 612 and 635 Ashbury, respectively. All are private homes now, so don't bother the current occupants.

Haight Street ★: The main retail strip is a kind of informal shopping mall of the off-beat, with an interesting collection of stores, cafés, restaurants, and bars. Since many shops are as unique inside as their storefronts suggest, wandering up and down the street until you expire from sensory overload is the best strategy. You'll find an especially large selection of funky clothing stores, with both new and used threads, including such places as **Daljeets** (1744 Haight), a punk-rock fashion haven that claims to have "The Largest Selection of Thi-Hi Boots." Music still plays an important role in the Haight. **Ameoba Music** (1855 Haight), **Reckless Records** (1401 Haight), and **Recycled Records** (1377 Haight) are three good outlets. For a bit of the unusual, check out the **Bound Together Book Collective** (1369 Haight).

The Castro ★

The Castro, the heart of San Francisco's gay community since the 1970s, is never a dull place to wander. Best of all, however, you won't need to worry about a strict agenda since there are no real "sights," per se. You'll find most of the stores, restaurants, and bars along Market, Castro, and 18th streets. The surrounding area has many well-tended Victorian homes with rainbow flags proudly displayed.

Harvey Milk Plaza: If you get to the Castro by MUNI, you will come up to street level at the corner of Market and Castro at Harvey Milk Plaza, named after the nation's first openly gay elected city official, who was assassinated along with Mayor George Moscone in 1978 by conservative and disgruntled ex-city supervisor Dan White. To this day, Harvey Milk remains a local hero, and the date of his assassination is always marked by a candlelight procession from Harvey Milk Plaza to City Hall, where the murder took place.

NAMES Project Foundation ★★: 2362A Market St. (Castro), 415/882-5500. For insight into the community spirit that has gathered force in the face of the AIDS crisis, pay a visit to the headquarters of the organization that sponsored the creation of a gigantic quilt made up of individual panels created in memory of AIDS victims by their lovers, friends, and families. Sections of the quilt are often on display around the country, and it has become too large to be exhibited as a whole. In the showroom, you can see thousands of individual panels and learn more about the quilt project. • Open M-Sa noon-7pm; Su noon-6pm. Free.

Twin Peaks Tavern: 401 Castro St. (Market). Known for being the first gay bar with a facade of windows, a good-bye kiss to the days when such places had to be tucked away in back alleys to avoid police raids. Today, the bar is better known by the young-and-beautiful set as the "glass coffin," for the older crowd that frequents this spot.

Castro Theater: 429 Castro St. (Market/18th St.), 415/621-6120. One of the city's favorite movie theaters, loved for its magnificent, over-the-top baroque interior and its unpredictable lineup.

Castro and 18th Streets: Known as the "gayest four corners in the world," there is never a dull moment on the southeast corner, dubbed Hibernia Beach for the bank that once stood here (now home to a Bank of America branch) and the shirtless men who tend to gather in front of it.

Castro and Market Streets: Many area stores capture the neighborhood flavor. At the indispensable **Cliff's Variety Store** (479 Castro) you can pick up any of your basic items, from a wrench to a red feather boa. Next door, **A Different Light** is the only bookstore in the city devoted solely to gay and lesbian literature. **Does Your Mother Know . . .** (4079 18th Street) offers a wide selection of cards for every occasion, except, strangely enough, for coming out to your parents. **The Midnight Sun** (4069 18th Street) is a popular gay video bar where a rapt audience watches *Melrose, 90210*, and anything else that comes across the oversized screens placed around the bar.

Along Market Street, innumerable restaurants, cafés, and shops have sprung up over the years, but the most popular of these is still the long-enduring **Café Flore** (2298 Market). This is the place to be seen reading Descartes or, if you're not into the brainy image, to put on an ultra-cool pair of sunglasses and go for the pretty look. Later in the evening, **The Café** (2367 Market) is a popular bar, especially good if you're up for dancing (see Bars & Clubs section). This stretch of Market is also one of the best places to scout for music, especially vinyl. Once you're stocked up on music, head to **Gauntlet** (2377 Market), where the staff will gladly assist you with all of your body piercing needs. Local restaurants cater to the late-night tendencies of their clientele, and there are several 24-hour eateries that will never turn you away. **Sparky's Diner** (242 Church) and **Bagdad Café** (2295 Market) offer good, greasy food at any hour.

The Mission ★

The Mission District, named for Mision San Francisco de Asis (aka Mission Dolores), was established as a Spanish settlement in 1776, four days before the signing of the Declaration of Independence. That spirit of freedom lives on in this neighborhood on the south side of San Francisco. Populated largely by families of Latin American descent, the Mission is also home to many artists, musicians, and a recent surge of gen-Xers drawn by the relatively low rents.

Although there are only a few formal tourist attractions, there are plenty of ways to enjoy the Mission: a window-shopping stroll along Valencia to visit the many thrift stores, sunbathing in the park, or maybe just having coffee in a hip café. The Mission is on the sunny side of San Francisco: when the summer fog rolls over the rest of the city, the Mission frequently still lies in full sun. The area isn't the city's safest, however, and visitors should be cautious at night, especially north of 16th Street and east of Mission Street.

Festivals for **Day of the Dead** happen around Halloween, complete with a drum-led procession through the streets (check with the Mission Cultural Center for details). **Carnaval** happens the last Sunday in May and fills the streets with costume-clad revelers swaying to music that could be live or from a DJ and from any nation. Contingents represent a mix of nations, including Brazil, Cuba, Haiti, Trinidad and Tobago, and the Bahamas.

Mission Dolores ★: Dolores and 16th sts., 415/621-8203. Built in 1791, this is the oldest building in San Francisco, with furnishings accumulated over the last 200 years. The cemetery is particularly captivating, as is the small collection of artifacts on display in the modest museum.

Murals ★★: A favorite neighborhood activity is viewing the more than 70 murals sited in various spots throughout the Mission. There's a concentration of excellent murals on 24th Street between Folsom and Potrero, with some of the best tucked away on **Balmy Alley**, a narrow lane next to the Mission Neighborhood Center (3013 24th Street). Don't miss the gripping mural painted, perhaps ironically, on **St. Peter's Church** (corner of 24th and Florida streets). In 1995, work by over 500 artists was completed on the magnificent mural lining two sides of the **Women's Building** (18th Street between Valencia and Guerrero). **Organized walking tours** are hosted by **Precita Eyes** (348 Precita). Stop in any time and, for a $1.50 donation, receive a map of the mural locations for a self-guided tour. Guided tours of the Mission's murals leave on Saturdays at 11am and 1pm ($5 adults, $4 seniors, $1 under 18). Call 415/285-2287 for additional tours.

Galeria de la Raza: 2857 24th St. (Bryant), 415/826-8009. Experience the local art scene on a smaller scale at this gallery, which shows local and international Latino artwork. The gallery's adjacent shop sells Mexican and South American folk art at reasonable prices.

Mission Cultural Center: 2868 Mission St. (24th St./25th St.), 415/821-1155. In addition to showing artwork, Mission Cultural Center itself is an object of art, covered with an enormous, vivid mural. This neighborhood center houses an active theater and a large gallery and offers dance classes from countries around the globe. Try some Brazilian samba or, if you are more inclined, the home arts classes will teach you how to re-cane and repaint your needy furniture.

Mission and Valencia Streets ★: Fruit and vegetable stands offering a rich selection of produce from all over the world line Mission and Valencia streets. Some of the best outlets are at Valencia and 22nd, Valencia and 16th, and Mission and 26th. The area is also home to some of the city's best and most diverse restaurants (see Restaurants section).

Mission nightlife is equally interesting, with many excellent bars, clubs, and cafés offering everything from a quiet game of pool to cutting-edge local music (see Bars & Clubs section). If you are in the mood for a movie, the **Roxie** (3117 16th St.) screens an interesting array of films. **Muddy's** (1304 Valencia), which is not to be confused with **Muddy Waters,** hosts a weekly Wednesday Night Game Night: Scrabble, checkers, you name it. You can bring your own board or settle into a match with a friend-not-yet-met—a great way to meet people if you're new in town.

Some local stores, in true San Francisco style, cater to unique tastes. Be sure to browse in **Modern Times Bookstore** (888 Valencia), which has a particularly good selection of books dealing with political and social issues. **Good Vibrations** (1210 Valencia) carries a selection of sensual accessories in a women-friendly, nurturing environment.

Thrift Stores ★: If these are a passion for you, you'll be spending most of your time in the Mission. **Captain Jack's** (866 Valencia) has an incredible selection of clothing, shoes, and accessories, while **Hocus Pocus** (900 Valencia) has more antiques, collectibles, and furnishings than you can imagine. We dare you to walk out empty-handed. **Classic Consignment** (867 Valencia), **Harrington Brothers Antiques** (599 Valencia), and **Upstairs Downstairs** (890 Valencia) primarily offer refinished 1920s to 1950s furnishings. **Sensacional** (3615 18th Street) has as-is furnishings at unbelievable prices. Don't be dismayed by the sign out front that says "This junk is for sale." There are treasures buried in that pile. **ThriftTown** (2101 Mission), though incredibly large, does not offer the competitive pricing you would expect from a Salvation Army. The selection is vast, however, with items ranging from wedding dresses to washing machines. **Gypsy Honeymoon** (1201 Guerrero) caters to a taste for the macabre in its furnishings and fashions. **Community Thrift** (625 Valencia) has everything you need to start a new house: toasters, coasters, and roasters at unbelievably thrifty prices along with furnishings, clothing, dishes, magazines, and more. Well worth a look, even if you are usually antithrift.

Other Neighborhoods

The area South of Market, **SoMa**, is home to **Yerba Buena Gardens ★★** between Third, Fourth, Howard, and Mission streets. Outside, lush lawns, water sculptures, pavilions, and benches mark the landscape, a perfect setting for a picnic while enjoying one of the many free alfresco performances. The buildings house theaters and art galleries. A large children's center and an imposing Sony entertainment complex are being constructed on the site. Many museums now surround the area, including the dramatic **San Francisco Museum of Modern Art (SFMOMA)**, **Ansel Adams Center for Photography,** and **Cartoon Art Museum** (see Museums section).

Twin Peaks ★★: Tour buses full of visitors come year-round to take in the spectacular **view** of the city (on a clear day) from the city's highest lookout point, at the top of Twin Peaks (take Twin Peaks Drive off of Portola Drive). From this vantage, you can see the Marin Headlands and Golden Gate Bridge to the north; downtown San Francisco, the bay, and Oakland to the east; and the San Mateo bridge to the south. Another beautiful and popular panorama of the city can be viewed from the pull-off on Portola Drive just down from the intersection of Burnett Avenue and Clipper Street. At sunrise and on clear evenings, professional photographers line up to capture the city's beauty for posterity and postcards.

Japantown ★: Post Street between Webster and Laguna sts. Many Japanese Americans lived here until they were interned during World War II, but the area never regained its original population. It is centered around the prominent **Japan Center** complex, a small, 1960s shopping center that houses many shops selling Japanese goods. The rather spare outdoor Peace Plaza is home to a large concrete pagoda. The block on Buchanan Street between Post and Sutter streets is a pedestrian mall. There are a number of Japanese restaurants and grocery stores in the vicinity, as well as the popular **Kabuki Movie Theater** and **Kabuki Hot Springs**. The Cherry Blossom Festival is held here in April.

MUSEUMS

Golden Gate Park is home to the M.H. de Young and Asian Art Museums and the Academy of Sciences. Museum frequenters note: membership in the **Museum Society** 415/750-3636 entitles you and a friend to a year's free admission to both the de Young and Asian Art Museums. Fort Mason houses several smaller museums that spotlight particular cultures, while the Yerba Buena Center for the Arts in the South of Market area is the city's new and comprehensive home for the arts.

Academy of Sciences: Tea Garden Dr., Golden Gate Park, SF, 415/750-7145. Morrison Planetarium: 415/750-7141. Laserium: 415/750-7138. San Francisco's main science museum. The attractions include a "safe quake," a simulation of the 1906 earthquake, a frozen great white shark, and the Discovery Room for Children, which is filled with interactive exhibits. Academy admission includes entry to the **Steinhart Aquarium**, located in the same building. Watch penguins, alligators, and thousands of other aquatic creatures cruise in tanks. Call for animal feeding schedules. The Academy also houses the **Morrison Planetarium**, which features celestially oriented planetarium shows and entertainment-oriented Laserium shows. Admission to Planetarium is separate. • Labor Day-Memorial Day, daily 10am-5pm; Memorial Day-Labor Day, daily 9am-6pm. $8.50 adults; $5.50 ages 12-17, students with ID, and seniors; $2 ages 4-11; children under 3 free. Free first W of month. Morrison Planetarium: General admission plus $2.50 adults; $1.25 ages 6-12 and seniors; children under 5 free. Laserium: F-Su evenings, call for times and shows. $6-$8 adults; $5-$6 ages 6-12 and seniors.

African-American Historical and Cultural Society: Bldg. C, Fort Mason (Buchanan at Marina Blvd.), SF, 415/441-0640. Displays African, African-American, and Caribbean artwork. • Museum and gallery: W-Su noon-5pm; first W of month noon-8pm. Donation appreciated.

Asian Art Museum: Tea Garden Dr., Golden Gate Park, SF, 415/668-8921. Located in the same building as the de Young, the Asian Art Museum contains an important permanent collection of paintings and ceramics from all Asian countries. Because of limited space, only a small portion of the collection is on display at a time, so exhibits are small and frequently rotated. The museum will move into the old Main Library when a large earthquake retrofit is completed. • W-Su 9:30am-5pm; first W of month 9:30am-8:45pm. $7 adults; $5 seniors; $4 ages 12-17; under age 12 free. Free first W of month.

Cable Car Museum: 1201 Mason St. (Washington), SF, 415/474-1887. A tiny museum which houses three antique cable cars, including the world's first (built in 1873), and the cable winding machinery that's still used to run the cars. • Daily 10am-5pm (summer until 6pm). Free.

California Palace of the Legion of Honor: Lincoln Park, 34th Ave. and Clement St., SF, 415/750-3600. Looking buffed and polished after a recent renovation, the Legion houses a collection of European art impressive in scope, yet manageable in size. Beaux Arts galleries lit by skylights gracefully frame works ranging from Medieval to Postimpressionist. Makes for a great afternoon for art lovers and is a must-see for any fan of Rodin sculptures. Downstairs, the Achenbach Foundation for Graphic Arts displays the Bay Area's largest print collection—frequently changing to protect the fragile works. • Tu-Su 9:30am-5pm. $7 adults; $5 seniors; $4 ages 12-17. Free second W of month.

Cartoon Art Museum: 814 Mission St., 2nd Fl. (4th St./5th St.), SF, 415/546-3922. A collection of newspaper strips, animation stills, comic books, and political cartoons illustrating the history of the craft, from a Hogarth engraving to present-day "funnies." • W-F 11am-5pm; Sa 10am-5pm; Su 1-5pm. $5 adults; $3 students and seniors; $2 children under 12; children under 5 free. Free first W of month.

Chinese Cultural Center: Holiday Inn, 750 Kearny St. (Washington), SF, 415/986-1822. Features changing exhibits of everything from Chinese-American history to calligraphy. Fun to visit during Chinese New Year. • Tu-Su 10am-4pm. Free.

Exploratorium: 3601 Lyon St. (Marina Blvd.), SF, 415/561-0360 (recorded information); Tactile Dome 415/561-0362. Located at the scenic Palace of Fine Arts (dangerously close to the road that leads towards the Golden Gate Bridge, check your map before going) the Exploratorium is an internationally acclaimed museum of science, art, and human perception. It features over 650 interactive exhibits, including a distorted room, an indoor tornado, and the popular Shadow Box—all designed to help people of all ages and backgrounds understand natural phenomena. • Labor Day-Memorial Day: Tu-Su 10am-5pm; W 10am-9:30pm. Memorial Day-Labor Day: Th-Tu 10am-6pm, W 10am-9pm. $9 adults; $7 seniors and students; $5 disabled and children 6-17; $2.50 children ages 3-5; free under age 3. First W of month free. Tactile Dome: $12 during museum hours (includes Exploratorium admission); $10 after hours Tu, Th, F. Reservations are necessary.

The Friends of Photography and Ansel Adams Center: 250 4th St. (Folsom/Howard), SF, 415/495-7000. Houses works by Adams and exhibits works by other photographers. • Tu-Su 11am-5pm; 11am-8pm first Th of month. $5 adults; $3 students; $2 ages 13-17 and seniors; children under 13 free.

Jewish Museum: 121 Steuart St. (Mission/Howard), SF, 415/543-8880. Features changing exhibits of Jewish art and artifacts from all over the world. The museum will move to Mission Street between Third and Fourth streets sometime in 2001. • Su-W 11am-5pm; Th 11am-8pm. $5 adults; $2.50 students and seniors. Free first M of month.

Mexican Museum: Bldg. D, Fort Mason (Buchanan at Marina Blvd.), SF, 415/441-0404. A collection numbering 9,000 works divided into galleries of pre-Hispanic, colonial, folk, Mexican, and Mexican-American art. • W-F noon-5pm; Sa-Su 11am-5pm; first W of month noon-7pm. $3 adults; $2 students and seniors; under age 10 free. Free first W of month.

Musée Mecanique: Cliff House, 1090 Point Lobos Ave. (Great Hwy.), SF, 415/386-1170. A re-creation of a turn-of-the-century arcade, where the mechanical attractions include fortune tellers, elaborate moving toothpick architecture constructed by Alcatraz inmates, and hysterical laughing ladies. (Warning: racist caricatures abound.) • M-F 11am-7pm; Sa-Su, holidays 10am-8pm. Free.

Museo Italo Americano: Bldg. C, Fort Mason (Buchanan at Marina Blvd.), SF, 415/673-2200. Contains a permanent collection of Italian and Italian-American modern art and presents four special exhibits a year. • W-Su noon-5pm. $2 adults; $1 students and seniors; free ages 12 and under.

Maritime National Historical Park: extends from Aquatic Park at Polk Street to Fisherman's Wharf at Taylor Street, SF, 415/556-3002. Museum: Beach St. and Polk St. A historic park encompassing parts of the northern waterfront. Within the park, the **Maritime Museum** at the northern foot of Polk Street houses models and photos of historical ships. Outside, at the **Hyde Street Pier**, explore three 19th-century ships—a sidewheel ferry, a lumber schooner, and a square rigger. • Museum: daily 10am-5pm. Free. Hyde Street Pier: October-May, daily 9:30am-5pm; June-September, daily 10am-6pm. $4 adults; $2 ages 12-17; free under 12 and seniors; $10 family pass.

M.H. de Young Memorial Museum: Tea Garden Dr., Golden Gate Park, SF, 415/750-3600. The de Young, 44 galleries strong, features a recently expanded collection of American art from the colonial period to the mid-20th century—the finest collection west of the Mississippi—along with exhibits featuring the arts and crafts of Africa, Oceania, the Américas, and England. The de Young also offers tours, workshops, children's classes, and occasional films, often free. • W-Su 9:30am-5pm; first W of month 9:30am-8:45pm. $7 adults; $5 seniors; $4 ages 12-17; free ages 11 and under. Free first W of month. Free Walkman-guided tours.

San Francisco Craft and Folk Art Museum: Bldg. A, Fort Mason (Buchanan at Marina Blvd.), SF, 415/775-0990. The only museum of its kind in Northern California, this San Francisco original hosts six exhibitions a year on subjects ranging from African-American quilt making to Haitian steel-drum sculpture. • Tu-F, Su 11am-5pm; Sa 10am-5pm. $3 adults; $1 seniors and ages 12-17; free ages 11 and under. Also free every Sa 10am-noon and first W of month 11am-7pm.

San Francisco Museum of Modern Art: 151 3rd St. (Mission/Howard), SF, 415/357-4000. The stunning museum near Yerba Buena Center in the SoMa district draws an incredible stream of visitors. Although the permanent collection includes works by virtually every major 20th-century artist, including Calder, Klee, Matisse, and Pollack, it doesn't yet live up to the world-class architecture, but it is expanding rapidly. Some of the most interesting pieces are by California artists such as Richard Diebenkorn and Wayne Thiebaud. The fascinating array of exhibits ranges from visions of futuristic cities created by Japan's leading architects to a pop sculpture of Michael Jackson and his chimpanzee, created by Jeff Koons. • Labor Day-Memorial Day: F-Tu 11am-6pm; Th 11am-9pm; Memorial Day-Labor Day F-Tu 10am-6pm; Th 10am-9pm. $8 adults; $5 seniors; $4 students. Half-price Th 6-9pm; free first Tu of month.

Tattoo Art Museum: 841 Columbus St. (Greenwich/Lombard), SF, 415/775-4991. The country's only museum devoted to body graphics displays tattoo equipment, flashes (advertisements), and exhibits on tattoo use in other cultures. • M-Th noon-9pm; F-Sa noon-10pm; Su noon-8pm. Free.

U.S.S. Pampanito: Pier 45, Fisherman's Wharf (Embarcadero at Taylor), SF, 415/929-0202. Explore a World War II submarine in this part of the National Maritime Historic Park. • Labor Day-Memorial Day: Su-Th 9am-6pm; F-Sa 9am-8pm. Memorial Day-Labor Day: daily 9am-8pm. $7 adults; $4 ages 6-12 and seniors; free ages 5 and under; $20 family rate.

Yerba Buena Center for the Arts: 701 Mission St. (3rd St.), SF, 415/978-ARTS (2787). The Center for the Arts gallery is bright, open, and spacious. There is no permanent collection, so exhibits change regularly. The gallery shares its elegant space with a screening room for documentaries, films, and video presentations; a café; and a gift shop selling goods made by local and international artisans. • Tu-Su 11am-6pm; first Th of month 11am-8pm. $5 adults; $3 students, seniors, and children. Children under 5 free. (More for special events.) Free first Th of month 6pm-8pm.

RESTAURANTS

Albona ★★★ $$ North Beach: 545 Francisco St. (Taylor/Mason), 415/441-1040. Named after the owner's hometown on the Istrian Peninsula (the point of land that sticks out across the Adriatic from Venice), this eatery serves a menu that meshes cuisines of Central Europe and Italy into a unique table. Delicacies include home-made ravioli stuffed with nuts and cheeses, fried gnocchi in a savory sauce with bits of sirloin, and lamb in pomegranate sauce. Everything is memorable here, including the service, which is very friendly. • Tu-Sa 5-10pm.

Angkor Wat ★★★ $$ Richmond: 4217 Geary Blvd. (6th Ave./7th Ave.), 415/221-7887. This is probably the only restaurant in San Francisco that serves a soup (*samlaw machhou kroeung krahorm*, chicken and pineapple simmered in lemongrass broth) for which the Pope's personal cook requested the recipe, after the Pontiff himself ate here on a visit. Host Charlie Sar, chef and owner of this beautifully decorated Cambodian palace, is effusive and eager to recommend dishes. Aside from the soup, which is near mandatory, recommendations include the gourmet duck curry and the incredible Cambodian five-spices shark. It's hard to go wrong with any dish. Classical Cambodian dancing is performed on Fridays and Saturdays. • M-Th 11am-2:30pm, 5-10pm; F-Sa 11am-2:30pm, 5-10:30pm; Su 5-10pm.

Appam ★★ $$ SoMa: 1261 Folsom St. (8th St./9th St.), 415/626-2798. Some of the better Indian food in the city is served at this elegant SoMa eatery. The dining room is dimly lit and romantic. Curries are prepared *dum phukt* style, cooked under a crust in a specially made clay pot that allows them to steam gently. Sit out back under the gazebo on warm evenings. • Daily 11am-11pm.

Aqua ★★★ $$$$ Financial District: 252 California St. (Front/Battery), 415/956-9662. This is one of the city's most glittery, stylish seafood restaurants. Enter the gleaming, mirrored dining room through an unmarked facade; you'll know you're in the right place by the fish-tail door handle and the glamorous patrons. Exquisitely prepared and beautifully presented fish is the order of the day. Try the lobster, potato gnocchi, or the grilled swordfish. Jacket and tie preferred for men. • M-F 11:30am-2:15pm, 5:30-10:30pm; Sa 5:30-10:30pm.

Beach Chalet ★ $$ Sunset: 1000 Great Hwy. (Fulton/Lincoln), 415/386-8439. Opened in 1997 at a long-dormant outpost on the western tip of Golden Gate Park, the Beach Chalet has quickly become a vital destination for well-scrubbed suburban-ites, tourists, and well-to-do thirtysomething professionals. The giant space, with its undulating moldings, exposed beams, and blonde wood fittings, affords diners an unimpeded view of Ocean Beach and the vast Pacific Ocean behind floor-to-ceiling plate-glass windows; the expansive bar area affords drinkers a view of the Chalet's giant copper brewing tanks. While the food won't keep you away, you'll come for the spectacular location. If in doubt, gravitate towards the fresh seafood dishes—the moist and flavorful grilled salmon is a good bet—the can't-miss buttermilk fried onion rings or brewpub mainstays like the Niman-Schell burger. Riskier choices include the unreliable pastas and steamed vegetable platter. Most of the house brews, from the light and fruity Churchyard Pale Ale to the heavier Pacific Porter, are solid choices. • M-Th 11:30am-10pm; F-Sa 11:30am-11pm; Su 10am-10pm.

Betelnut ★★ $$/$$$ Marina: 2026 Union St. (Buchanan/Webster), 415/929-8855. This riotously popular place is an Asian beer house. Grazing food, tidbits to accompa-ny drinks, a light lunch, a late-afternoon or late-night snack, or even dinner: all can be had here. Chinese, Thai, Japanese, and less frequently seen specialties from Malaysia and Singapore are all featured. Diners can sit at the sidewalk tables, in the lively bar, near the open kitchen, or in a spacious back room (where large groups are seated). • M-Th 11:30am-11pm; F-Sa 11:30-midnight; Su 11:30am-11pm.

Bix ★★ $$$ Financial District: 56 Gold St. (off Montgomery btwn. Pacific/Jackson), 415/433-6300. Located on a Jackson Square alley, this moody supper club fits perfectly into its quaint setting. Sidle up to the gleaming mahogany bar, order one of the city's best martinis, and check out the looming mural while you listen to the piano player tickle the ivories; you expect a swell guy named Bugsy to stroll by. The dining area in this compact, vertical space is split between a few downstairs tables and a small mezzanine overlooking the cocktail crowd. The food is secondary to the scene: good, but retro—a Waldorf salad can only be so exciting. The potato leek pancakes with smoked salmon is a reliable favorite, as are the panfried chicken and the grilled pork chop with mashed potatoes. • M-Th 11:30am-11pm; F 11:30am-midnight; Sa 5:30pm-midnight; Su 6-10pm.

Boulevard ★★★ **$$$$** SoMa: 1 Mission St. (Steuart), 415/543-6084. Another instant hit for the ubiquitous Pat Kuleto. The dramatic decor in the historic Audiffred Building overlooking the bay updates the Parisian brasserie with such trademark Kuleto touches as an open kitchen, alabaster lighting fixtures, and sweeping views. The French theme contrasts with chef Nancy Oakes' eclectic California cuisine. Dishes can be as simple as oven-roasted chicken or as elaborately wrought as roast duck breast with champagne Parmesan risotto, chanterelle mushrooms, roasted tomatoes, and a salad of duck cracklings and chervil. The large dining room and lively scene enhance the restaurant's celebratory feeling. • M-W 11:30am-10pm; Th-F 11:30am-10:30pm; Sa 5:30-10:30pm; Su 5:30-10pm.

Bruno's ★★★ **$$$** Mission: 2389 Mission St. (19th St./20th St.), 415/550-7455. Formerly a fabled Mission district political hangout, Bruno's has been reborn as a soigné '50s-style supper club featuring cocktail-dress-clad hostesses, circular red vinyl booths, and innovative California cooking. Start the evening with a martini and an order of oysters, then move on to braised lamb shank with truffled white-bean ravioli or delectable herb gnocchi with seared scallops and asparagus tips. After dinner, enjoy a cocktail at Bruno's nightclub, adjacent to the restaurant, offering live jazz nightly. • Tu-Th 6:30-11pm; F-Sa 6:30pm-midnight.

Buca Giovanni ★★★ **$$$** North Beach: 800 Greenwich St. (Columbus), 415/776-7766. An old-style northern Italian restaurant for people who eat pasta as a *secondo piatto*. The marvelous menu offers a wide range of salads, many unusual pastas, risotto, seafood, rabbit, game dishes, lamb, veal, and beef. Rabbit with grappa, prosciutto, and oyster mushrooms and lamb with black olives and capers exemplify dishes to tantalize the jaded palate. Count on everything being well prepared. Go with a hearty appetite. The below-street-level setting is cavelike (*buca* means "cave") but pleasant, and the Old World service is casually professional. • Tu-Su 5:30-10:30pm.

Café Claude ★★ **$** Union Square: 7 Claude Ln. (off Bush btwn. Grant/Kearny), 415/392-3505. So Gallic, from the music, to the food, to the charming waiters. The atmosphere is airy and open, with French posters and original art on the walls. On nice days, tables are set out in the alley for that Parisian sidewalk-café feel. The espresso bar serves a latte in a bowl, just like in the old country. For lunch or dinner, be sure to try the onion soup and huge Caesar salad, or such typical French standbys as a *croque monsieur* or a baguette sandwich. Don't miss glimpsing the antique zinc bar brought over from Paris. Well hidden but worth the search. • M-Sa 10am-10pm.

Café Jacqueline ★★ **$$$** North Beach: 1454 Grant Ave. (Green/Union), 415/981-5565. One of the city's more romantic eateries, with fresh flowers and candles on the tables. Jacqueline specializes in made-to-order soufflés. The spinach tends to be a bit watery, so go for the mushroom or the corn, ginger, and garlic special instead. And don't skip dessert! The chocolate-raspberry soufflé is beyond decadent. Soufflé production can be excruciatingly slow (order soup or salad to while away the time). Sadly, the wine list is painfully overpriced, as is the corkage for those who choose to bring their own. • W-Su 5:30-11pm.

Café Kati ★★★ **$$$** Japantown: 1963 Sutter St. (Fillmore/Webster), 415/775-7313. Make sure you're feeling daring when you venture to Café Kati, which bills itself as featuring cuisine that marries flavors and foods from the Asia-Pacific region with those of the West. Many of the offerings are exotic and mysterious, beginning with the *papadam* (a large crispy Indian cracker) and cucumber dipping sauce that arrive on your table in lieu of bread and butter. Curious appetizers such as mango rolls (wrapped in rice paper) and adventurous main courses such as a trio of "Hawaiian seafoods" (ask your waiter for an explanation) make you feel like a gastronomic Indiana Jones. The desserts, namely the "warm and gooey chocolate cake" (its real name) and the butterscotch pudding, are dramatically presented with tiaralike clouds of spun sugar crowning them. • Tu-Th 5:30-9:30pm; F-Sa 5:30-10pm; Su 5:30-9:30pm.

Café Marimba ★★ $ Marina: 2317 Chestnut St. (Scott/Divisadero), 415/776-1506. A sizzling mix of inspired Mexican dishes and Chestnut Street nightlife, Café Marimba is one of the see-and-be-seen spots in the Marina. The house drinks, like habanero martinis or Brazilian *batidas* (an alcoholic *agua fresca*), are potent but smooth and keep the crowd lively. Chips come with two kinds of homemade salsas, such as *rojo* and *el copil*. Main courses vary from light side dishes, including squash blossom quesadillas, to one of several hearty chicken moles. The side dishes of drunken beans, rice, and plantains and grilled corn are tasty and inexpensive. • M 5:30-10pm; Tu-Th 11:30am-10pm; F-Sa 11:30am-11pm; Su 11:30am-10pm.

Caffè delle Stelle ★★ $$ Civic Center: 395 Hayes St. (Gough), 415/252-1110 A popular spot in the ultracool Hayes Valley neighborhood, Caffè delle Stelle serves rustic Italian cuisine at reasonable prices. The modest interior feels like an authentic Italian trattoria and the eclectic clientele ranges from stylish Euro types to doggedly determined foodies. Order one of the unusual pasta dishes with a glass of rough country wine. • M-Th 11:30am-2:30pm, 5-10pm; F-Sa 11:30am-2:30pm, 5-10:30pm; Su 5-10pm.

Caffè Museo ★★ $ SoMa: 151 3rd St. (Mission/Howard), 415/357-4500. A casual street-level café in the spectacular Museum of Modern Art. Good breakfast and lunch dishes are served at fair prices. Like the museum, this café is a cut above, with lots of style. Try the panini (the orange-roasted chicken with caramelized onions is good), wonderful salads, and excellent pastries. No table service; you stand in line, order, and the food is delivered to your table. Also like the museum, it can be crowded on weekends. • M-Tu, F-Su 10am-6pm; Th 10am-9pm.

Campton Place ★★★ $$$$ Union Square: 340 Stockton St. (Post/Sutter), 415/781-5555. A beautiful restaurant in a beautiful hotel. The dining room is sumptuous and peaceful, the crowd rich and well dressed, and the food almost as good as the prices are high. The kitchen is renowned for what many think is the best breakfast in town, including some of the most memorable corned beef hash this side of the Pierre in New York. Also try the excellent version of eggs Benedict. Superb service. Jacket and tie recommended for dinner. • M-Th 7-10:30am, 11:30am-2pm, 6-10pm; F 7-10:30am, 11:30am-2pm, 5:30-10:30pm; Sa 8-11am, noon-2pm, 5:30-10:30pm; Su 8am-2pm, 6-9:30pm.

Carta ★★★ $$ Civic Center: 1772 Market St. (Gough/Octavia), 415/863-3516. Although the description—inconvenient location, dicey parking, casual interior, a menu based on the cuisine of a different single country or region each month—doesn't encourage you to drop everything and head there, please go to Carta! These people really know how to cook, and you'll enjoy dishes you'll never get elsewhere. Culinary venues have included Greece, Provence, and India. Minimal decoration in the small storefront, but prices are fair and service is good. A unique restaurant. • Tu-F noon-3pm, 5:30-11pm; Sa 5:30-11pm; Su 10am-3pm, 5:30-11pm.

Casa Aguila ★★ $$ Sunset: 1240 Noriega St. (19th Ave./20th Ave.), 415/661-5593. This Sunset District hole-in-the-wall serves up some of the tastiest Mexican grub in San Francisco. The portions are enormous, justifying the high prices. Try the pork enchiladas, the chiles rellenos, the tamales, the extra-fruity sangria—and anything else on the extensive menu, for that matter, since it's all good. The service is efficient and friendly, although on weekends the line can be long. • Daily 11:30am-3:30pm, 5-10pm.

Cassis Bistro ★★★ $$ Marina: 2120 Greenwich St. (Fillmore/Webster), 415/292-0770. This small neighborhood eatery, with its creamy walls and lavender-accented decor, feels sunny even in the evening. The French staffers wear jeans, although the clientele tends to be dressier. The menu includes steak, pastas, rabbit, fish, and toothsome specials. All the details are wonderful: the pesto sauce and vinaigrette are delectable, while the side dishes of ratatouille and a toss of potatoes with garlic are memorable. Try the duck with cassis and the shivery orange sherbet served in an orange skin. No credit cards. • Tu-Th 5:30-10pm; F-Sa 5:30-10:30pm.

Cha Cha Cha ★★★ $ Haight: 1801 Haight St. (Shrader), 415/386-5758. You *will* have to wait for a table—two hours is not uncommon—at this swinging Caribbean restaurant in the Haight, but it's a small inconvenience considering the quirky, palate-tingling food that comes out of the kitchen. Most items are tapas sized, so order a selection and share. Shrimp in creamy Cajun coconut sauce is sublime, as are fried plantains, seafood specials, and just about everything else on the menu. The kooky, witch-doctorish decor adds to the experience. The scene can be trying but it's still one of the city's best meals. • Su-Th 11:30am-4pm, 5-11pm; F-Sa 11:30am-4pm, 5-11:30pm.

Chez Panisse ★★★★ $$$$ East Bay: 1517 Shattuck Ave. (Cedar/Vine), Berkeley, 510/548-5525. It's *not* located in San Francisco, but it *is* one of the cooking world's most important restaurants. There's nothing that we can say about this mecca of California cuisine that hasn't been said at least three times before. Go at least once in your life to experience food touched by the talented hands of Alice Waters and her apprentices. Her preparations are deceptively simple—a salad of mixed greens, corn and garlic soup, salmon with Zinfandel butter—and made with the best ingredients done perfectly. The prix fixe menu changes daily, but you don't get to choose anything other than the day you go. You also don't have to decide what tip to leave: a service charge is added to the bill. Fortunately, service is usually outstanding. Reservations are absolutely necessary–far in advance on weekends. The café upstairs serves an à la carte lunch and dinner menu at lower prices. • M-Sa seatings at 6-6:30pm and 8:30-9:30pm.

Cypress Club ★★★ $$$ Financial District: 500 Jackson St. (Montgomery), 415/296-8555 A visiting Bostonian described the interior of this supper club as "biological punk." Strange, anthropomorphic shapes dominate the interior; a copper door frame resembles a pair of balloon-shaped legs, and curvy purple velvet banquettes have a Jetsonesque appeal. The menu includes luxurious, well-prepared fare such as seared paillard of venison, grilled vegetable sandwiches, and fabulous braised sweetbreads. If you're not springing for dinner, have a drink at the bar and observe the scene. • Su-Th 5:30-9:45pm; F-Sa 5:30-10:45pm.

Dol Ho ★★ ¢ Chinatown: 808 Pacific Ave. (Stockton/Powell), 415/392-2828. A classic dim sum dive, right in the heart of Chinatown, Dol Ho provides a good alternative to the large, glamorous, and more expensive restaurants dominating San Francisco's dumpling lunch scene. Most everything is good, from the steamed pork buns to the shrimp in translucent wrappers to the shark fin dumplings. The restaurant is small and popular with neighborhood locals. No credit cards. • Daily 7am-5pm.

Eliza's ★★ $ Civic Center: 205 Oak St. (Gough/Octavia), 415/621-4819 M-F 11am-3pm, 5-8:45pm; Sa 5-8:45pm • Potrero Hill: 1457 18th St. (Connecticut/Missouri), 415/648-9999. An unlikely name for a Chinese restaurant, but it doesn't fool those in search of the city's most civilized spot for well-prepared Asian fare. Eliza's delivers a host of appealing dishes with fresh ingredients and strong spices. Celery salad is a tasty and unusual appetizer. Main dishes include all the usuals plus lesser-known but successful offerings like minced chicken with deep-fried basil. • M-F 11am-3pm, 5-9:45pm; Sa 11am-9:45pm; Su noon-9:45pm.

Ella's ★★ $$ Laurel Heights: 500 Presidio Ave. (California), 415/441-5669. Chef Danny Wilser presents a gourmet adventure in every plate. His menus change weekly. Fresh-squeezed blood-orange juice with ginger, bacon omelet with arugula and sun-dried tomato ricotta, and lemon-ginger oatmeal have been stops along the search for the ultimate brunch. Lunch might include a mouthwatering romaine salad with grilled squash, olives, and goat cheese; grilled salmon; or a juicy burger on a home-made bun. The crowded dining room with huge mirrors and lots of windows provides for a rowdy see-and-be-seen scene. Reservations only for groups of eight or more, so expect to see a line at key hours. • M-F 7am-9pm; Sa-Su 9am-2pm.

Enrico's Café ★★ $$ North Beach: 504 Broadway (Kearny), 415/982-6223. Inside there is a bar where regulars who began drinking at Enrico's in its first incarnation still imbibe. Diners sit at marble-topped tables and banquettes along art-filled walls and eat delicious California-Italian meals, listen to live music, or just graze on small dishes like garlic mashed potatoes or cockles and mussels. The outdoor patio—San Francisco's first sidewalk café, heated with lamps against chilly summer nights—is a prime people-watching place. • M-Th 11:30am-11:30pm; F-Sa 11:30am-12:30am; Su 11:30am-11pm.

Eos ★★★ $$$ Haight: 901 Cole St. (Carl), 415/566-3063. At this bustling outpost of fusion cuisine, head chef Arnold Wong cooks in an open kitchen that, along with the rest of the sharp, stripped-down dining area (exposed pipes, wooden beams, and black matte tables are among the touches), feels like an artist's work space. Start with the appetizers, small and expensive but essential: the shiitake mushroom dumplings and rock shrimp cakes are exceptional. The best of the entrées are the organic skirt steak (marinated in Chimay ale), the tea-smoked duck breast, and the pan-roasted local salmon. Side dishes such as wasabi mashed potatoes point to Wong's ingenious mix of European and Asian tastes. Many excellent wines are available to complement the meal, or to enjoy at the adjoining wine bar. The staff is good, although they have trouble seating reserved tables promptly. • M-Sa 5:30-11pm; Su 5-11pm.

Esperpento ★★ $ Mission: 3295 22nd St. (Mission/Valencia), 415/282-8867. A bois-terous crowd flocks to this quirky, brightly painted Spanish tapas restaurant, so expect a wait if you go on a weekend night. Try the grilled squid, marinated pork, mussels in a red-pepper vinaigrette, or potatoes served with hot chile sauce—the perfect antidote to a foggy San Francisco evening. No credit cards. • M-Th 11am-3pm, 5-10pm; F-Sa 11am-3pm, 5-10:30pm.

Farallon ★★★ $$$ Union Square: 450 Post St. (Powell/Mason), 415/956-6969. With an ambiance that recalls "Octopus's Garden" and *20,000 Leagues Under the Sea*, Farallon manages to be both excessive and elegant at the same time. The decor ranges from corny (waterfront paintings) to understated (a curvaceous opalescent white dining area) to outrageous (jellyfish chandeliers and a caviar staircase). Still, the main dining room, with vaulted ceilings and tiled Neptune-themed murals, is an original and surprisingly charming place to dine. Naturally, seafood is the culinary theme, but this is a far cry from Fisherman's Wharf. Chef Mark Franz's complex starters and main dishes highlight fresh seafood in its many forms, often in unusual combinations. House-made items include fresh caviar and smoked salmon and sturgeon. The soups and vegetable dishes are as good as the main courses. There's a lengthy international wine list, a martini menu, and appealing nonalcoholic cocktails. The servers are smooth and attentive, if a bit opinionated. The tasting plate of candies and cookies is a satisfying choice after a great meal. Patrons wear ties and dresses for lunch, and reservations are essential. • M-Th 11:30am-2pm, 5:30pm-10pm; F-Sa 11:30am-2pm, 5:30pm-10:30pm; Su 11:30am-2:30pm, 5:30pm-9:30pm.

Firefly ★★★ $$$ Noe Valley: 4288 24th St. (Douglas), 415/821-7652. Few restaurants manage to combine Firefly's professionalism, in both the cooking and the service, with a relaxed neighborhood climate that includes country curtains, wall moldings, and a real colonial hutch. The food is eclectic and excellent. Appetizers such as grilled polenta or Thai salmon cakes are small for the price but tasty. Main courses are triumphs of presentation: try the pepper-seared top sirloin steak or the gigantic bayou gumbo with spiced duck breast. The decadent desserts—sorbet, shortcake, a towering ice cream brownie sundae—top it all off. A truly exceptional meal can be had here. • Daily 5:30-10:30pm.

Fleur de Lys ★★★★ $$$$ Union Square: 777 Sutter St. (Taylor/Jones), 415/673-7779. You might expect to be let down by a restaurant that has been heralded as one of San Francisco's shining stars. Experiencing Fleur de Lys firsthand, however, is enough to convert any cynic. Situated in a surprisingly seedy block of Sutter Street, the elegant interior, dimly lit to a velvety, romantic darkness, is a welcome oasis of luxury in an ultraurban landscape. Contemporary French fare is the specialty: standout items include a silky New York State foie gras and a smooth chilled cucumber soup with vodka sorbet and caviar as appetizers; salmon served with wild mushrooms and a classic cut of filet mignon are sure-bet pleasers for main courses. Desserts are the crowning glory of a Fleur de Lys feast. On one evening, the chocolate crème brûlée with caramelized banana was so delicious that it soothed the sting of the considerable bill that arrived soon afterward. Book your reservations for Friday and Saturday weeks in advance. Tie optional but jacket required for gentlemen. • M-Th 6-9:30pm; F-Sa 5:30-10:30pm.

Flying Saucer ★★★ $$$ Mission: 1000 Guerrero St. (22nd St.), 415/641-9955. Some of the most celestial food in San Francisco is served here in a Jetsons junk-store atmosphere. Choose from luxurious foie gras, homemade smoked oysters, or any of the other fabulous starters, and move on to a superb blackened catfish, ultrasophisticated duck confit, or house-smoked pork loin. Culinary accents are Asian, and the platter-sized dinner plates—two can easily share—come decked out with a dizzying array of garnishes, all delightfully seasoned with mysterious flavors. Out-of-this-world desserts like three sorbets on a macadamia nut shell arrive on huge plates dusted with sparkling blue sugar. • Tu-Sa 5:30-9:30pm.

42 degrees ★★★ $$$ China Basin: 235 16th St. (at Illinois off 3rd St.), 415/777-5558. James Moffat has turned the former Caffè Esprit into a sleek dinner spot serving California comfort food along with jazz music until midnight. The softly lit downstairs seating area is lined by an open kitchen along one wall and a deco bar along another. Giant roll-up warehouse doors in front open onto a patio where lunch is served during warm weather. The upstairs balcony offers enormous curved banquettes for festive small groups. The menu changes weekly, but generously portioned dinners might include roasted lamb chops heaped on celery root mashed potatoes or grilled salmon with white beans and chanterelle mushrooms. Grazers can pick from tapas-sized chalkboard specials such as herb-roasted potatoes with aioli or a charcuterie plate. • M-Tu 11:30am-3pm; W-Th 11:30am-3pm, 6-10:30pm; F 11:30am-3pm, 6-11pm; Sa 6-11pm.

Fringale ★★★ $$ SoMa: 570 4th St. (Bryant/Brannan), 415/543-0573. This sophisticated, sleek bistro located in the netherworld between Market Street and the CalTrain station is oh-so-French. The waiters speak in exaggerated accents (you may ask yourself, "Is this guy for real?"), the menu features classic French fare such as bouillabaisse and cassoulet, and you begin to feel like an Ugly American. But the food is very good, simple, and reasonably priced, and the scene is fun to observe. • M-F 11:30am-3pm, 5:30-10:30pm; Sa 5:30-10:30pm.

Globe ★★★ $$$ Financial District: 290 Pacific Ave. (Front/Battery), 415/391-4132. The city's movers and shakers have been dining at Globe ever since the nouveau-American bistro, located on the fringes of Jackson Square, opened its doors in 1997. The airy, narrow room—done up in the now familiar industrial-elegant style—sets the stage for Chef Joseph Manzare's winning culinary creations. The menu rotates regularly, but the food is consistently delicious and served in generous portions. Recent highlights include a hearty fennel and eggplant soup, succulent grilled salmon, a pork chop in a sweet-and-spicy cherry pepper ragout, and the otherworldly double-cut T-bone for two, which comes with some of the finest, buttery potato gratin you'll ever taste. Terrific desserts are on offer. The staff is professional and unobtrusive. Not surprisingly, reservations well in advance are a must. • M-F 11:30am-1am; Sa 6pm-1am.

223

Golden Turtle ★★ $$ Russian Hill: 2211 Van Ness Ave. (Broadway/Vallejo), 415/441-4419. The city's most celebrated Vietnamese food is served in this attractive dining room that's decorated with tree branches and twinkling lights. Try the imperial rolls stuffed with minced pork and shrimp and the five-spice chicken. You pay for the upscale setting. • Tu-Su 5-11pm.

Gourmet Carousel ★★ $ Pacific Heights: 1559 Franklin St. (Pine), 415/771-2044. Gourmet Carousel looks like a clean and basic Chinese restaurant. The food, however, is anything but basic. The Singaporean curry noodles arrive teeming with a tasty assortment of carrots, onions, celery, and tender shrimp and tossed with just the right amount of spicy yellow curry. Also try the pot stickers or egg rolls, crisp on the outside and full of crunchy vegetables. If good food isn't enough to get you to stop in, maybe low prices and large portions will win you over. • Tu-Sa 11am-9:30pm; Su 4-9:30pm.

Greens ★★★ $$ Marina: Ft. Mason, Bldg. A (Buchanan at Marina), 415/771-6222. Greens has been catering to vegetarians for over ten years from an airy dining room with a panoramic view of the Golden Gate Bridge. While it's vegetarian, you would hardly guess from the surprisingly rich creations—cheese and crème fraîche are kitchen favorites. The menu changes periodically, but you might find delectable corn fritters, a southwestern corn tart, or pasta and pizza. Excellent wine list. Saturday nights there's an expensive prix fixe menu. The to-go counter serves soups, creative salads, and sandwiches. • M 5:30-9:30pm; Tu-F 11:30am-2pm, 5:30-9:30pm; Sa 11:30am-2:30pm, 5:30-9:30pm; Su 10am-2pm. To-go counter M-F 8am-9:30pm; Sa 8am-4:30pm; Su 9:30am-3:30pm.

Hawthorne Lane ★★★ $$$$ SoMa: 22 Hawthorne St. (Howard/Folsom), 415/777-9779. The location is highly unlikely for one of the city's most celebrated eateries: the ground floor of the Crown Point Press building on an alley hidden between Second, Third, Howard, and Folsom streets. The food expands upon the East-West California cuisine the chefs developed at Postrio, from foie gras to grilled beef to halibut with cellophane noodles. A large bar area with tables makes it easy to sample starters such as tempura vegetables and Postrio-like gourmet pizzas without reserving a table in the dining room weeks in advance. (The bar allows you to order from the dining room menu as well.) The stylish, formal dining room offers good views of the beautiful artworks printed by Crown Point over the years. The outsized wine list matches the surroundings. • Restaurant: M-F 11:30am-1:45pm, 5:30-10pm; Sa-Su 5:30-10pm Bar/Café: Daily 11:30am-11pm.

Hayes Street Grill ★★ $$$ Civic Center: 320 Hayes St. (Franklin/Gough), 415/863-5545. Hayes Street is one of the city's best seafood restaurants. Order Chinese-menu style from a series of lists: first, pick your cooking method (grilled, sautéed, fried); then, choose the fish from the day's fresh offerings; finally, pick a sauce: herbed butter, tomatillo salsa, hollandaise. The salads are quite good, and the French fries are famous. The spare brasserie setting is clubby—brass rails, wood, forest green appointments—with professional service to match. • M-Th 11:30am-2pm, 5-9:30pm; F 11:30am-2pm, 5:30-10:30pm; Sa 5:30-10:30pm; Su 5-8:30pm.

Helmand ★★ $$ North Beach: 430 Broadway (Montgomery/Kearny), 415/362-0641. Afghani food in North Beach? Strange but true. The Beats would surely have approved of the excellent exotic food served at this pleasant spot. Start with the *kaddo borawni* (baby pumpkin served with yogurt and garlic sauce), and move on to *chopan* (grilled lamb served on flat bread). A large selection of vegetarian specialties will please nonmeat eaters. • Su-Th 5:30-10pm; F-Sa 5:30-11pm.

Home Plate ★★ $ Marina: 2274 Lombard St. (Steiner/Pierce), 415/922-4663. Home Plate attracts hoards of beautiful, hungry neighbors for weekend brunch. Put your name on the list, sit in the sun on the sidewalk, and watch traffic plow along Lombard Street, then crowd into a table in a bright, bare little room. Your endurance will be rewarded when you dive into the eggs Benedict, pancakes heaped with fresh fruit, turkey bacon and avocado omelet, or a similar delight. • Daily 7am-4pm.

The House ★★★ **$$** North Beach: 1230 Grant Ave. (Columbus), 415/986-8612 • Sunset: 1269 9th Ave. (Irving/Lincoln), 415/682-3898. East-West fusion cuisine on the border of Chinatown and North Beach? How perfect. Chef Larry Tse's masterful garlicky creations include a vibrant vegetable tempura, a light Caesar salad with seared bay scallops, and stir-fried calamari with bean paste noodles. Tse also has a sure hand with fresh fish; if grilled sea bass with a garlic-ginger-soy dipping sauce is on the menu, don't miss it. The slate floor, blond wood tables, brushed celadon walls, and mod dangling light fixtures give The House a casual, modern feel, but the restaurant can be very loud on a busy night. The second location in the Sunset is similar. • N. Beach: M-Th 11:30am-3pm, 5:30-10pm; F 11:30am-3pm, 5:30-11pm; Sa 5:30-11pm. • Sunset: M 11:30am-3pm; Tu-Th 11:30am-3pm, 5:30-10pm; F 11:30am-3pm, 5:30-11pm; Sa 5-11pm; Su 5-10pm.

House of Nanking ★★ **$** Chinatown: 919 Kearny St. (Jackson/Columbus), 415/421-1429. This riotously popular restaurant on the edge of Chinatown always has an hour-long line snaking outside. This is the kind of cramped dive where the owner tries to order for you and the wait is longer than the rushed meal. The crowds flock here for the garlicky renditions of Chinese specialties made safe for American tastes. No credit cards. • M-F 11am-10pm; Sa noon-10pm; Su 4-10pm.

Hunan Restaurant ★★ **$** Telegraph Hill: 924 Sansome St. (Broadway/Vallejo), 415/956-7727. • Financial Dist.: 674 Sacramento St. (Kearny/Montgomery), 415/788-2234. • SoMa: 1016 Bryant St. (8th St./9th St.), 415/861-5808. This is the restaurant that introduced Hunan food to the Bay Area. They pack them in, but the incendiary food remains high quality, especially the Chinese chicken salad and the harvest pork. The cavernous dining rooms at the Sansome Street location are nothing special, and service is abrupt at best, but the place is worth a visit. Two other branches spread the fire to weekday workers. • Tel. Hill: daily 11am-9:30pm. • Financial Dist.: M-F 9:30am-5:30pm. • SoMa: M-F 11:30am-9pm.

Jackson Fillmore Trattoria ★★★ **$$** Pacific Heights: 2506 Fillmore St. (Jackson), 415/346-5288 An inviting neighborhood place, highly recommended by loyal patrons. The decor is nothing special, just a storefront with white walls, basic furniture, and a friendly local clientele. The menu is rustic Italian with California touches. Risotto and a delicious *bruschetta* are good choices, although seafood is the best-seller here—don't miss the salmon in sage butter. Most tables seat four, and reservations are taken only for groups of three or more—highly recommended—so single diners and couples will have to wait for the chance table (you might end up sharing) or a seat at the counter. • M 5:30-10pm; Tu-Th 5:30-10:30pm; F-Sa 5:30-11pm; Su 5-10pm.

Kabuto Sushi ★★★ **$$** Richmond: 5116 Geary Blvd. (15th Ave./16th Ave.), 415/752-5652. A diverse crowd agrees that Kabuto has some of the best sushi in town. While there's plenty of seating in the spare dining room, many diners prefer waiting for a seat at the sushi bar, where they will be welcomed and entertained by owner-chef Sachio Kojima. This generous, creative soul will whip up all the usual stuff, as well as delightful creative combinations (not always on the menu). The menu also includes the usual array of cooked Japanese standards. • Tu-Sa 5:30-11pm.

Kate's Kitchen ★★ **$** Lower Haight: 471 Haight St. (Webster/Fillmore), 415/626-3984. This bare-bones Lower Haight eatery serves up some of the biggest and best breakfasts in town to a hip crowd of well-pierced slackers. Weekend mornings the sidewalk fills with the hungry and hungover waiting for a table and a heaping plate of some down-home specialty. The red flannel hash, with giant chunks of corned beef, looks more like a New England dinner. The famous cornmeal pancakes are huge. Homey soups and sandwiches carry the menu into the lunch hour. The linoleum floor, closely packed tables, and coolly casual staff make a relaxed beginning to the day. The persistent crowds are making consistency a problem. No credit cards. • M 9am-2:45pm; Tu 8am-2:45pm; W-F 9am-2:45pm; Sa-Su 9am-3:45pm.

Khan Toke Thai House ★★★ $$ Richmond: 5937 Geary Blvd. (23rd Ave./24th Ave.), 415/668-6654. One spoonful of Khan Toke's stratospheric chicken coconut soup and you'll know you're eating at a great Thai restaurant. You have to take off your shoes before entering the teakwood dining rooms and sit, in traditional style, on the floor surrounded by exotic decorations on the walls and real roses on the tables. Ambience aside, the real highlights are the tasty dishes: try the superb *rama long grong* (beef with spinach topped with peanut sauce), the subtle *yom pla muk* (squid with salad, chili, lemongrass, and mint leaves), or the pad Thai. Not surprisingly, a one-hour wait on weekend evenings is common. • Daily 5-10:45pm.

La Folie ★★★★ $$$$ Russian Hill: 2316 Polk St. (Green/Union), 415/776-5577. Transported to an outer *arrondissement* of Paris, you stumble into a charming storefront of blond wood and amiable music. Just as you order your aperitif, an *amuse bouche* of house-smoked salmon wrapped around a cayenne puff pastry twig arrives to tease your palate. Should you order the lobster and mango salad? *Mais oui*, because the menu is prix fixe and the location is upper Polk Street, so you can experience French cuisine without a plane trip. Stellar chef Roland Passot creates escapist evenings with his leisurely dinners of rare flavor and beauty. Each of your five courses arrives looking like a *plein air* painting and tasting like a dream. The setting is just a touch informal for the creative perfectionism of the food and solicitous service, but your only true folly in coming here may be picking up the hefty tab. • M-Sa 5:30-10pm.

La Taqueria ★★ ¢ Mission: 2889 Mission St. (24th St./25th St.), 415/285-7117. Perhaps the area's most beloved taqueria, always packed with lively neighborhood patrons from families to workers to young hipsters. They've been filling their excellent tacos, burritos, and quesadillas with house-made meats, salsas, and vegetables since long before the chains popularized fresh Mex. Standard taqueria decor. The sunny front patio offers a good view of street life. No credit cards. • Daily 11am-9pm.

Laghi ★★★ $$$ Richmond: 1801 Clement St. (19th Ave.), 415/386-6266. This popular Clement Street Italian restaurant looks ordinary, but the food and service are first-rate. You won't find better rabbit anywhere, and specialty dishes such as risotto with black truffles truly shine. The delicious bread and pasta are homemade by the chef's wife. The Italian wine list is very good and reasonably priced. • Tu-Su 5-9:30pm.

Lichee Garden ★★★ $ Chinatown: 1416 Powell St. (Broadway/Vallejo), 415/397-2290. One critic described Lichee Garden as a "Chinatown family club," and after a Sunday dinner surrounded by a riotous birthday party or two, you'll see why: It seems as if the whole neighborhood is here gathered around those large, round tables, sharing platters of some of the city's best Cantonese cooking. Seafood is the highlight, with delicious crab in ginger and scallion sauce, spicy salted prawn, and steamed fresh fish. Chow mein (try it panfried) and vegetable dishes are equally good. Hunan and Sichuan items are less reliable. • Daily 7am-9:30pm.

LuLu ★★★ $$ SoMa: 816 Folsom St. (4th St./5th St.), 415/495-5775. This grand café has captured the fancy of San Francisco's discriminating epicureans with its intriguing Provençal menu. The large, open dining room, done up in muted shades of blue and gray, encourages people watching. The food deserves your full attention, though, especially side dishes like olive-oil mashed potatoes and grilled asparagus with shaved Parmesan and lemon. Main dishes are equally alluring, in particular anything off the grill. And don't overlook the mussels cooked on an iron griddle. • Daily 11:30am-11pm.

Manora's Thai Cuisine ★★ $ SoMa: 1600 Folsom St. (12th St.), 415/861-6224. Manora's serves a full range of Thai specialties, with excellent seafood dishes and rich curries. Try such interesting specials as fried soft-shell crabs with tamarind sauce. Manora's has a perpetual crowd of SoMa party types waiting at the bar for one of the closely packed tables. • M-F 11:30am-2:30pm, 5:30-10:30pm; Sa-Su 5:30-10:30pm.

Masa's ★★★★ $$$$ Union Square: 648 Bush St. (Powell/Stockton), 415/989-7154. Just about perfect, and very expensive. Many call Masa's San Francisco's best restaurant. The deep red walls are a bit somber, but the food and the wines are still sparkling. The five-and seven-course menus ($70 and $75, respectively) are full of dishes that shimmer with imagination and thrill with deep flavors. Opt for the seven smallish tasting courses, which offer such choices as a succulent foie gras and a beautiful squab in its own juices. The service is impeccable. Jacket required. • Tu-Sa 6-9:30pm.

McCormick & Kuleto's Seafood ★★ $$$ Fisherman's Wharf: Ghirardelli Square, 900 North Point St. (Polk/Larkin), 415/929-1730. This huge restaurant has magnificent Golden Gate vistas. Upstairs, bar patrons can order an array of café food—crusty sourdough, old-fashioned shrimp cocktails, a wide selection of oysters. Downstairs, the more formal white-clothed dining room offers full dinners of typical pasta and seafood dishes. Simple fish dishes tend to be the best. • M-Sa 11:30am-11pm; Su 10:30am-11pm.

Mecca ★★★ $$$ Castro: 2029 Market St. (Dolores/14th St.), 415/621-7000. The Castro's techno-chic crowd has found its latest place of worship, flocking faithfully to Mecca's steel and zinc industrial-deco bar to imbibe creative cocktails and revel in the scene. And a scene it is—concrete beams and velvet curtains, chocolate leather banquettes and exposed cooling ducts, and a swirl of guests costumed in Armani and armor. If you can tear your eyes away from the striking patrons, you will be delighted by the food. From the open kitchen, Mecca turns out a well-edited menu with a luscious array of fresh flavors and tastes, including exquisite thin-crust pizzas and innovative main courses which include some excellent vegetarian selections. Desserts and house-made sorbets are memorable and well worth the caloric splurge. A pilgrimage to Mecca never seemed so decadent. Mealtime reservations are a must, but a full menu is served on a walk-in basis at the bar. • Su-W 6pm-11pm; Th-Sa 6pm-midnight.

Metropol ★★ $$ Financial District: 168 Sutter St. (Kearny/Montgomery), 415/732-7777. Klaus and Albert Rainer, former owners of the Hyde Street Bistro, have opened this sleek café catering to the downtown crowd. Lunch is quick and affordably gourmet: You order at the counter and are then politely escorted to a table, where your food will be served. Light choices include soups, salads, sandwiches, pastas, and calzones; finish your meal with an espresso and one of Klaus's famous Austrian desserts. Dinner is more formal and features substantial entrées such as roast pork loin with goat-cheese mashed potatoes and tomato-mushroom ragout, as well as lighter soup-salad-sandwich offerings (perfect for pre-theater dining). • M-F 7am-9pm; Sa noon-5pm.

Michelangelo Café ★★ $$ North Beach: 579 Columbus Ave. (Union/Green), 415/986-4058. Michelangelo offers customers authentic Italian-American style and a menu full of delicious renditions of such reliable favorites as prosciutto-wrapped melon, fettuccine with pesto, and shrimp scampi. Michelangelo also treats customers like family. (Much of the art on the cluttered walls looks to have been painted by family members.) Wine is served in ceramic pitchers, Botticelli-inspired faces glow from the tabletops, sauces leave you wanting more to taste (no matter how full you are), and biscotti and orange slices come with your coffee. Waiting lines are all too common. No credit cards. • M-Sa 5-11pm; Su 3-10pm.

Millennium ★★ $$ Civic Center: 246 McAllister St. (Hyde/Larkin), 415/487-9800. Specializing primarily in vegan cooking, which avoids all animal products, Millennium presents a menu filled with salads, vegetables, and numerous faux concoctions. Choose dishes such as grilled portobello mushrooms with sweet Moroccan dressing, a "steak" of soy or seitan in a mushroom and Marsala sauce, or an unambiguous macro (as in biotic) plate that includes a mushroom, bean, and onion stew with grains, tofu, broccoli, and house pickle. A list of organic wines completes the healthful menu. The bright, upscale dining room in the old Abigail Hotel features black-and-white floor tiles, sponged cream walls, and large floral arrangements. • Daily 5-9:30pm.

Mo's ★★ **$** North Beach: 1322 Grant Ave. (Vallejo/Green), 415/788-3779. Knowledgeable San Franciscans come to this modest eatery for one of the city's best burgers. Mo's grills seven-ounce slabs of prime chuck to perfection over an open flame for that backyard barbecue flavor. Other, equally delicious menu items have an international flavor: grilled chicken breast with Thai curry paste, Mediterranean lamb burger, grilled eggplant with pesto and Parmesan on focaccia. A thick shake goes perfectly with the spicy fries. Bare-bones diner decor. • M-Th 11am-10:30pm; F 11am-11:30pm; Sa 9am-11:30pm; Su 9am-10:30pm.

North India Restaurant ★★ **$$** Marina: 3131 Webster St. (Lombard), 415/931-1556. Popular consensus has it that North India serves the best tandooris around: mouth-watering, with the freshest ingredients, and imaginatively presented. It's best to stick to those regional specialties, since the curries tend to be thin. In addition, the portions are somewhat smaller than at other Indian restaurants. Still, there are a few deals, like the $12.95 prix fixe, which includes soup, *nan*, condiments, basmati rice, and an entrée. Most anyone will like the genteel atmosphere and hushed conversations, fine service, and the sight of cooks working at the tandoor oven. • M-F 11:30am-2:30pm, 5-10:30pm; Sa-Su 5-10:30pm.

One Market Restaurant ★★★ **$$$** SoMa: 1 Market St. (Steuart), 415/777-5577. Bradley Ogden and George Morrone's large venture in One Market Plaza overlooks the Embarcadero and, unlike Ogden's famed Lark Creek Inn, it has a somewhat corporate feel. The food is still great, though. The menu changes daily and might include grilled Norwegian salmon with artichoke ragout, grilled barbecued pork loin, or oak-grilled chicken breast with crispy wild mushrooms. • M-Th 11:30am-2pm, 5:30-9:30pm; F 11:30am-2pm, 5:30-10pm; Sa 5-10pm.

Palio d'Asti ★★★ **$$$** Financial Dist.: 640 Sacramento St. (Montgomery/Kearny), 415/395-9800. Named for the annual bareback horse races of Asti, Italy, which are celebrated in the restaurant's colorful hanging banners. The formal concrete-and-glass dining space includes stone columns and multileveled ceilings. Owner Gianni Fassio presents a changing lunch menu of hearty regional Italian specialties. For a real treat try the ravioli filled with Fontina cheese or braised rabbit; for lighter fare, order sautéed spinach, sun-dried tomatoes, and mozzarella on focaccia. Service is always excellent, making it a favorite with the business lunch crowd. • M-F 11:30am-2:30pm, 5:30-9pm.

Pane e Vino ★★★ **$$** Marina: 3011 Steiner St. (Union), 415/346-2111. This perfect neighborhood trattoria serves simple, classic Italian dishes like *vitello tonnato*, gnocchi, antipasto, and a great *tiramisù*. The interior is rustic and inviting. Service is friendly and professional. Reservations are essential, although you may still have to wait before being seated. • M-Th 11:30am-2:30pm, 5-10pm; F-Sa 11:30am-10:30pm; Su 5-10pm.

PlumpJack Café ★★★ **$$$** Marina: 3127 Fillmore St. (Filbert/Greenwich), 415/563-4755. San Francisco scions Bill Getty and Gavin Newsom named PlumpJack after their namesake wine shop (which is named for Gordon Getty's opera based on Shakespeare's greatest gourmand, PlumpJack Falstaff). Chef of the moment Maria Helm exhibits a deft hand with the California-Mediterranean dishes, especially her specialty risottos and stews. The extremely helpful staff will bring you generous tastes of any wine before you order off the retail-priced wine list and will guide you through the menu with skill. The pewter and gold leather banquettes offer a muted backdrop for the manicured socialites and gentlemen bankers who frequent this neighborhood haunt. • M-F 11:30am-2pm, 5:30-10pm; Sa 5:30-10pm.

Postrio ★★★★ **$$$$** Union Sq.: Prescott Hotel, 545 Post St. (Taylor/Mason), 415/776-7825. Strictly a splurge experience, Postrio has been a hit since the moment it opened. An upscale business crowd flocks here to sample celebrity chef Wolfgang Puck's cuisine. If you're a nobody (and odds are you fit this description) you may be relegated to a corner table and treated like a nuisance. But if you're a dedicated restaurant goer with a strong ego, this is a must-stop on your itinerary. The haute California cuisine with an Asian twist is superb (it should be, considering the prices); grab a table in the bar and try the gourmet pizza Puck is known for. Jacket and tie preferred for gentlemen at dinner. • M-W 7-10am, 11:30am-2pm, 5:30-10pm; Th-F 7-10am, 11:30am-2pm, 5:30-10:30pm; Sa 11am-2pm, 5:30-10:30pm; Su 9am-2pm, 5:30-10pm.

The Ramp ★ $ China Basin: 855 China Basin Blvd. (Mariposa off 3rd), 415/621-2378. The most popular of the several waterfront bars in the abandoned warehouse section of SoMa, The Ramp is San Francisco's premier postfraternal party spot. On weeknights, this vast, outdoor concrete slab of a bar is regularly booked for informal, semiprivate, very drunken dance parties. On weekend mornings it's the perfect post-blowout brunch place, serving generous portions of fried hangover food. Bring sunglasses, and be prepared to wait for a table. Weekday alfresco lunches are a less crowded, relaxing escape. • M-F 8am-3:30pm; Sa-Su 8am-4pm.

Rasselas ★★ $$ Pacific Heights: 2801 California St. (Divisadero), 415/567-5010. This spacious salon is better known for its live jazz and blues bands than for its exotic Ethiopian cuisine, but it's the best in San Francisco. The food is surprisingly light and healthy, once you get used to the mushy texture of such delicious specialties as *doro wat*—a spicy chicken stewlike dish, or the tasty *yatakelt kilikil*—vegetables sautéed in garlic and ginger. Meals are served with a salad and *injera*, a spongy bread used in place of silverware to scoop up the tasty concoctions. Since live music plays nightly, it's best to dine early. • Su-Th 5-10pm; F-Sa 5-11pm.

Rose Pistola ★★★ $$$ North Beach: 532 Columbus Ave. (Union/Green), 415/399-0499. Reed Hearon's sizzling venture has generated quite a buzz. Long waits are standard, and diners are advised to reserve a table a week in advance. Located in the heart of North Beach, the restaurant sports a bustling open kitchen, sleek lighting, and lots of dark, polished wood. Based on the cuisine of Liguria, Hearon's menu features warm, fresh focaccia, a salad of octopus, potato, and green beans, and outstanding meat entrées, including a roast suckling pig with polenta croutons. You can order seafood cooked in a variety of intriguing styles. • Su-Th 11:30am-midnight; F-Sa 11:30am-1am.

Rubicon ★★★ $$$$ Financial District: 558 Sacramento St. (Sansome/Montgomery), 415/434-4100 It's the food—the superb roast chicken, the excellent lamb shank, the wonderful herbs and intense flavors—that matters at this upscale, celebrity restaurant just off Montgomery Street, not the overtouted celeb investors—Francis Ford Coppola, Robin Williams, and Robert DeNiro—who rarely show up anyway. The narrow, two-story industrial brick space feels warmer downstairs; upstairs has a slightly Siberian air to it. Service is generally good. The wine list is extraordinary but high priced. • M-Th 11:30am-2:30pm, 5:30-10pm; F 11:30-2:30, 5:30-11pm; Sa 5:30-11pm.

Rumpus ★★★ $$ Union Square: 1 Tillman Pl. (off Grant btwn. Sutter/Post), 415/421-2300. An exciting American bistro only a block off Union Square. It's open late and the food is excellent and relatively inexpensive, especially at lunch. Try the succulent roast chicken, the lusty lamb shank, or the juicy veal chop; interesting appetizers include a piquant onion tart and tasty dolmas. Don't miss ordering some of the fine but less well-known wines featured here. • M-Th 11:30am-2:30pm, 5:30-10pm; F-Sa 11:30am-2:30pm, 5:30-11pm; Su 5:30-10pm.

Sanppo ★★ $ Japantown: 1702 Post St. (Buchanan), 415/346-3486. A Japantown standby, serving a complete range of Japanese specialties without sacrificing quality on any. Sushi and sashimi rely on clean, fresh fish and well-seasoned rice, while customers rave about the light and crunchy tempura. Generous portions and moderate prices—a bit higher for sushi—keep Sanppo among the more reasonable Japantown establishments. The dining room is split into two small sections by the partially open kitchen. When it's busy, small groups may have to share one of the large tables. Service can be somewhat disorganized. • Su-Th 11:30am-10pm; F-Sa 11:30-11pm.

Sanraku ★★ $$ Union Square: 704 Sutter St. (Taylor), 415/771-0803. The mirrored wall at this sleek downtown restaurant may fool you into thinking the interior is bigger than it is, but the persistent line of patrons waiting for a seat at one of the ten tables or the small sushi bar should set you straight. The delightfully fresh sushi, available in a variety of creative combinations, is no illusion, however. Other choices include teriyaki, tempura, and *donburi* (bowls of rice with meat served on top). Dinner prices can add up quickly, but lunch specials are reasonable. • M-F 11am-10pm; Sa-Su 4-10pm.

Scala's Bistro ★★★ $$ Union Square: 432 Powell St. (Sutter/Post), 415/395-8555. This stylish dining room in the Sir Francis Drake hotel was meant to look like it's been around for years: chiaroscuro murals, burnished dark wood booths deep enough to hide in, and a bustle of white-shirted waiters. The innovative Californian-Italian menu is deliberately more contemporary, with modern combinations like a seared ahi tuna salad, grilled mahi-mahi with preserved lemon and olive relish, and a variety of rustic pizzas. Most everything tastes delicious, and the portions verge on gargantuan. The location, mere steps away from Union Square's shopping delights, attracts a mature, monied crowd of ladies who lunch, even well into the dinner hour. • M-F 7am-midnight; Sa-Su 8am-midnight.

Sears Fine Food ★★ $ Union Square: 439 Powell St. (Sutter/Post), 415/986-1160. This San Francisco institution is world famous for its 18 little Swedish pancakes, and they really are good. You'll also find diner breakfast fare done the old-fashioned way: omelets (from ham and cheese to jelly), crisp, light and fluffy hash browns, huge slabs of ham. Ordering the pecan waffles with real maple syrup almost guarantees that the other folks at your table will be asking for samples. The decor is 1940s luncheonette. The professional waitresses in 1960s pink uniforms have been known to call patrons "Hon." Long lines are common, especially during summer, so check on the counter seats if you're starving: it's often possible to bypass the tourists and walk right in. Cash only. • Daily 6:30am-2:30pm.

The Slanted Door ★★★ $$ Mission: 584 Valencia St. (16th St./17th St.), 415/861-8032. One of the hottest eateries in the Mission, The Slanted Door, a high-ceilinged bilevel room decked out in light green walls, wooden floors, and quirky wall art, brilliantly melds Vietnamese and French styles. The food looks and tastes terrific. Sumptuous appetizers include the perfect Vietnamese crêpes or fresh spring rolls in peanut sauce. Entrée highlights range from incredibly sweet chicken simmered in caramel sauce and ginger to shrimp with glass noodles to pork stir-fried with jicama strips. Servings are fairly large and prices are surprisingly moderate. Service is pleasant and attentive. The only downside is that the wait to be seated can seem eternal (even with a reservation). • Tu-Su 11:30am-3:30pm, 5:30-10pm.

South Park Café ★★★ $$ SoMa: 108 South Park Ave. (2nd St./3rd St.), 415/495-7275. A classic French café. Pale yellow walls, morning sunlight, and European newspapers make this an attractive brunch spot. Or go during cocktail hour and sample the excellent tapas, which include golden fried potatoes with aioli and anchovy toasts. For dinner, try the fabulous mussels or the duck. • M-F 7:30am-10pm; Sa 6-10pm.

Stars ★★★ $$$$ Civic Center: 555 Golden Gate Ave. (Van Ness/Polk), 415/861-7827. San Francisco's much-loved grand café is as sizzling as ever. The glamorous dining room, redecorated with in a more austere Asian-influenced style, has star-shaped paper-lantern light fixtures and more modern appointments. Stars attracts a glittering crowd of sophisticates and a smattering of tourists, as well as folks celebrating a special occasion. Chef Ralf Marhencke has helped to put a new spin on the food: there's a spring onion and sweet corn chowder in season; tempura-style soft shell crab; and even Swiss raclette over potatoes. Entrées can include poached sea bass; breast of capon with a garlic-herb jus or an aged Angus steak with black pepper-Madeira sauce. The prix fixe lunches are a bargain for Stars: soup, salad, and beverage for $10.50; soup or salad, entrée, cookie, and beverage for $12.95. Don't miss the

"Dare to be Different Wine Bar" where you can taste flites of wine, with or without dinner. • M-F 11:30am-2pm, 5:30-10pm; Sa-Su 5:30-10pm.

Straits Café ★★★ $$ Richmond: 3300 Geary Blvd. (Parker), 415/668-1783. It looks like a hip European bistro, with wood shutters, airy lighting and smooth jazz playing over the sound system, but this café is known for its Singaporean menu, a blend of Indian, Malay, and Chinese dishes. The servings are on the small side given the price, so be sure to order appetizers. Start with *poh pia* (spring rolls), *kway pati* (stuffed pastry shells), or lamb soup; all are delicious. For the main course, the highlights include *ayam rendang*, a crisp chicken simmered in a dry curry sauce, and the mouth-watering *ikam panggang*, a grilled boneless trout wrapped in banana leaf that is generally acknowledged to be one of the best seafood dishes in the city. Service is cheerful and attentive. • Su-Th 11:30am-10pm; F-Sa 11:30am-11pm.

Suppenküche ★★ $$ Civic Center: 601 Hayes St. (Laguna), 415/252-9289. Suppenküche brings new respect to German cooking. Opened by a wandering German design student, this spare beer hall serves a range of unusual German brews on tap and by the bottle. Seating is family style around long pine tables, so expect to make a few friends through the course of the meal. For starters, there is always a vegetarian soup, and the house salad is a large portion of slaw and cut vegetables. The mains are authentic renditions of traditional dishes such as *sauerbraten* and *jager schnitzel*. They come with delicious accompaniments like spaetzle or panfried potatoes. The strudel will keep you coming back (reserve a serving in advance). • M-F 5-10pm; Sa-Su 10am-2:30pm, 5-10pm.

Tadich Grill ★★ $$$ Financial District: 240 California St. (Battery/Front), 415/391-1849. This California landmark has been a part of San Francisco dining for nearly a century and a half, and things are still done the old-fashioned way here. Brass, wood, and uniformed waiters help maintain the 1850s atmosphere; excellent old-style service and food complete the illusion. Choose a seat in the main dining room, at the long wooden counter, or in a private, curtained alcove reminiscent of cigar-filled back rooms. Fresh seafood has been the main draw all these years, and the food is still wonderful if a bit retro. Enjoy such timeless classics as oyster stew, broiled halibut steak, or the memorable calamari steak with garlic butter sauce. • M-F 11am-9:30pm; Sa 11:30am-9:30pm.

Taqueria San Jose ★★ ¢ Mission: 2830 Mission St. (24th St./25th St.), 415/282-0203. • Mission: 2839 Mission St. (24th St./25th St.), 415/282-0283. • North Beach: 2257 Mason St. (Francisco), 415/749-0826. The long list of well-prepared taco and burrito fillings includes the standard beef and chicken, plus authentic specialties such as *al pastor* (barbecued pork), chorizo sausage, and tongue. Each table has bowls of fresh, hand-cut tomato salsa loaded with bright green chili peppers and fiery tomatillo salsa. Wash it all down with excellent *aguas frescas* like *tamarindo* and *horchata*. The decor is typical taqueria: Formica tables, wall murals, and a loud jukebox. Cash only. • 2830 Mission: daily 8am-1am. • 2839 Mission: daily 8am-11pm. • North Beach: daily 10am-9pm.

Thep Phanom ★★★ $ Lower Haight: 400 Waller St. (Fillmore), 415/431-2526. Possessing one of the most pleasant and inviting interiors of any Thai restaurant in the Bay Area, Thep Phanom has a standout menu as well. A long list of tasty salad dishes provides more ways to get your vegetables than many Thai eateries, and the nightly specials board lists fresh, interesting offerings. One regular favorite is The Weeping Lady, a delectable combination of minced chicken, garlic, chilies, and fresh basil served over broiled Japanese eggplant. • Daily 5:30-10:30pm.

Ti Couz ★★ $ Mission: 3108 16th St. (Valencia/Guerrero), 415/252-7373. A charming Breton-style crêperie, Ti Couz serves an array of classic and delicious crêpes. With its white stucco walls crisscrossed with dark wood beams, French-country tables and chairs, and photographs of peasants from Brittany, Ti Couz is an enchanting spot to indulge your Gallic fantasies. Savory crêpe fillings range from ratatouille to Gruyère to salmon. The onion soup is excellent, as are the salads. Missing a dessert crêpe

here—Nutella, white chocolate, poached pears, fresh whipped cream—is a crime. •
M-F 11am-11pm; Sa 10am-11pm; Su 10am-10pm.

Tommaso's ★★ $$ North Beach: 1042 Kearny St. (Pacific/Broadway), 415/398-9696.
Don't be deterred by the sleazy strip joints as you hunt down this pizza joint, located
in the midst of San Francisco's finest collection of smut houses. Behind a heavy
wooden door and down a flight of stairs you'll find a dark, shadowy interior with
Italian wall murals. Traditional thin-crusted Italian pizzas have been cooked in the
wood-burning oven here for over 60 years. The fewer toppings the better, in order to
taste the wonderful tomato sauce. Be sure to try one of the cold vegetable salads
(asparagus, if it's in season). If you feel like dining with the locals, this is the place to
be. • Tu-Sa 5-10:45pm; Su 4-9:45pm.

Ton Kiang ★★ $ Richmond: 5821 Geary Blvd. (22nd Ave./23rd Ave.), 415/387-8273.
• Richmond: 3148 Geary Blvd. (Spruce), 415/752-4440. This pair of eateries special-
izes in Hakka cuisine (famous for wine sauces and claypot dishes) but the menu
includes dishes from all over China. Execution is consistently good. Choose from an
abundant list of seafood dishes: crab in black bean sauce, pepper-and-salt prawns,
and spicy Sichuan squid. Braised tofu specialties feature airy chunks of tofu, superior
fillings, and hearty sauces. Good vegetable dishes, too. Prices are a bit higher than
your average dive. The Spruce branch has the bright-red-and-gold-dragon-phoenix
Chinese restaurant look; the 22nd Avenue branch is more restrained, with carpeting
and pastel colors. The latter branch serves famous dim sum daily. • 22nd Ave.: M-Th
10:30am-10pm; F 10:30am-10:30pm; Sa 10am-10:30pm; Su 9am-10pm. • Spruce: M-
Th 11am-10pm; F-Su 11am-10:30pm.

2223 Market (No Name) ★★ $$$ Castro: 2223 Market St. (Sanchez/Noe), 415/431-
0692. This chicly unnamed place has been packing in a hip, prosperous Castro clien-
tele drawn to refined American cuisine: Even with a reservation, be prepared to wait
awhile (the kitchen can be slow). The appetizers are small and very expensive, but
the grilled prawns in pancetta, at least, are worth it at twice the price. Main courses
are better sized and include grilled ahi tuna, succulent Sonoma lamb, and juicy roasted chicken with outstanding onion rings. The wait staff, if you don't mind a firm
touch of Attitude, is tip-top. The sparse dining room, with dark wooden floors, ivory
walls, and warm utilitarian lighting, affects a Quaker-like humbleness, but the
cacophonous space makes conversation a trial. • M-Th 6-10pm; F 6pm-midnight; Sa
10am-2pm, 6pm-midnight; Su 10am-2pm, 6-10pm.

Universal Café ★★★ $$ Mission: 2814 19th St. (Bryant/Florida), 415/821-4608. This
sleek, stylish café started as a coffee roastery, but the zoning laws made it easier to
become a full-service restaurant. Open all day, the Universal switches from a café in
the day to a full-scale restaurant at night. The fresh-made soups and grilled sandwich-
es make a filling lunch; for dinner try one of the flatbread appetizers (either with
caramelized onions or *brandade* and tomatoes) and any of the grilled main courses. •
Tu-Sa 8am-10pm; Su 5:30-9:30pm.

Val 21 ★★ $$ Mission: 995 Valencia St. (21st St.), 415/821-6622. Although the menu
changes at this popular spot about every six weeks, you can always count on eggless
Caesar salad with seeded croutons and blackened chicken breast with plantains, black
beans, brown rice, and *salsa fresca*. Otherwise, the sky's the limit. Healthful ingredients
dominate at Val 21 (they usually offer a vegan main), and red meat is strictly *verboten*,
but the kitchen combines Asian, Latino, and good ol' American ingredients with glee-
ful abandon, and the cooks are not afraid of cream and butter. On weekends, the
design-studio hip dining room is filled with satisfied brunchers. • M-Th 5:30-9:30pm; F
5:30-10:30pm; Sa 10am-2pm, 5:30-10:30pm; Su 10am-2pm, 5:30-9:30pm.

Vertigo ★★★ $$$$ Financial District: 600 Montgomery St. (Clay), 415/433-7250.
Vertigo is located on the ground floor of the Transamerica Tower, and the dining
room makes the most of the dramatic location: diners may swoon like Jimmy Stewart
in Hitchcock's namesake classic when they gaze up at the pyramid through the sky-

lights. The crowd's energy bounces through the loud, multilevel space, creating a general feeling of joie de vivre. The cutting-edge California cuisine menu mingles French, Asian, and Italian influences in elaborately presented creations. Highlights include tuna carpaccio niçoise, grilled beef fillet in a red wine sauce, and braised sea bass. • M-F 11:30am-2:30pm, 5:30-10pm; Sa 5:30-10pm.

Vivande Porta Via ★★★ $$/**Vivande** ★★ $$$ Pacific Heights: 2125 Fillmore St. (Sacramento/California), 415/346-4430. • Civic Center: 670 Golden Gate Ave. (Van Ness/Franklin), 415/673-9245. Porta Via on Fillmore is actually a combination gourmet food store and Italian restaurant. A brick wall covered with beautiful, hand-painted Italian tiles lines one side of the cramped dining area, a deli counter the other. The food is imaginative and authoritatively Italian. Owner Carlo Middione is a noted writer on Italian cuisine, and his menus include wonderful pastas and risottos, excellent lamb chops, and a superb version of the classic Tuscan side dish of white beans with olive oil. You can purchase many of his ingredients—and even finished creations—to enjoy at home or on a picnic. The newer Vivande's space is so big that it lacks a certain heart and soul in spite of the inventive trattoria decor. Service can also be uneven. • Porta Via: daily 11:30am-10pm. • Daily 11:30am-2pm, 5-10pm.

Woodward's Garden ★★★ $$$ Mission: 1700 Mission St. (Duboce), 415/621-7122. Incongruous locale notwithstanding (it's located almost beneath the freeway), this unpretentious little restaurant serves up the most phenomenal California cuisine this side of Chez Panisse. Although the menu is limited and often changes, you'll be sure to find mouth-watering appetizers like grilled nectarines with Gorgonzola; enormous main dishes like pork chops with garlic mashed potatoes, apple slices and greens; and out-of-this-world desserts like blueberry and lemon crème brûlée. Add to this great wines, good service, and an unhurried atmosphere, and you'll easily forget what's outside the door. • W-Su dinner seatings at 6-6:30pm, 8-8:30pm.

Yank Sing ★★ $$ (Take-Out $) Financial District: 427 Battery St. (Clay/Washington), 415/781-1111. • SoMa: 49 Stevenson St. (1st St./2nd St.), 415/541-4949. One of San Francisco's most famous dim sum houses, Yank Sing has two locations giving easy lunch access to downtown workers. Sit in the restaurant's giant, white-tablecloth-formal dining room and choose elegantly presented, authentic specialties from roving carts. The upscale setting is perfect for lunch meetings or a romantic midday rendezvous. Efficient take-out operations offer fast food at low prices. Go early for the best selection. • Fin Dist.: M-F 11am-3pm; Sa-Su 10am-4pm. • SoMa: M-F 11am-3pm; Su 11am-2:30pm.

Yoyo Bistro ★★★ $$/$$$ Japantown: 1611 Post St. (Laguna), 415/922-7788. This superb restaurant, located in the Hotel Miyako, is a seductive mix of French and Japanese sensibilities. There are three different ways to eat in Yoyo's graceful, multi-leveled dining room: the main menu; the bistro menu, a simpler, scaled-down version of the main menu; and small plates, or *tsunami*. The *tsunami* plates are the star here. Outstanding choices are ginger pickled salmon with wasabi crème fraîche, ahi tuna tartare with pickled plum vinaigrette, and briny Kumamoto oysters topped with wasabi *mignonette*. The main menu presents intriguing interpretations of classic French bistro fare: bouillabaisse, roasted chicken, and duck breast cured with tangerine and star anise all satisfy. • Daily 6:30am-2:30pm, 5:30-10pm.

Yuet Lee ★★ $ Chinatown: 1300 Stockton St. (Broadway), 415/982-6020. • Mission: 3601 26th St. (Valencia/Guerrero), 415/550-8998. This place has all the hallmarks of a dive—bright lights, Formica tables, and brusque service—but the Cantonese seafood is arguably unmatched for freshness and flavor. Try the clams in black bean sauce—the city's best—the pepper-and-salt roast prawns, and any other seafood items on the menu. Also good are the vegetable dishes, Peking spareribs, and claypots. Alas, the soup, noodle, and other dishes are disappointing. Cash only in Chinatown. • Chinatown: W-M 11am-3am. • Mission: M, W-Th 11am-3pm; 5-9:30pm; F-Su 11am-3pm, 5-10:30pm.

Zarzuela ★★ $$ Russian Hill: 2000 Hyde St. (Union), 415/346-0800. The name derives from a Spanish musical variety show and is also the name of a Catalonian seafood stew. All the favorite hot and cold Spanish tapas dishes—salty ham, savory squid, *tortilla española*, chorizo—and main dishes such as paella and, naturally, zarzuela are served along with sangria and sherry in this bright, crowded restaurant right off the Hyde Street cable car line. There may be a slight wait during rush hours (they don't take reservations). • Tu-Th 5:30-10:30pm; F-Sa 5:30-11pm.

Zuni Café and Grill ★★★ $$$ Civic Center: 1658 Market St. (Gough/Franklin), 415/552-2522. A die-hard temple of Mediterranean cuisine frequented by the artsy set, with a few advertising and business types mixed in. It looks very New Mexico, with an adobe fireplace, a long copper bar, and lots of serapes thrown about. The best selection of oysters around. Interesting preparations include house-cured anchovies with Parmesan and celery, or a divine whole roast chicken for two served with Tuscan bread salad. Slow service with a bad attitude unless you're a regular. • Tu-Sa 11:30am-midnight; Su 11am-11pm.

PERFORMING ARTS

Great sources for finding out what's happening each night are Sunday's *San Francisco Examiner and Chronicle* "pink pages," the *Bay Guardian*, and the *SF Weekly*.

Classical Music and Opera

Grace Cathedral Concerts: 1100 California St. (Taylor), SF, 415/749-6350. Choral music, organ concerts, chamber, and other music is presented in the glorious surroundings of the cathedral. Some candlelit performances.

San Francisco Opera: 301 Van Ness Ave. (Grove), SF, 415/864-3330. One of the best opera companies in the world, and one of the oldest in the country. The ticket prices reflect this status: single seats run from about $20 to well over $100. Performances usually take place in the grand War Memorial Opera House, where the sound is good even in the least expensive seats far in the back and on the sides. Supertitles projected above the stage make it easy to follow the plots of foreign-language operas, and opera glasses are available for rent.

San Francisco Performances: 415/392-4400. Call this number for information on a variety of classical and modern concerts and dance performances at several venues.

San Francisco Symphony: Davies Symphony Hall, 201 Van Ness Ave. (Hayes/Grove), SF, 415/864-6000, 800/696-9689 from 408 area code. The excellent San Francisco Symphony performs a full and varied schedule and attracts several world-class soloists and guest conductors each season. Tickets cost around $26-$78, but you can also get nonreserved bench seats for $11-$13 behind the orchestra (facing the conductor) if the performance doesn't feature a chorus; discount tickets go on sale two hours prior to performance, and you can only buy two at a time. Student discounts of 50% are available on selected days. Acoustics are generally better in the center seats of elegant Davies Symphony Hall, which also plays host to some of the greatest orchestras in the world, including the Leipziger Gewandhaus Orchestra and the Boston Symphony. Tickets to guest orchestras usually cost more than San Francisco Symphony performances. Bay Area residents can also take advantage of the free summer performances given by the Symphony in Stern Grove.

Dance

San Francisco Ballet: 455 Franklin St. (Grove/Fulton), SF, 415/865-2000 for box office, 415/861-5600 for information. The War Memorial Opera House is home to the San Francisco Ballet, a major company and the oldest in the country. Uncritical audiences lap up the traditional favorites and romantic new pieces choreographed by Danish director Helgi Tommassen, but critics drool over the contemporary pieces by a variety of guest choreographers. The American Ballet Theater and other world-class touring ballet companies, such as the Kirov and Joffrey, also make frequent appearances at the Opera House. Tickets range from $10 in the balcony to $100 for box seats. Students and seniors can buy discounted tickets (if available) by calling the box office the morning of the performance. (Seniors can also buy discounted series tickets.) The ballet gives a free performance in Stern Grove during the summer.

Smuin Ballet: 415/978-ARTS (2787) for tickets, 415/664-8885 for information. Former director of the San Francisco Ballet, Michael Smuin, choreographs for this company, which performs at Yerba Buena Center for the Arts.

Theater

TIX Bay Area: Union Square, Stockton St. between Post and Geary sts., SF, 415/433-7827. This small kiosk is a full-service box office serving most of the city's theaters and performances. It also offers day-of-show, half-price tickets to many events. Half-price tickets are cash only, and any tickets for Sunday and Monday shows must be purchased by Saturday. • Tu-Th 11am-6pm; F-Sa 11am-7pm.

ACT (American Conservatory Theater): 450 Geary St. (Mason/Taylor), SF, 415/749-2228. San Francisco's premier theater company, ACT maintains the Stage Door Theater on Mason, the grandly renovated Geary Theater (on Geary) for major (often controversial) productions, and also presents staged readings. Famous alumni include Denzel Washington and Annette Bening.

Beach Blanket Babylon: 678 Beach St. (Hyde/Leavenworth), SF, 415/421-4222. This beloved San Francisco institution offers ever-changing, highly polished musical revues poking fun at contemporary popular culture. Reserve tickets far in advance.

Curran Theater: 445 Geary St. (Taylor/Mason), SF, 415/776-1999 for charge-by-phone tickets, 415/551-2000 for information. The Best of Broadway series brings traveling Broadway productions such as the never-ending *Phantom of the Opera* to the Curran.

Magic Theatre: Building D, Fort Mason Center, Laguna St. at Marina Blvd., SF, 415/441-8822. One of the best places to catch contemporary experimental theater in the city. Look for high-quality productions of works by playwrights like Sam Shepard (before *The Right Stuff*).

Midsummer Mozart: 415/392-4400 for sales, 415/954-0850 for information. A popular summertime series playing in various Bay Area locations. Performances are mostly, but not exclusively, Mozart.

Theatre Rhinoceros: 2926 16th St. (S. Van Ness/Capp), SF, 415/861-5079. San Francisco's premier gay theater.

Venues

Cowell Theatre: Fort Mason, Pier 2 (Marina Blvd. and Buchanan), SF, 415/441-FMTS (3687) for ticket sales, 415/441-3400 for information. Dance performances, comedies, and concerts.

Golden Gate Theatre: 1 Taylor St. (Market/6th St.), SF, 415/551-2000. Big, mainstream shows like Andrew Lloyd Webber's *Music of the Night*.

BARS & CLUBS

Even for a city of 720,000 residents, San Francisco has a mind-boggling number of bars and clubs. Some say it has the finest selection in the country. There are few types of night owls who are left unprovided for, whether tastes run upscale or downscale, crowded or quiet, bottled domestic beer or exotic mixed drinks, cool jazz or white-hot punk rock. The following is merely a sampling of what's out there and is, by no means, complete.

Great sources for finding out what's happening each night are Sunday's *San Francisco Examiner and Chronicle* "pink pages," the *Bay Guardian*, and the *SF Weekly*. You might want to call **BASS Tickets** at 510/762-2277 or 408/998-2277 for information on ticket availability for bigger shows and a listing of events. For a phone listing of hip hop, acid jazz, house, and other dance-oriented music—at both bars and roving parties—call the **Be-at-Line** 415/626-4087.

Alta Plaza Pacific Heights: 2301 Fillmore St. (Clay), 415/922-1444. What two venerable institutions disappeared in the late '80s, only to return, better than ever, in the mid-90s? The answer: civility and Alta Plaza, the bar of choice for the Pacific Heights button-down gay set. And the two go hand in hand. Alta Plaza is the place to meet a man you can bring home to mother, especially if she's the old-fashioned sort who appreciates a gentleman who minds his manners. Polished wood and stenciled walls form the backdrop to an elegant bar, cleverly set in front of a mirror that makes checking out your neighbor easier. Happy hour runs from 4 to 7pm, and the crowd is very friendly, very male, and delighted to be reviving the phrase "smart cocktails." The music can be a bit loud (mitigating factors: it's jazz and often live), and you may have to get a grip on your finances (those smooth Red Hook drafts are four bucks each), but if you're looking for a civilized gay bar, Alta Plaza's the place to see. And be seen.

Backflip Tenderloin: The Phoenix Hotel, 601 Eddy St. (Larkin), 415/771-FLIP (3547). If the crowds that flock here to see and be seen are any indication, Backflip, the city's hippest new restaurant-bar-hangout, is a more-than-worthy successor to Miss Pearl's Jam House, the nightspot that previously occupied this Phoenix Hotel space. It can't hurt that the '50s space-age-Jetsons interior is decorated within an inch of its life. Filled with a variety of synthetic materials bathed in blues, the room sports aquatic fountains, glittery padded booths and chaise lounges, sunken plastic chairs, numerous dark hideaways, wavy opaque glass and mirrored walls (make sure you don't bump into one), and a metallic bridge that separates the dining room from the doughnut-shaped bar. A cooler-than-thou bar staff dispenses regal cocktails—Cosmos, Greyhounds, and Belvedere Martinis (with a blue Italian liqueur)—along with a bunch of microbrews. Those who are underdressed here may feel sheepish, as the place is crawling with Beautiful People who all seem to know one another. Still, if you're on your way to or from a gig at the Great American Music Hall, this is a great spot to stop for a drink.

Bahia Cabana Upper Market: 1600 Market St. (Franklin), 415/861-4202. There's an entire world of culture partying at this Brazilian thatched-hut restaurant-cum-nightclub. You'll find bikini-clad, samba-stepping women on Saturday nights (which feature great samba and pagode bands like Entre Nos), and Wednesdays a multi-orientation crowd grooves to the American-European progressive/house-techno music while downing *caiparinhas* (the Brazilian version of the margarita). Club Charisma brings the "100 percent ritmo" of salsa, merengue, and Latin house every Friday—if you want to get into step, stop in for free salsa lessons the night before. In fact, it's a full-fledged, hard-core, dance-til-you-sweat party every night of the week.

Balboa Café and Grill Marina: 3199 Fillmore St. (Greenwich), 415/921-3944. This rectangular corner bar has been here since 1914, and it feels like a real saloon, with antique drop lighting, brass railings, and wood paneling. A big sofa sits in one corner and small tables line the windows; a more formal dining room is in back, with a menu that's overseen by the chef from the PlumpJack Café. Best of all, the beers are proudly displayed behind glass in lit refrigerators, making them seem like objects of worship. On Friday and Saturday nights, yuppies pack the place to overflowing, but the bar's elegance cannot be diminished by its location at the heart of the Triangle scene. On weeknights, Balboa becomes conducive to quiet, relaxed conversation.

The Beach Chalet Brewery Richmond: 1000 Great Highway (Fulton/Lincoln), 415/386-8439. The Beach Chalet, the combination visitors center and brew pub at the outer edge of Golden Gate Park, recently reopened after lying vacant for years. The owners have overhauled the broad-columned rectangular building, creating a beautiful art deco interior with a wavy ceiling pattern, exposed wooden beams and light woods, plus giant plate glass windows affording a spectacular ocean panorama. Seating options abound in the spacious bar area: choose from the long bar with the giant copper brewing tanks behind it, the high tables in the corner, the wicker chairs facing the ocean, or the long benches that separate the bar from the restaurant seating. Although the bar serves plenty of liquors and bottled beers, the spotlight is on the five brews made on the premises, from the light and fruity Churchyard Pale Ale to the medium Pacific Porter. Before or after drinks, head downstairs to the visitors center, past the mosaic tiles and the carved wooden banister, to see the beautifully restored WPA-era murals of San Francisco workers and the scale model of Golden Gate Park. With an unimpeded view of Ocean Beach and the vast Pacific, the Beach Chalet has already become a destination for plenty of well-scrubbed suburbanites, tourists, and well-to-do thirtysomething professionals: reservations are essential at the restaurant, and the bar is packed on weekend afternoons with a sporty, post-softball crowd. But if you don't have a car, it's one long MUNI ride to reach this windswept spot along the Great Highway.

Ben Butler Bar/Phineas T. Barnacle Cliff House Richmond: 1090 Point Lobos Ave. (Great Highway), 415/386-3330. These are the two most westerly bars in the entire city. That should be readily apparent upon entering their host building, the venerable Cliff House, an ugly-on-the-outside/pretty-on-the-inside tourist haunt that hangs precariously over the Pacific and whose large back windows provide a sweeping view of the water from Pacifica to Marin. The Ben Butler is the ritzier of the two, an elegant Victorian interior of plush carpeting, molded copper ceilings, and low-slung oak tables. Drinks are predictably expensive and include the house specialty, the Ocean Beach (vodka, peach schnapps, cranberry juice, and pineapple juice). Appetizers such as calamari are also available. Phineas T. Barnacle is a dowdier joint with a nautical theme that may remind you of a ride at Disneyland. It's an A-framed room done up in dark woods and brass railings, with more limited window seating that primarily offers views of the Marin Headlands in the background and the Sutro Baths in the foreground. The TV is tuned to sports, though heaven knows why anyone would come all the way out here just for that.

Bimbo's 365 Club North Beach: 1025 Columbus Ave. (Chestnut/Francisco), 415/474-0365. The living definition of swank, this cavernous nightclub/lounge was hip long before the current Cocktail Nation craze. Founded in 1931 by Agostino "Bimbo" Giontoli and still family-run, Bimbo's exquisite interior features red velvet curtains, a plush black-and-red diamond carpet, a garish nude painting, large candelabras, a giant mirrored disco ball—you get the picture. All this plus a separate barroom with a giant fishbowl and a white-stucco lobby with a plaster mermaid centerpiece. Bimbo's hosts diverse musical events most nights of the week, from avant-garde rock to soul and funk, and on special evenings, the world-famous Dolphina, otherwise known as the Girl in the Fishbowl, makes an appearance. The menu is limited, featuring bottled beer and a few unremarkable victuals, which is why you should order what everyone else orders—cocktails, cocktails, and more cocktails, preferably one of their reliable martinis. If attending a low-volume performance, try to get a spot up front near the stage, where the crowd is more attentive. Toward the back of the room the chatting is so loud you probably wouldn't hear a plane if it landed next to your table. Oh, and a couple more things: Be sure to tip the bathroom steward, and do dress up, even if it's just high casual.

Bix Financial District: 56 Gold St. (off Montgomery btwn. Pacific/Jackson), 415/433-6300. You probably can't get any closer to the feel of a classic supper club than at the swank Bix, an Art Deco bilevel space done up in gunmetal gray and tucked surreptitiously into a Jackson Square alleyway. At the long mahogany bar, urns of chilled champagne and a silver bowl of iced martini glasses sit poised for the after-five crowd. In an atmosphere that one of the owners calls "too sophisticated to be happy hour," mixed drinks and luxury wines by the glass are served to tired workers. A pricey gourmet menu is available to those who choose to dine at one of the intimate tables lining the walls on both floors. If that level of opulence doesn't appeal to your palate or your pocketbook, you can raid bowls of nuts at the bar. During dinner hours, the live jazz begins. Mary Stallings, Merrill Hoover, John Goodman, Benny Miller, and Don Asher are the regulars. The patrons—Pacific Heights nouveau riche, well-heeled tourists, architects and designers who work nearby, the usual assortment of movers and shakers—range in age from 20 to 80.

Blues Marina: 2125 Lombard St. (Fillmore/Steiner), 415/771-BLUE (2583). Although an unlikely setting for a cozy nightclub, Blues provides an inviting refuge from the Lombard Street clatter. Live acts play da blooz, R&B, and soul every night of the week. The cool atmosphere is in large part due to the decor: purple-velvet walls, white leather banquettes, a midnight blue linoleum bar, and an alcove shrine to Elvis complete with votive candles. A painting of questionable taste—a luxuriating woman with no clothes on—hangs above the bar, so some may wish to keep their eyes focused on the stage (and some may not). The crowd here is older and more mature than the usual Marina set, plus German and Japanese blues afficionados regularly stop by. Napa Red, Sierra Nevada, and the watery domestics are on tap. Special nights include Rockin' Rock-a-billy Thursdays, Grand Funk Fridays, and the acid-jazz-tinged Leopard Lounge on Sundays. Doors open at 8pm; cover charge after 9pm for the bands on Thursdays through Sundays.

Bottom of the Hill Potrero: 1233 17th St. (Texas), 415/621-4455. This small rock club at the far reaches of Potrero Hill attracts punters with its intelligent and prescient bookings. This is the best place to see local bands practice their craft and up-and-coming national acts before they move on to bigger venues. Also, it's usually the first place to see heavily hyped Britpop acts on their virgin U.S. tours. With its tiny raised stage and low ceilings, the intimate space turns even sold-out shows into intimate affairs, and the quirky cartoonish wall decor skews perspectives even before the drinking starts. There's a set of pool tables in the back room a few feet from the stage and an outdoor patio for catching a breath of fresh air. The kitchen serves very good burger-and-fries combos, along with other grub, and is now open until 11pm on gig nights. The rockin' all-you-can-eat barbecue on Sunday afternoons is legendary. Plenty of microbrews on tap.

Bruno's Mission: 2389 Mission St. (19th St./20th St.), 415/550-7455. Bruno's has been a Mission mainstay for ages, but since its renovation in 1995, the demographic profile has skewed to younger and hipper. Maybe that's because the place now looks like a cross between a 1960s bachelor pad and a suburban steakhouse. One-half of the place, with gorgeous rounded vinyl booths, is, in fact, a well-regarded restaurant. The other half is made up of a long bar with white Naugahyde stools and a colorfully lit lounge. There's live music six nights a week, featuring avant-jazz and various experimental combos of note (don't miss the Clubfoot Orchestra). Not surprisingly, it fills up on weekends, and if you're planning to make an evening of it (dinner and a show), reservations for the meal are absolutely essential.

The Café Castro: 2367 Market St. (Castro), 415/861-3846. A rock-solid institution of the Castro nightclub scene since its days as Café San Marco in the early 1980s, The Café continues to be the destination of choice for the twentysomething gay male crowd. Lesbians have been known to cry foul that gay men have taken over a bar that was largely their turf until the mid-'90s, and some straights decry the bar's "no straight kissing" policy (quickly renamed a "no deep kissing by anyone" policy when the bar was charged with discrimination). Nonetheless, both lesbians and straights are still found here in large numbers early in the evening; later on the crowd becomes almost exclusively male and gay. The large, generic-looking two-story night-club is divided into various sections—a dance floor, two pool tables, the bar, and a balcony that commands a prime view of the corner of Market and Castro below—with each attracting its own clique. Monday night is $1.25 domestic beer night and Tuesday is half-price well drinks night, but regulars still swear the best night to go is Thursday, when the weekend hasn't yet drawn the out-of-towners, but the city boys are out and about.

Café Du Nord Castro: 2170 Market St. (Church/Sanchez), 415/979-6545. Café Du Nord is a throwback to the days of dining and dancing, when martinis were clear, everyone smoked cigarettes, and "vintage clothing" meant hand-me-downs. There's a comfortable, well-used feeling about the nightclub: everything has a charming patina of wear, with no glitz or pomp or new paint to be seen. Dusty red velvet abounds as you descend the dramatically steep stairs into the spacious-yet-cozy bar. Beyond the bar is a smallish room, with little white-clothed tables and a stage in front of a real dance floor that gets plenty of use. There's music seven days a week in a delightfully wide range of styles. Learn to salsa dance for free on Tuesdays with Benny Velarde, enjoy the musical stylings of such retro swing acts as Lavay Smith and the Red Hot Skillet Lickers on Saturdays, and occasionally hear such legendary bluesmen as Charles Brown. Cover charge is unusually modest, $3 Sunday through Thursday and $5 on the weekends, with no cover before 8pm. Cocktails are $2 during happy hour (4-7pm daily). If you need a place to bring a date for dinner or to show off your Palm Beach suit, Café Du Nord should be on your A list.

Carnelian Room Financial District: Bank of America Building, 52nd Fl., 555 California St. (Kearny/Montgomery), 415/433-7500. Spectacular views of the city and the bay are the draw at this somewhat stuffy restaurant and lounge. Floor-to-ceiling picture windows meet at right angles and provide a dramatic, sweeping vista from bridge to bridge, plus Marin and the East Bay (come during Fleet Week, when the Blue Angels pilots blitz the surrounding skies, for an experience right out of a Schwarzenegger film). The cocktail lounge has the air of an exclusive social club from days of yore, done up in thick carpeting, leather padded chairs, and wood-paneled walls. You pay for the view, of course, and the service is particularly snooty here—there's a reception-ist's desk for visitors just past the gilded elegance of the elevator lobby, which should be a serious hint to either dress the part or booze it up at street level.

Dalva Mission: 3121 16th St. (Valencia/Guerrero), 415/252-7740. Dalva, a self-described "cocktails/jukebox/hideout" bar, is proof of two axioms: 1) Timing is everything, and 2) Location, location, location. Debuting a couple of years back, just as the 16th Street renaissance was approaching its apex, Dalva's darkly cool atmos-phere—narrow room, high ceiling, subdued lighting, walls painted in Mediterranean hues—has been drawing steady crowds since opening day. It's a perfect place to have a drink, whether before dinner (there should be a crossing guard controlling the traffic between here and Ti Couz across the street), or after a movie at the Roxie Cinema next door. Many people, of course, make an evening of it right here, since there's a myriad of drink choices: microbrews on tap, bush malt, Belgian ales, fine wines, and sweet Sangria, among others. Owing to the crowds and the acoustics of the room, it gets pretty noisy at night, when seating at the long bar or the high tables is hard to come by. (There is also a small, secluded back room with tables—usually occupied, alas—which looks like a clandestine meeting spot for the French Resistance.) If you come by very late, however, the crowd sometimes clears out. Anglophiles will appreciate the jukebox.

Deluxe Haight: 1511 Haight St. (Ashbury/Clayton), 415/552-6949. Small and swing-ing, with a beatnik attitude and a 1940s style—that's the Deluxe. Sit at the bar and chat up the hip, the groovy, and the not-necessarily-the-Haight-Street crowd. Stir your martini with an olive-clad toothpick. Sit back and let the sounds emanating from the tiny stage move you—owner Jay Johnson often does his best Frank Sinatra to the accompaniment of a jazz trio, or Steve and Patsy and other acts get the joint swinging and singing. You can also have a seat at a 1950s chrome tabletop and ask one of the friendly servers (who's working a 1940s fashion statement with peplum skirt, beehive hair, and three-inch pointy-toed pumps that would put Lucille Ball to shame) for a Cosmopolitan, a gin and tonic, or what some say is the best Bloody Mary in town. All told, a flashback San Francisco hot spot that's hip enough to make you hop.

DNA Lounge SoMa: 375 11th St. (Harrison/Folsom), 415/626-1409. How you feel about SoMa—whether you love it or hate it—depends a lot on how you feel about the 11th Street Scene, the nightclub ghetto between Folsom and Harrison that, on weekends at least, is a cacophony of nubile girls and studly boys who only know the word *party* as a verb. The DNA, a blacklit warehouse space that features a large stage, a horseshoe bar, and a recently remodeled perimeter balcony, is the epitome of that scene. Nakedly catering to the East Bay bridge-and-tunnel crowd with '70s cover bands like Grooveline (the erstwhile Friday-night house band), the management occasionally remembers the club's roots as an industrial hangout and invites edgy rock groups in for a show. The cover charge on weekends runs about $10, and drinks aren't cheap either. Rest assured, however, that all the A-list folks end up here one time or another, from the Artist Formerly Known as Prince to the Former Mayor again known as Frank Jordan.

Edinburgh Castle Tenderloin: 950 Geary St. (Larkin/Polk), 415/885-4074. Great Scot! The Edinburgh is not so much a castle as a veritable Viking beer hall, with a large bar and wooden booth area that sits under an enormous horseshoe balcony that overlooks everything. (They could have filmed the battle scenes from *Braveheart* here.) The crowd is young, hip, international, and literary. The latter trait is partially due to the many readings by Scottish authors that are held here, events that have included such luminaries as *Trainspotting* author Irvine Welsh. Pool tables and darts are available for sporting types, and there is a completely separate upstairs room that hosts rock and country bands in a casual, intimate space. For an authentic taste of the UK, order the mouthwatering fish-and-chips that are cooked across the street and delivered, wrapped in newspaper, to wherever your are standing or sitting. Twenty beers are on tap and, of course, some fine single-malt scotches are poured. Live music Wednesdays through Saturdays at 9:30pm.

El Rio Mission: 3158 Mission St. (Cesar Chavez/Valencia), 415/282-3325. Located in the netherworld between Bernal Heights and the Mission, this casual hangout, home to a diverse crowd, advertises itself as "your dive." Friendly servers and old-timers aside, the bar space itself is nothing special. The real drawing card here is the expansive outdoor patio—one of the best in the city—filled with tropical plants and strings of colored lights. On a warm night, it's a great place to sit and have a drink or listen to the great musical offerings: rock and salsa bands play Wednesdays, Fridays, and Saturdays. El Rio's famous margaritas are only $2 on Tuesday night's Margaritaville, while an occasional oyster special draws crowds on Friday nights. There are games, too, from a pool table (with tan felt) to indoor shuffleboard.

Elbo Room Mission: 647 Valencia St. (17th St./18th St.), 415/552-7788. One of the finest-looking nightspots in town, with a wavy Formica-topped bar, wooden arches, and candles to enhance the mood lighting. The long bar spans the length of the room downstairs, with cocktail tables set behind a hip-high wall, dividing the traffic from those sitting down. Beers on tap include Red Hook and Guinness. Liquor, like the heavenly Laphroaoig Scotch, is also abundant. Two pool tables anchor the back of this level. Upstairs, Elbo Room hosts bands playing everything from ambient jazz to rap/funk for a modest cover charge (usually no more than $5). An additional bar, pool table, and pinball machines occupy the back area, but the remainder of the room is solely for body gyrations. The ethnically diverse crowd, straight out of a Benetton ad, is twentysomething on average and heavy on the scenesters. If you're a hep cat, you can hang here comfortably. This lively outpost gets packed, so dress casual (jeans, T-shirts, skimpy dresses) and lightly. Tuesdays are for samba, Wednesdays feature jazz, and Fridays and Saturdays bring the funk. DJs spin funk and soul Monday and Thursday nights, with special live bands turning up occasionally as well, often to premiere their new CDs.

Elysium Café Mission: 2438 Mission St. (20th St./21st St.), 415/282-0337. Look for the blue lights wound around a tree for the entrance to the Mission's hottest new addition. The sophisticated decor is warm, inviting, and will keep the eye wandering. Overstuffed couches, armchairs, low coffee tables, and even a koi pond make for such comfort that the only thing missing seems to be hookah pipes. As the mixed crowd converse over long-stem cocktails and good Italian wines, ultrasmooth DJs enhance the mood, creating experimental soundscapes (everything from old-school jazz to Latin American standards). A full bar and kitchen complement the scene, and the Hell Damnation spareribs and haystack shoestring potatoes are highly recommended.

Endup SoMa: 401 6th St. (Harrison), 415/357-0827. A publication circulating through the local area for the past few years is entitled, *I Found God at the Endup*. True to its name, after a long nights' clubbing, when there is no place left to go, this is your place to Endup. Open almost all the time during the weekend, with different parties seemingly every few hours, including the infamous Saturday-night G Spot and Sunday Tea Dance—call their phone line for details. Huge space with an outdoor patio.

Harry Denton's Financial District: 161 Steuart St. (Mission/Howard), 415/882-1333. There really *is* a Harry Denton, and on fortuitous occasions he may be found working the crowd of beautiful people in this popular nightspot in the shadow of the Bay Bridge. Behind the velvet-curtained entrance and the Pamela Anderson Lee look-alike hostess, you'll find the city's swells dancing the night away to a live band cranking out disco and Motown hits. By about midnight, the compact black-and-white deco-tile dance floor and traditional wooden bar are jammed with Financial District suits and Bebe-clad twentysomething females reminiscent of Sande in *L.A. Story*. Despite the sheer numbers, the presence of Harry Denton the man gives the place a surprisingly intimate feel: San Francisco's own Casablanca meets Generation X. If you just can't wear your beat-up Levi's and Doc Martens one more night, slither into your sleekest black ensemble and slide on down to Harry's. He'll be waiting.

Harry Denton's Starlight Room Union Square: Sir Francis Drake Hotel, 21st Fl., 450 Powell St. (Post/Sutter), 415/395-8595. Much like the Top of the Mark up the hill, the Starlight Room harks back to an earlier gilded age when stylishness and elegance were a way of life. Walking into the opulent interior with its French doors, marble columns, silk drapes, burgundy velvet booths, plush carpeting, beveled mirrors, and crystal chandeliers, you easily sense the history of this place, even though it seems so fantastic as to be slightly unreal. Unlike most other hotel bars, this is really more a place for locals than for tourists, especially later in the evening, when a wide range of music sends everyone onto the dance floor. Wednesday night is the popular Indulgence dance party for the twentysomething crowd; Thursday night is R&B; and Friday and Saturday the effervescent Starlight Orchestra always packs the house. Most well drinks are under three bucks during happy hour (Monday to Friday, 5pm to 7pm) and a very reasonable four bucks the rest of the time; beers range from three to five dollars. Excellent buffets are also available. Last but not least, and free of charge, there are the spectacular views to the east, south, and west (sunset here is spectacular). A romantic bar in the true sense of the word.

Hi-Ball Lounge North Beach: 473 Broadway (Kearny/Montgomery), 415/397-9464. The key word here is *lounge*, as it reflects the '90s retro/cocktail revival trend among the city's young clubbers, a fad that shows no signs of passing anytime soon. The fashionable interior is one of red-velvet booths, circular candlelit tables, and dimmed lighting against darkly painted walls. The effect would look like a cliché, except that the Hi-Ball was one of the first places to jump on this particular bandwagon. As for the crowd, the preponderance of men in bowling shirts and women in baby-doll dresses drinking from Y-shaped glasses will tip anyone off to what sort of people hang out here. You can enjoy live jazz and swing music nightly, with dance lessons provided by the suave Johnny Swing on Sundays, Tuesdays, and Wednesdays. (Call 964-3654 for lesson information.)

Hotel Utah Saloon SoMa: 500 4th St. (Bryant), 415/421-8308. This old-fashioned bilevel bar still carries a hint of Wild West decor. But these days there's no hint of a cowboy, or a hotel, or Utah anywhere. Instead, you've got just bartenders behind a massive mahogany bar serving up good microbrewed pints, along with such delicious pub fare as vegetarian chili, chips, and spicy salsa. The small, creaky stage, which perfectly fits the intimacy of the place, hosts a wide variety of live acts—rock, pop, punk, country bands, and acoustic singer-songwriters. The cover charge is almost never more than $5, and open-mike Mondays, when the local talent often surpasses signed acts, are free. Use the quarters you save for the Buzz Ball machine, which dispenses chocolate-covered espresso beans.

Jazz at Pearl's North Beach: 256 Columbus Ave. (Broadway/Pacific), 415/291-8255. Situated in the heart of the very busy nightlife scene of North Beach is a real pearl of a place—a popular venue for small jazz combos as well as some larger groups. Bay Area talent such as Bruce Forman and the well-known Pete Escovedo appear often, playing between walls covered with large, black-and-white photographs of jazz legends. There is no cover charge, but there is a stiffly-enforced, two-beverage minimum weeknights—two drinks per set (9pm and 11pm) weekends. Most patrons are in their mid-30s, with a few more-mature music lovers mixed in. The dress code permits casual attire, although most people are gussied up for a night out. Appetizers, burgers, pizza, and sandwiches are available for noshing in the well-lit, tableclothed rooms, front and back. Windows, which open to the street, draw many outside spectators, and the melodious sounds can be heard a block away.

Jelly's China Basin: 295 China Basin St. (off Mission Rock), 415/495-3099. Jelly's, a diamond-in-the-rough club on the outskirts of the city at Pier 50, offers a great view of the city skyline, an outdoor patio overlooking the water, and a loud, pumping, dance-oriented ambience. It's primarily a party-for-rental hot spot, so the events change weekly, but the Sunday salsa jam can be counted on for a serious swing, and on the last Friday of every month the TamTam Queen rocks the house with African soukous, samba, soca, reggae, salsa, and merengue. If you catch wind that SpinCycle Productions is throwing one of their legendary party jams, don't miss it. The crowd changes depending upon the party but tends to be multicultural, open, and friendly. No matter what the night, there's always good music, great margaritas, and a good wine and beer selection.

Johnny Love's Russian Hill: 1500 Broadway (Polk), 415/931-8021. Early evening at Johnny Love's has the air of expectancy: awaiting the arrival of the infamous hordes of well-coiffed barhoppers, the live band, and Johnny himself. Infamous bartender Johnny Metheney, known for his uncanny ability to remember the name of every female that ever ordered a drink, opened this perennially popular spot several years ago, and the crowd continues to pour in. At least by legend if not by fact, this *is* the city's primary pickup joint for young urban professionals. The smooth, quick-handed bartenders revel in talking up the legend: last Monday's hip-hop night that resembled a weekend reverie, the Christmas party for the Raiderettes that featured bar-top dancing, the Saturday Johnny created a new drink and gave away free shots with every order all night long. The large space is divided by a central horseshoe bar, with leather banquettes for diners, a band stage and dance area, and plenty of drinking room. When all those are full, lots of people simply end up dancing on tabletops. (It's that kind of place.) The crimson-and-forest-green walls are studded with European alcohol posters and photographs featuring Johnny and celebrities ranging from Steve Young to Weird Al Yankovich. A band plays 1970s music on Saturday nights. The line to get in usually runs halfway down the block. Unspoken dress code: Oxford shirts and Dockers for men, clingy dresses or miniskirts for women. The cover charge and waiting line varies according to the entertainment. A permanent party, all week long.

Josie's Cabaret and Juice Joint Castro: 3583 16th St. (Market/Noe), 415/861-7933. This colorful neighborhood institution combines a small but amazingly well-stocked daytime café—breakfast, lunch, and dinner daily from 9:30am to 7pm—and the Castro's best-loved nighttime local stage. In its evening cabaret guise, Josie's features gay comedy and theater, from high drama to high camp, with cover charges that vary with the performance or event. While performances span the talent range, great ones occur often enough, and less acclaimed ones always have at least something to offer in the way of entertainment. (If you want to see a performance with an unobstructed view, get here early for a good seat. If you don't, you'll be sitting in the balcony and hearing the show but seeing a support beam.) The price of admission is reasonable, rarely over $10, and it's only $5 for the open-mike comedy on Monday nights. The staff is awfully nice and will wait on you toe and heel with a smile. (Don't be intimidated by their Haight Street fashion sense.) And although this is called a juice joint, rest assured that draft beer is also served. On a sunny day, check out the back patio, have a mimosa, and soak up those rays.

Julie's Supper Club SoMa: 1123 Folsom St. (7th St./8th St.), 415/861-0707. Julie Ring's landmark restaurant was not only one of the first SoMa hot spots, but also the center of the supper club revival phenomenon. Years later, this remains a popular place with those who were here when the scene started, as well as with recently legal-to-drink East Bay and South Bay clubbers. The decor and the atmosphere of the bar and main dining space is Jetsons–Space Age meets '50s diner, with a back room done up in an aquatic motif. Weekdays attract the typical SoMa types looking for a quick drink before heading to the latest digital/art/poetry happening. A small corner sound stage hosts live music on weekends (mostly jazz and swing), when the place starts to jump and revelers begin to make room for dancing. Unless you're just drinking, reservations are recommended for Fridays and Saturdays. As there is nothing like Julie's in most other parts of the country, this is a great place to take your less-sophisticated out-of-town friends. Trendy, sure, but Julie's Supper Club started the trend.

Last Day Saloon Richmond: 406 Clement St. (5th Ave./6th Ave.), 415/387-6343. Like a beacon, the Last Day Saloon's bright and hopping two-story interior draws in nightlifers adrift in the black quiet. The downstairs is straightforward sports bar, with longtime neighborhood residents drinking pints, listening to the jukebox, watching the pro league game of choice on TVs, and waiting for a turn at the pool tables. Upstairs, a sprawling room with tables in back and a sizable stage in front hosts the bands. The booking policy brings in lots of different types of mainstream music, from blues and rock to funk. Headlining weekend acts usually fill the room, while mostly just FOBs (Friends of the Band) turn up for the casual, less-crowded weeknights. History buffs will enjoy the wall covered with the names of the acts who have graced the stage. Yes, even Foghat once played here. Anchor and numerous other beers are on tap. There's a cover charge for the music.

Little Shamrock Sunset: 807 Lincoln Wy. (9th Ave./10th Ave.), 415/661-0060. Established in 1893, the Little Shamrock is the oldest Irish bar in the city as well as a wonderfully inviting place within walking distance of the Haight and the Inner Sunset, located directly across the street from Golden Gate Park. You might have the distinct sensation that you're paying a visit to someone's gracious home, from the bed of flowers outside the front windows to the sofas and love seats and cluttered-attic decor inside. The cheerful atmosphere encourages lingering, perhaps near the cozy fireplace on a cold night. Be warned that darts are taken *very* seriously here, and denizens of the clubby darts room, with its array of league trophies, do their best to intimidate neophytes. The rest of the crowd is very easygoing, however, and includes a nice mix of folks from different neighborhoods and different ages. Yes, they serve Guinness.

Lou's Pier 47 Fisherman's Wharf: 300 Jefferson St. (Jones), 415/675-0308. Lou's is considerably rowdier than nearby Tarantino's, owing to the fact that 17 bands—blues, rock, R&B, country—pass across its stage each week. The Bourbon Street-like ambience is furthered by what must be the world's longest happy hour: noon to 8pm on weekends (4 to 8pm on weeknights), a period during which folks pack the pink Formica bar and take up every seat at the closely arranged tables. There's a full snack bar, and the cover charge doesn't kick in until 8pm. Lou, the First Lady of Fisherman's Wharf, is often on hand if you'd like to chat. • Daily 4pm-2am (Restaurant open daily 6am-11pm)

Mad Dog in the Fog Lower Haight: 530 Haight St. (Fillmore/Steiner), 415/626-7279. There's so much to say about Mad Dog in the Fog, it's hard to know where to begin. First off, it's the premier Anglophile bar in town, a virtual England-on-Haight. The entire huge space (well, most of it anyway) is decorated with bar towels trumpeting various brands of ale, soccer club banners, and other touchingly British souvenirs. Secondly, the beer selection is wonderful, with lots of dee-lish imports in bottles (including the sublime Boddington's and Old Peculiar) and a respectable number on tap as well. Add to that darts and a lovely back garden and you've got a dynamite destination. Seating is plentiful, and the front room has a big window that opens onto life in the Lower Haight. Perhaps the best feature of the Mad Dog, however, is the trivia game held every Monday and Thursday. The same guy has been running it for some time (apparently he makes his living at it; more power to him), bellowing out questions over the din of the bar in a sometimes incomprehensible Irish brogue. If all this isn't enough—and it certainly should be—stop by at 5:30 or 6 some morning during Mad Dog's legendary live satellite screenings of major British football matches. Stick your head in the door, if it's even possible, and be rewarded by the sight of dozens of sports-crazed British expats clutching pints of Guinness, screaming at the telly at the tops of their lungs, pissed out of their minds at 6 in the morning. Bloody good.

The Make-Out Room Mission: 3225 22nd St. (Mission/Valencia), 415/647-2888. Half a block off of the perpetually up-and-coming Valencia corridor, The Make-Out Room is the ultimate in the current gentrificaton-with-an-edge wave. It's a place where the savvy bartenders have deemed tiny cocktail straws a superfluous drink garnish and raise an eyebrow at the uninitiated who ask for one. The regulars are generally drawn from the neighborhood genetic pool: goateed and/or pierced, cigarette smoking, and fluent in conversational multimediaese. The decor is a combination of utilitarian, minimalist, concrete-meets-lush, baroque, and garage sale. The back area has plenty of cocktail tables, while the front bar is lined with booths. Kudos to whoever dreamed up the idea of antlers placed sporadically along the walls. Bathrooms are small, but festooned with cheerfully bright paint. On occasion, The Make-Out Room is also a venue for live music, turning over the stage to ultra-alternative acts that hail from as far away as New Zealand. Comfortably active on weeknights, this place is packed on weekends. Bring a date, but be forewarned that he or she may be distracted by the attractive "scenery."

Nickie's BBQ Lower Haight: 460 Haight St. (Webster/Fillmore), 415/621-6508. If Nickie's looks way too small on the outside to be a dance club, that's because it is. The small, grubby, bare-bones room consists of little more than the bar and a few leather-padded booths; when the typically vibrant and diverse young Lower Haight crowd shows up, the whole place is a dance floor, and it's one nation under a groove. Each night there are different DJs and sounds. Monday features Grateful Dead jams; Tuesday it's world beat (with renowned spin-ster cheb i sabbah); Wednesday it's funk; Thursday it's groove jazz, soul, and Latin; and Friday and Saturday it's full-on '70s funk and soul. Although some say a decline in the quality of the music mix has brought an end to the sardine-packed, sweaty-bodied days of yore, this remains an excellent place to shake your booty, and the cover charge is never more than five bucks. Wide selection of domestic and imported beers. Pool tables downstairs. Take to heart the sign that says "Be Nice or Leave."

Noc Noc Lower Haight: 557 Haight St. (Fillmore/Steiner), 415/861-5811. Noc Noc possesses what is arguably the weirdest interior of any bar in the city, which is saying a lot. The painted, papier-mâché-surfaced walls are covered with sections of aircraft sheet metal, hieroglyphics, and obscure images of scary creatures. Tiny, silent TVs hang from the ceiling, showing blank blue screens (perhaps it's a subtle dig at sports bars). Throw pillows and squat, cramped seats are scattered among the various nooks and crannies. Basically, it's Dr. Who meets Dr. Seuss in San Francisco's equivalent of the bar from *Star Wars*. After being bombarded by all of these oddities, you'll find the tiny bar itself remarkably pedestrian and tame, featuring a small but solid beer selection, plus wines and pretzels. A DJ hidden behind a booth in the corner plays acid jazz and ambient music for the young, suitably hipster crowd. Come early if you don't want to end up standing all night.

Paradise Lounge/Transmission Theater SoMa: 1501 Folsom St. (11th St.), 415/861-6906. The Paradise is more like a house than a lounge, what with its numerous "spaces" separated by walls: the bar, the multiple performance stages, and the dark drinking corners. Six nights a week, a young, with-it crowd shows up to check out hip local bands and esoteric national acts, from grungy rock to country twang (although the emphasis is certainly on the former). Right next door, connected by a short hallway, is an additional warehouse-sized room called Transmission Theater. With its sprawling wooden floor, the Transmission looks like it should be hosting a square dance, but the art videos on large screens hanging from two of the walls betray the experimental, eclectic nature of the acts that play/perform here. Don't miss the craziness that ensues when Incredibly Strange Wrestling makes its occasional stop. The upper-loft area faces 11th Street, and is a good place to relax. During happy hour, which runs from 3 to 8pm, well drinks are $3.25, beers are $3; look for the occasional special offering $2 domestic beers.

Paragon Bar and Café Marina: 3251 Scott St. (Chestnut/Lombard), 415/922-2456. Before the recent remodeling, the Paragon fancied itself a hangout for frat boys and tanned Southern California surfer types who wanted to relive their pre-yuppie pasts. Now it has a more sophisticated feel, owing to the black-and-tan walls with sconces and moldings, the abstract artwork, the stone fireplace, and the hanging industrial light fixtures. The crowd has gotten older and more professional, but this is still the Marina, and the J. Crew/Gap/Banana Republic look predominates; no body piercings here. The revamped musical calendar leans towards the KFOG aesthetic, with lots of acoustic songwriters and retro rockers performing live Sunday through Wednesday, and a resident DJ spinning crowd-pleasing tunes the rest of the week. Food is served at the tables in the back of the room. Remains popular and packed on weekends.

Plough & Stars Richmond: 116 Clement St. (2nd Ave./3rd Ave.), 415/751-1122. A favorite with the Irish lads and lassies residing in the Richmond, the Plough & Stars is an authentic re-creation of an Eire pub. The dim lighting, sparse decoration, and unobtrusive stage at the back will remind any former backpacker of a rural County pub. Seating options include long, narrow, communal tables of dark wood as well as the crowded bar. A mellow, ruddy-faced crowd enjoys pool, darts, and Guinness, with traditional Irish folk music playing nightly at 9:15 (there's a $4 cover charge except on Sundays).

Radio Valencia Mission: 1199 Valencia St. (23rd St.), 415/826-1199. Radio Valencia is really more of a café-restaurant than a bar (and the healthy, homemade fare here is truly excellent), but it does become a club of sorts from Friday through Sunday nights. That's when the enlightened and sophisticated folks who run the place showcase a spectrum of live music—acoustic, bluegrass, and jazz improv—to entertain a suitably bohemian crowd of artists, writers, and Mission scenesters. Friday and Sunday nights are free, and the Saturday night jazz (shows at 7:30pm and 9pm) can be enjoyed for a nominal $3 cover charge. You can grab a seat at the tiny bar that serves a dozen beers on tap, or find an open table in this midsized storefront room. Check out the musical instruments suspended from the ceiling, the horse tapestries mounted on one wall, and the vinyl records (remember those?) stuck on the other. If you're wondering why the linoleum floor is fire-engine red, find someone here willing to tell you the now-legendary story behind it.

The Red Room Union Square: 827 Sutter St. (Jones/Leavenworth), 415/346-7666. The entrance door is red. The rows of bottles stacked from floor to ceiling are red. The walls are red. The floors are red. The leather couches are red. The leather chairs are red. The backless bar stools are red. The Formica-topped, semicircular bar is red. The giant plastic martini glass behind the bar is red. The straws are red. The bathrooms are red. Get the picture? This trendy watering hole is called the Red Room for a reason, and if that reason is not immediately apparent to you when you enter this mecca of hip on the edge of Nob Hill, you need a few more drinks. The crowd is very young and likes their cocktails with a twist of background lounge music. The bartenders are friendly and amazingly good-natured about working in such an monochromatic environment. This up-to-the-minute bar gets more than its share of novelty-seeking crowds, so come early, stay late, and leave any color-blind friends at home.

Sol y Luna Financial District: 475 Sacramento St. (Battery/Sansome), 415/296-8191. A lively Latin supper club sandwiched between two office buildings and done up in a sleek modernist/industrial decor, Sol y Luna is just getting going when the rest of the Financial District has packed up their briefcases and gone home for the night. On weekends, the crowd skews to the young and international, and the front patio becomes a crush of bodies. On Friday nights, house and Euro dance music blare from the speakers, and on Saturday nights there's a blowout flamenco show and salsa bands (reservations recommended). Live bands and DJs fill out the rest of the week's entertainment, with the occasional cigar night on Tuesday. Happy hour specials on both drinks (go for the pitcher of sangria) and Spanish tapas.

The Sound Factory SoMa: 525 Harrison St. (1st St./2nd St.), 415/243-9646. The Sound Factory, right near the entrance to the Bay Bridge, is a massive dance warehouse divided into several rooms each color coded by theme. The music varies depending on the night and the event, but the spectrum runs from near-Top 40 mainstream (for the bridge-and-tunnel crowd) to the rave-influenced house-jungle-ambient beats (for the psychedelic-shirts-and-baggy-pants crowd). All the rooms have a bar so thirst will never be an issue. They also have a thankfully efficient and reliable coat-check room—important because you'll work up a sweat dancing and freeze when you go outside in the chilly late-night air. Call ahead to check for special events or to find out which DJ will be appearing.

Storyville Haight: 1751 Fulton St. (Central/Masonic), 415/441-1751. Red velvet walls, black leather couches, gold deco sconces, glowing fireplaces, and old-time photos give Storyville the feel of the legendary jazz clubs of New York and the Fillmore. Here, African-Americans who had patronized the old joints mix with both jazz-loving professionals and younger people who are trying the supper club thing. (The crowd evolves as the evening progresses, starting older and getting younger.) There are two rooms: The Lounge in front is where, for the price of a drink, you can listen to the house band, featuring Don Pender and various others, play from 5pm until 8pm. The Showroom in the back offers both dining and the club's headliners. The acts are mostly solid, midlevel combos. The food celebrates the Louisiana kitchen with jambalaya, gumbo, and catfish on the menu, and a jazz brunch features eggs sardou, seafood omelets, and crayfish on brioche. Desserts include gooey chocolate pecan parfait and sweet potato crisp. No cover is charged most nights.

Tonga Room Nob Hill: Fairmont Hotel, 950 Mason St. (California/Sacramento), 415/772-5278. Every once in a while it becomes necessary for those who love kitsch to make a pilgrimage to the Tonga Room. Sure, there are plenty of other cheesy Polynesian bars in the city serving up globular glasses of sickeningly sweet drinks with tiny umbrellas as decoration. This one, however, is the king, and not merely because of its regal location on Nob Hill. The space, more of a hall than a room, features table seating beneath thatched-hut roofs, fake bamboo trees, and an enormous center pool with a floating stage, on which the groovy house band performs nightly. Best of all, every half hour there are simulated tropical storms, complete with lightning, thunder, and, yes, precipitation. It must be seen to be believed. The band performs a dinner show after 8pm, but the prices for both food and drinks may be prohibitive for some. The penurious are advised to go during happy hour (5 to 7pm), when the Mai Tais and daiquiris are discounted and an all-you-can-eat buffet is only $5.

Top of the Mark Nob Hill: Mark Hopkins Hotel, 19th Fl., 1 Nob Hill (California/Mason), 415/616-6916. Ever since it opened in 1939, atop the famed Mark Hopkins Hotel, the Top of the Mark has served as the quintessential place to take your out-of-town relatives or to have that big anniversary dinner. While the view remained as magnificent as ever, the atmosphere eventually began to feel a little, well, stodgy. Thus, the Mark remodeled and turned from an outdated corporate-'70s look to the soon-to-be-outdated Pottery Barn-'90s look of blonde wood furnishings, beaded candle holders, and wrought-iron chandeliers. Still, it's an improvement, especially with the addition of a raised dance floor in the center of the room, where salsa and swing bands now perform starting at 8:30 nightly. (If you prefer the Mark of old, come early; it remains a piano bar from 4pm to 8pm). Best of all, there are still two rows of tables lining the perimeter of the room, from which you can ooh and aah over San Francisco to your heart's content.

Tosca Café North Beach: 242 Columbus Ave. (Broadway/Pacific), 415/986-9651. Elegant without being pricey, refined without being stuffy, relaxed without being a dive, Tosca is the classiest bar in the city, at least when there's no room-shaking, rumbling bass coming from the Palladium disco next door. Matron Jeannette Etheredge's palace of good taste has dark walls, a high ceiling, faded floor tiles, giant red leather booths, Formica tables, a long wooden bar, and operatic arias playing in the background on the ancient jukebox. In this sepia-toned ambience, bottled beers like Anchor Steam are served, plus the usual array of cocktails as mixed by the professional bartenders—the house special is a potent coffee-free "cappuccino," and both the martinis and the cosmopolitans pack the requisite punch. The place gets quite crowded on weekends, drawing everyone from yuppies on a North Beach pub crawl to Swing Nation denizens decked out in vintage clothes. Come early; better yet, come early on weeknights, when there is no finer venue for hushed conversation. For what it's worth, actor Nicolas Cage has often been sighted here.

Up & Down Club SoMa: 1151 Folsom St. (7th St./8th St.), 415/626-2388. Two separate bars under one swell name, this has been a landmark spot for the new generation of jazz artists in the city during the 1990s—whatever one might think of the scene. The downstairs offers a sleek bar charmed by golden walls, candlelight, and a small stage showcasing various combos six nights a week. Upstairs is more of a "gimme a beer, Mac!" joint, with sticky-in-the-heat vinyl booths and a DJ pumping loud music—generally soul, hip-hop, funk, and acid jazz—for a too-small-by-half dance floor. The attractive patrons may be a reflection of and tribute to one of the club's owners, supermodel Christy Turlington, who is known to drop in on occasion. A dinner menu is available downstairs, and upstairs or downstairs can be rented for private parties.

PLACES TO STAY

Prices listed below show a general range covering singles, doubles, and suites. Prices at an establishment can vary dramatically depending on the room and the season. Always ask about specials: weekend, frequent flier, AAA, corporate, and so forth.

The Archbishops Mansion $$$ Western Addition: 1000 Fulton St. (Steiner), SF, 415/563-7872, 800/543-5820; fax 415/885-3193. One of the finest hotels of any size in San Francisco, the Archbishops Mansion is a popular place for honeymooners. Built in 1904 for the archbishop himself, this elegant mansion on Alamo Square features a beautiful French parlor, deep-stained wood cornices, oriental rugs galore, an enormous staircase lit by a stained-glass skylight, and a piano once owned by Noel Coward. The rooms have traditional fireplaces, partially canopied beds, and French antiques; the suites feature double tubs, lovely views, and sitting areas. A complimentary continental breakfast is brought to your room in the morning, and wine is served in the afternoon. Advance reservations recommended. $139-$419.

AYH Fort Mason Hostel ¢ Marina: 240 Fort Mason, Franklin St. at Bay St., SF, 415/771-7277. This budget-priced hostel, located in the Marina's Golden Gate National Recreation Area, overlooks the Golden Gate Bridge and is convenient to Fisherman's Wharf, the Marina, and Pacific Heights. Of course, you'll have to sleep in dormitory quarters and live with a few simple regulations, but it's worth it for the beautiful scenery. (There is also a hostel located near Union Square.) $17 a night for members and nonmembers.

Brady Acres $$ Union Sq.: 649 Jones St. (Post/Geary), SF, 415/929-8033, 800/627-2396. The name conjures up rural, homey imagery, and despite being three blocks from the bustle of Union Square, personable proprietor Deborah Liane Brady makes good on the promise of comfort in a cozy setting. The 25 recently remodeled studio rooms are individually (and tastefully) decorated, with enough cupboards and kitchen amenities (refrigerator, microwave, coffeemaker, toaster, plus utensils) to encourage cooking. Each studio also has a color TV, cassette player, and a private-line telephone with answering machine. The private baths are tiny but newly tiled and clean. An especially good choice for those staying a week, as special deals apply. $65-$95.

Campton Place $$$$ Union Sq.: 340 Stockton St. (Sutter), SF, 415/781-5555. This Union Square luxury hotel is renowned for its restaurant (celebrity chef Bradley Ogden established his reputation here) and for its tasteful, understated atmosphere. The Campton staff manages to create an intimate and romantic atmosphere that is quite a contrast to most large hotels in this area. $240-$360.

Chancellor Hotel $$$ Union Sq.: 433 Powell St. (Post/Sutter), SF, 415/362-2004, 800/428-4748; fax 415/362-1403. One hundred and twenty-seven pristine, stylish rooms, many with terrific views of the square, feature queen or twin beds with phones and private baths. There are also ceiling fans for those rare hot days. Neighborhood parking, complimentary health club, and a location that can't be beat make this an attractive choice. Call for special deals on "slow days" or off-season, which often include breakfast or free parking. $124-$139.

Dolores Park Inn $$ Castro: 3641 17th St. (Church/Dolores), SF, 415/621-0482. Former airline employee Bernie Vielwerth has run this gorgeous, ornate B&B since 1987. Chock full of fine antiques and Oriental rugs, the two-story Italianate Victorian mansion was built in 1874 by the Dorland family and features a subtropical garden in front, a sunny patio in back, and twin lion statues guarding the entry. No wonder celebrities like Tom Cruise have chosen to stay here. Rooms have queen-size beds, color TVs, clock radios, and shared baths. Full breakfast served. Two-night minimum stay. German and Spanish spoken. $89-$189.

The Fairmont Hotel $$$$ Nob Hill: 950 Mason St. (California/Sacramento), SF, 415/772-5000; fax 415/781-3929. The Fairmont Hotel, whose stone façade gained notoriety in the 1980s when it was used in the opening credits of the TV series *Hotel*, is routinely rated the best in San Francisco. If you judge a hotel by the common facilities, this is certainly true: The lobby is an impressive space, with golden marble columns, a grand staircase, world-class art, and plush red velvet chairs. The rooms, however, vary in size, degree of luxury, and view. Eight lounges and restaurants are scattered around the building, including the kitschy Tonga Room (see Bars section) and the top-floor Crown Restaurant, which is reached by riding a glass elevator with truly breathtaking views. Room rates begin at $229 and spiral upward from there.

Golden Gate Hotel $$ Union Sq.: 775 Bush St. (Powell/Mason), SF, 415/392-3702, 800/835-1118; fax 415/392-6202. Midway between Union Square and Nob Hill lies this cozy, 23-room B&B, which may be the best value in the city. Wicker furniture, brightly painted walls, antique claw-foot tubs, and an original 1913 birdcage elevator add to the ambiance, overseen by a friendly and helpful management. The European-style rooms with a double bed and separate bath are a real bargain; the larger queen or twin rooms include a private bath. Continental breakfast and afternoon tea are included. $99-$109.

Hotel Beresford $$ Union Sq.: 635 Sutter St. (Mason/Taylor), SF, 415/673-9900, 800/533-6533; fax 415/474-0449. This is one of the more underrated hotels in the city and an especially good deal for families, since children under 12 stay free. The warmly lit rooms have a subtle, tasteful decor with private bath, honor bar, phone, and color TV. Downstairs features a Victorian parlor and the White Horse Tavern, a startlingly authentic British pub. Continental breakfast is included, and there is an adjacent public garage. $109-$119 (family rates $129-$139). Discount for senior citizens and AAA members.

Hotel Triton $$$ Union Sq.: 342 Grant Ave. (Bush), SF, 415/394-0500, 800/433-6611; fax 415/394-0555. Interior-design buffs will think they've died and gone to heaven at the Hotel Triton, where every lamp, table, bed, and chair is a work of art. No two rooms are the same, and a typical one looks more Magritte than Motel 6. Beyond the off-the-charts hip quotient, it's full of amenities like honor bars, cable TVs, room service, valet parking, and an on-site health facility. The café and restaurant are on the ground floor. $159-$299 and up.

Hyatt-Regency $$$$ Embarcadero: Embarcadero Center Five, Drumm St. at Market St., SF, 415/788-1234, 800/233-1234. For business people operating in the financial district, the Hyatt-Regency Embarcadero offers a great location at the foot of Market and California Streets. The accommodating staff adds to the attraction of this architecturally appealing hotel. Although the neighborhood is dead at night, this is the easiest place to get a cab in the whole state. *Note:* Two other Hyatt hotels—the Park and the Grand—are located nearby. $210-$315.

The Mansions Hotel $$$ Pacific Heights: 2220 Sacramento St. (Laguna/Buchanan), SF, 415/929-9444. A singular lodging experience in a city full of interesting hotels, the Mansions is a century-old historical landmark that's quirky, cozy, opulent, packed with more "stuff" than a museum, and to top it all off, (apparently) haunted. Those staying here might never see the city because one could easily spend hours exploring all the common rooms: the restaurant featuring the largest continuous scene of stained glass ever created; the parlor full of historic documents; the International Pig Museum; the Billiard Room with a giant dollhouse against the wall; and the velvet-drenched Music Room, home to a nightly magic show performance (complimentary for guests). Barbra Streisand is one of many famous guests who have been taken in by the Mansions charms. Private baths. Limited number of TVs for in-room use. Breakfast included. Reservations recommended. Rooms $139-$279, expansive suites $225-$279.

Mark Hopkins Intercontinental Hotel $$$$ Nob Hill: 1 Nob Hill (California and Mason), SF, 415/392-3434; fax 415/616-6907. For sheer physical location, few hotels in the world rival the Mark Hopkins, which sits atop the peak of Nob Hill, an imposing L-shaped lion overlooking the city. The airy, chandeliered lobby is small but usually packed with business types or conventioneers (though the hotel has, in its storied history, hosted everyone from Judy Garland to Nikita Khruschev). The 390 guest rooms, many with outstanding views, have a functional but pleasant style, and come well equipped with color TV, mini-bar, and private bath. Limousine service, 24-hour room service, and an in-house fitness room are also available. Fourteen function rooms host various meetings. Glorious views and drinks can be had on the 19th floor at the world-famous Top of the Mark Lounge. Not surprisingly, you'll pay dearly for all this privilege: rooms start at $220, and the luxury suites can top a cool grand.

The Red Victorian $$ Haight: 1665 Haight St. (Cole), SF, 415/864-1978; fax 415/863-3293. The "Red Vic" Peace Center is a unique B&B, a tranquil oasis in the general chaos of the Upper Haight. For those who seek spiritual peace as well as a good night's rest, here are 18 guest rooms, each with its own theme and design—ranging from the tiny, economy Butterfly Room with its canopied double bed and corner sink (share the "Love Bath" outside), to the Redwood Forest Room with queen bed and private bath), to the Peacock Suite, an exceptionally large and popular spot for honeymooners. Continental breakfast is included, while walking tours and "life enhancement consultants" are also available. The smiling staff is wonderfully earnest. There's a minimum stay of two to three nights on weekends and holidays; big discounts for longer stays. $76-$200.

Sherman House $$$$ Pacific Heights: 2160 Green St. (Webster/Fillmore), SF, 415/563-3600. Built in 1876, this beautiful Victorian mansion located in tony Pacific Heights nicely survived both the 1906 and 1989 quakes. Luxuriously decorated rooms, a fine chef, and a professional, personable staff make this charming spot one of the city's most sought-after destinations. With only 12 rooms, the hotel recommends making reservations months in advance for popular weekends. $310-$775.

Sir Francis Drake Hotel $$$ Union Sq.: 450 Powell St. (Sutter), SF, 415/392-7755, 800/227-5480; fax 415/395-8559. A 1928 historic landmark that sits mere feet from Union Square, the Sir Francis Drake attracts business travelers as well as an international set. The dramatic staircase leading up to the glittering lobby of mirrors, marble, and chandeliers hints at the elegance within, but the rooms are relatively affordable given the location. Most feature cherry wood and mahogany furniture, air-conditioning, cable TV, telephones with voice mail, and a clock radio. Scala's Bistro is on the ground floor, and Harry Denton's Starlite Room, with its spectacular views of the city and the bay, is on the top floor. Reservations recommended. $165-$229.

Victorian Inn on the Park $$$ Western Addition: 301 Lyon St. (Fell), SF, 415/931-1830, 800/435-1967; fax 415/931-1830. This enormous Victorian across the street from the Panhandle features a warm atmosphere reminiscent of 1890s elegance (at 1990s prices). Guest rooms are simultaneously cozy and ample, full of touches like frilly lace curtains, Victorian furniture, and poster beds; each one includes a private bathroom, and TVs are provided by request. The common areas of the house are almost as interesting: dark hallways with deep red carpeting, a gloriously ornate sitting room and library, and an oak-paneled dining room where a generous continental breakfast is served each morning. The neighborhood, however, is somewhat nondescript. $124-$174.

White Swan Inn $$$ Union Sq.: 845 Bush St. (Mason/Taylor), SF, 415/775-1755, 800/999-9570; fax 415/775-5717. Part of a statewide collection of country inns, the White Swan's richly decorated Laura Ashley-style interior will make you'll swear you're in England instead of Nob Hill. Rooms are swathed in rose-printed wallpaper and feature mahogany poster beds, lace curtains, and mantle clocks over the fireplaces. A gracious staff serves a complimentary country breakfast in the elegant basement parlor, which is a adjacent to a wood-paneled library straight out of *Masterpiece Theatre*. Books, magazines, newspapers, afternoon tea, concierge, and countless other amenities are available. $150-$250; ask about special deals.

The Willows Inn $$ Castro: 710 14th St. (near Church/Market intersection), SF, 415/431-4770; fax 415/431-5295. Even though it's self-described as "gay-oriented," owing to its proximity to the Castro, this relaxing inn welcomes a diverse and international clientele with rustic willow furnishings and Laura Ashley bedding. Each room has a phone, alarm clock/radio, and robes to wear to the separate bath facilities. A healthy breakfast and a morning newspaper are brought to your room; sherry and chocolates are served at night. Off-street parking is available, and reservations are recommended for weekends, holidays, and the Gay Pride parade. $78-$125.

Getaways

MARIN ★★

Marin County is just north of San Francisco, extending from the Golden Gate Bridge up the coast to Bodega Bay and inland to the wine country. With the most hot tubs per capita in the United States, one of the highest per-capita income levels, and notable residents like the surviving members of the Grateful Dead and the principals at LucasFilms Productions, Marin has earned a reputation for being quintessentially Californian. It is also home to some of the most stunning scenery in the Bay Area. With such abundant open space and natural beauty, outdoor activities dominate the list of things to do in the county.

Basic Information

Golden Gate National Recreation Area: National Park Service, Fort Mason Building 201, Franklin and Bay sts., SF, 415/556-0560. • M-F 9:30am-4pm.

Marin County Visitors Bureau: 30 N. San Pedro Rd. #150 (Hwy 101), San Rafael, 415/472-7470. • M-F 9am-5pm.

Mill Valley Chamber of Commerce: 85 Throckmorton Ave. (Miller/Blithedale), Mill Valley, 415/388-9700. • M-Tu, Th-F 10am-4pm.

Sausalito Chamber of Commerce: Village Fair Shopping Center at 777 Bridgeway 4th Fl. (Caledonia), Sausalito, 415/332-0505. • M-F 11:30am-4pm.

Getting There

From the Peninsula, go to San Francisco and over the Golden Gate Bridge onto Hwy 101. Hwy 101 is the main traffic artery through Marin and a major commuter route into the San Francisco during rush hour. Traffic headed south on Hwy 101 can also get ugly on weekend evenings, when all of the hikers, picnickers, and wine tasters are heading back into the city. (A $3 bridge toll is collected from southbound traffic.) If you're in no hurry, Hwy 1, which clings to the coastline, is a scenic, if excruciatingly curvy and slow, alternative to Hwy 101.

Both Golden Gate Transit and Blue and Gold Fleet provide ferry service from San Francisco to Marin; bus service is provided by Golden Gate Transit. The schedules are geared to commuters' needs, and serve most Marin cities and towns, and even some beaches. San Francisco has a city bus, the number 76, which goes to the Marin Headlands on Sundays and some holidays. See Transportation chapter for more information on these companies and services.

Angel Island-Tiburon Ferry: 415/435-2131. Family-run ferry located at 21 Main Street in Tiburon. During summer, Ferries to Angel Island run M-F 10am-3pm; Sa-Su 10am-5pm; call for current off-season schedule. Round-trip tickets to Angel Island are $6 adults, $4 children ages 5-11, $1 bikes.

Greyhound Bus: 800/231-2222, 415/453-0795. There is a terminal in San Rafael at 850 Tamalpais Avenue.

Sights & Attractions

Marin Headlands ★★: Take Hwy 101 to Alexander Avenue, the first exit north of the Golden Gate Bridge. Go left under the highway and follow Conzelman Road up the hill. Encompassing most of the hills and valleys inland from the Pacific Coast north of the bridge, the Marin Headlands' grassy hills offer amazing views, while wildflowers and wildlife fill the valleys. The area is a war legacy, home to military installations active until the end of WWII. Battlements and bunkers still dot the hilltops.

Halfway up Conzelman Road, a dirt road on the left leads hikers and bikers down to **Kirby Cove,** a secluded beach almost under the bridge. If you'd like to camp here, you must make reservations by calling the **Park Service** at 415/561-4304. As you continue up Conzelman Road, bear left at the Y-intersection and continue to the top to reach **Battery 129**, a typical military relic. Hike up to the top of **Hawk Hill** for great views, but if it's a sunny weekend, expect a crowd. Continue on Conzelman west to **Point Bonita**. The still-functioning **Point Bonita Lighthouse** was one of the first to be built on the West Coast. It is open Sa-Su 12:30pm-3:30pm and for special guided tours; call the Headlands Visitors Center (see below) for schedules and reservations. The road past Point Bonita loops into Rodeo Valley, where you'll find **Rodeo Lagoon** (good for birding), **Rodeo Beach** (scenic but too rough to swim), and the **Marine Mammal Center** 415/289-SEAL (7325), a hospital for marine critters that allows visitors daily 10am to 4pm.

Marin Headlands Visitors Center: Bunker Rd., at the end of Rodeo Valley, 415/331-1540. The center houses engaging hands-on exhibits in the historic Fort Barry Chapel. A small store sells maps and books about the area.

Sausalito ★: Take Hwy 101 to Alexander Avenue and follow it into town. Sausalito lies across Hwy 101 from the Headlands. Originally a fishing village and then an artists' retreat, Sausalito is now a typical tourist town. Located on the edge of the bay, it has a marina and a main commercial street lined with a variety of coffeehouses, waterfront restaurants, galleries, and T-shirt shops. Ferry service operates between Sausalito and San Francisco (see Transportation chapter).

Downtown offers shops and a boardwalk. On the water a little north of town sits a fascinating collection of **houseboats**, more house than boat (locals call them floating homes). Nearby at 2100 Bridgeway, there's the **San Francisco Bay Model** (see Amusements below). Over Labor Day weekend, the Marin Ship Park is the site of the **Sausalito Arts Festival** (see below).

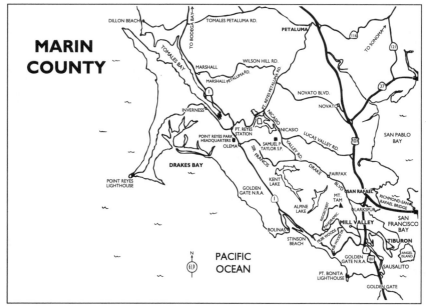

For adventurous types, Sausalito offers many water activities. **Sea Trek Adventures** launches ocean kayaks for tours of Sausalito harbor and beyond. Their Full Moon Tour is a favorite. If you prefer sailing, try **Cass' Rental Marina**. For more information, see the Sailing and Kayaking sections. If you would rather sit back and have someone do the sailing for you, the **Hawaiian Chieftain** 415/331-3214 is a large square-rigged top-sail ketch built in the style of the 1790s. The ship's offices are at 3020 Bridgeway #266. For a bird's eye view of Marin and the bay, stop by **San Francisco Seaplane Tours** 888/SEAPLANE (732-7526) just off Hwy 101, four miles north of the Golden Gate Bridge at the Shoreline Hwy. exit.

Sausalito Arts Festival: Marin Ship Park next to the Bay Model Visitors Center, 415/332-3555. This high-end juried arts and crafts festival features the work of almost 250 local, national, and international artists. Arts and crafts for sale include jewelry, ceramics, oil paintings, and photographs. Live music, children's entertainment and activities, and food booths are also featured. Held for three days over Labor Day weekend, the festival draws huge crowds.

Bay Area Discovery Museum: 557 East Fort Baker (off Alexander Ave.), Sausalito, 415/487-4398. Created solely with kids in mind, this museum, found under the north tower of the Golden Gate Bridge, features dozens of hands-on exhibits where children can engage in activities from rowing on a boat crew to exploring underneath a house. • School year Tu-Th 9am-4pm, F-Su 10am-5pm; Summer Tu-Su 10am-6pm. $7 adults; $6 children; free under age 1; first Th of each month free.

San Francisco Bay Model: 2100 Bridgeway, Sausalito, 415/332-3870. A working facsimile built by the Army Corps of Engineers to study the bay. • Tu-F 9am-4pm; Sa 10am-6pm. Free.

Tiburon ★: Take Hwy 101 to Tiburon Boulevard east. A small pay-parking lot at the very end of the road is the best place to ditch your car. If you're bicycling, follow the lovely bike path, which begins along Bridgeway in Sausalito and goes north along the bay to Tiburon Boulevard. A right turn leads you to town. There is also ferry service from San Francisco (see Transportation chapter). Spanish for "shark," Tiburon lies on a fin-shaped peninsula north of Sausalito. There isn't much in the way of tourist attractions; most people go to eat at one of the restaurants with a view of the bay and San Francisco (see Restaurants below). A small waterfront park has great views of San Francisco and inviting grass for picnics. The stores and galleries on **Ark Row** at the west end of Main Street will happily deplete your savings.

Mill Valley ★: Take Hwy 101 to Tiburon Boulevard/East Blithedale exit and go west, following the signs to downtown Mill Valley. Once home to the mill that processed the huge trees used to build San Francisco, Mill Valley is now quintessentially Marin: a hip bedroom community with cute cottage houses, good food, coffee, and lots happening in the arts. Each autumn the **Mill Valley Film Festival** 415/383-5256 brings the town to life. The town is also a convenient base of operations for expeditions to Mount Tam, which rises to the west. **Start to Finish Bicycles** 415/388-3500 at 116 Throckmorton Avenue in downtown Mill Valley rents mountain bikes for $35 to $50 a day for exploring the mountain.

Mount Tamalpais ★★: At 2,600 feet, Mount Tam dominates the landscape and offers spectacular views of the Bay Area, plus an enormous trail system. Within its vast expanse lie **Mount Tamalpais State Park** 415/388-2070, **Muir Woods National Monument** (see below), and the **Marin Municipal Water District** 415/924-4600 or 415/459-5267. The diverse terrain includes redwoods, oak, and grassland. A quick way to sample Mount Tam is to drive to the top. Take Hwy 101 to Hwy 1, bear right on Panoramic Highway, and follow the signs to Mount Tam and Muir Woods. At Pantoll Road, turn right and wind your way to the top. From the parking lot ($5 fee), walk up a short, steep dirt road for the ultimate view. Close to the summit you will find the **Sydney B. Cushing Memorial Theater**, a 5,000-seat outdoor amphitheater that hosts musical productions by the **Mountain Play Association** (see Arts & Entertainment below).

The extensive trail network on all sides of the mountain offers endless possibilities for exploring and lets you approach from any angle. (Some trailheads now require a $5 parking fee.) The excellent Olmstead Bros. map, *Trails of Mount Tamalpais and the Marin Headlands,* is available in most bike shops and bookstores. Limited camping is possible. Bikes can be rented in San Anselmo at **Caesar's Cyclery**, 29 San Anselmo Avenue, 415/258-9920. Keep in mind that bikes are allowed only on fire and paved roads and that speed limits and one-way routing are strictly enforced.

Muir Woods ★★: Take Hwy 101 to Hwy 1, bear right on Panoramic Highway, then turn left down Muir Woods Road. The park is about a mile down the road on your right, 415/388-2595. One of the only places you can find old-growth, coastal red-woods in Northern California, Muir Woods is the forest primeval. The towering, thousand-year-old trees block out most of the sunlight, leaving the narrow valley cool and tranquil. Muir Woods attracts its well-deserved crowd; you can avoid the throngs somewhat by going during the week or in the winter, when the creeks are filled with water. A short loop winds its way along a stream bed among towering redwoods; this walk of less than an hour is what most visitors choose to explore, so even on week-ends you can find solitude by taking the steeper trails away from the valley floor. A few trails are paved and wheel-chair accessible. Picnicking, biking, and camping are forbidden in the park. **The Visitors Center** is open daily from 9am to 6pm in the summer and until 5pm the rest of the year. Visitors over 17 pay a $2 entrance fee.

Muir Beach ★: Take Hwy 101 to Hwy 1 and follow the signs. After six miles on Hwy 1 you will see the **Pelican Inn**. To reach Muir Beach, turn left. This small beach is locat-ed in an isolated, semicircular cove cut into the cliffs. The surf is generally too rough for swimming. A small grassy area has some picnic tables and barbecue grills. The rugged hills in the background attract mountain bikers, hikers, and horseback riders.

Stinson Beach ★★: Follow directions to Muir Beach, but continue straight past the Pelican Inn for six miles and follow the signs to the left. Stinson is a very happening place; a wide spit of sand perfect for running, Frisbee, or sand castles. The parking lot has sheltered picnic spots, and a small settlement at the entrance includes shops and restaurants where you can fill out your picnic, rent a surfboard, or pop down oys-ters and beers under an umbrella. **Off the Beach Boats** 415/868-9445 rents open-top kayaks for experts to use in the surf and for the rest of us to use in Bolinas Lagoon; rates start at $15 for two hours, $27 all day. They also rent surfboards, boogie boards, and sailboats. Add a little culture to your day at the beach with a production of **Shakespeare at the Beach** (see Arts & Entertainment below). Be forewarned: Stinson Beach has a huge following, and on hot weekends traffic gets backed up for miles. You can avoid the crowds and find parking if you go early. Call ahead for fog, surf, and traffic information 415/868-1922 or 415/868-0942.

Point Reyes National Seashore ★★★: Take Hwy 101 to Sir Francis Drake Boulevard to Hwy 1, turn right and then immediately left, and follow the signs to the Park Headquarters. At the northern edge of Marin lies this spectacular park, ideal for hik-ing, camping, and beachcombing. The 75,000-acre expanse contains numerous well-marked trails through forest and coastal territory, while the ten-mile stretch of beach is full of caves, cliffs, waterfalls, and windy headlands.

Information is available at the **Bear Valley Visitors Center** 415/663-1092. The vis-itors center is a good place to pick up maps or walk through the exhibits on park wildlife before setting out. Nearby is the **Earthquake Trail**, a **Miwok Village** re-cre-ation, and **Morgan Horse Ranch**. The popular **Bear Valley Trail** leads hikers through four fairly flat miles to Arch Rock. From Arch Rock you can enjoy the beautiful view of the ocean, or take the lower trail to the beach and walk through Miller Cave if it's low tide. For a strenuous three-mile hike, take Bear Valley Trail to the Sky Trail, which ascends Mount Wittenberg, the highest point in Point Reyes. From there, you can continue down to the coast; then return either via the same route, or, to avoid Mount Wittenberg, along the beach to Arch Rock and back.

If you want to bike in Point Reyes, you can rent mountain bikes at **Trailhead Rentals** in Olema, 88 Bear Valley Rd., 415/663-1958. Weekday bike rentals are $6 for two hours or $20 per day; weekend rentals are $7.50 for two hours or $24 per day. Call ahead for reservations and information (only open during the summer). Tents, cameras, and binoculars can also be rented.

If you prefer horseback riding to mountain biking, there are a few ranches along Hwy 1 which rent horses. **Five Brooks Ranch Horse Rental** at 8001 Hwy 1 in Olema, 415/663-1570, offers guided trail rides and hay rides. They are conveniently located at the Five Brooks Trailhead entrance to the Point Reyes National Seashore. Reservations recommended.

Point Reyes Lighthouse ★★★: Take Sir Frances Drake Boulevard to the end. The lighthouse sits at the very tip of the Point Reyes peninsula. Bring binoculars to watch California gray whales during their biannual migrations in late November through early January and March through April. Sea lion sightings are more common. The lighthouse, located down a long set of stairs on a steep cliff, is open Th-M 10am-4:30pm; it is closed when the wind is too strong. The visitors center is open Th-M 10am-5pm. The weather can be cold, foggy, and extremely windy, but when it's clear, the **views** ★★★ are spectacular.

Drake's Bay Beach (watch for the left turn off Sir Francis Drake a few miles before the lighthouse) is located on the south side of the Point Reyes peninsula. The beach is backed by towering cream-colored cliffs. Along the way, you'll pass through the sleepy town of **Inverness**, which has bed-and-breakfasts, restaurants, and a grocery store.

Finally, **Tomales Bay** is a 15-mile inlet created by movement along the San Andreas Fault. A great way to explore the bay is by kayak. See Sea Kayaking section of Sports chapter for more information.

Places to Eat

Picnic Supplies

Boudin Bakery ¢: 1 Main St. (Tiburon Blvd.), Tiburon, 415/435-0777. Enjoy sourdough bread and sandwiches at the bright corner café, or eat them on the lawn outside enjoying the view of Angel Island. • M-F 6:30am-8pm; Sa 7am-10pm; Su 7am-8pm.

Johnson's Drake's Bay Oysters: 17171 Sir Francis Drake Blvd., turnoff 6 miles past Inverness on the way to the lighthouse, 415/669-1149. At this bayside oyster farm, you can see how oysters are cultivated, then buy some to take home. Shucked oysters are sold by the pint or the quart; oysters in the shell go by the dozen or the thousand.

Marin French Cheese Factory: Petaluma-Pt. Reyes Rd. (about 9 miles west of Novato), Petaluma, 707/762-6001. They make Camembert, Schloss, and Brie cheeses under the Rouge et Noir label; sold along with sandwiches and other picnic foods. The factory is set on a farm and offers a bucolic picnic area complete with a pond. Call for information about tours.

Mill Valley Market: 12 Corte Madera Ave. (Throckmorton), Mill Valley, 415/388-3222. This grocery store caters to well-heeled Mill Valley gourmets in search of excellent cheese, pâté, and such. Complete a picnic by choosing from their extensive bread and wine selections.

Restaurants & Cafés

Avenue Grill ★★ $$ 44 E. Blithedale Ave. (Sunnyside), Mill Valley, 415/388-6003. The Avenue Grill brought upscale American comfort food to Marin before it was commonplace, and still enjoys a loyal following despite claims of inconsistent execution. The large front windows brighten the convivial bistro setting, complete with requisite yellow walls and white tablecloths. On rainy days, turn to comfort foods like meat loaf with gravy and garlic mashed potatoes or barbecued honey-glazed pork loin with coleslaw. • Su-Th 5:30-10pm; F-Sa 5:30-11pm.

Bubba's Diner ★★ $$: 566 San Anselmo Ave. (Tunstead/Bridge), San Anselmo, 415/459-6862. This tiny diner has been a runaway success, drawing huge crowds willing to wait for a seat in a Naugahyde booth or at the counter. The menu focuses on authentic American comfort food. Tender pork chops with mashed potatoes show a refined touch, as does the hamburger served on a fresh-baked bun with homemade mayonnaise. Finish with a milk shake or apple pie. Breakfast offers some of the best food—don't miss the pancakes—and longest lines. • M, W-Th, Su 8am-2pm, 5:30-9pm; F 8am-2:30pm, 5:30-9:30pm; Sa 8am-2pm, 5:30-9:30pm.

Buckeye Roadhouse ★★ $$$: 15 Shoreline Hwy. (Hwy 101), Mill Valley, 415/331-2600. The Buckeye Roadhouse, along with Fog City Diner in San Francisco, Mustards Grill in Napa, and a growing list of others, is part of peripatetic chef Cindy Pawlcyn's burgeoning kitchen empire. It serves expensive new American cuisine—grilled pork chops with mashed potatoes, fantastic onion strings, strawberry short-cake—although not always as good as that found at some of her other outposts. If duck is on the menu, try it. The wait staff is professional, but highly sales oriented. Reservations highly recommended. • M-Th 11:30am-10:30pm; F-Sa 11:30am-11pm; Su 10:30am-10pm.

Caffè Trieste ★ ¢: 1000 Bridgeway (Caledonia), Sausalito, 415/332-7770. This suburban branch of the famous North Beach hangout serves the same fantastic, pricey cappuccino and cheesecake, plus decent pizza and pasta, in a cramped jumble of tiled tables. The low brick wall outside serves as a resting and posing point for the many bicyclists passing by. No credit cards. • Daily 7am-midnight.

Depot Bookstore and Café ★ ¢: 87 Throckmorton Ave. (Miller), Mill Valley, 415/383-2665. This tiny café, located in a charming old train station in the center of town, got the bookstore-café combination down before Borders and Barnes & Noble invaded. Inside you'll find a small, erudite bookstore and a basic café. If you take a table outside at which to devour your new book along with a latte and pastry, you'll have a view of local slackers playing hackey-sack on the square. • Su-M 7am-9pm; Tu 7am-10pm; Th 7am-9pm; F-Sa 7am-10pm; food until one-half hour before closing.

Dipsea Café ★ $: 200 Shoreline Hwy. (Tennessee Valley Rd.), Mill Valley, 415/381-0298. Most people come to this country cottage hall overlooking a breezy tidal inlet near the road to Tennessee Valley to enjoy home-cooked brunches, salads, and sandwiches. The walls are covered with pictures of the Dipsea Race, a grueling cross-country run from Mill Valley to Stinson Beach—and back for the Dipsea Double. Load up on carbs and give it a try. • M-F 7am-3pm; Sa-Su 7am-4pm.

Drake's Bay Beach Café ★ $: 1 Drake's Bay Beach Rd., Point Reyes National Seashore near lighthouse, 415/669-1297. Warm and cozy, serving fried, barbecued, and stewed Johnson's oysters, along with more typical seaside café favorites. • Daily 10am-6pm (closed Tu-W in winter).

Gray Whale Pub & Pizzeria ★ $: 12781 Sir Francis Drake Blvd., Inverness, 415/669-1244. Pizza, beer, coffee drinks, and a variety of cakes, pies, and pastries. • Summer M-F 11am-9pm; Sa-Su 8:30am-9pm (open daily during the rest of the year but with reduced hours).

Guaymas ★★ $$: 5 Main St. (Paradise/Tiburon Blvd.), Tiburon, 415/435-6300. Located in picturesque Tiburon, Guaymas is a little taste of Mexico on an American waterfront. Start with the *platillo de entremeses*, an assortment of South of the Border appetizers. An order of *camarones de Guaymas* delivers one pound of mesquite-grilled shrimp that have been marinated in lime juice and cilantro. The handmade tortillas and the margaritas are not to be missed. You can sit indoors or on the outdoor (heated in the winter) patio overlooking the water, for a meal or just drinks. Guaymas is also a good stopover when you are returning on the ferry from nearby Angel Island. Keep in mind that the wait can be long. • M-Th 11:30am-10pm; F-Sa 11:30am-11pm; Su 10:30am-10pm (open a half hour later in summer and closes a half hour earlier in winter).

Lark Creek Inn ★★★ $$$: 234 Magnolia Ave. (William), Larkspur, 415/924-7766. One of the most perfect places on earth. Situated in a Victorian house next to a wooded brook, the rustic dining room is understated and charming, the service is flawless, and the food is heavenly home cooking elevated to new heights: Yankee pot roast; oak-barbecued country spareribs with roasted potatoes, red garlic, and coleslaw; and homemade butterscotch pudding. Plus the best Sunday brunch ever. (The only distraction is the shameless hawking of Lark Creek Inn memorabilia on the menu.) Reservations a must on weekends. • M-Th 11:30am-2pm, 5:30-9:30pm; F 11:30am-2pm, 5-10pm; Sa 5-10pm; Su 10am-2pm, 5-9pm.

Left Bank ★★★ $$: 507 Magnolia St., (Ward), Larkspur, 415/927-3331. This is the second restaurant of chef Roland Passot, whose La Folie in San Francisco has been consistently rated one the city's best for years. In keeping with the locale, this Marin venture is a large, casual brasserie—yellow walls, French posters, white tablecloths, and all. Simple classics dominate the menu: steak with *pommes frites,* roast chicken, duck confit, steamed mussels. The large patio makes a lovely al fresco dining spot. The reasonably priced wines match the affordable food. Reservations recommended. • Su-M 11:30am-10pm; Tu-Th 11:30am-11pm; F-Sa 11:30am-midnight.

Manka's Inverness Lodge ★★★ $$$: 30 Callendar Wy. (take Sir Francis Drake to Argyle), Inverness, 415/669-1034. Manka's California wild-game menu draws rave reviews for the excellent renditions of venison, elk, and wild boar, much of it cooked over an open grill. In keeping with its seaside locale, seafood is also excellent. The building is an old hunting lodge that captures the feel with roaring fires, overstuffed chairs, and board games from another era. Reservations recommended. • Daily 6-9pm.

Marin Brewing Company ★ $: 1809 Larkspur Landing Cir. (Sir Francis Drake), Larkspur Landing, 415/461-4677. This large, immensely successful brew pub offers high-quality microbrews and a varied menu ranging from wood-fired pizza to Asian salads to pub grub. Located in the Larkspur Landing Shopping Center across from the ferry terminal, it attracts a loud after-work crowd. Reservations recommended if you want to bypass the bar on the way to your table. • Daily 11:30am-midnight.

Mikayla at Casa Madrona ★★ $$$$: 801 Bridgeway (Caledonia), Sausalito, 415/331-5888. Casa Madrona's most noteworthy feature is the spectacular view of San Francisco Bay and the city itself. The food, a mix of California and Continental, is also quite good. Start with polenta in a wild mushroom sauce, then move on to grilled salmon with balsamic vinaigrette, striped bass with leek cream sauce, or rack of lamb. Meals are served in a romantic dining room. The perfect spot for a Sunday brunch, the room has a tropical theme and a retractable roof for sunshine without blustery breezes. • M-Sa 6-9:30pm; Su 10:15am-2:15pm, 6-9:30pm.

Mountain Home Inn ★★ $$: 810 Panoramic Hwy. (Hwy 1), Mill Valley, 415/381-9000. On the slopes of Mount Tamalpais, the rustic Mountain Home Inn feeds hungry hikers and tourists great breakfasts on the weekends and dinners all week. Enjoy the view from the outdoor deck during the day and position yourself near the cozy fireplace in the evening. You pay for the wonderful atmosphere, but the food is pretty good, especially the outdoor brunch. Brunch is not served when the weather is bad. Reservations recommended. • Daily 11:30am-3:30pm, 5:30-9pm.

Parkside Café and Snack Bar ★★ $: 43 Arenal Ave. (Calle del Mar), Stinson Beach, 415/868-1272. The Parkside Café is closer to the beach than any of the other Stinson Beach restaurants. In keeping with the local architectural canon, it's a small cottage with a large patio that appeals to the beach-bound crowd. Food is a cut above that offered by the neighbors and consists of basic but fresh breakfasts and lunches, with inexpensive family-style Italian and seafood dinners. A snack bar dispenses burgers and fries to those who can't wait to start tanning. • Tu-W 7:30am-2pm; Th-M 7:30am-2pm, 5-9:30pm.

Pelican Inn ★ $$$: 10 Pacific Wy. (Hwy 1 at Muir Beach turnoff), 415/383-6000. A rambling Tudor-style bed and breakfast with an authentic British pub and rather formal dining room (tall folks will have to hunch down to avoid the low-timbered beams). Stop for a pint and some darts on your way back from the beach. Unfortunately, the food is as authentically British as the architecture: bangers and eggs, shepherd's pie, prime rib, and the like. On Sundays a lunch buffet is served. Be sure to wander the lovely gardens. Reservations only for groups of six or more. • Tu-Th 11am-3pm, 6-9pm; F 11am-3pm, 5:30-9:30pm; Sa 11:30am-3:30pm, 5:30-9:30pm; Su 11:30am-3:30pm, 5:30-9pm.

Rice Table ★★ $$: 1617 4th St. (G St.), San Rafael, 415/456-1808. Indonesian food doesn't share the same high recognition level that Thai or Vietnamese food does in America, but this immensely popular restaurant is doing its part to change that. Many of the dishes on the short menu are familiar from other Southeast Asian restaurants: the ubiquitous *satay* skewered meat and chicken with peanut sauce, *lumpia* spring rolls, and hearty curries. *Rijstaffel*, a banquet of sampler dishes with rice, will look familiar to those who've been to Amsterdam, where this former colony's cooking enjoys a large following. The authentic batik decorations in the rattan-lined room will make Deadheads feel at home. • W-Sa 5:30-10pm; Su 5-9pm.

Royal Thai ★★ $$: 610 3rd St. (Irwin), San Rafael, 415/485-1074. One of Marin County's most beloved restaurants, Royal Thai fits traditional Thai restaurant charm into a cozy Victorian house. The encyclopedic menu features an extensive range of dishes. Most dishes are pretty good, although the pad Thai is a standout. • M-F 11am-2:30pm, 5-10pm; Sa-Su 5-10pm.

Sam's Anchor Café ★★ $$: 27 Main St. (Tiburon Blvd.), Tiburon, 415/435-4527. Sam's is famous for the huge waterfront deck—featured in the movie *Nine Months*—where the Corona beer crowd comes to hang out and scarf burgers, fries, and deep-fried seafood. Its location also makes it a popular place for yachters to dock for snacks. It's the place to go for people watching and flirting on a sunny day. At night, the seafood menu gets more expensive, but not necessarily better. Look for familiar combinations of pasta, steak, seafood, and chicken. • M-Th 11am-10pm; F 11am-10:30pm; Sa 10am-10:30pm; Su 9:30am-10pm.

Sand Dollar ★ $$: 3458 Hwy 1, Stinson Beach, 415/868-0434. Quite the all-American beach restaurant with sandwiches, burgers, seafood, and pasta. The cozy bar inside is a local hangout—the gossip is juicier than the food—while the patio can be a scene for postfraternal San Francisco singles. Sit in the sun, sip a beer, and slurp some local oysters while you admire tan lines. • M-Th 11:30am-3pm, 5:30-9pm; F-Sa 11:30am-3pm, 5:30-9:30pm; Su 11am-3pm, 5:30-9:30pm.

Station House Café ★★ $$: 11180 Hwy 1 (2nd St.), Point Reyes Station, 415/663-1515. Warm and homey, the Station House Café is a favorite for wholesome preparations featuring local ingredients, especially fresh seafood and delicious brunches. Some of the kitchen's classics include steamed mussels, barbecued oysters, and corn bread. The country-casual dining room is a welcoming spot for hungry hikers returning from a day in the park. The garden is perfect for dining al fresco. Reservations suggested on weekends. • Su-Th 8am-9pm; F-Sa 8am-10pm.

Stinson Beach Grill ★ $$: 3465 Hwy 1, Stinson Beach, 415/868-2002. Burgers, seafood, and Southwest and Italian cuisines are all served in a beach house with a big deck. The food is passable, but most people come for the relaxing beach-hangout atmosphere after roasting in the sun or freezing in the fog. • M-Sa 11:30am-8:30pm; Su 11am-9pm.

Sushi Ran ★★★ $$: 107 Caledonia St. (Turney), Sausalito, (415) 332-3620. Without a doubt, Sushi Ran is the best sushi bar in Marin, and possibly the whole Bay Area. Though the restaurant is a well-guarded secret, you'll still wait up to an hour for a table on weekend nights. Don't be deterred, though; just get a bottle of warm sake or a large Japanese beer and linger on the patio until space opens up. Situated next to the newly refurbished Marin Theater, it's a great place for a bite before or after a movie. Bring a full wallet, because it's not cheap. Reservations essential. • M-F 11:45am-2:30pm, 5:30-11pm; Sa 5:30-11pm; Su 5-10:30pm.

Sweden House Bakery ★ $: 35 Main St. (Tiburon Blvd.), Tiburon, 415/435-9767. Delicious, authentic, and pricey Swedish baked goods are available here, plus substantial breakfasts and sandwiches. Try the Swedish pancakes (rolled crêpes) served with lingonberries, or French toast made with Swedish limpa bread, apple butter, walnuts, sour cream, and syrup. The small waterfront patio offers a saner alternative to Sam's and Guaymas. • M-F 8am-5pm; Sa-Su 8am-7pm (later in summer).

Taqueria La Quinta ★ ¢: 11285 Hwy 1 (3rd St.), Point Reyes Station, 415/663-8868. Point Reyes Station is an unlikely place for a budget-priced burrito shop, but here it is. It's not a Mission district taqueria—the clean interior is almost upscale—but it does a pretty good job with the basic soft tacos, burritos, and tostadas, and it's cheap and quick. No credit cards. • Su-M, W-Sa 11am-8pm

Thep Lela ★★★ $$: 411 Strawberry Village, Mill Valley, 415/383-3444. Surprise! Some of the best Thai food in the Bay Area is served in this strip mall eatery. While the location may be suburban, the restaurant itself is exotically decorated with ornate wood carvings, a mural of a Thai village, and low tables (with a hole cut in the floor). The brilliantly dressed waiters are gracious and efficient. The chefs have perfected the Thai art of blending sour, salty, spicy, and herbal flavors. Subtly flavored dishes include yellow, red, or green curry with your choice of meat, seafood, or tofu. The pad eggplant with shrimp is delicious, and the coconut milk soup earns rave reviews. Reservations recommended; if the restaurant is full, ask the staff to set up a table for you on the sidewalk. • M-Sa 11am-3pm, 5-10pm; Su 5-10pm

Tutto Mare ★★ $$: 9 Main St. (Tiburon Blvd.), Tiburon, 415/435-4747. Similar to neighboring Guaymas, but with an Italian fishing village theme. Sporting the same impressive views and outdoor deck, Tutto Mare appears to enjoy an equally enthusiastic following. The restaurant is split between the starkly casual downstairs "taverna," where diners pick from a limited menu of wood-fired pizzas, salads, and shellfish, and a more formal upstairs space with a full menu. The menu features many unusual seafood and pasta dishes such as spaghetti with a cuttlefish ink sauce and tortellini filled with sardines, currants, fennel, and pine nuts. The food can be inconsistent. • M-Th 11:30am-10:30pm; F 11:30am-11pm; Sa 11am-11pm; Su 11am-10:30pm.

Arts & Entertainment

Marin County Civic Center: 3501 Civic Center Dr. (N. San Pedro Rd. exit off Hwy 101), San Rafael, 415/499-6400, box office/events information 415/472-3500. This Frank Lloyd Wright–designed municipal center houses county government offices, a theater, and the Marin Veterans Memorial Auditorium. All of the performing arts are showcased here. This is the home of the **Marin Symphony**, the **Marin Opera Company**, the **Marin Ballet's** perennial production of "The Nutcracker," and the Golden Gate Geographic Travel Film Series.

Mountain Play Association: E. Ridgecrest Blvd., on Mount Tam, 415/383-1100. Close to the summit of Mount Tam is the **Sydney B. Cushing Memorial Theater**, a 5,000-seat outdoor amphitheater that hosts excellent musical productions by the **Mountain Play Association** in May and June—call for dates. Advance ticket purchases are usually necessary.

Shakespeare at the Beach: 415/868-9500. Next to the post office in Stinson Beach. Dress warmly and bring a picnic to one of the weekend evening performances during the summer.

Places to Stay

Camping & Hostels

Camping is available on most of the public lands in Marin. Many of the sites are walk-in, and most require reservations, sometimes months in advance.

AYH Point Reyes Youth Hostel: Limantour Rd., Point Reyes National Seashore, 415/663-8811. Located two miles from the ocean in a secluded valley near hiking trails and the estuary. You'll probably want to cook your own food here, but shop before you arrive, since the stores are an eight-mile trek from the hostel. Call for reservation information 7:30am-9:30am; 4:30pm-9:30pm. $12 adults, $6 children.

Marin State Parks District Office: 7665 Redwood Blvd., Suite 150, Novato, 415/893-1580. Supervises local state parks: Samuel Taylor, Angel Island, and Mount Tamalpais. For reservations, call Park.Net CA (see below). Open M-F 8am-5pm.

Park.Net CA: 800/444-PARK (7275). Takes state park reservations two days to seven months in advance. www.park-net.com.

Point Reyes National Seashore: Bear Valley Visitors Center, Bear Valley Rd. just west of Olema, 415/663-8054. Backpack sites only. Coast Camp is shortest hike (two miles each way). Wildcat Camp is also near the beach. Glen Camp and Sky Camp lie inland. Reservations required; call M-F 9am-2pm up to 2 months in advance. Free.

Samuel Taylor State Park: Sir Francis Drake Blvd., Lagunitas, 415/488-9897. Typical state park car camping: closely packed loops under the trees, plenty of facilities. Ranger kiosk open Su-Th 8am-8:30pm; F-Sa 8am-10pm. For reservations, call Park.Net CA (see above).

Steep Ravine Environmental Cabins: Mount Tamalpais State Park, Hwy 1, 1 mi. south of Stinson Beach. Rustic cabins on bluff overlooking ocean, with platform beds, woodstoves, and pit toilets. Water nearby, but no electricity. Camping allowed. (For reservations, call Park.Net CA (see above). $35 per cabin, $10 per campsite.

Hotels, Motels, Bed & Breakfasts, and Houses

Marin has a bounty of bed and breakfasts, quaint inns, and charming hotels. While it would be nice to drive around until you find one that catches your eye, reality is that they book up quickly, especially in the summer and on weekends. Make sure you have a reservation before you arrive—the following referral and reservations lines will help you find a place to your liking.

Bear Valley Inn Bed and Breakfast $$: 88 Bear Valley Rd., Olema, 415/663-1777. Three-room Victorian ranch house in Olema one-half mile from the Point Reyes National Seashore. The staff promises to pamper guests with great food and old-fashioned hospitality. Rents mountain bikes, too. $85-$135; $10 off midweek.

Bed & Breakfast Exchange of Marin: 45 Entrata, San Anselmo, 415/485-1971. Referrals and reservations for homestays, private cottages, and small inns.

Blackthorne Inn $$$$: 266 Vallejo Ave., Inverness, 415/663-8621. A unique lodging experience in a beautiful handcrafted tree house, complete with fireman's pole and spiral staircase, tucked in a secluded wooded canyon adjacent to the park. There are five rooms, a deck, a hot tub, and a full breakfast served every morning. Hiking trails are nearby. $175-$225.

Casa Madrona $$$: 801 Bridgeway, Sausalito, 415/332-0502. Deluxe, (mostly) historic inn built into hill above town. $138-$269.

Coastal Getaways: 415/485-2678. Lists availability only.

Coastal Lodging of West Marin: 415/663-1351. Referrals and reservations for bed and breakfasts in Point Reyes.

Fairwinds Farm Bed & Breakfast Cottage $$: Balboa Rd. off Hwy 1, Inverness, 415/633-9454. The cozy wood cottage will sleep up to eight—kids would love the loft. A fireplace and down comforters ward off the chilly fog which stalks Inverness Ridge. Demand for the cabin was so great that the family now rents their son Dan's room (don't worry, he's left home). His diploma and portrait still hang on the wall. Barnyard animals and cats napping in the sun next to the hot tub complete the idyllic scene. Call for reservations and directions. Cabin $135; Dan's Room $91.

Inns of Marin: 70 2nd St., Point Reyes Station, 415/663-2000, 800/887-2880. Lodging referrals and reservations for Point Reyes National Seashore.

Inverness Lodge/Manka's $$$: Corner of Callendar and Argyle rds., Inverness, 415/669-1034. Hunting lodge–style rooms and cabins, some with decks overlooking Tomales Bay. $135-$365; breakfast extra.

Mountain Home Inn $$$: 810 Panoramic Hwy., above Mill Valley, 415/381-9000. Charming old lodge on slopes of Mount Tam. Some rooms offer fireplace and Jacuzzi. $139-$259.

Pelican Inn $$$$: Hwy 1, Muir Beach, 415/383-6000. Cozy, English-style pub at entrance to Muir Beach. $173-$198 (includes full English breakfast); call 4 to 6 months in advance for Sa reservations!

Ten Inverness Way $$$: 10 Inverness Way, Inverness, 415/669-1648. Built in 1904, a quaint four-room inn with a stone fireplace, a hot tub, a sun room, and a flower garden. Full breakfast is served. $145-$180.

West Marin Vacation Rentals: 11150 Sir Francis Drake Blvd., Point Reyes Station, 415/663-1776, 800/540-1776. Vacation home rentals.

MENDOCINO ★★

Mendocino is the jewel in the crown of the Northern California coast. Built on a wide bluff that juts out into the ocean, the town enjoys dramatic views of the gorgeous, rocky coastline on three sides. Mendocino looks like a Maine fishing village, with its white, New England-style houses and clapboard church. In keeping with this old-fashioned charm, few establishments post their street numbers, so pick up a good map before exploring. Throughout the summer and on holiday weekends, the community fills with tourists, so off-season visits are the most pleasant (and less likely to be fogbound), though many visitors' services may be closed during mid-week.

Ten miles north of Mendocino is **Fort Bragg**, a large town catering to the lumber industry. Fort Bragg lacks the charm of its southern neighbor, but provides many of the everyday practicalities that are either unavailable or high-priced in Mendocino.

Fort Bragg-Mendocino Chamber of Commerce: 800/726-2780, 707/964-3153.

Getting There

To see as much as possible, take Hwy 1 in one direction and Hwy 101 the other. (Avoid following the former northward in the late afternoon—the sun can be a formidable adversary.) The most scenic route from San Francisco is to take the San Anselmo/Sir Francis Drake exit off Hwy 101 and go west on Sir Francis Drake Boulevard until it intersects Hwy 1 in Olema. From there, it's about three hours to Mendocino (see the *Inland Mendocino* section for inland directions, a somewhat quicker route). Without a car, your best bet is to rely on **Mendocino Transit Authority** 800/696-4MTA (4682) or 707/462-5765, which provides bus service to, from, and along the Mendocino coast; service includes a daily bus to Santa Rosa where you can use Golden Gate Transit or Amtrak buses to reach San Francisco (see Transportation chapter for more information on these companies).

Sights and Attractions

Parks and Preserves ★★

For information about these and other parks, contact the visitor center at Russian Gulch State Park (see below), open M-F 8am-5pm.

Mendocino Headlands State Park ★: General information 707/937-5804; Fort House Visitors Center 707/937-5397. The Headlands wrap around the southwest side of the town, providing a spectacular landscape of sea stacks sculpted by dramatic waves. This spot is great for hiking, tide-pooling, and whale watching.

Van Damme State Park ★: Hwy 1 about 3 mi. south of Mendocino, 707/937-4016. This park is made up of 1,800 acres covered with redwood trees and offers excellent camping (with a popular 71-site campground), a small beach for swimming, and several hiking trails that wind through pygmy forests, dense fern thickets, and a bog (the 2.5 mile Fern Canyon Trail is best). This park is especially popular with abalone divers. $5.

Russian Gulch State Park ★: Hwy 1 about 1.5 mi. north of Mendocino, 707/937-5804. Home to the **Devil's Punch Bowl**, a blowhole that sends the surf shooting skyward when the ocean is stirred up. Camping is available (30 sites), and from the park's headlands overlooking a wide bay, you can observe migrating whales in the winter. $5.

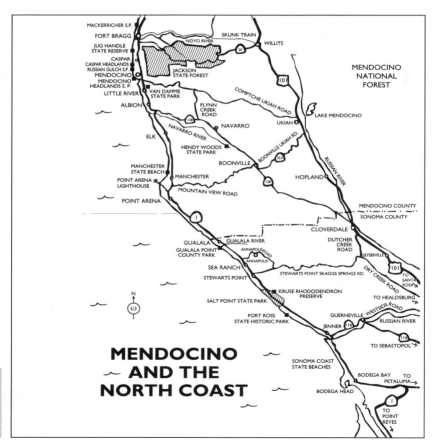

**MENDOCINO
~ AND THE
NORTH COAST**

Jug Handle State Reserve ★: Hwy 1 about 3 mi. north of Mendocino. Home to the "ecological staircase trail" that traces the geological and natural history of the area, from the beach to the redwoods. Here you can study 100-foot terraces carved by ocean waves, with each "step" 100,000 years older than the one below.

Mendocino Coast Botanical Gardens ★★: 18220 N. Hwy 1 about 7 mi. north of Mendocino, 707/964-4352. This 17-acre park is an ideal place to explore the ecologi-cally-rich coastal environment. You can enjoy the well-manicured gardens (with over 10,000 plant varieties) and spectacular bluff views in an hour's stroll, but spend an afternoon if you have time. $6.

MacKerricher State Park ★: Hwy 1 about 3 mi. north of Fort Bragg. This is the largest coastal state park in the area, featuring one of northern California's lengthiest beach-es, stretches of wildflower fields, and a freshwater lagoon. Take the short trail to Laguna Point, where migrating whales can be spotted from December through April; it's also a good vantage point to watch harbor seals playing. MacKerricher also features a 140-site campground, complete with full bathroom facilities and beach access. $5.

Other Activities ★

Catch a Canoe & Bicycles, Too! ★: Just south of Mendocino at Comptche-Ukiah Road, 707/937-0273. Rents and sells mountain bikes, canoes, and kayaks. Canoe trips from their dock on the Big River estuary provide glimpses of otters and blue herons, as well as secluded picnic spots along the river banks. Tandem canoes or kayaks rent for $16/hour or $44 /day.

Charter Boats ★: Several sport-fishing and whale-watching charter boats are anchored in **Noyo Harbor**, just south of Fort Bragg. Optimal whale watching occurs between December and March. The best fishing is during the summer and fall when the salmon are running. Many of the boats go out twice a day. Try **Anchor Charters** 707/964-3854 with rates starting at $45 per person for fishing excursions (including poles and bait) and $20 per person for a two-hour whale watching trip (only during whale migration season).

Ricochet Ridge Ranch ★: 24201 N. Hwy 1 about 3 mi. north of Fort Bragg across from MacKerricher State Park, 707/964-7669. Ricochet leads two-hour group horse-back trips on the beach as well as private rides. Rides start at $35/person.

Skunk Train ★: Foot of Laurel St., Fort Bragg, 707/964-6371. A good foggy day activi-ty is a ride on the aptly-named Skunk Train, which pulls out of Fort Bragg from the California Western Railroad depot for a 40-mile scenic journey through towering red-wood forests and over precarious gulches to Willits—where the skies could be cloud-free. The train makes day-long runs ($35 adults, $18 ages 3-11), as well as half-day trips ($25 adults, $13 ages 3-11). Advance reservations suggested.

Hot Tubs and Saunas ★: The local idiom for hot-tubbing on the North Coast is "soak." Beneath a renovated water tower next door to Café Beaujolais, **Sweetwater Gardens**, 955 Ukiah St., 707/937-4140 offers massages for the hike-weary and private hot tubs for $12/hr per person. For end-of-the-day bonding, there's an enormous group tub where, for $8 per person, you can soak as long as you want. Bring your own towels and save a buck. • Open M-Th 2pm-11pm; F-Su noon-11pm.

Places to Eat

Albion River Inn ★★ $$$: 3790 Hwy 1, Albion, 707/937-1919. Diners come for the excellent meals and the panoramic views of the Pacific. Dishes tend toward simple preparations of fresh local ingredients—such as grilled salmon, roast chicken, and gar-lic mashed potatoes. Reservations recommended. • Su-Th 5:30-9pm; F-Sa 5-9:30pm.

D'Aurelio & Sons ★ $: 438 S. Franklin St. (Chestnut, behind Rite-Aid), Fort Bragg, 707/964-4227. Good Italian food at reasonable prices. No credit cards. • Daily 5-9pm.

Ledford House ★ $$: 3000 N. Hwy 1, Albion, 707/937-0282. The dining room offers great vistas of the coast from its perch on Salmon Point. House specialties are country French: rack of lamb, roast duck, and so forth, all in rich sauces. Romantic diners will want to sit by a window to bill and coo and enjoy the view. • W-Su 5-9pm.

Little River Inn ★ $$: 7751 Hwy 1, Little River, 707/937-5942. An inn with a good reputation for its casual restaurant, and a long porch where you can sip a drink and watch the sunset with no obligation to dine later. Basic dishes might include red snapper with butter, lemon, and parsley, or charbroiled breast of chicken marinated in fresh ginger and soy sauce. The Swedish hotcakes are popular at breakfast. • M-Sa 7:30-10:30am, 6-8:45pm; Su 7:30am-1pm, 6-8:45pm.

Little River Restaurant ★★ $$$: 7750 N. Hwy 1 (attached to the market and post office), Little River, 707/937-4945. Among the better coastside eateries, the Little River Restaurant serves sumptuous meals in a cozy atmosphere. Preparations taking advantage of fresh local ingredients include poached salmon with tarragon cream sauce, broiled quail with hazelnut-port sauce, and steamed mussels. You give up the spectacular views found at other establishments, but the first-class food is delicious compensation. The dining room seats only about a dozen, so reservations are a must. No credit cards. • Seatings at 6pm and 8:30pm; winter F-M; summer F-Tu.

MacCallum House Restaurant/Grey Whale Bar & Café ★★ $$$: 45020 Albion St. (Lansing), Mendocino, 707/937-5763. A B&B that serves memorable meals. The dining area is split between the comfortable dining room and somewhat cramped café. Both share a menu of well-executed California cuisine. Hearty soups like seafood chowder and innovative pastas are the menu highlights. Entrées feature typical North Coast items like wild salmon and free-range chicken. Reservations recommended. • F-Tu 5:30-9pm (in summer, usually open earlier and close later).

Mendo Burgers ★ $: 10483 Lansing St. (Ukiah), Mendocino, 707/937-1111. Serves every kind of burger under the sun, including veggie, beef, chicken, fish, and turkey versions. • Daily 11am-7pm.

Mendocino Bakery & Café ★ ¢: 10485 Lansing St. (Ukiah), Mendocino, 707/937-0836. The pastries here are every bit as fresh as the local gossip you're bound to catch a whiff of at this local favorite. • Daily 7:30am-8pm.

Mendocino Café ★ $: 10451 Lansing St. (Albion), Mendocino, 707/937-2422. You can find some stellar offerings at reasonable prices here, although the waits can be long (reservations only for groups of five or more). The husband-and-wife owners comb the globe for new tastes which they successfully inject into their California cuisine repertoire. The place boasts a sunny deck to boot. • M-Th 11am-4pm, 5-9:30pm; F 11am-4pm, 5-10pm; Sa 10am-4pm, 5-10pm; Su 10am-4pm, 5-9pm.

Mendocino Market ¢: 699 Ukiah St., Mendocino, 707/937-FISH/3474. Locals' choice for deli supplies and sandwiches. • Daily 10am-6:30pm.

Moosse Café ★★ $$: 390 Kasten St. (Albion), Mendocino, 707/937-4323. Of course, in a place originally named the Chocolate Moosse Café, the desserts are sure to be decadently delicious. But this quaint restaurant also serves excellent appetizers and entrees. The mainly American menu includes salads, savory soups, pasta, and comfort foods such as roast chicken and short ribs. Lunch can be taken in Adirondack chairs in the front yard, and all dishes can be toted for a picnic in a park. No credit cards. • M-Sa 11:30am-4pm, 5:30-9:30pm; Su 9:30am-4pm, 5:30-9pm.

North Coast Brewing Co. ★ $: 444 N. Main St. (Pine/Main), Fort Bragg, 707/964-3400. This local brew pub serves excellent, freshly brewed beer; sample their renowned Red Seal ale. The food tends toward pub-grub standards like fish and chips, chili, and burgers. • Su, Tu-Th noon-9:30pm; F-Sa noon-10pm (bar open until 11pm).

Tote Fête ¢: 10450 Lansing St., Mendocino, 707/937-3383. Gourmet picnic fixings. • M-Sa 10:30-7pm; Su 10:30am-4pm.

Places to Stay

Since condo developments don't exist in the Mendocino architectural canon, and hotel chains have been banished, bed-and-breakfasts and quaint inns have a monopoly on accommodations. **Mendocino Coast Reservations** 707/937-1913 handles bookings for about 20 B&Bs and a number of vacation homes in the area. For a comprehensive list of all lodging possibilities, contact the **Fort Bragg-Mendocino Coast Chamber of Commerce** at 800/726-2780, they'll mail you brochures galore.

Most of the parks listed in the Parks & Preserves section above allow camping, though policies vary between different parks, and reservations are highly recommended. Call **Park.Net** 800/444-PARK (7275) or **Mendocino State Park Headquarters** 707/937-5804.

Albion River Inn $$/$$$$: 3790 Hwy 1, Albion, 707/937-1919. A gracious inn located on a bluff overlooking the Albion River. Twenty cottages on the river's edge offer deluxe accommodations, most with decks and some with Jacuzzis. $170-$260.

Brewery Gulch Inn $$: 9350 Hwy 1, 1 mi. south of Mendocino, 707/937-4752. Recognizable by the water tank on Hwy 1, this place is set amidst beautiful gardens. $85-$135.

Cypress Cove $$$: 4520 Chapman Dr., Mendocino, 707/937-1456. Offering a view of Mendocino Bay and the town itself, each of these two modern suites offers a deck, fireplace, and kitchenette. They are superbly located one mile south of town, very convenient to outdoor activities such as golf and canoe rentals. $170-$190.

Glendeven Inn $$$: 8221 N. Hwy 1, Little River, 800/822-4536, 707/937-0083. A rustic country inn with well-kept grounds, hearty breakfasts, and an adjacent gallery with shows by local artists. $100-$200.

Heritage House $$$/$$$$: 5200 N. Hwy 1, Little River, 707/937-5885. This historic B & B—popularized in the film *Same Time Next Year*—is located in a sprawling but spruced-up farmhouse with cottages dotted around it. The rather formal dining room caters primarily to guests, although the Heritage House now offers lodging without meals. Cottages $125-$350 ($243-$468 inclusive of meals).

Inn at Schoolhouse Creek $$: 7051 N. Hwy 1, Little River, 707/937-5525. Located south of town on Hwy 1, with three lodge rooms and two cottages which sleep four. $100-$160.

John Dougherty House $$$: 571 Ukiah St. (Kasten), Mendocino, 707/937-5266. A taste of New England, this 1867 Cape Cod-style house is located right in the midst of Mendocino village. The antiques are an elegant touch. $95-$205.

Jug Handle Farm & Nature Center ¢: 15501 Hwy 1 about 4 mi. north of Mendocino, 707/964-4630, 707/964-9912. The real lodging bargain in the Mendocino area is this spacious red farmhouse. They provide simple accommodations indoors, as well as campsites and primitive cabins nearby, for $18 to $25 per person per night ($12 to $15 with a student ID). Bring bedding or sleeping bags, towels, and anything else you might need. Bathrooms and showers are provided, and there is a kitchen available for guests' use. Everyone who spends the night is asked to perform an hour of work, which can mean chopping wood, sweeping, or gardening; guests can avoid the work by paying an extra $5 per night. Call ahead for reservations.

MacCallum House Inn $$$: 45020 Albion St. (Kasten/Lansing), Mendocino, 707/937-0289. An interesting B&B, part of which occupies a restored barn. $75-$180.

McElroy's Inn $$: 998 Main St. (Evergreen), Mendocino, 707/937-1734. A low-priced B&B located in the heart of town. $70-$110.

Mendocino Farmhouse $$: Comptche-Ukiah Rd., off Hwy 1, Mendocino, 707/937-0241. This inland B&B offers privacy and a break from the fog. $85-$130.

Mendocino Hotel $$/$$$$: 45080 Main St. (Lansing/Kasten), Mendocino, 800/548-0513, 707/937-0511. A large Victorian establishment with high-end offerings. $85-$275.

Mendocino Village Inn $$: 44860 Main St. (Evergreen/Howard), Mendocino, 707/937-0246. A cozy choice, this 1882 Victorian looks like it was transplanted right from Martha's Vineyard. $65-$90.

Reed Manor $$$$: Little Lake St. and Palette Dr., Mendocino, 707/937-5446. A recent construction (1990), this lodge offers its own breed of elegant accommodations. Some rooms have balconies overlooking either the ocean or the inn's lovely garden. $175-$350.

Sea Gull Inn $$: 44594 Albion St. (Lansing/Howard), Mendocino, 707/937-5204. A charming, centrally-located hostelry with inexpensive accommodations in downtown Mendocino. $40-$150.

Stanford Inn by the Sea/Big River Lodge $$$: Comptche-Ukiah Rd., off Hwy 1, Mendocino, 800/331-8884 or 707/937-5615. The best features of a B&B with the amenities of a larger hotel, including an indoor pool and hot tub, and resident llamas. Each room has a fireplace and TV. $215-$275.

Whitegate Inn $$$: 499 Howard St. (Ukiah), Mendocino, 707/937-4892. This romantic inn offers little details that make a stay memorable: flowers, fruit, and chocolates in each guest room; wine and hors d'oeuvres every evening in the parlor. $119-$229.

Sonoma & Mendocino Coasts ★★

The coastline from Marin County to southern Mendocino County is sparsely populated, but dotted with state parks, public beaches, and a good supply of offbeat restaurants and lodgings. Hwy 1 rolls through the bucolic farms and pastures that border the **Pt. Reyes National Seashore,** and up along **Bodega Bay,** the setting for Alfred Hitchcock's *The Birds*. **Bodega Head** is known as a fine whale-sighting promontory in the wintertime.

Sonoma Coast State Beaches ★★: Once you've reached Bodega Bay, sandy beaches punctuate the coast every few miles and make inviting rest stops. For more information on Bodega Bay and the Sonoma Coast State Beaches, contact the **Salmon Creek Ranger Station** at 707/875-3483.

Salt Point State Park ★: 25050 Hwy 1, Jenner, 707/847-3221. Further north you'll find a primal landscape that is just beginning to recover from a recent fire. The park has a campsite ($5 per night) popular with abalone divers. Within the park is the **Kruse Rhododendron State Preserve ★★**, with 300-plus acres of wild rhododendrons (they're particularly spectacular in April and May). Look for the entrance on the east side of Hwy 1.

The Sea Ranch: 888/732-7262, 707/785-2371. An award-winning planned community with vacation homes for rent throughout the year. Close to the ocean, the **Sea Ranch Lodge** at 60 Sea Walk Drive also has rooms if you're not into group housing; tariffs run between $140 and $205.

Gualala: A bit further north, this town (pronounced wah-la-la) is the area's commercial center. Activities in the Gualala vicinity include bike riding, wine tasting, and sea kayaking. **Adventure Rents** 45450 Hwy 1 (just north of the Chevron station in the middle of Gualala), 707/884-4386, rents bikes ($30/day) and kayaks (single kayaks rent for $30/day, doubles for $60/day). During summer they are generally open daily 10am to 5:30pm, but you should call ahead to confirm that they are not out in the field. The **Annapolis Winery,** 26055 Soda Springs Rd., 707/886-5460, is set back seven miles in the hills high above the wind and fog. You'll find complimentary tastings and picnic grounds with a sunny view of the coast. Open Daily noon to 5pm.

Places to Eat

Roadhouse Café ★ $: 6061 Hwy 1, Elk, 707/877-3285. Locals come to this unprepossessing eatery—it's attached to the owner's husband's auto repair shop—for inexpensive, hearty breakfasts and lunches. No credit cards. • Summer: Th-Su 9am-3pm, 6-9pm (call for winter hours).

St. Orres ★★★ $$$: 36601 S. Hwy 1, Gualala, 707/884-3303. An eye-catching onion dome sits atop the towering, three-story wall of windows that dominates the dramatic dining hall in this inn. The French-meets-California cuisine relies heavily on complex game dishes like medallions of venison sauced with huckleberries and Zinfandel, and wild boar stuffed with dates and walnuts and served with apple ginger chutney. If you're looking for something less carnivorous, choose from lighter dishes that might include mussels on black pasta or a grilled vegetable tart. The wine list is excellent. Make reservations well in advance, but if you get stuck with a late hour, come early anyway to catch the sunset from the porch. No credit cards. Reservations recommended. • Su-F 6-8pm; Sa 8:15-10pm.

Places to Stay

Elk Cove Inn $$$: 6300 S. Hwy 1, Elk, 707/877-3321. This 1883 Victorian house features ocean views (there are also four freestanding cabins near the main building) and private access to an adjacent state beach. $98-$278.

Greenwood Pier Inn $$$: 5928 Hwy 1, Elk, 707/877-9997. A cluster of cottages perched above a cut in the ocean cliffs. Gorgeous gardens and dazzling views complement the eclectic decor. $110-$235.

St. Orres $$/$$$: 36601 S. Hwy 1, Gualala, 707/884-3303. The Russian-looking restaurant also offers inexpensive rooms and rustic, secluded cabins. $60-$150.

Sandpiper House Inn $$$: 5520 S. Hwy 1, Elk, 707/877-3587. A charming 1916 ocean-front home, this inn offers private beach access and afternoon tea. $130-$220.

This is it! $$: Off Hwy 1 on Mtn. View Rd. btwn. Pt. Arena and Manchester State Beach, 707/882-2320. A cottage in the redwoods with its own kitchenette and hot tub. $75.

Inland Mendocino ★

The other route to Mendocino involves more cross-country driving but the trip is about an hour shorter than the coastal trip. Stay on Hwy 101 to Cloverdale, where you pick up Hwy 128. This road winds through vineyards, serene golden hills, and redwoods as it cuts across the Anderson Valley. Once Hwy 128 hits the coast, it's just another ten miles north on Hwy 1 to Mendocino. To go to Hopland, continue on Hwy 101 past Cloverdale for about 15 miles. To then reach Mendocino, either backtrack to Cloverdale or continue north on Hwy 101 to Lakeport, where you follow Hwy 253 west until it meets Hwy 128 in Boonville.

Restaurants and Hotels

Boonville Hotel ★★ $$$: 14050 Hwy 128 (Lambert), Boonville, 707/895-2210. This Victorian-era hotel sports a lively, informal restaurant overlooking gardens. During the day, they dish up a taqueria menu. At night, the kitchen serves an inventive menu that celebrates California cuisine. Light eaters can enjoy gourmet pizzas, while those looking for more formal offerings will enjoy chicken breast with corn tomatillo red pepper salsa. Don't miss the rack of lamb when it is featured. Reservations recommended. • M 6-8:45pm; W-Su 11:30-2:30pm, 6-9pm.

Buckhorn Saloon (Anderson Valley Brewing Company) ★ $: 14081 Hwy 128, Boonville, 707/895-BEER (2337). Some scruffy locals add authenticity to this stalwart tavern, although the large redwood deck is a far cry from a grubby saloon. The Buckhorn is famous for serving some of the best microbrewed beer around. The country lunches and dinners—burgers, fish and chips, fresh fish—are well suited to the house libations. • Summer: M-F 11am-9pm; Sa-Su 11am-10pm; Winter closed Wed.

Mendocino Brewing Company ★ $: 13351 S. Hwy 101, Hopland, 707/744-1361. This brew pub is home to the ever-popular Red Tail Ale, as well as such other ornithological derivatives as Black Hawk Stout and Peregrine Pale Ale. With a laid-back, wisteria-draped, beer-garden atmosphere, this establishment has good bar food and music on Saturday nights. For dessert, stop next door at the Cheesecake Lady for a delicious slice of their namesake specialty. • Daily 11am-9pm; bar Su-Th until 11pm; F until midnight; Sa until 2am.

MONTEREY, CARMEL, & BIG SUR ★★

Monterey & Pacific Grove ★★

Monterey is home to the famous Cannery Row and the Monterey Bay Aquarium, as well as the many special events it hosts every year—including golf tournaments and jazz, blues, Dixieland, and squid festivals. The town also celebrates the famous people who once called the area home, including John Steinbeck and Robinson Jeffers.

Next to Monterey on the tip of its eponymous peninsula sits the city of Pacific Grove. Founded by Methodists in 1875, Pacific Grove has the distinction of being the last dry town in California, with alcohol legal only since 1969. It is nicknamed "Butterfly City, USA" because thousands of migrating monarch butterflies winter here.

Monterey Peninsula Chamber of Commerce: 380 Alvarado St. (Franklin), Monterey, 408/649-1770. 24-hour information hotline. • Office open M-F 8:30am-5pm.

Tourist Information: 408/624-1711; room reservations 800/847-8066.

Getting There

Depending on traffic, it takes from one to one and a half hours to get to Monterey from San Jose; tack on another 15 minutes if you're going to Carmel and an additional half hour to reach the heart of Big Sur. There are two routes: the first is I-280 to Hwy 17 south to Santa Cruz, then Hwy 1 south. This drive takes a little longer, but it is more scenic and there are other attractions along the way. A quicker alternative is to take Hwy 101 south to Hwy 156 south through Castroville, then Hwy 1 south.

Sights and Attractions

Cannery Row ★: Along the waterfront off Lighthouse Rd. just west of the Presidio, Monterey. Once known as the sardine capital of the world, Cannery Row is the street immortalized in John Steinbeck's novel of the same name. In 1945, Monterey's 19 canneries packed more than 235,000 tons of fish. Cannery Row still stands—but in its current incarnation as a shopping bazaar, now it's tourists that are packed together like sardines. A principal attraction is the Monterey Bay Aquarium (see below). Nearby sights include an historic carousel, wax museum, and **Fisherman's Wharf,** just off Del Monte Avenue. Some of the many restaurants and shops there have been operated by the same families for generations. From December to early April, whale-watching tours depart from the wharf for close-up views of the migrating sea mammals.

Monterey Bay Aquarium ★★★: 886 Cannery Row, Monterey, 408/648-4888; advance tickets 800/756-3737. This state-of-the-art wonder provides a comprehensive view of the bay, from the sloughs to the deep sea. To the left of the entrance is the **California Kelp Forest** exhibit; don't miss feeding time at this 335,000-gallon tank. Though you'll have plenty of company with all the international visitors, the mesmerizing petting pools and special exhibits of jellyfish and schools of silvery sardines will prove unforgettable. The latest addition to the aquarium is the **Outer Bay** exhibition, designed to simulate open ocean conditions in an enormous tank with tuna, ocean sunfish, and stingrays. Outside, take in the beauty of the bay itself and watch sea otters lounge on the rocks. • Daily 9:30am-6pm. $14.95 adults; $11.95 seniors, students, ages 13-17; $6.95 ages 3-12.

Monterey State Historic Park ★★: Around Custom House Plaza, Lighthouse Rd. and Del Monte Ave., Monterey, 408/649-7118. This park manages a collection of historic structures located throughout the city. Stop by the headquarters at 20 Custom House Plaza behind Fisherman's Wharf for a free, self-guided tour map and listing of each

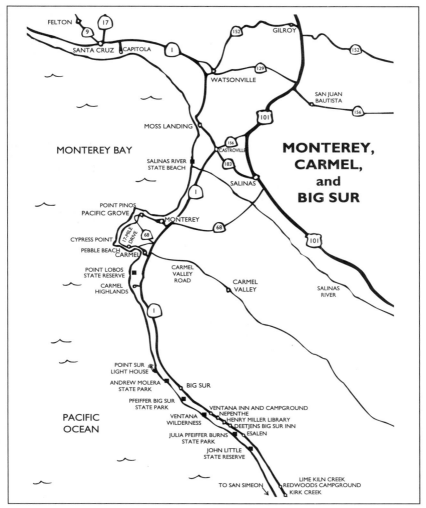

building's hours. Included on the tour are several fine old adobes, some with beautiful patios and gardens from the early whaling days of the city when it was still owned by the King of Spain. A $5 two-day pass covers admission to four houses. A $2 walking tour leaves daily from Stanton Center on the Plaza at 10:15am, 12:30pm, and 2:30pm.

Maritime Museum ★: Stanton Center, Custom House Plaza, Monterey, 408/373-2469. Displays artifacts from Monterey's whaling days. • Daily 10am-5pm. $5.

Monterey Peninsula Museum of Art ★: 559 Pacific St. (Madison), Monterey, 408/372-5477. Has a diverse collection with an excellent selection of Western art, including several Charles M. Russell cowboy statues. • W-Sa 11am-5pm (third Th of the month until 7:30pm); Su 1-4pm. Free.

Colton Hall ★: Friendly Plaza, Pacific and Jefferson sts., Monterey, 408/646-5640. An architectural gem well worth visiting, this is where California's first constitution was crafted in 1849.

Pacific Grove ★★: On the way to Pacific Grove, check out Ocean View Boulevard, also known as **Three-Mile Drive ★★** (begin at Cannery Row past the aquarium) for one of the best views of the region. Continuing beyond the aquarium you'll find the **American Tin Cannery**, 125 Ocean View, 408/372-1442, with over 40 factory outlets. Further along the coast are **Shoreline Park**, **Marine Gardens Park**, and **Lover's Point Beach**, all great spots to picnic. Follow the ocean to **Point Piños Lighthouse and Museum**—408/375-4450 for private tours; 408/648-3116 for group tours—the oldest operating lighthouse on the West Coast. Open to the public for tours Th-Su 1-4pm. **Doc's Great Tidepool**, a favored spot for microcosmic marine exploration, is at the base of the lighthouse. Check out more tide pools, as well as wind-sculpted cypress trees, at **Asilomar State Beach**.

Pacific Grove Museum of Natural History ★: Central and Forest aves. (turn on Forest from Lighthouse), Pacific Grove, 408/648-3116. One of the finest natural history museums in the country, it highlights local species, including sea otters and over 400 varieties of birds; be sure to visit the Butterfly Tree. • Tu-Su 10am-5pm. Free.

17-Mile Drive ★★: 408/649-8500. You can get to this renowned attraction from Sunset Drive in Pacific Grove, Hwy 1 south of Monterey, or Ocean Avenue in Carmel. The famed scenery of this drive includes fancy houses, (many of them featured in Alfred Hitchcock films), the golf courses in exclusive **Pebble Beach**, the picturesque lone cypress, and Crocker Grove, a 13-acre pine and cypress natural reserve. $7.25/car (refundable if you eat, play golf, shop, etc. along the way—keep any receipts). You'll see enough romantic rocks and crashing waves to last you a lifetime.

Outdoor Activities ★

Monterey's **scuba diving ★★** is ranked among the best in Northern California, and there are plenty of local dive shops ready to serve your needs. **Sea kayaking ★★** is also very popular here, and there are several places that rent boats and offer tours. See Sports chapter for more information.

Boat Charters ★: Monterey Sport Fishing, 96 Fisherman's Wharf (Del Monte), 408/372-2203, has various deep-sea fishing packages and also offers a 45-minute sightseeing cruise of Monterey Bay ($7 per person, weekends only) and seasonal whale-watching trips. **Randy's Fishing Trips**, 66 Fisherman's Wharf, 408/372-7440, also offers numerous excursions.

Bicycle/Moped Rental ★: For the land-bound, biking and mopeding are popular and fun. **Monterey Moped Adventures**, 1250 Del Monte at Fisherman's Wharf, 408/373-2696, has both bikes and mopeds for rent (open weekends only). **Joselyn's**, 638 Lighthouse Avenue (Hoffman/Prescott), 408/649-8520), is another source for bicycle rentals. **Bay Bikes**, 640 Wave Street, 408/646-9090 rents mountain bikes and surreys—four-person pedal bikes. You can take off right behind the store on a bike path that follows the coast to Pacific Grove and 17-Mile Drive.

Golf Courses ★★★

The Monterey area is a mecca for world-class golf courses. See Golfing section.

Places to Eat

Amarin Thai Cuisine ★ $: 807 Cannery Row, Monterey, 408/373-8811. Traditional Thai specialties like *satay*, pad Thai, and curries, at decent prices in a casual atmosphere. • Daily 11am-9pm.

Clock Garden ★ $: 565 Abrego St. (Pearl), Monterey, 408/375-6100. A great place to eat breakfast outdoors. The food is imaginative, delicious, and reasonably priced. • M-F 11am-3:30pm, 5-9pm; F-Sa 11am-3:30pm, 5-10pm.

Fandango's ★★ $$: 223 17th St. (Lighthouse), Pacific Grove 408/372-3456. Multiple fireplaces and bars, plus plenty of fresh flowers heighten the warmth of this Mediterranean restaurant with a major wine list and textbook versions of paella and bouillabaisse. • Daily 11am-3pm, 5-9:30pm.

The Fishwife at Asilomar Beach ★★ $$: 1996½ Sunset Dr. (Fillmore), Pacific Grove, 408/375-7107. Seafood with a Caribbean flair. • M-F 11am-10pm; Sa 10am-10pm; Su 9am-10pm.

Fresh Cream ★★ $$$: Heritage Plaza, Building 100, 408/375-9798. A spiral staircase leads to bar and dining rooms of this showroom for French and California cuisine. Amazing crème brûlée and excellent poultry and seafood dishes. Great artwork on the walls is another plus. • Daily 6-9pm (later if busy).

Gianni's Pizza ★ $: 725 Lighthouse Ave., Monterey, 408/649-1500. The best pizza in Monterey—worth the wait. • Su-Th 4-10pm; F-Sa 11:30am-11pm.

Monterey's Fish House ★★ $$: 2114 Del Monte Ave. (Casa Verde), Monterey, 408/373-4647. An East Coast–style seafood restaurant—basic but good. Grilled or blended with pasta, the fish is fresh and tasty. • M-F 11:30am-2:30pm, 5:30-9:30pm; Sa-Su 5:30-9:30pm.

Montrio ★★ $$$: 414 Calle Principal (Franklin), Monterey, 408/648-8880. This former firehouse houses a pleasant restaurant serving first-rate California cuisine. Look for well-executed standards such as seared ahi tuna salad and grilled mahi mahi. • M-Th 11:30am-10pm; F-Sa 11:30am-11pm; Su noon-10pm.

O'Kane's Irish Pub ★ $: 97 Prescott St. (Wave), Monterey, 408/375-7564. Irish hospitality is in abundance here. A better-than-average pub scene. • Daily 11am-midnight.

Old Bath House Restaurant ★★ $$$: 620 Ocean View Blvd. (17th), Pacific Grove, 408/375-5195. One of Pacific Grove's finest restaurants, it serves steak, chicken, seafood, and killer desserts in a charming Victorian overlooking the ocean. A top place for romantic dining and for feasting on turn-of-the-century antiques and decor. • M-F 5pm-midnight; Sa 4-11pm; Su 3-11pm.

Pepper's Mexicali Café ★★ $: 170 Forest Ave. (Central), Pacific Grove, 408/373-6892. Good, authentic Mexican fare. • M, W-Sa 11:30am-10pm; Su 4-10pm.

Phil's Fish House & Eatery ★ $: 7640 Sandholdt Rd., Moss Landing, 408/633-2152. Just north of Monterey, Phil's is one of the only eateries in minuscule Moss Landing. Run with Sicilian warmth by its exuberant owner, Phil's turns out consummate seafood salads and pastas and is a treasure trove of fresh catches from the bay. Bring an ice chest and buy some Monterey spot prawns to barbecue over mesquite. • Daily M-Th 8:30am-8pm, F-Sa 8:30am-9pm, Su 8:30am-7pm.

Roy's at Pebble Beach ★★★ $$$$: The Inn at Spanish Bay, 2700 17-Mile Dr., Pebble Beach, 408/647-7423. Much acclaimed East-West cuisine from superstar chef Roy Yamaguchi. Never mind the great views, this is the kind of LA-style restaurant where all the glamorous fun is inside. Reservations recommended. • Daily 6:30am-10pm.

Spadaro's ★★ $$: 429 Alvarado St., Monterey, 408/372-8881. Excellent Italian food served up with a spectacular view. • Daily 11am-2:30pm, 5-10pm.

Taqueria del Mar ★ ¢: 530 Lighthouse Ave., Pacific Grove, 408/372-7887. Awesome burritos and other great Mexican dishes. • M-Sa 11:30am-8pm; Su 11:30am-4pm.

Tarpy's Roadhouse ★★ $$: Hwy 68 and Canyon Del Rey Rd., Monterey 408/647-1444. Housed in a turn-of-the-century ranch house, this is a local legend for serious game dishes, two-fisted American cuisine, and gracious courtyard dining. Comfort food abounds, as do the throngs of local diners. • Daily 11:30am-10pm.

The Tinnery ★ $$: 631 Ocean View Blvd. (17th), Pacific Grove, 408/646-1040. A bar featuring live entertainment nightly, and plenty of seafood. Also offers complete breakfasts. • M-F 8am-10pm; Sa-Su 8am-1am. Happy hour 4pm-6pm and 11pm-1am.

Toastie's Café ★ $: 702 Lighthouse Ave., Pacific Grove, 408/373-7543. A great place for breakfast. • M 6am-3pm; Tu-Sa 6am-3pm, 5-9pm; Su 7am-2pm.

Warehouse Restaurant ★★ $$: 640 Wave St. (Prescott), Cannery Row, Monterey, 408/375-1921. A very good Italian restaurant. • M-Th noon-10pm; F-Sa noon-11pm; Su 10am-10pm.

Whaling Station Inn ★★ $$$: 763 Wave St. (Prescott), Monterey, 408/373-3778. Elegant setting for an excellent continental meal. • Daily 5-10pm.

Places to Stay

A midweek or off-season stay can be substantially cheaper.

Andril Fireplace Cottages $$: 569 Asilomar Blvd. (Finex), Pacific Grove, 408/375-0994. Cottages with fully equipped kitchens and fireplaces, set among the pines. $80-$110.

Asilomar Conference Center $$: 800 Asilomar Blvd. (Crocker), Monterey, 408/372-8016. A historical landmark, right on the beach. Primarily for large groups; single rooms available. Reservations taken up to 30 days in advance. Breakfast included. $70-$90.

Beachcomber Inn $$: 1996 Sunset Dr. (Fillmore), Pacific Grove, 408/373-4769. Heated pool; a few rooms have kitchen facilities. Free bicycle rental and continental breakfast. $60-$118.

Best Western Lighthouse Lodge $$$: 1150 Lighthouse Ave. (Fillmore), Pacific Grove, 408/655-2111. A great view of (what else?) the lighthouse; Jacuzzis and in-room fireplaces. $79-$119; suites $185.

Californian Motel $$: 2042 N. Fremont St., Monterey, 408/372-5851. Some rooms have kitchens, and there's a pool and whirlpool. $49-$109.

Colton Inn $$$: 707 Pacific St. (Madison), Monterey, 408/649-6500. Rooms come with balconies, fireplaces, and whirlpool tubs. $77-$210.

Jabberwock $$$: 598 Laine St. (Hoffman), Monterey, 408/372-4777. A 1911 post-Victorian decorated in an *Alice in Wonderland* theme. Complimentary hors d'oeuvres and wine are served in the evening; milk and cookies await you at bedtime. $100-$175.

Martine Inn $$$: 255 Ocean View Blvd. (3rd/5th), Pacific Grove, 408/373-3388. A grand Mediterranean mansion overlooking the crashing surf. Full breakfast and afternoon wine and hors d'oeuvres included. $125-$250.

Merritt House $$$: 386 Pacific St. (Franklin), Monterey, 408/646-9686. A charming historic adobe with 25 adjoining new units. All rooms have fireplaces. Breakfast included. $120-$200.

Monterey Bay Inn $$$: 242 Cannery Row (Lighthouse), Monterey, 408/373-6242, 800/424-6242. A great location on the bay, plus a rooftop hot tub with a panoramic view. $119-$319.

Pacific Grove Motel $$: Lighthouse and Grove Acre aves., Pacific Grove, 408/372-3218. Centrally located, with a pool and hot tub. Refrigerators in each room. $59-$139.

Sand Dollar Inn $$: 755 Abrego St. (Fremont), Monterey, 408/372-7551. Offers a pool and spa, and includes continental breakfast. $64-$104.

Spindrift Inn $$$: 652 Cannery Row, Monterey, 408/646-8900, 800/424-6242. Pamper yourself with goose-down feather beds, fireplaces, and a rooftop garden. Complimentary continental breakfast and wine and cheese. $99-$179 for city views; $209-$289 for ocean views.

Terrace Oaks Inn $$: 1095 Lighthouse Ave., Pacific Grove, 408/373-4382. Standard, reasonably priced lodging. $60-$85.

Carmel ★

Carmel is located on Hwy 1 just south of Monterey, and is known for its array of excellent restaurants, shops, and romantic inns and bed-and-breakfasts. Accordingly, most restaurants and hotels cater to those travelers with big bank accounts. Parking is very limited in the downtown area. Local ordinances prohibit house numbers and parking meters—but you can still get a ticket from the vigilant police.

Sights and Attractions

For more activities in the area, check out the **Sunset Cultural Center**, 408/624-3996, located on San Carlos Street between Eighth and Ninth, or pick up a copy of the *Monterey Peninsula Review*, a free weekly newspaper that lists of the week's events.

Ocean Avenue ★: Carmel's main street is a window-shopper's delight, with countless specialty shops, art galleries, and boutiques. An art colony gone berserk (and a bit sour), you can't walk down a street in Carmel without encountering at least three galleries. Art lovers should investigate **Carmel Art Association Galleries** 408/624-6176 on Dolores Street between Fifth and Sixth, which tastefully displays the work of local artists and hosts major traveling exhibits.

City Beach ★★: At the foot of Ocean Avenue, the town meets the sea, explaining the downtown area's official name, Carmel-by-the-Sea. Beautiful to look at, but rough for swimming. You'll find a less populated stretch of beach south on Scenic Road.

Tor House ★: 26304 Ocean View Ave., or off Stewart Way off Scenic Rd., 408/624-1813; F-Sa call docent office, 408/624-1840. The house of poet Robinson Jeffers. Jeffers built the home from rocks he carried up from the beach. Open only for guided tours given Fridays and Saturdays hourly between 10am and 3pm; reservations are suggested. No children under 12 allowed. Adults $7; children $2.

Carmel Mission ★★: 3080 Rio Rd. (west of Hwy 1), 408/624-3600. For a dose of California history, drop by the this mission, which has a baroque stone church completed in 1797, three museums, and fabulous gardens. Across the street is **Mission Trail Park**, 35 acres ready and waiting for hikers and mountain bikers.

Places to Eat

Flaherty's ★★ $$: 6th St. between San Carlos and Dolores, Carmel, 408/624-0311. Known as the best seafood place in town; expect to wait if you don't get there very early. • Daily 5:30am-10pm; oyster bar from 11:30am-10pm.

Flying Fish Grill ★★ $$$: Mission St. between Ocean and 7th, Carmel, 408/625-1962. An intimate, upscale Japanese restaurant that isn't afraid to experiment with Western influences in its menu (desserts include crème brûlée). • Daily 5-10pm.

Friar Tucks ★ $: 5th Avenue and Dolores, Carmel, 408/624-4274. One of the best breakfast deals around. The food is delicious, and the publike atmosphere lends itself well to the basic lunches. • Daily 6:30am-2pm.

Hog's Breath Inn ★ $$: San Carlos St. between 5th and 6th, Carmel, 408/625-1044. This Clint Eastwood-owned establishment is moody, low-lit, and woody inside, but the outdoor patio is cheery and social, sporting multiple fireplaces and a bar. Free hors d'oeuvres buffet 4pm to 6pm. A top place for well-made cocktails. • Daily 11:30am-3pm, 5-10pm.

Katy's Cottage ★ $: Lincoln between Ocean and 7th, Carmel 408/625-6260. A local landmark, Katy's caters to home-cooked comforts, long on all-day breakfasts baked by the mother of all cooks. It's a pretty place with fireplace and fresh ideas about soups and salads, as well as classics like French toast and eggs Benedict. • Tu-Sa 7:30am-3pm, 5-10pm.

Rio Grill ★★★ $$: Rio Rd. at Hwy 1, Carmel, 408/625-5436. One of the original sources of California cuisine, the Rio serves impeccable New American ideas, mesquite-grilled everything accentuated with unusual fresh herbs and vegetables. Great daily specials, wines by the glass, and microbrews. Very popular with everybody. • M-Th 11:30am-10pm; F-Su 11:30am-11pm.

Places to Stay

Carmel Mission Ranch $$$: 26270 Dolores St., Carmel, 408/624-6436. A rustic place replete with goats and grazing sheep, narrowly saved from condominium hell by none other than Clint Eastwood. Many cottages and rooms offer views of the ocean; continental breakfast included. $95-$250.

Carmel Valley Inn $$: Corner of Los Laureles Grade Rd. and Carmel Valley Rd., Carmel, 408/659-3131, 800/541-3113. Tennis courts, swimming pool, and hot tub. $69-$149.

Green Lantern $$: 7th and Casanova, Carmel, 408/624-4392. Romantic rooms at reasonable prices. $75-$189.

Lincoln Green Inn $$$: Carmelo, between 15th and 16th, Carmel, 408/624-1880. Excellent spot for couples and families. Cottages sleep four; almost all have fireplaces and full kitchens. $135 & up.

Pine Inn $$$: Ocean Ave. between Lincoln and Monteverde, Carmel, 408/624-3851. "Carmel-Victorian" decor. Some rooms have ocean views. $100-$205.

Big Sur ★★★

Stretching along the mountains from Carmel south to San Simeon is the majestic coastline known as Big Sur. Seventy miles of cliff-hanging S-curves and switchbacks make up this part of the Pacific Coast Highway that runs perilously close to the ocean, with plenty of pull-offs to take in the **views ★★★**. The town of Big Sur is located about midway along the drive, but most people use "Big Sur" as a collective term for the whole magnificent landscape. There are several good camping areas, a few restaurants, and plenty of views and trails for hiking.

Big Sur Chamber of Commerce: P.O. Box 87, Big Sur CA, 93920, 408/667-2100.

Big Sur Station: Hwy 1, one-half mi. south of Pfeiffer-Big Sur State Park, 408/667-2423. A multi-agency ranger station with lots of information and maps for national forests and state parks. Also the place to go for Ventana Wilderness permits. • Daily 8am-6pm.

Pfeiffer-Big Sur State Park: 408/667-2315. For information about Andrew Molera State Park, Garrapata State Park, Julia Pfeiffer Burns State Park, Pfeiffer-Big Sur State Park, and Point Sur Lighthouse State Park.

Sights and Attractions

The state and national parks offer plenty of opportunities for the solitude that first drew writer Henry Miller to Big Sur in the 1940s.

Point Lobos State Reserve ★★★: Hwy 1, 3.5 mi. south of Carmel, 408/624-4909. More than 1,250 magnificent acres of natural coastal and inland habitat. Hike along the reserve's numerous coastal and wilderness trails, check out the tide pools, or take a nature tour. Parking is very limited, so get there early; when the park is full you have to wait until a car exits before you can enter. Many consider this one of the most beautiful spots on earth. A hike along the necklace of gemlike cove beaches explains why. • Daily 9am-7pm; gate closes at 6:30pm (7pm in summer). $7.

Garrapata State Park ★: Hwy 1 about 6 mi. south of Carmel. There's a nice beach here and some high ground from which to watch whales in the winter, but there are few facilities and heavy winds.

Point Sur Lighthouse State Park ★: Hwy 1 about 19 mi. south of Carmel, 408/625-4419, 408/625-2006. This dramatically situated, historic lighthouse is maintained by the Coast Guard and can only be visited as part of a tour. Tours last over two hours, and visits by small children and the unfit are discouraged (some climbing required). Arrive at the gate early, since people are not permitted to enter or even wait outside the lighthouse if they miss the tour. • Tours Sa 10am, 2pm; Su 10am; also some Wednesday, sunset, and full-moon tours. Adults $5; children $3.

Andrew Molera State Park ★: Hwy 1 about 22 mi. south of Carmel. Features a two-mile beach, a coastal sanctuary for seabirds, and walk-in campsites a few hundred yards from the dirt parking lot. Inside the campground, **Molera Trail Rides** 408/625-8664, has two-hour rides at daybreak, afternoon, and sunset for $40-$55.

Pfeiffer-Big Sur State Park ★: Hwy 1 about 25 mi. south of Carmel on the east side of the highway, 408/667-2315. The trails leading up into the mountains offer spectacular views of the Big Sur River gorge and the valley below, including the 60-foot **Pfeiffer Falls**. Provides access to Ventana Wilderness. $6.

Ventana Wilderness ★★: Access from Pfeiffer-Big Sur State Park. Inland from the state park is the largest protected area in Big Sur. Visitors need to have a free permit to hike, build fires, or camp within the preserve. These can be obtained, along with maps, at the **Big Sur Station** (see above).

Pfeiffer Beach ★: Hwy 1 about 26 mi. south of Carmel. This small, popular cove is a good place to explore sea caves and watch divers.

Henry Miller Memorial Library ★: Hwy 1 about 28 mi. south of Carmel, 408/667-2574. The unimposing wood structure houses Miller memorabilia—books, paintings, and photographs of Miller's friends and assorted wives.

Julia Pfeiffer Burns State Park ★: Hwy 1 about 36 mi. south of Carmel, 408/667-2315. This park boasts the only California waterfall that drops directly into the sea. There are also walk-in campsites with limited facilities. Other state parks further south include **Lime Kiln State Park**, where you can spend about an hour or two hiking to ancient lime kilns, and then cool off in the waterfall. The park also has camping and beach access. $5.

Esalen Institute ★: Hwy 1 about 40 mi. south of Carmel, 408/667-3000. Formerly a symbol of the 60s counterculture, but now a New Age retreat that bills itself as a "center to encourage work in the humanities and sciences that promotes human values and potentials." The beautiful encampment and cliffside baths are open to the curious public 1am-3:30am (yes, that's the wee hours of the morning), and reservations are required; call 408/667-3047.

Restaurants and Entertainment

Big Sur Lodge ★ $: Hwy 1, Pfeiffer-Big Sur State Park, 408/667-2171, 800/424-4787. A rustic spot next to the Big Sur Campground. The food is much better than is found at typical park concessionaires, particularly the fresh-baked pies. • Daily 7am-10pm.

Center Deli ¢: Hwy 1, next to the post office, 408/667-2225. A good place to pick up a sandwich and some fixings, but there is no seating on-site. • Daily 8am-8pm.

Coast Gallery Café ★ ¢: Hwy 1, 3 mi. south of Nepenthe, 408/667-2301. Hot and cold sandwiches and a great view. • Daily 9am-5pm.

Deetjen's Big Sur Inn Restaurant ★★ $$: Hwy 1, 408/667-2378. Wonderful brunches and dinners served in a country setting. Dinner reservations recommended. • Daily 8-11:30am, 6-8:30pm.

Fernwood Burger Bar ★ $: Hwy 1, 26 mi. south of Carmel, 408/667-2422. A hopping place with occasional live music blasting through the redwoods. • Daily noon-10pm.

Nepenthe ★★ $$$/$$$$: Hwy 1, 30 mi. south of Carmel, 408/667-2345. Once the haunt of literary loafer Henry Miller and stars Liz Taylor and Richard Burton, today's famous diners include the likes of Jane Fonda and Ted Turner. Exceptional views, of course, which greatly outdo the food. No reservations. • Daily 11:30am-10pm.

Post Ranch Inn ★★★ $$$$: Hwy 1, across from Ventana Inn, 408/667-2200. An expensive, near-the-ocean experience of delicious California cuisine and phenomenal views. Reservations required. • M-F 5:30-9:30pm; Sa-Su noon-2pm, 5:30-9:30pm.

Ventana Inn ★★★ $$$$: Hwy 1, 28 mi. S. of Carmel, 408/667-2331 or 408/624-4812. Breathtaking views and prices to match, but if you decide to splurge you won't be disappointed. Coffee or tea on the deck gives a great overlook of the ocean. • Daily 11am-3pm, 6-9:30pm.

Places to Stay

Park.Net.CA: 800/444-7275. State park campground reservations. www.park-net.com.

Big Sur Campground and Cabins $/$$: Hwy 1, next to the River Inn, 408/667-2322. Campgrounds and cabins, some with kitchens, nestled among the redwoods. Campsites $22 for two, $3 for each additional person; tent cabins $40 for two, $10 each additional; cabins $88-$143.

Big Sur Lodge $$: Located in Pfeiffer-Big Sur State Park, 408/667-3100, 800/424-4787 for reservations. Choose from 61 cottage-style rooms with either a deck or a porch. Some with kitchens and fireplaces. $79-$179.

Big Sur River Inn $$: Hwy 1, 25 mi. south of Carmel, 408/667-2700. The first business you'll encounter in Big Sur Valley, with nice, clean, simple rooms. $88-$160.

Bottchers Gap Campground ¢: North of the Point Sur Lighthouse, Palo Colorado Rd. (Big Sur Station). Limited services and a first-come, first-served policy. $5.

Deetjen's Big Sur Inn $$: Hwy 1, 408/667-2377. It's hard to imagine a more picturesque inn with its garden, ever-stoked fire, and hearty, inventive breakfasts. Two months' advance reservations recommended; call noon-4pm. $66-$121 and up.

Esalen Institute $$: Hwy 1, 408/667-3000. Private or shared bunk-bed rooms available; meals included. Pool and hot tub. Reservations taken only a week in advance. $70-$125.

Fernwood Motel & Campground $/$$: Hwy 1 around 26 mi. south of Carmel, 408/667-2422. Campsites for two $21, $5 each additional person (add $2 for electrical hookup); rooms $55-$74.

Highland's Inn $$$$: Hwy 1, south of Carmel, 800/682-4811, 408/624-3801. Rustic elegance abounds at this vintage resort draped across a hillside overlooking the swirling Carmel tidepools. Close to Point Lobos, at the gateway to Big Sur, this stylish spot offers wood-burning fireplaces, Jacuzzis, and balconies—many rooms with full kitchen and breakfast area. Great in-house restaurant, bar, and public rooms with stone fireplaces. $290-$475.

Kirk Creek Campgrounds ¢: Hwy 1, 15 mi. south of the Esalen Institute, 408/385-5434 (U.S. National Forest Service). Policy is first come, first served at these campsites set on an open bluff above the ocean—go early in the afternoon, they usually fill up fast. Water, but no showers, phones, or electricity. $16.

Lime Kiln State Park: Hwy 1 about 55 mi. south of Carmel, 408/667-2403. Situated in a canyon and surrounded by good hiking trails. Flush toilets and beach access. Advance reservations are a must and are handled through **Park.Net** at 800/444-PARK (7275). $20-$25/site. www.park-net.com.

Post Ranch Inn $$$$: Hwy 1, 408/667-2200. The newest resort in Big Sur. Its luxurious rooms are appointed with private fireplaces, Jacuzzis, and wet bars. The inn features neorustic lodgepole architecture among the redwoods, spectacular views, and plentiful spa services. $265-$525.

Ripplewood Resort $$: Hwy 1, 408/667-2282. Some of these 16 well-kept cabins (nine of which are on the Big Sur River) have kitchens, fireplaces, and decks. $45-$80.

Riverside Campground & Cabins $/$$: Hwy 1, located on the Big Sur River, 408/667-2414. No kitchens or fireplaces. Campsites $24 for two people, add $3 each additional person; cabins $45-$90.

Ventana Campground $: Hwy 1, 408/667-2688. On the grounds of the Ventana Inn, so you're within reach of a meal or drink if those freeze-dried dinners aren't cutting it. $25 for two people. Reservations required, ten days' notice, and $25 deposit.

Ventana Inn $$$$: Hwy 1 about 30 mi. south of Carmel, 408/667-2331, 408/624-4812. A woodsy retreat, considered to be one of the finest in Northern California. Located high above the ocean, this sprawling, ranchlike compound is luxurious without being pretentious. Clothing-optional hot tubs and sun-bathing areas are only a sampling of the amenities available. Roughing it with style. $195-$550.

PENINSULA COAST ★★

The wild and woolly Peninsula coast that begins just south of San Francisco is replete with rolling hills, fields of artichokes, and gorgeous rugged beaches that draw surfers and beachcombers from far and wide. Sleepy towns like Pescadero, filled with ramshackle barns and Depression-era architecture, are more reminiscent of Tom Joad than Steve Jobs.

General Information

Half Moon Bay Chamber of Commerce: 520 Kelly Ave., Half Moon Bay, 650/726-5202.

California State Parks District Office: 95 Kelly Ave., Half Moon Bay, 650/330-6300. Manages state beaches along coast.

Pacifica to Half Moon Bay ★

If you need a break from sunny, warm weather, visit fog-bound Pacifica. To get to Pacifica, one of the first coastal towns south of San Francisco, take I-280 to Hwy 1 south. *Warning:* Hwy 1 normally continues south to Moss Beach and Half Moon Bay, but heavy rains can close the Devil's Slide portion of the road between San Pedro

Point and Montara Beach (sometimes for months). When this happens, you must take I-280 to Hwy 92 west to Half Moon Bay to Hwy 1 north to reach Moss Beach and the surrounding area.

Beaches ★★: Pacifica is first and foremost a beach community. It offers both town-infused, commercial beach areas like San Pedro Point and rocky, secluded inlets such as the mysterious Gray Whale Cove.

Sharp Park State Beach: The first Sharp Park Boulevard exit will bring you to this popular family park, with a sandy beach and a picnic and barbecue area.

Rockaway Beach: Farther south on Hwy 1, you'll encounter the turn-off for Rockaway Beach and the strip of hotels and restaurants that abuts it. The beach area is small, framed by two outcroppings of rock, and is known to actually disappear during heavy rains. Most of the patrons of Rockaway are hotel guests or diners, though on sunny days a fair number of families can appear, and with good reason; Rockaway oozes convenience, with numerous free parking lots, large bathroom and changing facilities, and a number of decent eating establishments lining the road to the beach.

San Pedro Point: Pacifica's largest and most frequented beach, this area is a favorite with boogie-boarders and surfers. From the highway, the landmark that distinguishes San Pedro Point is the enormous, neon-trimmed Taco Bell that sits just beyond the sand overlooking the ocean. It's been called the prettiest fast food restaurant in the world; nevertheless, it presents one of a number of eyesores along the

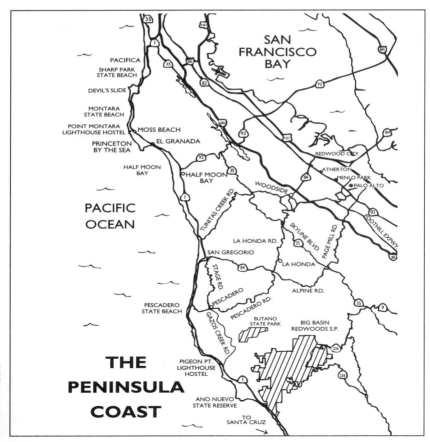

water here. Pacifica surfer kids and some families compose the crowd, and the beach itself is fairly uninteresting, located in a commercial area and thus devoid of wildlife. It's a good place for beach sports and wading. There is a small bathroom facility, but be warned: the surfer dudes here have been known to forgo the bathroom and shed their wetsuits in one of the two parking lots.

Gray Whale Cove: Drive slowly along the "Devil's Slide" area of Hwy 1 or you might miss the tiny left-side parking lot for this beautiful little beach area. A fairly steep stairway and a path down the cliffs leads you to a secluded stretch of sand where sunbathing—usually *sans* clothing—is the primary activity. There is a $5 admission fee, collected by a concessionaire who apparently shows up only when the day looks promising. Gray Whale Cove is clean and lovely, framed by beds of native dune plants and wildflowers. If you dig the seclusion but public nudity isn't for you, stick to the south end of the beach, where the few clothed beachcombers tend to congregate.

Montara Beach: This long, narrow stretch of sand is the perfect place for a romantic stroll by the water. Approximately two miles long, Montara is lined with cavelike depressions in the low, rocky cliffs, providing semiprivate areas for enjoying the beach in seclusion. You can get to the water by way of one of two steep paths leading down from the parking lots on the bluff, and a small, undesirable bathroom facility is located at the southern lot.

Fitzgerald Marine Reserve ★: Off Cypress Ave., Moss Beach, 650/728-3584. Hidden in Moss Beach, a tiny burg along the coast, is this vast and fascinating reserve. Its 30 acres of exposed reef at low tide make it one of the best places to explore tidepools on the coast. Adjacent to the Marine Reserve, in Princeton-by-the-Sea, is **Pillar Point Harbor**, embarkation point for deep-sea fishing and whale-watching tours. A fresh fish market and several seafood restaurants are also located at the harbor.

Restaurants and Entertainment

Barbara's Fishtrap ★★ $$: 281 Capistrano Rd. (off Hwy 1), Princeton-by-the-Sea, 650/728-7049. Some of the freshest fish, grilled or fried, on the San Mateo coast. While your California sensibilities steer you to the grilled fare, you won't be able to resist Barbara's great fried fish and tempura-style vegetables. Two can easily share the Fishtrap special, a heaping potpourri of fried calamari, scallops, shrimp, rockfish, and vegetables. The fish and chips are perfectly done in the English style. Sitting on a pier, the restaurant's large windows overlook the harbor. A suitably nautical theme dominates inside, with cheery blue-and-white-checkered tablecloths. Prices may seem a bit high but the food is well worth it. No credit cards. • Su-Th 11am-9:30pm; F-Sa 11am-10pm (hours shorter during winter)

Café Classique ★ ¢: 107 Sevilla Ave. (Ave. Alhambra), El Granada, 650/726-9775. A popular gathering place in El Granada for morning cappuccino and freshly baked muffins and scones. Both are available in flavors savory (like artichoke and red pepper) or sweet (how about raspberry with white chocolate?). Café Classique is also open for light meals (pastas and salads). • Daily 7am-3pm.

Chart House ★★ $$$: 8150 Cabrillo Hwy. aka Hwy 1 (2nd), Montara Beach, 650/728-7366. Good, simple food, attentive service, and a spectacular sunset view of the beach make the Chart House a popular dinner destination with locals and tourists alike. The restaurant buys its excellent beef from Omaha; prime rib and "baseball sirloin teriyaki" (the tenderest part of the sirloin) are the best things on the menu. • M-F 5-9pm; Sa-Su 4-9:30pm.

El Gran Amigo ★ ¢: 2448 Hwy 1 (California/Virginia), Moss Beach, 650/728-3815. Three Amigos' sister taqueria in Moss Beach. A constant flow of faithful regulars and tourists comes for the delicious, inexpensive burritos—don't miss the *chile verde* version. No credit cards. • Daily 10:30am-10:30pm.

Moss Beach Distillery ★★ $$$: Beach Way (off Hwy 1 at Ocean Blvd.), Moss Beach, 650/728-5595. The sign on Hwy 1 sums up the appeal of this Prohibition-era road-house: View, Food, Ghost. The restaurant boasts a large bar and deck area with a gorgeous view of the sunset over the Pacific (blankets and heaters are provided). Young crowds mob the patio on sunny weekend afternoons. As you may have guessed, food isn't the main attraction. Mesquite-grilled fresh fish is the highlight of the menu, and there is plenty of pasta. And yes, there is a ghost in residence: the "blue lady" even starred on an episode of *Unsolved Mysteries.* • M-Sa noon-9pm; Su 10am-2:30pm, 4:30pm-9pm (hours longer during summer).

Nick's ★★ $$: 100 Rockaway Beach (Hwy 1), Pacifica, 650/359-3900. Nick's is a veritable time machine, taking you back to an era when wooden pelicans and stuffed swordfish were the decor of choice for seafood restaurants. Overlooking an unremarkable stretch of Rockaway Beach, the restaurant's seating consists of several Naugahyde booths, which are almost always filled, and a few white-clothed tables, which are almost always empty. The menu covers all the traditional seafood bases, from a crab salad sandwich to shrimp scampi. Most of the dishes, while far from creative, are well-prepared. Most of Nick's fried dishes are surprisingly light and tasty, particularly the calamari. After your meal, visit the adjacent lounge for a rousing evening of line dancing, complete with live music and lessons. • M-F 9am-10pm; Sa-Su 8am-10:30pm.

Playa de Acapulco ★ $: 145 Rockaway Beach, Pacifica, 650/359-3800. Serves cheap Mexican food. • M, W-F 4-8:30pm; Sa-Su noon-9pm.

Village Green ★ $: 89 Portola Ave. (Obispo/Coronado), El Granada, 650/726-3690. El Granada is an unlikely setting for an authentic English teahouse. The full English breakfasts are hearty and authentic, featuring such things as perfectly poached eggs, scones with lemon curd, and great fried potatoes. At lunch traditional English fare, such as bangers and mash, are served. No credit cards. • M-Tu, Th-F 9am-3pm; Sa-Su 9am-4pm.

Places to Stay

Point Montara Lighthouse Hostel ¢: Hwy 1 at 16th St., Montara, 650/728-7177. Check-in 4:30-9:30pm, closed 9:30am-4:30pm. A very interesting, inexpensive option featuring an outdoor hot tub and a functioning lighthouse. Rooms are booked weeks, if not months, in advance. $8 for American Youth Hostel members, $10 for nonmembers.

Half Moon Bay ★★

Half Moon Bay is the only incorporated city between Pacifica and Santa Cruz. This commercial center of the Peninsula coastline is currently experiencing a bit of a boom, resulting in growth at a rapid clip. Host of the enormously popular Half Moon Bay Pumpkin Festival every October, the town is the center of a rich agricultural economy that encompasses everything from brussels sprouts to Christmas trees. To get there, take I-280 to Hwy 92 west. Hwy 92 cuts through the middle of town and ends at Hwy 1; beaches lie both north and south of that intersection.

Main Street ★: Originally known as Spanishtown, Half Moon Bay has a sleepy, historic Main Street lined with shops, restaurants, and inns. **The Spanishtown Historical Society/Half Moon Bay Jail** 650/726-7084 at 505 Johnston Street offers walking tours on weekend afternoons (Sa-Su 1-4pm) that start at the old jail; reservations are recommended. It's definitely worth stopping on Main Street to check out the interesting stores and **galleries**.

If you haven't brought your bike, visit **The Bicyclery** 650/726-6000 at 101 Main Street. For $6 an hour, the friendly people at this bicycle store will supply you with mountain or road bikes, helmets, and locks. They're open M-F 9:30am-6:30pm; Sa 10am-5pm; Su 11am-5pm.

Beaches ★★: Beaches span the entire length of Hwy 1, but one of the largest continuous sandy stretches comprises the Half Moon Bay State Beach. Because of the town's tourist industry, this beach can be crowded, and a few less convenient areas just south of town will provide a more private beach experience.

Half Moon Bay State Beach 650/726-8820. There are many access points to this large stretch of beach along Hwy 1, but the main entrance on **Francis Beach** is just south of Hwy 92 at Kelly Avenue. This beach is also the only one in the area that allows overnight camping. There's a $5 charge for parking your car during the day (see Places to Stay section below for camping information) but this fee also entitles you to park at any of the state parks on the coast. Other beaches around the area include **Elmar, Venice** 650/726-5550, **Dunes, Naples, and Miramar,** each of which has a different personality and facilities, so check out a few sites before setting up for the day.

Redondo Beach: To access this small stretch of sand, take Redondo Beach Road, a lengthy, poorly paved turn-off just south of Hwy 92. Redondo is pretty and somewhat secluded, with a collection of rocks emerging from the shore and framing the sandy beach area. To get there, take a quick, steep scramble down the low cliffs that provide a feeling of privacy found here. Difficult access (as well as a lack of facilities—no bathrooms or picnic tables) keeps the crowds down.

Cowell Ranch Beach: Cowell Ranch is a working farm along the coast that dates to the gold rush days and now opens its beach area to the public. The beach is accessed by way of a half-mile trail from the parking lot, and thus it is not a popular spot for families or picnickers seeking the more convenient beach experience. The trail to the beach area is gorgeous, set amidst meadows of high grasses and coastal trees. Once you reach the stairway that leads to the sand, look south, where a harbor seal preserve can be viewed from the cliffs.

Sea Horse Ranch/Friendly Acres Ranch ★: 1828 Cabrillo Hwy. aka Hwy 1, one mile north of Hwy 92, 650/726-8550. These twin local stables offer horse rentals and guides that will take you for an hour-and-a-half trip along the coast for $35 (or one hour for $25 or two hours for $40). The stables offer trail and beach rides for all levels of riding ability and are open daily from 8am-6pm.

Obester Winery ★: 12341 San Mateo Rd. aka Hwy 92, 1.5 miles east of Hwy 1, 650/726-9463. Obester makes a nice Sauvignon Blanc that you can taste on the spot or save for a picnic. They also produce their own mustard, olive oil, and herbal vinegars. Open daily 10am-5pm. The surrounding area along Hwy 92 as you come into Half Moon Bay is replete with **nurseries,** offering everything from fresh-cut flowers to shrubs and trees. It's a great place to browse for new additions to your yard or window box.

Restaurants and Entertainment

Cunha's Country Store ¢: 448 Main St. (Kelly/Mill), Half Moon Bay, 650/726-4071. Huge, cheap sandwiches, and everything from Jell-O to wild mushroom pasta. • M-Sa 8am-8pm; Su 8am-7pm.

Flying Fish Grill ★ $: 99 San Mateo Rd. (Corner of Hwy. 1 and Main St.), Half Moon Bay, 650/712-1125. Standard fried fish and chips and interesting grilled seafood. • Tu-F 11am-8pm; Sa-Su 11am-8:30pm.

Half Moon Bay Coffee Company ★ ¢: 315 Main St. (Hwy 92), Half Moon Bay, 650/726-1994. The home of huge slices of amazing pie. • M-F 6:30am-9pm; Sa-Su 7:30am-10pm.

LA DI DA ★ ¢: 500-C Purisima Rd., Half Moon Bay, 650/726-1663. This popular stop has a wacky approach to coffee, an offbeat selection of artwork, and live entertainment. • M-W 6am-6pm; Th-F 7am-6pm; Sa 11am-1pm; Su 8am-6pm.

McCoffee ★ ¢: 522 Main St. (Kelly), Half Moon Bay, 650/726-6241. A good local joint to nurse espresso. • M-F 7am-6pm; Sa 8am-6pm; Su 9am-6pm.

Miramar Beach Inn ★★ $$: 131 Mirada Rd. (Magellan off Hwy 1), Half Moon Bay, 650/726-9053. Right next to the ocean, this rugged beach dining hall offers a good selection of seafood, steaks, and pasta dishes. Stick to the basics, especially the salmon, and you won't be disappointed. An historic roadhouse dating back to Prohibition that keeps the roar of the '20s alive. In fact, word has it that this is *the* place to party on the coastside, especially if you're over 30. • M-F 11:30am-3:30pm, 5:30-9pm; Sa 11am-3:30pm, 5-10pm; Su 10am-3:30pm, 5-10pm (hours vary depending on business).

Pasta Moon ★★ $$: 315 Main St. (Hwy 92/Mill), Half Moon Bay, 650/726-5125. One of the better restaurants along the coast, Pasta Moon is cozy and quaint, albeit a bit cramped, with small town hospitality. Start with the assorted antipasti plate, which might include generous servings of grilled eggplant, roasted peppers, frittata, and more. Pastas are always a good bet, as are the seafood dishes. • M-Th 11:30am-2:30pm, 5:30-9:30pm; F 11:30am-2:30pm, 5:30-10pm; Sa noon-3pm, 5:30-10pm; Su noon-3pm, 5:30-9:30pm.

San Benito House ★★ $$$ (Deli $): 356 Main St. (Mill), Half Moon Bay, 650/726-3425. A delightful restaurant inside a historic inn in downtown Half Moon Bay. At lunch, deli sandwiches made with bread from the restaurant's oven make for an instant picnic. Candlelit dinners go beyond the standard slap-up seashore fare with imaginative California cuisine: grilled salmon on a bed of rice with gazpacho vinaigrette or roast chicken stuffed with hazelnuts, thyme, and mushrooms topped with orange cranberry *demi-glace*. • Th-Su 5:30-9pm. Deli 11am-3pm.

Sushi Main Street ★★★ $$: 696 Mill St. (Main), Half Moon Bay, 650/726-6336. A hidden gem of a restaurant in Half Moon Bay. It's the coastside's only sushi choice, so it's fortunate that the fish is extremely fresh, creatively prepared, and inexpensive. Among the more inventive concoctions is the California-inspired tuna roll with macadamia nuts and avocado served with the chef's special sauce. • M-Sa 11:30am-2:30pm, 5-9pm; Su 5-9pm.

3 Amigos Taqueria ★ ¢: 200 Cabrillo Hwy. aka Hwy 1 (Kelly), Half Moon Bay, 650/726-6080. A fast-food atmosphere and Mexican specialties. Cash only. • Daily 10am-10pm.

Two Fools ★★ $: 408 Main St. (Kelly/Mill), Half Moon Bay, 650/712-1222. A casual atmosphere and stylishly prepared and presented salads, sandwiches, rotisserie chicken, and fish. Brunch and lunch fare includes healthy burritos with black beans and potatoes. Specials change daily, but you'll have such choices as an elegant meat loaf with tomatoes and caramelized onions on a homemade bun. The dinner menu focuses on hearty food to take out or eat in: fried chicken, shiitake mushroom stuffing, and great mashed potatoes. • M 11am-2pm; Tu-F 11am-9pm; Sa-Su 8am-9pm.

Places to Stay

Francis Beach Campground, Half Moon Bay State Beach ¢: Hwy 1 just south of Hwy 92 at Kelly Ave., Half Moon Bay, 650/726-8820. There are 51 individual campsites located on the low bluff above the beach, all given out on a first-come first-served basis. You sign up on a waiting list starting at 8:30am and check back in the afternoon to see if you got a site. $16/campsite.

Cypress Inn $$$: 407 Mirada Rd. (Magellan off Hwy 1), Half Moon Bay, 650/726-6002, 800/83-BEACH (832-3224). A cozy eight-room Santa Fe–style hideaway. Each room is impressively equipped with a fireplace and French doors that open onto a private deck with a view of the ocean. $150-$275.

Mill Rose Inn $$$: 615 Mill St., Half Moon Bay, 650/726-9794. A romantic inn with attentive service. Enjoy an inviting English-country-garden setting. Separate entrances, private Jacuzzis, fluffy featherbeds, fireplaces, champagne breakfasts, VCRs, and phones complete this luxurious picture. $165-$285.

Old Thyme Inn $$: 779 Main St., Half Moon Bay, 650/726-1616. This charming downtown inn is cheerful and upbeat, with stuffed animals on every bed, and rooms named and decorated in an herbal theme. Weekdays $95-$165; weekends $110-$220.

San Gregorio to Año Nuevo ★★

Beaches ★★: This stretch of coastline is a gorgeous drive as well as a great place to appreciate the natural habitat of the area. The rolling hills that frame these beaches are quintessential Northern California coast, with crooked evergreens leaning over the cliffs and a smattering of wildflowers in sunset colors. Admission to all beaches is $5, but one fee entitles you to park at any of the state parks on the coast for the whole day.

San Gregorio Beach: Although this popular area can draw crowds on weekends and holidays, it's a lovely spot that offers something for all types of beachgoers. Picnickers can enjoy a barbecue at the edge of one of the low cliffs, while those interested in walking can stroll along the dunes or take off down the miles of coastline that San Gregorio accesses. Local ocean birds—mostly seagulls, with the occasional more interesting specimen—populate a large, rather bizarre pond that's accumulated just at the foot of the cliffs, a good place for kids to search the water's edge for tiny sand crabs. The bathrooms and changing rooms here are the nicest on the San Mateo Coast, in themselves worth the trip.

Pomponio Beach: This smaller state beach is another great spot for picnics, where you can choose a table secluded in the dunes or on a cliff over the water. Appropriate to this beach, which is less crowded than its northern neighbor, the cliffwalks here are more private than those at San Gregorio, popular with nature enthusiasts (purple needlegrass, a rare and beautiful native plant, grows in abundance along the hills here). Surf-fishermen frequent Pomponio, and the eastern portion of the hills overlooking the beach is a working cattle ranch. Bathroom facilities are small but adequate.

Pescadero Beach: Park at the intersection of Pescadero Road and Hwy 1 and you'll come upon a wide vista of this entire area, an absolutely stunning state park as well as a fun place to hang for a day. The beach is a two-mile stretch of sand and interesting rock outcroppings; craggy boulders that dot the shoreline provide places to explore tidepools and venture out over the water at low tide. Three parking lots create easy access to the beach and offer picnic and barbecue areas, though these can be crowded and somewhat unpleasant on weekends. The beach is next to the 587-acre **Pescadero Marsh Natural Preserve**, and guided nature walks beginning at the second parking lot are offered on weekends, or you can explore the trails on your own. The marsh, a resting place for migratory birds during late fall and early spring, is an ideal place for bird-watching.

Pebble Beach: Although not ideal for sunbathing or wading, as the sandy area is tiny and quite pebbly (hence the name), Pebble Beach is a beautiful picnic spot. Enveloped by rolling dunes, the beach consists of rock formations that at low tide are great for searching for tidepool animals (crab skeletons litter the tiny beach area). It's less crowded than Fitzgerald Marine Preserve, the coast's most famous tidepooling area, and free guided tidepool programs are offered monthly through the state park service. A nature trail leads to Bean Hollow State Beach, and during the spring an abundance of wildflowers can make this walk particularly beautiful.

Bean Hollow State Beach: Although this beach is also quite rocky, the small stretch of sand here is quite suitable for sunbathing and sand castles. A picnic area atop the bluff provides an excellent view of the graceful marsh birds that frequent the area, gliding over the water in formation. A climb onto the rocks below the bluffs can reveal a view of the neighboring harbor seal rookery. Bean Hollow can draw a crowd on weekends, though it's a better bet for privacy than the larger Pescadero Beach.

Butano State Park ★★: Cloverdale Rd., south of Pescadero, 650/879-2040. If you're interested in a hike through the redwoods away from the coast, come here. This stretch of forest was lightly logged in the 1880s, and it features a stand of old-growth redwoods. Follow the Doe Ridge Trail for a hike through virgin timber. The facilities include walk-in and trail campsites, often full in spring and summer; advance reservations are a must (car/walk-in sites handled by **Park.Net**, 800-444-7275, www.park-net.com; trail sites reserved through park office). $5 per vehicle.

Año Nuevo Reserve ★★★: Hwy 1 about 30 mi. south of Half Moon Bay, 650/879-0227, 650/879-2025. By far the most interesting coastal area south of Half Moon Bay, and perhaps on the entire Peninsula. This area is home to enormous elephant seals that range from 8 to 18 feet long and can weigh as much as two and a half tons. The female seals come on shore in December to give birth, and then mate again while the male seals battle to establish breeding rights. Stellar sea lions and harbor seals breed on the beaches here at other times of the year, so it's always worth a visit. During the December to March breeding season, the reserve is only open to guided tours led by park rangers; advance reservations are a must (handled by **Park.Net**, 800/444-7275 or www.park-net.com). $5/vehicle.

Coastways U-Pick Ranch ★: across from Año Nuevo, 650/879-0414. A farm where you can pick kiwifruits, olallieberries, and so forth, depending on the time of year. Enjoy your produce in the ranch's nice picnic area. Call first for harvest schedule.

Big Basin Redwood State Park ★★: Hwy 1 about 32 mi. south of Half Moon Bay, 408/338-8860, 408/425-1218. This part of Big Basin marks one end of the Skyline-to-the-Sea trail that begins at Waddell Beach and runs through the park to the top of the Santa Cruz Mountains on Skyline Drive. From the mountain headquarters on Hwy 236, there's easy access to Big Basin's many other trails, which wind through miles of forest and along creeks and waterfalls. The park has some campgrounds, and the old logging roads make for great mountain biking. The inland part of Big Basin can be reached by taking Hwy 85 to Hwy 9, and then following Hwy 236 into the park. $6 vehicle.

Restaurants and Entertainment

Duarte's Tavern ★★ $$: 202 Stage Rd. (Pescadero Creek Rd.), Pescadero, 650/879-0464. Pescadero's most celebrated saloon for over a century. Now a respectable family seafood restaurant, the famous artichoke and green chili soups, garden-grown vegetables, delicious local seafood, and great pie give this place its well-deserved reputation as a wonderful stop back in time. If you're not in the mood for a full meal, sit at the counter and soak up the 1950s atmosphere over a piece of olallieberry pie and a cup of coffee. Reservations recommended on weekends. • Daily 7am-9pm.

Norm's Market ¢: 287 Stage Rd. (Pescadero Creek Rd.), Pescadero, 650/879-0147. Great picnic fixings, fresh-baked bread, and an extensive wine cellar. M-Sa 10am-7pm; Su 10am-6pm.

Phipps Ranch ¢: 2700 Pescadero Creek Rd., Pescadero, 650/879-0787. Seasonal produce, pick-your-own berries, and a petting zoo. This is a curious and charmingly ramshackle spread, where you can purchase weird, heirloom dried beans and seeds. • Daily 10am-7pm (closed Thanksgiving and the week between Christmas and New Year's Day).

San Gregorio General Store $: Hwy 84 and Stage Rd., San Gregorio, 650/726-0565. Everything you'll ever need—a bar, bookstore, and music hall all in one. Bluegrass and Irish music starts weekends at 2pm. • Daily 9am-6pm (often later weekends).

Taquería de Amigos ★ ¢: 1999 Pescadero Creek Rd. (Stage), Pescadero, 650/879-0232. Don't be discouraged by the unglamorous location of this little taqueria (in a gas station mini-mart across from the famed Duarte's Tavern). Taqueria de Amigos is a tasty and inexpensive alternative when the wait at its renowned neighbor is longer than you (or your appetite) can tolerate. Relax at one of the several Formica tables and sample the warm, crispy tortilla chips and fresh chunky salsa. Try a huge, delicious chicken enchilada, but avoid the greasy quesadillas. For dessert, choose from the racks of colorful, homemade Mexican baked goods. No credit cards. • Daily 6am-10pm.

Places to Stay

Pigeon Point Lighthouse Hostel ¢: Pigeon Point Rd. and Hwy 1, Pescadero, 650/879-0633. Made up of four buildings next to the still-functioning lighthouse, this hostel can house up to 50 people overnight. Reservations recommended since rooms are often booked months in advance. Check-in is from 4:30pm to 9:30pm; desk is closed from 9:30am to 4:30pm. $12 for American Youth Hostel members, $15 for nonmembers.

SANTA CRUZ ★★

Idyllic Santa Cruz is southwest of the urban sprawl of the Bay Area, in redwood-covered hills that roll down to the sandy shores of the Pacific. With both the mountains and the ocean, Santa Cruz has unparalleled beauty and unlimited potential for outdoor activities. Far more than just a beach town, Santa Cruz offers a refreshing and peaceful atmosphere for all, a blend of the best of Northern and Southern California.

State Parks District Office: 408/429-2850.

Santa Cruz Chamber of Commerce: 408/423-1111.

Santa Cruz Visitors' Council: 701 Front St., Santa Cruz, 408/425-1234. • M-Sa 9am-5pm; Su 10am-4pm.

Downtown Information: 1126 Pacific Ave., Santa Cruz, 408/459-9486. • Daily 10-8.

Getting There

The easiest way to get to Santa Cruz is by car. The most direct route is I-280 south to Hwy 17 west, which ends in Santa Cruz. (For a slight shortcut, from I-280 take Hwy 85 to Hwy 17 west.) For a more scenic drive, take I-280 to Hwy 92 west to Hwy 1 south, a steep road that winds along the coast all the way to Santa Cruz.

The best method for getting to Santa Cruz sans car is to take CalTrain to the San Jose stop at 65 Cahill St. You should find a bus stop by the station where you can board the Amtrak bus called the "Santa Cruz Connector." For $5 ($8 round-trip) the bus will take you to the Metro Center in downtown Santa Cruz. **Metro** 408/425-8600 provides Santa Cruz public transit, so you can then transfer to another bus depending on your final destination. The city of Santa Cruz has discontinued its free Beach Shuttle service. Instead, you can take bus #7 to the beach ($1/ride, $3/day pass).

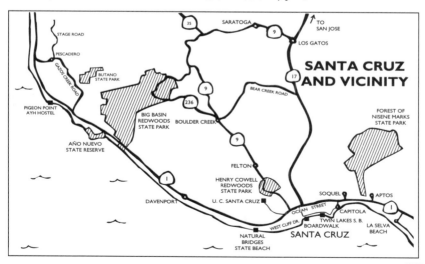

Sights and Attractions

Santa Cruz Beach Boardwalk ★★: Beach St. at Riverside Ave., 408/423-5590. The Boardwalk is a Coney Island-type amusement park—California's oldest—with a hair-raising, old-fashioned wooden roller coaster, a vintage, 85-year-old merry-go-round, and perhaps best of all, a collection of pinball machines and video games that includes all those classics which everyone else seems to have gotten rid of (Remember Joust?). New state-of-the-art rides, like the vertiginous Typhoon, can curl your hair. The old rides can still offer a thrill—not the least because of their age—and are accompanied by the usual assortment of cotton candy and carnival games. Cool off on the beach between rides. $17.95 day pass, individual rides $1.50-$3 each.

UC Santa Cruz ★: High St. at Bay Dr. on the hill above town. Central operator 408/459-0111. Don't miss wandering around the redwood-shaded campus of UCSC. It is one of the smaller UC schools, and has perhaps the most beautiful campus of all the schools. Enjoy the beautiful views of Monterey Bay from the athletic field, and the scent of both forest and ocean. The innovative **Shakespeare Santa Cruz** 408/459-2121 summer festival of plays, held in a wooded grove on the campus from July to September, shouldn't be missed. These interpretations of Shakespeare's plays are nontraditional and humorous, filled with drag queens and cross-gender casting. Bring a blanket, a jug of wine, and a picnic. The truly adventurous should ask a student how to find the **caves** located just across the Empire Grade.

Downtown Santa Cruz ★: Downtown centers around the outdoor **Pacific Garden Mall,** Pacific Ave. at Lincoln St., and offers a variety of intriguing bookstores, used-record stores, new-age crystal shops, as well as interesting cafés and restaurants. The atmosphere is upbeat—it's recovered from the devastating 1989 earthquake—but the number of languishing hippies and prepubescent panhandlers may at times make you think you're in the Haight. Book lovers will enjoy **Bookshop Santa Cruz** 408/423-0900 at 1520 Pacific Ave. (Mission), which has been in business since the 1960s and has everything from bestsellers to a gay and lesbian bulletin board. It also has a boho in-store café, Georgiana's that serves great pastries, fine light meals, and bracing espressos. They're open daily 9am-11pm. Later in the day, visit **Kiva Hot Tubs** at 702 Water Street 408/429-1142, which offers two outdoor tubs in a garden setting, as well as a dry redwood sauna. Two private tubs are also available. Clothing is optional; they're open Su-Th noon-11pm, F-Sa noon-midnight. Su 9am-noon it's reserved for women only.

Outdoor Activities ★★

Beaches ★★★: The sandy beaches of Santa Cruz draw crowds from far and wide, especially on the weekends. If crowds and cotton candy aren't your thing, skip the Boardwalk and head across the San Lorenzo River toward Santa Cruz Harbor. **Seabright Beach ★★★** and **Twin Lakes State Beach ★★★** are two of the many pleasant places to enjoy the sand and sun, offering some of the best ocean swimming and bodysurfing in northern California. If you continue east from these beaches, you'll eventually come to **Capitola**, California's first seaside resort. Capitola is quaint, clean, and has great beachside shopping; however, during the summer it can be just as crowded as Santa Cruz. This is a great place to people-watch and take advantage of many fine small seafood houses along the atmospheric Esplanade.

Heading west from the Boardwalk on West Cliff Drive, watch for the **Lighthouse Surfing Museum** 408/429-3429 at Lighthouse Point, marked by a statue of a young surfer dude. They're open M, W-F noon-4pm, Sa-Su noon-5pm. Lighthouse Point is a great place to watch the surfers below chop through the world-class waves of **Steamer Lane,** or try the waves yourself. Surfing equipment and lessons are available at the north end of the boardwalk at **Cowell's Beach and Bikini**, 109 Beach St. 408/427-2355. Just west of the Lighthouse, people gather daily at **It's Beach** to drum and dance at sunset. Continuing west from the point along West Cliff Drive, you'll find beautiful natural rock formations at **Natural Bridges State Beach** ★ 408/423-4609, which is small and pretty, but has much colder, rougher water than the beaches to the east. Official parking is $6 ($5 seniors, $3 disabled); street parking outside the entrance is free but crowded. Dogs ($1 admission) are allowed in the picnic area but not on the beach.

Bike Path ★: A flat section of asphalt along West Cliff Drive between Natural Bridges and Capitola is perfect for rollerbladers, bikers, and joggers—no cars and lots of coastal scenery. Bring your bike. Rollerblades are available for rent at **Go Skate Surf and Sport**, at 601 Beach Street (Riverside) 408/425-8578, open 10am-6pm daily (summer until 7pm), or rent a bike at **Pacific Avenue Cycles**, 709 Pacific Ave. 408/423-1314.

Sea Kayaking ★: If you'd like to try a hand at sea kayaking, stop by **Venture Quest Kayak Rentals**, 125 Beach St. 408/427-2267, open W-F 10am-5pm, Sa-Su noon-5pm, where they offer kayak rentals, lessons, and guided kayak tours of the area. **Adventure Sports**, 303 Potrero St. (River), 408/458-DO-IT (3648), also rents kayaks along with other water toys. Beginners are required to take an introductory class in basic paddling and safety before going out in an enclosed boat.

The Forest of Nisene Marks State Park ★: Aptos Creek Rd. off Soquel Dr. off Hwy 1, Aptos. With 10,000 acres of undeveloped, pristine redwood wilderness, this park has good hiking and challenging mountain biking trails.

Hwy 9 ★: Take a drive up Hwy 9 or Felton Empire Road to enjoy the redwoods and the small hippie towns along the way, such as **Felton**, **Ben Lomond**, and **Boulder Creek**. Another attraction in the Santa Cruz mountains is the wacky **Mystery Spot** ★, at 1953 North Branciforte Drive 408/423-8897, a "natural phenomenon" where all laws of gravity are forgotten, balls roll uphill, and other bizarre events take place. Admission is $4, $2 for kids (free under 5), and includes a bumper sticker; they're open 9am-8pm. About 30 minutes north of Santa Cruz on Hwy 236 lies **Big Basin Redwoods State Park** (see Peninsula Parks), with hiking, camping, and the gorgeous Berry Creek Falls. It was California's first State Park and its giant virgins are among the oldest living things on earth.

Wineries ★

The Santa Cruz area, with almost two dozen wineries but without the crowds of Napa Valley, is a great destination for wine tasting.

Bargetto Winery: 3535-A N. Main St., Soquel, 408/475-2258. Their tasting room is casual and packed with gourmet "foodstuffs." Enjoy the view of wooded Soquel Creek while you taste. The staff is passionate about their wines and loves to make recommendations. Bargetto is known for its fruit wines, such as olallieberry and apricot. Be sure to try the Chaucer's Mead. • M-Sa 9am-5pm; Su 11am-5pm; tours M-F 11am or 2pm.

Bonny Doon: 10 Pine Flat Rd., Santa Cruz, 408/425-3625. Wins honors for its Italian-style wines; winemaker Randall Graham is one of the infamous "Rhône Rangers". • Sep. 15-Apr. 15: Th-M noon-5pm. Apr. 16-Sep. 14: daily noon-5pm.

David Bruce Winery: 21439 Bear Creek Rd., Los Gatos, 408/354-4214. Great winery for picnics; outstanding Pinot Noirs. • Daily noon-5pm.

Devlin Wine Cellars: 3801 Park Ave., Soquel, 408/476-7288. Located on a 30-acre estate overlooking Monterey Bay. Try the champagne. • Sa-Su noon-5pm.

Hallcrest Vineyards: 379 Felton Empire Rd., Felton, 408/335-4441. Specializes in organic wines. • Daily 11am-5:30pm.

Storrs Winery: 35 Potrero St., Santa Cruz, 408/458-5030. Run by a husband-and-wife team who are both award-winning wine makers; specializing in Santa Cruz Mountain estate Chardonnays. • F-M noon-5pm.

Restaurants and Entertainment

The Bagelry ¢: 320A Cedar St. (Laurel/Maple), Santa Cruz, 408/429-8049. Fresh, inexpensive bagels made on the premises. Try the "slugs": large, misshapen bagels weighed down by "everything" (poppy and sesame seeds, onion, you name it). • M-F 6:30am-5:30pm; Sa 7:30am-5:30pm; Su 7:30am-4pm.

Aldo's Café ★★★ $$: 841 Almar Ave. (Mission/Ingalls), Santa Cruz 408/429-9982. New and sleek, this smart bistro anchoring one end of a busy Westside shopping mall serves sensuous pastas, creative salads and excellent steaks. A winning, cosmopolitan ambiance. • Tu-Th 5-9:30pm; F 5-10pm; Sa 11:30am-2pm, 5-10pm; Su 9:30am-1:30pm, 5-9:30pm.

Benten ★★ $$: 1541 Pacific Ave. (Locust/Water), Santa Cruz, 408/425-7079. A cozy, clean place serving great Japanese food. • M, W-F 11:30am-2:30pm, 5:30-9pm; Sa-Su 12:30-9pm.

The Blue Lagoon: 923 Pacific Ave. (Maple/Elm), Santa Cruz, 408/423-7117. Behind the mirrored facade is a small, hopping dance club playing the latest techno and rave for a mostly gay and bisexual crowd. (But all are welcome.)

Caffè Lido ★ ¢: 110 Monterey Ave. (Esplanade), Capitola, 408/475-6544. Well-placed windows capture the afternoon sun and fill the main room with light. Rich desserts and strong espresso. • W-Th, Su 11:30am-9pm, F-Sa 11:30am-10pm.

Caffè Pergolesi ★ ¢: 418 Cedar St. (Elm), Santa Cruz, 408/426-1775. Bearing the name "Dr. Miller's," this artsy, Victorian house is the UCSC slacker place for desserts, espresso, and Indian Chai. (The owners scored on those dark-wood church pews in the side room.) Definitely an only-in-Santa-Cruz experience. There's a large, shady deck for whiling the hours away. • Daily 8am-midnight.

The Catalyst ★ $: 1011 Pacific Garden Mall (Pacific at Walnut), Santa Cruz, 408/423-1338. The light, airy atrium is perfect for brunch. (Glance around. See all those plants? This used to be *the* fern bar in the 1970s). At night this is still the happening place. Play pool upstairs or check out the band in the back (anything from acoustic rock to hillbilly blues). The greatest names in rock still hit this place at the beginning of world tours. This was the town's bowling alley in the 1950s. The stage sits where the pins used to fall. • Cover charge $1 and up; 21 and over. Shows start around 9:30pm.

El Palomar ★★★ $: Pacific Garden Mall (Pacific at Walnut), in the Palomar Hotel, Santa Cruz 408/425-7575. Housed in the beautifully restored ballroom of this Deco hotel gem is one of the area's top Mexican eateries. A lively bar and innovative taco cantina add to the main action—creatively sauced Latin seafoods, definitive refried beans and margaritas. Don't miss the housemade soft corn tortillas. • M-Th 11am-3pm; F 11am-3pm, 5-10:30pm; Sa 11am-10:30; Su 10am-10pm. 5-10pm. Taco bar & cantina open daily 11am-10pm.

Espresso Royale Café ★ ¢: 1545 Pacific Ave. (Front/Water), Santa Cruz, 408/429-9804. A great café with a peaceful garden courtyard to offset that coffee buzz. Hang with your laptop and check out the ever-changing art installations. Don't leave without trying the India Joze biscotti. • M-F 7am-midnight; Sa-Su 7am-midnight.

The Fog Bank ★ $: 211 Esplanade (Stockton), Capitola, 408/462-1881. A casual bar scene for grabbing a burger or sandwich. Sit at the outdoor bar to best survey the beach scene. • M-F 10am-11pm; Sa-Su 9am-2am.

India Joze ★★ $: Art Center, 1001 Center St. (Union/Water), Santa Cruz, 408/427-3554. Your friends will tire of hearing you rave about this place after your meal here. (Yes, the food is that good.) An extremely original restaurant serving spicy and eclectic Middle Eastern and Asian cuisine. For added fun, the menu changes weekly. (And remember: leave room for the chocolate truffles.) • M-Sa 11:30am-2:30pm, 5:30-9:30pm; Su 10am-2:30pm, 5:30-9pm. Caffè Beppe serves light snacks daily 2:30-5:30pm.

Kuumbwa Jazz Center: 320-2 E. Cedar St. (Broadway), Santa Cruz, 408/427-2227. A jazz bar popular with older locals and those "in-the-know." The small venue lends an intimacy to performances. • Cover $5 and up. Call for showtimes and scheduling.

Mr. Toots Coffeehouse ★ ¢: 221 Esplanade (Wharf), Capitola, 408/475-3679. A comfortable, earthy hang-out with live jazz/classical guitar nightly. Slouch around on garage-sale couches, get intellectual at the long study table, or head for the balcony out back and trip on the waves. • Su-Th 8am-11pm; F-Sa 7:30am-midnight.

New Leaf ¢: 1134 Pacific Ave. (Front), Santa Cruz, 408/425-5323. This small, well-stocked organic grocery and deli makes a fine place to pick up picnic fixings before heading to the beach or the hills. • Daily 9am-9pm.

Omei ★★★ $: 2316 Mission St. aka Hwy 1 (Fair/Swift), Santa Cruz, 408/425-8458. It doesn't look like much from the parking lot, but once inside, you'll find this romantic setting offers delicious, innovative Chinese food. The red oil dumplings are legendary, as are any of the sensuous sea bass dishes. The menu—which showcases locally made wines—changes seasonally. • M-Th 11:30am-2pm, 5-9pm; F 11:30am-2pm, 5-10pm; Sa 5-10pm; Su 5-9:30pm.

Oswald ★★★ $$$: 1547 Pacific Ave. (Locust/Water), Santa Cruz, 408/423-7427. Sophisticated bistro setting gives rise to some top-quality new American cooking, long on seasonal produce-fueled salads, succulent grilled and roasted meats, and opulent desserts. A smart place filled with a smart crowd. • Daily 5:30pm-10pm.

The Red Room: 1003 Cedar St. (Soquel), Santa Cruz, 408/425-0591. It's actually two rooms, complete with dance floor, bar, live music, and hoards of slacker-types on weekends.

Ristorante Avanti ★★★ $: 1711 Mission St. aka Hwy 1 (Bay/Palm), Santa Cruz 408/427-0135. Popular with University professors and visiting celebrities, this laid-back trattoria offers sensitive, seasonal dishes—local seafoods, fine pastas, organic salads, and a fun wine bar for sampling new vintages. • M-Th Su 8am-2pm, 5-9pm; F-Sa 8am-2pm, 5-9:30pm.

Royal Taj ★ $: 270 Soquel Ave. (Ocean/River), Santa Cruz, 408/427-2400. Reasonably priced Indian food served in peaceful and comfortable surroundings. A short walk from downtown. • Daily 11:30am-2:30pm, 5:30-10pm.

Santa Cruz Brewing Company and Front Street Pub ★★ $: 516 Front St. (Soquel), Santa Cruz, 408/429-8838. Great beer on tap, all brewed on the premises, and a better than average pub menu. Live music some nights. • Su-Tu 11:30am-11pm; W-Sa 11:30am-midnight.

Santa Cruz Coffee Roasting Company ★ ¢: 1330 Pacific Ave. (Soquel), Santa Cruz, 408/459-0100. One of the original cafés downtown. Grab a cup of (individually brewed) joe and check out the scene from their patio. • M-Th 6am-11pm; Sa-Su 6:30-midnight.

Seabright Brewery ★ $$: 519 Seabright Ave. (E. Cliff), Santa Cruz, 408/426-2739. Good place for drinks and outdoor dining. During warm days, the outdoor patio is jammed with rollerbladers, mountain bikers, beach goers, and locals who quaff steins, swap stories, and (possibly) exchange phone numbers. • Daily 11:30am-11:30pm.

Shadowbrook ★★ $$$: 1750 Wharf Rd. (Capitola Rd.), Capitola, 408/475-1511. A town classic. Always voted the city's "most romantic" dining spot. Take the single-car funicular from the upper terrace down to the restaurant. Or walk through the intriguing, garden-lined paths that lead to the dining room entrance. Even though this place has "special occasion" written all over it, the menu of updated continental standards is well executed. Seafood dishes especially can be outstanding. • M-Th 5:30-9pm; F 5-9:30pm; Sa 4-10:30pm; Su 10am-2:15pm, 4-9pm.

Tacos Moreno ★ $: 1053 Water St. (Morrison), Santa Cruz, 408/429-6095. Inexpensive family-style Mexican food. One of the most authentic taquerias this side of San Francisco's Mission district. Amazing carnita*s* and *al pastor*. Cash only. • Daily 11am-8pm.

Zachary's Restaurant ★★ $: 819 Pacific Ave. (Laurel/Maple), Santa Cruz, 408/427-0646. Popular place with great healthy breakfasts. You may have to wait as long as an hour on the weekend, but the curry-tofu scramble is well worth it. • Tu-Su 7am-2:30pm.

Whale City Bakery Bar & Grill ★ $: Hwy 1 (12 mi. north of Santa Cruz), Davenport 408/423-9803. Have breakfast with surfers, mountain men, and German tourists, then stay to linger over a lunch of cheeseburgers and beer. With a trail leading to the beach just across the highway, this place is an institution. • Daily 6am-8pm.

Places to Stay

Camping & Hostels

Park.Net State Parks Camping Reservations: 800/444-7275. www.park-net.com.

New Brighton State Beach $: 408/475-4850. From Santa Cruz, take Hwy 1 south to beach exit. This is a great wooded park with separate facilities for car and bike campers. $17 Su-Th, $18 F-Sa; extra cars $6; hikers and bikers $3, dogs $1. Day use $6.

Santa Cruz American Youth Hostel $: 321 Main St. (2nd/3rd), Santa Cruz, 408/423-8304. Dubbed "the friendliest hostel in the West," this small, charming, post-Victorian house attracts foreign travelers and backpackers in the summer. The hostel is a 10-minute walk from the downtown bus stop and has parking. $12. Call 8-10am or 5-10pm to reach a person instead of a message for reservations.

Hotels, Motels, and B&Bs

Babbling Brook Bed and Breakfast Inn $$$: 1025 Laurel St. (California), Santa Cruz, 408/427-2437. A restored country inn with 12 rooms, all boasting private baths and French decor. Fireplaces, private decks, and a garden stream contribute to the romantic setting. Located near the beach, shops, and boardwalk. $145-$195.

Cliff Crest Bed and Breakfast Inn $$$: 407 Cliff St. (2nd/3rd), Santa Cruz, 408/427-2609. A Queen Anne-style house with five rooms, one with a fireplace. Full breakfast is served in the rooms or the solarium, and wine and cheese are offered in the evenings. $95-$150.

The Darling House $$$: 314 West Cliff Dr. (Gharkey), Santa Cruz, 408/458-1958. An eight-room oceanside mansion dating from 1910, with antique furnishings. Continental breakfast is served in the dining rooms, and most rooms have a shared bath. Great views looking out onto the Monterey Bay and mountains beyond. $95-$225.

Inn Cal $$: 370 Ocean St. (Broadway), Santa Cruz, 408/458-9220. It's 10 minutes from the Boardwalk, and has all the comforts of home (color TV, air conditioning, and telephones) but is a bit noisy due to the location. $35-$100.

Sea & Sand Inn $$$: 201 West Cliff Dr. (Bay), Santa Cruz 408/427-3400. A splendid location hanging out over the surfing lanes of Cowells Beach, with a great view across the Monterey Bay, it features attractive oceanview rooms and a setting within easy walking of the Wharf and Boardwalk. Su-Th $119-$239; F-Sa $139-$299.

Terrace Court $$$: 125 Beach St. (Front), Santa Cruz, 408/423-3031. A most excellent location directly across from the wharf. Rent a room on one of the two terraces facing the ocean. (Or stay in a poolside unit with a kitchenette.) The husband-and-wife management team will treat you like family. Summer $105-$165; winter $90-$140.

TAHOE ★★

Lake Tahoe, the second deepest lake in the United States, is the center of the region known to many simply as "Tahoe." Rand McNally has named the area "America's Number One Resort Area," and justifiably so—there's skiing and snowboarding in the winter; hiking, camping, biking, water sports, and other outdoor activities in the summer; and gambling on the Nevada side year-round.

Most people divide the area into North Lake and South Lake. South Lake centers around the adjacent towns South Lake Tahoe, California and Stateline, Nevada. This area embodies the honky-tonk hustle of Stateline's casinos, although it still offers outdoor activities in the lovely Desolation Wilderness and many state parks nearby. North Lake Tahoe commercial activity is less concentrated. Hotels, restaurants, and stores spread out along the lake from the low-key resort town Tahoe City to pricey Incline Village (aka Income Village) and extend far from the lake to the Truckee-Donner Lake area. North Lake evokes a mixture of old-West history and modern strip malls.

General Information

Road Conditions: California 800/427-ROAD (7623). Nevada 702/793-1313.

South Lake Tahoe Chamber of Commerce: 3066 L. Tahoe Blvd. (Lyons), South Lake Tahoe, 530/541-5255. Visitor information. • M-Sa 9am-5:30pm.

South Lake Tahoe Visitors Authority: 800/AT-TAHOE (288-2463). Lodging reservations.

North Lake Tahoe Resort Association: 245 N. Lake Boulevard, Tahoe City, 530/583-3494, 800/TAHOE4U (824-6348). Visitor information: daily 8am-5pm. Lodging reservations: 800/822-5959. • M-F 6:30am-8pm; Sa-Su 9am-4pm.

North Lake Tahoe Chamber of Commerce: 530/581-8736 or 530/581-6900.

U.S. Forest Service Visitor Information: Hwy 89, 3 mi. north of the "Y" in S. Lake Tahoe, 530/573-2674. • Summer daily 8am-5:30pm; fall Sa-Su only; closed Nov-May.

Getting There

When driving, take I-80 east to Sacramento; turn onto Hwy 50 to South Lake Tahoe or continue on I-80 toward Truckee and the North Shore. Reno is another 35 miles past Truckee. It can snow heavily without much warning at any time of the year; always carry chains. Also avoid leaving the Bay Area any time near 5pm on Friday.

Greyhound (central reservations 800/231-2222 or Stateline, Nevada terminal 702/588-4645) runs a few daily buses to South Lake Tahoe, Truckee, and Reno from San Francisco; the one-way fare is around $27. **Amtrak** 800/872-7245 runs from Oakland and San Jose to South Lake, Truckee, and Reno. Most trips involve a train to Sacramento and a bus to your destination, but an occasional train offering spectacular views goes all the way to Truckee and Reno (reservations required for this train). The one-way fare to South Lake is around $30, to Truckee around $25 (during certain promotions, round-trip fares are almost the same as one-way). **South Lake Tahoe Airport** 530/542-6180 is tiny and is currently without commercial service. The airport is a short cab or shuttle-bus ride from South Lake Tahoe. There are frequent flights into **Reno-Tahoe Airport** 702/328-6400, but it's an hour from Lake Tahoe, so you may have to rent a car or take a shuttle; try the **Tahoe Casino Express** 800/446-6128, **Tours Unlimited** 530/546-1355, **Budget Chauffeur** 800/426-5644, or **Aerotrans** 702/786-2376.

Once in Tahoe, **TART**, Tahoe Area Regional Transit 530/581-6365, offers bus service through the North Lake area, including winter ski area shuttles (ski and bike accessible). **STAGE**, South Tahoe Area Ground Express, 530/573-2080, serves the South Lake Tahoe area with buses, tourist trolleys, and a shuttle service for those far from bus lines called Bus Plus.

Skiing & Snowboarding ★★

Because the Sierra is the first mountain range in from the coast, storms bring heavy, wet snows that are measured in feet, not inches. It's reasonable to expect skiable snow from December to May. However, snowfall varies dramatically. During a bad year, ski areas might get 200 inches of snow, while during a good year they might get 600 inches.

The region offers a wide variety of skiing options, from huge resorts to tiny mom-and-pop hills. Tahoe also has many good cross-country ski resorts. **Royal Gorge** claims to be the largest in the United States. Many downhill resorts have trails, as do **Claire Tappaan Lodge** and **Alpine Skills Institute**. Many people prefer free "backwoods" skiing—you can often spot the trailhead by the cars parked on the side of the road. Many parking areas are part of California State Parks Sno-Park program, and require a permit; check with a local sports shop or call State Parks, 530/541-3030. Stop in at any outdoors store for advice and trail maps. In addition to shops at ski areas, there are rental shops in Truckee, Tahoe City, and South Lake.

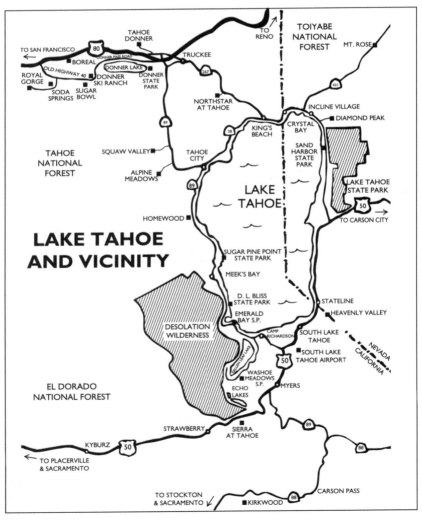

Ski Club Hotline: 510/827-4303. Lists phone numbers of various Bay Area ski clubs.

Alpine Meadows: Off Hwy 89 between Truckee and Tahoe City, 530/583-4232, 800/441-4423. The "other" large area in North Lake, but much smaller than Squaw. Offers ample variety, including steep chutes accessed by climbing. Well-sheltered in stormy weather. The last area to close in the spring. A local favorite, in part because of candid snow reports and retro feel. 1,553' vert. $47 adult.

Boreal Ski Area: Just off I-80 at Boreal/Castle Peak exit, 530/426-3666, 530/426-1114. A short, wide area that offers a good variety of runs for beginners and interme-diates as well as night skiing. Right off highway on top of Donner pass, so it's conve-nient and gets lots of snow. Popular with snowboarders and families. Also owns **Soda Springs,** a tiny area off Hwy 40 near Norden. 600' vert. $28 adult.

Diamond Peak at Ski Incline: Off Hwy 28, Incline Village, Nevada, 702/832-1126. 24-hour ski information: 702/831-3211. Summer phone 702/832-117. Medium-sized area just across the state line. It's a bit harder to reach (which means smaller crowds) and can have good snow when other areas are lacking. Recently increased its skiable terrain, adding numerous expert runs at the top of the mountain. Cross-country area. 1,840' vert. $38 adult.

Donner Ski Ranch: Old Hwy 40 about 6 mi. from I-80 Soda Springs/Norden exit, 530/426-3635. Mom-and-pop sized, but offers some good intermediate terrain, a homey atmosphere, and night skiing. 750' vert. $23 adult.

Heavenly Valley: Ski Run Blvd. from Hwy 50 in South Lake Tahoe or Tramway Dr. off Kingsbury Grade east of Stateline, 530/541-1330, 702/586-7000. Huge resort claiming the most skiable terrain of any resort in the United States. Experts prefer the Nevada side. It also offers great views and is just minutes from the casinos and accommodations in Stateline. Suffers from overcrowding and a confusing trail net-work. 3,600' vert. $49 adult.

Homewood: Hwy 89, 6 mi. south of Tahoe City, 530/525-2992, 530/525-2900. Small area—although bigger than what you see from the road—with mostly intermediate runs and classic postcard views of Lake Tahoe. It may be the best place to ski on the weekends and is definitely an ideal place to learn to snowboard. 1,650' vert. $35 adult.

Kirkwood Ski and Summer Resort: Hwy 88 from the Central Valley, or ½ hour south of South Lake Tahoe off Hwy 89, 209/258-6000, 415/989-SNOW (7669). Good-sized ski area with diverse terrain, including radical steeps and smaller crowds. High base elevation leads to drier snow. Cross country. 2,000' vert. $43 adult.

Mt. Rose Ski Resort: Rt. 431 near Incline Village, Nevada, 702/849-0704, 800/SKI-ROSE/754-7673. Another Medium-sized area across the state line offering a surpris-ing amount of challenging terrain. Good on powder days. 1,450' vert. $38 adult.

Northstar-at-Tahoe: Hwy 267 between Truckee and Kings Beach, 800/GO-NORTH (466-6784), 530/562-1010, 530/562-1330. Large, planned resort with the motto, "Northstar has it all," including luxury condominiums, cross-country, and a golf course. Medium-sized ski area with many beginner and intermediate cruising runs (locals call it Flatstar). 2,200' vert. $46 adult.

Royal Gorge: Off Old Hwy 40 from I-80 Soda Springs/Norden exit, 530/426-3871. Huge cross-country ski area, with well-groomed tracks for kick-and-glide and skating. Serves all levels from beginners to competitive racers. Full-service lodge with rentals, lessons, and underfriendly employees. $19.50 adult.

Sierra at Tahoe: Off Hwy 50 between Echo Summit and South Lake Tahoe, 530/659-7453. A good-sized ski area that provides bowl skiing for intermediates and a nurtur-ing atmosphere for beginners. 2,212' vert. $43 adult.

Squaw Valley: Hwy 89 between Tahoe City and Truckee, 530/583-6985, 530/583-6955. Squaw Valley is huge, offering everything from serious cliff jumping to gentle bunny hills. There's even a mountain-top outdoor skating rink, swimming pool, and bungee jumping. But be prepared for long lift lines on weekends, steep ticket prices, and a glitzy scene. The upper lifts are often closed on windy days. Squaw employees wear buttons that say "We Care," but everyone knows they don't. 2,850' vert. $48 adult.

Sugar Bowl Ski Resort: Old Hwy 40 about three miles from I-80 Soda Springs/Norden exit, 530/426-3651. Medium-sized area with varied terrain. Ridge-top location draws good snow coverage. A recent expansion added road access to the Mr. Judah base area—good for those who don't like riding the creaky old gondola to the base lodge. Slow, old lifts stop a lot. 1,500' vert. $47 adult.

Tahoe Donner: Northwoods Blvd., north of I-80 from first Truckee exit, 530/587-9444, tickets 530/587-9400, snow report 530/587-9494. Tiny area associated with sub-division offering limited beginner and intermediate skiing. Family-oriented. Excellent cross-country area. $26 adult.

Warm-Weather Activities ★★

Parks and Beaches ★★

Much of the area around Lake Tahoe is public land; either State Park, National Forest, or local park. Most of the parks are open from approximately Memorial Day through Labor Day, weather permitting. **Donner Memorial State Park** 530/582-7894, off I-80 on Donner Pass Road near Truckee, lies on the edge of **Donner Lake**. It's a beautiful spot for a short visit or camping, and there's even a museum which tells the Donner Party's grisly story—stranded pioneers reduced to cannibalism—open daily 9am to 5pm year-round. Off Hwy 89 along the west side of the lake, you'll find three state parks: **Sugar Pine Point** 530/525-7982, **D. L. Bliss** 530/525-7277, and **Emerald Bay** ★★ 530/541-3030, home to shoreline beaches, camping, and trails. While at Emerald Bay, visit the Scandinavian mansion Vikingsholm. In **Lake Tahoe Nevada State Park** 702-831-0494 on the northeastern side of Lake Tahoe, you'll find **Sand Harbor**, a beautiful beach with shallow water that warms up enough for swimming. During the summer, Sand Harbor often hosts theater or music performances on its outdoor stage.

Desolation Wilderness ★★★: along the southwest side of Lake Tahoe, 530/573-2600. This magnificent area's austere beauty has much to offer day hikers and backpackers. There are four primary entry points: Emerald Bay and Fallen Leaf Lake off Hwy 89, and Echo Lake and Horsetail Falls off Hwy 50. It's one of California's most popular wilderness areas, so you won't find total solitude on the trail during summer week-ends, but you will find crystal clear lakes nestled under ragged peaks and plenty of memorable vistas.

Aquatic Sports ★

Because Lake Tahoe is so large, it is always cold—the warmest it gets is 65 degrees—but never freezes over. However, the brave still swim, ski, sail, and otherwise indulge in the lake. Donner Lake is also cold, but popular for skiing and fishing.

Jet ski and boat rentals are a popular way to get out on the water for a few pricey hours. Reservations are recommended. On Tahoe's north shore, Kings Beach and Tahoe City have the most active marinas. In King's Beach, try **North Tahoe Marina** 530/546-8248, located at the Kings Beach marina (just west of Hwy 267), or **King's Beach Aquasports** 530/546-AQUA (2782), on the east side of King's Beach. **Tahoe Paddle and Oar** 530/581-3029, at the North Tahoe Beach Center across from Hwy 267, rents a variety of nonmotorized water toys. In the center of Tahoe City, try **Lighthouse Watersports Center** 530/583-6000, located in the marina behind Safeway, and **Tahoe Water Adventures** 530/583-3225, located across from the Lakehouse Mall. On the west shore south of Tahoe City with locations in Sunnyside and Homewood, **High Sierra Water Ski School** 530/583-7417 and 530/525-1214, has a variety of boats, including sailboats. In South Lake Tahoe, head for Timber Cove Marina on Lakeshore Boulevard at Park Avenue just west of the state line, where you'll find the **South Lake Tahoe Marina** 530/541-6626, **Timber Cove Marina** 530/542-4472 or 530/544-2942 for jet skis and power boats, and **Kayak Tahoe** 530/544-2011 for kayaks. For a more relaxed exploration of the lake, hop on the glass-bottomed **Tahoe Queen** 530/541-3364 or 800/23-TAHOE (238-2463), at Hwy 50 and Ski Run Boulevard. They offer daily Emerald Bay cruises and sunset dinner-dance trips. The Emerald Bay trip costs about $16 for adults; the sunset cruise costs $16 or $28 including dinner.

Mountain Biking ★★★

There are a number of excellent rides throughout the Tahoe hills, free from all the rules and regulations prevalent in the Bay Area. Most Tahoe bike stores can give you advice on their favorite rides, but you can choose from an endless supply of fire roads. Serious riders should ask about the Flume Trail. Most of the bigger ski areas listed above open their trails to bikes in summer and offer bike rentals and even lift service (start with Squaw Valley and Northstar).

Rentals are available at those ski areas and at bike stores in Tahoe City, Truckee, and South Lake for about $20-$25/day. In downtown Tahoe City, try **Olympic Bicycle Shop** 530/581-2500 at 620 North Lake Boulevard (just west of the Boatworks Mall) for higher performance gear or **Porter's Ski & Sport** 530/583-2314 across the street at 501 North Lake Boulevard for basic bikes. Porter's has a second location in the Lucky Shopping Center on Hwy 89 just south of I-80. In South Lake Tahoe, bike rentals are available at **Tahoe Cyclery** 530/541-2726, located at 3552 Hwy 50, **Anderson's** 530/541-0500, located at 645 Emerald Bay Road (aka Hwy 89) at 13th Street, and **Sierra Cycleworks** 530/541-7505 at 3430 Hwy 50.

Gambling ★

Nevada's casinos conspicuously mark the border between that state and California. (Remember that you must be 21 to get in.) Tahoe's casinos can offer some great deals (Reno's are the best!) including moderate room and meal prices and cheap entertainment in their lounges. Look for all-you-can-eat buffet specials for $5 or less.

On the south shore, **Caesar's**, **Harrah's**, and the other big-name casinos cater to visitors with more cash—they raise the minimum betting limits throughout the night. If you're looking to test the waters with small bets, find a $2 or $3 blackjack table at **Harvey's** or the **Horizon**—friendly, low-key places. Most casinos on the north shore are in Crystal Bay, Nevada. The biggest club on the north shore, however, is the **Hyatt**, which is off by itself in Incline Village.

Caesar's: 55 Hwy 50, Stateline, NV, 702/588-3515, 800/648-3353.

Crystal Bay: 14 Hwy 28, Crystal Bay, NV, 702/831-0512.

Harrah's: Hwy 50, Stateline, NV, 702/588-6611, 800/648-3773.

Harvey's: Hwy 50, Stateline, NV, 800/648-3361.

Horizon Resort Hotel Casino: Hwy 50, Stateline, NV, 702/588-6211, 800/648-3322.

Hyatt Regency Lake Tahoe Resort and Casino: 111 Country Club Dr. (at Lakeshore Dr.), Incline Village, NV, 702/831-1111, 800/233-1234.

Tahoe Biltmore Lodge and Casino: 5 Hwy 28, Crystal Bay, NV, 702/831-0660, 800/BILTMORE (245-8667).

Restaurants and Entertainment

The Beacon ★★ $$: 1900 Jamieson Beach Rd. (off Hwy 89 at Camp Richardson), South Lake Tahoe, 530/541-0630. Standard California fare along with its signature Rum Runner cocktail in a beachfront location. • Daily 10am-10pm.

Bridge Tender ★ $: 30 W. Lake Blvd. aka Hwy 89, Tahoe City, 530/583-3342. Live trees grow through the roof, and outdoor seating overlooks Fanny Bridge. Burgers, fries, and other pub grub. • Daily 11am-11pm; bar open until 2am.

Cantina Los Tres Hombres ★ $: 765 Emerald Bay Rd. aka Hwy 89, South Lake Tahoe, 530/544-1233. Margaritas and Mexican food. • Su-Th 11:30am-9:30pm; F-Sa 11:30am-10:30pm.

Chart House ★★ $$$: 392 Kingsbury Grade, Stateline, NV, 702/588-6276. Well-done surf-and-turf with great views of the lake. • Su-F 5:30-10pm; Sa 5-10:30pm.

Christy Hill ★★★ $$$$: 115 Grove St. (off N. Lake Blvd. near marina), Tahoe City, 530/583-8551. Creative California cuisine considered by many to be the finest in Tahoe. The multilevel dining room is located in a simply furnished house—lots of pink and gray—with the decorative emphasis on the spectacular lake views. • Tu-Su 5:30-9:30pm.

Donner Lake Kitchen ★ $: 13720 Donner Pass Rd., Truckee (behind Donner Pines Store along Donner Lake), 530/587-3119. Popular local diner for home-style and Mexican breakfasts and lunches. Love the velvet paintings. Cash only. • Daily 7am-2pm.

Fire Sign Café ★★ $: 1785 W. Lake Blvd. aka Hwy 89, Tahoe Park (2 mi. south of Tahoe City), 530/583-0871. A great spot for breakfast or a healthy lunch. Pleasant patio. • Daily 7am-3pm.

Frank's Restaurant ★ $: 1207 Emerald Bay Rd. aka Hwy 89, South Lake Tahoe, 530/544-3434. An amazing place for home-cooked breakfast. • M-Sa 6am-2pm; Su 7am-2pm.

La Hacienda del Lago ★ $: Boatworks Mall, 760 N. Lake Blvd. aka Hwy 28, Tahoe City, 530/583-0358. Tasty Mexican food and free-flowing margaritas at this festive local hangout. Happening night life. • Summer daily 11:30am-10pm. Winter daily 4-10pm.

Heidi's ★ $: 3485 Lake Tahoe Blvd. aka Hwy 50, South Lake Tahoe, 530/544-8113. They claim to serve "the best breakfast you'll ever have." Good lunches, too. • Daily 7am-2pm.

Jake's on the Lake ★★ $$: Boatworks Mall, 780 N. Lake Blvd. aka Hwy 28, Tahoe City, 530/583-0188. A swinging night spot ("snakes on the make"), with surprisingly good American food, especially seafood and pasta. • Su-Th 11:30am-10pm; F-Sa 11:30am-10:30pm.

Lake Tahoe Pizza Co. ★ $: 1168 Emerald Bay Rd. aka Hwy 50 and Hwy 89, just south of the Y, South Lake Tahoe, 530/544-1919. Fantastic pizza place. • Daily 4-10pm.

O.B.'s Pub and Restaurant ★ $$/$$$: 10046 Commercial Row, Truckee, 530/587-4164. A favorite among locals. Large, dark saloon serving a range of hearty American food from burgers to pasta to grilled salmon. • Daily 11:30am-10pm.

The Passage ★★★ $$$: Truckee Hotel, 1007 Bridge St. (at Commercial), Truckee, 530/587-7619. Creatively prepared and presented California cuisine in a historic, candlelit dining room. Game specials can be superb. • M-Th 11:30am-9:30pm; F-Sa 11:30am-10pm; Su 10am-9:30pm.

River Ranch Lodging and Dining ★★ $$/$$$: 2285 River Rd. (Hwy 89 at Alpine Meadows Rd.), Tahoe City, 530/583-4264. Dark and cozy restaurant near Alpine Meadows with good basic food and great views of the Truckee River. If you don't want a serious meal, get a burger by the fireplace in the bar or out on the patio. • Patio Su-Th noon-3pm; F-Sa 11:30am-5pm. Dining Room Su-Th 6-9:30pm; F-Sa 5:30-10pm.

Rosie's Café ★ $$: 571 North Lake Blvd. (Hwy 28), Tahoe City, 530/583-8504. Eclectic, healthy menu in country saloon setting. Particularly good breakfasts. • Daily 6:30am-2:30pm, 5:30-10pm.

Squeeze Inn ★ $: 10060 Commercial Row, Truckee, 530/587-9814. Very popular local spot for great omelets (limitless variety of options), as well as other breakfast and lunch dishes. No credit cards. • Daily 7am-2pm.

Sunnyside Resort ★ $$: 1850 West Lake Blvd. aka Hwy 89, Tahoe City, 530/583-7200. Sports a large deck on the lake and standard sandwich and burger fare. Especially pleasant for summer brunch. • M-Th 11am-10pm; F-Sa 11am-10:30pm; Su 9am-10pm (no breakfast and shorter dinner hours during winter).

Truckee Trattoria ★★ $$: Gateway Shopping Center, Hwy 89 at Old Hwy 40, Truckee, 530/582-1266. Surprising find in a Safeway strip mall. Bright and clean setting for light California and Italian cuisine. Special entrées shine more than pastas. Liberal corkage policy. Reservations recommended. • Su, W-Su 5-9pm.

Wolfdale's ★★★ $$$: 640 N. Lake Blvd., Tahoe City, 530/583-5700. Highly regarded Asian-California vegetarian cuisine. Reservations recommended. • Dinner W-M 6-whenever; nightly during summer.

Za's ★ $/$$: 395 N. Lake Blvd. aka Hwy 28, Tahoe City, 530/583-1812. A tiny local's favorite where the waitstaff remembers regulars. Za's bills itself as a simple Italian restaurant, and lives up to it with hearty basic pasta, calzone, and pizza laden with garlic. Hidden behind Pete & Peter's bar. • Su-Th 4:30-9:30pm; F-Sa 4:30-10pm.

Places to Stay

In addition to the places listed below, try the North and South Tahoe Visitors Bureaus, Chambers of Commerce, and Central Reservations numbers listed under *General Information* for places to stay; they handle house and condo rentals, hotels, or inns. Also, **casinos** frequently offer good deals on weekend packages, figuring what you don't cough up in lodging you'll spend on gambling. **Renting houses** for a week or weekend is a good option for groups. Central Reservations' numbers should be able to handle short-term rentals. Many groups rent a house for the entire ski season. Tahoe realty companies have listings of available properties for short-term or seasonal rentals. The best bets for luxury accommodations are renting a nice condo (or house) or staying in one of the more upscale casinos such as the Hyatt.

Camping

Camping is available on most of the public lands around Tahoe, including the parks listed above. Most campgrounds are only open late spring and summer, although **Sugar Pine Point** and **Grover Hot Springs State Park** are both available for year-round camping. If you intend to camp in organized campgrounds between May and September, make reservations well in advance.

Park.Net: 800/444-7275. State Park campground reservations. www.park-net.com.

Biospherics: 800/280-2267. Forest Service campground reservations.

Camp Richardson $/$$: Hwy 89, 2 mi. north of Hwy 50, South Lake Tahoe, 530/541-1801. Private development with an 83-acre campground on the south shore that boasts 112 campsites with hot showers, a beach, a marina, and Nordic skiing in the winter. Lodging includes an inn as well as cabins (minimum one-week rental during summer). Campsites $19, lodge $64-90, cabins $546/week and up.

Hotels, Motels, and B&Bs

Alpine Skills International Lodge $/$$: Old Hwy 40 off I-80 at Norden/Soda Springs exit, 530/426-9108. A mountaineering school that offers bunk-and-breakfast accommodations. Lodge open full-time Thanksgiving-mid-April; during course times June-September; closed spring and fall. $24 bunk bed; $75 double-occupancy room.

Best Western Truckee Tahoe $$: 11331 Hwy 267, 1.5 mi. south of Truckee, 530/587-4525. Basic, clean, and comfortable, with pool, Jacuzzi, sauna, and skimpy continental breakfast. $84-$101.

Clair Tappaan Lodge $: Old Hwy 40 off I-80 at Norden/Soda Springs exit, 530/426-3632. Run by the Sierra Club, this huge old building has dormitory-style rooms; price includes family-style meals. $33-$37/Sierra Club members, $37-$39/nonmembers.

Donner Country Inn $$: 10070 Gregory Place (Donner Lake Rd. at Donner Pass Rd.), Truckee, 530/587-5574. Tiny, unassuming motel has comfortable rooms—some with wood-burning stoves. Minimum two night stay. $95.

Loch Leven Lodge $$: 13855 Donner Pass Rd., along Donner Lake, Truckee, 530/587-3773. Lakeside lodge with a big deck and hot tubs. Some rooms have fireplaces or kitchenettes. Cash or checks only. $66-$136.

Squaw Valley Central Reservations: 800/545-4350. Handles reservations for Squaw Valley and beyond. **Resort at Squaw Creek $$$$** is the newest, most deluxe property, while the PlumpJack Inn is newly upgraded; there are other, older facilities. Also handles condos and houses. $149-$325.

Super 8 Lodge $$: 11506 Deerfield Dr. (off Hwy 89 just south of I-80), Truckee, 530/587-8888. Not charming, but convenient, with Jacuzzi and sauna. $76-$104.

Tahoe City Travelodge $$: 455 N. Lake Blvd., Tahoe City, 530/583-3766, 800/255-3050. Basic, clean, and comfortable, with pool. In town. $78-$121.

Trade Winds Motel $: 944 Friday Ave., Stateline, NV, 800/628-1829. Two blocks from the casinos. Coffee makers, and a year-round spa and pool are included. $48-$98.

Truckee Hotel $$: 10007 Bridge St. (at Commercial Row), Truckee, 530/587-4444, 800/659-6921. A country-quaint historic building with reasonable prices (especially for European-style rooms). Breakfast included. $85-$100.

WINE COUNTRY ★★

The Napa and Sonoma Valleys are renowned as much for their scenic beauty as for their award-winning wines. In the Napa Valley, vineyards are scattered along a 35-mile stretch of land between the towns of Napa to the south and Calistoga (home of the hot springs and the bottled water) to the north. In between are Yountville, Rutherford, Oakville, and St. Helena—all quaint communities. The Sonoma Valley is less traveled than its neighbor, but is home to many quality wineries and other points of interest in the towns of Sonoma and Kenwood, and the small settlements in the Russian River Valley. Couples favor the region's numerous bed-and-breakfasts and intimate restaurants, which make for romantic (though often pricey) weekend retreats. For a most enjoyable visit, try to avoid going in summer, when temperatures regularly top 100 degrees, other tourists clog the streets, and lodging prices skyrocket. Spring can be lush and fragrant, fall brings the excitement of the harvest, and winter offers peaceful seclusion (and off-season discount accommodations).

Napa ★★

Until Spanish explorers arrived in 1823, the Nappa Indian tribe inhabited the Napa Valley. American farmers began settling the region in the 1830s, and in 1833, George Calvert Yount (Yountville's namesake) planted the first vineyard in the valley. It was Charles Krug, however, who brought Riesling grapes to the area in 1861, launching the wine business in earnest.

Calistoga Chamber of Commerce: 1458 Lincoln Ave. #9 (Lincoln/Fairway), Calistoga, 707/942-6333. • M-F 10am-5pm; Sa 10am-3pm; Su 11am-4pm.

Napa Valley Conference & Visitors Bureau: 1310 Napa Town Center Mall, (downtown off 1st between Main and Franklin sts.), Napa, 707/226-7459. • Daily 9am-5pm.

St. Helena Chamber of Commerce: 1010a Main St., St. Helena, 707/963-4456. • M-Sa 10am-5pm.

Getting There

By car, follow Hwy 101 north over the Golden Gate Bridge. From Hwy 101, take Hwy 37 east to Hwy 121, to Hwy 29 north, which runs the length of the valley from Napa to Calistoga. It's about a one-hour drive from the Golden Gate Bridge to the city of Napa. For a less crowded route through the Napa Valley, travel along the Silverado Trail, which runs parallel to Hwy 29. Along this road you'll find a host of smaller wineries tucked into the wooded mountains that form Napa's eastern border. These wineries may be hard to find if you're not paying attention to the small blue road signs, but if you tear yourself away from the quiet beauty of the valley, you'll find them—many of them.

Napa City Bus: 1151 Pearl St. (Main/Coombs), Napa, 707/255-7631. • Office M-F 8am-5pm; Sa 10am-3pm. Buses run M-F 6:30am-7:30pm; Sa 7:30am-6pm.

Getting Around

You probably don't need to be told again that drinking and driving isn't a good idea. Also, the roads near wineries are heavily policed. To avoid a ticket or an accident, consider one of these alternatives to a designated driver.

Bau Limousines: 999 S. Novato Blvd. (Redwood), Novato, 707/257-0887. This service has Towne Cars, stretch limos, and a luxury bus for larger groups. They will customize a wine tour to your liking. Rates are $45 per hour—ask about specials when you call. Reservations recommended.

Classic Cadillac Limousine Services: 1837 Tanen St. (Soscol), Napa, 707/252-2339. Tour Napa in style in a vintage Cadillac (their 1949 Caddy was featured in *The Godfather*). Drivers dress in period uniforms, and rates are about $60 per hour with a three-hour minimum. Reservations recommended.

Napa Valley Wine Train: 1275 McKinstry St. (1st/Soscol), Napa, 707/253-2111. Although the train only stops at one winery on the wine tour, you will see plenty of the wine country on the three-hour round-trip from Napa to St. Helena.

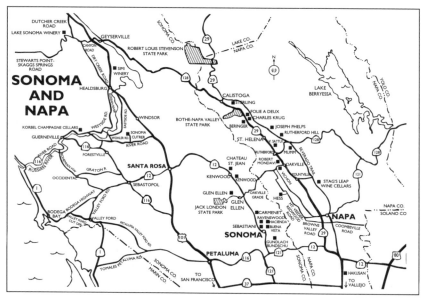

Napa Valley Wineries ★★

Many of Napa's wineries offer extensive, informative tours, and most charge a nominal fee for both the tour and tasting. Seasoned visitors take a comprehensive tour at one of the big wineries and then head to the smaller, less-crowded wineries that have free tastings and unique wines not readily available in stores. The following list is just a sampling; while you visit, pick up one of the many free brochures listing other wineries galore.

Beringer Wine Estates: 2000 Main St. aka Hwy 29, St. Helena, 707/963-7115, 707/963-4812. Guided tours of the winery's caves and historic Germanic mansion, where tasting and purchasing take place. Tasting is complimentary (for a fee you can sample reserve wines). • Tours daily 9:30am-5pm. Tasting 10am-5:30pm.

Charles Krug Winery: 2800 Main St. aka Hwy 29, St. Helena, 707/963-5057. The valley's first winery, and a must-visit for its extensive, entertaining tour. Group tours by appointment. • Tasting daily 10:30am-5:30pm. $3 including glass (free on Wednesday). Tours Th-M 11:30am, 1:30pm, 3:30pm. $3 (includes tasting).

Domaine Chandon: 1 California Dr. (Hwy 29), Yountville, 707/944-2280. The place to visit if you get a kick from champagne—more accurately, sparkling wine. This vineyard is owned and operated by the French vintners Moet et Chandon, makers of Dom Perignon. Group tours by reservation. • Free tours daily 11am-5pm (W-Su in winter). Tasting M-Tu 10am-6pm; W-Su 10am-8pm. $8 including glass.

Hakusan Sake Gardens: One Executive Way (Hwy 12/Hwy 37), Napa, 707/258-6160. For a change of drink, visit this place for sake and a stroll in a beautiful Japanese garden. • Daily 10am-5pm for self-guided tours and tasting ($1 for four kinds of sake).

Hess Collection Winery: 4411 Redwood Rd. (Hwy 29), Napa, 707/255-1144. A self-guided tour of this renovated historic building and its immaculate premises, replete with an impressive contemporary art collection (in essence, a small museum) distinguish a visit to this winery. The wines also win many awards. Tasting $3; museum free. • Daily 10am-4pm for tours and tasting.

Joseph Phelps Vineyard: 200 Taplin Rd. (Silverado Trail), St. Helena, 707/963-2745, 800/707-5789. Informative tours and generous samples at one of the best-designed vineyards in the valley. Tours and tastings by appointment only. • M-Sa 9am-5pm; Su 10am-4pm.

La Familia de Robert Mondavi (formerly Vichon Winery): 1595 Oakville Grade (Hwy 29), Oakville, 707/944-2811. A new Mondavi-owned winery that produces Italian-varietal wines and offers complimentary tasting. The shady picnic grounds that overlook the valley make this a nice place to stop for lunch, but they ask that you purchase a bottle of their vino in exchange for the setting. • Daily 10am-4:30pm.

Mumm Napa Valley: 8445 Silverado Trail (Rutherford Cross), Rutherford, 707/942-3434. The new kids on the champagne-makers' block, this winery offers enlightening tours every hour 11am-4pm (until 3pm in winter). To taste the wine you must purchase a glass or bottle of the bubbly—hardly a chore. • Daily 10:30am-6pm (10am-5pm in winter).

Robert Mondavi Winery: 7801 St. Helena Hwy. aka Hwy 29 (Oakville Cross), Oakville, 707/259-9463, 800/MONDAVI. A good place for first-time visitors to the valley, featuring a thorough, one-hour tour of the facilities. The tours are free (except for special tours), but you may have to wait quite a while to join one, since they fill up quickly (reservations suggested). You must take the tour to partake of the complimentary tastes of regular wines, and reserve wine tasting is charged by the glass. Throughout the summer months, the winery is the site of a program of concerts and events. • Daily 9am-5pm and in the winter until 4:30pm; hourly tours summer 10am-4pm and in the winter 9:30am-4:30pm. Concert and event information: 707/963-9617, ext. 6100.

Rutherford Hill Winery: 200 Rutherford Hill Rd. (off the Silverado Trail), Rutherford, 707/963-7194. While the 30-minute tours here are free, you'll have to ante up for a barrel tasting of the outstanding Merlots. The $4 fee includes a keepsake glass. • Tasting and sales daily 10am-5pm. Tours M-F 11:30am, 1:30pm, and 3:30pm, Sa-Su 11:30am, 12:30pm, 1:30pm, 2:30pm, 3:30pm, and 4:30pm. Only three tours a day during the winter.

Stag's Leap Wine Cellars: 5766 Silverado Trail (Yountville Cross/Oakville Cross), Napa, 707/944-2020. A small, unassuming place with great Cabernets and Chardonnays. Tastings are held throughout the day for $5 and include a glass. Free nonalcoholic beverages for designated drivers. • Daily 10am-4:30pm; tours by appointment only.

Sterling Vineyards: 1111 Dunaweal Ln. (Hwy 128), Calistoga, 707/942-3344 Accessible to visitors by aerial tram; the views and scenery from this hilltop winery are amazing. Tasting and tram ride included in the $6 visitor fee ($3 for ages 3-18, free under 3). Self-guided tours. • Daily 10:30am-4:30pm.

Other Attractions ★

Hot Air Balloons ★: Take to the skies in a hot air balloon for a panoramic view of the valley. Though not for the frugal or the acrophobic, ballooning has become a popular and romantic tourist activity. Balloons typically depart at dawn, and most companies provide a champagne brunch afterward. Try **Above the West Ballooning** 707/944-8638 and 800/NAPA-SKY (627-2759) in Yountville, or **Bonaventura Balloon Company** 707/944-2822 and 800/FLY-NAPA (359-6272) in Napa. Flights are about $195 per person. Reservations are recommended.

Horseback Riding ★: Landlubbers take heart—you can also see the countryside on horseback on a guided trail ride with **Sonoma Cattle Company**, 707/996-8566. They operate concessions at three area parks: Bothe-Napa Valley State Park (see below), Sugarloaf Ridge State Park, and Jack London State Park (the latter two are in Sonoma). A 90-minute ride at Bothe costs $40, while two-hour treks at the other parks costs $45. Reservations are recommended on the weekend.

Bicycle Rentals ★: Athletic types may want to bring bikes and cycle through the flats of the valley. If you lack a bike or a way to transport your own, you can rent wheels at **St. Helena Cyclery**, 1156 Main St. aka Hwy 29 (Spring), St. Helena, 707/963-7736. Located in the heart of Napa Valley, it rents hybrids (a combination of a mountain and a road bike) for $7 per hour, $25 per business day. Prices include a lock, helmet, saddlebag, and water-bottle rack. • M-Sa 9:30am-5:30pm; Su 10am-5pm.

Bryan's Napa Valley Cyclery 4080 Byway East (Trowler), Napa, 707/255-3377, rents road bikes and hybrids for $7 per hour, $22 for an entire day. All-day guided cycle tours along the Silverado Trail are also available for groups of two to ten riders for $85 per person. Tours include bike rentals, and visits to three or four wineries with tastings and lunch. Make reservations at least four days in advance. • M-F 9:30am-5pm; Sa 9:30am-6pm.

Bothe-Napa Valley State Park ★: Hwy 29 between St. Helena and Calistoga, 707/942-4575. This park offers 1,800 acres of hiking amid redwoods, oaks, and wildflowers, as well as picnicking and a swimming pool. Camping is $15-$16(see Places to Stay below). $5 day-use fee.

Robert Louis Stevenson State Park ★: Hwy 29, 4.5 mi. north of St. Helena, 707/942-4575. Among the attractions at this park are an abandoned silver mine and the bunkhouse where the writer spent his honeymoon in 1880 and collected material for his novel *Silverado Springs*. There are no comfort facilities in the park (not even water or restrooms), but even so, make the climb to the 2,960-foot summit of **Mount St. Helena** (rumored to have been Stevenson's inspiration for Spyglass Hill in Treasure Island) for the breathtaking **view ★★** of the Bay Area and the Sierra Nevada. Free.

Silverado Museum ★: 1490 Library Ln. (Adams), St. Helena, 707/963-3757. True Stevenson aficionados can also visit this museum, which is filled with manuscript notes and other memorabilia. The museum is located in the library in downtown St. Helena, so you can bone up on the author's works while you're there. • Tu-Su noon-4pm.

Taking the waters ★★: Don't leave Napa Valley without paying a visit to one of the many Calistoga spas and mineral baths. Indulgences range from basic mud and mineral baths to extras like herbal facials, acupressure, and manicures. The staff at **Calistoga Village Inn and Spa**, 1880 Lincoln Ave. aka Hwy 29 (Silverado Trail), Calistoga, 707/942-0991, will pamper you at reasonable prices, as will **Dr. Wilkinson's** 1507 Lincoln Ave. (Fairview), Calistoga, 707/942-4102, which offers a two-hour mud bath/massage package for just $89. Overnight accommodations are available on the premises, but you don't have to be a guest to use the spa facilities—though you do need a reservation.

Old Faithful Geyser ★★: Hwy 29 to 1299 Tubbs Ln. (just north of Calistoga), 707/942-6463. En route to the healing baths of Calistoga, take a detour to watch a different kind of steam bath. This natural wonder spews a 60-foot jet of boiling water into the air approximately every 40 minutes (emissions can vary quite a bit depending on the water level). • Daily 9am-6pm. Admission $6, seniors $5, ages 6-12 years $2, and under 6 free.

Places to Eat

Auberge du Soleil ★★ $$$$: 180 Rutherford Hill Rd. (off Silverado Trail), Rutherford, 707/963-1211. Auberge du Soleil is one of the most luxurious and expensive resorts in Napa Valley. In keeping with the sunny name, it's done up in a Southwest-meets-south-of-France style with lots of stucco and sports impressive views of the surrounding hills and dales, especially from the terrace. An afternoon drink on the patio lets you taste the luxury without committing to dine here. The California cuisine offers the popular blend of local ingredients with diverse influences. Reservations recommended. • M-Th 7-11am, 11:30am-2:30pm, 6-9:30pm; F-Su 7-11am, 11:30am-2:30pm, 5:30-9:30pm.

Bistro Don Giovanni ★★ $$: 4110 Hwy 29 (Salvador), Napa, 707/224-3300. Piatti veterans Donna and Giovanni Scala have filled this large modern space with patrons hungry for their their lusty Italian cooking. In addition to the ubiquitous wood-fired pizzas, the menu includes creative focaccia sandwiches (served with homemade potato chips and aioli), hearty pasta dishes (*pappardelle* with rabbit stew should warm your soul), roast chicken, and braised lamb shanks. Sit on the porch with a view of the vineyards, wash down your meal with a hearty red wine, and soak up the Mediterranean ambience. A recent renovation adds to the charm as does the herb garden. Reservations recommended. • Su-Th 11:30am-10pm; F-Sa 11:30am-11pm.

Brava Terrace ★★★ $$$: 3010 Hwy 29 (Lodi), St. Helena, 707/963-9300. Fred Halpert is yet another big city chef who's successfully moved north to enjoy the good life in Napa Valley. He's made the best of the new locale, creating a restaurant with a delightful namesake terrace overlooking a shady brook, a perfect spot for enjoying his delicious French-California cuisine on warm days. Inside, the airy dining room combines old-style wooden floors and a rustic stone fireplace with modern track lighting and bright tile accents. The menu mixes French classics such as cassoulet with Cal-Italian standards like risotto, light pastas, grilled vegetables, and even barbecue. Save room for dessert. Reservations highly recommended. • Daily noon-9pm (Nov-April closed W).

Catahoula ★★★ $$$: 1457 Lincoln Ave. (Washington), Calistoga, 707/942-2275. Owner-chef Jan Birnbaum escaped the constraints of big-city restaurants when he left San Francisco's Campton Place to open his own dining room in downtown Calistoga. This whimsical country venture assumes a canine theme—Catahoula is the state dog of Birnbaum's Louisiana birthplace—with photos of dogs on the walls, food in dog shapes, and a chic junkyard art motif. His Southern menu takes mentor Paul Prudhomme's food uptown. Listed along with gumbo you'll find a crispy duck confit salad with honey tangerines and candied onions. Definitely order dessert. Reservations recommended. • M-Th 5:30-10pm; F-Su 8:30am-10:30pm (shorter in winter).

The Diner ★★ $: 6476 Washington St. (California), Yountville, 707/944-2626. This Diner serves up food a good deal more progressive than the retro diner decor would suggest. Delectable favorites include banana pecan waffles and pancakes, French toast, huevos rancheros, and omelets. Some people come just for the crispy potato pancakes with homemade applesauce. Lunch and dinner turn back the clock to when California was a Mexican colony, serving excellent Mexican-American favorites—burritos, tacos, tostadas—plus sandwiches. No credit cards. Reservations only for groups of six or more. • Tu-Su 8am-3pm, 5:30-9pm.

Domaine Chandon ★★★ $$$: 1 California Dr. (Hwy 29), Yountville, 707/944-2892. As you might imagine, this winery, owned by the makers of Dom Perignon, makes the kind of special occasion food that goes with champagne (or even *méthode champenoise* sparkling wine). The first gourmet restaurant in the Wine Country, Chandon continues to cling to its French heritage, although local trends have crept into the menu. The kitchen turns out to-die-for renditions of such starters as smoked salmon, smoked trout, and duck rillettes with greens. Sweetbreads on lentils in an herb cream sauce, grilled rabbit, and potato-cheese ravioli in wild mushroom sauce are available for red wine aficionados. Elegant lunches take best advantage of the outdoor patio while dinner is served in the modern California redwood-enrobed dining room. Reservations essential, especially for dinner. • May-Sept. M-Tu 11:30am-2:30pm; W-Su 11:30am-2:30pm, 6-9:30pm; reduced hours during the winter.

Foothill Café ★★ $$: J&P Shopping Ctr., 2766 Old Sonoma Rd. (Foothill), Napa, 707/252-6178. This low-profile eatery is an enigma. Tucked into the back corner of a strip mall, this wonderful place was founded by a former sous chef at Masa's in San Francisco who wanted to provide first-class food for Napa Valley residents at less than first-class prices. It offers a limited menu of mostly barbecued and grilled items; the ribs are excellent, but don't miss anything that comes out of the oak oven, or the fresh fish specials. The wine list is reasonably priced and varied, featuring vintages from the smaller wineries in the Carneros region. The bare, gray space is not much to look at, and service can be amateurish, but it all enhances the locals-only orientation. • W-Su 4:30-9:30pm.

French Laundry ★★★★ $$$$: 6640 Washington St. (Creek), Yountville, 707/944-2380. This charming stone building on a side street in Yountville doesn't even have a sign, but determined gourmets quickly turned it into one of Northern California's premier destination restaurants. Celebrity chef Thomas Keller's wittily worded menu yields a surfeit of riches, and despite the prix fixe format, he offers at least four choices for each course, with substitutions and additional courses upon request, including a vegetarian menu. The portions are Lilliputian, the prices gargantuan, but the culinary feats are worthy of all of the fuss and finance. A spectacular set of wine choices makes for more decisions, but it would be difficult to make a wrong choice with the chef's consistent skill and flair. You may be taken to the cleaners at The French Laundry, but this is one meal that's worth the shirt off your back. Prepare to linger for the evening, French style. Book weekend reservations months in advance. • June-October daily 5:30-9:30pm; F-Su noon-1:30pm; closed Monday November-May.

Giugni's ¢: 1227 Main St. aka Hwy 29 (Spring/Hunt), St. Helena, 707/963-3421. A good place for sandwiches, which can be eaten in the back room. • Daily 9am-5pm.

Mustards Grill ★★★ $$: 7399 St. Helena Hwy. aka Hwy 29 (Yountville Cross), Yountville, 707/944-2424. This upscale roadhouse, operated by the owners of San Francisco's Fog City Diner, has established itself as one of the most popular and well-known restaurants in the valley. Order crispy golden onion rings or sample nouvelle

California cuisine—barbecued ribs, Asian marinated flank steak, or smoked duck with a coconut-almond sauce—while you survey the always-bustling scene. Easily the best burger in the valley. Reservations recommended. • Su-F 11:30am-9:30pm; Sa 11:30am-10pm.

Oakville Grocery Co. $: 7856 St. Helena Hwy. (Hwy 29/Oakville Cross), Oakville, 707/944-8802. The gourmet's choice for picnic fixings. • Daily 9am-6pm.

Ristorante Piatti ★★ $$: 6480 Washington St. (Oak), Yountville, 707/944-2070. A branch of this locally based chain of lively trattorias. The simple, bright dining rooms are casual and relaxed. Food tends to light preparations of Italian favorites. Try the ravioli in lemon sauce, the delightful mushroom risotto, or anything off the grill. Wood-fired pizzas are justifiably popular. Consistency has been a problem as the chain has grown. Wine prices are on the high side. Reservations recommended. • Summer: M-Th 11:30am-10pm; F-Su 11:30am-11pm. Winter: M-Th until 9pm; F-Su until 10pm.

Showley's ★★★ $$$: 1327 Railroad Ave. (Hunt/Adams), St. Helena, 707/963-1200. Based on the number of unlabeled bottles on the tables around you, you can safely bet you're dining among the gentry of wine country at Showley's. Local vintners and their guests love to while away the evenings in the courtyard under the fig tree, comparing cabernets and savoring quintessential California food with a Mediterranean flair. The Showley family's personal touches are much in evidence here, both in the understated decor and the appealing menu, which tends toward the Provençal and Tuscan in its flavors and presentation. The lamb shanks are a house specialty. Reservations recommended. • Tu-Su 11:30am-3pm, 6-10pm.

Terra ★★★★ $$$: 1345 Railroad Ave. (Hunt/Adams), St. Helena, 707/963-8931. An elegant, sophisticated eatery perfect for a special dinner. The rustic stone building establishes a warm, intimate tone for chef Hiro Sone's fabulous cuisine. Raves keep coming for innovative combinations like duck liver wontons with wild mushroom sauce, duck breast with sun-dried cherries, or salmon in miso sauce. Sone's wife, Lissa Doumani, oversees the excellent desserts and service. The wine list is oriented toward splurges. Reservations recommended. • Su-M, W-Th 6-9pm; F-Sa 6-10pm.

Tra Vigne ★★ $$$: 1050 Charter Oak Ave. (Hwy 29), St. Helena, 707/963-4444. Don't pass up a delicious Italian meal with a California accent in this airy dining room, or on the sylvan patio. Mustards Grill's suave Italian sibling, Tra Vigne is sure to impress guests—even those from the big city. High-tech accouterments and soaring ceilings give the rustic, old stone building a trendy touch. The similarly cutting-edge menu includes gourmet pizzas, rustic pastas, and hearty meat dishes. Sometimes the food is more style than substance, but it's still a favorite with visitors. Cantinetta Tra Vigne serves up pizza, sandwiches, and picnic fixings café-style or to go. Reservations recommended. • Su-Th 11:30am-10pm; F-Sa 11:30am-10:30pm.

Wappo Bar Bistro ★★ $$: 1226-B Washington St. (Lincoln), Calistoga, 707/942-4712. The name comes from a local Native American tribe, but the eclectic cuisine comes from all over the world. Mix New World specialties like chiles rellenos and empanadas with such old-country favorites as paella and Moroccan stew. The rustic interior with exposed wooden beams, rough wooden furniture, and tile floor has refreshingly few decorative flourishes. In true Wine Country fashion, a beautiful garden patio awaits fair-weather diners. • M, Th-Su 11:30am-2:30pm, 6-9:30pm; W 11:30-2:30pm.

Places to Stay

For more information and reservations, call **Napa Valley Reservations Unlimited** 707/252-1985, located at 1819 Tanen Street in Napa, open M-F 9am-5pm. If you want to stay over a summer weekend, you may need to make reservations as far as two months in advance.

Auberge du Soleil $$$$: 180 Rutherford Hill Rd. (off Silverado Trail), Rutherford, 707/963-1211. The place to go for very special occasions. Located in a secluded olive grove, rooms come with the works—fireplaces, terraces, sofas, king-size beds, and resplendent bathrooms. Facilities include a pool, hot tub, spa, and tennis. $350-$2000.

Bothe-Napa Valley State Park ¢: 3801 St. Helena Hwy. N. aka Hwy 29, St. Helena, 707/942-4575. Call Park.Net for reservations: 800/444-PARK (7275), www.park-net.com. Facilities include hot water, restrooms, and showers. $15-$16 per campsite, $5 per extra vehicle.

Calistoga Ranch Campground ¢: 580 Lommel Rd. (Silverado Trail), Calistoga, 707/942-6565. A cheap stay, with showers available. Tent sites with elevated barbecue and picnic table $19 for four people, $5 each additional adult and $2.50 for each additional child. 28-day maximum stay.

Calistoga Spa and Hot Springs $$: 1006 Washington St. (Lincoln), Calistoga, 707/942-6269. Frequent discounts are offered—inquire when making reservations. Appointments must be made for the spa, which offers mud and mineral baths, massages, and steam blanket wraps. With bath, kitchenette $87-$132.

Calistoga Village Inn and Spa $$: 1880 Lincoln Ave. (Silverado Trail), Calistoga, 707/942-0991. Sunken tubs, geothermal baths, whirlpools, and a swimming pool are included in the reasonable rates. With private bath $79-$159. No minimum stay.

Mountain Home Ranch $/$$: 3400 Mountain Home Ranch Rd. (off Petrified Forest Rd.), Calistoga, 707/942-6616. Find seclusion at this rustic resort. Set on over 300 acres in the mountains above Calistoga with its own natural sulfur spring, two swimming pools, tennis, volleyball, fishing, hiking trails, and a wisteria-draped family picnic area. Accommodations are available in the historic main lodge or in private cabins. Perfect for family escapes. $60-$130.

Napa Town & Country Fairgrounds ¢: 575 3rd St. (Silverado Trail), Napa, 707/253-4900. RV campground. Water and electricity included. No reservations. Campsites $15.

Pink Mansion $$$: 1415 Foothill Blvd. (Lincoln), Calistoga, 707/942-0558. An elegant, restored mansion with in-house wine tasting and an indoor pool filled with local waters. Full breakfast included. $135-$225.

Shady Oaks Country Inn $$$: 399 Zinfandel Ln. (Hwy 29/Silverado Trail), St. Helena, 707/963-1190. A quiet, romantic setting. Gourmet champagne breakfasts and wine and hors d'oeuvres every night add to the charm. $159-$190.

Triple S Ranch $: 4600 Mountain Home Ranch Rd. (off Petrified Forest Rd.), Calistoga, 707/942-6730. Nine cabins located near the Old Faithful Geyser of California and numerous hiking trails—a true bargain for a double room. $42-$54.

Sonoma ★★★

When George Yount and Charles Krug were establishing Napa Valley as a wine-growing region, neighboring Sonoma County was undergoing chaotic times. The Russian, Mexican, and American governments were engaged in fierce territorial skirmishes over the region until the United States finally took possession of Sonoma and its riches. Nowadays, the peaceful vineyards and scenic landscapes give little indication of the area's tumultuous past. Wineries in Sonoma County are centered in the Sonoma Valley, which is in the southern part of the county, and in northern Sonoma County around the town of Healdsburg and the Russian River Valley. Exploration of Sonoma requires an investigator's eye—the treasures abound, but you'll have to look a bit harder to find them, which makes it a more relaxed escape than Napa.

Sonoma Convention & Visitors Bureau: 5000 Roberts Lake Rd. #A (Golf Course Dr.), Rohnert Park, 707/935-0758, 707/586-8100. Maps, brochures, and information on the wineries, including a tasting guide. • M-F 8am-5pm.

Sonoma Valley Visitors Bureau: 453 1st St. E. (Napa/Spain), Sonoma, 707/996-1090. Maps of Sonoma County. • Daily 9am-7pm; winter 9am-5pm.

Getting There

The most direct route to the Sonoma Valley is via Hwy 101 across the Golden Gate Bridge. Continue on 101 to visit Healdsburg, Santa Rosa, and Sebastopol. If you want to head straight for the town of Sonoma, Hwy 37 to Hwy 121 to Hwy 12 is the quickest route. Sonoma is approximately one hour's drive from the Golden Gate Bridge.

Sonoma Wineries ★★

The vineyards of Napa may have brought California's wine country to prominence, but Sonoma is where it all began. Stories about the exact origins of the Golden State's wine business differ, but it seems to have taken root in 1823 at the vineyards of the Sonoma Mission. Wine making spread with arrival of the Hungarian immigrant Agoston Haraszthy, who brought thousands of vines back from Europe in 1861. The vineyards of Sonoma Valley and Northern Sonoma County still have a lot to offer to both the wine connoisseur and the dilettante, and unlike Napa, most wineries offer free tasting (although fewer tours and fancy visitor centers). When traveling through Sonoma, bear in mind that most of the wineries are not directly on the highway; keep your eyes open for the turnoffs, and don't hesitate to venture off into the countryside.

Buena Vista Historical Winery: 18000 Old Winery Rd. (Napa), Sonoma, 707/938-1266. Self-guided tours through the historic stone winery, picnic spots, and a wine museum and gallery are some of the attractions beyond the internationally-acclaimed bottlings. • Daily 10:30am-4:30pm; winter 10:30am-4pm. Guided tour daily at 2pm.

Carmenet Vineyard: 1700 Moon Mountain Dr. (Hwy 12), Sonoma, 707/996-5870. Tours and tastings are by appointment only—well worth the call. The vista of the Mayacamas Mountains, the underground aging caves, the Sauvignon Blanc, and the Cabernet are all outstanding reasons for a visit. • Make an appointment for a tour and tasting M-Th 7am-5:30pm; F-Su 9am-4pm.

Chateau St. Jean: 8555 Sonoma Hwy. aka Hwy 12, Kenwood, 707/833-4134. The 1920s-inspired tasting room, complimentary tastings, and picnic area make this a pleasant option. • Daily 10am-4:30pm.

Benzinger Family Winery: 1883 London Ranch Rd. (Arnold), Glen Ellen, 707/935-4046. This ranch was once owned by General Vallejo and more recently was home to Glen Ellen Winery. Tasting for some varieties is gratis, others are $5 per glass. There's a free motorized tram tour of the vineyards, and picnic spots among the redwoods are inviting. • Tastings daily 10am-5pm; tours daily 11:30-3:30pm.

Gundlach-Bundschu Winery: 2000 Denmark St. (Napa), Sonoma, 707/938-5277. A small, family-run winery known for its Merlot. Self-guided tours. • Daily 11am-4:30pm.

Kenwood Vineyards: 9592 Sonoma Hwy.aka Hwy 12 (Warm Springs), Kenwood, 707/833-5891. Some of the excellent vintages made here are the product of grapes still grown on Jack London's estate in Glen Ellen. Comprehensive 30-45 minute tours are by appointment. (Staff permitting, a free, 15-minute mini-tour is available on a walk-in basis.) Tour participants receive a 20 percent discount on wine purchases. Tasting is complimentary and many weekends feature food and wine pairings. • Daily 10am-4:30pm.

Korbel Champagne Cellars: 13250 River Rd. (14 miles west of Hwy 101), Guerneville, 707/887-2294. To get your fill of bubbles, brandy, and wine, visit this century-old winery. The picturesque place resembles a castle tucked away in the redwoods. There is a new deli and market and a few picnic tables. • Complimentary tasting and tours daily 10am-3pm; hours vary by season.

Lake Sonoma Winery: 9990 Dry Creek Rd. (Dutcher Creek), Geyserville, 707/431-1550. Its proximity to Warm Springs Dam and the Lake Sonoma Recreation Area make this a worthwhile to stop for the scenic views alone. An in-house deli offers fixings to accompany the family-produced vino for a picnic on the grounds. • Daily 10am-5pm.

Ravenswood Vintners: 18701 Gehricke Rd. (Lovall Valley), Sonoma, 707/938-1960. Noted for its big red vintages—their souvenir bumper sticker proclaims "No Wimpy Wines"—traditional production techniques, and summer weekend barbecues, this is a good place for a taste and a snack. Tours by appointment only. • Daily 10am-4:30pm.

Simi Winery: 16275 Healdsburg Ave. (Dry Creek), Healdsburg, 707/433-6981. Two Italian immigrants began making wine here in 1876 and built the beautiful stone building in 1890. Now owned by the same French company as prestigious Moet-Hennessey, Simi offers three excellent guided tours per day, and tasting and picnicking on the grounds. • Tasting daily 10am-4:30pm; tours at 11am, 1pm, 3pm.

Viansa Winery: 25200 Arnold Dr. aka Hwy 121, Sonoma, 707/935-4700. Ringed by outdoor picnic tables, this hilltop Mediterranean-style villa overlooks acres of vineyards. Complimentary wine tasting, plus an Italian food marketplace featuring terrific oils, spices, and dips, all of which can be liberally sampled. • Daily 10am-5pm.

Other Attractions ★

Sonoma Historic Park ★: Sonoma Plaza at 1st, Spain, and Napa sts., 707/938-1519. A good place to start exploring is in the town of Sonoma, where many of the historic battles for control of the region took place. Sonoma Plaza was laid out in 1834 by General Mariano Guadalupe Vallejo, the Mexican commander charged with keeping the territory out of the hands of the Russians. Several historical landmarks comprise the park and are also sprinkled among the shops and restaurants that now line the square. Whichever monument you visit first, you will have to buy a ticket (adults $2, children $1), that is good for admittance to all the other sites. These include: **Sonoma Mission**, the last of the great California missions; the remaining portion of General Vallejo's first home, **La Casa Grande Indian Servants' Quarters**; the **Sonoma Barracks**, where Vallejo's troops were housed; and **Lachryma Montis**, the General's second, even more stately home. • Daily 10am-5pm.

Sonoma Cheese Factory ★: 2 W. Spain St. (1st), Sonoma, 707/938-5225. This fragrant store also fronts the Plaza, marking the spot Sonoma Jack cheese has been made from the same recipe since 1931. Kids especially like to watch the cheesemaking process. • M-F 8:30am-5:30pm; Sa-Su 8:30am-6:30pm.

Jack London State Historic Park ★: 2400 London Ranch Rd., Glen Ellen, 707/938-5216. Heading north from Sonoma, be sure to visit Jack London State Historic Park, the writer's former ranch. Hiking and riding trails—horse rentals are available from Sonoma Cattle Company, 707/996-8566—crisscross the ranch past old barns, pigpens, and the charred remains of Wolf House, which was to be London's home but was destroyed by fire shortly before he could move in. **The House of Happy Walls** was built by London's widow, Charmian, and now houses many of his manuscripts, notes, and personal effects. • Daily 9:30am-7pm; winter until 5pm. Museum daily 10am-5pm. Cottage Sa-Su 12:30-4:30pm. Park entrance $6 per vehicle, $5 for seniors.

Snoopy's Gallery and Gift Shop: 1665 W. Steele Ln. (Range/Hardys), Santa Rosa, 707/546-3385. Before concluding that Sonoma County is too much like history class, recapture part of your childhood by visiting this emporium, owned and operated by the clever beagle's creator, Charles Schultz. This gallery boasts the world's largest collection of Peanuts memorabilia. • Daily 10am-6pm.

Bike Rental ★★: If you'd like to cycle your way around the area, **Rincon Cyclery** 707/538-0868 rents mountain bikes for $7 per hour (two-hour minimum), or $25 per day. Not too far from the bike trails of Annadel State Park, the shop is located at 4927 Sonoma Hwy 12 (at Middle Rincon) and is open M-F 10am-6pm; Sa 9am-6pm; Su

10am-5pm. You can also rent hybrid and tandem bikes at the **Spoke Folk Cyclery**, 249 Center St., Healdsburg, 707/433-7171. Rates are $7 per hour, $25 for the day. Hours are M, W-F 10am-6pm; Sa 10am-5pm; Su 11am-4pm.

Hot Air Ballooning ★: Sonoma has its share of hot air balloon operators eager to take you up for a champagne breakfast flight. **Above the Wine Country Balloons & Tours** 707/829-7695, 800/759-5638 ends its flights with a tasty gourmet brunch. Rides cost about $175 per person, and reservations are required.

Canoe Rentals ★: Near Healdsburg, the Russian River's placid waters and forested banks are the perfect setting for a leisurely day of canoeing, swimming, and picnicking. Be warned, however: some folks come for a bucolic retreat, others to party their brains out. **Trowbridge Recreation**, 20 Healdsburg Ave. (S. University), Healdsburg, 707/433-7247, organizes canoe, kayak, and camping trips along the Russian River for groups. Trowbridge also rents canoes and kayaks: one day with a canoe is $39 and must be reserved in advance. You can also rent from **Burke's Canoe Trips** at 8600 River Rd. (Mirabel/River), Forestville, 707/887-1222 and paddle the ten miles to Guerneville; bring a picnic lunch and make a day of it. A shuttle will take you back to Forestville. Two-person canoes rent for $35. Pick up canoes 9-10am. Weekend reservations are required

Places to Eat

Bistro Ralph ★★★ $$$: 109 Plaza St. (Healdsburg/Center), Healdsburg, 707/433-1380. Chef Ralph Tingle broke the old Italian restaurant monopoly on the square in Healdsburg when he opened this updated French-American bistro. He does an excellent job at featuring seasonal local ingredients and seafood. Salmon might be made into cakes with sweet mustard sauce and capers, halibut might come steamed and topped with pesto, while grilled leg of lamb might come simply *au jus*. Deep-fried items like French fries and Sichuan pepper calamari are delightfully greaseless. Service is highly variable. Reservations recommended. • M-F 11:30am-2:30pm, 5:30-9:30pm; Sa-Su 5:30-9:30.

Café Lolo ★★ $$$: 620 5th St. (Mendocino/D St.), Santa Rosa, 707/576-7822. Café Chef Michael Quigley came over from Napa's Meadowood Resort, bringing California cuisine in tow. Carrot soup comes seasoned with ginger and cilantro, roast duck is served with a rhubarb chutney and mushrooms, and fettuccine accompanies steamed mussels. The small dining room, with little on the white walls but a large, gold-framed mirror, is cozy and intimate—a perfect special-occasion restaurant. The limited wine list has very reasonable prices. Reservations recommended. • M-F 11:30am-2pm, 5:30-10pm; Sa 5:30-10pm.

Catelli's The Rex ★★ $$: 21047 Geyserville Ave. (off Hwy 128), Geyserville, 707/433-6000. North Beach fare in Geyserville. Located in the heart of downtown, The Rex (as it is usually called) serves family-style Italian dinners with a touch of class. Soup or salad and a side of pasta (choice of four different sauces) come with the main courses. Reservations recommended. • Tu-F noon-2pm, 5:30-8:30pm; Sa 5-9pm; Su 5-8:30pm.

Della Santina's ★★ $$: 133 E. Napa St. (1st St. E.), Sonoma, 707/935-0576. This small, simple Italian restaurant is run by the same family that heads up Corte Madera's Marin Joe's. The food is more upscale, with the menu split between competently executed, basic pastas—lasagna bolognese, cannelloni Florentine, tortellini pesto, gnocchi in tomato sauce—and wonderful spit-roasted meats and fowl. A mixed grill allows you to choose three of the juicy, aromatic meats, which include chicken, pork loin, turkey breast, rabbit, duck, and veal. A good escape from the increasingly complicated menus dominating this region. Local winery types come for a basic business lunch. The wine list is small and short on low-priced entries. Not long ago, Della Santina moved a few doors down the street and now offers a wonderful patio. Reservations recommended. • Daily 11am-3pm, 5-9:30pm.

The General's Daughter ★ **$$:** 400 W. Spain St. (4th St. W.), Sonoma, 707/938-4004. This attractive Sonoma newcomer occupies a beautifully restored Victorian. The elegant setting will probably get more attention than the country food. The everyday offerings—soups, salads, steak and potatoes—rely on fresh ingredients, and might come as a relief after too many eclectic menus. Service can be perky but amateurish. • M-Th 11:30am-2:30pm, 5:30-9:30pm; F 11:30am-2:30pm, 5:30-10:30pm; Sa 11am-2:30pm, 5:30-10:30pm; Su 11am-2:30pm, 5:30-9:30pm.

La Casa ★ **$:** 121 E. Spain St. (1st St. E./2nd St. E.), Sonoma, 707/996-3406. This popular downtown spot serves passable Mexican food in an authentic Cal-Mex setting: dark wood, hand-painted tiles, the works. Wash down tacos and burritos with a tasty margarita and enjoy the low-key atmosphere. Reservations recommended. • Daily 11:30am-10pm (Cantina menu until midnight).

Lisa Hemenway's ★★★ **$$:** 714 Village Ct., Montgomery Village (Farmers Ln./Sonoma Ave.), Santa Rosa, 707/526-5111. It's hard to believe such a delightful gourmet restaurant could be hidden in such a labyrinthine shopping mall. Nevertheless, Lisa Hemenway, a John Ash veteran who's been inspired by world travel, has created a venue well suited to special-occasion dining. The light and airy dining room allows celebrants to relax without distraction and enjoy the eclectic cuisine based on fresh local ingredients. Start with crab cakes, oysters on the half shell, or a duck quesadilla, then enjoy Mongolian-style pork, vegetable tamales, or chicken breast with sun-dried cherries. Fill your picnic basket next door at Lisa Hemenway's Tote Cuisine. Reservations recommended. • M-Su 11:30am-3pm, 5:30pm-9:30pm.

Ravenous ★★ **$:** 117 North St. (Center/Healdsburg), Healdsburg, 707/431-1770. This bird's nest of a restaurant, tucked into the recently dolled up Raven movie theater, is a film buff's and foodie's delight. This tiny gem is classic Sonoma, with a chalkboard menu and an intense chef in full view, creating some wonderful pasta and grilled dishes with locally grown ingredients and a lot of imagination. A short but stellar wine list offers interesting selections, desserts are wonderful, and the service can be good if the kitchen is not too swamped. Your problem will be getting a reservation—this is a local hangout, with diners starting to line up at 5pm. Keep Ravenous a secret? Nevermore. No credit cards. • Su, W-Th 11:30am-2:30pm, 5-9pm; F-Sa 11:30am-2:30pm, 5-9:30pm.

Ristorante Piatti ★★ **$$$:** 405 1st St. W. (W. Spain St./W. Napa St.), Sonoma, 707/996-2351. A breezy, modern Italian restaurant, twin to the Napa original. • M-Th 11:30am-10pm; F-Su 11:30am-11pm; winter, M-Th until 9pm, F-Su until 10pm.

Singletree Inn ★★ **$:** 165 Healdsburg Ave. (Mill), Healdsburg, 707/433-8263. Great cheap eats for breakfast. Good for fueling up before a long day of exploring or cycling. • Daily 7am-3pm.

World Famous Hamburger Ranch and Pasta Farm ★★ **$:** 31195 Redwood Hwy. N. (Hwy 128 West), Cloverdale, 707/894-5616. No infusions, no exotica. Nothing but good food, with something for every palate: famous burgers, basic pastas, grilled cheese sandwiches. Summertime outdoor barbecues make a perfect family outing. Wines are basic, but good local beer is served. • Daily 7am-9pm; F-Sa until 10pm in summer.

Places to Stay

Camping

Lake Sonoma/Warm Springs Dam ¢**:** 3333 Skaggs Springs Rd. (Dry Creek), Geyserville, 707/433-9483. Drive-in campsites include access to hot showers. Drive-in sites $14 per night per vehicle; boat-in and backpacker sites $8. All sites first come, first served.

Spring Lake Park ¢**:** 5390 Montgomery Dr., between Howarth Park and Annadel State Park, Santa Rosa 707/539-8092, 707/539-8082. Campsites include access to hot showers. Sites $15, $5 extra vehicle. Reservations for May-September accepted beginning in January, and must be made two weeks in advance; unreserved sites available first come, first served.

Sugarloaf Ridge State Park ¢: 2605 Adobe Canyon Rd., Kenwood, 707/833-5712. Reservations essential on weekends; call Park.Net 800/444-PARK (7275). www.park-net.com. Sites $15-$16.

Hotels, Motels, and B&Bs

Best Western Garden Inn $$: 1500 Santa Rosa Ave., Santa Rosa, 707/546-4031, 800/528-1234. Landscaped grounds with two swimming pools. $75-$87.

Best Western Hillside Inn $$: 2901 4th St. (Farmers/Hwy 12), Santa Rosa, 707/546-9353, 800/528-1234. Rooms with kitchens and two-bedroom family units. $65.

Glenelly Inn $$$: 5131 Warm Springs Rd. (Arnold/Henno), Glen Ellen, 707/996-6720. Eight rooms with private baths and entrances, a garden, and an outdoor Jacuzzi. $115-$150.

Grape Leaf Inn $$$: 539 Johnson St. (Grant), Healdsburg, 707/433-8140. Seven rooms with private baths, whirlpool tubs for two, full breakfast in the morning, and wine and cheese at night. $95-$165.

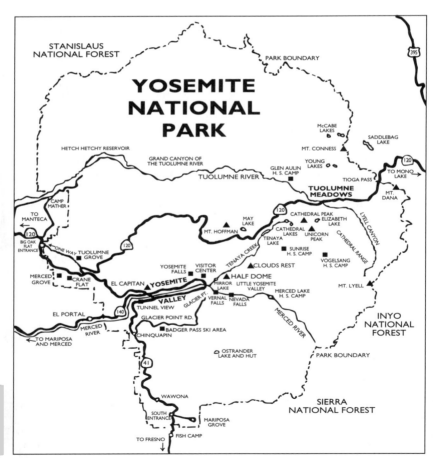

Madrona Manor $$$$: 1001 Westside Rd. (W. Dry Creek/Westside), Healdsburg, 707/433-4231. All 21 rooms have private baths; some have fireplaces. Enjoy the pool and gourmet restaurant. $155-$255.

Raford House $$$: 10630 Wohler Rd. (Eastside), Healdsburg, 707/887-9573. An authentic Victorian farmhouse, complete with period furnishings, set on a hill among the vineyards. The seven guest rooms are cozy and private, and views from the deck are spectacular. $120-$155.

Santa Rosa Motor Inn $: 1800 Santa Rosa Ave. (Colghan), Santa Rosa, 707/523-3480. Standard, clean, and Spartan motel rooms. $40-$65.

Sonoma Mission Inn & Spa $$$$: 18140 Sonoma Hwy. aka Hwy 12, Boyes Hot Springs, 707/938-9000, 800/862-4945. This sprawling landmark offers all the amenities and pampering you'd expect of a big luxury hotel. The rooms are rather small, but expect to spend most of your time by the pool, in the spa, or on a golf or tennis course. (Unless you book a spa package, you must pay $15-$25 extra to use spa facilities, although use of the main pool is included with all room rates.) $185-$750.

YOSEMITE ★★★

Famous throughout the world, Yosemite National Park has stupendous scenery, challenging hikes, and unfortunately, hordes of tourists—three and a half million a year. Yosemite Valley, the park's best-known attraction, inspired photographers Ansel Adams and Galen Rowell and Sierra Club founder, naturalist John Muir. Sheer granite cliffs rise 3,000 feet above this scenic valley. Cascading down these cliffs are waterfalls that rank among the world's highest, most spectacular, and most visited—it isn't unheard of to be caught in traffic on a busy summer weekend. Try to see the valley in the spring (April or May) when the waterfalls are raging, the flowers are blooming, and free parking spots aren't as elusive as deer. In the summer, Tuolumne Meadows in the northern area of the park is an outstanding and less crowded place for walking, hiking, or climbing. In the fall, you can explore the Mist Trail without being trampled. The backcountry skiing in Yosemite is among the best in the Sierra, and there's both a touring center and a downhill area at Badger Pass in the southern area of the park.

When contacting the park for information or reservations, please note that the National Park Service manages the park, but most businesses within the park (lodges, restaurants, rentals) are operated by Yosemite Concession Services, a private business.

Yosemite National Park: P. O. Box 577, Yosemite, CA 95389; Operator/Recorded Announcements 209/372-0200, 372-0264, 372-0209; Public Information 209/372-0265; Wilderness Center 209/372-0285; Permit Information 209/372-0310; Wilderness Permit Reservations 209/372-0740. • M-F 9am-4pm.

Backcountry Stations: Yosemite Valley 209/372-0308. Tuolumne 209/372-0309. • Su-F 7:30am-7:30pm; Sa 6:30am-7:30pm.

Tuolumne Visitors Center: Tuolumne Meadows, 209/372-0263. • 9am-7pm daily.

Yosemite Concession Services: 209/372-1000.

Yosemite Valley Visitors Center: 209/372-0299. • Daily 8am-8pm summer, 9am-5pm winter.

Getting There

By car, plan on driving three and one-half hours to Yosemite Valley. Take I-580 toward Livermore, then I-205 east toward Stockton. I-205 runs into Hwy 120 East, which you follow all the way to Yosemite. Pay attention to the signs or you'll lose Hwy 120: there's a tricky stretch where Hwys 108 and 120 split; you'll have to take a right turn to stay on Hwy 120, which heads toward Chinese Camp, Groveland, Buck Meadows, and Yosemite.

GETAWAYS

Entrance to the park is $20 per vehicle valid for seven days. If you arrive by foot, bus, bicycle, motorcycle, or horse, the entrance fee is $10 and also valid for seven days. A Yosemite annual pass is $40.

Other mountain byways that enter the park from the west and south give you scenic driving options through alternate park entrances. Hwy 140 enters through the town of El Portal, and Hwy 41 enters through the towns of Fish Camp and Mariposa. If you are lucky enough to enter on 41 at sunset, the view from the Wawona Tunnel is breathtaking.

If you're using public transportation, you'll have to be patient. **Via Yosemite**, 209/722-0366, runs buses from Merced and Fresno Air Terminal to Yosemite (four times daily; $48 round-trip from Fresno; $38 round-trip from Merced). You can get to Merced and Fresno from the Bay Area by **Greyhound** 800/231-2222 or **Amtrak** 800/872-7245 bus.

Yosemite Valley ★★

Yosemite Valley, for all its splendor, is basically a human zoo—more Disneyland than natural escape. The best sightseeing is on the trails, so whether you hike, bike, ride, or ski, get away from the roads. All road signs and the park map (available at the entrance stations) lead you to the day-use parking lot in **Curry Village**, home to much of the valley's lodging and plenty of food concessions and shops. When exploring Yosemite Valley, park your car in Curry Village and take the free and frequent **shuttle bus** to the Visitors Center and all other valley destinations.

General Sightseeing

El Capitan ★★★: As you drive into the valley, the first dramatic sight is this sheer rock wall, towering well over 3,000 feet above the valley. (The best view spot is actually from a meadow located on the north side of the road exiting the valley.) The rock is nirvana for serious rock climbers who spend days hauling themselves up to the top (if you get close to the base, look out for climber waste).

Yosemite Village: The administrative center of the park. Timid visitors might start by dropping by the **Visitors Center** to learn about what they should experience outside. Guided nature walks also leave from here. The **Ansel Adams Gallery** 209/372-4413, a tribute to the photographer who made the park so famous, is open from 8:30am to 6:30pm in the summer, and 9am to 6pm in the winter.

Yosemite Concession Services offers a **guided bus tour**. Obtain more information at any of the information desks located at Yosemite Lodge, Curry Village, the Ahwahnee Hotel, and next to the Village Store, or by calling 209/372-1240. Advance reservations are required. On the night of a full moon and for two nights before, night tours through the valley floor are offered.

The Ahwahnee Hotel ★: A national historic landmark with lavish rooms and high rates, this hotel is well worth a look-in, if only for a walk through the grand common rooms. Built from native stones and logs, the hotel has an impressive fireplace, a huge dining hall with exposed log beams, and big windows to take in the sweeping vistas.

Glacier Point ★★★: If you'd prefer to see the valley from a different perspective, drive, bus, bike, or hike (see below) from the valley to Glacier Point, where you'll have a bird's-eye view of the valley and Half Dome. If you are traveling by road, on the way back be sure to stop at **Tunnel View ★★★** (a turnout at the eastern end of the Wawona Tunnel) and gaze at the valley's cliffs and waterfalls and the Sierra in the distance.

Hiking, Riding, & Climbing ★★★

Mist Trail ★★: This trail, which leads to Vernal Falls, got its name because the spray from the river it follows frequently soaks it and its travelers (making the ground slick). You can start your hike from Curry Village or take a shuttle bus to Happy Isles and start there. You can take a hike of any length; the trail follows a sparkling river up a scenic valley, so you don't have to get to any peak destination to make it worth your while. **Vernal Falls ★★** is a three-mile round trip, perfect for a half day. Though the trail is very popular, and initially paved like a freeway, it's well worth the effort. If you have the better part of a day, the Mist Trail continues past Vernal Falls to **Nevada Falls ★★**, a seven-mile round trip. The extra climb gives you views of a second, bigger waterfall and the valley. From Nevada Falls, you have the option of returning to the valley via a loop trail; unfortunately, the loop trail is heavily used by horses, which makes hiking less desirable.

Yosemite Falls ★★★: An even shorter walk is to the bottom of Yosemite Falls, only about half a mile, round trip. It doesn't sound like much, but it's impressive to stand at the base of the pounding water as it surges and sprays. During a full moon, when the falls are raging, one can even see "moonbows," or lunar rainbows, at the base of the falls. On a busy summer day it's not uncommon to see 20 tour buses parked at this trailhead across from the Yosemite Lodge, but don't be daunted—it's the only place for buses to park in the valley.

An enjoyable, but much more ambitious hike is to the **top of Yosemite Falls ★★★**, 6.6 miles round trip. Continuing to **Yosemite Point ★★★** puts you on the rim above the valley with a great view of Half Dome. The trail is steep—it climbs over 3,000 vertical feet—and gives a good workout, so bring adequate food, water, and clothing.

Glacier Point ★★★: If you're feeling very ambitious, hike up to Glacier Point for breathtaking views. The trailhead is on the southern road in the valley, west of the Chapel. Like the climb to Yosemite Point, this hike is a serious challenge. You can enjoy a less strenuous trip if you take the shuttle bus up to Glacier Point and hike back to the valley. An interesting bit of trivia to contemplate as you hike: The summer of 1996, an enormous chunk of rock fell from Glacier Point into the valley causing massive winds and killing one person.

Half Dome ★★★: If you're truly hard core, hike Half Dome by the cables route—not an undertaking for the fainthearted. It's 16 miles round trip with a vertical gain of over 5,000 feet. The last half-mile is so steep that the Park Service has installed cables and steps. (Lightning storms are not uncommon; avoid being up there in a storm.) Start very early and bring warm, windproof clothing, lots of food and water, and rain gear.

Backpacking ★★★: The advantage of going on a multiday hike is that once you leave the valley, the crowds thin rapidly. The number of routes is virtually limitless, so buy a good topographic map and have some fun planning. Remember, all overnight trips in the park require a free permit, available at the backcountry stations around the park. Also, some trails have summer quotas, so call ahead for information on limits and reservations. Always hang your food in a tree or rent a bear box, lest the bears hold a midnight feast with your breakfast (most camping stores and rangers can explain the details). An enjoyable two- or three-day outing is a trek up the Mist Trail to Little Yosemite Valley. From camp you can do a day trip up Half Dome, or for an even longer trip, continue over Clouds Rest for one of the best views in the park.

In the summer, a hiker's shuttle runs once a day from the valley to Tuolumne and back. It leaves the valley hotels around 8am, arrives in Tuolumne about two hours later, and continues all the way to Lee Vining on the east side of the park. It returns in the afternoon, stops in Tuolumne at 4pm, and returns to the valley by 6pm. See the Wilderness Office or the Visitors Center for times and reservations.

Bike Rentals: If you'd prefer to see the valley on your own but don't have the time for a tour on foot, Curry Village 209/372-1000 rents bikes seasonally; open daily 8:30am-5:45pm. **Yosemite Lodge** offers year-round rentals as does **Lodge Bike Rentals**, across from parking lot for Yosemite Falls. They're open from 8:30am to 5:45pm daily, with the last rental out at 4:45pm; call 209/372-1208 for details. Ride the eight miles of bike trails in the valley or venture onto the main road out of the valley. A popular and easy destination is **Mirror Lake ★** and Meadow, where you can gaze straight up at the massive, sheer cliff of Half Dome's north side and see what remains of the lake (a fair amount during the spring runoff, very little in the late fall). For some strange reason, you're required to walk the last quarter of a mile (a bit of an uphill).

Horseback Riding: If you give yourself at least a half day, why not saddle up? Curry Stables 209/372-8348 runs horse trips around the valley. This is a good option for folks who want a little adventure but are intimidated by the length or altitude gain in the trails.

Rock Climbing ★★★: Yosemite is one of the most challenging and scenic places to rock climb in the world, as the international mix of climbers in the park can attest (look for many of them at the Sunnyside campground). **The Yosemite Mountaineering School** 209/372-8344 offers excellent classes for first-time climbers—call for schedules and rates. Numerous books describe the many challenging routes in Yosemite. If you're a hard-core climber, scale El Capitan by the Nose Route, giving yourself five days. Don't forget to leave your fear behind.

Tuolumne Meadows ★★★

Unlike the valley, where temperatures can soar into the 90s (and the crowds seemingly into the millions), Tuolumne's altitude (8,000 feet) keeps the temperature bearable in the summer, and there are fewer people milling about. There are no "attractions," but hiking the trails around the heart of Tuolumne Meadows, watching birds of prey, enjoying the flora and fauna, and peering at the brightly clad climbers can be beautiful. A shuttle bus even allows you to park at the main lot and spend the day unencumbered by your automobile. **Tioga Road** crosses Tuolumne Meadows, leading to **Tioga Pass** on its way east to Mono Lake. The road is usually open June-November, depending on snowfall. **Olmstead Point ★★★,** located near the midpoint of Tioga Road, offers one of the park's best viewpoints looking down a dramatic valley towards Half Dome.

Hiking & Climbing ★★★: Hiking options from Tioga Road are virtually limitless. You should get a good, topographic trail map and have some fun (the USGS Tuolumne Meadows quad map is good, although private-company maps are often printed on durable plastic and show trail mileages). When planning a trip, keep in mind that you'll find more solitude if you avoid the "High Sierra Camps," semi-permanent villages with lots of people and horses. For all overnight trips, you need a permit (available at the Tuolumne Wilderness Office near the Tuolumne Meadows lodge). Also, bring enough cord and stuff sacks to hang your food at night or rent a bear box from the park—it's bulky, but it requires less strategic planning.

Young's Lakes is a long day or overnight hike. It can be a bit crowded but offers great views of the lakes, Ragged Peak, and Mt. Conness. Equine packers frequent the lakes, so pick another destination if you don't like horses. From Young's Lakes there's a Class 2 scramble leading up Mt. Conness. There's also a harder route (Class 2 to 3) from the other side, starting from Saddlebag Lake.

Mt. Hoffman offers one of the best views in Tuolumne. There's a moderately challenging trail from May Lake. **Elizabeth Lake** is popular and offers great views of the Clark Range and the Sierra. **Cathedral Peak** is a Class 4 climb, but it's reasonable for experienced rock climbers and provides great views. **Unicorn Peak** is a Class 3 scramble. **The Grand Canyon of the Tuolumne River** is spectacular in the spring and early summer when the water is high. You can reach it from Glen Aulin High Sierra Camp.

To get to **Mt. Dana**, a half-day climb, follow the footpath that runs from Tioga Pass (on Hwy 120 toward the east side). Ice climbers may want to try a scenic, if not too challenging, 40-degree ice route on the northeast side. **Mt. Lyell**, the highest peak in the park, is a nice two-day, Class 3 climb. An ice ax, crampons, and a rope are advisable. To get to the base camp, hike up the beautiful **Lyell Canyon**, a worth-while trip in itself.

Other Areas ★

Yosemite is also home to three **Sequoia Groves ★★**. Sequoia trees, wide-bodied cousins of the taller but less massive coastal redwood trees, are the largest living things on earth and Yosemite houses some splendid specimens. **Tuolumne and Merced Groves ★** are near the Big Oak Flat entrance, on Hwy 120, and include the famous drive-through tree. The other grove is **Mariposa Grove ★★**, in the Wawona Basin (the southern part of the park on Hwy 41). A tour bus will take you the final distance from the Mariposa Grove parking lot to the giant sequoias. This is an amazing place for a long walk and a picnic. **Wawona** is a much quieter area than the valley; you can also hike into Wawona Point and Chilnualna Falls.

Seasonal Activities ★

In the early spring when the waters are high, the Merced River, which runs down Yosemite Valley, offers exciting **rafting**. There are innumerable lakes and rivers in Yosemite, all open for **fishing**. New environmental rules only allow sport fishing in the Merced. The Mountain Shop in Curry Village and the camping store next to the supermarket sell fishing licenses and gear.

In the winter, there's **downhill skiing** at Badger Pass. The terrain is limited, but the views are priceless. The **cross-country skiing**, however, is excellent. Beginners enjoy the road out to Glacier Point, which is closed to cars in the winter and groomed daily. The trip all the way to Glacier Point is challenging—a long but reasonable day for well-conditioned skiers. Off this road, side trails lead to **Ostrander Hut** (a possible overnight—call the Wilderness Center at 209/372-0740 for reservations), Dewey Point, and the back of the ski area offer ungroomed skiing. For real outback skiing, try a multiday trip into Tuolumne Meadows. From the Bay Area, the quickest access is via the Snow Creek Trail that starts in Yosemite Valley (Tioga Pass Road is closed in winter).

Places to Eat

While there are several options for eating in and around the park, you may want to consider bringing your own food, a particularly good plan if you're heading for the back country. High prices and crowds are often more ominous than your appetite. But if you really need that hot meal and the camp stove isn't lighting, a foray into the eateries in the park will reward you with sustenance—after a wait in line.

Ahwahnee Dining Room ★★ $$$: Ahwahnee Hotel, 209/372-1488. This is a one of the priciest meals in the area, and one of the best. Dinner is a relatively formal affair with California-Continental cuisine. If you think it's the perfect place for a holiday get-together, make plans *very* far in advance. • Daily 7am-10:30am, 11:30am-3:30pm, 5:30pm-9pm.

Curry Village Cafeteria ¢: The good news is that this cafeteria is centrally located in Curry Village. The bad news is that so are the crowds. Think of it as a trip back to summer camp or a college dorm. • Daily 7am-10:30pm (Summer), 7am-8pm (Winter).

Degnan's Deli ¢: Yosemite Village, 209/372-1454. Good snacks and pizzas. The grill upstairs is the best deal in town. • Daily 7am-10:30pm (Summer), 7am-8pm (Winter).

Yosemite Lodge: ¢ 209/372-1265. Varied cafeteria offerings. •Daily 6:30am-10pm, 11:30am-3:45pm, 4:30pm-8pm. • Also within the lodge: **Garden Terrace $** 209/372-1269. • Buffet lunch and dinner. • Daily noon-8pm. • **Mountain Room Broiler $$$** 209/372-1281. Quality food at sequoia-sized prices. • Daily 5pm-8:30pm.

Places to Stay

Camping

For overnights on the trail, contact the **Wilderness Office** for free wilderness backpacking permits. For car camping, there are two types of campgrounds in the park: walk-ins (first come, first served) and those that require a reservation. The walk-ins tend to be filled to capacity in the peak season, so it's quite a gamble; try this option to get a site only if you are stuck with no other options. The best way to get a site is to be at the campground in the early morning on a weekday and grab a site just as someone is vacating it. The walk-in sites are **Hetch Hetchy, Tenaya** (on a lake close to Tuolumne Meadows), and **Sunnyside** (a climbers' hangout). From June 1 to September 15, there's a 7-day limit for Valley sites, and a 14-day limit outside the valley. At all other times of the year there's a 30-day limit. All sites are $15 per car/tent except Sunnyside which is $3 per person—walk-ins only.

Reservation campgrounds are handled through a special **Park.Net** office, which can be rather difficult to deal with. Reservations can be made no sooner than eight weeks beforehand, a task best done early in the morning. The campgrounds in the valley are **Upper Pines, North Pines, Lower Pines, Upper River, and Lower River.** They're all roughly the same. The best campgrounds along Tioga Pass Road in order of preference and distance from Tuolumne Meadows are **Tuolumne, Porcupine Flat, Yosemite Creek, White Wolf, Tamarack Creek, and Hodgdon Meadow**. Three more options in the park are **Crane Flat** (on the Big Oak Flat Road), **Bridalveil Creek** (on the road to Glacier point), and **Wawona**.

Park.Net (National Park campground reservations): 800/436-PARK/7275. www.park-net.com.

Yosemite Association: 5020 El Portal Rd., El Portal, 209/379-2646, hut reservations 209/372-0740. Mailing address: P.O. Box 230, El Portal, CA 95318. Manages Ostrander Hut reservations.

Lodging

Ahwahnee Hotel $$$$: Yosemite Park, 209/372-1406. Rugged luxury, spectacular views, and conveniently located right in the Valley. $265 rooms, $450-$750 suites.

Buck Meadows Lodge $$: Hwy 120, Buck Meadows, 209/962-6366. Located 30 miles from the park. May through October double rooms $99 and family rooms $109.

Cedar Lodge Resort $$: Hwy 140, El Portal, 209/379-2612. Just outside park. $85-$399.

Mariposa Inn $$: Hwy 140, Mariposa, 209/966-4676. Located 43 miles from the park in downtown Mariposa, this six-room historic inn features a rear garden veranda and elegant design. Summer $84-$97; Winter $72-$83.

Tenaya Lodge $$$: Hwy 41, 2 mi. from the south entrance of the park, 209/683-6555. Good restaurants, a convenient location, and clean, simple lodging. $129-$239.

The Redwoods $$/$$$: Wawona, 209/375-6666. Books private homes for vacation rentals, with one- to six-room rentals available. Summer $110-$438; Winter $82-$325.

Yosemite Concession Services: Reservations 209/252-4848. Handles reservations for all park lodging except camping. Includes **Ahwahnee Hotel, Yosemite Lodge, Wawona Hotel, White Wolf Lodge,** and the wood cabins and tent **cabins in Curry Village.**

Yosemite West $$: 209/372-4240. Rents studio and loft condos year-round. Located near Chinquapin, which is inside the park between the Valley and Glacier Point. $79-$129 for two; $10 for each additional person.

INDEX